Fodor's

ROME

WELCOME TO ROME

Italy's vibrant capital lives in the present, but no other city on earth evokes its past so powerfully. For over 2,500 years, emperors, popes, artists, and common citizens have left their mark here. Archaeological remains from ancient Rome, art-stuffed churches, and the treasures of Vatican City vie for your attention, but Rome is also a wonderful place to practice the Italian-perfected *il dolce far niente,* the sweet art of idleness. Your most memorable experiences may include sitting at a caffè in the Campo de' Fiori or strolling in a beguiling piazza.

TOP REASONS TO GO

★ **History:** The Colosseum and the Forum are just two amazing archaeological musts.

★ **Food:** From pasta and pizza to innovative fare, great meals at trattorias or enotecas.

★ **Art:** Works by Michelangelo, Raphael, Bernini, and Caravaggio dazzle around the city.

★ **Churches:** Places of worship from the Byzantine to baroque eras hold artistic bounty.

★ **Landmarks:** The Pantheon, St. Peter's Basilica, the Spanish Steps—to name only a few.

★ **Shopping:** Chic boutiques around Piazza di Spagna, flea-market finds in Trastevere.

Fodor's ROME

Editors: Caroline Trefler (lead editor); Joanna G. Cantor, Heidi Johansen, Denise Leto

Editorial Contributors: Nicole Arriaga, Erica Firpo, Dana Klitzberg, Amanda Ruggeri, Margaret Stenhouse

Production Editor: Evangelos Vasilakis

10th Edition

ISBN 978-0-8041-4263-2

ISSN 276-2560

PRINTED IN THE UNITED STATES OF AMERICA

10 9 8 7 6 5 4 3 2 1

CONTENTS

Fodor's Features

CONTENTS

MAPS

ABOUT THIS GUIDE

Fodor's Ratings

Everything in this guide is worth doing—we don't cover what isn't—but exceptional sights, hotels, and restaurants are recognized with additional accolades. **Fodor's Choice★** indicates our top recommendations; ★ highlights places we deem highly recommended; and **Best Bets** call attention to notable hotels and restaurants in various categories. Care to nominate a new place? Visit Fodors.com/contact-us.

Trip Costs

We list prices wherever possible to help you budget well. Hotel and restaurant price categories from **$** to **$$$$** are noted alongside each recommendation. For hotels, we include the lowest cost of a standard double room in high season. For restaurants, we cite the average price of a main course at dinner or, if dinner isn't served, at lunch. For attractions, we always list adult admission fees; discounts are usually available for children, students, and senior citizens.

Hotels

Our local writers vet every hotel to recommend the best overnights in each price category, from budget to expensive. Unless otherwise specified, you can expect private bath, phone, and TV in your room. For expanded hotel reviews, facilities, and deals visit Fodors.com.

Restaurants

Unless we state otherwise, restaurants are open for lunch and dinner daily. We mention dress code only when there's a specific requirement and reservations only when they're essential or not accepted. To make restaurant reservations, visit Fodors.com.

Credit Cards

The hotels and restaurants in this guide typically accept credit cards. If not, we'll say so.

Top Picks

★ Fodor's Choice

Listings

- ✉ Address
- Branch address
- ☎ Telephone
- Fax
- Website
- E-mail
- Admission fee
- Open/closed times
- M Subway
- Directions or Map coordinates

Hotels & Restaurants

- Hotel
- Number of rooms
- Meal plans
- ✕ Restaurant
- Reservations
- Dress code
- No credit cards
- $ Price

Other

- ⇨ See also
- Take note
- Golf facilities

EXPERIENCE ROME

ROME TODAY

Rome the Eternal is 25 centuries old and constantly reinventing itself. The glories of Ancient Rome, the pomp of the Renaissance Papacy, and the futuristic architecture of the 20th and 21st centuries all blend miraculously into a harmonious whole. You can get Wi-Fi in the shadow of 2,000-year-old ruins. It's this fusion of old and new and the casual way that Romans live with their weighty history that make this city unique.

It's not the Roma your mother knew.

No, in many ways it's better! Much of the historic center has been pedestrianized or has had its access limited to residents, public transport, and taxis, so you can now stroll around areas like the Pantheon, the Trevi Fountain, and the Spanish Steps without having to dodge a constant stream of traffic. A radical change for Italy is that smoking is now banned in all public places, including restaurants and pubs. And central areas such as Monti, Testaccio, and San Lorenzo have become gentrified or arty-chic, so you can extend your sightseeing range to spots your mother wouldn't have dreamed of visiting.

Multiculturalism

Spend a day in Rome's Esquilino neighborhood and you'll see just how cosmopolitan the Eternal City is becoming. Once famous for its fruit and vegetable market at Piazza Vittorio, the area has fast become a multiethnic stomping ground, with a vast choice of Chinese, Indian, African, and Middle Eastern restaurants. The now world-famous Orchestra di Piazza Vittorio, made up of 16 musicians from North Africa, South America, the Caribbean, Eastern Europe, and Italy, got its start in this ramshackle district just steps away from Rome's Termini station and now performs at festivals around the world. It's worth noting, too, that Rome, the stronghold of Roman Catholicism is also home to Europe's largest Islamic mosque. Near the elegant Parioli district, north of the city, it opened its doors in 1995 and welcomes visitors of all faiths.

A new metro line

Romans are anxiously awaiting the completion of the new Metro C subway line, which will cut through the city center at Piazza Venezia and link with both the A and the B lines at Ottaviano for St. Peter's and the Colosseum, respectively. Expected to considerably ease

WHAT ROMANS ARE TALKING ABOUT

Over morning cappuccinos Romans love to talk about traffic, whether it's the potholes that never seem to be repaired, or the fact that the roads around the Colosseum are now closed to traffic. Carpooling is also up for debate. A new scheme to encourage ridesharing puts car owners and potential passengers in touch with each other, online and through smartphones and tablets.

The city is also abuzz with talk about 2013's Oscar-winning film *The Great Beauty*. Italy's last award was for 1997's *Life Is Beautiful* and Romans are hopeful that Cinecittà studios—now virtually a museum—will start churning out masterpieces like in Fellini's day. Stay tuned.

on-surface traffic congestion, the new line progresses slowly because every time a shaft is sunk in Roman ground, some important archaeological site comes to light and all work halts while it is investigated. The planned station at Piazza Torre Argentina, in fact, had to be canceled due to the wealth of material uncovered. Rome also has a new bridge. The grandiose new "Ponte della Musica" bridge by Tiber River has now "bridged the gap" between the worlds of sports and music and arts: it connects the Foro Italico area (home to Rome's stunning Stadio Olimpico and Stadio dei Marmi) with the Flaminio district (where the Parco della Musica and the MAXXI museum are located). Designed by British star-engineer Buro Happold, the eco-friendly ponte can be used by pedestrians, cyclists, and electric buses.

New rails

Italo, Italy's first private railway, now gives rail travelers an alternative to the state-run Trenitalia. Italo leaves from the newly restructured Tiburtino station (not from Termini) and connects most of Italy's major cities. Its technological gem is the high-speed Frecciarossa 1000 (Red Arrow 1000), which can reach a top speed of 225 mph. For shorter journeys, you'll have to settle for the regional rail network where, alas, things haven't moved forward much in decades. In compensation, fares are cheap.

Politics

Romans love to talk about politics, especially national politics and it should be interesting to see how the Italians embrace their new young prime minister, Matteo Renzi. When he was sworn in, in February 2014, he was just 39 years old (and previously the mayor of Florence). His center-left politics should be the talk of the town in coming years.

Also in the news these days is the avant-garde (some would say bizarre) new conference center called La Nuvola (the Cloud), by architect Massimiliano Fuksas. The plan is that it will "float" like a plastic cloud in a steel cage. Construction on the project, however, has been postponed several times.

Romans know how to live it up, and the nightlife scene continues to expand. The latest "It" neighborhood is San Lorenzo, near the Termini train station. Rome's "Left Bank" district is filled with students and a young bohemian crowd, thanks to its close proximity to La Sapienza University. Pigneto, a bit farther from the train station, is the latest student hangout.

WHAT'S WHERE

The following numbers refer to chapters in the book.

3 Ancient Rome. No other archaeological park in the world has so compact a nucleus of fabled sights.

4 The Vatican. A separate state, the residence of the Pope draws millions to St. Peter's Basilica and the Vatican Museums.

5 Piazza Navona, Campo de' Fiori, and the Jewish Ghetto. The Piazza Navona and Campo de' Fiori are busy meeting points in central Rome, surrounded by restaurants, cafés, and shops. The Pantheon is nearby, too. The Jewish Ghetto is the historic center of Jewish life in Rome and is still home to many Jewish restaurants.

6 Piazza di Spagna. The Spanish Steps are iconic, and the area nearby is wonderful for strolling chic fashion boutiques. The Trevi Fountain is a short walk away.

7 Repubblica and Quirinale. These areas bustle with local business but are also home to several worthwhile churches and sights, including the Bernini's Baroque Sant'Andrea al Quirinale. The Palazzo del Quirinale, home to Italy's president, crowns the Quirinal hill, which is Rome's tallest.

8 Villa Borghese, Piazza del Popolo, and Flaminio. The Villa Borghese, Rome's vast "Central Park" is home to dazzling museums, from the 17th-century Galleria Borghese to the National Gallery of Modern Art. The nearby Piazza del Popolo is prime people-watching territory, and convenient for seeing works by Caravaggio and Raphael in Santa Maria del Popolo. Flaminio is farther north.

9 Trastevere. Rome's "Greenwich Village" attracts locals and visitors for its restaurants and wine bars. Janiculum Hill offers an incomparable view of Rome.

10 Aventino and Testaccio. These neighborhoods are off the usual tourist track but have all the vibrancy of true Rome. Aventino is a posh residential area; Testaccio is more working class and has a happening nightlife.

11 Monti, Esquilino, Celio, San Lorenzo, San Giovanni, and the Appian Way. Near Termini station, these are some of Rome's least touristy and best-loved neighborhoods, with plenty of ancient sights and spectacular churches, as well as Monti's artisanal shops, trattorias, and high-end boutiques. The Via Appia Antica leads past the landmark church of Domine Quo Vadis to the catacombs.

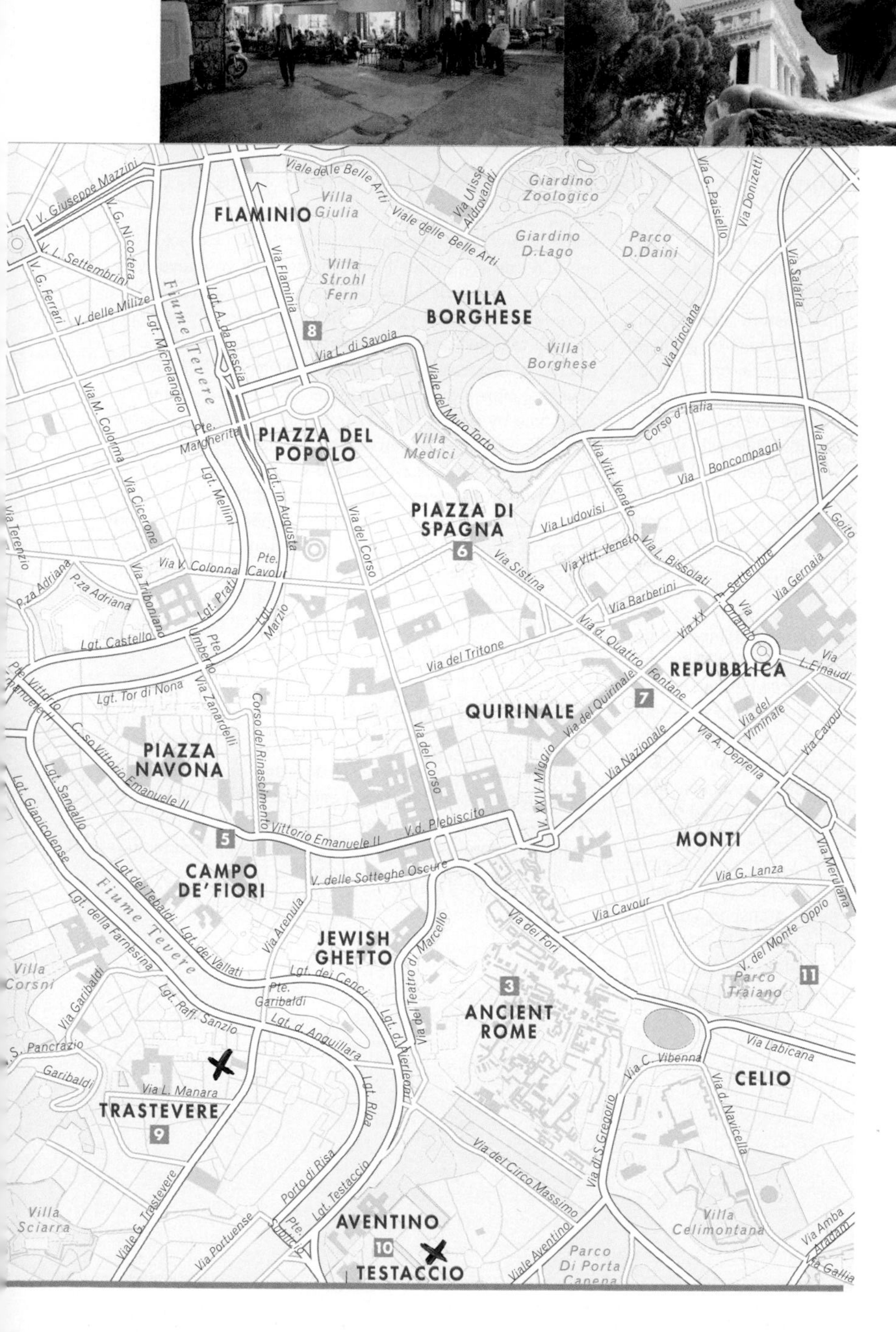
FLAMINIO
VILLA BORGHESE
PIAZZA DEL POPOLO
PIAZZA DI SPAGNA
REPUBBLICA
QUIRINALE
PIAZZA NAVONA
MONTI
CAMPO DE' FIORI
JEWISH GHETTO
ANCIENT ROME
CELIO
TRASTEVERE
AVENTINO
TESTACCIO
8
6
7
5
3
11
9
10
Giardino Zoologico
Giardino D.Lago
Parco D.Daini
Villa Giulia
Villa Strohl Fern
Villa Borghese
Villa Medici
Fiume Tevere
Villa Corsni
Parco Traiano
Villa Sciarra
Villa Celimontana
Parco Di Porta Capena
Viale delle Belle Arti
Via Ulisse Aldrovandi
Via G. Paisiello
Via Donizetti
Via Salaria
V. Giuseppe Mazzini
V. G. Nicotera
V. L. Settembrini
V. G. Ferrari
V. delle Milizie
Lgt. Michelangelo
Lgt. A. da Brescia
Via Flaminia
Via L. di Savoia
Viale del Muro Torto
Via Pinciana
Corso d'Italia
Via Piave
Via Boncompagni
Via Vitt. Veneto
Via Ludovisi
V. Goito
Via M. Colonna
Pte. Margherita
Lgt. Mellini
Lgt. in Augusta
Via del Corso
Via Cicerone
Via Terenzio
Via V. Colonna
Pte. Cavour
Via Sistina
Via L. Bissolati
Via XX Settembre
Via Gernaia
P.za Adriana
Via Triboniano
Lgt. Prati
Lgt. Marzio
Via Barberini
Via Orlando
Lgt. Castello
Pte. Umberto
Via del Tritone
Via d. Quattro Fontane
Via L. Einaudi
Pte. Vittorio Emanuele II
Lgt. Tor di Nona
Via Zanardelli
Corso del Rinascimento
Via del Quirinale
Via del Viminale
Via Cavour
Via Nazionale
Via A. Depretis
C.so Vittorio Emanuele II
Via XXIV Maggio
Lgt. Gianicolense
Lgt. Sangallo
Vittorio Emanuele II
V.d. Plebiscito
Via Merulana
Lgt. dei Tebaldi
V. delle Botteghe Oscure
Via G. Lanza
Lgt. della Farnesina
Via Arenula
Via dei Fori
V. del Monte Oppio
Lgt. dei Vallati
Lgt. dei Cenci
Via del Teatro di Marcello
Via Garibaldi
Lgt. Raff. Sanzio
Pte. Garibaldi
Lgt. d. Anguillara
Lgt. d. Pierleoni
Via Labicana
S. Pancrazio
Garibaldi
Via L. Manara
Lgt. Ripa
Via C. Vibenna
Via di S. Gregorio
Via d. Navicella
Via del Circo Massimo
Porto di Risa
Lgt. Testaccio
Viale G. Trastevere
Via Portuense
Pte. Sublicio
Viale Aventino
Via Amba Aradam
Via Gallia

ROME PLANNER

Getting Around

Fortunately for tourists, many of Rome's main attractions are concentrated in the *centro storico* (historic center) and can be covered on foot. In addition, Rome has a good network of public transport, both above and below ground. The Metro A line will take you to Termini station, the Trevi Fountain (Barberini stop), the Spanish Steps (Spagna stop), St. Peter's (Ottaviano), and the Vatican Museums (Cipro), to name a few.

Single tickets (BIT) for the bus and metro cost €1.50 and must be purchased before boarding. They are available at Termini station, from automatic ticket machines in metro stations, and most newsstands. These tickets can be used on all city buses and trams for 100 minutes or for a single metro ride. A day pass (BIG) covering all public transport costs €6, while a weekly ticket (CIS) is €24. Children under 10 travel free on all public transport.

Making the Most of Your Time

Rome wasn't built in a day, so you shouldn't expect to see it in one either. But if that's all the time you have, you can get a taste that will whet your appetite for a future, more leisurely trip. If you're a first-time visitor, the Vatican and the remains of ancient Rome are must-sees. Both require at least half a day; a good strategy is to devote your first morning to one and your second to the other. Save time by purchasing "skip the line" passes, available for St. Peter's, the Vatican Museums, and the Colosseum. These cost €24.90, €27.50, and €19,90, respectively, if purchased from street booths, and less if you buy online. Leave the afternoons for exploring the neighborhoods that comprise Baroque Rome and the shopping district around the Spanish Steps and Via Condotti. Among the sights, Galleria Borghese and the church of San Clemente are particularly worthwhile, and Trastevere and the Ghetto make for great roaming.

Discounts and Deals

In addition to the one-day, three-day, and seven-day public transport passes, a three-day Roma Pass (€34 🌐 *www.romapass.it*) covers unlimited use of buses, trams, and the Metro, plus free admission to two museums or archaeological sites of your choice and discounted entrance to others.

Hop-On, Hop-Off Bus

Rome has its own "hop-on, hop-off" sightseeing buses. The Trambus Open Roma 110 bus leaves every 15 minutes daily 8:30–7:30 from Piazza dei Cinquecento (at the main Termini station), with a two-hour loop including the Colosseum, Piazza Navona, St. Peter's, and the Trevi Fountain. One-day tickets are €15, two-day tickets are €20; children under 10 ride free. A two-day family ticket good for two adults and two children ages 10–17 costs €50. The Archeobus (€12, family pass €40) runs March–November on Fridays, Saturdays, and Sundays. It departs every 20 minutes from the Piazza dei Cinquecento and heads out to the Via Appia Antica, the Colosseum, and the catacombs. Tickets for both can also be purchased ahead of time online (🌐 *www.trambusopen.com*).

Roman Hours

On Sunday, Rome virtually shuts down on its official day of rest. Meanwhile, state museums and exhibition halls, plus many restaurants are closed Monday. Daily food shop hours generally run from 10 to 1, then 4 until 7:30 or 8, but other stores in the center usually observe continuous opening hours. Pharmacies tend to close for the lunch break and keep night hours (*ora rio notturno)* in rotation. As for churches, most open at 8 or 9 in the morning, close from noon to 3 or 4, then reopen until 6:30 or 7. St. Peter's, however, has continuous hours from 7 to 7 (until 6 in the fall and winter), and the Vatican Museums are open on Monday but closed Sunday (except for the last one of the month).

When to Go

Spring and fall are the best times to visit, with mild temperatures and many sunny days. Summers are often sweltering. In July and August, come if you like, but learn to do as the Romans do—get up and out early, seek refuge from the afternoon heat, resume activities in early evening, and stay up late to enjoy the nighttime breeze.

Come August, many shops and restaurants close as locals head out for vacation. Remember that air-conditioning is still a relatively rare phenomenon in this city. Roman winters are relatively mild, with persistent rainy spells.

Tourist Information

The Department of Tourism in Rome, called Roma Capitale, launched a new single phone number that tourists can call for cultural happenings and events, ticket sales, and other visitor information (☎ *06/0608* 🌐 *www.turismoroma.it*). Roma Capitale also staffs green information kiosks (with multilingual personnel) near important sights as well as at Termini station and Leonardo da Vinci Airport. These kiosks, called Tourist Information Sites (Punti Informativi Turistici, or PIT), can be found at:

Castel S. Angelo, Lungotevere Vaticano; 9:30–7.

Cinque Lune, Piazza delle Cinque Lune (Piazza Navona); 9:30–7.

Fiumicino, Aeroporto Leonardo Da Vinci–Arrivi Internazionali Terminal C; 9–7:30.

Minghetti, Via Marco Minghetti (corner of Via del Corso); 9:30–7.

Nazionale, Via Nazionale (Palazzo delle Esposizioni); 9:30–7.

Santa Maria Maggiore, at Via dell'Olmata; 9:30–7.

Termini, Stazione Termini, at Via Giovanni Giolitti 34; 8–8.

Trastevere, on Piazza Sidney Sonnino; 9:30–7.

ROME TOP ATTRACTIONS

Roman Forum

(A) This fabled labyrinth of ruins variously served as a political playground, a commerce mart, and a place where justice was dispensed during the days of the emperors (500 BC to AD 400). Today, the Forum is a silent ruin—*sic transit gloria mundi* (so passes away the glory of the world).

The Colosseum

(B) Legend has it that as long as the Colosseum stands, Rome will stand; and when Rome falls, so will the world. One of the Seven Wonders of the World, the mammoth amphitheater was begun by Emperor Vespasian and inaugurated by Titus in the year 80.

The Pantheon

(C) Constructed to honor all pagan gods, this best-preserved temple of ancient Rome was rebuilt in the 2nd century AD by Emperor Hadrian and has survived intact because it was consecrated as a Christian church. Its dome is still considered an architectural marvel.

Piazza Navona

(D) You couldn't concoct a more Roman street scene: crowded café tables at street level, wrought-iron balconies above, and, at the center of this urban "living room," Bernini's spectacular Fountain of the Four Rivers and Borromini's super-theatrical Sant'Agnese.

Vatican City

Though its population numbers only in the few hundreds, the Vatican—home base for the Catholic Church and the papacy—makes up for them with the millions who visit each year.

St. Peter's Basilica

(E) Every year, millions of pilgrims flock to the world's most important Catholic church to marvel at Michelangelo's cupola, the *Pietà,* and Bernini's papal altar.

The Spanish Steps

(F) Byron, Shelley, and Keats all drew inspiration from this magnificent *scalinata,* constructed in 1723. Connecting the ritzy shops at the bottom with the ritzy hotels at the top, this is one of Rome's liveliest spots, with tourists and locals congregating on the steps and around the fountain at their base. The steps face west, so sunsets offer great photo ops.

Trastevere

(G) Located just across the Tiber River, this time-stained, charming villagelike neighborhood is a maze of jumbled alleyways, traditional Roman trattorias, cobblestone streets, and medieval houses, though today the happening area is often described as Rome's Brooklyn. The area also has one of the oldest churches in Rome—Santa Maria in Trastevere.

Trevi Fountain

(H) One of the few fountains in Rome that's actually more absorbing than the people crowding around it, the Fontana di Trevi was designed by Nicola Salvi in 1732—and immortalized in *La Dolce Vita.* This granddaddy of all fountains may be your ticket back to Rome—that is, if you throw a coin into it.

Galleria Borghese

(I) Only the best could satisfy the aesthetic taste of Cardinal Scipione Borghese, whose holdings evoke the essence of Baroque Rome. Spectacularly frescoed ceilings and multihue marble walls frame great Bernini sculptures and paintings by Titian and Raphael.

MUSEUM OVERVIEW

Major Museums

At the top of every first-time visitor's priority list, the **Vatican Museums** include the Borgia papal apartments and the frescoed Raphael Rooms; legendary works by Leonardo, Raphael, and Caravaggio; and of course Michelangelo's sublime *Last Judgment* and Sistine ceiling. Rome's second most popular museum is the Galleria Borghese, set in the vast Villa Borghese Park. The Gallery has some of Bernini's most famous sculpture groups, as well as works by Raphael and Titian. The Palazzo dei Conservatori has some of the classical world's most famous bronze sculptures, while the Museo Nazionale Etrusco di Villa Giulia contains the most important collection of Etruscan art and antiquities in Italy.

Museums of Antiquities

The two **Musei Capitolini** (the Palazzo dei Conservatori is one) stand atop the Capitoline Hill, where Michelangelo set the equestrian statue of Marcus Aurelius in the square he had designed. The City of Rome has gathered so much stuff over the centuries that it needs four separate museums to house it all: **Palazzo Altemps, Palazzo Massimo alle Terme, Terme di Diocleziano,** and **Crypta Balbi,** collectively known as the **Musei Nazionale Romano.** The **Museo dei Fori Imperiali,** inside the ruins of Trajan's Market, offers a privileged view of Trajan's Column. Crowning the Palatine hill, the **Museo Palatino** incorporates the rooms of the surprisingly humble House of Augustus. For something unusual, head for the **Centrale Montemartini,** where 400 ancient Roman statues stand among the machinery of a historic electric power station.

Great Art Collections

Palazzo Barberini houses Rafael's La Fornarina, the baker's daughter who was the artist's mistress and perhaps his secret wife. The same lovely girl modeled for his frescos in **Villa Farnesina,** commissioned by millionaire banker Agostino Chigi. Palazzo Corsini belonged to Pope Clement XII's nephew, who put together a huge collection of Old Masters. The magnificent 17th-century **Palazzo Doria-Pamphilj,** the only palace-museum still owned by the original family, has one of the most important collections of Old Masters in Rome. Enjoy the optical illusion in **Palazzo Spada,** where Borromini created a trick trompe l'oeil gallery. **Villa Torlonia** has three separate museums, including a collection of rare Art Nouveau stained glass, while **Palazzo Venezia** houses medieval and renaissance artifacts in bronze, enamel, marble, and ceramic.

Modern and Contemporary Art Galleries

Rome's top contemporary art museum is the **MAXXI,** followed by the **Galleria d'Arte Moderna,** which has a large collection of 19th- and 20th-century art. American art dealer Larry Gagosian's **Gagosian Gallery** has a branch in Rome.

House Museums

The **Museo Atelier Canova Tadolini** is crammed with plaster casts and preparatory models of his work. In the town house of Napoléon's niece, the **Napoleonic Museum** has a charming collection of Empire-style memorabilia. **Museo Mario Praz** is stuffed with the acquisitions of the art critic and collector. The **Keats-Shelley House** is a poignant insight into the last months of the life of the English Romantic poet John Keats.

TOP CHURCHES IN ROME

There are many, many churches in Rome and, in addition to being places of worship, many of them double as museums, full of amazing works of art and objects of high craftsmanship.

The Tiber Trail

St. Peter's Basilica, the world's most important Catholic church and a treasure house of art, tops most visitors' lists, with Michelangelo's *Pietà* and Bernini's papal altar. One of Rome's oldest churches, **Santa Maria in Trastevere,** is decorated with glittering mosaics. Stick your hand in the Bocca della Verità at the 12th-century Romanesque church of **Santa Maria in Cosmedin.**

Baroque Splendor

Many of Rome's most interesting churches cluster in the Baroque center near the Pantheon and Piazza Navona, such as Borromini's **Sant'Agnese in Agone**; the Jesuit church **Sant'Ignazio,** with its stunning trompe d'oeil dome; and Rome's only Gothic church, **Santa Maria sopra Minerva,** with Michelangelo's *Risen Christ*.

Layers of History

San Giovanni in Laterano, first built by Constantine, is the Cathedral Church of Rome and the official seat of the pope. The present 12th-century church of **San Clemente** is built over another 4th-century church, underneath which stands a well-preserved pagan Temple to Mithras. **Santa Maria del Popolo** contains works by Raphael, Carracci, Caravaggio, and Bernini. **Santa Maria in Aracoeli** occupies the spot where the Temple of Juno crowned the summit of the Capitoline Hill.

Other Churches

Santa Maria della Vittoria holds Bernini's masterpiece, The Ecstasy of Saint Teresa. Michelangelo's colossal *Moses* is housed in **San Pietro** in Vincoli. Caravaggio's celebrated frescoes on the life of St. Matthew are in **San Luigi dei Francesi.** The 4th-century **Santa Maria Maggiore** is one of the four great basilicas of Rome.

ROME LIKE A LOCAL

"When in Rome, do as the Romans do." The phrase may be clichéd, but it's advice worth taking: Romans know how to live life to the fullest, indulging in the simplest pleasures and doing so with style. Put yourself in their shoes (Fendi, preferably) and be a Roman for a day.

Il Mercato

If you're looking to rub shoulders with real Romans, there's no better place to do it than at the local open-air food market, where vendors turn the practice of selling the region's freshest produce into a grand theatrical performance. The most popular market is the Campo de' Fiori, Rome's oldest food market. Nowadays, you'll find craft and clothing stands among the food stalls to add to the local color, as well as pricey gastronomic specialties.

La Piazza

For Italians young and old, *la piazza* serves as a meeting place—for making dinner plans, people-watching, and catching up with friends. The Piazza di Spagna is a favored spot for Italian boys looking to meet American girls. The Campo de' Fiori is a bustling marketplace by day; by night, the piazza turns into a popular hangout for Romans and foreigners lured by its pubs, cheap eateries, and street cafés. The Piazza Navona and the Piazza del Rotonda, in front of the Pantheon, are also excellent hangouts.

L'Aperitivo

The Milanese invented it, but the Romans perfected *l'aperitivo*. Similar to "happy hour" (but without the drink specials), this is a time to meet up with friends and colleagues for drinks after work or on weekends. Hours are usually 7–9 pm. The aperitif experience can sometimes be an economic alternative to dinner, as it often includes an all-you-can-eat appetizer buffet of finger foods, sandwiches, and pasta salads.

Il Caffè

If there's something Romans certainly can't live without, it's *il caffè* (espresso), and there is no shortage of coffee bars to satisfy the craving. Real Italian espresso is a thimble-full of aromatic black liquid, prepared by a barista—you can have it *stretto* (concentrated), *doppio* (double), *all'americano* (water added), *macchiato* (with a drop of milk foam), *marocchino* (with a drop of cream and a sprinkling of cocoa), or even sinfully *corretto* (with a drop of grappa). A cappuccino is espresso with steamed milk and foam. In summer, order a *caffè shakerato* (freshly made espresso shaken briskly with sugar and ice, to form a froth when poured) or a *caffè freddo* (iced espresso).

Il Gelato

Italian gelato is tastier and lighter than American ice cream and traditionally made with only the freshest ingredients. Most places allow you up to three flavors (even on a small cone) and portions are usually quite generous. Typical flavors are *crema* (plain cream), *nocciola* (hazelnut), pistachio, chocolate, and a vast choice of fruit flavors. Or hunt down the latest and greatest flavors, such as *cioccolato con peperoncino* (chocolate with chilies).

La Passeggiata

A favorite Roman pastime is *la passeggiata* (literally, the promenade). Especially on weekends in the late afternoon and early evening, couples, families, and packs of teenagers stroll up and down Rome's main streets and piazzas. It's a ritual of exchanged news and gossip, window-shopping, flirting, and gelato eating that adds up to a uniquely Italian experience. A top promenade is the Via del Corso.

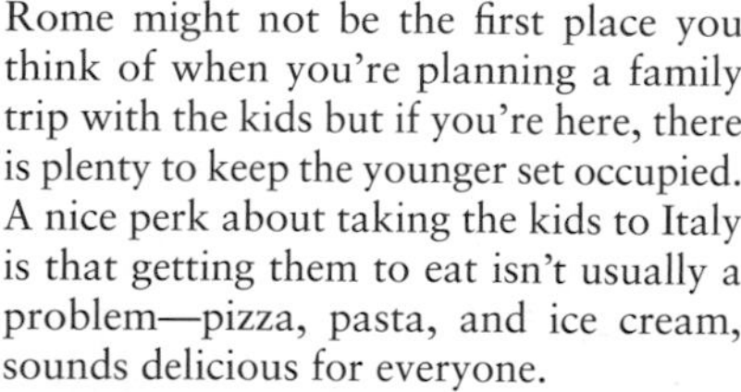

ROME WITH KIDS

Rome might not be the first place you think of when you're planning a family trip with the kids but if you're here, there is plenty to keep the younger set occupied. A nice perk about taking the kids to Italy is that getting them to eat isn't usually a problem—pizza, pasta, and ice cream, sounds delicious for everyone.

Archaeology

If your kids are into archaeology or gladiators, traipsing the ruins of ancient Rome can provide hours of entertainment. What child can resist climbing the giant steps of the **Colosseum**? Taking a photo with one of those kitschy gladiators in front of the Colosseum will win some smiles and give your child a great souvenir to show off at home. Some of these Russell Crow lookalikes have helmets and cloaks for tourists to try on and a sword to brandish into the bargain. Remember to bargain the "photo fee" beforehand. It shouldn't be more than €5.

Get Into the Movies

At **Cinecittà** movie studios, you can stroll down the 19th-century Broadway set made for Martin Scorsese's *Gangs of New York* and explore the life-size plasterboard Roman Forum.

Explore the Parks

Take little ones to see the Teatrino Pulcinello's open-air **puppet show** weekdays on the Janiculum hill or the San Carlino puppet theater weekends on the Pincio Terrace in Villa **Borghese Park.** The park is also home to other kid-orientated attractions such as the **Biopark** (zoo), with over 1,000 animals in peaceful landscaped surroundings. Rent a bike (on the Pincio at Viale dell'Orologio or at Piazzale M. Cervantes near the zoo) and explore the vast Borghese estate.

Shivers Down the Spine

The catacombs are spooky enough to wipe the bored look off your teenager's face. The best is the **Catacombe di San Callisto** on the Via Appia Antica. Kids can't fail to be impressed by the labyrinth of dark corridors and grisly tales of Christian martyrs. The **Capuchin Crypt** under Santa Maria della Concezione contains the skulls and bones of 3,700 friars arranged all over the walls and ceiling in fanciful patterns. Take the kids to the Bocca della Verità (Mouth of Truth) at **Santa Maria in Cosmedin,** but warn them that it bites off liars' hands!

I Nasoni

The public water fountains in Rome are free (and safe) to drink from . . . if you can figure out how to do it without getting wet! The cast iron fountains' nose-shaped spouts point downward, making getting a simple drink a fun challenge.

GREAT ITINERARIES

Rome is jam-packed with things to do and see. These are some of our suggested itineraries. ⇨ *For more ideas, see the Rome's Best Walks chapter.* Make sure to leave yourself time to just wander and get the feel of the city as well.

Rome 101

Rome wasn't built in a day, but if that's all you have to see it, take a deep breath, strap on some stylish comfy sneakers, and grab a cappuccino to help you get an early start. Get ready for a spectacular sunrise-to-sunset spree of the Ancient City.

Begin by exploring Rome's most beautiful neighborhood, Vecchia Roma (Old Rome), the area around Piazza Navona. Start out on Via del Corso, the big avenue that runs into Piazza Venezia, the traffic hub of the historic center.

A block apart are two opulently over-the-top monuments that show off Rome at its Baroque best: the church of Sant'Ignazio and the princely Palazzo Doria Pamphilj, aglitter with great Old Master paintings. Mid-morning, head west a few blocks to find the granddaddy of monuments, the fabled Pantheon, still looking like Emperor Hadrian might arrive shortly. A few blocks north is San Luigi dei Francesi, home to the greatest Caravaggio paintings in the world.

Just before lunch, saunter a block or so westward into beyond-beautiful Piazza Navona, studded with Bernini fountains. Then take Via Cucagna (at the piazza's south end) and continue several blocks toward Campo de' Fiori's open-air food market (for some lunch-on-the-run fixings). A great place to stop for a cheap and quick panino or a slice of pizza is Forno Campo de' Fiori (✉ *Campo de' Fiori* 22).

Two more blocks toward the Tiber brings you to one of the most romantic streets of Rome, Via Giulia, laid out by Pope Julius II in the early 16th century. Walk past 10 blocks of Renaissance palazzos and ivy-draped antiques shops to take a bus (from the stop near the Tiber) over to the Vatican.

Gape at St. Peter's Basilica, then hit the treasure-filled Vatican Museums (Sistine Chapel) in the early afternoon—during lunch, the crowds empty out! Wander for about two hours and then head for the Ottaviano stop near the museum and Metro your way to the Colosseo stop.

Climb up into the Colosseum and picture it full of screaming toga-clad citizens enjoying the spectacle of gladiators in mortal combat. Follow Via dei Fori Imperiali to the entrance of the Roman Forum. Photograph yourself giving a "Friends, Romans, Countrymen" oration (complete with upraised hand) on one of the marble fragments. At sunset, the Forum closes but the floodlights come on.

March down the forum's Via Sacra—people walked here centuries before Christ—and back out into Via dei Fori Imperiali where you will head around "the wedding cake," the looming Vittorio Emanuele Monument (Il Vittoriano), to the Campidoglio. Here, on the Capitoline Hill, tour the great ancient Roman art treasures of the Musei Capitolini (which is open most nights until 8), and snap the view from the terrace over the spotlit Forum.

After dinner, hail a cab—or take a long passeggiata walk down *La Dolce Vita* memory lane—to the Trevi Fountain, a gorgeous sight at night. Needless to say, toss a coin in to ensure your return trip back to Rome.

Temples Through Time: Religious Rome

Making a trip to Rome and not going to see the Vatican Museums or St. Peter's Basilica is almost like breaking one of the Ten Commandments. If you head out early enough (yes, 7 am), you might get a jump on the line for the Vatican Museums, where one of the world's grandest and most comprehensive collections of artwork is stored. Even better, book tickets online at 🌐 *bigliettteriamusei.vatican.va* beforehand, and you get to skip the line, period (tickets cost slightly more—€20 instead of €16—but it saves you headaches). Once you've conquered both, take the Metro from Ottaviano to Piazza del Popolo (Metro stop: Flaminio), where Santa Maria del Popolo is not to be missed for its famous chapels decorated by Raphael and Caravaggio.

Head south along the Corso for about 10 blocks toward Sant'Ignazio, an eye-popping example of Baroque Rome, with its amazing "Oh, I can't believe my eyes" optical illusion of a dome. Take Via Sant'Ignazio to Via Piè di Marmo, which will lead you to Piazza della Minerva, where Bernini's elephant obelisk monument lies in wait. Take in the adjacent Gothic-style Santa Maria sopra Minerva, best known for Michelangelo's *Risen Christ*.

Then make your way south to Corso Vittorio Emanuele and the bus piazza at Largo Argentina where you'll take Tram No. 8 to picturesque Trastevere, one of Rome's quaintest quarters. Make your way through a series of winding cobblestoned alleyways and piazzas toward the famed Piazza Santa Maria in Trastevere, where one of Rome's oldest churches—Santa Maria in Trastevere—stands. Dedicated to the Virgin Mary, the church has a fine display of glimmering gilded mosaics covering what is perhaps Rome's most spectacular nave.

Retail Therapy: Shop-'Til-You-Drop Rome

For serious shoppers, there's no better place to treat yourself to some retail therapy than the network of elegant streets at the Spanish Steps. If money is no question, Rome's Via dei Condotti (Metro A stop: Spagna) is *paradiso*. VIPs can continue their shopping spree down streets Via del Babuino for fabled antique furniture and fine jewelry, and Via Frattina for exclusive boutiques. Even if you're penny-pinching, window-shopping can be just as fun as you make your way down to the more affordable Via del Corso. Department-store-style shopping can be done in the Galleria Alberto Sordi halfway along the Corso, or at COIN in Termini station.

If vintage is your thing, head toward Piazza Navona and down Via del Governo Vecchio, where an assortment of vintage consignment shops features high-end clothing, handbags, and accessories.

Now that you've blown your shopping budget, it's time for real bargain-shopping Roman style. For rock-bottom bargains try the city's open air and flea markets. Rome's largest and most famous are markets on Via Sannio in San Giovanni (Monday–Saturday only) and the Porta Portese market (Sunday only) in Trastevere.

The market on Via Sannio specializes in new and used clothing, shoes, and accessories. The Porta Portese market sells everything but the kitchen sink: clothes, souvenirs, antiques, housewares, and knickknacks galore.

FREE AND ALMOST FREE

Rome may be on the fast track to becoming one of the most expensive cities in Europe; however, in compensation, there is a slew of free and inexpensive things to do in the *Città Eterna* that won't break the bank. For a quick look at a range of low-cost activities, check out the Comune di Roma's tourism website (🌐 *www.turismoroma.it*).

Art and Archaeological Sites

Where other than Roman churches can you admire so many works by such masters as Caravaggio, Tintoretto, Michelangelo, and Raphael for free? It doesn't cost anything to take in the celebrated Roman fountains or enter the Pantheon to gaze at the famous dome and pay homage at Raphael's tomb. During the *Settimana della Cultura*, or Cultural Week (usually held in spring), many of the major archaeological sites and museums in and around Rome waive their entrance fees. Check out 🌐 *www.beniculturali.it* for exact dates and listings. In autumn, Rome holds White Nights when many museums and sites are open in the evenings free of charge. The Vatican Museums are free on the last Sunday of every month (only open, however, until 12:30, and there is usually a huge line up).

Music and Performances

Rome's summer season (L'Estate Romana) offers a vast program of free or low-cost events June to mid-September, including open-air concerts ranging from pop to classical. Rome's parks, the Tiber Island, and many major piazzas become impromptu venues for street artists, cinema under the stars, food festivals, and musical and theatrical performances, many of which are free. Throughout the year, many of Rome's historic churches host free recitals and chamber music concerts that are not widely advertised. Look out for flyers in hotels, on café counters, or stuck to lampposts. Check the website 🌐 *www.turismoroma.it* or phone ☎ *06/0608* for information. *Wanted in Rome* magazine (online and in print) is a good source of information about events in English.

Unofficial Sightseeing

For a cheap version of the Hop-Off, Hop-On tour, board the N3 tram that trundles through Trastevere and the Aventine, past the Colosseum, San Giovanni, and the museums of the Belle Arti in the Villa Borghese park. You get 100 minutes of travel for a mere €1.50 bus ticket. And don't forget people-watching. For the price of an espresso, you can sit for hours at a piazza café. Entertainment is guaranteed.

ROMANTIC ROME

Whether you're looking for love or hoping to rekindle the romance, there's no better place to do so than the Eternal City. Ah yes, it certainly seems that love lurks behind every street corner, park bench, and monument. And if you don't find the abundance of public displays of affection off-putting, you'll be sure to find scores of places to steal both that first and ultimo *bacio* (kiss).

Set the Mood

If you really want to impress that special him or her, book a couple of seats at Rome's plush opera house where you can hold hands and wax sentimental over the sad fate of Violetta or Mimi. In summer, opera under the stars in the ruins of the Baths of Caracalla is dramatic and lovely. Don't forget a glass of Italian bubbly from the bar during the interval.

Capture the Fleeting Moment

Visit the Non-Catholic Cemetery at the Piramide, final resting place of a number of noted artists, most famously English poets. Stroll in this lovely peaceful garden under the cypresses and umbrella pines and pause at the grave of the romantic poet John Keats, buried with the letters from his only love—"Bright Star" Fanny Brawne—pressed to his heart. What better incentive to seize the fleeting moment?

Count the Stars at the Zodiaco

Make a nighttime trip up Monte Mario to the Zodiaco terrace, where the lights of Rome are spread out below like a carpet of stars. You won't be alone as this is a favorite spot for young Italian couples who arrive in droves on their scooters, but you may well be the only foreigner.

Throw Your Coin in . . . Another Fountain

If you don't feel like elbowing your way through the crowds at the Trevi Fountain, take your beloved for a magical stroll through Trastevere and up to the lesser-known Acqua Paola Fountain on the top of Janiculum Hill. Admire the angels, monsters, and dragons adorning the monumental facade, exquisitely floodlit at night, and toss your coins together into the wide water-filled basin.

Where to Take the Plunge

You've decided to make it official. Where better to exchange your vows than in the Garden of the Oranges on the Aventine hill? This lovely little park on a terrace high above the Tiber has a view over the rooftops and monuments of Rome. And speaking of churches, consider the beautiful 5th-century church of Santa Sabina right next door if you have a Roman wedding in mind. But if you prefer a nonreligious ceremony, no problem: Rome has a charming deconsecrated church opposite the Baths of Caracalla especially for civil weddings.

ITALIAN ART 101

Gianlorenzo Bernini (1598–1680) ushered in the Italian Baroque; you'll see his work, especially sculpture but also architecture, everywhere you turn, from the colonnade of St. Peter's to the stupendous Fountain of the Four Rivers in Piazza Navona. He was the first to succeed in capturing the softness of flesh in marble: see the goddess struggle desperately with the grim God of the Underworld in The Rape of Proserpina, in Galleria Borghese. His masterpiece, *The Ecstasy of Saint Teresa*, is at the church of Santa Maria della Vittoria. Many of the more conservative members of the clergy were shocked when this work was unveiled, and it is not hard to see why.

Francesco Borromini (1599–1667), a leading Baroque architect, was Bernini's eternal rival. The two started their working lives together as assistants to Carlo Maderno. When Maderno died, Borromini, who was introverted and depressive, expected to take over as chief architect of St. Peter's, but the Pope gave the job to personable, charming Bernini instead. Borromini's personal masterpiece is the Church of San Carlo alle Quattro Fontane. Borromini eventually killed himself, consumed with frustration and jealousy because Bernini's Fountain of the Four Rivers in Piazza Navona had totally overshadowed his own work on the facade of the Church of Sant'Agnese in Agone, opposite.

Caravaggio (1571–1610), known as "the Damned" because of his mutinous and dissolute character, was an innovator who changed the concept of painting, introducing the effects of chiaroscuro (light and dark) to create atmosphere and convey moods. Some of his most famous works are three masterpieces dedicated to St. Matthew, in the Church of San Luigi dei Francesi near Piazza Navona; many of his other celebrated paintings are in Galleria Borghese. Caravaggio incurred the wrath of the establishment because he portrayed the saints as ordinary people with careworn faces, dirty feet, and ragged clothing, as in *The Crucifixion of St. Peter* in the Church of Santa Maria del Popolo.

Michelangelo (1475–1564) is the uncontested giant of the Renaissance, celebrated in his lifetime and regarded with awe and reverence today. He saw himself as a sculptor but (unwillingly) turned his hand to the colossal job of frescoing the Sistine Chapel ceiling, achieving one of the world's greatest masterpieces, equaled only by his *Last Judgment*. To appreciate his genius as a sculptor, see his powerful *Moses* in the church of San Pietro in Vincoli, a total contrast to his delicate and sensitive *Pietà* in St. Peter's.

Raphael (1483–1520), a master of the High Renaissance known during his brief lifetime as the "Divine Raphael," is considered to have achieved levels of perfection seldom approached by other artists. His Madonnas are infused with spirituality and calm, his compositions are models of balance and harmony. He was 25 when he began painting the four rooms in the Vatican Palace that are now known by his name. Perhaps his most famous portrait is *La Fornarina*, featuring the baker's daughter who was his lover and perhaps his wife, on view in Palazzo Barberini.

ROME'S BEST WALKS

Baroque Rome, Trastevere, and the Roman Forum

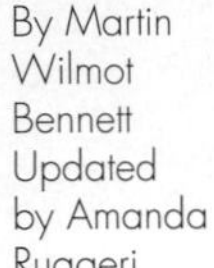

By Martin Wilmot Bennett
Updated by Amanda Ruggeri

With more masterpieces per square foot than any other city in the world, Rome presents a particular challenge for visitors: just as they are beginning to feel hopelessly smitten by the spell of the city, they realize they don't have the time—let alone the stamina—to see more than a fraction of its treasures. Rome may not have been built in a day, but neither can it be seen in one day, or even two or three. As the Italian author Silvio Negro once put it: *Roma, non basta una vita* ("Rome, a lifetime is not enough").

It can be wise to start out knowing this, and to have a focused itinerary. To provide just that, here are three strolls that introduce you to especially evocative stretches of the city: Vecchia Roma, where Rome's bravura Baroque style sets the city's tone; Trastevere—Rome's Greenwich Village—and the picturesque Tiber Island; and the Roman Forum, where the glory that was (and is) Rome is best captured.

Along the way, terra-cotta-hued palaces, Baroque squares, and time-stained ruins will present an unfolding panorama of color upon color—an endlessly varied palette that makes Rome into one of Europe's most enjoyable cities for walking. Forget about deadly earnest treks through marble miles of museum corridors and get ready to immerse yourself in some of Italy's best "street theater."

In addition, these three tours of clustered sightseeing capture quintessential Rome while allowing roamers to make minidiscoveries of their own. Use these itineraries as suggestions to keep you on track as you explore both the famous sights and those off the beaten path. Remember that people who stop for a *caffè* (coffee) get more out of these breaks than those who breathlessly try to make every second count. So be Nero-esque in your rambles and fiddle while you roam.

ENJOYING THE GILT: A STROLL THROUGH THE BAROQUE QUARTER

The most important clue to the Romans is their Baroque art—not its artistic technicalities, but its spirit. When you understand that, you'll no longer be a stranger in Rome. Flagrantly emotional, heavily expressive, and sensuously visual, the 17th-century artistic movement known as the Baroque was born in Rome, the creation of four geniuses, Gian Lorenzo Bernini, Francesco Borromini, Annibale Caracci, and Caravaggio. Ranging from the austere drama found in Caravaggio's painted altarpieces to the jewel-encrusted, gold-on-gold decoration of 17th-century Roman palace decoration, the Baroque sought to both shock and delight by upsetting the placid, "correct" rules of the Renaissance masters. By appealing to the emotions, it became a powerful weapon in the hands of the Counter-Reformation. Although this walk passes such sights as the Pantheon—ancient Rome's most perfectly preserved building—it's mainly an excursion into the 16th and 17th centuries, when Baroque art triumphed in Rome.

We wend our way through one of Rome's most beautiful districts—Vecchia Roma (Old Rome), a romantic nickname given to the areas around Piazza Navona and the Campo de' Fiori. Thick with narrow streets with curious names, airy Baroque piazzas, and picturesque courtyards, and occupying the horn of land that pushes the Tiber westward toward the Vatican, this has been an integral part of the city since ancient times. For centuries, artisans and shopkeepers toiled in the shadow of the huge palaces built to consolidate the power and prestige of the leading figures in the papal court who lived and worked here. The greatest artists flocked here to get commissions. Today, artisans still live hereabouts but their numbers are diminishing as the district becomes one of Rome's ritziest.

FROM EARTHLY TO HEAVENLY GLORY

We begin just off the main thoroughfare of Rome, the Via del Corso, about four blocks northwest of Piazza Venezia's traffic hub. Heading up the Corso, make a left turn down tiny Via Montecatini to emerge into the delightful proportions of the ocher and stone **Piazza di Sant'Ignazio.** Any lack in size of this square is made up for in theatricality. Indeed, a Rococo theater set was exactly what its architect, Filippo Raguzzini, had in mind when he designed it in 1727. The exits and entrances these days, however, are by carabinieri, not actors, the main building "backstage" being a police station. With perfectly matching concave facades, two other buildings make up "the wings." It's a rare example of the *barocchetto*—that is, the "cute" Baroque—a term that demonstrates how Italian art critics have a name for everything.

At one time the chapel of the gigantic Collegio Romano, the church of **Sant'Ignazio**—on your left—was Rome's largest Jesuit church. Honoring the order's founding saint, it is famous for its over-the-top Baroque spectacle—few churches are as gilt-encrusted, jewel-studded, or stupendously stuccoed. This is the 17th-century Counter-Reformation pulling out all the stops: religion as supreme theater.

Walk down the vast nave and position yourself on the yellow marble disc on the floor and prepare to be transported heavenward. Soaring above you, courtesy of painter-priest Fra Andrea Pozzo, is a frescoed *Allegory of the Missionary Work of the Jesuits* (1691–94). While an angel holds the Jesuit battle motto HIS (*In Hoc Signo Vinces*)—"In this sign we conquer"—just below, upward, ever upward, soars Saint Ignatius in triumph, trailed by a cast of thousands. A masterly use of perspective opens giddying vistas where clouds and humans interact until the forces of gravity seem to flounder. *Diavolerie*—"fiendish tricks"—a commentator of the time called such wonders. To rephrase a hopefully not too sacrilegious modern essay: Not until *Superman* comics does anything get close.

Looking back toward the entrance door, notice how the painted columns—continuations more or less of their real marble equivalents below—seem to rise straight into heaven. Now walk 20 yards back toward the door, and gaze again. And experience an optical earthquake: Those straight columns have tilted 60 degrees. Believe it or not, the whole towering edifice of classic arches, columns, and cornices from the windows upward is entirely flat.

Time to walk down the nave and admire the massive dome—although it is anything but. Dome, windows, the golden light, they're all illusion—all that majestic space is in reality flat as the top of a drum, mere paint masterfully applied across a round canvas 17 meters in diameter in trompe l'oeil fashion. Funds for a real dome ran out, so Pozzo created the less costly but arguably no less marvelous "flat" version here. Another disc set in the marble floor marks the spot where his deception takes maximum effect.

GOD'S LITTLE MASCOT

Head out of the church, turning left to find Via S. Ignazio, then left again to Via Pie' di Marmo, which leads into Piazza Santa Caterina di Siena and the Piazza della Minerva. Here stands Santa Maria sopra Minerva, the only major church in Rome built in Gothic style, and famous as the home of Michelangelo's *Risen Christ*. But the object of our delight is right on the piazza: the **Obelisk of Santa Maria sopra Minerva,** an astounding conceit of an obelisk astride an elephant, masterfully designed by Gian Lorenzo Bernini. The obelisk is a soaring emblem for theology and the vertiginous weight of knowledge, the beast beneath embodying that which is needed to support it—a mind that is both humble and robust, and never, thank heaven, beyond a jest, even when at its own expense.

Straight ahead is the curving, brick-bound mass of the **Pantheon,** the most complete building surviving from antiquity, and a great influence on Baroque architects. Follow Via della Minerva to Piazza della Rotonda and go to the north end of the square to get an overall view of the temple's columned portico: it once bore two Baroque bell towers of Bernini's design but, after being ridiculed for their similarity to "donkey's ears," they were demolished. Enjoy the piazza and side streets, where you will find a busy café and shopping scene.

Returning to the Piazza della Rotunda, continue northward on Via della Maddalena and proceed into Piazza della Maddelena. In the corner is the excellent Gelateria Pasqualetti. Meanwhile, in front is the Rococo facade of the church of **S. Maria Maddalena,** its curly and concave stone appearing as malleable as the ice cream that you may have just eaten,

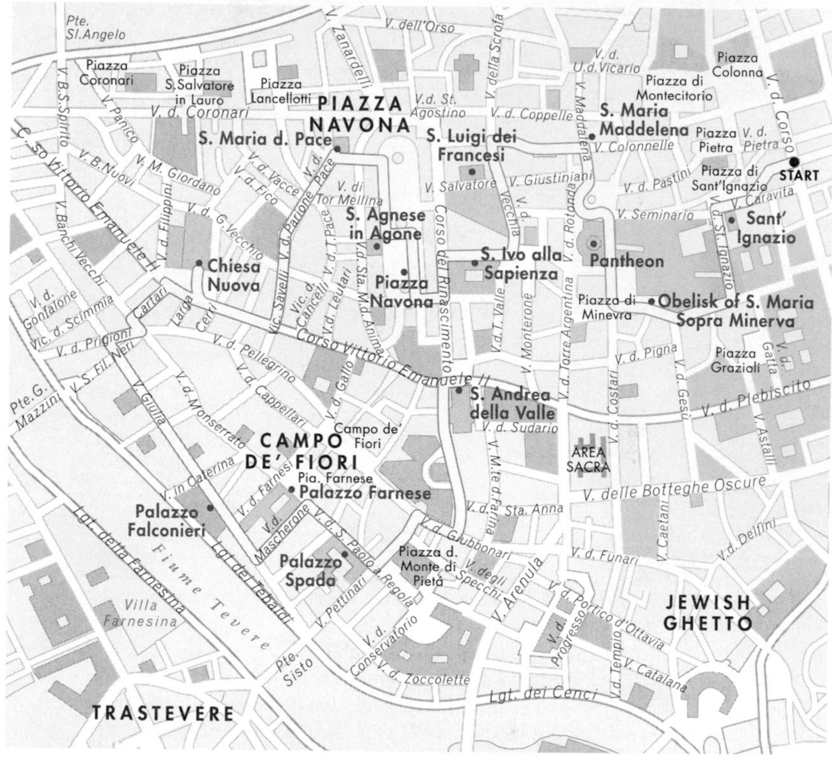

Why Go?:	Rome gave birth to the Baroque—the lavish, eye-popping style that revolutionized Europe in the 17th century—and this walk shows off Rome's Baroque at its best.
Good in the 'Hood:	Marveling at Bernini fountains, time-traveling back to the 17th century, watching the world pass by on Piazza Navona, and Rome's best cup of coffee.
Highlights:	Caravaggio paintings at San Luigi dei Francesci, Sant'Ignazio, Via Giulia, Palazzo Farnese, and Piazza Navona.
Where to Start:	Piazza di Sant'Ignazio, a few blocks north of Piazza Venezia (turn left off the Corso on Via Montecatina to access the piazza); take Bus 40 or 64 to Piazza Venezia or Bus No. 122 down the Corso to get here.
Where to Stop:	For a caffeine fix, make a stop at Sant'Eustachio il Caffè—regarded by many as serving up the best coffee in Rome—just around the corner from the Pantheon at Piazza di Sant'Eustachio 82. Unless you want to pay the somewhat exorbitant fees for sitting at one of the outdoor tables, common for cafés in the center, take your coffee as the Romans do—at the bar inside.
Time:	Four to six hours, depending on your pace.
Best Time to Go:	Get an early start, around 9 am, and you'll be able to visit most of the churches before they close for their midday siesta at noon.
Worst Time to Go:	If the weather is inclement or gray, wait for a sunnier day.

No need to pack bottled Pellegrino on your walks—just savor the refreshing water from city fountains along the way, as Romans have done for centuries.

a gelato for the eyes. Inside the church observe how the late-17th-century Baroque twists and meanders into the 18th-century Rococo style. Marble work was seldom given such ornate or sumptuous treatment, and here is often gilded as well, as is the magnificent organ loft.

Head to Via Pozzo delle Cornacchia, directly opposite the church facade, and take it one block to the looming church across the square, **San Luigi dei Francesi**—the church of Rome's French community. In the left-side chapel closest to the altar are the masterpieces painted by Caravaggio on the life and martyrdom of Saint Matthew—these three gigantic paintings had the same effect on 17th-century art that Picasso's *Demoiselles d'Avignon* had on 20th-century artists. Illuminated in Caravaggio's landmark chiaroscuro (light and shadow) style, these are works unrivaled for emotional spectacle. The artist's warts-and-all drama was a deeply original response to the Counter-Reformation writings by St. Carlo Borromeo and the result is Baroque at its sublime best.

THE STING OF WISDOM

Continue south on Via della Dogana Vecchia to Piazza di Sant'Eustachio. As culture-vulture exhaustion may be setting in, it's time for a coffee. There's no better place than Il Caffè, which, a true Roman will tell you, serves the best coffee in Rome, if not the universe. Inside the bar a cup costs only €1; outside, the price triples, but then, up on your left, the best available view of S. Ivo's dome is thrown in. **Sant'Ivo alla Sapienza** is considered by many to be Francesco Borromini's most astounding building. To get another look at the bizarre pinnacle crowning its dome (the church's rear entrance is on Piazza Sant'Eustachio), head down Via del Salvatore and turn left on Corso del Rinascimento to Number

40. Here a grand courtyard view of the church reveals Borromini—Bernini's great rival—at the dizzying top of his form.

Admire the church's concave facade and follow your gaze upward to see how Borromini mixes concave and convex shapes like a conjurer in stone. This performance is topped first with the many-niched lantern, and then the spiraling, so-called *puntiglione,* or giant stinger. Some suggest Borromini was inspired by that ziggurat of ziggurats—the Tower of Babel, featured in many paintings of the time. A more popular theory cites the sting of a bee, and indeed the nickname means just that. This would also square with the building having been begun under Pope Urban VIII of the Barberini family, whose three-bee'd crest is much in evidence all over Rome. Neatly enough, the bee is also a symbol of wisdom and this palace of Sapienza was once the hoary home of the University of Rome.

WORD OF MOUTH

"I love walking Rome. Keep in mind, though, that estimated times do not include stops for cappuccini, gelati, shopping and/or all those moments where you want to just take all of this amazing city in." —LucieV

THE QUEEN OF PIAZZAS

Leaving the courtyard, follow all the crowds one block to reach that showstopper of Baroque Rome, **Piazza Navona.** The crown jewel of the *centro storico* (historical center), this showcases Bernini's extravagant Fontana dei Quattro Fiumi, whose statues represent the four corners of the earth and, in turn, the world's great rivers. Emperor Domitian's stadium once stood on this site, hence the piazza's unusual oval shape. Before someone figured out that the piazza's church of **Sant'Agnese in Agone** was designed prior to the fountain, common belief held that Bernini's fountain-figures were poised as if looking in horror at the inferior creation of Borromini, Bernini's rival. For lunch, grab a ringside café seat and take in the piazza spectacle—this is some of the most delicious scenery on view in Europe.

After lunch, escape the madding crowds by exiting the piazza on the little *vicolo* (alleyway) to the right of the church complex, Via di Tor Millina, to turn right on Via di S. Maria dell'Anima. Continue to the soaring bell tower of the church of S. Maria dell'Anima, then make a sharp left up a narrow alley to emerge on pretty Piazza della Pace. The centerpiece of one of the city's cutest streetscapes is the church of **Santa Maria della Pace,** commissioned by the great Chigi-family art patron, Pope Alexander VII. Although there are two great Renaissance treasures inside—Raphael's *Sibyls* and Bramante's cloister—the Baroque masterstroke here is the church facade, designed in 1657 by Pietro da Cortona to fit into the tiny *piazzina,* created to accommodate the 18th-century carriages of fashionable parishioners.

GRAND PALAZZOS COME IN THREES

Take the street leading to the church, Via della Pace (past the always chic Antico Caffè delle Pace), and continue a few blocks south down to the big avenue, Corso Vittorio Emmanuele II. Turn right a couple of blocks to reach the Chiesa Nuova, another of Rome's great Counter-Reformation churches (with magnificent Rubens paintings inside), and, directly to the left, Borromini's Oratorio dei Filippini. Head across the

DID YOU KNOW?

Andrea Pozzo's eye-popping Sant'Ignazio 1694 ceiling fresco set the standard for trompe l'oeil aerial perspective and made it all the rage in Europe.

Corso another two blocks toward the Tiber along Via D. Cartari and turn left on Via Giulia, often called Rome's most beautiful street. While laid out—as a ruler-straight processional to St. Peter's—by Michelangelo's patron, Pope Julius II, it is lined with numerous Baroque palaces (Palazzo Sachetti, at No. 66, is still home to one of Rome's princeliest families). At No. 1 is **Palazzo Falconieri,** probably Borromini's most regal palace and now home to the Hungarian academy—note the architect's rooftop belvedere adorned with the family "falcons."

COUNTING NOSES

For some merriment around the Piazza della Rotonda, head to Via de' Pastini 99, where you'll meet not one Pinocchio but several hundreds, still or animated, from life- to pocket-size. The artisans responsible are the Bartolucci, and this family keeps Pinocchio not just alive and well, but multiplying to a dizzying degree.

2

Looming over everything else is the massive **Palazzo Farnese,** a Renaissance masterpiece topped off by Michelangelo himself. You can tour the palace (today the French Embassy) in English on Wednesday at 5 pm. (⇨ *See write-up of palace in Navona section for details*). Inside is the fabled Galleria, with frescoes painted by Annibale Carracci. These florid depictions of gods and goddesses were among the first painted in the Baroque style and were staggeringly influential.

If you can't get into the Farnese, no problem. Just a block to the south is the grand **Palazzo Spada.** The rich exterior trim of painted frescoes on the top story hint at the splendors within: grand salons nearly wallpapered with Old Master paintings capture the opulent, 17th-century version of *Lifestyles of the Rich and Famous.*

But don't miss the *colonnato prospettico* in the small courtyard between the library and the palace cortile. While the colonnaded tunnel, with a mythological figure in marble at the far end, seems to extend for 50 feet, it is actually only one-third that length.

Due to anamorphic deformation used as a trick by the designer, once thought to be Borromini himself (now seen as the work of Giovanni Maria da Bitono), the columns at the far end are only two feet high!

PUCCINI'S CHOICE

For the finale, head four blocks northward along Via Biscione back to the Corso Vittorio Emmanuele. Landmarking the famous Baroque church of **Sant'Andrea della Valle** is the highest dome in Rome (after St. Peter's).

Designed by Carlo Maderno, the nave is adorned with 17th-century frescoes by Lanfranco, making this one of the earliest ceilings in full Baroque fig.

Richly marbled chapels flank the nave, the setting Puccini chose for Act I of his opera *Tosca.* The arias sung by Floria Tosca and her lover Cavaradossi (load it on your iPod) strike exactly the right note to conclude this tour of Rome.

TRASTEVERE: THE VILLAGE WITHIN THE CITY

Charming, cobblestoned Trastevere is often called the Brooklyn of Rome. Staunchly resisting the tides of change for centuries, the off-the-beaten-path district was known—until the millionaires and chichi real estate agents arrived a decade ago—as "the real Rome." It's heavily populated by *romani di Roma*—those born and bred in the Eternal City for at least three generations—who call themselves the only true Romans. To brook no arguments, they named their charming July fete the *Festa de Noantri*: the "Festival of We Others," as the people of Trastevere pugnaciously labeled themselves so as to be distinguished from "Voiantri," the "you others" of the rest of Rome or anywhere else.

A MIDSUMMER NIGHT'S DREAM

Rome's most charming festival begins on the first Saturday after July 16, when a statue of the Madonna is dressed in precious clothes and jewels and transported from the church of Sant'Agata to the church of San Crisogono. The eight days it remains there signal a local holiday: Trastevere streets are hung with colored lights and lanterns and everyone joins in festive merriment, complete with open-air singing contests, *cocomero* (watermelon) vendors, public dances, and *stornellatori* (quip makers) passing from table to table.

In fact, the Trasteverini have always been proud and combative, a breed apart. Dating back to republican times when it hosted both Jewish and Syriac communities as well as assorted slaves and sailors, the area was only incorporated into the "Urbs" (or city proper) by Emperor Augustus in 7 BC. By the Middle Ages, Trastevere still wasn't considered truly part of Rome, and the "foreigners" who populated its maze of alleys and piazzas fought bitterly to obtain recognition for the neighborhood as a *rione (district)*, or official district of the city. In the 14th century the Trasteverini won out and became full-fledged Romans, while stoutly maintaining their separate identity.

It's been the case ever since. Trastevere has always attracted "outsiders," and those have included celebrated artists and artisans. Raphael's model and mistress, the dark-eyed Fornarina (literally, "the baker's daughter"), is believed to have been a Trasteverina. The artist reportedly took time off from painting the *Galatea* in the nearby Villa Farnesina to woo the winsome girl at the tavern now occupied by the district's most toothsome restaurant, Romolo's. Long cocooned from "the strange disease of modern life," the district these days has been colonized with trendy boutiques and discos. Today, it's newly hip with actors and alternative thinkers. No matter: tourists still love the place, with good reason. Long considered Rome's "Greenwich Village," Trastevere remains a delight for dialecticians, biscuit eaters, winebibbers, and book browsers alike.

TIBER'S ISLAND

The best gateway to Trastevere turns out to be one of Rome's most picturesque: the Ponte Fabricio over the **Isola Tiberina,** the island wedged between Trastevere and the Campo area. As you stride over Rome's

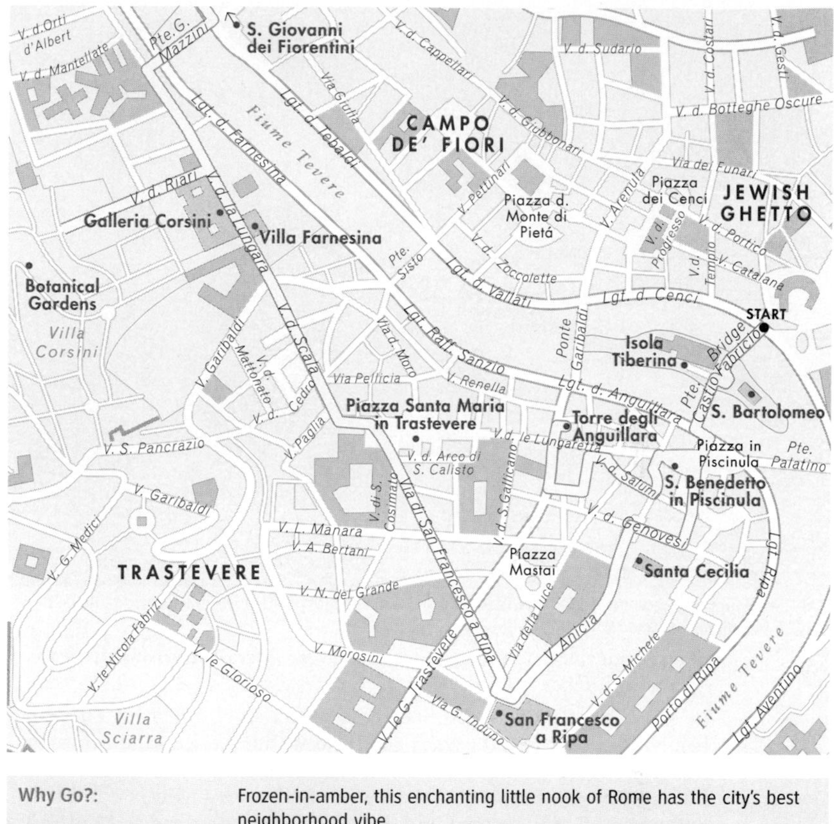

Why Go?:	Frozen-in-amber, this enchanting little nook of Rome has the city's best neighborhood vibe.
Good in the 'Hood:	Chilling out in Piazza Santa Maria in Trastavere, walking in Raphael's footsteps, roaming "Middle-Age"-d alleyways, lunching on Romolo's gorgeous terrace.
Highlights:	Mosaic splendor at Santa Maria in Trastevere, tiny Piazza in Piscinula, picturesque Isola Tiberina, Bernini's Blessed Ludovica Albertoni.
Where to Start:	Isola Tiberina (Tiber Island), accessed via bus from Largo Torre Argentina—get off near the Jewish Ghetto area, a few blocks from the Isola.
Where to Stop:	Make a gelato stop at Via della Lungaretta, where I Fior di Luna, a local institution, serves up scoops made using only the freshest, best-quality ingredients. Via della Lungara heads north to the Principe Amadeo bridge, where you can take No. 64 bus back to the city center.
Time:	Three to five hours, depending on your pace.
Best Time to Go:	The afternoon light here is best, but some churches, including almost all of Rome's smaller ones, close from about noon to 4 pm.
Worst Time to Go:	As the sun sets, hipster crowds arrive—Trastevere has a completely different vibe at night.

(above) The Ponte Cestio connects the Isola Tiberina with Trastevere; (opposite) the Ponte Fabricio—Rome's oldest (AD 62)—links the island with the Jewish Ghetto.

oldest bridge, let's not forget that Trastevere, literally translated, means "across the Tiber."

In Rome every stone worth its weight has a story attached. The one behind the Tiber Island, writes ancient historian Livy, is that Etruscan leader Tarquin, on his banishment, left behind a crop of grain in the Campo Marzio. For various superstitious reasons this was uprooted, put in baskets, and thrown into the Tiber for good riddance. Mud and sediment did the rest. The resulting island was eventually walled in the shape of a ship, ready to take on board another myth: allegedly this is where Aesculapius, god of medicine, landed from Greece (or his serpent double did). Whichever, the medical tradition continues to this day in the Hospital of Fratebenefratelli, the large building to your right. For one of Rome's most unique ancient survivals, head (in the opposite direction) down the embankment to the island's southern tip to the **ancient "stone prow"** carved with medicine's serpent. Take in the 18th-century facade of the church of **San Bartolomeo,** built above Aesculapius's Temple. Off to the right is what some call the world's most beautiful movie theater, the open-air Cinema d'Isola di Tiberina (which operates during the summer festival of Estate Romana). Cross the bridge—the Ponte Cestio (dated 26 BC)—to get to Trastevere proper.

MEDIEVAL NOOKS AND CRANNIES

You're now on the Lungotevere riverside road but continue for another block into the district to hit **Piazza in Piscinula** (from *piscina,* pool), one of Rome's most time-stained squares, home to **S. Benedetto in Piscinula,** a 17th-century church with a much earlier campanile, one of the smallest and cutest in Rome. Here St. Benedict, the founder of Western monasticism, once had a cell. The church has recently been restored by the

Brazilian "Heralds of the Gospel" who, in resplendent uniform, are there on Sunday to greet visitors and worshippers alike. The multicolor 12th-century floor is a wonder in itself. On the opposite flank of the square is the 14th-century **Casa dei Mattei,** replete with cross-mullioned windows and loggias.

History nestles quietly in every nook and cranny off the square, but opt for the charming incline at the northern end, the **Via dell'Arco dei Tolomei,** graced with a medieval house built over an arch. One block north, let history take a rest in Via della Luce at a bakeshop par excellence—just look for the sign "Biscotti." Several blocks farther north, the "Middle-Aged" want to detour up to Piazza Belli, where they'll find one of the largest medieval structures in Trastevere, the **Torre degli Anguillara,** a much-restored mini-fortress whose main tower dates from the 13th century.

Back under the Tolomei arch, this street leads into the Via dei Salumi and one block leftward brings you to **Via dell'Atleta,** with a number of picturesque medieval houses. Via dell'Atleta runs into **Via dei Genovesi,** which commemorates the Genovese sailors who thronged Trastevere when it was the papal harbor in the 15th century. These gents roomed in the vicinity of the 15th-century church of San Giovanni dei Genovesi, which has an extraordinary cloister. Whether Christopher Columbus ever stayed here is not recorded, but the dates would fit. Meanwhile, at a ring of the bell (at No. 12 Via Anicia), the cloister is still visitable every afternoon 3–6.

SAINTLY PORTRAITS IN STONE

Via dei Genovesi leads directly to one of the district's majestic medieval landmarks, the church of **Santa Cecilia,** which was built atop the Roman house of this martyr and patron saint of music. In 1599 her sarcophagus was found, her body inside miraculously intact. Sculptor Stefano Maderno was summoned to attest in stone to what he saw, and sketched before decomposition set in. In a robe-turned-shroud the saint lies on her side, head turned away, across her neck a deep gash, which she's supposed to have survived for three days after suffocation in a steam bath had left her not only unscathed but singing (all this sent Marquis de Sade into rather dubious raptures). With its almost mystically white marble, the work has a haunting quality that few statues can match. But the greatest treasure can be seen only if you exit and ring the bell on the left: for €3 a nun will show you to an elevator that ascends to a *Christ in Judgment* by Pietro Cavallini, whom art historians believe was Giotto's master. Painted in 1293, the frescoes are remarkably intact.

TIME-TESTED TASTE TREAT

On the right of Ponte Cestio you will see the beloved kiosk of "La Gratachecca del 1915." Using recipes going back to ancient Roman times, its variety of ice crushes are famous enough locally to cause lines 100 feet long in summer.

Leaving the church, turn left and walk down Via Anicia several blocks to Piazza S. Francesco d'Assisi and **San Francesco a Ripa.** The fourth chapel on the left features Bernini's eye-knocking statue of the *Blessed Ludovica Albertoni,* a Franciscan nun whose body is buried beneath the altar. It has been remarked that the Baroque, at its most effective, served not just to educate but to sweep you off your feet. Here's an example. Marble pillow, folds, and drapery in abundance, all set off the deathbed agony and ecstasy of the nun—her provocative gesture of clutching at her breast is actually an allusion to the "milk of charity."

MAJESTIC SANTA MARIA

We now set off for the walk's northern half by heading up Via di San Francesco a Ripa, one of Trastevere's main shopping strips. But this dreary stretch actually enhances the delight at finding, at the end of the street, **Santa Maria in Trastevere,** famously set on one of Rome's dreamiest piazzas. Noted for its fountain and café, it is the photogenic heart of the rione. Fellini evidently thought the same, making it a supporting star of his film *Roma.*

Staring down at you from the 12th-century church facade are the famed medieval frescoes of the Wise and Foolish Virgins. Dramatically spotlit at night, these young ladies refer to the "miraculous" discovery of oil here in 39 BC. In the mosaic, the Virgin is set between the wise virgins and two foolish ones—the latters' crownless heads bowed with shame at having left their lamps empty, the flame extinguished. In the church's presbytery the *fons olii* marks the spot from whence the oil originally flowed.

Thanks to its gilded ceiling, shimmering mosaics, and vast dimensions, the church nave echoes the spectacle of an ancient Roman basilica—the columns are said to have come from the Baths of Caracalla. The church's main wonder, however, must be the golden mosaics behind the altar. The famous mosaics of Pietro Cavallini depict episodes in the life of the Virgin so often revisited during the Renaissance. With its use of perspective, the work—completed in 1291—is seen as something of a watershed between the old, static Byzantine style and the more modern techniques soon to be taken up by Giotto. This is the very dawn of Western art.

WHEREFORE ART THOU, ROMOLO?

No visit to Trastevere is complete without a visit to its landmark restaurant, Romolo (✉ *Via di Porta Settimiana 8*), not far from the Villa Farnesina. Haunted by the spirit of Raphael—who wooed his Fornarina here—it has Rome's prettiest garden terrace, menus embellished by Miró, and scrumptious specialties, like the chef's famous artichoke sauce.

The piazza outside is the very heart of the Trastevere rione. With its elegant raised fountain and sidewalk café, this is one of Rome's most beloved outdoor "living rooms," open to all comers. Through innumerable generations, this piazza has seen the comings and goings of tourists and travelers, intellectuals and artists, who lounge on the steps of the fountain or lunch at Sabatini's, whose food has seen much better days but whose real estate, with its tables set up directly in front of the fountain, is among Rome's most coveted. Here the paths of Trastevere's residents intersect repeatedly during the day; they pause, gathering in clusters to talk animatedly in the broad accent of Rome or in a score of foreign languages. At night, it's the center of Trastevere's action, with street festivals, musicians, and gamboling dogs vying for attention from the throngs of people taking the evening air.

RAPHAEL WAS HERE

Directly north of the church is Piazza di S. Egidio (the small but piquant Museo di Trastevere is here) and then you enter Via della Lungara, where, several blocks along on the right, the **Villa Farnesina** stands (hours are 9–2 daily, except Sunday). Originally built by papal banker and high-roller Agostino "Il Magnifico" Chigi, this is Rome at its High Renaissance best.

Enter the Loggia di Galatea to find, across the ceiling, Peruzzi's 1511 horoscope of the papal banker, presumably not foretelling the family's eventual bankruptcy and the selling off of the same property (and horoscope) to the wealthy Farnese family. Off left, next to the wall, sits Sebastiano di Piombo's depiction of one-eyed giant *Polyphemus* with staff and giant panpipes; this is what, just next door, Raphael's *Galatea* is listening to in her shell-chassis, paddle-wheeled chariot. With the countermovement of its iconic putti, nymphs, sea gods, and dolphins, this legendary image became a hallmark of Renaissance harmony.

In the next room, also—or at least mostly—decorated by Raphael, is the *Marriage of Cupid and Psyche*. After provoking the jealousy of Venus, Psyche has to overcome a number of trials before being deemed fit to drink the cup of immortality and marry Cupid. Here, of course, is an alter ego for Agostino Chigi. The paintings are made still more wonderful by Giovanni da Udine's depictions of flower and fruit separating one from the other as if it were a giant *pergolato* (or arbor)—gods float

Pull up a café seat and settle down to enjoy the daily spectacle that is the Piazza di Santa Maria in Trastevere—one of Rome's favorite "living rooms."

at every angle while ornithologists will delight in spotting Raphael's repertoire of bird species. Climbing upstairs one passes through Peruzzi's Hall of Perspectives to Chigi's private rooms. Here, in Il Sodoma's *Alexander's Wedding,* Roxanna is being lovingly undressed by a bevy of cupids. Note the one so overexcited he attempts a somersault like a footballer after a winning goal.

QUEEN CHRISTINA AT HOME

Directly across the street from the Villa Farnesina is the **Galleria Corsini** (⏲ *Tues.–Sun., 8:30–2*), entered via a gigantic stone staircase right out of a Piranesi print. This was formerly the palazzo of pipe-smoking Christina of Sweden, immortalized by Greta Garbo on the silver screen and to whom history, that old gossip, attaches the label, "Queen without a realm, Christian without a faith, and a woman without shame." Her artistic taste is indisputable.

The second room alone contains a magnificent Rubens, Van Dyck's *Madonna of the Straw,* an Andrea del Sarto, and then, courtesy of Hans Hoffman, surely the hare of all hares. Worth the price of admission alone is Caravaggio's *John the Baptist.* In other rooms, for aficionados of high-class gore, there's Salvator Rosa's *Prometheus,* the vulture *in flagrante* and on Prometheus's face a scream to rival Munch. A visit to the **Botanical Gardens** that stretch behind the galleria is well worth a visit, if just to restore a sense of calm after all that Baroque bloodletting.

To get back to central Rome, continue on up Via della Lungara (past the church of Giacomo Apostolo, which has a fine Bernini inside) and cross over the Ponte Mazzini. Taking advantage of one of the bus stops by the Tiber, you can take any number of buses, including the famous No. 64, back to the centro historico.

ROME OF THE EMPERORS: A ROMAN FORUM WALK

Taking in the famous vista of the Roman Forum from the terraces of the Capitoline Hill, you have probably already cast your eyes down and across two millennia of history in a single glance. Here, in one fabled panorama, are the world's most striking and significant concentrations of historic remains. From this hilltop aerie, however, the erstwhile heart of ancient Rome looks like one gigantic jigsaw puzzle, the last piece being the Colosseum, looming in the distance. Historians soon realized that the Forum's big chunks of weathered marble were the very seeds of our civilization and early-20th-century archaeologists moved in to weed it and reap: in the process, they uncovered the very heart of the ancient Roman Empire. While it is fine to just let your mind contemplate the scattered pieces of the once-impressive whole, it is even better to go exploring to decipher the significance of the Forum's noble fragments. This walk does precisely that.

WORLD'S MIGHTIEST HEIRLOOM

To kick things off, we start just south of the Forum at ancient Rome's hallmark monument, the **Colosseum** (with its handy Colosseo Metro stop). Convincingly austere, the Colosseum is the Eternal City's yardstick of eternity. Weighing in at 100,000 tons, it must be the world's mightiest heirloom. A special road having been built to transport the Travertine stone from nearby Tivoli—these quarries are still there to this day—the building was begun under the emperor Titus Flavius Vespasianus (aka Vespasian) and named the Flavian Amphitheater after his family. His son Titus, according to his father's will, inherited the task of finishing it in AD 80 while his other son, Domitian, built the gladiatorial schools on the adjacent Colle Oppio.

One rationale for the building was that Rome's only previous amphitheater, the Theater of Taurus, had been destroyed in the great fire of AD 64. Another was that the new version would erase memories of wicked Nero, who had privatized a vast swath of land near the public Forum for his private palace, the so-called Domus Aurea. In fact, the Colosseum was positioned directly over a former lake in Nero's gardens, and nearby would have towered the 110-foot-high, colossal statue of Nero himself. In one of history's ironic twists, the term *Flavian amphitheater* never caught on.

A typical day at the Colosseum? The card would usually begin with a wild-beast hunt, then a pause for lunch, during which the sparse crowd was entertained with tamer displays by jugglers, magicians, and acrobats, along with third-tier fights involving "lesser" combatants, such as the Christians. Then, much gorier, would come the main event: the gladiators. The death rates among them have been much debated—30,000 is one estimate.

The building could evidently be filled in as little as 10 minutes, thanks to the 80 entrance archways. Nowadays, you can take one of the elevators upstairs to level one (the uppermost levels are closed for excavation) to spy the extensive subterranean passageways that used to funnel all the unlucky animals and gladiators into the arena.

ANCIENT ARCHES TELL THE TALE

Leaving the Colosseum behind, admire the **Arch of Constantine,** standing just to the north of the arena. The largest and best preserved of Rome's triumphal arches, it was erected in AD 315 to celebrate the victory of the emperor Constantine (280–337) over Maxentius—it was shortly after this battle that Constantine converted Rome to Christianity. Something of an amalgam historically, it features carved depictions of the triumphs of emperors Trajan, Marcus Aurelius, and Hadrian as well, a cost-cutting recycling that indicates the empire was no longer quite what it once was. You have to walk down Via dei Fori Imperiali to the only Forum entrance, located about halfway down the street from the Colosseum and across from Via Cavour, to enter the Forum. From there, you can take a left up the ancient Via Sacra to start at the Forum's southwestern point with the **Temple of Venus and Roma.** In part it was proudly designed by would-be architect Hadrian—at least until the true professional Apollodurus pointed out that with Hadrian's measurements the goddess risked bumping her head on the apse, a piece of advice for which he was repaid with banishment. Off to your left, on the spur of hillside jutting from the Palatine Hill, stands the famed **Arch of Titus.** Completed by his brother, and successor, Domitian in AD 81, the arch in one frieze shows the Roman soldiery carrying away booty—Moses's candelabra, silver trumpets, an altar table—from the destruction of the Temple in Jerusalem 10 years earlier. On the other side there is Titus on the same Via Sacra, in this case being charioted toward the Capitol after the campaign in Palestine begun by his father Vespasian. Through the arch, photograph the great vista of the entire Forum as it stretches toward the distant Capitoline Hill.

MASSIVE MAXENTIUS

After doubling back down the Via Sacra, make sure to take in the massive **Basilica of Maxentius,** or the third of it left standing. Heavily damaged during Alaric's sack of Rome in 410, it had been founded by Maxentius in 306–10, then completed by Constantine the Great, Maxentius's archenemy, at the battle of the Milvian Bridge. The three remaining side vaults give an idea of the building's scale; also to how, through their use of brick and barrel vaulting, the Romans had freed themselves from the tyranny of gravity. Here once stood—or sat rather—the surrealistically large head and other body fragments of Constantine (now in the outside courtyard of the Palazzo dei Conservatori), the first Christian emperor. Rome's first Christian basilica, San Giovanni in Laterano, originated many of the features used in the basilica here. Not surprisingly this most majestic of ruins was much admired and studied by the great Renaissance architects and painters alike—in Raphael's *School of Athens* the background edifice is surely a depiction of what you are seeing here. Today, the basilica is the site of wonderful concerts in summer and the occasional dramatized trial of this or that emperor (e.g., Nero and Tiberius).

TEMPLES STILL STANDING TALL

Resuming your walk back toward the Capitoline Hill, the next building is the **Temple of Romulus.** The Romulus here is not Rome's founder but the son of Emperor Maxentius. Apart from the Pantheon, this is the only Roman temple to remain entirely intact—so intact even the lock in the original bronze doors is said to still function. This is due to its having subsequently been used, at least until the late 19th century, as the atrium of a Christian church above. The stonework across the

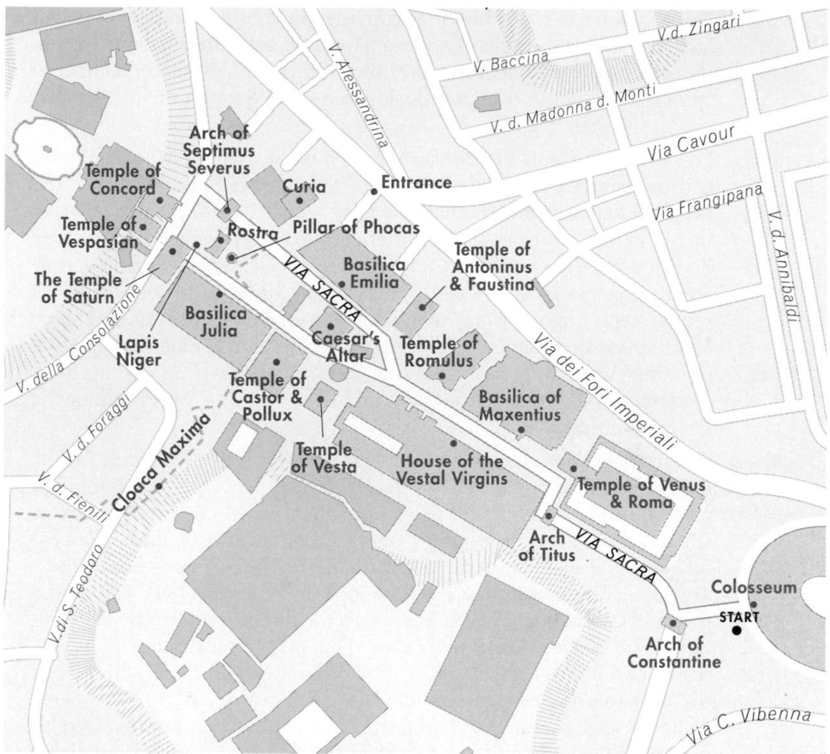

Why Go?:	Ancient Rome's "Times Square," this Forum was the civic core of the city and is the best place to experience the ageless romance of the Eternal City.
Good in the 'Hood:	Walking in the footsteps of Julius Caesar, Mark Antony, St. Paul, and Nero; picnicking in the peaceful gardens of the Palatine, home of the emperors; photographing Colosseum "gladiators."
Highlights:	Arches of Septimus Severus, Titus, and Constantine; the Colosseum; the Via Sacra; the Roman Forum.
Where to Start:	Piazza del Colosseo, with its handy Colosseo Metro stop.
Where to Stop:	Northern edge of the Roman Forum, near the Temple of Vespasian and the exit to Via di San Teodoro, leading to the Capitoline Hill.
Time:	Two to five hours, depending on your pace.
Best Time to Go:	Either right when the Colosseum opens (8:30 am) or in the mid-afternoon to avoid the heat and direct sun.
Worst Time to Go:	Midday, when the sun is high and merciless—remember, there are no roofs and few trees to shelter under at these archaeological sites. Crowds are at their thickest after 10 am.

lintel is as perfect as when it was made, as are the two porphyry pillars. For an inside view of the same temple and, until a century ago, the attached church atrium, enter the Church of Cosma and Damiano from the Via dei Fori Imperiali side and peer through the glass at the end of the main chapel.

Proof of how deeply buried the Forum was throughout Medieval times can be seen in the wonderful pillars of the next building down, the **Temple of Antoninus and Faustina,** his wife. Those stains reaching halfway up are in fact centuries-old soil marks. Further evidence of the sinking Forum are the doors of the 13th-century church above—note how they seem to hang almost in midair. Now a full 30 feet above the temple's rebuilt steps, originally they would, of course, have been at ground level. Here we see an example of the Christian world not so much supplanting the pagan world as growing out of it. Meanwhile, there against the blue, read the words "Divo Antonino" and "Diva Faustina," proclaiming the couple's self-ordained "divination."

A CAESAR AMONG CAESARS

Continue your walk toward the Capitoline Hill by strolling by the largely vanished **Basilica Emilia.** To the left, however, is the Temple of Caesar, sometimes referred to as **Caesar's Altar,** where, after his assassination from 23 knife wounds, Caesar's body was brought hotfoot for cremation. Peep behind the low wall and now in Caesar's honor there are flowers instead of flames. Now look up and head over, just across the road known as the Vicus Tuscus, to the three wonderfully white pillars of the **Temple of Castor and Pollux.** This was reconstructed by Augustus to pay homage to the twin sons of Jupiter and Leda who helped the Roman army to victory back in the 5th century BC. The emperor Caligula, says Suetonius, "had part of the temple incorporated into his palace as his own vestibule. Often he would stand between the divine brothers displaying himself for worship by those visiting the temple."

To this temple's right sits the **Basilica Julia.** After the death of Julius Caesar, all chaos broke loose in Rome and preluded another long bout of civil war. This ended with the victory of Augustus who, ever the dutiful stepson, had this massive basilica completed in his father's honor. Pitted with column marks, a rectangular piece of the ground remains. As with other Roman basilicas, the place was more judicial in nature, swarming, according to Pliny, with 180 judges and a plague of lawyers. Look carefully at the flooring and you might still spy a chessboard carved into the marble, perhaps by a bored litigant.

HAUNT OF THE VESTAL VIRGINS

Backtrack a bit along the Via Sacra past the Temple of Castor and Pollux to the circular **Temple of Vesta.** In a tradition going back to an age when fire was a precious commodity, the famous vestal virgins kept the fire of Rome burning here. Of the original 20 columns only 3 remain, behind which stretch the vast remains of the **House of the Vestal Virgins.** Privileged in many ways—they had front-row seats in the Colosseum and rights of deciding life and death for poor gladiators, for example—they were also under a 30-year-long vow of chastity. As everyone knows, the notorious punishment for breaking their vow was being buried alive. But it is time to turn back and press on with our walk. Crossing the central square and walking back toward the towering Capitoline Hill,

See you later, gladiator: the Colosseum hosted gladiatorial combats for centuries and up to 30,000 may have tragically perished in its arena.

you are now entering the midsection of the open area of the Forum proper; you can see to your left the **Pillar of Phocas.** The last monument to be built on the by now largely abandoned Forum was this column, erected by an otherwise forgotten Byzantine emperor. In 1813, on the orders of Pope Pius VII, the area was excavated, with the assumption that the column belonged to the Temple of Jove Custode. Then, at the base, surfaced the inscription, describing how it had been erected in 608 to the Christian emperor from the east on his bequeathing the Pantheon to the Roman Church.

A BURIAL TOO SOON

The long stone platform presiding over this area is the famous **Rostra.** *Forum* comes from an old Latin word meaning "to meet," and it was from here that Rome's political elite would address the people. Indeed, this is where, with some help from Shakespeare, Mark Antony would have pronounced his rabble-rousing "I come to bury Caesar, not to praise him." The name Rostra dates to the custom of adorning the platform with prows of captured ships following an early naval victory off Antium/Anzio in 338 BC.

Going back even farther is, on the other side of the Via Sacra, the so-called **Lapis Niger,** or Black Stone, which marks the site of a Temple to Romulus. The small sanctuary underneath goes back to the 6th century BC as does a strange column with the oldest Latin inscription yet known, cursing all those who profaned the place—irreverent archaeologists take note!

Altogether mightier in scale is the **Curia**—the Senate house of ancient Rome—nearby. Not the building of the earlier republican period, this is a version rebuilt by Diocletian and in turn rebuilt in 1937. Here sat the

300 members of Senate, then rendered largely powerless by Diocletian. Originally decorating the nearby rostra, the two friezes show the much earlier emperor Trajan. Meanwhile the porphyry statue without a head has been attributed to Trajan also. But there is a neater theory: with the turnover in emperors reaching to as many as six per year and porphyry being almost priceless, the head was replaceable by whatever emperor happened to be in power.

HEADS AND TALES

Continue back down the Via Sacra, where towers one of the Forum's extant spectaculars, the **Arch of Septimus Severus.** Built by his sons, it celebrates Septimus's campaign against the Parthians and the ensuing influx into Rome of booty and slaves. A number of these, their hands tied behind them, are depicted. Also on view is the murderous Caracalla, son number two, though the head of his elder brother Gaeta has, Stalin-fashion, been erased. Sadly, many other heads have also had a Caracalla done on them by the erosive fumes of Roman traffic.

Continuing left and up the Via Sacra, you reach the base of the celebrated **Temple of Saturn.** Now the name of a planet, Saturn was then as close to the earth as you can get, the word originating from *sero*—"to sow." Saturn was originally a corn god, first worshipped in Magna Grecia, then allowed, so goes the patriotic myth, to settle in Rome by the city's presiding deity, Janus. That Saturn was the God of Plenty in more than an agricultural sense is also attested to by the fact that beneath the floor was kept the wealth of the Roman treasury.

Position yourself below the easternmost two of the eight columns of Egyptian marble and peer upward as they reach higher than a rocket at Cape Canaveral and are every bit as majestic.

HAIL AND FAREWELL

Meanwhile, up ahead ascends the last stretch of the Via Sacra—the so-called Clivus Capitolinus. On the left is the **Temple of Vespasian.**

Bowing to the powerful nature of time, now only three splendid columns remain. Next door once stood the **Temple of Concord.**

Built back in republican times, it celebrated the peace between the oft-warring patricians and plebs, the two cardinal elements in the winning formula of SPQR—in other words the patrician Senate (S) and the people (PQ). A few stones mark the spot—and the last piece in the Forum's monumental jigsaw.

For a better sense of the whole—a sort of archaeological gestalt—take the steps alongside to ascend to the Campidoglio, the Capitoline Hill, where vistas from the piazza balconies will put your two or three past hours of walking into panoramic context.

You cannot help but ponder on the truth of *sic transit Gloria* ("glory passes away")—a similar view by moonlight inspired Edward Gibbon to embark on his epic *Decline and Fall of the Roman Empire.*

3

ANCIENT ROME

Campidoglio, Roman Forum, Imperial Fora, Colosseum

GETTING ORIENTED

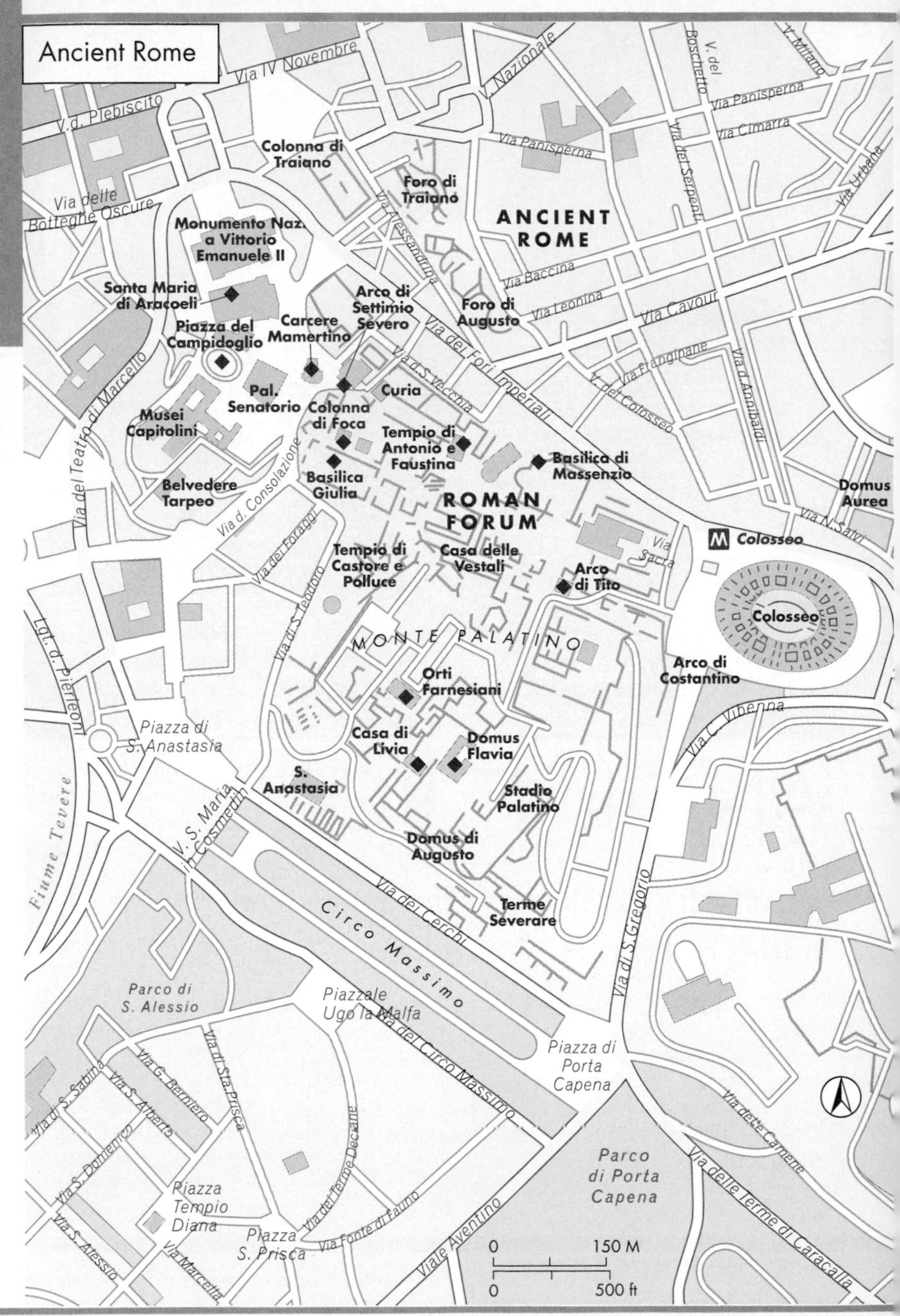

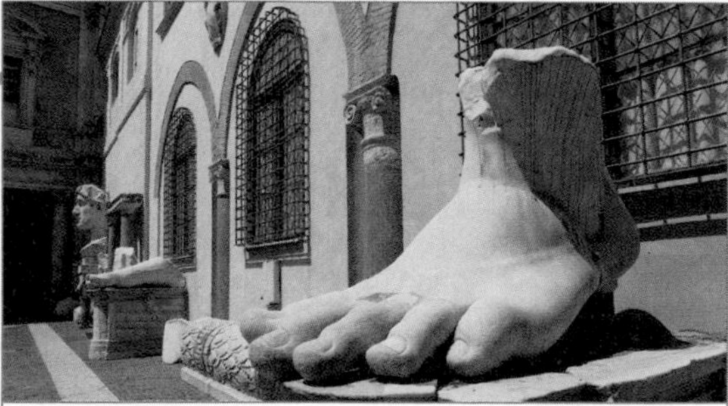

TOP REASONS TO GO

The Colosseum: Clamber up the stands to the emperor's box, and imagine the gory games as Trajan saw them.

The Roman Forum: Walk through the crumbling, romantic ruins, a trip back 2,000 years to the heart of one of the greatest empires the world has ever seen.

Sunset: Watch the sun go down over ancient and Renaissance Rome from the back of the Campidoglio, the best view in town.

Capitoline Museums: Look eye-to-eye with the ancients—the busts of emperors and philosophers are more real than ideal.

Caffè Capitolino: Sip Prosecco on the terrace of the Palazzo Caffarelli—part of the Musei Capitolini complex—while you take in a Cinerama scene of Roman rooftops.

MAKING THE MOST OF YOUR TIME

This area might be relatively compact, but it's rich with history. Real history buffs should give themselves a full day to see all of it, including an hour in the Colosseum, an hour or more in the Forum, and two hours in the Capitoline Museums. Even for ancient Rome experts, taking a tour can be particularly helpful, as a good guide can bring the piles of rubble and ruins to life in a way that no written explanation can. Just be sure to book a guide in advance instead of picking up one of those trying to shill their expertise on-site. The longest line in Rome, aside from the one at the Vatican museums, is at the Colosseum, so be sure to follow the tips in this guide. Even so, you'll still find the interior quite crowded, particularly in high season. Consider going either immediately when it opens (at 8:30 am) or later in the afternoon, when many tour buses have started to depart. Also keep in mind that there is little to no shade in the Forum, so it gets extremely hot and dusty under the direct sun of the summertime—another reason to either go early or start late!

GETTING HERE

The Colosseo Metro station is right across from the Colosseum proper and a short walk from both the Roman and imperial forums, as well as the Palatine Hill. Hoofing from the very heart of the historic center will take about 20 minutes, much of it along the wide and busy Via dei Fori Imperiali. The little electric Bus No. 117 from the center or No. 175 from Termini will also deliver you to the Colosseum's doorstep. Any of the following buses will take you to or near the Roman Forum: Nos. 60, 75, 85, 95, and 175.

QUICK BITES

Antico Caffè del Brasile. Since 1908, this caffè in the heart of Monti has been a local favorite. Even Pope John Paul II was a fan: As a student, he regularly grabbed coffee here. Come for a pick-me-up—including not only the caffé's own coffee blends, but chocolates and pastries, too. $ *Average main: €2* ✉ *Via dei Serpenti 23, Monti* ☎ *06/4882319.*

Divin Ostilia. Relax over a glass of wine at this *enoteca* (wine bar), just a block from the Colosseum. Sit outside or grab a table in the warm, cozy interior. Although you can find better dinner entrées elsewhere, the wine selection is excellent and the snacks (like the cheese plate or bruschetta) are good bets, too. $ *Average main: €10* ✉ *Via Ostilia 4, Monti* ☎ *06/70496526* M *Colosseo.*

Sightseeing ★★★★★
Nightlife ★★
Dining ★★
Lodging ★★★
Shopping ★

If you ever wanted to feel like the Caesars—with all of ancient Rome (literally) at your feet—simply head to Michelangelo's famed Piazza del Campidoglio. There, make a beeline for the terrace flanking the side of the center building, the Palazzo Senatorio, Rome's ceremonial city hall. From this balcony atop the Capitoline Hill you can take in a panorama that seems like a remnant of some forgotten Cecil B. DeMille movie spectacular.

Updated by Amanda Ruggeri

Looming before you is the entire Roman Forum, the *caput mundi*—the center of the known world for centuries and where many of the world's most important events in the past 2,500 years happened. Here, all Rome shouted as one, "Caesar has been murdered," and crowded to hear Mark Antony's eulogy for the fallen leader. Here, legend has it that St. Paul traversed the Forum en route to his audience with Nero. Here, Roman law and powerful armies were created, keeping the barbarian world at bay for a millennium. And here the Roman emperors staged the biggest blowout extravaganzas ever mounted for the entire population of a city, outdoing even Elizabeth Taylor's Forum entry in *Cleopatra*.

But after a more than 27-century-long parade of pageantry, you'll find that much has changed in this area. The rubble-scape of marble fragments scattered over the Forum area makes all but students of archaeology ask: Is this the grandeur that was Rome? It's not surprising that Shelley and Gibbon once reflected on the sense of *sic transit gloria mundi*—"thus pass the glories of the world." Yet spectacular monuments—the Arch of Septimius Severus, the Palatine Hill, and the Colosseum (looming in the background), among them—remind us that this was indeed the birthplace of much of Western civilization.

Before the Christian era, before the emperors, before the powerful republic that ruled the ancient seas, Rome was founded on seven hills. Two of them, the Capitoline and the Palatine, surround the Roman Forum, where the Romans of the later Republic and Imperial ages worshipped deities, debated politics, and wheeled and dealed. It's all history now, but this remains one of the world's most striking and significant concentrations of ancient remains: an emphatic reminder of the genius and power that made Rome the fountainhead of the Western world.

THE CAMPIDOGLIO

Your first taste of ancient Rome should start from a point that embodies some of Rome's earliest and greatest moments: the Campidoglio. Here, on the Capitoline Hill (which towers over the traffic hub of Piazza Venezia), a meditative Edward Gibbon was inspired to write his 1764 classic, *The History of the Decline and Fall of the Roman Empire.* Of Rome's famous seven hills, the Capitoline is the smallest and most sacred. It has always been the seat of Rome's government, and its Latin name is echoed in the designation of the national and state capitol buildings of every country in the world.

TOP ATTRACTIONS

Fodor's Choice ★ **Musei Capitolini.** Surpassed in size and richness only by the Musei Vaticani, this immense collection was the first public museum in the world. A greatest-hits collection of Roman art through the ages, from the ancients to the baroque, it is housed in the twin Museo Capitolino and Palazzo dei Conservatori that bookend Michelangelo's famous piazza. Here, you'll find some of antiquity's most famous sculptures, such as the poignant *Dying Gaul,* the regal *Capitoline Venus,* the *Esquiline Venus* (identified as possibly another Mediterranean beauty, Cleopatra herself), and the *Lupa Capitolina*, the symbol of Rome. Although some pieces in the collection—which was first assembled by Sixtus IV (1414–84), one of the earliest of the Renaissance popes—may excite only archaeologists and art historians, others are unforgettable, including the original bronze statue of Marcus Aurelius whose copy sits in the piazza.

Buy your ticket and enter the museums on the right of the piazza (as you face the center Palazzo Senatorio), into the building known as the Palazzo dei Conservatori. Before picking up a useful free map from the cloakroom, you cannot miss some of the biggest body parts ever: that giant head, foot, elbow, and imperially raised finger across the courtyard are what remains of the fabled seated statue of Constantine, which once filled the Basilica of Maxentius, his defeated rival (and the other body parts were of wood, lest the figure collapse under its own weight). Constantine believed that Rome's future lay with Christianity and such immense effigies were much in vogue in the latter days of the Roman Empire. Take the stairs up past a series of intricately detailed ancient marble reliefs to the resplendent Salone dei Orazi e Curiazi (Salon of Horatii and Curatii) on the first floor. The ceremonial hall is decorated with a magnificent gilt ceiling, carved wooden doors, and 16th-century frescoes depicting the history of ancient Rome. At both ends of the hall are statues of the Baroque era's most charismatic popes: a marble Urban VIII (1568–1644) by Gian Lorenzo Bernini (1598–1680) and a bronze Innocent X (1574–1655) by Bernini's rival, Algardi (1595–1654).

THE CAMPIDOGLIO

⌧ *Piazza dei Campidoglio, incorporating the Palazzo Senatorio and the two Capitoline Museums, the Palazzo Nuovo, and the Palazzo dei Conservatori, Jewish Ghetto.*

TIPS

■ The piazza centerpiece is the legendary equestrian statue of Emperor Marcus Aurelius but, as of 1999, a copy took up residence here when the actual 2nd-century AD statue moved to a new wing in the surrounding Musei Capitolini. The Sala Marco Aurelio and its glass room also protect a gold-plated Hercules along with more massive body parts, this time bronze, of what might be Constantine or that of his son Constans II (archaeologists are still undecided).

■ While there are great views of the Roman Forum from the terrace balconies on either side of the Palazzo Senatorio, the best view may be from the Tabularium, the arcade balcony below the Senatorio building and accessed with admission to the Musei Capitolini. The museum also has the Terrazza Caffarelli, featuring a restaurant with a magical view looking toward Trastevere and St. Peter's.

Spectacularly transformed by Michelangelo's late-Renaissance designs, the Campidoglio was once the epicenter of the Roman Empire, the place where the city's first shrines stood, including its most sacred, the Temple of Jupiter.

Originally, the Capitoline Hill consisted of two peaks: the Capitolium and the Arx (where Santa Maria in Aracoeli now stands). The hollow between them was known as the Asylum. Here, prospective settlers once came to seek the protection of Romulus, legendary first king of Rome—hence the term "asylum." Later, during the Republic, in 78 BC, the Tabularium, or Hall of Records, was erected here.

By the Middle Ages, however, the Capitoline had become an unkempt hill strewn with ancient rubble.

In preparation for the impending visit of Charles V in 1536, triumphant after the empire's victory over the Moors, his host, Pope Paul III Farnese, decided that the Holy Roman Emperor should follow the route of the emperors, climaxing at the Campidoglio.

But the pope was embarrassed by the decrepit goat pasture the hill had become and commanded Michelangelo to restore the site to glory; he added a third palace along with Renaissance-style facades and a grand paved piazza.

Newly excavated ancient sculptures, designed to impress the visiting emperor, were installed in the palaces, and the piazza was ornamented with the giant stone figures of the Discouri and the ancient Roman equestrian statue of Emperor Marcus Aurelius (original now in Musei Capitolini)—the latter a visual reference to the corresponding glory of Charles V and the ancient emperor.

Proceeding to the collection of ancient sculpture, the first room contains the exquisite "Spinario": Proving that the most everyday action can be as poetic as any imperial bust, a small boy in the act of removing a thorn becomes unwittingly immortalized. Nearby is the rather eerie glass-eyed bust of Junius Brutus, first Roman Consul. Farther along is a separate room devoted to the renowned symbol of Rome, the Capitoline Wolf, a 5th-century BC Etruscan bronze, the Romulus and Remus below being late additions by Antonio Pollaiolo (15th century). Donated by Sixtus IV, the work came to symbolize Roman unity.

Marcus Aurelius Statue

The heart of the museum, however, is the Exedra of Marcus Aurelius (Sala Marco Aurelio), a large, airy room with skylights and high windows, which showcases the spectacular original bronze statue of the Roman emperor whose copy sits in the piazza below. Created in the 2nd century AD, the statue should have been melted down like so many other bronze statues of emperors after the decline of Rome, but this one is thought to have survived because it was mistaken for the Christian emperor Constantine. To the right the room segues into the area of the Temple of Jupiter, with its original ruins rising organically into the museum space. A reconstruction of the temple and Capitol Hill from the Bronze Age to present day makes for a fascinating glance through the ages. Some of the pottery and bones on display were dug up from as early as the 12th century BC, recasting Romulus and Remus as Johnny-come-latelies.

Off left are rooms dedicated to statuary from the so-called Horti, or the gardens of ancient Rome's great and mega-rich. From the Horti Lamiani is the Venere Esquilina doing her hair. (Look for the fingers at the back, at the end of the missing arms.) Believe it or not, you might be gazing at the young Cleopatra invited to Rome by Julius Caesar. Or so say some experts—a further clue is the asp. In the same room is an extraordinary bust of the Emperor Commodus, seen here as Hercules and unearthed in the late 1800s during building work for the new capital. On the top floor the museum's pinacoteca, or painting gallery, has some noted Baroque masterpieces, including Caravaggio's *The Fortune Teller* (1595) and *St. John the Baptist* (1602; albeit, given the ram, some critics see here a representation of Isaac, the pose this time influenced by Michelangelo's "Ignudi"), Peter Paul Rubens's (1577–1640) *Romulus and Remus* (1614), and Pietro da Cortona's sumptuous portrait of Pope Urban VIII (1627). Adjacent to the Palazzo dei Conservatori is **Palazzo Caffarelli,** which holds temporary exhibitions. Here, set on the Piazzale Caffarelli, the new Caffè Capitolino offers a spectacular vista over Rome (looking toward St. Peter's); it is open daily, except Monday, 9 to 7.

To reach the Palazzo Nuovo section of the museum (the palace on the left-hand side of the Campidoglio), take the stairs or elevator to the basement of the Palazzo dei Conservatori, where an underground corridor called the Galleria Congiunzione holds a poignant collection of ancient gravestones. But before going up into Palazzo Nuovo, be sure to take the detour to the right to the Tabularium Gallery with its unparalleled view over the Forum.

Room of the Emperors

Inside the Palazzo Nuovo on the stairs you find yourself immediately dwarfed by Mars in full military rig and lion-topped sandals. Upstairs is the noted Sala degli Imperatori, lined with busts of Roman emperors, along with the Sala dei Filosofi, where busts of philosophers sit in judgment—a fascinating who's who of the ancient world, and a must-see of the museum. Although many ancient Roman treasures were merely copies of Greek originals, portraiture was one area in which the Romans took precedence. Within these serried ranks are 48 Roman emperors, ranging from Augustus to Theodosius (AD 346–395). On one console, you'll see the handsomely austere Augustus, who "found Rome a city of brick and left it one of marble." On another rests Claudius "the stutterer," an indefatigable builder brought vividly to life in the history-based novel *I, Claudius*, by Robert Graves. Also in this company is Nero, one of the most notorious emperors, who built for himself the fabled Domus Aurea. And, of course, there are the standout baddies: cruel Caligula (AD 12–41) and Caracalla (AD 186–217), and the dissolute, eerily modern boy-emperor, Heliogabalus (AD 203–222). In the adjacent Great Hall, be sure to take in the 16 resplendently restored marble statues. Nearby are rooms filled with masterpieces, including the legendary *Dying Gaul*, *The Red Faun* from Hadrian's Villa, and a *Cupid and Psyche*—each worth almost a museum to itself. Downstairs near the exit is the gigantic, reclining figure of Oceanus, found in the Roman Forum and later dubbed Marforio, one of Rome's famous "talking statues" to which citizens from the 1500s to the 1900s affixed anonymous satirical verses and notes of political protest. ✉ *Piazza del Campidoglio, Jewish Ghetto* ☎ *06/0608* 🌐 *www.museicapitolini.org* 🎫 *€13; audio guide €6* 🕙 *Tues.–Sun. 9–8* Ⓜ *Bus 44, 63, 64, 81, 95, 85, 492.*

THAT FACE, THAT FACE!

As a stroll through the Room of the Emperors will reveal, the Romans generally preferred the "warts and all" school of representation (unlike the Greeks, whose portraits were idealized). A prime example is the brutally realistic bust of Commodus (AD 161–192), the emperor-gladiator. Movie lovers will want to search out this bust: he was the inspiration for the character portrayed by Christopher Plummer in *The Fall of the Roman Empire* and by Joaquin Phoenix in *Gladiator.*

Santa Maria di Aracoeli. Sitting atop its 124 steps—"the grandest loafing place of mankind," as Henry James put it, and the spot on which Gibbon was inspired to write his great history of the decline and fall of the Roman empire—Santa Maria di Aracoeli perches on the north slope of the Capitoline Hill. You can also access the church using a less challenging staircase from Michelangelo's piazza. The church rests on the site of the temple of Juno Moneta (Admonishing Juno), which also housed the Roman mint (hence the origin of the word "money"). According to legend, it was here that the Sibyl, a prophetess, predicted to Augustus the coming of a Redeemer. The emperor supposedly responded by erecting an altar, the Ara Coeli (Altar of Heaven). This was eventually

CLOSE UP

An Emperor Cheat Sheet

OCTAVIAN, or Caesar Augustus, was Rome's first emperor (27 BC–AD 14). While it upended the republic once and for all, his rule began a 200-year peace known as the Pax Romana.

The name of **NERO** (AD 54–68) lives in infamy as a violent persecutor of Christians . . . and as the murderer of his wife, his mother, and countless others. Although it's not certain whether he actually fiddled as Rome burned in AD 64, he was well known as an actor.

DOMITIAN (AD 81–96) declared himself "Dominus et Deus," Lord and God. He stripped away power from the Senate, and as a result after his death he suffered "Damnatio Memoriae"—the Senate had his name and image erased from all public records.

TRAJAN (AD 98–117), the first Roman emperor to be born outside Italy (in southern Spain), enlarged the empire's boundaries to include modern-day Romania, Armenia, and Upper Mesopotamia.

HADRIAN (AD 117–138) designed and rebuilt the Pantheon, constructed a majestic villa at Tivoli, and initiated myriad other constructions, including the famed wall across Britain.

MARCUS AURELIUS (AD 161–180) is remembered as a humanitarian emperor, a Stoic philosopher whose *Meditations* are still read today. Nonetheless, he was devoted to expansion and an aggressive leader of the empire.

CONSTANTINE I (AD 306–337) made his mark by legalizing Christianity, an act that changed the course of history, legitimizing the once-banned religion and paving the way for the papacy in Rome.

replaced by a Benedictine monastery then church, which passed in 1250 to the Franciscans, who restored and enlarged it in Romanesque-Gothic style. Today, the Aracoeli is best known for the **Santa Bambino,** a much-revered olive-wood figure of the Christ Child (today a copy of the 15th-century original stolen in 1994 and as yet unfound). At Christmas, everyone pays homage to the Bambi Gesù as children recite poems from a miniature pulpit. In true Roman style, the church interior is a historical hodgepodge—classical columns and large marble fragments from pagan buildings, as well as a 13th-century Cosmatesque pavement. The richly gilded Renaissance ceiling commemorates the naval victory at Lepanto in 1571 over the Turks. The first chapel on the right is noteworthy for Pinturicchio's frescoes of San Bernardino of Siena (1486). ✉ *Via del Teatro di Marcello, on top of steep stairway, Jewish Ghetto* ☎ *06/69763838* ⏲ *Oct.–Apr., daily 9–5:30; May–Sept., daily 9–6:30* Ⓜ *Bus 44, 160, 170, 175, 186.*

WORTH NOTING

Belvedere Tarpeo. In ancient Roman times, traitors were hurled from here to their deaths. In the 18th and 19th centuries, the Tarpeian Rock became a popular stop for people making the Grand Tour, because of the view it gave of the Palatine Hill. Today, the Belvedere viewing point has been long shuttered for restoration, but you can proceed a short walk down to Via di Monte Tarpeio, where the view is spectacular enough. It was on this rock that, in the 7th century BC, Tarpeia betrayed the Roman citadel to the early Romans' sworn enemies, the Sabines, only asking in return to be given the heavy gold bracelets the Sabines wore on their left arm. The scornful Sabines did indeed shower her with their gold . . . then added the crushing weight of their heavy shields, also carried on their left arms. ✉ *Via del Tempio di Giove, Jewish Ghetto.*

Carcere Mamertino (*Mamertine Prison*). The Mamertino has two subterranean cells where Rome's enemies, most famously the Goth, Jugurtha, and the indomitable Gaul, Vercingetorix, were imprisoned and died, of either starvation or strangulation. In the lower cell, legend has it that St. Peter himself was held prisoner and that he miraculously brought forth a spring of water to baptize his jailers. A church, San Giuseppe dei Falegnami, now stands over the prison. A recent restoration of the cells installed a multimedia show, to mixed reviews. The automated tour focuses on the Christian history of the cell, and the audio is more fluffy than historical, making this stop a must-see only for those who really must see the place where Peter and Paul once (according to myth) stood. ✉ *Via del Tulliano, Monti* ☎ *06/698961* 🌐 *www.operaromanapellegrinaggi.org* 🎟 *€5* 🕒 *Summer, daily 9–7; winter, daily 9–5.*

Palazzo Senatorio. During the Middle Ages this city hall looked like the medieval town halls you can see in Tuscan hill towns, part fortress and part assembly hall. The building was entirely rebuilt in the 1500s as part of Michelangelo's revamping of the Campidoglio for Pope Paul III; the master's design was adapted by later architects, who wisely left the front staircase as the focus of the facade. The ancient statue of Minerva at the center was renamed the Goddess Rome, and the river gods (the River Tigris remodeled to symbolize the Tiber, to the right, and the Nile, to the left) were hauled over from the Terme di Costantino on the Quirinal Hill. Today, it is the regional seat of Rome's Comune administration and is not open to the public. ✉ *Piazza del Campidoglio, Jewish Ghetto.*

THE ROMAN FORUM

Fodor's Choice ★ **The Roman Forum.** From the entrance on Via dei Fori Imperali, descend into the extraordinary archaeological complex that is the Foro Romano. Before the 1st century, when the Roman Republic gave over to hedonistic imperial Rome, this was the heart of the empire. The Forum began life as a marshy valley between the Capitoline and Palatine hills—a valley crossed by a mud track and used as a cemetery by Iron Age settlers. Over the years a market center and some huts were established here, and after the land was drained in the 6th century BC, the site eventually became a political, religious, and commercial center: the Forum.

Hundreds of years of plunder reduced the Forum to its current desolate state. But this enormous area was once Rome's pulsating heart, filled with stately and extravagant temples, palaces, and shops, and crowded with people from all corners of the empire. Adding to today's confusion is the fact that the Forum developed over many centuries; what you see today are not the ruins from just one period but from a span of almost 900 years, from about 500 BC to AD 400. Nonetheless, the enduring romance of the place, with its lonely columns and great broken fragments of sculpted marble and stone, makes for a quintessential Roman experience.

There is always a line at the Colosseum ticket office for the combined Colosseum/Palatine/Forum ticket, but in high season, lines sometimes also form at the Forum and Palatine entrances. **■ TIP→ Those who don't want to risk waiting in line can now book their tickets online in advance, for a €1.50 surcharge, at www.coopculture.it.** ✉ *Entrance at Via dei Fori Imperiali, Monti* ☎ *06/39967700* 🌐 *www.coopculture.it* 🎫 *€12 (combined ticket with the Colosseum and Palatine Hill, if used within 2 days); audio guide €5* ⏱ *Jan.–Feb. 15, daily 8:30–4:30; Feb. 16–Mar. 15, daily 8:30–5; Mar. 16–last Sat. in Mar., daily 8:30–5:30; last Sun. in Mar.–Aug., daily 8:30–7:15; Sept., daily 8:30–7; Oct. 1–last Sat. in Oct., daily 8:30–6:30; last Sun. in Oct.–Dec., daily 8:30–4:30* Ⓜ *Colosseo.*

3

TOP ATTRACTIONS

Fodor's Choice ★

Arco di Settimio Severo (*Arch of Septimius Severus*). One of the grandest triumphal arches erected by a Roman emperor, this richly decorated monument was built in AD 203 to celebrate Severus's victory over the Parthians. It was once topped by a bronze statuary group of a chariot drawn by four or perhaps as many as six life-size horses. Masterpieces of Roman statuary, the stone reliefs on the arch were probably based on huge painted panels depicting the event, a kind of visual report on his foreign campaigns that would have been displayed during the emperor's triumphal parade in Rome to impress his subjects (and, like all statuary back then, were painted in florid, lifelike colors). ✉ *West end of Foro Romano, Monti.*

Arco di Tito (*Arch of Titus*). Standing at the northern approach to the Palatine Hill on the Via Sacra, this triumphal arch was erected in AD 81 to celebrate the sack of Jerusalem 10 years earlier, after the great Jewish revolt. The superb view of the Colosseum from the arch reminds us that it was the emperor Titus who helped finish the vast amphitheater, begun earlier by his father, Vespasian. Under the arch are two great sculpted reliefs, both showing scenes from Titus's triumphal parade along this very Via Sacra. You still can make out the spoils of war plundered from Herod's Temple, including a gigantic seven-branched candelabrum (menorah) and silver trumpets. During his sacking of Jerusalem, Titus killed or deported most of the Jewish population, thus initiating the Jewish diaspora—an event that would have historical consequences for millennia. ✉ *East end of Via Sacra, Monti.*

Basilica di Massenzio (*Basilica of Maxentius*). Only about one-third of the original of this gigantic basilica (or meeting hall) remains, so you can imagine what a wonder this building was when erected. Today, its great arched vaults still dominate the north side of the Via Sacra. Begun under the emperor Maxentius about AD 306, the edifice was a center of judicial and commercial activity, the last of its kind to be built in Rome. Over the centuries, like so many Roman monuments, it was exploited as a quarry for building materials and was stripped of its sumptuous marble and stucco decorations. Its coffered vaults, like the coffering inside the Pantheon's dome, later were copied by many Renaissance artists and architects. ✉ *Via Sacra, Monti.*

Comitium. The open space in front of the Curia was the political hub of ancient Rome. Julius Caesar had rearranged the Comitium, moving the Curia to its current site and transferring the imperial **Rostra,** the podium from which orators spoke to the people (decorated originally with the prows of captured ships, or *rostra,* the source for the term "rostrum"), to a spot just south of the Arch of Septimius Severus. It was from this location that Mark Antony delivered his funeral address in Caesar's honor. On the left of the Rostra stands what remains of the **Tempio di Saturno,** which served as ancient Rome's state treasury. ✉ *West end of Foro Romano, Monti.*

Curia. This large brick structure next to the Arch of Septimius Severus, built during Diocletian's reign in the late 3rd century AD, is the Forum's best-preserved building—thanks largely to having been turned into a church in the 7th century. By the time the Curia was built, the Senate, which met here, had lost practically all of the power and prestige that it had possessed during the Republican era. Still, the Curia appears much as the original Senate house would have looked. Today, the Curia generally is open only if there's an exhibit inside; luckily, that's not infrequent. Definitely peek inside if it's open, and don't miss the original, intricate floor of marble and porphyry, done in *opus sectile.* ✉ *Via Sacra, northwest corner of Foro Romano, Monti.*

Tempio di Castore e Polluce. The sole three remaining Corinthian columns of this temple beautifully evoke the former, elegant grandeur of the Forum. This temple was dedicated in 484 BC to Castor and Pollux, the twin brothers of Helen of Troy who carried to Rome the news of victory at Lake Regillus, southeast of Rome—the definitive defeat of the deposed Tarquin dynasty. The twins flew on their fabulous white steeds 20 km (12 miles) to the city to bring the news to the people before mortal messengers could arrive. Rebuilt over the centuries before Christ, the temple suffered a major fire and was reconstructed by Emperor Tiberius in 12 BC, the date of the three standing columns. ✉ *West of House of the Vestals, Monti.*

Tempio di Vesta. While just a fragment of the original building, the remnant of this temple shows the sophisticated elegance that architecture

THE RISE AND FALL OF ANCIENT ROME

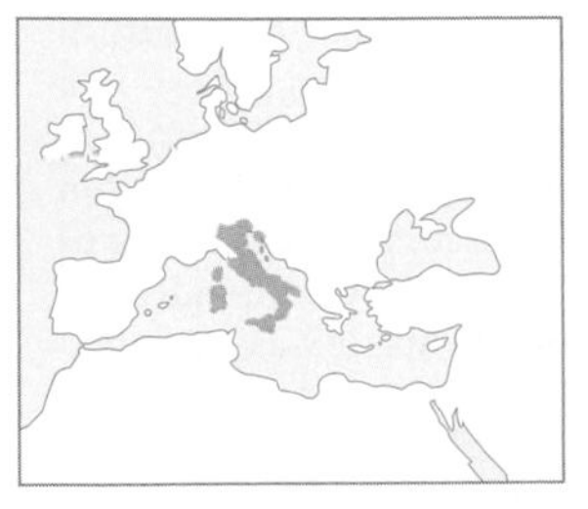

ca. 800 BC	Rise of Etruscan city-states.
510	Foundation of the Roman Republic; expulsion of Etruscans from Roman territory.
343	Roman conquest of Greek colonies in Campania.
264–241	First Punic War (with Carthage): increased naval power helps Rome gain control of southern Italy and then Sicily.
218–200	Second Punic War: Hannibal's attempted conquest of Italy, using elephants, is eventually crushed.

achieved under the later Empire. Set off by florid Corinthian columns, the circular tholos was rebuilt by Emperor Septimius Severus when he restored this temple around AD 205. Dedicated to Vesta—the goddess of the hearth—the highly privileged vestal virgins kept the sacred vestal flame alive. Next to the temple, the **Casa delle Vestali**, which reopened after restoration in 2011, gives a glimpse of the splendor in which the women lived out their 30-year vows of chastity. Marble statues of the vestals and fragments of mosaic pavement line the garden courtyard, which once would have been surrounded by lofty colonnades and at least 50 rooms. Chosen when they were between 6 and 10 years old, the six vestal virgins dedicated the next 30 years of their lives to keeping the sacred fire, a tradition that dated back to the very earliest days of Rome, when guarding the community's precious fire was essential to its well-being. Their standing in Rome was considerable; among women, they were second in rank only to the empress. Their intercession could save a condemned man, and they did, in fact, rescue Julius Caesar from the lethal vengeance of his enemy Sulla. The virgins were handsomely maintained by the state, but if they allowed the sacred fire to go out, they were scourged by the high priest, and if they broke their vows of celibacy, they were buried alive (a punishment doled out only a handful of times throughout the cult's 1,000-year history). The vestal virgins were one of the last of ancient Rome's institutions to die out, enduring to the end of the 4th century AD, even after Rome's emperors had become Christian. ⊠ *South side of Via Sacra, Monti.*

Via Sacra. The celebrated basalt-paved road that loops through the Roman Forum, lined with temples and shrines, was also the traditional route of religious and triumphal processions. Pick your way across the paving stones, some rutted with the ironclad wheels of Roman wagons, to walk in the footsteps of Caesar and Antony. ⊠ *Monti.*

WORTH NOTING

Basilica Emilia. Once a great colonnaded hall, this served as a meeting place for merchants and a kind of community center of the 2nd century BC; Augustus rebuilt it in the 1st century AD. A spot on one of the basilica's preserved pieces of floor, immediately to the right as you enter the Forum, testifies to one of Rome's more harrowing moments—and to the hall's purpose. That's where bronze coins melted, leaving behind green

150 BC	Roman Forum begins to take shape as the principal civic center in Italy.
146	Third Punic War: Rome razes city of Carthage and emerges as the dominant Mediterranean force.
133	Rome rules entire Mediterranean Basin except Egypt.
49	Julius Caesar conquers Gaul.
44	Julius Caesar is assassinated.
27	Rome's Imperial Age begins; Octavian (now named Augustus) becomes the first emperor and is later deified. The Augustan Age is celebrated in the works of Virgil (70 BC–AD 19), Ovid (43 BC–AD 17), Livy (59 BC–AD 17), and Horace (65–8 BC).

stains, when Rome was sacked and the basilica burned by the Visigoths in 410 AD. The term "basilica" refers not to the purpose of a church, but to the particular architectural form developed by the Romans. A rectangular hall flanked by colonnades, it could serve as a court of law or a center for business and commerce. ✉ *On right as you descend into Roman Forum from Via dei Fori Imperiali entrance, Monti.*

Basilica Giulia. The Basilica Giulia owes its name to Julius Caesar, who ordered its construction; it was later completed by his adopted heir Augustus. One of several such basilicas in the center of Rome, it was where the Centumviri, the hundred-or-so judges forming the civil court, met to hear cases. The open space between the Basilica Emilia and this basilica was the heart of the Forum proper, prototype of Italy's famous piazzas, and the center of civic and social activity in ancient Rome. ✉ *Via Sacra, Monti.*

Colonna di Foca (*Column of Phocas*). The last monument to be added to the Forum was erected in AD 608 in honor of a Byzantine emperor who had donated the Pantheon to Pope Boniface IV. It stands 44 feet high and remains in good condition. ✉ *West end of Foro Romano, Monti.*

Santa Francesca Romana. This church, a 10th-century edifice with a Renaissance facade, is dedicated to the patron saint of motorists; on her feast day, March 9, cars and taxis crowd the Via dei Fori Imperali below for a special blessing—a cardinal and carabinieri on hand plus a special siren to start off the ceremony. The incomparable setting continues to be a favorite for weddings. ✉ *Piazza di Santa Francesca Romana, next to Colosseum, Monti.*

Santa Maria Antiqua. The earliest Christian site in the Forum was originally part of an imperial temple, before it was converted into a church some time in the 5th or 6th century. Within are some exceptional but faded 7th- and 8th-century frescoes of the early church fathers, saints, and popes; the styles vary from typically classical to Oriental, reflecting the empire's expansion eastward. Largely destroyed in a 9th-century earthquake, the church was abandoned only to be rebuilt in 1617, then knocked down again in 1900 following excavation work on the Forum. The church had been closed to visitors since 1980, but its repair was taken on as a World Heritage Monuments fund project in 2006. The Early Christian frescoes have been restored, and Rome's Culture

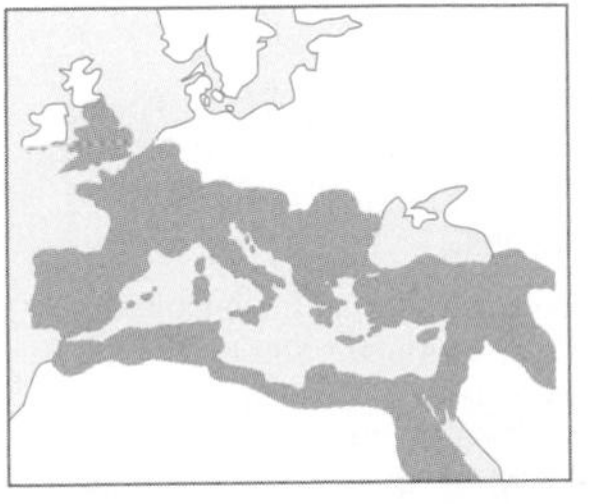

43 AD	Rome invades Britain.
50	Rome is the largest city in the world, with a population of a million.
65	Emperor Nero begins the persecution of Christians in the Empire; Saints Peter and Paul are executed.
70–80	Vespasian builds the Colosseum.
98–117	Trajan's military successes are celebrated with his Baths (98), Forum (110), and Column (113); the Roman Empire reaches its apogee.

Ministry announced that it would start opening to visitors three days a week in spring 2014. ✉ *South of Tempio di Castore and Polluce, at foot of Palatine Hill, Monti.*

Tempio di Antonino e Faustina. Erected by the Senate in honor of Faustina, deified wife of emperor Antoninus Pius (AD 138–161), Hadrian's successor, this temple was rededicated to the emperor as well upon his death. Because it was transformed into a church, it's one of the best-preserved ancient structures in the Forum. ✉ *North of Via Sacra, Monti.*

Tempio di Cesare. Built by Augustus, Caesar's successor, the temple stands over the spot where Julius Caesar's body was cremated. A pyre was improvised by grief-crazed citizens who kept the flames going with their own possessions. ✉ *Between 2 forks of Via Sacra, Monti.*

Tempio di Venere e Roma. Once Rome's largest and possibly cleverest temple (it was dedicated to Venus and Rome or, in Latin, to "amor" and "Roma"), this temple was begun by Hadrian in AD 121 and finished 20 years later. The recent restoration took even longer—some 25 years—and finally ended in 2010, meaning the public can visit the temple once again. ✉ *East of Arco di Tito, Monti.*

Tempio di Vespasiano. All that remains of Vespasian's temple are three graceful Corinthian columns. They marked the site of the Forum through the centuries while the rest was hidden beneath overgrown rubble. Nearby is the ruined platform that was the **Tempio di Concordia.** ✉ *West end of Foro Romano, Monti.*

THE PALATINE HILL

Palatine Hill. Just beyond the Arch of Titus, the Clivus Palatinus gently rises to the heights of the **Colle Palatino** (Palatine Hill)—the oldest inhabited site in Rome. Despite its location overlooking the Forum's traffic and attendant noise, the Palatine was the most coveted address for ancient Rome's rich and famous. More than a few of the Twelve Caesars called the Palatine home, including Caligula, who was murdered in the still-standing and unnerving (even today) tunnel, the Cryptoporticus. The palace of Tiberius was the first to be built here; others followed, notably the gigantic extravaganza constructed for Emperor Domitian. But perhaps the most famous lodging goes back to

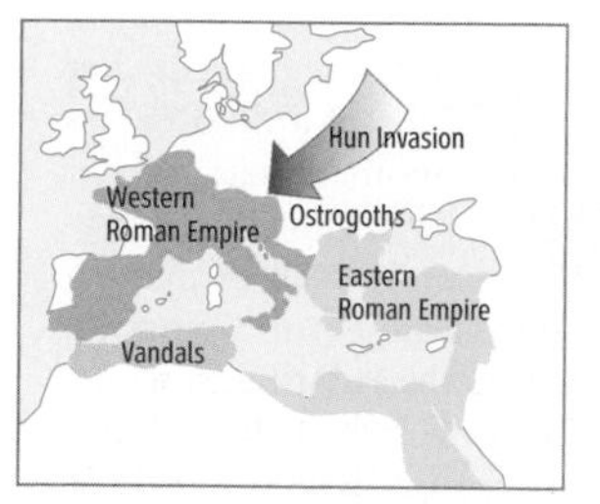

238 AD	The first wave of Germanic invasions penetrates Italy.
293	Diocletian reorganizes the Empire into West and East.
330	Constantine founds a new Imperial capital (Constantinople) in the East.
410	Rome is sacked by Visigoths.
476	The last Roman emperor, Romulus Augustus, is deposed. The western Roman Empire falls.

Rome's very beginning. Once upon a time, skeptics thought Romulus was a myth. Then, about a century ago, Rome's greatest archaeologist, Rodolfo Lanciani, excavated a site on the hill and uncovered the remains of an Iron Age settlement dating back to the 9th century BC, supporting the belief that Romulus, founder of Rome, lived here. In fall 2007, archaeologists unearthed a sacred sanctuary dedicated to Romulus and Remus set beneath the House of Augustus near the Palatine Hill. This sanctuary is now being renovated.

During the Republican era, the Palatino became the "Beverly Hills" of ancient Rome. Hortensius, Cicero, Catiline, Crassus, and Agrippa all had homes here. Augustus was born on the hill; the House of Livia, reserved for Augustus's wife, is today the hill's best-preserved structure. To visit the ruins of the Palatine (some scholars think this name gave rise to our term "palace") in roughly chronological order, start from the southeast area facing the Aventine. ✉ *Entrances at Piazza del Colosseo and Via di San Gregorio 30, Monti* ☎ *06/39967700* 🌐 *www.coopculture.it* 🎫 *€12 (combined ticket with the Colosseum and Roman Forum, if used within 2 days)* ⏲ *Daily 8:30 am–one hour before sunset* Ⓜ *Colosseo.*

TOP ATTRACTIONS

Casa di Augustus (*House of Augustus*). First discovered in the 1970s and only opened in 2006, this was the residence of the great Emperor Augustus (27 BC–14 AD)—before he became great (archaeologists have recently found two courtyards rather than one, though, in the style of Rome's ancient Greek kings, suggesting Augustus maintained this house after his ascension to prominence). The house here dates to the time when Augustus was known merely as Octavian, before the death of, and Octavian's adoption by, his great uncle Julius Caesar. Four rooms have exquisite examples of Roman wall decorative frescoes (so precious that only five people at a time are admitted). Startlingly vivid and detailed are the depictions of a narrow stage with side doors and some striking comic theater masks. ✉ *Northwest crest of Palatino, Monti* ☎ *06/39967700* 🌐 *www.coopculture.it* ⏲ *Apr.–Oct., Mon., Wed., Thurs., and weekends 8:30–1:30; Nov.–mid-Feb., Mon., Wed., and weekends 11–4; mid-Feb.–mid-Mar., Mon., Wed., and weekends 11–4.30; last 2 wks in Mar., Mon., Wed., and weekends 11–5.*

Casa di Livia (*House of Livia*). First excavated in 1839, this house was identifiable from the name inscribed on a lead pipe, Iulia Augusta. In other words, it belonged to the notorious Livia that—according to Robert Graves's *I, Claudius*—made a career of dispatching half of the Roman imperial family. (There's actually very little evidence for such claims.) She was the wife of Rome's first, and possibly greatest, emperor, Augustus. He married Livia when she was six months pregnant by her previous husband, whom Augustus "encouraged" to get a divorce. As empress, Livia became a role model for Roman women, serving her husband faithfully, shunning excessive displays of wealth, and managing her household. But she also had real influence: As well as playing politics behind the scenes, she even had the rare honor (for a woman) of being in charge of her own finances. Here, atop the Palatine, is where she made her private retreat and living quarters. The delicate, delightful frescoes reflect the sophisticated taste of wealthy Romans, whose

The "Bel Air" of ancient Rome, the Palatine Hill was the address of choice of Cicero, Agrippa, and the emperors Tiberius, Caligula, and Domitian.

love of beauty and theatrical conception of nature were revived by their descendants in the Renaissance Age. While closed at the time of this writing, the House of Livia will sometimes open for brief periods, so check by phoning or online at www.coopculture.it. ✉ *Northwest crest of Palatino, Monti* ☎ *06/39967700* 🌐 *www.coopculture.it.*

Circo Massimo (*Circus Maximus*). From the belvedere of the Domus Flavia, you can see the Circus Maximus, the giant arena where more than 300,000 spectators watched chariot races while the emperor looked on from this very spot. Ancient Rome's oldest and largest racetrack lies in a natural hollow between two hills. The oval course stretches about 650 yards from end to end; on certain occasions, there were as many as 24 chariot races a day and competitions could last for 15 days. The charioteers could amass fortunes rather like the sports stars of today (the Portuguese Diocles—one of many such "miliari"—is said to have totted up winnings of 35 million sesterci). The noise and the excitement of the crowd must have reached astonishing levels as the charioteers competed in teams, each with its own colors—the Reds, the Blues, etc. Betting also provided Rome's majority of unemployed with a potentially lucrative occupation. The central ridge was the site of two Egyptian obelisks (now in Piazza del Popolo and Piazza San Giovanni in Laterano). Picture the great chariot race scene from MGM's *Ben-Hur* and you have an inkling of what this all looked like. ✉ *Valley between Palatine and Aventine hills, Aventino* Ⓜ *Circo Massimo.*

Domus Augustana. In the Palazzi Imperiali complex, this palace, named for the "August" emperor, consisted of private apartments for Emperor Domitian and his family. Here Domitian—Master and God as he liked

Continued on page 78

ANCIENT ROME: ROME WASN'T BUILT IN A DAY

by Robert I. C. Fisher

RE-CREATING THE ANCIENT CITY

Time has reduced ancient Rome to fields of silent ruins, but the powerful impact of what happened here, of the genius and power that made Rome the center of the Western world, echoes across the millennia. In this one compact area of the city, you can step back into the Rome of Cicero, Julius Caesar, and Virgil. You can walk along the streets they knew, cool off in the shade of the Colosseum that loomed over the city, and see the sculptures poised over their piazzas.

Today, this part of Rome, more than any other, is a perfect example of the layering of historic eras, the overlapping of ages, of religions, of a past that is very much a part of the present.

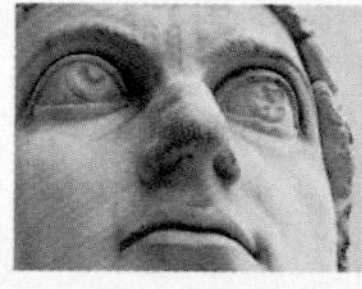

Although it has been the capital of the Republic of Italy only since 1946, Rome has been the capital of *something* for more than 2,500 years, and it shows. The magnificent ruins of the Palatine Hill, the ancient complexity of the Forum, the Renaissance harmony of the Campidoglio—all are part of Rome's identity as one of the world's most enduring seats of government.

This is not to say that it's been an easy 2½ millennia. The Vandal hordes of the 3rd century, the Goth sacks of the Middle Ages, the excavations of a modern-day Mussolini, and today's modern citizens—all played a part in transforming Rome into a city of fragments. Semi-preserved ruins of ancient forums, basilicas, stadiums, baths, and temples are strewn across the city like remnants of some Cecil B. DeMille movie set. Even if you walk into the Termini McDonalds, you'll find three chunks of the 4th century BC Servian Wall. No wonder first-time visitors feel that the only thing more intimidating than crossing a Roman intersection at rush hour is trying to make sense of the layout of ancient Rome.

The following pages detail how the new Rome overlaps the old, showing how the modern city is crammed with details of all the city's ageless walls and ancient sites, even though some of them now lie hidden underneath the earth. Written in these rocks is the story of the emperors, the city's greatest builders. Thanks in large part to their dreams of glory—combined with their architectural megalomania—Imperial Rome became the fountainhead of Western civilization.

Colosseum; (top) Head of Emperor Constantine, Musei Capitolini

THE WAY ROME WAS

Circus Maximus: Atop the Palatine Hill, the emperor's royal box looked down on the races and games of this vast stadium—most Early Christians met their untimely end here, not in the Colosseum.

Capitoline Hill (Campidoglio): Most important of Rome's original seven hills, and home to the Temple of Jupiter, the "capital" hill was strategically located high above the Tiber and became the hub of the Roman Republic.

Palatine Hill (Palatino): The birthplace of Rome, settled by Romulus and Remus, the Palatine ultimately became Rome's

Rome in the Year 300 AD

"Beverly Hills" for it was home to Cicero, Julius Caesar, and a dozen Emperors.

Roman Forum: Downtown ancient Rome, this was the political heart of the Republic and Empire—the place for processions, tribunals, law courts, and orations, it was here that Mark Antony buried Caesar and Cleopatra made her triumphant entry.

Colosseum: Gladiators fought for the chance to live another day on the floor before 50,000 spectators in this giant arena, built in a mere eight years and inaugurated in AD 80.

Domus Aurea: Nero's "Golden House," a sprawling example of the excesses of Imperial Rome, once comprised 150 rooms, some shimmering with gold.

THEY CAME, THEY SAW, THEY BUILT

Remember the triumphal scene in the 2000 film *Gladiator*? Awesome expanses of pristine marble, a cast of thousands in gold-lavished costumes, and close-ups of Joaquin Phoenix (playing Emperor Commodus) on his way to the Colosseum: Rome à la Hollywood. But behind all the marble splendor seen in the film lies an eight-centuries-long trail that extends back from Imperial Rome to a tiny village of mud huts along the Tiber river.

Museo della Civiltà Romana's model of Imperial Rome

ROMULUS GOES TO TOWN

Legend has it that Rome was founded by Romulus and Remus, twin sons of the god Mars. Upon being abandoned in infancy by a wicked uncle, they were taken up and suckled by a she-wolf living on a bank of the Tiber. (Ancient gossip says the wolf was actually a woman nicknamed Lupa for her multiple infidelities to her shepherd husband.)

As young men, Romulus and Remus returned in 753 BC to the hallowed spot to found a city but came to blows during its building, ending in the death of Remus—which is how the city became Roma, not Rema.

Where myth ends, archaeology takes over. In 2007, Roman excavators uncovered a cavernous sanctuary dedicated to the brothers situated in the valley between the Palatine and Capitoline (Campidoglio) hills in central Rome. Often transformed into "islands" when the Tiber river overflowed, these two hills soon famously expanded to include seven hills, including the Esquiline, Viminale, Celian, Quirinale, and Aventine.

SIMPLY MARBLE-LOUS

Up to 510 BC, the style of the fledging city had been set by the fun-loving, sophisticated Etruscans—Rome was to adopt their vestal virgins, household gods, and gladiatorial games. Later, when the Republic took over the city (509 BC–27 BC), the austere values promulgated by its democratic Senate eventually fell to the power-mad triumvirate of Crassus, Pompey, and Julius Caesar, who waved away any detractors—including Rome's main power-players, the patrician Senators and the populist Tribunes—by invoking the godlike sovereignty of emperorship.

Republican Rome's city was badly planned, in fact not planned at all, and the great contribution of the Emperor Augustus—who took over when his stepfather Caesar was assassinated in 43 BC—was to commence serious town planning, with results far surpassing even his own claim that he "found Rome brick and left it marble." Which was only fitting, as floridly colored marbles began to flow into Rome from all of the Mediterranean provinces he had conquered (including obelisks transported from Egypt to flaunt his victory over Cleopatra).

Via Sacra in the Roman Forum with the Temple of Saturn in the foreground and the Basilica Julia on the right.

A FUNNY THING HAPPENED ON THE WAY TO THE ROMAN FORUM

It was during Augustus's 40-year-long peaceful reign that Rome began its transition from glorified provincial capital into great city. While excavations have shown that the area of the Roman Forum was in use as a burial ground as far back as the 10th century BC, the importance of the Forum area as the political, commercial, and social center of Rome and, by extension, of the whole ancient world, grew immeasurably during Imperial times. The majestic ruins still extant are remnants of the massive complex of markets, civic buildings, and temples that dominated the city center in its heyday.

After Rome gained "empire" status, however, the original Forum was inadequate to handle the burden of the many trials and meetings required to run Western civilization, so Julius Caesar built a new forum. This apparently started a trend, as over the next 200-plus years (43 BC–AD 180), four different emperors—Augustus, Domitian, Vespasian, and Trajan—did the same. Oddly enough, the Roman Forum became four different Forums. They grew, in part, thanks to the Great Fire of AD 64, which Nero did not set but for which he took credit for laying waste to shabbier districts to build new ones.

For half a millennium, the Roman Forum area became the heart and soul of a worldwide empire, which eventually extended from Britain to Constantinople. Unfortunately, another thousand years of looting, sacking, and decay means you have to use your vivid imagination to see the glory that once was.

■ TIP→ For a step-by-step tour of the Roman Forum, see the "Rome's Best Walks" chapter.

WHERE ALL ROADS LEAD

Even if you don't dig ruins, a visit to the archaeological ruins in and around the Roman Forum is a must. Rome's foundation as a world capital and crossroads of culture are to be found here, literally. Overlapped with Rome's current streets, this map shows the main monuments of the Roman Forum (in tan) as they originally stood.

Basilica Julia

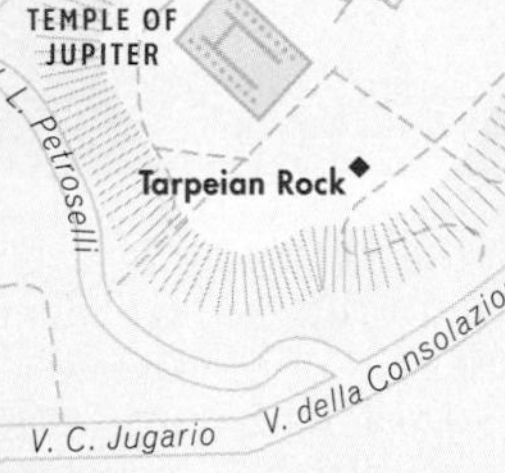

Temple of Antoninus and Faustina

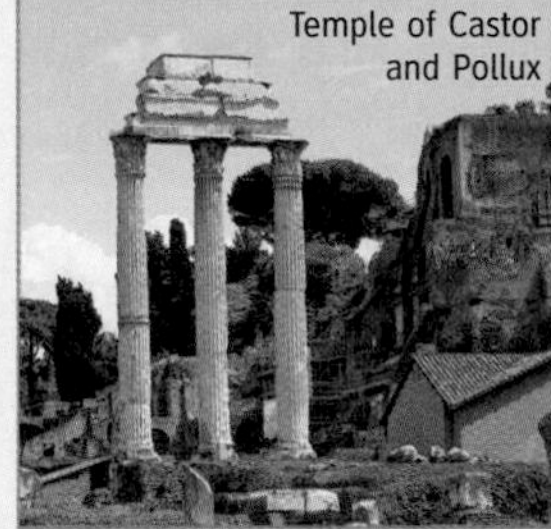
Temple of Castor and Pollux

Domitian's Palace

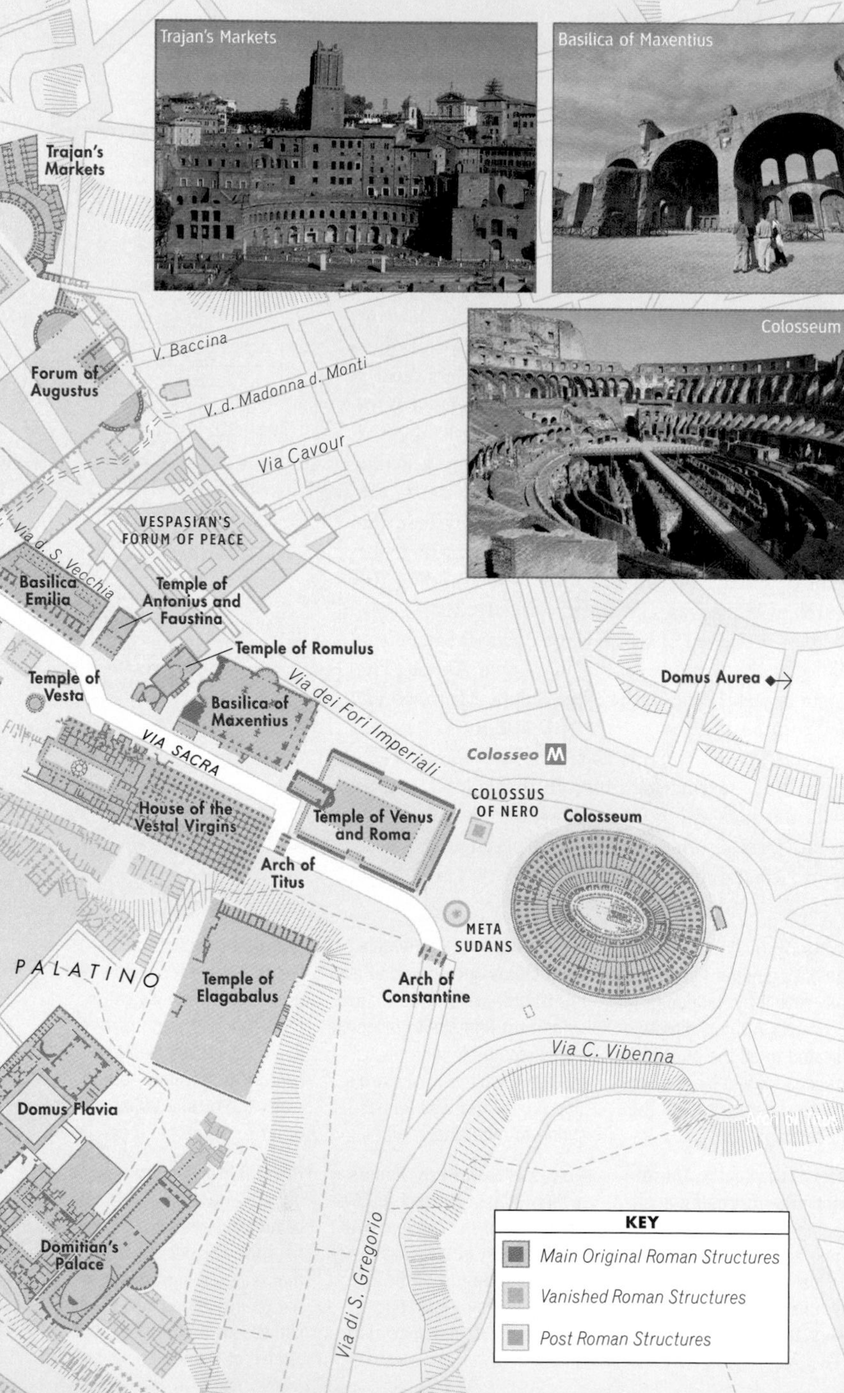
Trajan's Markets
Basilica of Maxentius
Colosseum
Trajan's Markets
Forum of Augustus
V. Baccina
V. d. Madonna d. Monti
Via Cavour
VESPASIAN'S FORUM OF PEACE
Via d. S. Vecchia
Basilica Emilia
Temple of Antonius and Faustina
Temple of Romulus
Temple of Vesta
Basilica of Maxentius
Via dei Fori Imperiali
Domus Aurea
Colosseo
VIA SACRA
House of the Vestal Virgins
Temple of Venus and Roma
COLOSSUS OF NERO
Colosseum
Arch of Titus
META SUDANS
PALATINO
Temple of Elagabalus
Arch of Constantine
Via C. Vibenna
Domus Flavia
Domitian's Palace
Via di S. Gregorio
KEY
Main Original Roman Structures
Vanished Roman Structures
Post Roman Structures

URBIS ROMÆ: THE EXPANDING CITY

Today's Campitelli district—the historic area comprising the Forums and the Colosseum—was, in fact, a relatively small part of the ancient city. From the center around the Forum, the old city dramatically grew outwards and in AD 7, the emperor Augustus organized ancient Rome into 14 *regiones,* administrative divisions that were the forerunners of today's historic *rioni* (districts). Rome's first city walls went up in the 6th century BC when King Servius Tullius built an eight-mile ring. As the city's borders greatly expanded, however, the outlaying areas needed extra protection. This became a dire necessity in the 3rd century when Germanic tribes arrived to sack Rome while Emperor Aurelian was fighting wars on the southern border of the empire. Fueled by fear, the emperor commissioned an 11-mile bulwark to be built of brick between 271 and 275. Studding the Aurelian Walls were 380 towers and 18 main gates, the best preserved of which is the Porta di San Sebastiano, at the entrance to the Via Appia Antica. The Porta is now home to the Museo delle Mura (✉ *Via di Porta San Sebastiano 18* ☎ *06/060608* 🌐 *www.museodellemuraroma.it* 🎫 *Open Tues.–Sun., 9–2*), a small but fascinating museum that allows you to walk the ancient ramparts today; take Bus No. 118 to the Porta. From the walls' lofty perch you can see great vistas of the timeless Appian Way.

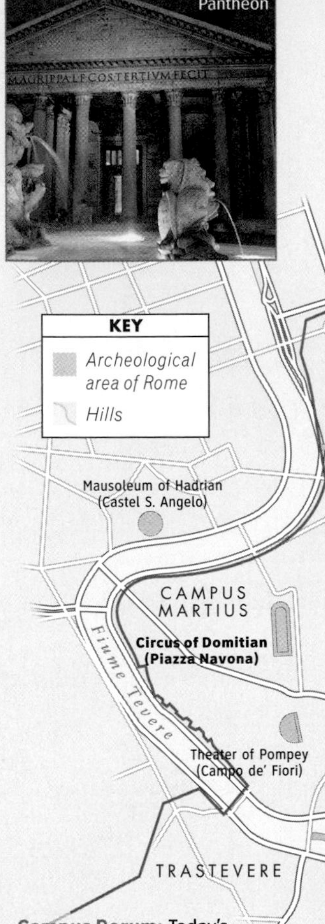

Pantheon: Built in 27 BC by Augustus's general Agrippa and totally rebuilt by Hadrian in the 2nd century AD, this temple, dedicated to all the pagan gods, was topped by the largest dome ever built (until the 20th century).

Baths of Caracalla: These gigantic thermal baths, a stunning example of ancient Roman architecture, were more than just a place to bathe—they functioned somewhat like today's swank athletic clubs.

Isola Tiberina: The Temple of Aesculapius once presided over this island—which was shaped by ancient Romans to resemble a ship, complete with obelisk mast and (still visible) marble ship prow—and was Rome's shrine to medicine.

Circus of Domitian: Rome's present Piazza Navona follows the shape of this ancient oval stadium built in 96 AD—houses now stand on top of the *cavea,* the original stone seating, which held 30,000 spectators.

Campus Borum: Today's Piazza della Bocca della Verità was ancient Rome's cattle market and the site of two beautifully preserved 2nd century BC temples, one dedicated to Fortuna Virilis, the other to Hercules.

Porta di San Sebastiano: The largest extant gate of the 3rd-century Aurelian Walls, located near the ancient aqueduct that once brought water to the nearby Baths of Caracalla, showcases the most beautiful stretch of Rome's ancient walls.

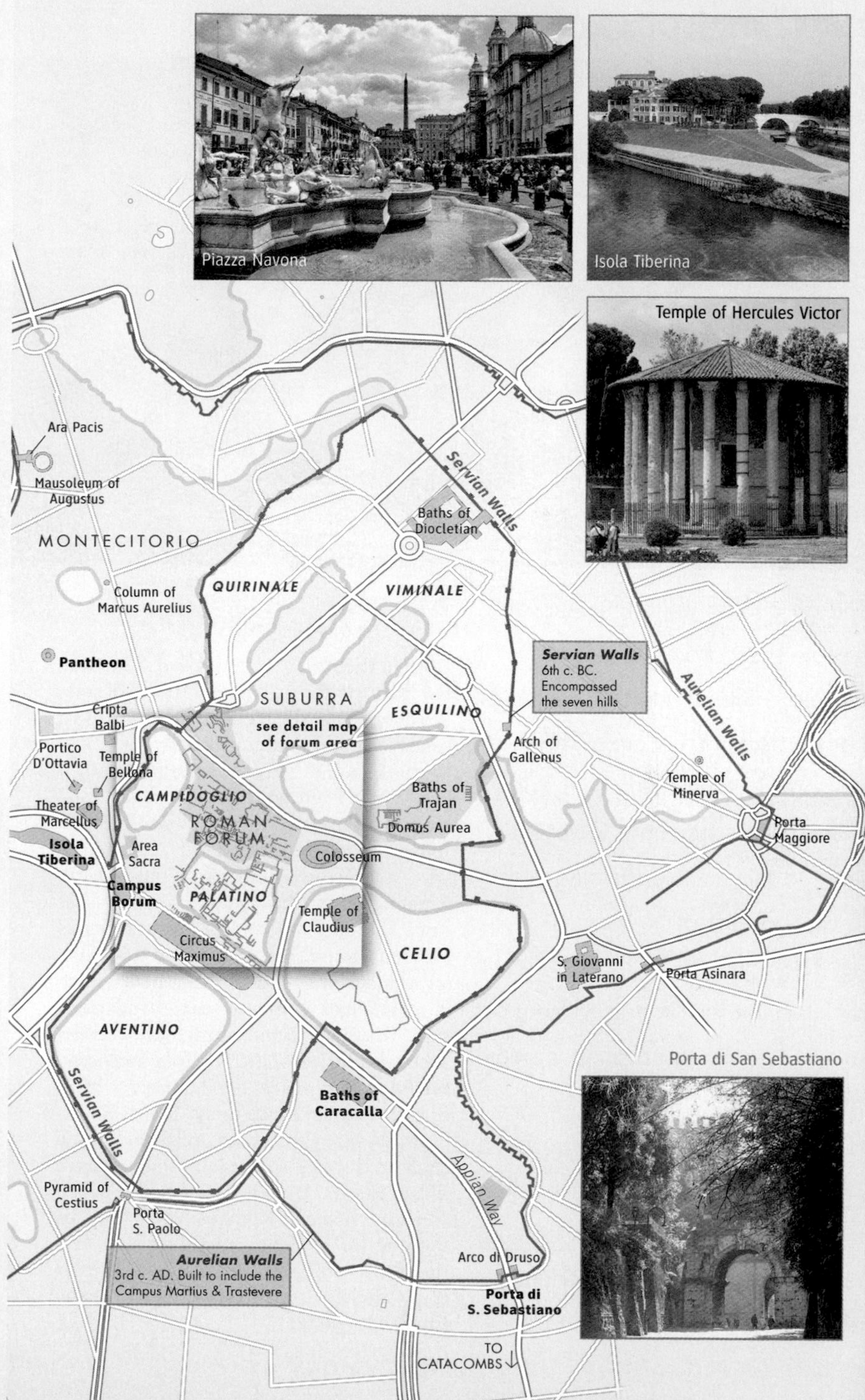
Piazza Navona
Isola Tiberina
Temple of Hercules Victor
Ara Pacis
Mausoleum of Augustus
MONTECITORIO
Column of Marcus Aurelius
Pantheon
QUIRINALE
VIMINALE
Servian Walls
Baths of Diocletian
Servian Walls
6th c. BC.
Encompassed the seven hills
Aurelian Walls
SUBURRA
ESQUILINO
Cripta Balbi
see detail map of forum area
Portico D'Ottavia
Temple of Bellona
Arch of Gallenus
Temple of Minerva
Theater of Marcellus
CAMPIDOGLIO
ROMAN FORUM
Baths of Trajan
Domus Aurea
Porta Maggiore
Isola Tiberina
Area Sacra
Colosseum
Campus Borum
PALATINO
Temple of Claudius
Circus Maximus
CELIO
S. Giovanni in Laterano
Porta Asinara
AVENTINO
Porta di San Sebastiano
Servian Walls
Baths of Caracalla
Appian Way
Pyramid of Cestius
Porta S. Paolo
Aurelian Walls
3rd c. AD. Built to include the Campus Martius & Trastevere
Arco di Druso
Porta di S. Sebastiano
TO CATACOMBS

BUILDING BLOCKS OF THE EMPERORS

Vespasian's Colosseum

The oft quoted remark of Augustus, that he found Rome brick and left it marble, omits a vital ingredient of Roman building: concrete. The sheer size and spectacle of ancient Rome's most famous buildings owe everything to this humble building block. Its use was one of the Romans' greatest contributions to the history of architecture, for it ennabled them not only to create vast arches, domes, and vaults—undreamed of before—but also to build at a scale and size never before attempted. The fall of the Roman empire ultimately arrived, but great architectural monuments remain to remind us of its glory.

THE ARCH

VESPASIAN'S COLOSSEUM

Born in Riete, Titus Flavius Vespasian was the first of the new, military emperors. A down-to-earth countryman, with a realistic sense of humor, his dying words "I think I am in the process of becoming a god" have lived on. Along with generally restoring the city, which had burned down under Nero, he started the Colosseum, (his son, Titus, finished it, in AD 80). Erected upon the swampy marsh that once held the *stagnum*, or lake, of Nero's Golden House, the Colosseum was vast; its dimensions underscored how much Romans had come to value audacious size. The main architectural motif was the arch—hundreds of them in four ascending birthday tiers, each tier adorned with a different style of column: Doric, Ionic, Corinthian, Corinthian pilaster. Inside each arch was a statue (all of which have disappeared). Under these arches, called *fornices,* ancient Romans were fond of looking for bedfellows (so famously said the great poet Ovid), so much so that these arches gave a new word to the English language.

ero's Domus Aurea

Hadrian's Pantheon

THE VAULT
NERO'S DOMUS AUREA

Most notorious of the emperors, but by no means the worst, Nero had domestic and foreign policies that were popular at first. However, his increasing megalomania was apparent in the size of his Domus Aurea, the "Golden House," so huge that the cry went up "All Rome has become a villa." Taking advantage of the Great Fire of AD 64, Nero wanted to re-create his seaside villa at Baia (outside Naples) right in the middle of Rome, building a vast palace of polychrome marble with a dining room with perforated ivory ceilings so that diners could be showered with flowers and perfume (designed by Fabullus, Nero's decorator). But the masterstrokes were the gigantic vaulted rooms—the Room of the Owls and the octagonal-shaped center room—designed by Nero's architects, Severus and Celer. Greek post-and-lintel architecture was banished for these highly dramatic spaces created by soaring vaults. You can still tour the ruins of Nero's "villa" but his 120-foot-high colossal bronze statue gave way to make room for the Colosseum.

THE DOME
HADRIAN'S PANTHEON

The concrete Roman dome at its most impressive can be seen in the Pantheon (around AD125), a massive construction 141 feet across. It is a fascinating feat of both design and engineering, for it is modeled on a sphere, the height of the supporting walls being equal to the radius of the dome. Larger than Saint Peter's, this dome of domes was constructed by the greatest Imperial builder of them all, the Emperor Hadrian. Poised on top of the dome's mighty concrete ring, the five levels of trapezoid-shaped coffers represent the course of the five then-known planets and their concentric spheres. Then, ruling over them, comes the sun, represented symbolically and literally by the so-called oculus—the giant "eye" open to the sky at the top. The heavenly symmetry is further paralleled by the coffers themselves: 28 to each row, the number of lunar cycles. In the center of each would have shone a small bronze star. All of the dome's famous gilt trim was stripped away by the Barberini popes in the 17th centuty, who melted it down to decorate the Vatican.

to be called—would retire to dismember flies (at least according to Suetonius). ✉ *Southern crest of Palatino, Monti.*

Domus Flavia. Domitian used this palace in the Palazzi Imperiali complex for official functions and ceremonies. Also called Palazzo dei Flavi, it included a basilica where the emperor could hold judiciary hearings. There were also a large audience hall, a peristyle (a columned courtyard), and the imperial triclinium (dining room), the latter set in a sunken declivity overlooking the Circus Maximus—some of its mosaic floors and stone banquettes are still in place. Domitian had the walls and courtyards of this and the adjoining Domus Augustana covered with the shiniest marble, to act as mirrors to alert him to any knife in the back. They failed in their purpose. He died in a palace plot, engineered, some say, by his wife Domitia. ✉ *Southern crest of Palatino, Monti.*

WORTH NOTING

Museo Palatino. The Palatine Museum charts the history of the hill from Archaic times with quaint models of early villages (ground floor) through to Roman times (ground and upper floors). On display in Room V are painted terra-cotta moldings and sculptural decorations from various temples (notably the Temple of Apollo Actiacus, whose name derives from the god to whom Octavian attributed his victory at Actium; the severed heads of the Medusa in the terra-cotta panels symbolize the defeated Queen of Egypt). Upon request, museum staff will accompany visitors to see the 16th-century frescoes of the Loggia Mattei. Portions of the paintings have been returned here from the Metropolitan Museum of Art in New York City. In the same building are frescoes detached from the Aula Isaica, one of the chambers belonging to the House of Augustus. ✉ *Northwest crest of Palatino, Monti* 🌐 *www.museopalatino.com* 🎫 *€12 (combined ticket with the Colosseum, Roman Forum, and Imperial Forums, if used within 2 days)* ⏲ *Daily 8:30–4* Ⓜ *Colosseo.*

Orti Farnesiani. Alessandro Farnese, a nephew of Pope Paul III, commissioned the 16th-century architect Vignola to lay out this archetypal Italian garden over the ruins of the Palace of Tiberius, up a few steps from the House of Livia. This was yet another example of the Renaissance renewing an ancient Roman tradition. To paraphrase the poet Martial, the statue-studded gardens of the Flavian Palace were such as to make even an Egyptian potentate turn green with envy. ✉ *Monte Palatino, Monti.*

Stadio Palatino. Domitian may have created this vast, open space adjoining his palace as a private hippodrome, or simply as a sunken garden. It also may have been used to stage games and other amusements for the emperor's benefit. ✉ *Southeast crest of Palatino, Monti.*

THE IMPERIAL FORUMS

Imperial Forums. A complex of five grandly conceived squares flanked with colonnades and temples, the Fori Imperiali (Imperial Fora) formed the magnificent monumental core of ancient Rome, together with the original Roman Forum. Excavations at the start of the 21st century have revealed more of the Imperial Fora than seen in nearly a thousand years.

From Piazza del Colosseo, head northwest on Via dei Fori Imperiali toward Piazza Venezia. Now that the road has closed to private traffic, it's a bit less chaotic and more pleasant for pedestrians—thanks to a 2013 decree by Rome's new mayor, it is buses and taxis only, much to the annoyance of many locals. (It also closes to all traffic every Sunday.) On the walls to your left, maps in marble and bronze put up by Benito Mussolini show the extent of the Roman Republic and Empire. The dictator's own dreams of empire led him to construct this avenue, cutting brutally through the Imperial Fora, so that he would have a suitable venue for parades celebrating his expected military triumphs. Among the Fori Imperiali along the avenue you can see the Foro di Cesare (Forum of Caesar) and the Foro di Augusto (Forum of Augustus). The grandest of all the Imperial Fora was the Foro di Traiano (Forum of Trajan), with its huge semicircular Mercati Traianei and the Colonna di Traiano (Trajan's Column). You can walk through part of Trajan's Markets on the new promenade, which opened in 2013 after a long restoration, or at the new Museo dei Fori Imperiali, which presents the Imperial Forums and shows how they would have been used, through both ancient fragments and artifacts and modern multimedia. On very rare occasions, guided tours of the Imperial Forums may be offered (check with the tourist office). The fora also are illuminated at night. ✉ *Via dei Fori Imperiali, Monti* ☎ *06/0608* 🌐 *www.mercatiditraiano.it* 🎫 *Museum €9.50* ⏲ *Museum Tues.–Sun. 9–7* Ⓜ *Colosseo.*

TOP ATTRACTIONS

Colonna di Traiano (*Trajan's Column*). The remarkable series of reliefs spiraling up this column celebrate the emperor's victories over the Dacians in today's Romania. It has stood in this spot since AD 113. The scenes on the column are an important primary source for information on the Roman army and its tactics. An inscription on the base declares that the column was erected in Trajan's honor and that its height corresponds to the height of the hill that was razed to create a level area for the grandiose Foro di Traiano. The emperor's ashes, no longer here, were kept in a golden urn in a chamber at the column's base; his statue stood atop the column until 1587, when the pope had it replaced with a statue of St. Peter. ✉ *Via del Foro di Traiano, Monti.*

Foro di Traiano (*Forum of Trajan*). Of all the Imperial Fora complexes, Trajan's was the grandest and most imposing, a veritable city unto itself. Designed by architect Apollodorus of Damascus, it comprised a vast basilica (at the time of writing closed for restoration), two libraries, and a colonnade laid out around the square, all once covered with rich marble ornamentation. Adjoining the forum were the **Mercati Traianei** (Trajan's markets), a huge, multilevel brick complex of shops, walkways, and terraces that was essentially an ancient shopping mall. The **Museo dei Fori Imperiali** (Imperial Forums Museum) opened in 2007, taking advantage of the forum's soaring, vaulted spaces to showcase archaeological fragments and sculptures while presenting a video recreation of the original complex. In addition, the series of terraced rooms offers an impressive overview of the entire forum. **■ TIP→ A new, pedestrian-only passageway alongside Via dei Fori Imperiali also allows for an excellent, and free, view of the forum.**

To build a complex of this magnitude, Apollodorus and his patron clearly had to have great confidence, not to mention almost unlimited means and cheap labor at their disposal—this readily provided by captives from Trajan's Dacian wars. Formerly thought to be the Roman equivalent of a multipurpose commercial center, with shops, taverns, and depots, the site is now believed to be more of an administrative complex for storing and regulating Rome's enormous food supplies. They also contained two semicircular lecture halls, one at either end, which were likely associated with the libraries in Trajan's Forum. The markets' architectural centerpiece is the enormous curved wall, or *hexedra,* that shores up the side of the Quirinal Hill exposed by Apollodorus's gangs of laborers. Covered galleries and streets were constructed at various levels, following the hexedra's curves and giving the complex a strikingly modern appearance.

A CLASSY LOOKOUT

The exit of the Palatino leads to the Arch of Titus, where you turn east toward the Colosseum and the Arco di Costantino. Cross Piazza del Colosseo and stroll through the park on the Colle Oppio (Oppian Hill), the site of Trajan's baths and of Nero's Golden House. The park here has some great views over the Colosseum; one of the best vantage points is from Via Nicola Salvi, which climbs uphill from the Colosseum. Around dusk, camera snatchers can appear so keep one eye on your Nikon, one eye on the view.

As you enter the markets, a large, vaulted hall stands in front of you. Two stories of shops or offices rise up on either side. It's thought that they were an administrative center for food handouts to the city's poor. Head for the flight of steps at the far end that leads down to Via Biberatica. (*Bibere* is Latin for "to drink," and the shops that open onto the street are believed to have been taverns.) Then head back to the three tiers of shops/offices that line the upper levels of the great hexedra and look out over the remains of the forum. Empty and bare today, the cubicles were once ancient Rome's busiest market stalls. Though it seems to be part of the market, the **Torre delle Milizie** (Tower of the Militia), the tall brick tower, which is a prominent feature of Rome's skyline, was built in the early 1200s. ✉ *Entrance:, Via IV Novembre 94, Monti* ☎ *06/0608* 🌐 *www.mercatiditraiano.it* 🎫 *€9.50* ⏲ *Tues.–Sun. 9–7 (ticket office closes at 6)* Ⓜ *Bus 85, 175, 186, 810, 850, H, 64, 70.*

Fodor's Choice ★ **Santi Cosma e Damiano.** Home to one of the most striking Early Christian mosaics in the world, this church was adapted in the 6th century from two ancient buildings: the library in Vespasian's Forum of Peace and a hall of the Temple of Romulus (dedicated to the son of Maxentius and at Christmas the setting for a Christmas crib). In the apse is the famous AD 530 mosaic of Christ in Glory. It reveals how popes at the time strove to re-create the splendor of imperial audience halls into Christian churches: Christ wears a gold, Roman-style toga, and his pose recalls that of an emperor addressing his subjects. He floats on a blue sky streaked with a flaming sunset—a miracle of tesserae mosaic-work. To his side are the figures of Sts. Peter and Paul, who present Cosmas and Damian, two Syrian benefactors whose charity was such that they were branded Christians and condemned to death. Beneath this awe-inspiring work is an enchanting mosaic frieze of holy lambs. ✉ *Via in Miranda 11, Monti* ☎ *06/6920441* ⏲ *Daily 9–1 and 3–7* Ⓜ *Bus 85, 850, 87, 571.*

WORTH NOTING

Foro di Augusto (*Forum of Augustus*). These ruins, along with those of the **Foro di Nerva,** on the northeast side of Via dei Fori Imperiali, give only a hint of what must have been impressive edifices. ✉ *Via dei Fori Imperiali, Monti* Ⓜ *Colosseo.*

Foro di Cesare (*Forum of Caesar*). To try to rival the original Roman Forum, Julius Caesar had this forum built in the middle of the 1st century BC. Each year without fail, on the Ides of March, an unknown hand lays a bouquet at the foot of Caesar's statue. ✉ *Via dei Fori Imperiali, Monti* ☎ *06/0608.*

3

THE COLOSSEUM AND ENVIRONS

Legend has it that as long as the Colosseum stands, Rome will stand; and when Rome falls, so will the world. No visit to Rome is complete without a trip to the obstinate oval that has been the iconic symbol of the city for centuries. Looming over a group of the Roman Empire's most magnificent monuments to imperial wealth and power, the Colosseo was the gigantic sports arena built by Vespasian and Titus. To its west stands the Arch of Constantine, a majestic, ornate triumphal arch, built solely as a tribute to the emperor Constantine; victorious armies purportedly marched under it on their return from war. On the eastern side of the Colosseum, hidden under the Colle Oppio, is Nero's opulent Domus Aurea, a palace that stands as testimony to the lavish lifestyles of the emperors—unfortunately, closed, once again, for restoration after rainwater caused part of the roof to collapse in 2010.

TOP ATTRACTIONS

Arco di Costantino (*Arch of Constantine*). This majestic arch was erected in AD 315 to commemorate Constantine's victory over Maxentius at the Milvian Bridge. It was just before this battle, in AD 312, that Constantine—the emperor who converted Rome to Christianity—had a vision of a cross in the heavens and heard the words "In this sign thou shalt conquer." Many of the rich marble decorations for the arch were scavenged from earlier monuments, both saving money and allying Constantine with the greatest emperors of the past. It is easy to picture ranks of Roman legionnaires marching under the great barrel vault. ✉ *Piazza del Colosseo, Monti* Ⓜ *Colosseo.*

Fodor's Choice ★

The Colosseum. The most spectacular extant edifice of ancient Rome, the Colosseo has a history that is half gore, half glory. Here, before 50,000 spectators, gladiators would salute the emperor and cry *Ave, imperator, morituri te salutant* ("Hail, emperor, men soon to die salute thee"); it is said that when one day they heard the emperor Claudius respond, "or maybe not," they became so offended that they called a strike.

Scene of countless Hollywood spectacles—Deborah Kerr besieged by lions in *Quo Vadis*, Victor Mature laying down his arms in *Demetrius and the Gladiators*, and Russell Crowe fighting an emperor in

Hollywood got it wrong, historians got it right: plenty of gladiators died in the Colosseum but early Christians only met their tragic fate in the nearby Circus Maximus arena.

a computer-generated stadium in *Gladiator*, to name just a few—the Colosseum still awes onlookers today with its power and might.

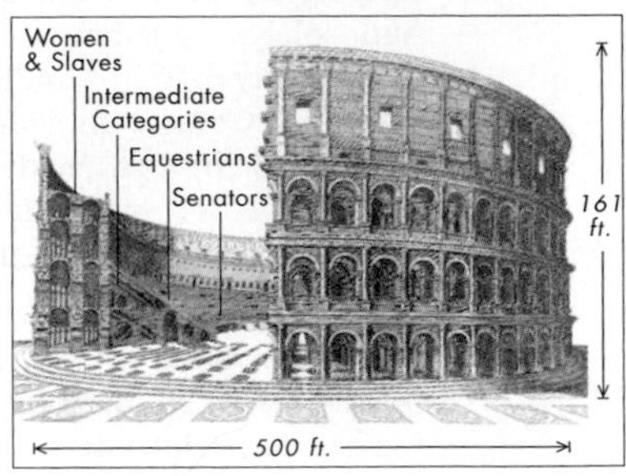

Designed by order of the Flavian emperor Vespasian in AD 72, the Colosseum was inaugurated by Titus eight years later with a program of games lasting 100 days.

Such shows were a quick way to political popularity—or, to put it another way, a people that yawns is ripe for revolt.

The arena has a circumference of 573 yards and was faced with travertine from nearby Tivoli. Its construction was a remarkable feat of engineering, for it stands on marshy terrain reclaimed by draining an artificial lake on the grounds of Nero's Domus Aurea.

Originally known as the Flavian amphitheater, it came to be called the Colosseo because it stood on the site of the Colossus of Nero, a 115-foot-tall gilded bronze statue of the emperor that once towered here.

Inside, senators had marble seats up front and the Vestal Virgins took the ringside position, while the plebs sat in wooden tiers at the back, then the masses above on the top tier. Over all was the amazing velarium, an ingenious system of sail-like awnings rigged on ropes and maneuvered by sailors from the imperial fleet, who would unfurl them to protect the arena's occupants from sun or rain.

Once inside, take the steep stairs or elevator up to the second floor, where you can get a bird's-eye view of the hypogeum: the subterranean passageways that were the architectural engine rooms that made the slaughter above proceed like clockwork. In a scene prefiguring something from Dante's *Inferno*, hundreds of beasts would wait to be eventually launched via a series of slave-powered hoists and lifts into the bloodthirsty sand of the arena above. The newly restored hypogeum, along with the third level of the Colosseum, reopened to much acclaim in fall 2010 (visitable only via a prebooked, guided tour). Since then, however, it's open and shut, depending on the season and recent rains. Check the Pierreci website for its current state.

Legend has it that as long as the Colosseum stands, Rome will stand; and when Rome falls, so will the world... not that the prophecy deterred Renaissance princes (and even a pope) from using the Colosseum as a quarry. In the 19th century, poets came to view the arena by moonlight; today, mellow golden spotlights make the arena a spectacular sight.

TIPS

Are there ways to beat the big ticket lines at the Colosseum? Yes and no. First off, if you go to the Roman Forum, a couple of hundred yards down Via dei Fori Imperiali on your left, or to the Palatine, down Via di San Gregorio, the €12 ticket you purchase there includes admission to the Colosseum and, even better, lets you jump to the head of the *looooooong* line. Another way is to buy the Romapass (🌐 *www.romapass.it*) ticket, which includes the Colosseo. Or you can book a ticket in advance through 🌐 *www.coopculture.it* (for a €1.50 surcharge), the main ticket-reservation service for many Italian cultural sights. Finally, you can book another tour online with a company (do your research to make sure it's reputable) that lets you "skip the line."

No matter what, however, avoid the tours that are being sold on-the-spot right around the Colosseum, including on the piazza and just outside of the metro. It's all part of a fairly disreputable system that goes on both there and at the Vatican. While the (usually young and English-speaking) "sellers" themselves vary and often work for different companies, their big selling point is always the same: You can skip the line. Although this makes them tempting if you haven't come up with any other game plan, be aware that the tour guides tend to be dry or, due to heavy accents, all but incomprehensible, the tour groups huge, and the tour itself rushed. Plan on an alternative way to get past the line so you don't fall into the last-minute-tour trap.

The exhibition space upstairs often features fascinating temporary exhibitions, included in your ticket price. A bookshop is also on-site.

Thumbs Down

Although the Colosseum had 80 entrances, it only had one exit named after the Roman goddess of death—the Porta Libitinaria—which was how dead gladiators were trundled out of the arena. Historians state that most of these warriors did survive to fight another day. If the die was cast, however, the rule was a victorious gladiator was the person to decide to take his opponent's life. He was often spurred on by the audience and the emperor—*pollice verso* meant the downturned thumb. Gladiatorial combat, or *munera*, is now traced back to the funeral rites of the early Etruscans when prisoners of war would sometimes be sacrificed to placate the spirits of the underworld. Rome's City Council, in conjunction with Amnesty International, tries to make amends for these horrors by floodlighting the Colosseum by night every time a death sentence is commuted or a country votes to abolish capital punishment. As well as the sellers pushing tours on the piazza outside the Colosseum, you'll come across muscled men who call themselves the "gladiators." They're actually dressed as Roman centurions, but that doesn't stop them from posing for pictures with tourists—and then insisting on a €5, €10, or even higher price afterwards. If you just have to get that photo op with a sword on your neck, make sure you set the price with the "gladiator" beforehand. ✉ *Piazza del Colosseo, Monti* ☎ *06/39967700* 🌐 *www.pierreci.it* 🎟 *€12 (combined ticket with the Roman Forum, Palatine Hill, and Imperial Forums, if used within 2 days)* ⏲ *Daily 8:30–1 hr before sunset* Ⓜ *Colosseo. Bus 117, 75, 81, 673, 175, 204.*

WORTH NOTING

Domus Aurea (*Golden House of Nero*). Legend has it that Nero famously fiddled while Rome burned. Fancying himself a great actor and poet, he played, as it turns out, his harp to accompany his recital of "The Destruction of Troy" while gazing at the flames of Rome's catastrophic fire of AD 64. Anti-Neronian historians propagandized that Nero, in fact, had set the Great Fire to clear out a vast tract of the city center to build his new palace. Today's historians discount this as historical folderol (going so far as to point to the fact that there was a full moon on the evening of July 19, hardly the propitious occasion to commit arson). But legend or not, Nero did get to build his new palace, the extravagant Domus Aurea (Golden House)—a vast "suburban villa" that was inspired by the emperor's pleasure palace at Baia on the Bay of Naples. His new digs were huge and sumptuous, with a facade of pure gold, seawater piped into the baths, decorations of mother-of-pearl, fretted ivory, and other precious materials, and vast gardens. It was said that after completing this gigantic house, Nero exclaimed, "Now I can live like a human being!" Unfortunately, following damage due to flooding in December 2008, the Domus is closed for restorations once again. ✉ *Via della Domus Aurea, Monti* ☎ *06/39967700 information about possible future openings* Ⓜ *Colosseo.*

Museo delle Mura. Rome's first walls were erected in the 6th century BC but the ancient city greatly expanded over the next few centuries. In the 3rd century AD, Emperor Aurelian commissioned an 11-mile wall to protect the southern border of the empire. Studding the Aurelian Walls were 380 towers and 18 main gates, the best preserved of which is the Porta di San Sebastiono, at the entrance to the Via Appia Antica. The Porta is home to a small museum that allows visitors to walk the ancient ramparts. Take Bus No. 118 to the Porta. There are wonderful views of the Appian Way from the walls. ✉ *Via di Porta San Sebastiano, Via Appia Antica* ☎ *06/39060608* 🌐 *www.en.museodellemuraroma.it* 🎟 *€6* ⏲ *Daily 9 am–9 pm.*

4

THE VATICAN

GETTING ORIENTED

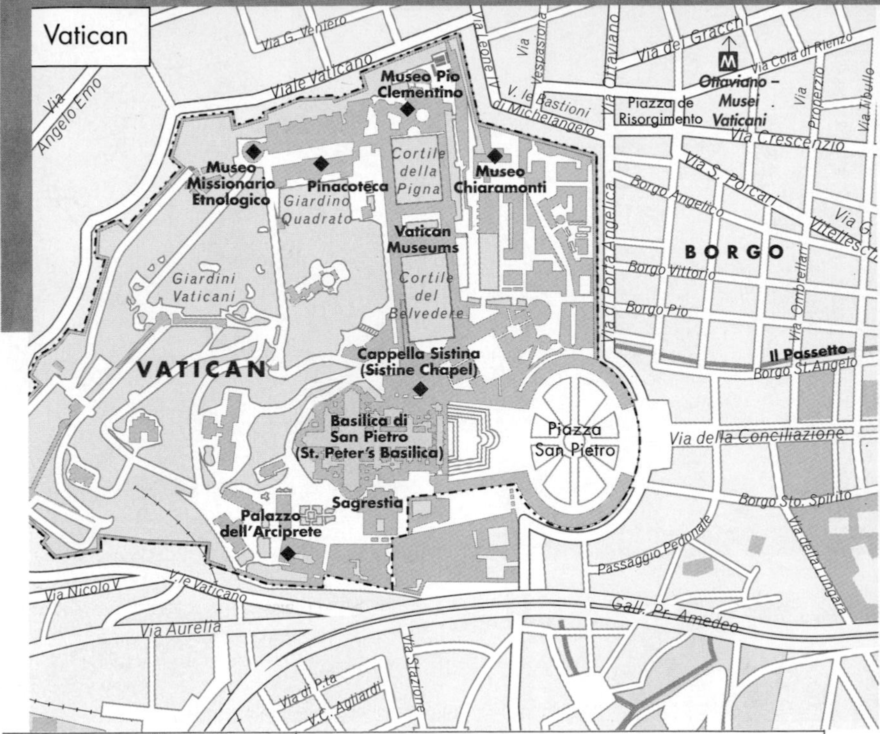

GETTING HERE

Metro stops Cipro or Ottaviano (Musei Vaticani) will get you within about a 10-minute walk of the entrance to the Vatican Museums. Or, from Termini station, the No. 40 Express or the famously crowded No. 64 will take you to Piazza San Pietro. Both routes swing past Largo Argentina, where you can also get the 571 or 46.

A leisurely meander from the historic center across the exquisite Ponte Sant'Angelo footbridge will take about a half hour.

HOW TO BEAT THOSE LONG LINES

Home to the Sistine Chapel and the Raphael rooms, the Vatican Museums are among the most congested of all Rome's attractions.

For years, people thought the best way to get a jump on the crowds was to be at the front entrance when it opened at 8:30 am, particularly on the last Sunday of the month when entrance is free (other Sundays the museums are closed).

The problem was that everyone else had the same idea. Result: Rome's version of the Calgary stampede.

Instead, the best way to avoid long lines is to arrive between noon and 2, when lines will be very short or even nonexistent, except Sundays when admissions close at 12:30. Even better is to schedule your visit during the Wednesday Papal Mass, held in the piazza of St. Peter's or at Aula Paolo Sesto. This is usually 10:30 am—to see the pope's calendar, log on to: 🌐 *www.vatican.va*. Finally, you can purchase your ticket in advance online for an extra €4.

Or book a tour, either with the Vatican Museums directly or with a private agency that guarantees a skip-the-line entrance. The Vatican's own guided tour of the museums and Sistine Chapel, which can be booked online, costs €32 and lasts two hours.

All this with the proviso that, traditionally, in July the pope is away on holiday in Val d'Aosta, then in August to mid-September moves to Castel Gandolfo, papal masses being held there instead.

Hours for the Vatican Museums now run 9–4 (last entrance) and exit by 6 (including Saturdays).

The last Sunday of the month, when entrance is free, hours are 9–2 (last entrance at 12:30).

The Museums close the first three Sundays of every month; other dates of closures include January 1 and 6, February 11, March 19, Easter and Easter Monday, May 1, June 29, August 14 and 15, November 1, and December 8, 25, and 26.

TOP REASONS TO GO

Michelangelo's Sistine Ceiling: The most sublime example of artistry in the world, this 10,000-square-foot fresco took the artist four long, neck-craning years to finish.

St. Peter's Dome: Climb the claustrophobic and twisting Renaissance stairs to the very top for a view that you will really feel you've earned (or take the elevator on the right of the main church portico).

Papal Blessing: Join the singing, flag-waving throngs from around the world at the Wednesday general audience on St. Peter's Square (October–June only, weather permitting).

Vatican Museums: Savor one of the Western world's best art collections—from the Apollo Belvedere to Raphael's *Transfiguration*, this is pure Masterpiece Theater. Taken all together, culture here approaches critical mass.

St. Peter's Basilica: Stand in awe of both the seat of world Catholicism and a Renaissance masterwork.

Sightseeing
★★★★★
Nightlife
★★
Dining
★★★
Lodging
★★★
Shopping
★★

For many, a visit to the Vatican is one of the top reasons to visit Rome, and it is a vast and majestic place, jam-packed with things to see, so it's best to plan ahead. Borgo and Prati are the neighborhoods immediately surrounding the Vatican and it's worth noting that while the Vatican might be a priority, these neighborhoods are not the best places to choose a hotel as they're quite far from other top sights in the city.

THE VATICAN

Updated by Amanda Ruggeri

Climbing the steps to St. Peter's Basilica feels monumental, like a journey that has reached its climactic end. Swiss Guards stand at attention, spears at their sides, as you pass through the gates. Suddenly, all is cool and dark . . . and you are dwarfed by a gargantuan hall and its magnificence. Above is a ceiling so high it must lead to heaven itself. Great, shining marble figures of saints frozen mid-whirl loom from niches and corners. And at the end, a throne, for an unseen king whose greatness (it is implied) must mirror the greatness of his palace. For this basilica is a palace, the dazzling center of power for a king and a place of supplication for his subjects. Whether his kingdom is earthly or otherwise may be in the eye of the beholder.

For good Catholics and sinners alike, the Vatican is an exercise in spirituality, requiring patience but delivering joy. Some come here to savor a heavenly Michelangelo fresco—others to find their soul. But what all visitors share, for a few hours, is an awe-inspiring landscape that offers a famous sight for every taste. Rooms decorated by Raphael, antique sculptures like the Apollo Belvedere, famous paintings by Giotto and Bellini, and, perhaps most of all, the Sistine Chapel: for the lover of beauty, few places are as historically important as this epitome of faith and grandeur.

The story of this area's importance dates back to the 1st century, when St. Peter, known (albeit retroactively) as the first pope, was buried here. The first basilica in his honor rose in this spot under Emperor Constantine, the first Christian emperor of Rome, some 250 years later. It wasn't until the Middle Ages, however, that the papacy decided to make this area not only a major spiritual center, but the spot from which they would wield temporal power, as well. Today, it's difficult not to be reminded of that worldly power when you glimpse the massive walls surrounding Vatican City—a sign that you're entering an independent, sovereign state, established by the Lateran Treaty of 1929 between the Holy See and Mussolini's government.

Vatican City covers 108 acres on a hill west of the Tiber and is separated from the city on all sides, except at Piazza di San Pietro, by high walls. Within the walls, about 1,000 people are permanent residents. The Vatican has its own daily newspaper (*L'Osservatore Romano*), issues its own stamps, mints its own coins, and has its own postal system (one run, people say thankfully, by the Swiss). Within its territory are administrative and foreign offices, a pharmacy, banks, an astronomical observatory, a print shop, a mosaic school and art restoration institute, a tiny train station, a supermarket, a small department store, and several gas stations. The sovereign of this little state is the pope, Francis, elected in March 2013 after his predecessor, Benedict XVI, stepped down (the first time a pope has given up office since 1415). His main role is as spiritual leader to the world's Catholic community.

Today, there are two principal reasons for sightseeing at the Vatican. One is to visit the Basilica di San Pietro, the most overwhelming architectural achievement of the Renaissance; the other is to visit the Vatican Museums, which contain collections of staggering richness and diversity. Here at the Vatican great artists are honored almost as much as any holy power: the paintings, frescoes, sculptures, and buildings are as much monuments to their genius as to the Catholic Church.

Inside the basilica—breathtaking both for its sheer size and for its extravagant interior—are artistic masterpieces including Michelangelo's *Pietà* and Bernini's great bronze *baldacchino* (canopy) over the main altar. The Vatican Museums, their entrance a 10-minute walk from the piazza, hold endless collections of many of the greatest works of Western art. The Laocoön, Leonardo's *St. Jerome*, and Raphael's *Transfiguration* all are here. The Sistine Chapel, accessible only through the museums, is Michelangelo's magnificent artistic legacy and his ceiling is the High Renaissance in excelsis, in more ways than one.

TOP ATTRACTIONS

Fodor's Choice ★ **Basilica di San Pietro.** The world's largest church, built over the tomb of St. Peter, is the most imposing and breathtaking architectural achievement of the Renaissance (although much of the lavish interior dates to the Baroque). The physical statistics are impressive: it covers 18,000 square yards, runs 212 yards in length, and is surmounted by a dome that rises 435 feet and measures 138 feet across its base. Its history is equally impressive. No fewer than five of Italy's greatest artists—Bramante,

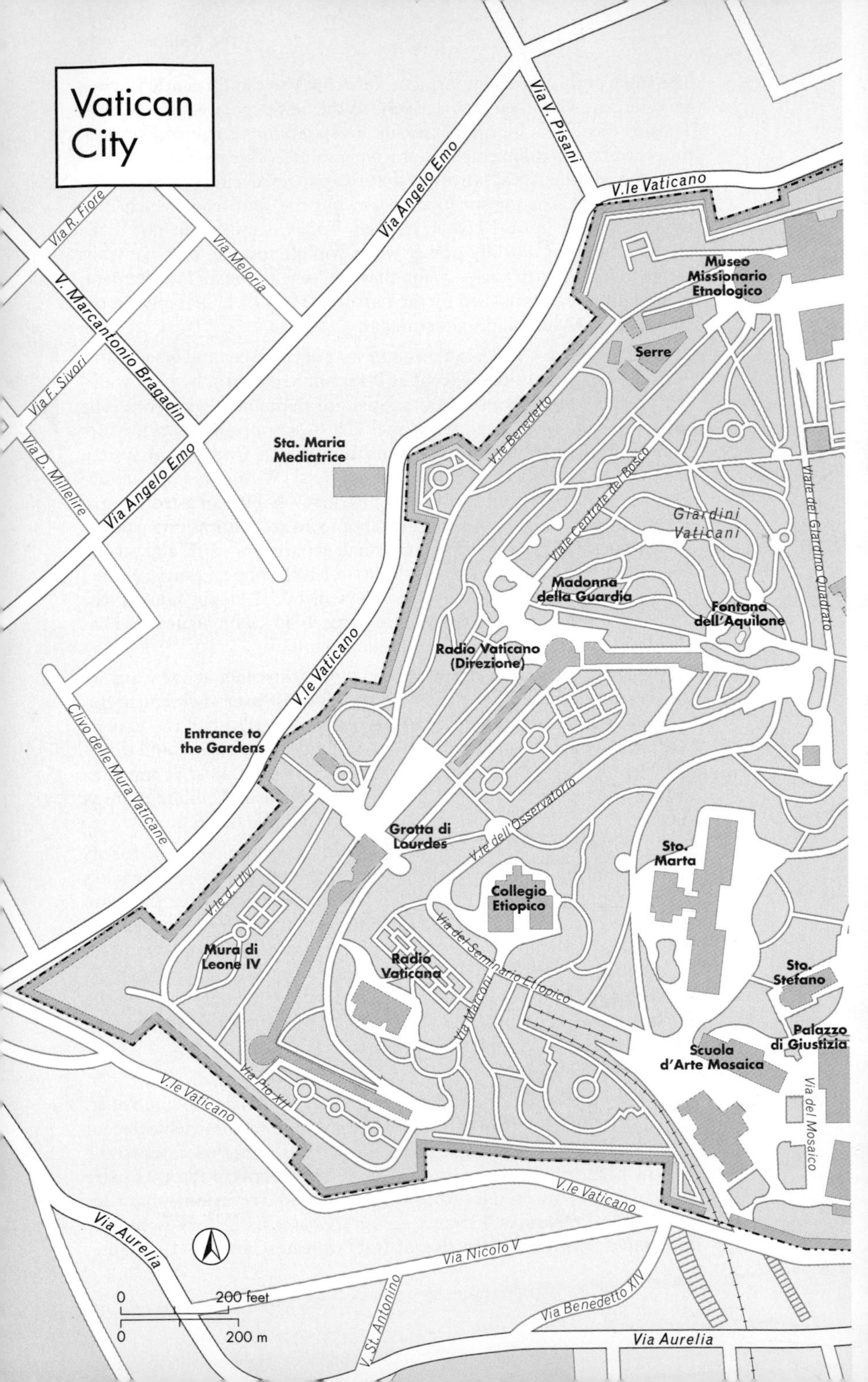

Vatican City
Via V. Pisani
V.le Vaticano
Via Angelo Emo
Via R. Fiore
Via Meloria
V. Marcantonio Bragadin
Via F. Sivori
Via D. Millelire
Museo Missionario Etnologico
Serre
V.le Benedetto
Sta. Maria Mediatrice
Viale Centrale del Bosco
Giardini Vaticani
Viale del Giardino Quadrato
Madonna della Guardia
Fontana dell'Aquilone
Radio Vaticano (Direzione)
Entrance to the Gardens
Clivo delle Mura Vaticane
Grotta di Lourdes
V.le dell'Osservatorio
Sto. Marta
V.le d. Ulivi
Collegio Etiopico
Via del Seminario Etiopico
Mura di Leone IV
Radio Vaticana
Sto. Stefano
Via Marconi
Palazzo di Giustizia
Scuola d'Arte Mosaica
Via del Mosaico
Via Pio XII
V.le Vaticano
V.le Vaticano
Via Aurelia
Via Nicolo V
Via St. Antonino
Via Benedetto XIV
Via Aurelia
0
200 feet
0
200 m

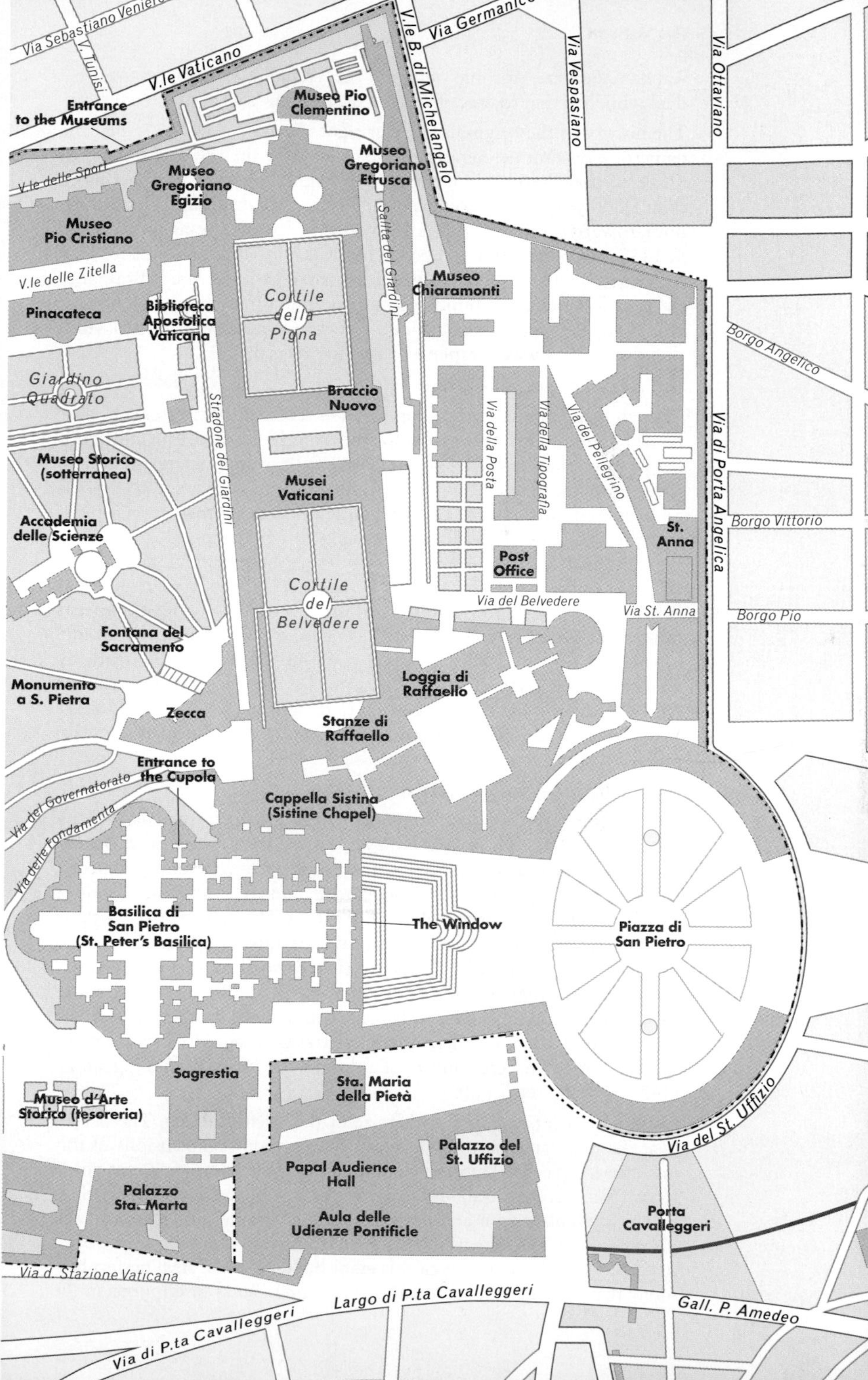
Via Sebastiano Veniero
V. Tunisi
V.le Vaticano
Via Germanico
V.le B. di Michelangelo
Via Vespasiano
Via Ottaviano
Entrance to the Museums
Museo Pio Clementino
Museo Gregoriano Etrusca
V.le delle Sport
Museo Gregoriano Egizio
Museo Pio Cristiano
Salita del Giardini
V.le delle Zitella
Museo Chiaramonti
Cortile della Pigna
Pinacateca
Biblioteca Apostolica Vaticana
Borgo Angelico
Giardino Quadrato
Braccio Nuovo
Stradone del Giardini
Via della Posta
Via della Tipografia
Via del Pellegrino
Via di Porta Angelica
Museo Storico (sotterranea)
Musei Vaticani
Accademia delle Scienze
St. Anna
Borgo Vittorio
Post Office
Cortile del Belvedere
Via del Belvedere
Via St. Anna
Borgo Pio
Fontana del Sacramento
Loggia di Raffaello
Monumento a S. Pietra
Zecca
Stanze di Raffaello
Entrance to the Cupola
Via del Governatorato
Cappella Sistina (Sistine Chapel)
Via delle Fondamenta
Basilica di San Pietro (St. Peter's Basilica)
The Window
Piazza di San Pietro
Sagrestia
Sta. Maria della Pietà
Museo d'Arte Storico (tesoreria)
Via del St. Uffizio
Palazzo del St. Uffizio
Papal Audience Hall
Palazzo Sta. Marta
Aula delle Udienze Pontificle
Porta Cavalleggeri
Via d. Stazione Vaticana
Largo di P.ta Cavalleggeri
Gall. P. Amedeo
Via di P.ta Cavalleggeri

Raphael, Peruzzi, Antonio Sangallo the Younger, and Michelangelo—died while striving to erect this new St. Peter's.

The history of the original St. Peter's goes back to AD 349, when the emperor Constantine completed a basilica over the site of the tomb of St. Peter, the Church's first pope. The original church stood for more than 1,000 years, undergoing a number of restorations and alterations, until, toward the middle of the 15th century, it was verging on collapse. In 1452 a reconstruction job began but was quickly abandoned for lack of money. In 1503, Pope Julius II instructed the architect Bramante to raze all the existing buildings and to build a new basilica, one that would surpass even Constantine's for grandeur. It wasn't until 1626 that the basilica was completed and consecrated.

St. Peter's Crossing and Dome

Though Bramante made little progress in rebuilding St. Peter's, he succeeded in outlining a basic plan for the church. He also, crucially, built the piers of the crossings—the massive pillars supporting the dome. After Bramante's death in 1514, Raphael, the Sangallos, and Peruzzi all proposed, at one time or another, variations on the original plan. In 1546, however, Pope Paul III turned to Michelangelo and forced the aging artist to complete the building. Michelangelo returned to Bramante's first idea of having a centralized Greek-cross plan—that is, with the "arms" of the church all the same length—and completed most of the exterior architecture except for the dome and the facade. His design for the dome, however, was modified after his death by Giacomo della Porta (his dome was much taller in proportion). Pope Paul V wanted a Latin-cross church (a church with one "arm" longer than the rest), so Carlo Maderno lengthened one of the arms to create a longer central nave.

Works by Giotto and Filarete

As you climb the shallow steps up to the great church, flanked by the statues of Sts. Peter and Paul, you'll see the **Loggia delle Benedizioni** (Benediction Loggia) over the central portal. This is the balcony where newly elected popes are proclaimed, and where they stand to give their apostolic blessing on solemn feast days. The vault of the vestibule is encrusted with rich stuccowork, and the mosaic above the central entrance to the portico is a much-restored work by the 14th-century painter Giotto that was in the original basilica. The bronze doors of the main entrance also were salvaged from the old basilica. The sculptor Filarete worked on them for 12 years; they show scenes from the martyrdom of St. Peter and St. Paul, and the life of Pope Eugene IV (1431–47), Filarete's patron.

Pause a moment to appraise the size of the great building. The people near the main altar seem dwarfed by the incredible dimensions of this immense temple. The statues, the pillars, and the holy-water stoups borne by colossal cherubs are all imposing. Walk over to where the cherub clings to a pier and place your arm across the sole of the cherub's foot; you will discover that it's as long as the distance from your fingers to your elbow. It's because the proportions of this giant building are in such perfect harmony that its vastness may escape you at first. Brass inscriptions in the

Basilica di San Pietro

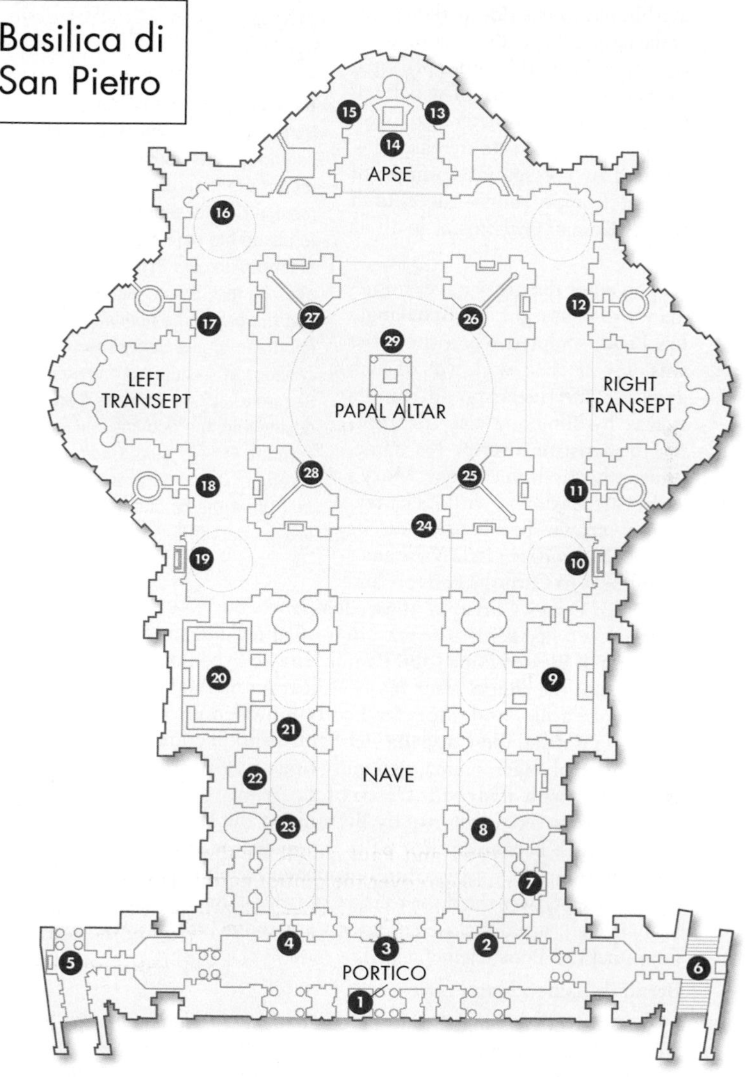

Alexander VII tomb **17**
Baldacchino **29**
Central Door **3**
Chapel of the Choir **20**
Chapel of the Column; altar & tomb of St. Leo **16**
Chapel of the Most Holy Sacrament **9**
Chapel of the Pietà; Pietà (Michelangelo) **7**
Chapel of the Presentation; John XXIII monument **22**
Charlemagne **5**
Christina of Sweden monument.................. **8**
Clement XIII monument ... **12**
Clementina Sobieski monument, opp. Pillar of the last Stuarts; Exit from Cupola **23**
Clementine Chapel; (under altar: St. Gregory the Great tomb) **19**
Emperor Constantine **6**
Entrance to Cupola **11**
Gregorian Chapel **10**
Holy Door **2**
Innocent VIII tomb **21**
Manzù Door **4**
Paul III tomb **15**
Pius V monument (below: entrance to Sacristy) **18**
St. Andrew **28**
St. Helen **26**
St. Longinus; entrance to crypt **25**
St. Peter **24**
Throne of St. Peter **14**
Urban VIII tomb **13**
The Veronica **27**
Vestibule: The Ship, Giotto mosaics **1**

marble pavement down the center of the nave indicate the approximate lengths of the world's other principal Christian churches, all of which fall far short of the 186-meter span of St. Peter's Basilica. In its megascale—inspired by the spatial volumes of ancient Roman ruins—the church reflects Roman *grandiosità* in all its majesty.

> **IT'S ALWAYS WHO YOU KNOW**
>
> The story goes that Bernini's Barberini patron, Pope Urban VIII, had no qualms about stripping the bronze from the Pantheon to provide Bernini with the material to create the gigantic bronze *baldacchino* over St. Peter's main altar. (In fact, Bernini already had the bronze he needed; the Pantheon bronze instead went to cannons at Castel Sant'Angelo.) Regardless of the bronze's final destination, the Romans reacted with the famous quip: *Quod non fecerunt barbari, fecerunt Barberini* ("What the barbarians didn't do, the Barberini did").

As you enter the great nave, immediately to your right. is **Michelangelo's *Pietà*,** sculpted when the artist was only 25. The work was of such genius, some rivals spread rumors it was by someone else, prompting the artist to inscribe his name, unusually for him, across Mary's sash. Farther down, with its heavyweight crown barely denting its marble cushion, is Carlo Fontana's monument to Catholic convert and abdicated Queen Christina of Sweden (who's buried in the Grotte Vaticane below). Just across the way, in the **Cappella di San Sebastiano,** lies the **tomb of Blessed Pope John Paul II.** The beloved pope's remains were moved into the chapel after his beatification on May 1, 2011. Exquisite bronze grilles and doors by Borromini open into the third chapel in the right aisle, the **Cappella del Santissimo Sacramento** (Chapel of the Most Holy Sacrament), generally open to visitors only from 7 am to 8:30 am, with a Baroque fresco of the Trinity by Pietro da Cortona. The lovely carved angels are by Bernini. At the last pillar on the right (the pier with Bernini's statue of St. Longinus) is a bronze statue of St. Peter, whose right foot is ritually touched by lines of pilgrims. In the right transept, over the door to the **Cappella di San Michele** (Chapel of St. Michael), usually closed, Canova created a brooding Neoclassical monument to Pope Clement XIII.

Bernini's Baldacchino

In the central crossing, Bernini's great bronze *baldacchino*—a huge, spiral-columned canopy—rises high over the *altare papale* (papal altar). At 100,000 pounds, it's said to be the largest, heaviest bronze object in the world. Circling the baldacchino are four larger-than-life statues of saints whose relics the Vatican has; the one of St. Longinus, holding the spear that pierced Christ's side, is another Bernini masterpiece. Meanwhile, Bernini designed the splendid gilt-bronze **Cattedra di San Pietro** (throne of St. Peter) in the apse above the main altar to contain a wooden and ivory chair that St. Peter himself is said to have used, though in fact it doesn't date from farther back than medieval times. (You can see a copy of the chair in the treasury.) Above, Bernini placed a window of thin alabaster sheets that diffuses a golden light around the dove, symbol of the Holy Spirit, in the center.

Two of the major papal funeral monuments in St. Peter's Basilica are on either side of the apse and unfortunately are usually only dimly lighted. To the right is the **tomb of Pope Urban VIII**; to the left is the **tomb of Pope Paul III**. Paul's tomb is of an earlier date, designed between 1551 and 1575 by Giacomo della Porta, the architect who completed the dome of St. Peter's Basilica after Michelangelo's death. Many believed the nude figure of Justice to be a portrait of the pope's beautiful sister, Giulia. The charms of this alluring figure were such that in the 19th century, it was thought that she should no longer be allowed to distract worshippers from their prayers, and she was thenceforth clad in marble drapery. It was in emulation of this splendid late-Renaissance work that Urban VIII ordered Bernini to design his tomb. The real star here, however, is *la Bella Morte* ("Beautiful Death") who, all bone and elbows, dispatches the deceased pope above to a register of blue-black marble. The **tomb of Pope Alexander VII**, also designed by Bernini, stands to the left of the altar as you look up the nave, behind the farthest pier of the crossing. This may be the most haunting memorial in the basilica, thanks to another frightening skeletonized figure of Death, holding an hourglass in its upraised hand to tell the pope his time is up. Pope Alexander, however, was well prepared, having kept a coffin (also designed by Bernini) in his bedroom and made a habit of dining off plates embossed with skulls.

Subsidiary Attractions

Under the Pope Pius V monument, the entrance to the sacristy also leads to the **Museo Storico-Artistico e Tesoro** (*Historical-Artistic Museum and Treasury; 06/69881840, €10 includes audio guide, Apr.–Sept., daily 9–6:15; Oct.–Mar., daily 9–5:15*), a small collection of Vatican treasures. They range from the massive and beautifully sculptured 15th-century tomb of Pope Sixtus IV by Pollaiuolo, which you can view from above, to a jeweled cross dating from the 6th century and a marble tabernacle by Donatello. Continue on down the left nave past Algardi's **tomb of St. Leo**. The handsome bronze grilles in the **Cappella del Coro** (Chapel of the Choir) were designed by Borromini to complement those opposite in the Cappella del Santissimo Sacramento. The next pillar holds a rearrangement of the Pollaiuolo brothers' monument to Pope Innocent VIII, the only major tomb to have been transferred from the old basilica. Lacking in bulk compared to many of its Baroque counterparts, it more than makes up in Renaissance elegance. The next chapel contains the handsome bronze monument to Pope John XXIII by contemporary sculptor Emilio Greco. On the last pier in this nave stands a monument by the late-18th-century Venetian sculptor Canova to the ill-fated Stuarts—the 18th-century Roman Catholic claimants to the British throne, who were long exiled in Rome and some of whom are buried in the crypt below.

Above, the vast sweep of the basilica's dome is the cynosure of all eyes. Proceed to the right side of the Basilica's vestibule; from here, you can either take the elevator or climb the long flight of shallow stairs to the roof (*06/69883462, elevator €7, stairs €5; Apr.–Sept., daily 8–6; Oct.–Mar., daily 8–5; on a Papal Audience Wed., opens after the audience finishes, about noon; closed during ceremonies in piazza*). From here, you'll see a surreal landscape of vast, sloping terraces, punctuated by domes. The roof affords unusual perspectives both on the dome above and the piazza below. The terrace is equipped with the inevitable souvenir shop and restrooms. A short flight of stairs leads to the entrance of the *tamburo* (drum)—the base of the dome—where, appropriately enough, there's a bust of Michelangelo, the dome's principal designer. Within the drum, another short ramp and staircase give access to the gallery encircling the base of the dome. (You also have the option of taking an elevator to this point.) From here, you have a dove's-eye view of the interior of the church. If you're overly energetic, you can take the stairs that wind around the elevator to reach the roof.

Only if you're of stout heart and strong lungs should you then make the taxing climb from the drum of the dome up to the *lanterna* (lantern) at the dome's very apex. A narrow, seemingly interminable staircase follows the curve of the dome between inner and outer shells, finally releasing you into the cramped space of the lantern balcony for an absolutely gorgeous panorama of Rome and the countryside on a clear day. There's also a nearly complete view of the palaces, courtyards, and gardens of the Vatican. Be aware, however, that it's a tiring, slightly claustrophobic climb. There's one stairway for going up and a different one for coming down, so you can't change your mind halfway and turn back. ✉ *Piazza di San Pietro* ⏲ *Apr.–Sept., daily 7–7; Oct.–Mar., daily 7–6:30; closed during the papal audience in St. Peter's Square on Wed. mornings until about noon* Ⓜ *Ottaviano–San Pietro.*

Necropoli Vaticana (*Vatican Necropolis*). With advance notice you can take a 1¼-hour guided tour in English of the Vatican Necropolis, under the basilica, which gives a rare glimpse of Early Christian Roman burial customs and a closer look at the tomb of St. Peter. Apply by fax or e-mail at least 2–3 weeks in advance, specifying the number of people in the group (all must be age 15 or older), preferred language, preferred time, available dates, and your contact information in Rome. ✉ *Piazza di San Pietro* ☎ *06/69885318* 📠 *06/69873017* ✎ *scavi@fsp.va* 🌐 *www.vatican.va* 🎟 *€12* ⏲ *Ufficio Scavi Mon.–Sat. 9–6, visits 9–3:30* Ⓜ *Ottaviano-San Pietro.*

Grotte Vaticane (*Vatican Grottoes*). The entrance to the Grotte Vaticane is to the right of the Basilica's main entrance. The crypt, lined with marble-faced chapels and tombs occupying the area of Constantine's basilica, stands over what is believed to be the tomb of St. Peter himself, flanked by two angels and visible through glass. Among the most beautiful tombs leading up to it are that of Borgia pope Calixtus III with its carving of the Risen Christ, and the tomb of Paul II featuring angels carved by Renaissance great Mino da Fiesole. ✉ *Piazza di San Pietro* 🎟 *Free* ⏲ *Weekdays and Sat. 9–4, Sun. 1:30–3:30; closed while the papal audience takes place in St. Peter's Square, until about noon on Wed.*

NEED A BREAK?

Insalata Ricca. About halfway between the Vatican Museums and St. Peter's Basilica, Insalata Ricca offers no-nonsense light meals: pasta, salads, pizza, and the like. While unremarkable, keep it in mind on a hot

CLOSE UP

Meet the Pope

Piazza San Pietro is the scene of large papal audiences as well as special commemorations, masses, and beatification ceremonies. When he's in Rome, the pope makes an appearance every Sunday at noon (call the Vatican Information office to find out if the pope is in town and the exact time) at the window of the Vatican Palace. He addresses the crowd and blesses all present. The pope also holds mass audiences in the square on Wednesday morning about 10:30 am; for a seat, a ticket is necessary. In the winter and inclement circumstances, the audience is held in an indoor audience hall adjacent to the basilica (Aula Paolo Sesto). During summer, while the pope is vacationing at Castel Gandolfo in the Castelli Romani hills outside Rome, he gives a talk and blessing from a balcony of the papal palace there. For admission to an audience, apply for free tickets by phone or fax in advance, indicating the date you prefer, the language you speak, and the hotel in which you will stay.

You also can apply for tickets at the Prefettura della Casa Pontifice, either by fax (39 06/69885863) or by going to the office on Tuesday between 3 and 7 or on the morning of the audience between 7 and 10. You can reach the office through the Portone di Bronzo (Bronze Door) at the end of the right-hand colonnade. Or you can arrange your tickets for free for Wednesday general audiences (although not for the papal mass) through the Santa Susanna American Church (*Via XX Settembre 15, near Termini* *06/69001821*). The best way is to fill out a booking form directly online at *www.santasusanna.org/popeVatican/tickets.html*. You can pick up your tickets on Tuesday between 5 pm and 6:30 pm only.

day—its air-conditioning is the best in the neighborhood. ***Piazza Risorgimento 6, Borgo*** ***06/39730387*** ***insalataricca.it*** **M** ***Ottaviano.***

Fodor's Choice ★ **Cappella Sistina** (*Sistine Chapel*). In 1508, the redoubtable Pope Julius II commissioned Michelangelo to fresco the more than 10,000 square feet of the Sistine Chapel's ceiling. (*Sistine,* by the way, is simply the adjective from *Sixtus,* in reference to Pope Sixtus IV, who commissioned the chapel itself.) The task took four years, and it's said that for many years afterward Michelangelo couldn't read anything without holding it over his head. The result, however, was the greatest artwork of the Renaissance. A pair of binoculars helps greatly, as does a small mirror—hold the mirror facing the ceiling and look down to study the reflection.

Before the chapel was consecrated in 1483, its lower walls were decorated by famed artists including Botticelli, Ghirlandaio, Perugino, Signorelli, and Pinturicchio. They painted scenes from the life of Moses on one wall and episodes from the life of Christ on the other. Later, Julius II, dissatisfied with the simple vault decoration—stars painted on the ceiling—decided to call in Michelangelo. At the time, Michelangelo was carving Julius II's resplendent tomb, a project that never came near completion. He had no desire to give the project up to paint a ceiling, considering the task unworthy of him. Julius was not, however, a man to be trifled with, and Michelangelo reluctantly began work. See our special photo feature, "Agony and Ecstasy: The Sistine Ceiling," for the complete backstory.

More than 20 years later, Michelangelo was called on again, this time by the Farnese pope Paul III, to add to the chapel's decoration by painting the *Last Judgment* on the wall over the altar. The subject was well suited to the aging and embittered artist, who had been deeply moved by the horrendous Sack of Rome in 1527 and the confusions and disturbances of the Reformation. The painting stirred up controversy even before it was unveiled in 1541, shocking many Vatican officials, especially one Biagio di Cesena, who criticized its "indecent" nudes. Michelangelo retaliated by painting Biagio's face on Minos, judge of the underworld—the figure with donkey's ears in the lower right-hand corner of the work. Biagio pleaded with Pope Paul to have Michelangelo erase his portrait, but the pontiff replied that while he could intercede for those in purgatory, he had no power over hell. As if to sign this, his late great fresco, Michelangelo painted his own face on the flayed-off human skin in St. Bartholomew's hand.

■ **TIP→ The best way to avoid long lines is to arrive between noon and 2, when lines will be very short or even nonexistent, except Sundays when admissions close at 12:30. Even better is to schedule your visit during the Wednesday Papal Mass, held in the piazza of St. Peter's or at Aula Paolo Sesto, usually 10:30 am.** ✉ *Vatican Palace; entry only through Musei Vaticani* 🌐 *mv.vatican.va* ⏲ *Mon.–Sat. 9–6 (last entrance at 4), last Sun. of month 9–12:30. Closed Jan. 1 and 6, Feb. 11, Mar. 19, Easter and Easter Monday, May 1, June 29, Aug. 14 and 15, Nov. 1, and Dec. 8, 25, and 26.*

Fodor's Choice ★ **Musei Vaticani** (*Vatican Museums*). Other than the pope and his papal court, the occupants of the Vatican are some of the most famous artworks in the world. The museums that contain them are part of the **Vatican Palace,** residence of the popes since 1377. The palace consists of an estimated 1,400 rooms, chapels, and galleries. The pope and his household occupy only a small part of the palace; most of the rest is given over to the Vatican Library and Museums. Beyond the glories of the Sistine Chapel, the collection is so extraordinarily rich you may just wish to skim the surface, but few will want to miss out on the great antique sculptures, Raphael Rooms, and the Old Master paintings, such as Leonardo da Vinci's *St. Jerome.*

Subsidiary Museums

Among the collections on the way to the chapel, the **Egyptian Museum** (in which Room II reproduces an underground chamber tomb of the Valley of Kings) is well worth a stop. The **Chiaramonti Museum** was organized by the Neoclassical sculptor Canova and contains almost 1,000 copies of classical sculpture. The gems of the Vatican's sculpture collection are in the **Pio-Clementino Museum,** however. Just off the hall in Room X, you can find the Apoxyomenos (Scraper), a beautiful 1st-century AD copy of the famous bronze statue of an athlete. There are other even more famous pieces in the **Octagonal Courtyard,** where Pope Julius II installed the pick of his private collection. On the left stands the celebrated Apollo Belvedere. In the far corner, on the same side of the courtyard, is the Laocoön group. Found on Rome's Esquiline Hill in 1506, this antique sculpture group influenced Renaissance artists perhaps more than any other.

In the **Hall of the Muses,** the Belvedere Torso occupies center stage: this is a fragment of a 1st-century BC statue, probably of Hercules, all rippling muscles and classical dignity, much admired by Michelangelo. The lovely Neoclassical room of the **Rotonda** has an ancient mosaic pavement and a huge porphyry basin from Nero's palace.

ART AND FAITH

Presiding over the great nave of St. Peter's is Michelangelo's legendary *Pietà.* Could you question whether this moving work, sculpted when the artist was only 22, owes more to man's art than to a man's faith? Perhaps as we contemplate this masterpiece we are able to understand a little better that art and faith sometimes partake of the same impulse.

The room on the Greek-cross plan contains two fine porphyry sarcophagi (burial caskets), one for St. Constantia and one for St. Helena, daughter and mother of the emperor Constantine, respectively.

Upstairs is an **Etruscan Museum**, an **Antiquarium**, with Roman originals; and the domed **Sala della Biga**, with an ancient chariot. In addition, there are the **Candelabra Gallery** and the **Tapestry Gallery**, with tapestries designed by Raphael's students. The incredibly long **Gallery of Maps,** frescoed with 40 maps of Italy and the papal territories, was commissioned by Pope Gregory XIII in 1580. Nearby is the **Apartment of Pius V.**

The Raphael Rooms

Rivaling the Sistine Chapel for artistic interest—and for the number of visitors—are the recently restored **Stanze di Raffaello** (Raphael Rooms). Pope Julius II moved into this suite in 1507, four years after his election. Reluctant to continue living in the Borgia apartments downstairs, with their memories of his ill-famed predecessor Alexander VI, he called in Raphael to decorate his new quarters. When people talk about the Italian High Renaissance—thought to be the very pinnacle of Western art—it's probably Raphael's frescoes they're thinking about.

The **Stanza della Segnatura,** the first to be frescoed, was painted almost entirely by Raphael himself (his assistants painted much of the other rooms). The theme of the room, which may broadly be said to be "enlightenment," reflects the fact that this was meant to be Julius's private library. Instead, it was used mainly as a room for signing documents, hence "*segnatura*" (signature). Theology triumphs in the fresco known as the *Disputa,* or *Debate on the Holy Sacrament,* on the wall in front of you as you enter. Opposite, the *School of Athens* glorifies philosophy in its greatest exponents. Plato (likely a portrait of Leonardo da Vinci), in the center, debates a point with Aristotle. The pensive, gloomy figure on the stairs is thought to be modeled after Michelangelo, who was painting the Sistine ceiling at the same time Raphael was working here. Michelangelo does not appear in preparatory drawings, so Raphael may have added his fellow artist's portrait after admiring

For St. Peter's, Michelangelo originally designed a dome much higher than the one ultimately built and designed by his follower Giacomo della Porta.

his work. In the foreground on the right, the figure with the compass is Euclid, depicted as the architect Bramante; on the far right, the handsome youth just behind the white-clad older man is Raphael himself. Over the window on the left is Mt. Parnassus, the abode of the Muses, with Apollo, famous poets (many of them likenesses of Raphael's contemporaries), and the Muses themselves. In the lunette over the window opposite, Raphael painted figures representing and alluding to the Cardinal and Theological Virtues, and subjects showing the establishment of written codes of law. Beautiful personifications of the four subject areas, Theology, Poetry, Philosophy, and Jurisprudence, are painted in circular pictures on the ceiling above.

However, the rooms aren't arranged chronologically. Today, for crowd-management purposes, you head down an outdoor gallery to loop back through them; as you go, look across the way to see, very far away, the Pinecone Courtyard near where you entered the museums. The first "Raphael Room" is the **Hall of Constantine**—actually decorated by Giulio Romano and Raphael's other assistants after the master's untimely death in 1520. The frescoes represent various scenes from the life of Emperor Constantine, including the epic-sized *Battle of the Milvian Bridge*. Guided by three low-flying angels, Constantine charges to victory as his rival Maxentius drowns in the river below.

The **Room of Heliodorus** is a private antechamber. Working on the theme of Divine Providence's miraculous intervention in defense of the faith, Raphael depicted Leo the Great's encounter with Attila; it's on the wall in front of you as you enter. The *Expulsion of Heliodorus from the Temple of Jerusalem,* opposite, refers to Pope Julius II's attempt to exert

CLOSE UP

Tips for Visiting the Vatican

To enter the Musei Vaticani (Vatican Museums), the Sistine Chapel, and the Basilica di San Pietro you must comply with the Vatican's dress code, or you may be turned away by the implacable custodians stationed at the doors. (Also no penknives, which will show up under the metal detector.) For both men and women, shorts and tank tops are taboo, as are miniskirts and other revealing clothing. Wear a jacket or shawl over sleeveless tops, and avoid T-shirts with writing or pictures that could risk giving offense.

If you opt to start at the Musei Vaticani, note that the entrance on Viale Vaticano (there's a separate exit on the same street) can be reached by Bus No. 49 from Piazza Cavour, which stops right in front; on foot from Piazza del Risorgimento (Bus 81 or Tram 19); or a brief walk from the Via Cipro–Musei Vaticani stop on Metro line A.

The collections of the museums are immense, covering about 7 km (4½ miles) of displays. To economize on time and effort, once you've seen the frescoes in the Raphael rooms, you can skip much of the modern religious art in good conscience, and get on with your tour.

You can rent a taped, if somewhat dry, commentary in English explaining the Sistine Chapel and the Raphael rooms.

You cannot take any photographs in the Sistine Chapel. Elsewhere, you're free to photograph what you like, barring use of flash, tripod, or other special equipment, for which permission must be obtained.

With some 20,000 visitors a day, lines at the entrance to the Cappella Sistina (Sistine Chapel) can move slowly, as custodians block further entrance when the room becomes crowded. It may be possible to exit the museums from the Sistine Chapel into St. Peter's, saving further legwork. A sign at the entrance to the museums indicates whether the "For Tour Groups" exit is open. While visitors in the past could use this by following an exiting tour group, lately the guards there have been sterner on this practice. Be aware, too, that the Sistine Chapel is a holy place; loud talking and other excessive noise is frowned upon and can get you shushed.

papal power to expel the French from Italy. The pope himself appears on the left, watching the scene. On the window wall, the *Liberation of St. Peter* is one of Raphael's best-known and most effective works.

After the Room of the Signature, the last room is the **Room of the Borgo Fire.** The final room painted in Raphael's lifetime, it was executed mainly by Giulio Romano, who worked from Raphael's drawings for the new pope, Leo X. It was used for the meetings of the Segnatura Gratiae et Iustitiae, the Holy See's highest court. The frescoes depict stories of previous popes called Leo, the best of them showing the great fire in the Borgo (the neighborhood between the Vatican and Castel Sant'Angelo) that threatened to destroy the original St. Peter's Basilica in AD 847; miraculously, Pope Leo IV extinguished it with the sign of the cross. The other frescoes show the coronation of Charlemagne by Leo III in St. Peter's Basilica, the *Oath of Leo III*, and a naval battle with the Saracens at Ostia in AD 849, after which Pope Leo IV showed clemency to the defeated.

The tiny **Chapel of Nicholas V** is rarely open. But if you can access it, do: one of the Renaissance's greatest gems, it's aglow with Fra Angelico (1395–1455) frescoes of episodes from the life of St. Stephen (above) and St. Lawrence (below). If it weren't under the same roof as Raphael's and Michelangelo's works, it would undoubtedly draw greater attention.

Downstairs, enter the recently restored **Borgia apartments,** where some of the Vatican's most fascinating historical figures are depicted on elaborately painted ceilings. Pinturicchio designed the frescoes at the end of the 15th century, though the paintings were greatly retouched in later centuries. It's generally believed that Cesare Borgia murdered his sister Lucrezia's husband, Alphonse of Aragon, in the Room of the Sibyl. In the Room of the Saints, Pinturicchio painted his self-portrait in the figure to the left of the possible portrait of the architect Antonio da Sangallo. (His profession is made clear by the fact that he holds a T-square.) The lovely St. Catherine of Alexandria is said to represent Lucrezia Borgia herself.

SOMETHING IN PAPAL PURPLE?

If you've come to the Eternal City looking for ecclesiastical garb or religious memorabilia, you'll hit gold in the shops near the Vatican on Via Porta Angelica. A celestial array of pope portraits, postcards, figurines, and even snow globes can be had for low prices. The pious can have their purchases blessed at a papal audience; blasphemers can put pope stickers on their cars. Lay shoppers may want to stick to the windows.

In the frescoed exhibition halls, the **Vatican Library** displays precious illuminated manuscripts and documents from its vast collections. The **Aldobrandini Marriage Room** contains beautiful ancient frescoes of a Roman nuptial rite, named for their subsequent owner, Cardinal Aldobrandini. The **Braccio Nuovo** (New Wing) holds an additional collection of ancient Greek and Roman statues, the most famous of which is the Augustus of Prima Porta, in the fourth niche from the end on the left. It's considered a faithful likeness of the emperor Augustus, who was 40 years old at the time. Note the workmanship in the reliefs on his armor.

The Vatican Pinacoteca

Equally celebrated are the works on view in the **Pinacoteca** (Picture Gallery). These often world-famous paintings, almost exclusively of religious subjects, are arranged in chronological order, beginning with works of the 12th and 13th centuries. Room II has a marvelous Giotto triptych, painted on both sides, which formerly stood on the high altar in the old St. Peter's. In Room III you'll see Madonnas by the Florentine 15th-century painters Fra Angelico and Filippo Lippi. Room VIII contains some of Raphael's greatest creations, including the exceptional *Transfiguration,* the *Coronation of the Virgin,* and the *Foligno Madonna,* as well as the tapestries that Raphael designed to hang in the Sistine Chapel. The next room contains Leonardo's beautiful (though unfinished) *St. Jerome* and a Bellini *Pietà*. A highlight for many is

Caravaggio's gigantic *Deposition*, in Room XII. In the courtyard outside the Pinacoteca you can admire a beautiful view of the dome of St. Peter's, as well as the reliefs from the base of the now-destroyed column of Antoninus Pius. A fitting finale to your Vatican visit can be found in the **Museo Pio Cristiano** (Museum of Christian Antiquities), where the most famous piece is the 3rd-century AD statue called the Good Shepherd, much reproduced as a devotional image.

VATICAN MUSEUMS TOP 10

Michelangelo's Sistine ceiling

Raphael rooms

Apollo Belvedere

Leonardo's *St. Jerome*

Laocoön

Caravaggio's *Deposition*

Raphael's *Transfiguration*

Aldobrandini Marriage

The Good Shepherd

Belvedere Torso

■ TIP→ The best way to avoid long lines into the museums, which can be three hours long in high season, is to arrive between noon and 2, when lines are short, except Sundays when admissions close at 12:30. Or schedule your visit during the Wednesday Papal Mass, held in the piazza of St. Peter's or at Aula Paolo Sesto, usually 10:30 am. You can also book your ticket in advance online (🌐 *biglietteriamusei.vatican.va*); there is a €4 surcharge.

For those interested in guided visits to the Vatican Museums, tours are €26 to €37, including entrance tickets, and can also be booked online. Other offerings include a regular two-hour guided tour of the Vatican gardens and the semiregular Friday night openings, allowing visitors to the museums until 11 pm; call or check online to confirm. For more information, call *06/69884676* or go to 🌐 *mv.vatican.va*. For information on tours, call *06/69883145* or *06/69884676*; visually impaired visitors can arrange tactile tours by calling *06/69884947*. Wheelchairs are available (free) and can be booked in advance by emailing *accoglienza.musei@scv.va* or by request at the "Special Permits" desk in the entrance hall.

■ TIP→ Ushers at the entrance of St. Peter's and sometimes the Vatican Museums will bar entry to people with bare knees or bare shoulders. ✉ *Viale Vaticano, near intersection with Via Leone IV* 🌐 *www.mv.vatican.va* 🎫 *€16; free last Sun. of month* ⏲ *Mon.–Sat. 9–6 (last entrance at 4), last Sun. of month 9–12:30* ⏲ *Closed Jan. 1 and 6, Feb. 11, Mar. 19, Easter and Easter Monday, May 1, June 29, Aug. 14 and 15, Nov. 1, and Dec. 8, 25, and 26* Ⓜ *Cipro–Musei Vaticani or Ottaviano–San Pietro. Bus 64, 40.*

NEED A BREAK?

Hostaria Dino e Toni. Many of the restaurants near the Vatican are touristy and terrible, so this eatery stands out. At Hostaria Dino e Toni you can dine on typical Roman fare, fresh from the nearby outdoor market on Via Andrea Doria, and pizza. It's closed Sunday. ✉ ***Via Leone IV 60, Prati*** ☎ ***06/39733284*** Ⓜ ***Ottaviano.***

CLOSE UP

Tips on Touring the Vatican Museums

Remember that the Vatican's museum complex is humongous—only after walking through what seems like miles of galleries do you see the entrance to the Sistine Chapel (which cannot be entered from St. Peter's Basilica directly). Most people—especially those who rent an audio guide and must return it to the main desk—tour the complex, see the Sistine, then trudge back to the main museum entrance, itself a 15-minute walk from St. Peter's Square.

That said, there is an "insider" way to exit directly from the Sistine Chapel to St. Peter's Basilica: Look for the "tour groups only" door on the right as you face the rear of the chapel and, when a group exits, go with the flow and follow them. This will deposit you on the porch of St. Peter's Basilica. While this served as a sly trick for years, guards and guides both have gotten stricter about the practice, meaning you might be the victim of a stern guard or a head count that leaves you in the cold. Also note that if you run to the Sistine Chapel, then do the "short-cut" exit into the basilica, you will have missed the rest of the Vatican Museum collection.

Plans are afoot to broaden the sidewalk leading to the museum, to install electronic information panels, and also to build a streamlined roof to protect people in the line up from sun or rain (until then, umbrellas are recommended). Another possibility is to visit in the evening. This experiment began in 2009 and has been running intermittently ever since, with the Vatican opening on many Friday evenings from 7 to 11. While the major hits, like the Sistine Chapel, are usually open during these special evenings, many more off-the-beaten-path rooms and galleries are not. Reservations are essential (and possible over the Internet at *www.vatican.va*).

WORTH NOTING

Giardini Vaticani (*Vatican Gardens*). Neatly trimmed lawns and flower beds extend over the hills behind St. Peter's Basilica, an area dotted with some interesting constructions and other, duller ones that serve as office buildings. The Vatican Gardens occupy almost 40 acres of land on the Vatican hill. The gardens include a formal Italian garden, a flowering French garden, a romantic English landscape, and a small forest; there's also the little-used Vatican railroad station, which now houses a museum of coins and stamps made in the Vatican, and the Torre di San Giovanni (Tower of St. John), restored by Pope John XXIII as a retreat for work, and now used as a residence for distinguished guests.

To visit the gardens, you must take a two-hour walking tour with an official Vatican guide (make sure to wear good walking shoes). *For Vatican tour, Centro Servizi, south side of Piazza San Pietro 06/69883145 Vatican tour mv.vatican.va €32 for 2-hour tour (includes €16 entrance ticket to Vatican museums) Tours daily except Wed. and Sun.* M *Ottaviano-San Pietro.*

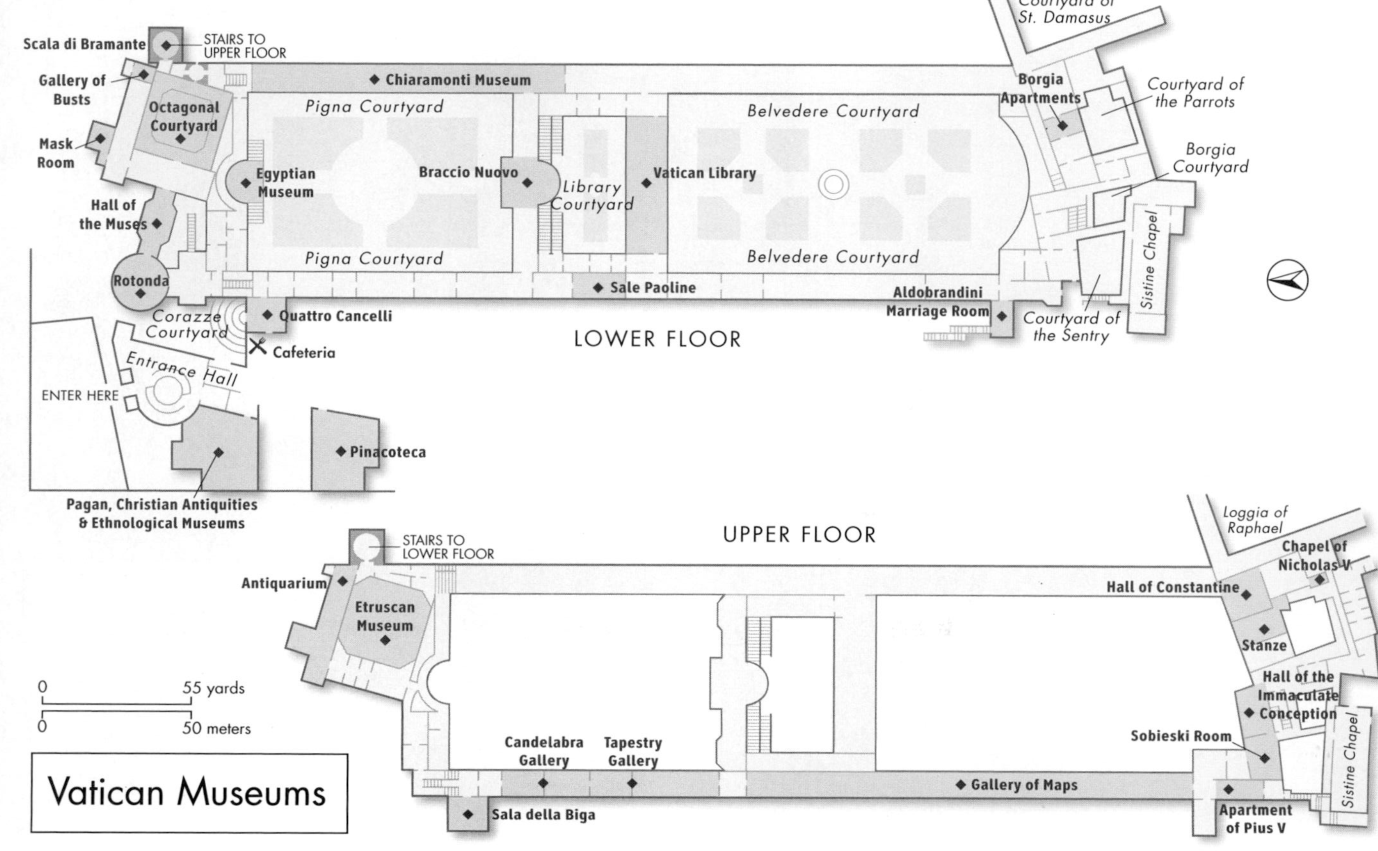
Vatican Museums
LOWER FLOOR
Scala di Bramante
STAIRS TO UPPER FLOOR
Gallery of Busts
Octagonal Courtyard
Mask Room
Hall of the Muses
Rotonda
Corazze Courtyard
Entrance Hall
ENTER HERE
Quattro Cancelli
Cafeteria
Pagan, Christian Antiquities & Ethnological Museums
Pinacoteca
Chiaramonti Museum
Pigna Courtyard
Egyptian Museum
Braccio Nuovo
Pigna Courtyard
Library Courtyard
Vatican Library
Sale Paoline
Belvedere Courtyard
Belvedere Courtyard
Aldobrandini Marriage Room
Courtyard of St. Damasus
Borgia Apartments
Courtyard of the Parrots
Borgia Courtyard
Sistine Chapel
Courtyard of the Sentry
UPPER FLOOR
STAIRS TO LOWER FLOOR
Antiquarium
Etruscan Museum
Candelabra Gallery
Tapestry Gallery
Sala della Biga
Gallery of Maps
Loggia of Raphael
Chapel of Nicholas V
Hall of Constantine
Stanze
Hall of the Immaculate Conception
Sobieski Room
Sistine Chapel
Apartment of Pius V
0 55 yards
0 50 meters

DID YOU KNOW?

Designed to be Hadrian's tomb, the Castel Sant'Angelo was originally topped by a marble-sheathed tumulus and crowned by a gigantic bronze of the emperor in his chariot.

BORGO

Between the Vatican and the once-moated bulk of Castel Sant'Angelo—erstwhile mausoleum of Emperor Hadrian and now an imposing relic of medieval Rome—is the old Borgo neighborhood, whose workaday charm has largely succumbed to gentrification. Be wary of the tourist trap lunch spots and souvenir shops right outside the Vatican walls.

LAW AND ORDER, 16TH-CENTURY STYLE

The Raphael room frescoes represent all the revolutionary characteristics of High Renaissance art: naturalism (Raphael's figures lack the awkwardness that pictures painted only a few years earlier still contained); humanism (the idea that man is the most noble and admirable of God's creatures); and a profound interest in the ancient world, the result of the 15th-century rediscovery of archaeology and classical antiquity. The frescoes in this room virtually dared its occupants to aspire to the highest ideas of law and learning—an amazing feat for an artist not yet 30.

WORTH NOTING

FAMILY **Castel Sant'Angelo.** Between the Tiber and the Vatican, this circular and medieval "castle" has long been one of Rome's most distinctive landmarks. Opera-lovers know it as the setting for the final scene of Puccini's *Tosca*; at the opera's end, the tempestuous diva throws herself from the rampart on the upper terrace. In fact, the structure began life many centuries before as a mausoleum for the emperor Hadrian. Started in AD 135, it was completed by the emperor's successor, Antoninus Pius, about five years later. It initially consisted of a great square base topped by a marble-clad cylinder on which was planted a ring of cypress trees. Above them towered a gigantic statue of Hadrian. From the mid-6th century the building became a fortress, a place of refuge for popes during wars and sieges. Its name dates from 590, when Pope Gregory the Great, during a procession to plead for the end of a plague, saw an angel standing on the summit of the castle, sheathing his sword. Taking this as a sign that the plague was at an end, the pope built a small chapel at the top, placing a statue next to it to celebrate his vision.

Enter the building through the original Roman door of Hadrian's tomb. From here, you pass through a courtyard enclosed in the base of the classical monument. You enter a vaulted brick corridor that hints at grim punishments in dank cells. On the right, a spiral ramp leads up to the chamber in which Hadrian's ashes were kept. Where the ramp ends, the Borgia pope Alexander VI's staircase begins. Part of it consisted of a wooden drawbridge, which could isolate the upper part of the castle completely. The staircase ends at the Cortile dell'Angelo, a courtyard that has become the resting place of neatly piled stone cannonballs as well as the marble angel that stood above the castle. (It was replaced by a bronze sculpture in 1753.) In the rooms off the Cortile dell'Angelo, look for the **Cappella di Papa Leone X** (Chapel of Pope Leo X), with a facade by Michelangelo.

PIAZZA DI SAN PIETRO

✉ *West end of Via della Conciliazione* ☎ *06/69881662* 🕓 *Daily 6:30 am–11 pm (midnight during Christmas)* Ⓜ *Cipro–Musei Vaticani or Ottaviano–San Pietro.*

TIPS

■ Officially called Informazioni per turisti e pellegrini, the Main Information Office is just left of the basilica as you face it, a few doors down from the Braccio di Carlo Magno bookshop. On the south side of the Piazza Pio XII is another Vatican bookshop, which contains the Libreria Benedetto XVI.

■ Public toilets are near the Information Office, under the colonnade, and outside the exit of the crypt.

Mostly enclosed within high walls that recall the papacy's stormy history, the Vatican opens the spectacular arms of Bernini's colonnade to embrace the world only at St. Peter's Square, scene of the pope's public appearances. One of Bernini's most spectacular masterpieces, the elliptical Piazza di San Pietro was completed in 1667 after only 11 years' work and holds 400,000 people.

Surrounded by a pair of quadruple colonnades, it is gloriously studded with 140 statues of saints and martyrs. Look for the two disks set into the piazza's pavement on either side of the central obelisk. If you stand on either disk, a trick of perspective makes the colonnades look like a single row of columns.

Bernini had an even grander visual effect in mind when he designed the square. By opening up this immense, airy, and luminous space in a neighborhood of narrow, shadowy streets, he created a contrast that would surprise and impress anyone who emerged from the darkness into the light, in a characteristically Baroque metaphor.

At the piazza center, the 85-foot-high Egyptian obelisk was brought to Rome by Caligula in AD 37 and moved here in 1586 by Pope Sixtus V. The emblem at the top of the obelisk is the Chigi star, in honor of Pope Alexander VII, a member of the powerful Chigi family, who commissioned the piazza.

Alexander demanded that Bernini make the pope visible to as many people as possible from the Benediction Loggia and to provide a covered passageway for papal processions.

Continued on page 120

HEAVEN'S ABOVE:
THE SISTINE CEILING

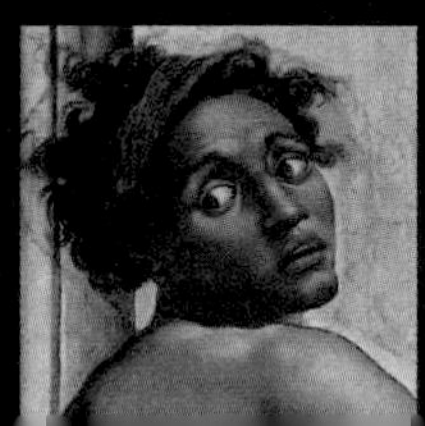

Forming lines that are probably longer than those waiting to pass through the Pearly Gates, hordes of visitors arrive at the Sistine Chapel daily to view what may be the world's most sublime example of artistry:

Michelangelo: *The Creation of Adam*, Sistine Chapel, The Vatican, circa 1511.

Michelangelo's Sistine Ceiling. To paint this 12,000-square-foot barrel vault, it took four years, 343 frescoed figures, and a titanic battle of wits between the artist and Pope Julius II. While in its typical fashion, Hollywood focused on the element of agony, not ecstasy, involved in the saga of creation, a recently completed restoration of the ceiling has revolutionized our appreciation of the masterpiece of masterpieces.

By Martin Wilmot Bennett

View of the Cappella Sistina

MICHELANGELO'S MISSION IMPOSSIBLE

Designed to match the proportions of Solomon's Temple described in the Old Testament, the Sistine Chapel is named after Pope Sixtus VI, who commissioned it as a place of worship for himself and as the venue where new popes could be elected. Before Michelangelo, the barrel-vaulted ceiling was an expanse of azure fretted with golden stars. Then, in 1504, an ugly crack appeared. Bramante, the architect, managed do some patchwork using iron rods, but when signs of a fissure remained, the new Pope Julius II summoned Michelangelo to cover it with a fresco 135 feet long and 44 feet wide.

Taking in the entire span of the ceiling, the theme connecting the various participants in this painted universe could be said to be mankind's anguished waiting. The majestic panel depicting the Creation of Adam leads, through the stages of the Fall and the expulsion from Eden, to the tragedy of Noah found naked and mocked by his own sons; throughout all runs the underlying need for man's redemption. Witnessing all from the side and end walls, a chorus of ancient Prophets and Sibyls peer anxiously forward, awaiting the Redeemer who will come to save both the Jews and the Gentiles.

APOCALYPSE NOW

The sweetness and pathos of his Pietà, carved by Michelangelo only ten years earlier, have been left behind. The new work foretells an apocalypse, its congregation of doomed sinners facing the wrath of heaven through hanging, beheading, crucifixion, flood, and plague. Michelangelo, by nature a misanthrope, was already filled with visions of doom thanks to the fiery orations of Savonarola, whose thunderous preachments he had heard before leaving his hometown of Florence. Vasari, the 16th-century art historian, coined the word "terrabilità" to describe Michelangelo's tension-ridden style, a rare case of a single word being worth a thousand pictures.

Michelangelo wound up using a *Reader's Digest* condensed version of the stories from Genesis, with the dramatis personae overseen by a punitive and terrifying God. In real life, poor Michelangelo answered to a flesh-and-blood taskmaster who was almost as vengeful: Pope Julius II. Less vicar of Christ than latter-day Caesar, he was intent on uniting Italy under the power of the Vatican, and was eager to do so by any means, including riding into pitched battle. Yet this "warrior pope" considered his most formidable adversary to be Michelangelo. Applying a form of blackmail, Julius threatened to wage war on Michelangelo's Florence, to which the artist had fled after Julius canceled a commission for a grand papal tomb unless Michelangelo agreed to return to Rome and take up the task of painting the Sistine Chapel ceiling.

MICHELANGELO, SCULPTOR

A sculptor first and foremost, however, Michelangelo considered painting an inferior genre—"for rascals and sissies" as he put it. Second, there was the sheer scope of the task, leading Michelangelo to suspect he'd been set up by a rival, Bramante, chief architect of the new St. Peter's Basilica. As Michelangelo was also a master architect, he regarded this fresco commission as a Renaissance mission-impossible. Pope Julius's powerful will prevailed—and six years later the work of the Sistine Ceiling was complete. Irving Stone's famous novel *The Agony and the Ecstasy*—and the granitic 1965 film that followed—chart this epic battle between artist and pope.

THINGS ARE LOOKING UP

To enhance your viewing of the ceiling, bring along opera-glasses, binoculars, or just a mirror (to prevent your neck from becoming bent like Michelangelo's). Note that no photos are permitted. Insiders know the only time to get the chapel to yourself is during the papal blessings and public audiences held in St. Peter's Square. Failing that, get there during lunch hour. Admission and entry to the Sistine Chapel is only through the Musei Vaticani (Vatican Museums).

SCHEMATIC OF THE SISTINE CEILING

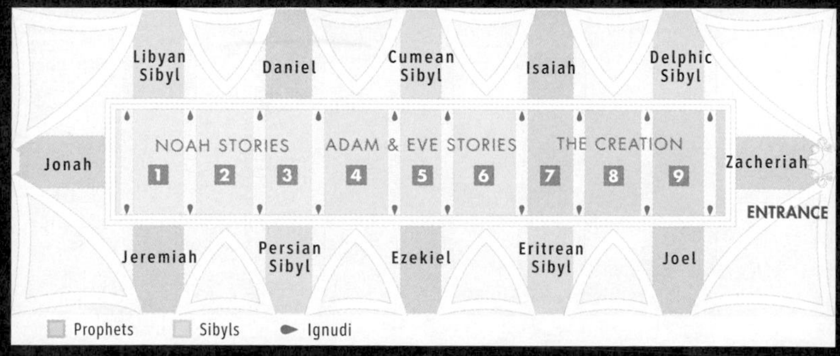

PAINTING THE BIBLE

The ceiling's biblical symbols were ideated by three Vatican theologians, Cardinal Alidosi, Egidio da Viterbo, and Giovanni Rafanelli, along with Michelangelo.

As for the ceiling's painted "framework," this *quadratura* alludes to Roman triumphal arches because Pope Julius II was fond of mounting "triumphal entries" into his conquered cities (in imitation of Christ's procession into Jerusalem on Palm Sunday).

THE CENTER PANELS

Prophet turned art-critic or, perhaps doubling as ourselves, the ideal viewer, Jonah the prophet (painted at the altar end) gazes up at the

Creation, or Michelangelo's version of it.

1 The first of three scenes taken from the Book of Genesis: God separates Light from Darkness.

2 God creates the sun and a craterless pre-Galilean moon while the panel's other half offers an unprecedented rear view of the Almighty creating the vegetable world.

3 In the panel showing God separating the Waters from the Heavens, the Creator tumbles towards us as in a self-made whirlwind.

4 Pausing for breath, next admire probably Western Art's most famous image—God giving life to Adam.

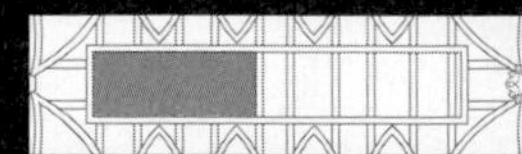

5 The Creation of Eve from Adam's rib leads to the sixth panel.

6 In a sort of diptych divided by the trunk of the Tree of Knowledge of Good and Evil, Michelangelo retells the Temptation and the Fall.

7 Illustrating Man's fallen nature, the last three panels narrate, in un-chronological order, the Flood. In the first Noah offers a pre-Flood sacrifice of thanks.

8 Damaged by an explosion in 1794, next comes Michelangelo's version of Flood itself.

9 Finally, above the monumental Jonah, you can just make out the small, wretched figure of Noah, lying drunk—in pose, the shrunken antitype of the majestic Adam five panels down the wall.

THE CREATION OF ADAM

Michelangelo's Adam was partly inspired by the Creation scenes Michelangelo had studied in the sculpted doors of Jacopo della Quercia in Bologna and Lorenzo Ghiberti's Doors of Paradise in Florence. Yet in Michelangelo's version Adam's hand hangs limp, waiting God's touch to impart the spark of life. Facing his Creation, the Creator—looking a bit like the pagan god Jupiter—is for the first time ever depicted as horizontal, mirroring the Biblical "in his own likeness." Decades after its completion, a crack began to appear, amputating Adam's fingertips. Believe it or not, the most famous fingers in Western art are the handiwork, at least in part, of one Domenico Carnevale.

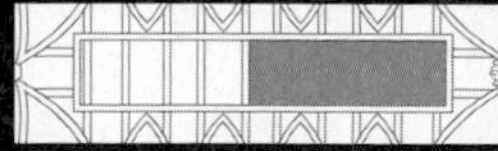

9

GOD IS IN THE DETAILS

Ezekiel

Jeremiah

Ignudi

Cumaean Sibyl

Libyan Sibyl

Ignudi

PROPHETS & SIBYLS

Uniting the pagan and pre-Christian worlds of antiquity, below the central painted panels sit seven Prophets and five of their Classical equivalents, the Sibyls, while the lunettes feature Christ's ancestors as listed in Matthew's Gospel.

Ezekiel & the Cumaean Sibyl

Illustrating Hebrew and pagan worlds are Ezekiel, his body and beard straining sideways, full of prophetic tension, and the Cumaean Sibyl, as impressive for her majestic ugliness as the other four sibyls are for their beauty. Look closely at the angels attending the scary prophetess to see how one of them, in Italian-fashion, is "giving the thumb"—then, as today, considered an obcene gesture.

Jeremiah & the Libyan Sibyl

The doomy-faced Jeremiah is taken to be a self portrait of the long-suffering Michelangelo himself while opposite, showing the artist's range, is the almost playful Libyan Sibyl, about on the point of tripping over as her tunic catches on the plinth while she reaches to put her book of prophecy back on its shelf.

THOSE SCANDALOUS "IGNUDI"

The immediate function of the ceiling's naked giants, the *"ignudi"*—Michelangelo's own coinage—is to carry the shields celebrating famous Israelite victories and so, indirectly, those of bellicose Pope Julius. Some refer to them as angels without wings, yet the passion in their faces seem all too human, fear and anxiety of a pagan world awaiting its overthrow in its very redemption. Historians note that the famed ancient sculpture of *Laocoon and His Sons*—a writhing nude grouping—was excavated in Rome recently. The iconographic tradition of the "ascetic athlete"—a figure of virtue—was also known at this time. Other critics see them as an excuse for Michelangelo to paint his favorite male models, discreetly filtered through the homoerotic optic of Platonic Love, a current trend taken up by Florentine philosophers like Poliziano.

THE SISTINE CEILING REBORN

In 2003, a twenty-year restoration of Michelangelo's frescoes was finally completed. After more than 500 time-stained years of candle-smoke, applied varnishes, and salt mold were removed, the world acclaimed a revolutionary "new" Michelangelo. Gone were the dark shadows and gloomy hues considered so "Michelangelesque." In their place were an array of pink raspberries, sherbet greens, and *changeant* tangerines—a palette even the Impressionist painters might have considered gaudy. Or, as one critic put it, "Michelangelo on Prozac." Some felt there was a gain in definition, but a loss in shadows and underpainting. For the most part, art historians hailed the new look, proclaiming it the long-lost antecedent for the acidic Mannerist colors that emerged in Italian art in the 1520s. Artists, however, remain scandalized, finding the evocative subtlety of the Renaissance master replaced by a paint-by-numbers version.

But with much of Michelangelo's overpainting removed, it is easier to track his changing artistic style. Halfway through, Michelangelo decided his earlier panels were too busy and, beginning with the *Creation of Adam*, he painted much larger figures and simpler compositions. Another factor was, undoubtedly, the sheer physical difficulty of the execution. Michelangelo left a sonnet describing with stoical humor the contortions to which his body was subjected daily: for almost four years, he had to stand with aching, bending back just under the ceiling, paint dripping in his face, a worse position in many ways than the false Hollywood image of Michelangelo on his back. Compared to the first executed of the main panels, *The Flood* (which took forty days to paint, just as the biblical flood did), the last of the center panels, *God separating Light from Darkness*, was almost miraculously the work of a single day. Michelangelo's brush had come to obey the same time frame as the Creator himself, a proof of how far the so-called "sculptor" had mastered his technique.

In the courtyard named for Pope Alexander VI, a wellhead bears the Borgia coat of arms. The courtyard is surrounded by gloomy cells and huge storerooms that could hold great quantities of oil and grain in case of siege. Benvenuto Cellini, the rowdy 16th-century Florentine goldsmith, sculptor, and boastful autobiographer, spent some time in Castel Sant'Angelo's foul prisons; so did Giordano Bruno, a heretical monk who was later burned at the stake in Campo de' Fiori, and Beatrice Cenci, accused of patricide and incest and executed just across Ponte Sant'Angelo.

Take the stairs at the far end of the courtyard to the open terrace for a view of the Passetto, the fortified corridor connecting Castel Sant'Angelo with the Vatican, which featured in the book and 2009 film *Angels and Demons* (it's possible to request a visit; call for more information). Pope Clement VII used the Passetto to make his way safely to the castle during the Sack of Rome in 1527. Near here is a caffè for refreshments. Continue your walk along the perimeter of the tower and climb the few stairs to the *appartamento papale* (papal apartment). As if times of crisis were no object, the Sala Paolina (Pauline Room), the first you enter, was decorated in the 16th century by Pierino del Vaga and assistants with lavish frescoes of scenes from the Old Testament and the lives of St. Paul and Alexander the Great. Look for the trompe l'oeil door with a figure climbing the stairs. From another false door, a black-clad figure peers into the room. This is believed to be a portrait of an illegitimate son of the powerful Orsini family. Out on the upper terrace, at the feet of the bronze angel, take in a magnificent view of the city below. ✉ *Lungotevere Castello 50, Borgo* ☎ *06/6819111 Central line, 06/6896003 Tickets* 🌐 *www.castelsantangelo.com* 🎫 *€10.50* 🕒 *Tues.–Sun. 9–7:30* Ⓜ *Lepanto.*

Ponte Sant'Angelo. Angels designed by Baroque master Bernini line the most beautiful of central Rome's 20-odd bridges. Bernini himself carved only two of the angels (those with the scroll and the crown of thorns), both of which were moved to the church of Sant'Andrea delle Fratte shortly afterward due to the wishes of the Bernini family. Though copies, the angels on the bridge today convey forcefully the grace and characteristic sense of movement—a key element of Baroque sculpture—of Bernini's best work. Originally built in AD 133–134, the Ponte Elio, as it was originally called, was a bridge over the Tiber to Hadrian's Mausoleum. Pope Gregory changed the bridge's name after he had a vision of an angel sheathing its sword to signal the ending of the plague of 590. In medieval times, continuing its sacral function, the bridge became an important element in funneling pilgrims toward St. Peter's. As such, in 1667 Pope Clement IX commissioned Bernini to design 10 angels bearing the symbols of the Passion, turning the bridge into a sort of Via Crucis. ✉ *Between Lungotevere Castello and Lungotevere Altoviti, Borgo* Ⓜ *Ottaviano.*

PRATI

Outside the Vatican walls, but a slightly upriver from the Borgo neighborhood, Prati is starting to come into its own as a foodie destination.

5

PIAZZA NAVONA, CAMPO DE' FIORI, AND THE JEWISH GHETTO

with the Pantheon

GETTING ORIENTED

Piazza Navona, Campo de' Fiori, and the Jewish Ghetto

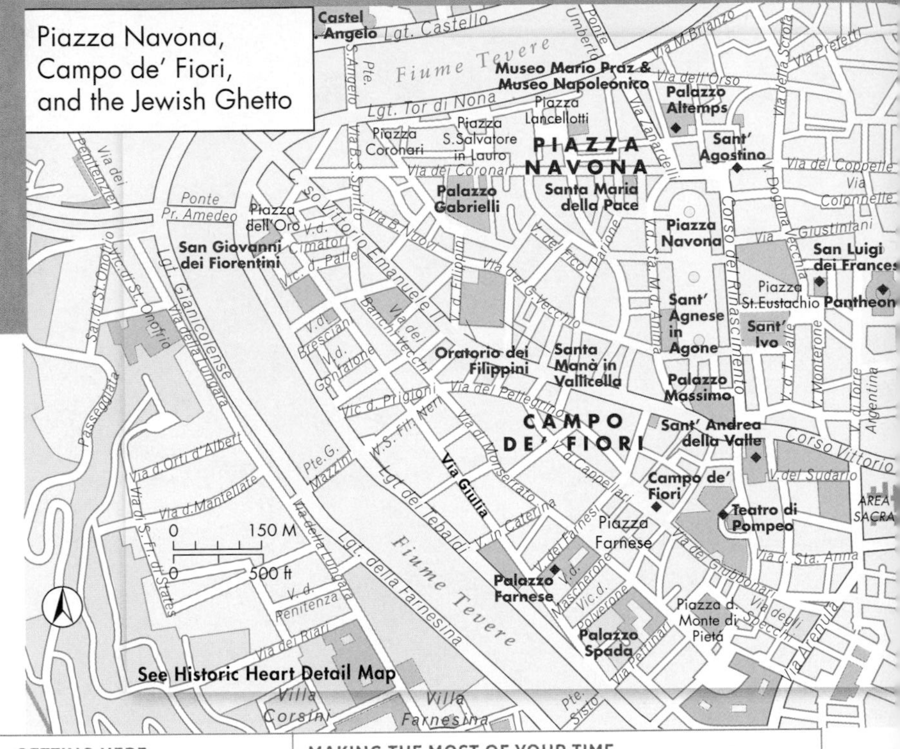

GETTING HERE	MAKING THE MOST OF YOUR TIME
The Piazza Navona and Campo de' Fiori are an easy walk from the Vatican or Trastevere, or a half-hour amble from the Spanish Steps. From Termini or the Vatican, take the No. 40 Express or the No. 64, to Largo Torre Argentina, a 10-minute stroll to either piazza. The No. 116 winds from Via Veneto past the Spanish Steps to Campo de' Fiori. From the Vatican or Spanish Steps, it's a 30-minute walk to the Jewish Ghetto, or take the No. 40 Express or the No. 64 bus from Termini to Largo Torre Argentina.	Start at Campo de' Fiori, where the popular market takes place every morning from Monday to Saturday. The cobblestone streets that stretch out from the square are still lined with artisanal workshops. Wind your way west through the Jewish Ghetto, the historic home of Rome's once-vibrant Jewish community (and a good place for lunch); don't miss the area around the Portico d'Ottavia, with some of the city's most atmospheric ruins. Heading north will take you across busy Corso Vittorio Emanuele toward the Pantheon. Duck into the piazza of Santa Maria Sopra Minerva, which contains Rome's most delightful Baroque conceit, the 17th-century elephant obelisk memorial designed by Bernini, and pop into the church, with the only Gothic interior in Rome. Straight ahead is one of the wonders of the world, the ancient Pantheon, with that postcard icon, Piazza Navona, just a few blocks to the west. You could spend about five hours to explore, not counting breaks—but taking breaks is what this area is all about.

TOP REASONS TO GO

Piazza Navona: This is the city's most glorious piazza—the showcase for Rome's exuberant Baroque style. Savor how Bernini's fantastic fountain is set off by the curves and steeples of Borromini's church of Sant'Agnese.

Caravaggio: Feel the power of 17th-century Rome's rebel artist in three of his finest paintings, at the church of San Luigi dei Francesi.

The Pantheon: Gaze up to the heavens through the dome of Rome's best-preserved ancient temple—could this be the world's only architecturally perfect building?

Campo de' Fiori: Stroll through the morning market for a taste of the sweet life.

Via Giulia: Lined with regal palaces—still home to some of Rome's *princeliest* families—this is a Renaissance-era diorama you can walk through.

Portico d'Ottavia: This famed ancient Roman landmark casts a spell over Rome's time-stained Ghetto Ebraico (Jewish Ghetto).

QUICK BITES

Cul de Sac. Steps from Piazza Navona, Cul de Sac was one of the first wine bars in Rome. Today, it offers small plates of Italian specialties—as well as a good wine list and outdoor seating (on a nice day, be prepared to wait for a table!). ✉ *Piazza Pasquino 73, Piazza Navona* ☎ *06/68801094.*

Giolitti. The Pantheon area is ice-cream heaven, with some of Rome's best gelaterias within a few steps of each other. But for many Romans, a scoop at Giolitti, which opened in 1900, is tradition. The scene at the counter often looks like the storming of the Bastille. Remember to pay the cashier first, and hand the stub to the counter-person when you order your cone. Giolitti also has a good snack counter. ✉ *Via Uffizi del Vicario 40, Around Piazza Navona* ☎ *06/6991243* 🌐 *www.giolitti.it* 🕒 *Daily 7 am–2 am.*

Sightseeing ★★★★★
Nightlife ★★★★
Dining ★★★
Lodging ★★★★★
Shopping ★★★★

The area around Piazza Navona, Campo de' Fiori, and the Jewish Ghetto is one of the city's most beautiful, liveliest, and atmospheric neighborhoods. More than almost anywhere else in Rome, this is an area worth getting lost in, with cobblestone side streets and artisanal shops often located just around the corner from the piazzas and sights that crowd with tourists (and the establishments that cater to them).

PIAZZA NAVONA

Updated by Amanda Ruggeri

In terms of sheer sensual enjoyment—from a mouthwatering range of restaurants and cafés to the ornate Baroque settings—it's tough to top this area of Rome. Just a few blocks, and some 1,200 years, separate the two main showstoppers: Piazza Navona and the Pantheon. The first is the most beautiful Baroque piazza in the world, which serves as the open-air salon for this quarter of Rome. As if this is not grandeur enough, across Corso di Rinascimento—and more than a millennium away—is the Pantheon, the grandest extant building still standing from ancient Rome. Even today, it's topped by the world's largest unreinforced concrete dome. Near the same massive hub, Bernini's delightful elephant obelisk shows small can also be beautiful. And beautiful is the word to describe this entire area, one that is packed with Baroque wonders, charming stores, and very happy sightseers.

TOP ATTRACTIONS

Fodor's Choice ★ **Palazzo Altemps.** Containing some of the finest ancient Roman statues in the world, the collection here formerly made up the core of the Museo Nazionale Romano. As of 1995, it was moved to these new, suitably grander digs. The palace's sober exterior belies a magnificence that appears as soon as you walk into the majestic courtyard, studded with statues and covered in part by a retractable awning. The restored interior hints at the Roman lifestyle of the 16th through

18th centuries while showcasing the most illustrious pieces from the Museo Nazionale, including the Ludovisi family collection. In the frescoed salons you can see the *Galata,* a poignant work portraying a barbarian warrior who chooses death for himself and his wife rather than humiliation by the enemy. Another highlight is the large Ludovisi sarcophagus, magnificently carved from marble. In a place of honor is the Ludovisi Throne, which shows a goddess emerging from the sea and being helped by her acolytes. For centuries this was heralded as one of the most sublime Greek sculptures but, today, at least one authoritative art historian considers it a colossally overrated fake. Look for the framed explanations of the exhibits that detail (in English) how and exactly where Renaissance sculptors, Bernini among them, added missing pieces to the classical works. In the lavishly frescoed Loggia stand busts of the Caesars. In the wing once occupied by early-20th-century poet Gabriele D'Annunzio (who married into the Altemps family), three rooms host the museum's Egyptian collection. ✉ *Piazza Sant'Apollinare 46, Piazza Navona* ☎ *06/39967700* 🌐 *www.coopculture.it* 🎫 *€7, includes three other Museo Nazionale Romano sites (Crypta Balbi, Palazzo Massimo, Museo Diocleziano); €10 if any one of them has an exhibit* ⏲ *Tues.–Sun. 9–7:45 (ticket office closes 1 hr before)* Ⓜ *Bus 70, 81, 87, 116T, 186, 492, 628.*

5

Fodor's Choice ★ **Pantheon.** One of the wonders of the ancient world, this onetime pagan temple, a marvel of architectural harmony and proportion, is the best-preserved ancient building in Rome. It was entirely rebuilt by the emperor Hadrian around AD 120 on the site of an earlier pantheon (from the Greek *pan,* all, and *theon,* gods) erected in 27 BC by Augustus's general Agrippa. It's thought that the majestic circular building was actually designed *by* Hadrian, as were many of the temples, palaces, and lakes of his enormous villa at Tivoli. Hadrian nonetheless retained the inscription over the entrance from the original building (today, unfortunately, replaced with modern letters) that named Agrippa as the builder. This caused enormous confusion among historians until, in 1892, a French architect discovered that all the bricks used in the Pantheon dated from Hadrian's time.

The most striking thing about the Pantheon is not its size, immense though it is (until 1960 the dome was the largest ever built), nor even the phenomenal technical difficulties posed by so vast a construction; rather, it's the remarkable unity of the building. You don't have to look far to find the reason for this harmony: the diameter described by the dome is exactly equal to its height. It's the use of such simple mathematical balance that gives classical architecture its characteristic sense of proportion and its nobility and why some call it the world's only architecturally perfect building. The great opening at the apex of the dome, the oculus, is nearly 30 feet in diameter and was the temple's only source of light. It was intended to symbolize the "all-seeing eye of heaven."

To do the interior justice defied even Byron. He piles up adjectives, but none seems to fit: "Simple, erect, severe, austere, sublime." Not surprising, perhaps, when describing a dome 141 feet high and the same across. Although little is known for sure about the Pantheon's

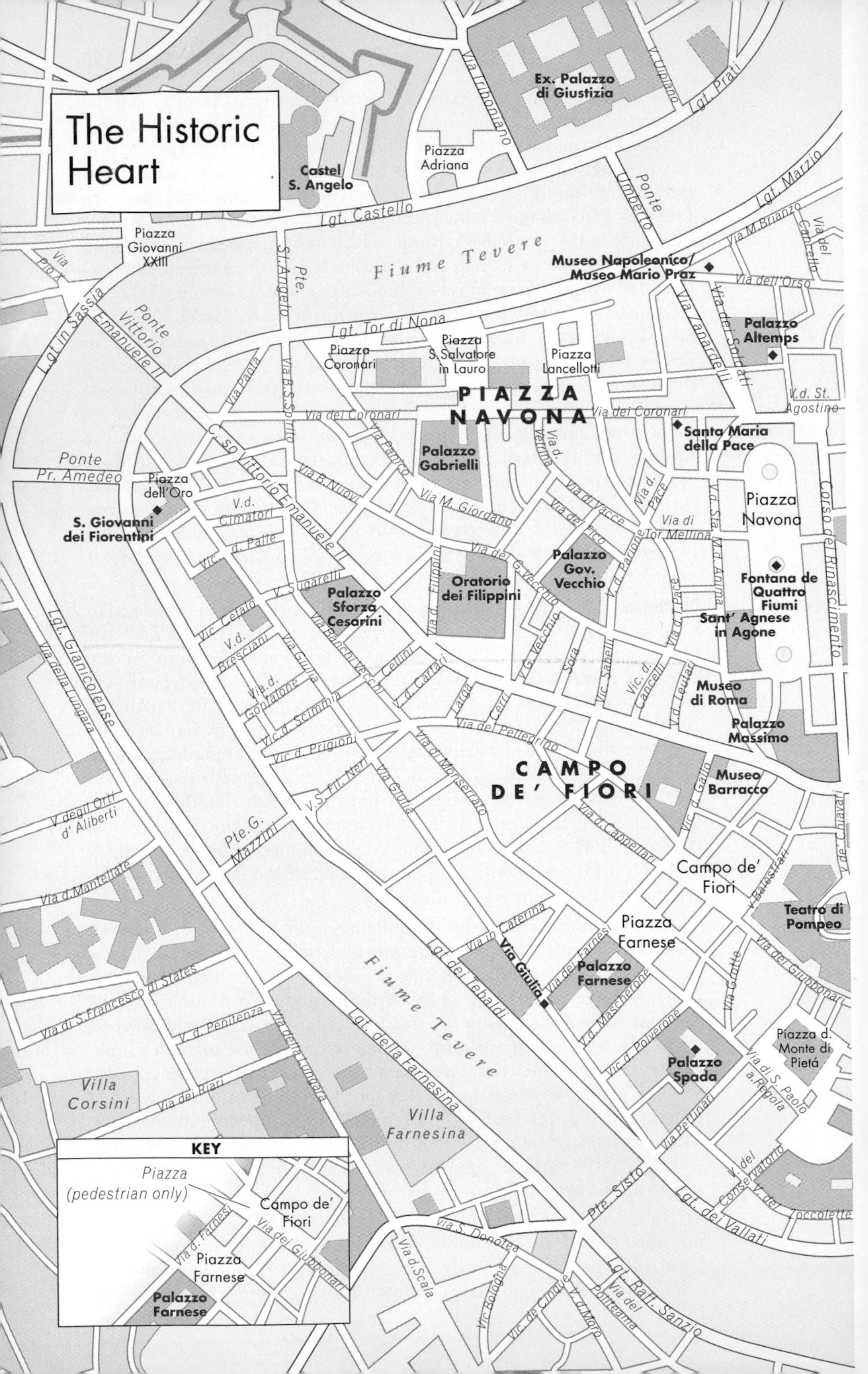
The Historic Heart
Castel S. Angelo
Piazza Adriana
Via Triboniano
Ex. Palazzo di Giustizia
V. Ulpiano
Lgt. Prati
Lgt. Castello
Ponte Umberto
Lgt. Marzio
Piazza Giovanni XXIII
Via Pio X
Pte. S. Angelo
Fiume Tevere
Museo Napoleonico/ Museo Mario Praz
Via M. Brianzo
Via del Cancello
Via dell'Orso
Lgt. in Sassia
Ponte Vittorio Emanuele II
Lgt. Tor di Nona
Piazza Coronari
Piazza S.Salvatore in Lauro
Piazza Lancellotti
Via Zanardelli
Via dei Soldati
Palazzo Altemps
Via Paola
Via B.S. Spirito
PIAZZA NAVONA
Via dei Coronari
V.d. St. Agostino
Santa Maria della Pace
Via Panico
Palazzo Gabrielli
Via d. Vetrina
Ponte Pr. Amedeo
Piazza dell'Oro
C.so Vittorio Emanuele II
Via B. Nuovi
Via M. Giordano
Via di Vacce
Via d. Pace
Piazza Navona
Corso del Rinascimento
S. Giovanni dei Fiorentini
V.d. Cimatori
Vic. d. Palle
Via del Fico
Via di Tor Mellina
V.d. Sta. M.d. Anima
Palazzo Gov. Vecchio
Via dei G. Vecchio
Via d. Filippini
Oratorio dei Filippini
V. d. Parione
Fontana de Quattro Fiumi
V. Sugarelli
Palazzo Sforza Cesarini
Sant' Agnese in Agone
Vic. Cefalo
V.d. Bresciani
Via Giulia
Via Banchi Vecchi
Cellini
V. d. Cartari
Via d. T. Pace
Lgt. Gianicolense
Via della Lungara
Via d. Gonfalone
Vic. d. Scimmia
Larga
Cerri
V. G. Vecchio
Sora
Vic. Sabelli
Vic. d. Cancelli
V. d. Leutari
Museo di Roma
Via del Pellegrino
Palazzo Massimo
Vic. d. Prigioni
Via di Monserrato
CAMPO DE' FIORI
Museo Barracco
V.S. Fil. Neri
Via Giulia
Vic. d. Gallo
V. degli Orti d' Aliberti
Pte. G. Mazzini
Via d. Cappellari
V. de' Chiavari
Campo de' Fiori
Via d. Mantellate
V. Balestrari
Teatro di Pompeo
Via in Caterina
Piazza Farnese
Via Giulia
Via dei Farnesi
Palazzo Farnese
Lgt. dei Tebaldi
Via dei Giubbonari
Via di S.Francesco di Sales
V.d. Mascherone
Via Grotte
Via di S. Penitenza
Via della Lungara
Lgt. della Farnesina
Vic. d. Polverone
Palazzo Spada
Piazza d. Monte di Pietá
Villa Corsini
Via dei Riari
Via di S. Paolo a. Regola
Villa Farnesina
Via Pettinari
Pte. Sisto
V. del Conservatorio
V. del Zoccolette
Lgt. dei Vallati
Via S. Dorotea
Via d. Scala
Vic. Bologna
Vic. de Cinque
V. d. Moro
Via del Politeama
Lgt. Raff. Sanzio
KEY
Piazza (pedestrian only)
Campo de' Fiori
Via d. Farnesi
Via dei Giubbonari
Piazza Farnese
Palazzo Farnese

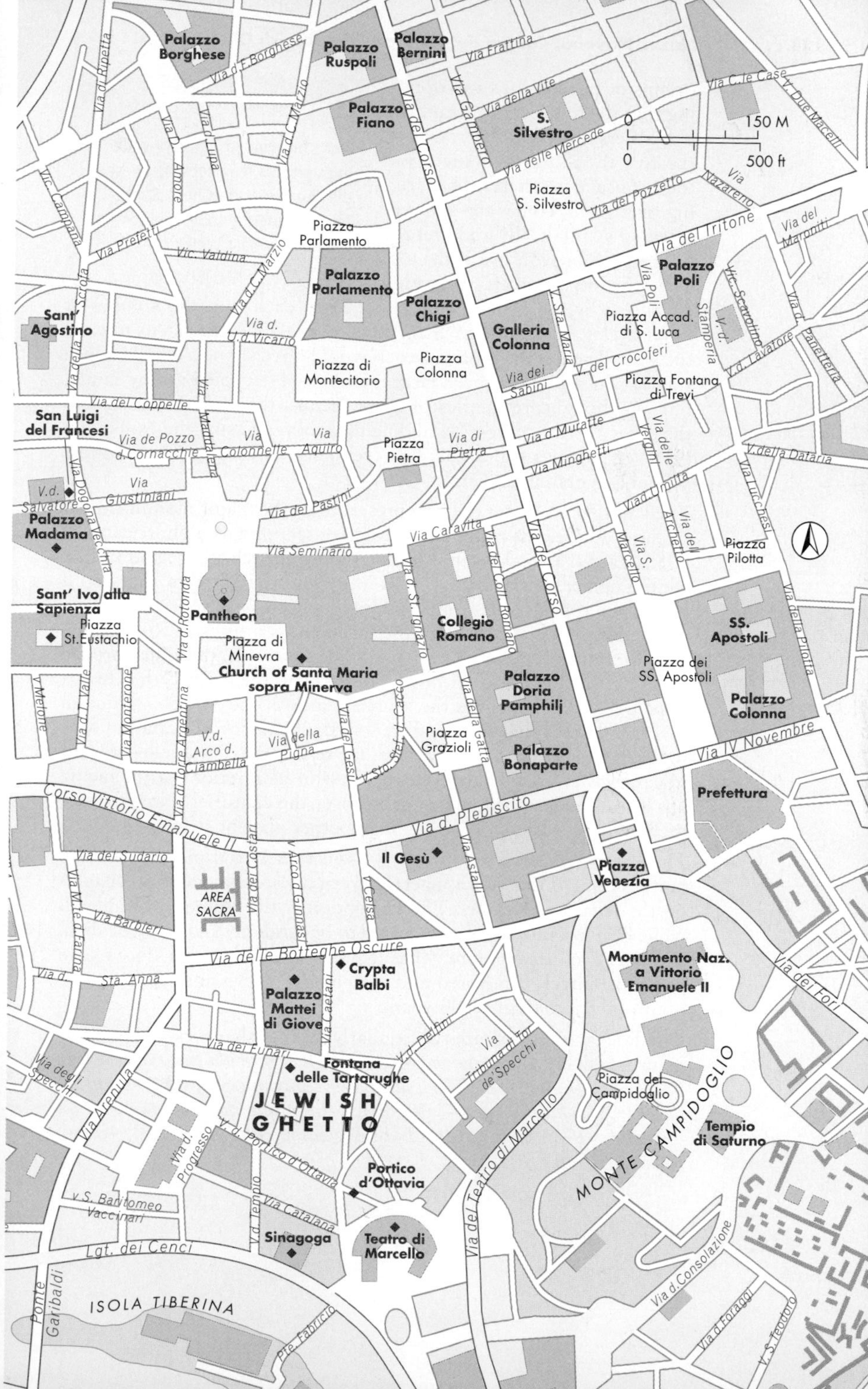

Palazzo Borghese
Palazzo Ruspoli
Palazzo Bernini
Via Frattina
Via d.F. Borghese
Via di Ripetta
Via d.C. Marzio
Palazzo Fiano
Via del Corso
Via Gambero
Via della Vite
S. Silvestro
Via delle Mercede
Via C.le Case
V. Due Macelli
0
150 M
0
500 ft
Via D. Amore
Via d. Lupa
Vic. Campana
Piazza S. Silvestro
Via del Pozzetto
Via Nazareno
Via Prefetti
Piazza Parlamento
Vic. Valdina
Via del Tritone
Via del Maroniti
Palazzo Parlamento
Palazzo Chigi
Palazzo Poli
Via della Scrofa
Via d.C. Marzio
Sant' Agostino
Via d. U.d.Vicario
V. Sta. Maria
Via Poli
Piazza Accad. di S. Luca
Stamperia
Vic. Scavolino
V.d. Lavatore
Via d. Panetteria
Galleria Colonna
Piazza di Montecitorio
Piazza Colonna
V. del Crocoferi
Via dei Sabini
Piazza Fontana di Trevi
Via del Coppelle
Via Maddalena
San Luigi del Francesi
Via de Pozzo d.Cornacchie
Via Colonnelle
Via Aquiro
Piazza Pietra
Via di Pietra
Via d. Muratte
Via delle Vergini
Via Minghetti
V. della Dataria
Via Giustiniani
V.d. Salvatore
Via Dogana Vecchia
Via del Pastini
Via d. Umiltà
Via dell Archetto
Via Lucchesi
Palazzo Madama
Via Caravita
Via del Coll. Romano
Via del Corso
Via S. Marcello
Piazza Pilotta
Via Seminario
Via d. St. Ignazio
Sant' Ivo alla Sapienza
Via d. Rotonda
Pantheon
Collegio Romano
SS. Apostoli
Via della Pilotta
Piazza St.Eustachio
Piazza di Minevra
Church of Santa Maria sopra Minerva
Piazza dei SS. Apostoli
Palazzo Doria Pamphilj
V. Melone
Via d. T. Valle
Via Monterone
Via di Torre Argentina
V.d. Arco d. Ciambella
Via della Pigna
Via del Gesù
V. Sto. Stef. d. Cacco
Piazza Grazioli
Via della Gatta
Palazzo Colonna
Palazzo Bonaparte
Via IV Novembre
Prefettura
Corso Vittorio Emanuele II
Via d. Plebiscito
Via del Sudario
Via M.te d. Farina
Via dei Cestari
V. Arco d. Ginnasi
V. Celsa
Il Gesù
Via Astalli
Piazza Venezia
AREA SACRA
Via Barbieri
Via delle Botteghe Oscure
Via d. Sta. Anna
Crypta Balbi
Palazzo Mattei di Giove
Via Caetani
Monumento Naz. a Vittorio Emanuele II
Via dei Fori
Via dei Funari
V. d. Delfini
Via Tribuna di Tor de' Specchi
Via degli Specchi
Via Arenula
Fontana delle Tartarughe
JEWISH GHETTO
Piazza del Campidoglio
Tempio di Saturno
MONTE CAMPIDOGLIO
Via d. Progresso
V. d. Portico d'Ottavia
Via del Teatro di Marcello
Portico d'Ottavia
v. S. Baritomeo Vaccinari
V.d. Tempio
Via Catalana
Sinagoga
Teatro di Marcello
Lgt. dei Cenci
Via d. Consolazione
Ponte Garibaldi
ISOLA TIBERINA
Pte. Fabricio
Via d. Foraggi
V. S. Teodoro

origins or purpose, it's worth noting that the five levels of trapezoidal coffers represent the course of the five then-known planets and their concentric spheres. Then, ruling over them, comes the sun represented symbolically and literally by the 30-foot-wide eye at the top. The heavenly symmetry is further paralleled by the coffers themselves: 28 to each row, the number of lunar cycles. Note how each coffer takes five planetary steps toward the wall. Then in the center of each would have shone a small bronze star. Down below the seven large niches were occupied not by saints, but, it's thought, by statues of Mars, Venus, the deified Caesar, and the other "astral deities," including the moon and sun, the "sol invictus." (Academics still argue, however, about which gods were most probably worshipped here.)

ITINERARY TIP

For a full guided itinerary walk through this magical quarter, see the "Enjoying the Gilt: A Stroll Through the Baroque Quarter" in the Rome's Best Walks chapter.

The Pantheon is by far the best preserved of the major monuments of imperial Rome, the result of it being consecrated as a church in AD 608. (It's still a working and Mass-holding church today, and it's the church name, the Basilica of Saint Mary and the Martyrs, that you'll see on the official signs.) No building, church or not, escaped some degree of plundering through the turbulent centuries of Rome's history after the fall of the empire. In 655, for example, the gilded bronze covering the dome was stripped. Similarly, in the early 17th century, Pope Urban VIII removed the bronze beams of the portico. Although the legend holds that the metal went to the *baldacchino* (canopy) over the high altar at St. Peter's Basilica, the reality may be worse—it went to cannons at Castel Sant'Angelo. Most of its interior marble facing has also been stripped and replaced over the centuries. Nonetheless, the Pantheon suffered less than many other ancient structures.

The Pantheon is one of the city's important burial places. Its most famous tomb is that of Raphael (between the second and third chapels on the left as you enter). The inscription reads "Here lies Raphael; while he lived, mother Nature feared to be outdone; and when he died, she feared to die with him." The temple's original bronze doors have remained intact, if restored and even melted down and recast at one point, for more than 1,800 years.

One-hour tours (€10) are run regularly in English; check at the information desk on your right as you enter. ✉ *Piazza della Rotonda, Piazza Navona* ☎ *06/68300230* 🌐 *www.pantheonroma.com* 🎫 *Free; audio guides €5* 🕒 *Mon.–Sat. 9–7:30, Sun. 9–6, public holidays that fall on a weekday 9–1* Ⓜ *Closest bus hub: Argentina (Bus 40, 85, 53, 46, 64, 87, 571; Tram 8).*

PIAZZA NAVONA

✉ *Junction of Via della Cuccagna, Corsia Agonale, Via di Sant'Agnese, and Via Agonale.*

TIPS

■ On the eve of Epiphany (the night of January 5), Piazza Navona's toy fair explodes in joyful conclusion, with much noise and rowdiness to encourage la Befana, an old woman who brings toys to good children and pieces of coal (represented by similar-looking candy) to the naughty. Dealers also set up before Christmas to selltrinkets and presepio (crèche) figures.

■ If you want a caffè with one of the most beautiful views in Rome the Piazza Navona is lined with cafés so you can pick and choose. Just be aware that the restaurants here are geared toward tourists, so while it's a beautiful place for a coffee, you can find cheaper, more authentic, and much better meals elsewhere.

Here, everything that makes Rome unique is compressed into one beautiful Baroque piazza. Always camera-ready, Piazza Navona has Bernini sculptures, three gorgeous fountains, a magnificently Baroque church (Sant'Agnese in Agone), and, best of all, the excitement of so many people strolling, admiring the fountains, and enjoying the view.

The piazza has been an entertainment venue for Romans ever since being built over Domitian's circus (pieces of the arena are still visible near adjacent Piazza Sant'Apollinare). Although undoubtedly more touristy today, the square still has the carefree air of the days when it was the scene of medieval jousts and 17th-century carnivals. Today, it's the site of a lively Christmas "Befana" fair.

The piazza still looks much as it did during the 17th century, after the Pamphili pope Innocent X decided to make it over into a monument to his family to rival the Barberini's palace at the Quattro Fontane.

At center stage is the Fontana dei Quattro Fiumi, created for Innocent X by Bernini in 1651. Bernini's powerful figures of the four rivers represent the four corners of the world: the Nile; the Ganges; the Danube; and the Plata, with its hand raised. One story has it that the figure of the Nile—the figure closest to Sant' Agnese in Agone—hides its head because it can't bear to look upon the church's "inferior" facade designed by Francesco Borromini, Bernini's rival. In fact, the facade was built after the fountain, and the statue hides its head because it represents a river whose source was then unknown (for more on Bernini and Borromini, see our special photo feature in Chapter 7).

NEED A BREAK?

Tazza d'Oro. On the east corner of the Pantheon's piazza, the Tazza d'Oro coffee bar (no tables, no frills) is the place for serious coffee drinkers. Indulge in their *granita di caffè con panna* (coffee ice with whipped cream). ✉ ***Via degli Orfani 86, Around Piazza Navona*** 🌐 ***www.tazzadorocoffeeshop.com.***

Fodor's Choice ★ **San Luigi dei Francesi.** A pilgrimage spot for art lovers everywhere, San Luigi's Contarelli Chapel is adorned with three stunningly dramatic works by Caravaggio (1571–1610), the Baroque master of the heightened approach to light and dark. At the altar end of the left nave, they were commissioned for San Luigi, the official church of Rome's French colony (San Luigi is St. Louis, patron of France). The inevitable coin machine will light up his *Calling of St. Matthew, Matthew and the Angel,* and *Matthew's Martyrdom,* seen from left to right, and Caravaggio's mastery of light takes it from there. When painted, they caused considerable consternation to the clergy of San Luigi, who thought the artist's dramatically realistic approach was scandalously disrespectful. A first version of the altarpiece was rejected; the priests were not particularly happy with the other two, either. Time has fully vindicated Caravaggio's patron, Cardinal Francesco del Monte, who secured the commission for these works and stoutly defended them. They're now recognized to be among the world's greatest paintings. ✉ *Piazza San Luigi dei Francesi, Piazza Navona* ☎ *06/688271* 🌐 *www.saintlouis-rome.net* ⏲ *Fri.–Wed. 10–12:30 and 3–7; Thurs. 10–12:30* Ⓜ *Bus 40, 87.*

Sant'Agnese in Agone. The quintessence of Baroque architecture, this church has a facade that remains a wonderfully rich mélange of bell towers, concave spaces, and dovetailed stone and marble, the creation of Francesco Borromini (1599–1667), a contemporary and rival of Bernini. Next to his new Pamphilj family palace, Pope Innocent X had the adjacent chapel expanded into this full-fledged church. The work was first assigned to the architect Rainaldi. However, Donna Olimpia, the pope's famously domineering sister, became increasingly impatient with how the work was going and brought in Borromini, whose wonderful concave entrance has the magical effect of making the dome appear much larger than it actually is. The name of this church comes from *agona,* the source of the word *navona* and a corruption of the Latin *agonalis,* describing the type of games held there in Roman times. The saint associated with the church is Agnes, who was martyred here in the piazza's forerunner, the Stadium of Domitian. As she was stripped nude before the crowd, her hair miraculously grew to maintain her modesty before she was killed. The interior is a marvel of modular Baroque space and is ornamented by giant marble reliefs sculpted by Raggi and Ferrata. ✉ *Piazza Navona, Piazza Navona* ☎ *06/68192134* 🌐 *www.santagneseinagone.org* ⏲ *Tues.–Sat. 9:30–12:30 and 3:30–7, Sun. and holidays 9–1 and 4–8* Ⓜ *Bus 87, 40, 64.*

Santa Maria della Pace. In 1656, Pietro da Cortona (1596–1669) was commissioned by Pope Alexander VII to enlarge the tiny Piazza della Pace in front of the 15th-century church of Santa Maria (to accommodate the carriages of its wealthy parishioners). His architectural solution was to design a new church facade complete with semicircular portico, demolish a few buildings here and there to create a more spacious approach to the church, add arches to give architectural unity to the piazza, and then complete it with a series of bijou-size palaces. The result was one of Rome's most delightful little architectural stage sets. Within are two great Renaissance treasures: Raphael's fresco above the first altar on your right depicts the *Four Sibyls*, almost exact, if more relaxed, replicas of Michelangelo's. The fine decorations of the Cesi Chapel, second on the right, were designed in the mid-16th century by Sangallo. Opposite is Peruzzi's wonderful fresco of the *Madonna and Child*. Meanwhile, the octagon below the dome is something of an art gallery in itself with works by Cavalliere Arpino, Orazio Gentileschi, and others as Cozzo's *Eternity* fills the lantern above. Behind the church proper is its cloister, designed by Bramante (architect of St. Peter's) as the very first expression of High Renaissance style in Rome. At times, the cloister is the venue for modern art shows and, thanks to the Caffè alla Pace, the little piazza has become the core of a trendy caffè scene. ✉ *Via Arco della Pace 5, Piazza Navona* ☎ *06/6861156* ⏲ *Mon., Wed., and Sat. 9–11:50* Ⓜ *Bus 87, 40, 64.*

Santa Maria sopra Minerva. The name of the church reveals that it was built *sopra* (over) the ruins of a temple of Minerva, ancient goddess of wisdom. Erected in 1280 by the Dominicans on severe Italian Gothic lines, it has undergone a number of more or less happy restorations to the interior. Certainly, as the city's major Gothic church, it provides a refreshing contrast to Baroque flamboyance. Have a €1 coin handy to illuminate the **Cappella Carafa** in the right transept, where Filippino Lippi's (1457–1504) glowing frescoes are well worth the small investment, opening up the deepest azure expanse of sky where musical angels hover around the Virgin. Under the main altar is the tomb of St. Catherine of Siena, one of Italy's patron saints. Left of the altar you'll find Michelangelo's *Risen Christ* and the tomb of the gentle artist Fra Angelico. Bernini's unusual and little-known monument to the Blessed Maria Raggi is on the fifth pier from the door on the left as you leave the church. In front of the church, the little obelisk-bearing elephant carved by Bernini is perhaps the city's most charming sculpture. An inscription on the base of **Bernini's Elephant Obelisk,** which was recently cleaned and restored, references the church's ancient patroness, reading something to the effect that it takes a strong mind to sustain solid wisdom. ✉ *Piazza della Minerva, Piazza Navona* ☎ *06/6793926* 🌐 *www.basilicaminerva.it* ⏲ *Weekdays 7:10–7, weekends 8–noon and 2–7.*

Sant'Ivo alla Sapienza. The main facade of this eccentric Baroque church, probably Borromini's best, is on the stately courtyard of an austere building that once housed Rome's university. Sant'Ivo has what must surely be one of the most delightful domes in all of Rome—a golden spiral said to have been inspired by a bee's stinger (for more information on Borromini, see our special photo feature, "Baroque and Desperate: The Tragic Rivalry of Bernini and Borromini" in Chapter 6). The bee symbol is a reminder that Borromini built the church on commission from the Barberini pope Urban VIII (a swarm of bees figure on the Barberini family crest). The interior, open only for three hours on Sunday, is worth a look, especially if you share Borromini's taste for complex mathematical architectural idiosyncrasies. "I didn't take up architecture solely to be a copyist," Borromini once said. Sant'Ivo is certainly the proof. ✉ *Corso Rinascimento 40, Piazza Navona* ☎ *06/6864987* 🌐 *060608.it* ⏲ *Sept.–June., Sun. 9–noon* Ⓜ *Bus 130, 116, 186, 492, 30, 70, 81, 87.*

WORTH NOTING

Museo Mario Praz. On the top floor of the Palazzo Primoli—the same building (separate entrance) that houses the Museo Napoleonico—is one of Rome's most unusual museums. As if in amber, the apartment in which the famous Italian essayist Mario Praz lived is preserved intact, decorated with a lifetime's accumulation of delightful Baroque and Neoclassical art and antiques arranged and rearranged to create symmetries that take the visitor by surprise like the best trompe d'oeil. As author of *The Romantic Sensibility* and *A History of Interior Decoration*, Praz was fabled for his taste for the arcane and the bizarre; here his reputation for the same lives on. ✉ *Via Zanardelli 1, Piazza Navona* ☎ *06/6861089* 🌐 *www.museopraz.beniculturali.it* 🎫 *Free* ⏲ *Tues.–Sun. 9–2 and 2:30–7:30 (ticket office closes 1 hr before closing)* Ⓜ *Bus 492, 70, 628, 81, 116.*

Museo Napoleonico. Housed in an opulent collection of velvet-and-crystal salons that hauntingly capture the fragile charm of early-19th-century Rome, this small museum in the Palazzo Primoli contains a specialized and rich collection of Napoléon memorabilia, including a bust by Canova of the general's sister, Pauline Borghese (as well as a plaster cast of her left bust). You may well ask why this outpost of Napoléon is in Rome, but in 1809 the French emperor had made a grab for Rome, kidnapping Pope Pius VII and proclaiming his young son the King of Rome. All came to naught a few years later, when the emperor was routed off his French throne. Upstairs is the Museo Mario Praz. ✉ *Palazzo Primoli, Piazza di Ponte Umberto I, Piazza Navona* ☎ *06/68806286* 🌐 *www.museonapoleonico.it* 🎫 *€8* ⏲ *Tues.–Sun. 10–6* Ⓜ *Bus 70, 30, 81, 628, 492.*

Piazza di Pasquino. This tiny piazza takes its name from the figure in the corner, the remnant of an old Roman statue depicting Menelaus. The statue underwent a name change in the 16th century when Pasquino, a cobbler or barber (and part-time satirist), started writing comments around the base. The habit caught on; soon everyone was doing it. The most loquacious of Rome's "talking statues," its lack of arms or face is more than made up for with commentary of any topic of the day. ✉ *Piazza di Pasquino, Piazza Navona.*

Sant'Agostino. Caravaggio's celebrated *Madonna of the Pilgrims*—which scandalized all of Rome because a kneeling pilgrim is pictured, all too realistically for the era's tastes, with dirt on the soles of his feet, with the Madonna standing in a less than majestic pose in a dilapidated doorway—is in the first chapel on the left. At the third column down the nave, admire Raphael's blue-robed *Isaiah*, said to be inspired by Michelangelo's prophets on the Sistine ceiling (Raphael, with the help of Bramante, had taken the odd peek at the master's original against strict orders of secrecy). Directly below is Sansovino's Leonardo-influenced sculpture, *St. Anne and the Madonna with Child.* As you leave, in a niche just inside the door, is the sculpted *Madonna and Child,* known to the Romans as the "Madonna del Parto" (of Childbirth) and piled high with ex-votos. The artist is Jacopo Tatti, also sometimes confusingly known as Sansovino after his master. ✉ *Piazza Sant'Agostino, Piazza Navona* ☎ *06/68801962* ⏲ *Daily 7:30–noon and 4–7:30.*

Santa Maria in Vallicella/Chiesa Nuova. This church, also known as Chiesa Nuova (New Church), was built toward the end of the 16th century at the urging of Philip Neri, and like Il Gesù is a product of the fervor of the Counter-Reformation. It has a sturdy Baroque interior, all white and gold, with ceiling frescoes by Pietro da Cortona depicting a miracle reputed to have occurred during the church's construction: the Virgin and strong-armed angels hold up the broken roof to prevent it crashing down onto the congregation below. The Church is most famed for its three magnificent altarpieces by Rubens. ✉ *Piazza della Chiesa Nuova, Corso Vittorio Emanuele II, Piazza Navona* ☎ *06/6875289* 🌐 *www.vallicella.org* ⏲ *Daily 7:30–noon and 4:30–7.*

CAMPO DE' FIORI

In the mornings, Campo de' Fiori, an evocative piazza ringed by medieval palazzi, is one of the city's most popular markets. While the market, like the square, is no longer a mainly local haunt—some stalls now hawk souvenirs and T-shirts, and tour groups are as common as bag-toting nonnas—it remains one of the most beloved, and bustling, institutions in the center. In the evening until past midnight, outdoor bars and restaurants transform this humble square into a hot spot.

TOP ATTRACTIONS

Campo de' Fiori. A bustling marketplace in the morning (Mon.–Sat. 8 am–1 pm) and a trendy meeting place the rest of the day (and night), this piazza has plenty of earthy charm. By sunset, all the fish, fruit, and flower vendors disappear and this so-called *piazza trasformista* takes on another identity, becoming a circus of bars particularly favored by study-abroads, tourists, and young expats (for the full scoop, see our special photo feature, "Life is a Piazza"). Brooding over the piazza is a hooded statue of the philosopher Giordano Bruno, who was burned at the stake here in 1600 for heresy. His was the first of the executions that drew Roman crowds to Campo de' Fiori in the 17th century. ✉ *Intersection of Via dei Baullari, Via Giubbonari, Via del Pellegrino, and Piazza della Cancelleria, Campo de' Fiori.*

Il Gesù. The mother church of the Jesuits in Rome is the prototype of all Counter-Reformation churches. Considered the first fully Baroque church, it has spectacular interior that tells a lot about an era of religious triumph and turmoil. Its architecture (the overall design was by Vignola, the facade by della Porta) influenced ecclesiastical building in Rome for more than a century and was exported by the Jesuits throughout the rest of Europe. Though consecrated as early as 1584, the interior of the church wasn't decorated for another 100 years. It was originally

Continued on page 139

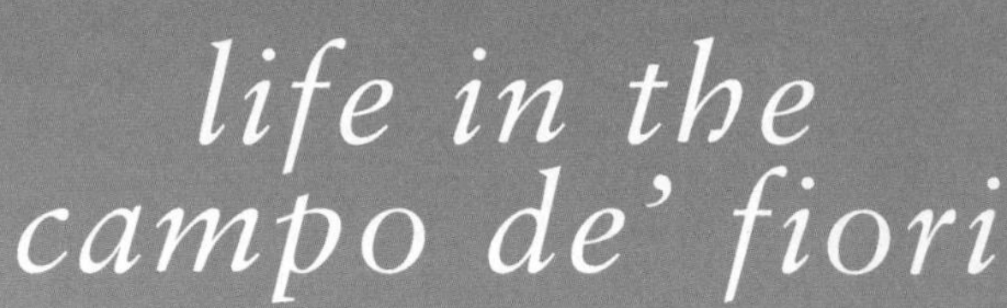

life in the campo de' fiori

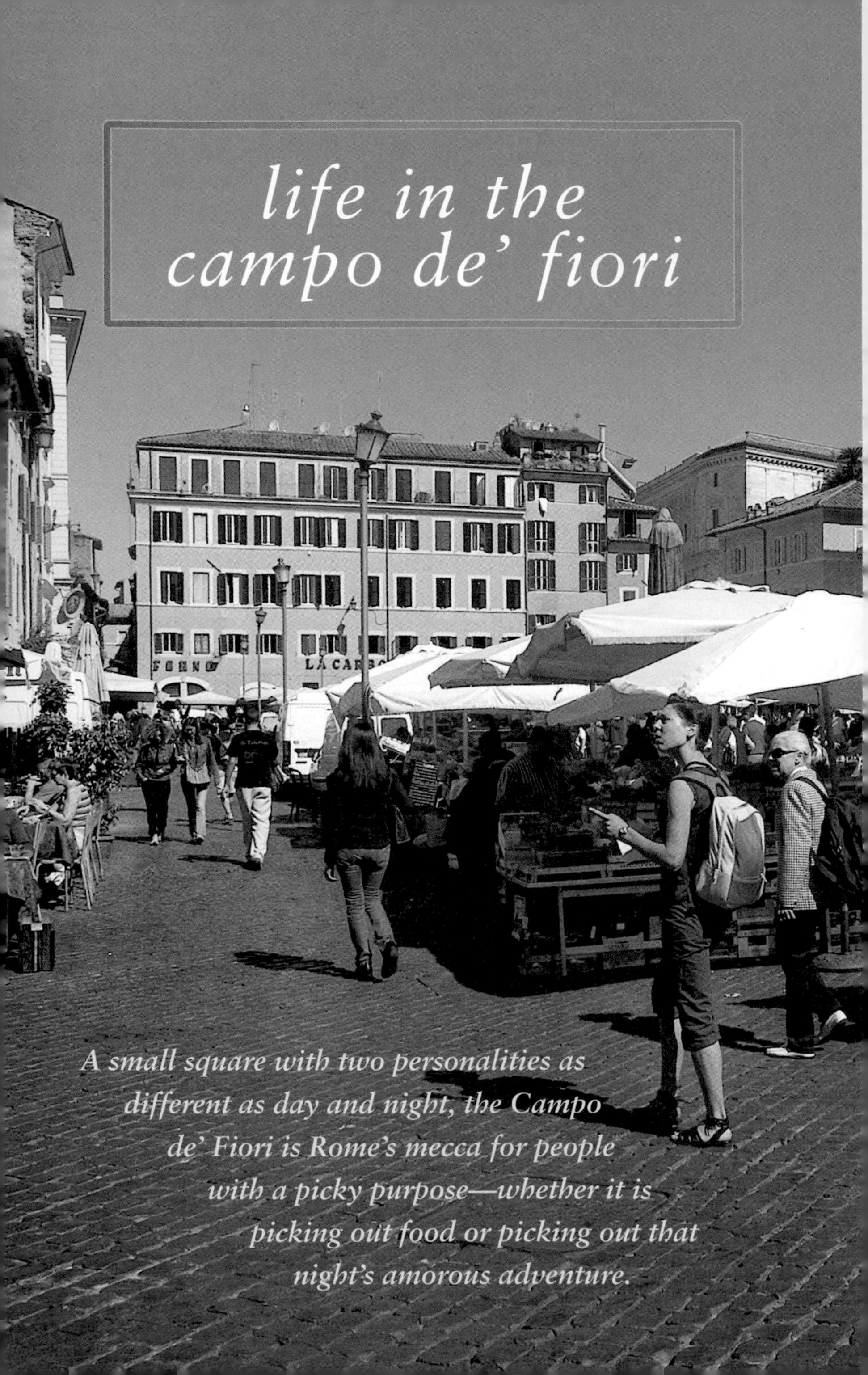

A small square with two personalities as different as day and night, the Campo de' Fiori is Rome's mecca for people with a picky purpose—whether it is picking out food or picking out that night's amorous adventure.

You can explore the Colosseum until your ears ring with roars of wild beasts, and make the rounds of churches until visions of angels dance in your head. But you won't know Rome until you have paused to appreciate the loveliness and vibrancy of the cityscape, perhaps from a table on one of Rome's beautiful squares. The Campo de' Fiori is particularly well endowed with such ringside seats, for here you can enjoy the show 24/7.

The Campo is heavily foot trafficked at any given hour, whether for its sunlit market stalls or its moon-shadowed cobblestones. If you only have 24 hours in Rome (and especially if the past 20 have been dedicated to sightseeing), take a breather here and inhale a truly Roman social scene, no matter what time of day or night.

In the daytime, the piazza is a buzzing produce market where ancient vendors shout out the day's specialties and caffè-goers gossip behind newspapers while enjoying the morning's cappuccino. In the late afternoon, the Campo de' Fiori transforms into the ultimate hang-out with overflowing bars, caffès, and restaurants filled with locals and tourists all vying for the perfect seat to check out passersby.

Campo life is decidedly without pause. The only moment of repose happens in the very wee hours of the morning when the remaining stragglers start the stumble home and just before the produce-filled mini-trucks begin their magnificent march in to the square. At any given hour, you will always find something going on in Campo, the "living room" of today's Rome.

By Erica Firpo

24 HOURS IN THE CAMPO DE' FIORI

5–6 am **The Flight of the Bumble-Bees:** *Ape* ("bee" in Italian) trucks file into the Campo to unload the day's goods. These mini-trucks are very cute, no? *Ao! Claudia che sta a fa?!* ("Hey, Claudia how ya doin'"), Daniele yells across to Claudia as market guys and gals joke around. Good lessons in Roman slang.

7–8 am **The Calm before the Storm:** The only time the Campo seems a bit sluggish, as stands have just opened, shoppers have yet to arrive, and everyone is just waking up. Market locals gather before heading off to work and school.

9–10 am **The Herd:** Tourists arrive. The locals take their "Pausa" coffee break while shops and late-opening caffès set up.

11–12 am **The Eye of the Storm:** Everyone is taking photos—photos of food, market-goers, vendors, models, caffè-goers, anything.

1–2 pm **Pranzo:** Lunchtime in the Campo. Everyone is looking for an outdoor table. Meanwhile, the vendors start to pack up.

3–4 pm **The Denoument:** The Campo is officially shutting down, marked by the notable odor of Campo refuse and the loud din of the cleaning trucks. This is perhaps the absolute worst time to be in Campo. When the trucks depart, they leave the square to parents and toddlers.

5–6 pm **Gelato Time:** Shoppers and strollers replace replace market-goers. The first of Campo's many musicians begin warming up for the evening's concert. Favorites always include: "Guantanamera," "My Way," and "Volare."

7–8 pm Happy Hours: The pre-aperitivi people enjoy the cocktail before the cocktails. Always good for the punctual. By 6 aperitivi have been served. Are you "in" or "out"? Outside means picking any of the umbrella *tavoli* that line the piazza. If you prefer to be on the sly, try an indoor *enoteca*. Late-comers arrive for a last sip of wine before deciding where to dine.

9–10 pm Dining Hour: Dining in Rome is an all-evening experience. It's common custom to argue for a half-hour about the perfect restaurant.

11 pm–12 am After-dinner Drinks: Everyone moves back to the Campo for a drink (or many). Drunkenness can include catcalls, stiletto falls, volleyed soccer balls, and the cops (polizia or carabinieri, take your pick).

1–2 am Time to Go Home: Bars begin to shut down, with lingering kisses and hugs ("Dude, I love you!"). Clean-up crews come back. The din returns, this time as trucks clean up broken bottles and plastic cups.

3–4 am Some stragglers are still hanging around. For the first time Campo de' Fiori is silent, to the delight of the residents around it. They have to hurry… because the Ape (see 5 am) are pressing to get back in.

THE COGNOSCENTI'S CAMPO

WHAT TO KNOW

No longer a simple flower market, from Monday through Saturday mornings the Campo de' Fiori is Rome's most famous produce market. This is where you'll find standard Italian favorites (like Pacchino tomatoes, peppers, and eggplant), as well as seasonal delicacies such as *puntarelle* (a variety of chicory) and Roman artichokes. There are also meat, regional cheese, and home-grown honey vendors. The *bancarelle* (tchotchke stands) sell T-shirts, purses, bangles, and cookware; sometimes they're good for souvenir shopping.

This is one of the best places for people-watching in Rome so hang out for a while. The many bars and cafés may look different but all have very similar menus and similar food. Mornings mean coffee and pastries; in the evening there is wine, beer, and mixed drinks. Most also have Wi-Fi.

A word of advice: leave the high heels at home—the uneven cobblestones can be treacherous.

It's worth noting that the Camp de' Fiori and the adjacent Piazza Farnese have two of the best newspaper kiosks for international publications; so if you want something to read while you sip your coffee, stop by.

intended that the interior be left plain to the point of austerity—but, when it was finally embellished, no expense was spared. Its interior drips with gold and lapis lazuli, gold and precious marbles, gold and more gold, all covered by a fantastically painted ceiling by Baciccia. Unfortunately, the church is also one of Rome's most crepuscular, so its visual magnificence is considerably dulled by lack of light.

The architectural significance of Il Gesù extends far beyond the splendid interior. The first of the great Counter-Reformation churches, it was put up after the Council of Trent (1545–63) had signaled the determination of the Roman Catholic Church to fight back against the Reformed Protestant heretics of northern Europe. The church decided to do so through the use of overwhelming pomp and majesty, in its effort to woo believers. As a harbinger of ecclesiastical spectacle, Il Gesù spawned imitations throughout Italy and the other Catholic countries of Europe as well as the Americas.

The most striking element is the ceiling, which is covered with frescoes that swirl down from on high to merge with painted stucco figures at the base, the illusion of space in the two-dimensional painting becoming the reality of three dimensions in the sculpted figures. Baciccia, their painter, achieved extraordinary effects in these frescoes, especially in the *Triumph of the Holy Name of Jesus,* over the nave. Here, the figures representing evil cast out of heaven seem to be hurtling down onto the observer. For details, the spectacle is best viewed through a specially tilted mirror in the nave.

The founder of the Jesuit order himself is buried in the Chapel of St. Ignatius, in the left-hand transept. This is surely the most sumptuous Baroque altar in Rome; as is typical, the enormous globe of lapis lazuli that crowns it is really only a shell of lapis over a stucco base—after all, Baroque decoration prides itself on achieving stunning effects and illusions. The heavy bronze altar rail by architect Carlo Fontana is in keeping with the surrounding opulence. ✉ *Piazza del Ges, off Via del Plebiscito, Campo de' Fiori* ☎ *06/697001* 🌐 *www.chiesadelgesu.org* 🕒 *Daily 7–12:30 and 4–7:45.*

Fodor's Choice ★ **Palazzo Farnese.** The most beautiful Renaissance palace in Rome, the Palazzo Farnese is fabled for the Galleria Carracci, whose ceiling is to the Baroque age what the Sistine ceiling is to the Renaissance. The Farnese family rose to great power and wealth during the Renaissance, in part because of the favor Pope Alexander VI showed to the beautiful Giulia Farnese. The massive palace was begun when, with Alexander's aid, Giulia's brother became cardinal; it was further enlarged on his election as Pope Paul III in 1534. The uppermost frieze decorations and main window overlooking the piazza are the work of Michelangelo, who also designed part of the courtyard, as well as the graceful arch over Via Giulia at the back. The facade on Piazza Farnese has recently been cleaned, further revealing geometrical brick configurations that have long been thought to hold some occult meaning. When looking up at the palace, try to catch a glimpse of the splendid frescoed ceilings, including the **Galleria Carracci** vault painted by Annibale Carracci between 1597 and 1604. The Carracci gallery depicts the loves of the gods, a supremely pagan theme that the artist painted in a swirling style that announced the birth of the Baroque. Other opulent salons are among the largest in Rome, including the Salon of Hercules, which has an overpowering replica of the ancient *Farnese Hercules* front and center. The French Embassy, which occupies the palace, offers weekly tours in English; be sure to book at least eight days in advance (book online at 🌐 *www.inventerrome.com*) and bring photo ID. ✉ *French Embassy, Servizio Culturale, Piazza Farnese 67, Campo de' Fiori* ☎ *06/686011* 🎫 *€5* 🕒 *By tours only (no children under 10); English tour Wed. at 5.*

Palazzo Spada. In this neighborhood of huge, austere palaces, Palazzo Spada strikes an almost frivolous note, with its upper stories covered with stuccos and statues and its pretty ornament-encrusted courtyard. While the palazzo houses an impressive collection of Old Master paintings, it is most famous for its trompe l'oeil garden gallery, a delightful example of the sort of architectural games rich Romans of the 17th century found irresistible. Even if you don't go into the gallery, step into the courtyard and look through the glass window of the library to the colonnaded corridor in the adjacent courtyard. See—or seem to see—Borromini's 8-meter-long gallery quadrupled in depth, a sort of optical telescope taking the Renaissance's art of perspective to another level, as it stretches out for a great distance with a large statue at the end. In fact the distance is an illusion: the corridor grows progressively narrower and the columns progressively smaller as they near the statue, which is just 2 feet tall. The Baroque prided itself on special effects, and this is rightly one of the most famous. It long was thought that Borromini was responsible for this ruse; it's now known that it was designed by an Augustinian priest, Giovanni Maria da Bitonto. Upstairs is a seignorial picture gallery with the paintings shown as they would have been, piled on top of each other clear to the ceiling. Outstanding works include Brueghel's Landscape with Windmills, Titian's Musician, and Andrea del Sarto's *Visitation*. Look for the fact-sheets that have descriptive notes about the objects in each room. ✉ *Piazza Capo di Ferro 13, Campo de' Fiori* ☎ *06/6861158* 🌐 *www.galleriaborghese.it* 🎫 *€5* 🕒 *Tues.–Sun. 8:30–7:30.*

Sant'Andrea della Valle. Topped by the highest dome in Rome (designed by Maderno) after St. Peter's, this huge and imposing 17th-century church is remarkably balanced in design. Fortunately, its facade, which had been turned a sooty gray from pollution, has been cleaned to a near-sparkling white. Use the handy mirror that's provided to examine the early-17th-century frescoes by Domenichino in the choir vault and those by Lanfranco in the dome. One of the earliest ceilings done in full Baroque style, its upward vortex was influenced by Correggio's dome in Parma, of which Lanfranco was also a citizen. (Bring a few coins to light the paintings, which can be very dim.) The three massive paintings of Saint Andrew's martyrdom are by Maria Preti (1650–51). Richly marbled and decorated chapels flank the nave, and in such a space, Puccini set the first act of *Tosca*. ✉ *Piazza Vidoni 6, Corso Vittorio Emanuele II, Campo de' Fiori* ☎ *06/6861339* 🌐 *www.sant-andrea-roma.it* 🕒 *Daily 7:30–12:30 and 4:30–7:30.*

Fodor's Choice ★ **Via Giulia.** Still a Renaissance-era diorama and one of Rome's most exclusive addresses, Via Giulia was the first street in Rome since ancient times to be laid out in a straight line. Named for Pope Julius II (of Sistine Chapel fame) who commissioned it in the early 1500s as part of a scheme to open up a grandiose approach to St. Peter's Basilica (using funds from the taxation of prostitutes), it became flanked with elegant churches and palaces. Though the pope's plans to change the face of the city were only partially completed, Via Giulia became an important thoroughfare in Renaissance Rome. Today, after more than four centuries, it remains the "salon of Rome," address of choice for Roman aristocrats. A stroll will reveal elegant palaces and old churches (one, **San Eligio,** at No. 18, reputedly designed by Raphael himself). The area around Via Giulia is a wonderful section to wander through and get the feel of daily life as carried on in a centuries-old setting. Among the buildings that merit your attention are **Palazzo Sacchetti** (Via Giulia 66), with an imposing stone portal (inside are some of Rome's grandest state rooms, still, after 300 years, the private quarters of the Marchesi Sacchetti), and the forbidding brick building that housed the **Carceri Nuove** (New Prison; Via Giulia 52), Rome's prison for more than two centuries and now the offices of Direzione Nazionale Antimafia. Near the bridge that arches over the southern end of Via Giulia is the church of **Santa Maria dell'Orazione e Morte** (Holy Mary of Prayer and Death), with stone skulls on its door. These are a symbol of a confraternity that was charged with burying the bodies of the unidentified dead found in the city streets. Home since 1927 to the Hungarian Academy, the **Palazzo Falconieri** (*Via Giulia 1* ☎ *06/6889671*) was designed by Borromini—note the architect's roof-top belvedere adorned with statues of the family "falcons," best viewed from around the block along the Tiber embankment. With a prior booking and €5 fee, you can visit the Borromini-designed salons and loggia. Remnant of a master plan by Michelangelo, the arch over the street was meant to link massive Palazzo Farnese, on the east side of Via Giulia, with the building across the street and a bridge to the Villa Farnesina, directly across the river. Finally, on the right and rather green with age, dribbles that star of many a postcard, the Fontana del Mascherone. ✉ *Between Piazza dell'Oro and Piazza San Vincenzo Palloti, Campo de' Fiori.*

WORTH NOTING

San Giovanni dei Fiorentini. Imbued with the supreme grace of the Florentine Renaissance, this often-overlooked church dedicated to Florence's patron saint, John the Baptist, stands in what was the heart of the Florentine colony in Rome's *centro storico*. Many of these Florentines were goldsmiths, bankers, and money changers who contributed to the building of the church. Talented goldsmith and sculptor Benvenuto Cellini of Florence, known for his vindictive nature as much as for his genius, lived nearby. Although the church was designed by Sansovino, Raphael (yes, he was also an architect) was among those who competed for this commission. Today, the church interior makes you feel you have wandered inside a perfect Renaissance space. Borromini executed a splendid altar for the Falconieri family chapel in the choir. He's buried under the dome, despite the fact that those who committed suicide normally were refused a Christian burial. ✉ *Via*

5

Accaioli 2, Piazza dell'Oro, Campo de' Fiori ☎ *06/68892059* ⏲ *Daily 7–noon and 5–7.*

JEWISH GHETTO

Although today most of Rome's Jews live outside the Ghetto, the area remains the spiritual and cultural home of Jewish Rome, and that heritage permeates its small commercial area of Judaica shops, kosher bakeries, and restaurants. The Jewish Ghetto was established by papal decree in the 16th century. It was by definition a closed community, where Roman Jews lived under lock and key until Italian unification in 1870. In 1943–44, the already small Jewish population there was decimated by deportations.

The turn-of-the-20th-century synagogue, with its museum dedicated to the history of Jewish Rome, is a must for understanding the Ghetto. Tight, teeming alleys lead from there up to Giacomo della Porta's unmistakable Turtle Fountain; nearby is the picture-perfect Palazzo Mattei. Via Portico d'Ottavia is a walk through the olden days. Most businesses in the Ghetto observe the Jewish Sabbath, so it's a ghost town on Saturdays. At its east end, the street leads down to a path past the 1st-century Teatro di Marcello. Separating the Ghetto and Trastevere is the Tiber River, but they are connected by one of the world's prettiest "bridges"—the Isola Tiberina (Tiber Island). Cross the river by using the Ponte Fabricio, the oldest bridge in Rome.

TOP ATTRACTIONS

Crypta Balbi. The fourth component of the magnificent collections of the Museo Nazionale Romano and visitable on the same ticket, this museum is unusual in its equitable apportioning of Rome's archaeological cake: a slice of Roman history—the crypt being part of the Balbus Theater complex (13 BC)—but also a slice of the largely vanished medieval Rome that once stood on top. The written explanations accompanying the well-lit exhibits are also excellent, making this museum much visited by teachers and schools. ✉ *Via delle Botteghe Oscure 31, Jewish Ghetto* ☎ *06/39967700* 🌐 *www.coopculture.it* 💳 *€7 (including 3-day access to 3 sister museums)* Ⓜ *Bus 64, 40, and Tram 8 from Trastevere.*

Fodor's Choice ★ **Palazzo Mattei di Giove.** Graceful and opulent, the arcaded, multistory courtyard of this palazzo is a masterpiece of turn-of-the-17th-century style. Designed by Carlo Maderno, it is a veritable panoply of sculpted busts, heroic statues, sculpted reliefs, and Paleo-Christian epigrams, all collected by Marchese Asdrubale Mattei. Have your Nikon ready as Roman and Renaissance heads cross glances across the ages. Inside are various scholarly institutes, including the Centro Studi Americani (Center for American Studies 🌐 *centrostudiamericani.org*), which also contains a library of American books. Various salons are decorated with frescoes by Cortona, Lanfranco, and Domenichino. ✉ *Via Michelangelo Caetani 32, other entrance in Via dei Funari, Jewish Ghetto* ☎ *06/68801613 Centro Studi Americani.*

Portico d'Ottavia. Looming over the Ghetto district, this huge porticoed enclosure, with a few surviving columns, comprises one of its most picturesque set pieces, with the time-stained church of Sant'Angelo in Pescheria built right into its ruins. Named by Augustus in honor of his sister Octavia, it was originally 390 feet wide and 433 feet long, encompassed two temples, a meeting hall, and a library, and served as a kind of grandiose entrance foyer for the adjacent Teatro di Marcello. The ruins of the portico became Rome's *pescheria* (fish market) during the Middle Ages. A stone plaque on a pillar, a relic of that time, admonishes in Latin that the head of any fish surpassing the length of the plaque was to be cut off "up to the first fin" and given to the city fathers or else the vendor was to pay a fine of 10 gold florins. The heads were used to make fish soup and were considered a great delicacy. After restoration, the lovely medieval church of Sant'Angelo in Pescheria has reopened to the public *(Wed., Sat., and first Mon. of the month 2–5; 06/68801819).* ✉ *Via Tribuna di Campitelli 6, Jewish Ghetto.*

NEED A BREAK?

Franco e Cristina. This stand-up pizza joint has some of the thinnest, crispiest pizza in town. ✉ ***Via Portico d'Ottavia 5, Jewish Ghetto.***

5

Teatro di Marcello. Begun by Julius Caesar and completed by the emperor Augustus in AD 13, this was Rome's first permanent building dedicated to drama; it held 20,000 spectators. Like other Roman monuments, it was transformed into a fortress during the Middle Ages. During the Renaissance, it was converted into a residence by the Savelli, one of the city's noble families. The small archaeological zone is used as a summer venue for open-air classical music and lyrical concerts. ✉ *Via del Teatro di Marcello, Jewish Ghetto* ☎ *06/87131590 for concert information* 🌐 *www.tempietto.it.*

WORTH NOTING

Fontana delle Tartarughe. Designed by Giacomo della Porta in 1581 and sculpted by Taddeo Landini, this 16th-century fountain, set in venerable Piazza Mattei, is Rome's most charming. The focus of the fountain is four bronze boys, each grasping a dolphin spouting water into a marble shell. Bronze turtles held in the boys' hands drink from the upper basin. The turtles are thought to have been added in the 17th century by Bernini. ✉ *Piazza Mattei, Jewish Ghetto.*

Sinagoga. This aluminum-roof synagogue has been the city's largest Jewish temple and a Roman landmark since its 1904 construction. At the back the Jewish Museum, with its precious ritual objects and other exhibits, documents the uninterrupted presence of a Jewish community for nearly 22 centuries. Until the 13th century the Jews were esteemed citizens of Rome. Among them were the bankers and physicians to the popes, who had themselves given permission for the construction of synagogues. But later, popes of the Counter-Reformation revoked this tolerance, confining the Jews to the Ghetto and imposing a series of restrictions, some of which were enforced as late as 1870. For security reasons, guided visits are mandatory; entrance to the synagogue is through the museum located in Via Catalana (*Largo 16 Ottobre 1943*). ✉ *Lungotevere Cenci 15, Jewish Ghetto* ☎ *06/68400661* 🌐 *www.museoebraico.roma.it* 🎫 *€11* 🕙 *Mid-Sept.–mid-June, Sun.–Thurs. 10–4:15, Fri. 9–1:15; mid-June–mid-Sept., Sun.–Thurs. 10–6:15, Fri. 10–3:15* Ⓜ *Bus 46, 64, 87; Tram 8.*

6

PIAZZA DI SPAGNA

GETTING ORIENTED

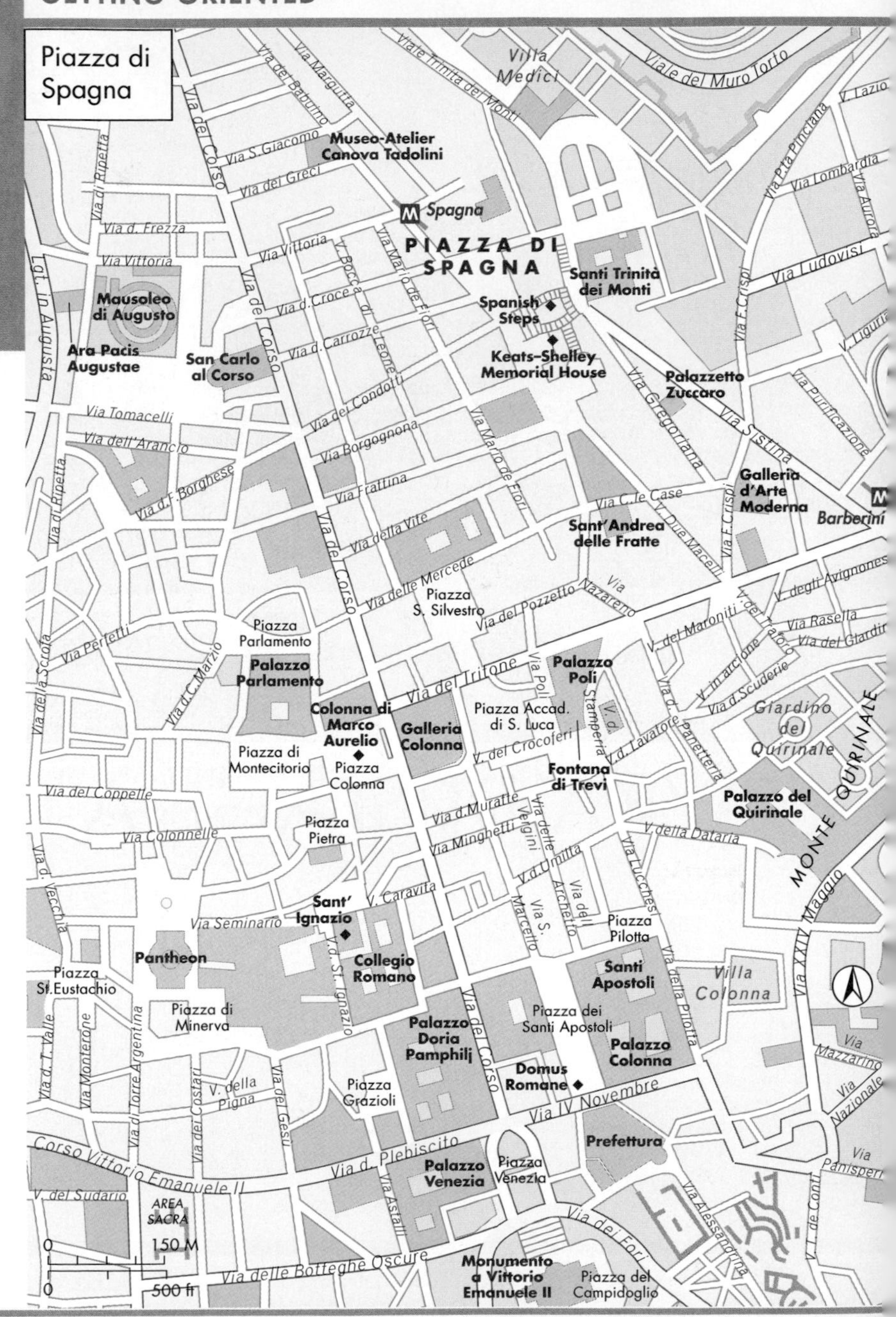

TOP REASONS TO GO

Trevi Fountain: In the pantheon of waterworks, this is Elvis—overblown, flashy, and reliably thronged by legions of fans.

The Spanish Steps: Sprawl seductively on the world's most celebrated stairway—everyone's doing it.

See Heaven: Stand beneath the stupendous ceiling of San Ignazio—Rome's most splendiferous Baroque church—and, courtesy of painter-priest Fra Andrea Pozzo, prepare to be transported heavenward.

Lifestyles of the Rich and Famous: Visit the Palazzo Doria Pamphilj and the Palazzo Colonna for an intimate look at the homes of Rome's 17th-century grandees.

Luxe Shopping on Via Condotti: You can get from Bulgari to Gucci to Valentino to Ferragamo with no effort at all.

MAKING THE MOST OF YOUR TIME

This neighborhood is chock-full of postcard-worthy sights, including the Spanish Steps, the Trevi Fountain, and the Victor Emanuel monument (Monumento Emanuele II)—which means a rewarding walk, but plenty of tourists. Consider starting early or taking an evening stroll, when many of the area's must-sees (including the Trevi Fountain) are lit up. Shoppers flock to Via del Corso, though in recent years, the street has been given over mostly to multinational chains; poke through the backstreets instead (Rome's swankiest boutiques and designers are on Via del Babuino and the surrounding streets).

GETTING HERE

The Piazza di Spagna is a short walk from Piazza del Popolo, the Pantheon, and the Trevi Fountain. One of Rome's handiest subway stations, Spagna, is tucked just left of the steps. Buses No. 117 (from the Colosseum) and No. 119 (from Piazza del Popolo) hum through the area; the latter tootles up Via del Balbuino, famed for its shops.

QUICK BITES

Caffè Ciampini. Just off the Corso in San Lorenzo in Lucina, a jewel of a piazza, sits this turn-of-the-century tearoom-gelateria-café. Stand at the elegant bar for a quick espresso, or shell out the extra euros to sit outdoors under a big umbrella, lingering over an aperitivo and the plateful of yummy hors d'oeuvres that come with it. ✉ *Piazza San Lorenzo in Lucina 29, Piazza di Spagna* ☎ *06/6876606* 🌐 *www.ciampini.com.*

Colline Emiliane. Around the corner from Piazza Barberini, this tiny, family-run trattoria serves up something different: excellent dishes from Emilia-Romagna, which some say is the best food region in Italy. It's popular with tourists and locals, so make a reservation for dinner. ✉ *Via degli Avignonesi 22, Piazza di Spagna* ☎ *06/4817538* Ⓜ *Barberini.*

La Campana. Thought to be the oldest restaurant in Rome (a document dates it back to 1518), La Campana is well liked for its honest Roman cuisine, slightly upmarket feel, and moderate prices. This is the place to have one of the best *coda alla vaccinara* (oxtail) in Rome, along with other specialties like saltimbocca and pasta *all'amatriciana* (a classic Roman tomato sauce). ✉ *Vicolo della Campana 18, Piazza Navona* ☎ *06/6875273* 🌐 *www.ristorantelacampana.com* ⏲ *Closed Mon.*

Sightseeing ★★★★★
Nightlife ★
Dining ★★★★★
Lodging ★★★★★
Shopping ★★★★★

In spirit, and in fact, this area of Rome is grandiose. The overblown Vittoriano monument, the labyrinthine treasure-chest palaces of Rome's surviving aristocracy, even the diamond-draped denizens of Via Condotti all embody the exuberant ego of a city at the center of its own universe. Here's where you'll see ladies in furs, and you can walk through a thousand snapshots as you climb the famous Spanish Steps.

Updated by Amanda Ruggeri

At the top of everyone's sightseeing list is the great Baroque confection of the Trevi Fountain. Since pickpockets favor this tourist-heavy spot, be particularly aware as you withdraw that wallet to keep your throw from being very expensive indeed. Once you've chucked in your change, follow the crowds and get ready to take some serious time to explore this neighborhood.

If Rome has a Main Street, it's Via del Corso, which is often jammed with swarms of Roman teenagers, in from the city's outlying districts for a ritual stroll that resembles a strutting migration of lemmings in blue jeans. Along this thoroughfare it's easy to forget that the gray and stolid atmosphere comes partially from the enormous palaces lining both sides of the street. Many were built over the past 300 years by princely families who wanted to secure front-row seats for the frantic antics of Carnevale. But once you step past entrances here, you'll discover some of Rome's grandest 17th- and 18th-century treasures, including Baroque ballrooms, glittering churches, and great Old Master paintings.

Via del Corso begins at noisy, chaotic Piazza Venezia, the imperial-size hub of all this ostentation, presided over by the Vittoriano, also known as the Altare della Patria (Altar of the Nation), or, less piously, as the "typewriter," the "wedding cake," or the Eighth Hill of Rome. Sitting grandly off the avenue are the Palazzo Doria-Pamphilj and the Palazzo Colonna—two of the city's great art collections housed in magnificent family palaces.

Extending just east of Via del Corso, but miles away in style, Piazza di Spagna and its surrounding streets are where the elite meet. Piazza di Spagna's main draw, however, remains the 18th-century Spanish Steps, which connect ritzy shops at the bottom of the hill with ritzy hotels (and one lovely church) at the top. The reward for climbing the *scalinata* is a dizzying view of central Rome. Because the steps face west, the views are especially good around sunset.

TOP ATTRACTIONS

Fodor's Choice ★ **Ara Pacis Augustae** (*Altar of Augustan Peace*). This vibrant monument of the imperial age has been housed in one of Rome's newest architectural landmarks: a gleaming, rectangular glass-and-travertine structure designed by American architect Richard Meier. Overlooking the Tiber on one side and the ruins of the marble-clad **Mausoleo di Augusto** (Mausoleum of Augustus), on the other, the result is a serene, luminous oasis right in Rome's center. Opened in 2006, after a decade of bitter controversy over the monument's relocation, the altar itself dates back to 13 BC; it was commissioned to celebrate the Pax Romana, the era of peace ushered in by Augustus's military victories. It is covered with spectacular and moving relief sculptures. Like all ancient Roman monuments of this type, you have to imagine them painted in vibrant colors, now long gone. The reliefs on the short sides show myths associated with Rome's founding and glory; the long sides display a procession of the imperial family. It's fun to play "who's who"—although half of his body is missing, Augustus is identifiable as the first full figure at the procession's head on the south-side frieze—but academics still argue over exact identifications. ✉ *Lungotevere in Augusta, Piazza di Spagna* ☎ *06/0608* 🌐 *www.arapacis.it* 🎫 *€10* ⏲ *Tues.–Sun. 9–7 (last admission 1 hr before closing)* Ⓜ *Flaminio (Piazza del Popolo).*

Keats-Shelley Memorial House. Sent to Rome in a last-ditch attempt to treat his consumption, English Romantic poet John Keats lived—and died—in this house at the foot of the Spanish Steps. At that point, this was the heart of the colorful bohemian quarter of Rome that was especially favored by the English. Keats had become celebrated through such poems as "Ode to a Nightingale" and "She Walks in Beauty," but his trip to Rome was fruitless. He breathed his last here on February 23, 1821, aged only 25, forevermore the epitome of the doomed poet. In this "Casina di Keats," you can visit his rooms, although all his furnishings were burned after his death as a sanitary measure by the local authorities. You'll also find a rather quaint collection of memorabilia of English literary figures of the period—Lord Byron, Percy Bysshe Shelley, Joseph Severn, and Leigh Hunt as well as Keats—and an exhaustive library of works on the Romantics. ✉ *Piazza di Spagna 26, Piazza di Spagna* ☎ *06/6784235* 🌐 *www.keats-shelley-house.org* 🎫 *€5* ⏲ *Weekdays and Sat. 10–1 and 2–6* Ⓜ *Spagna.*

Le Domus Romane di Palazzo Valentini. If you find your imagination stretching to picture Rome as it was two millennia ago, make sure to check out this "new" ancient site just a stone's throw from Piazza Venezia. As commonly done in Renaissance-era Rome, 16th-century builders filled in the ancient structures with landfill, using them as foundations for Palazzo Valentini. Unwittingly, the builders also preserved the ruins

CLOSE UP

Rome's Fountains

Anyone who's thrown a coin backward over a shoulder into the Fontana di Trevi to ensure a return to Rome appreciates the magic of the city's fountains.

From the magnificence of the Fontana dei Quattro Fiumi in Piazza Navona to the graceful caprice of the Fontana delle Tartarughe in the Jewish Ghetto, the water-spouting sculptures seem as essential to the piazzas they inhabit as the cobblestones and ocher buildings that surround them.

Rome's original fountains date back to ancient times, when they were part of the city's remarkable aqueduct system.

But from AD 537 to 1562 the waterworks were in disrepair and the city's fountains lay dry and crumbling. Romans were left to draw their water from the Tiber and from wells.

During the Renaissance, the popes brought running water back to the city as a means of currying political favor.

To mark the restoration of the Virgin Aqueduct, architect Giacomo della Porta designed 18 unassuming, functional fountains.

Each consisted of a large basin with two or three levels of smaller basins in the center, which were built and placed throughout the city at points along the water line.

Although nearly all of della Porta's fountains remain, their spare Renaissance design is virtually unrecognizable. With the Baroque era, most were elaborately redecorated with dolphins, obelisks, and sea monsters.

Of this next generation of Baroque fountaineers, the most famous is Gian Lorenzo Bernini.

Bernini's writhing, muscular creatures of myth adorn most of Rome's most visible fountains, including the Fontana di Trevi (perhaps named for the three streets—*tre vie*—that converge at its piazza); the Fontana del Nettuno, with its tritons, in Piazza Barberini; and, in Piazza Navona, the Fontana dei Quattro Fiumi, whose hulking figures represent the four great rivers of the known world: the Nile, the Ganges, the Danube, and the Plata.

The most common type of fountain in Rome is a kind rarely noted by visitors: the small, inconspicuous drinking fountains that burble away from side-street walls, old stone niches, and fire hydrant–like installations on street corners.

You can drink this water. Many of these *fontanelle* even have pipes fitted with a little hole from which water shoots up when you hold your hand under the main spout.

To combine the glorious Roman fountain with a drink of water, head to Piazza di Spagna, where the Barcaccia fountain is outfitted with spouts from which you can wet your whistle.

beneath, which archaeologists rediscovered in 2007 excavations. It took another three years for the two opulent, Imperial-era villas to open to the public on a regular basis.

Descending below Palazzo Valentini, which has been the seat of the *Provincia* of Rome since 1873, is like walking into another world. Not only are the villas luxurious and well preserved, still retaining their beautiful mosaics, inlaid marble floors, and staircases, but—unlike any other site in Rome—the ruins have been made to "come alive" through multimedia. Sophisticated light shows re-create what it all would have looked like while a dramatic, automated voiceover accompanies you as you walk through the rooms, pointing out cool finds (the heating system for the private baths, the mysterious fragment of a statue, the porcelain dumped here when part of the site became a dump in the Renaissance) and evidence of tragedy (the burn layer from a fire that ripped through the home). If it sounds corny, hold your skepticism: It's an effectively done, excellent way to actually "experience" the villa as ancient Romans would have—and learn a lot about ancient Rome in the process. A multimedia presentation halfway through also shows you what central Rome would have looked like 2,000 years ago.

The multimedia tour takes about an hour. There are limited spots, so book in advance over the phone, online, or by stopping by in person; make sure you book the English tour. The tour should be enjoyable for older children, but little ones might be afraid of how dark the rooms can be. ✉ *Via IV Novembre 119/A, Monti* ☎ *06/32810* 🌐 *www.palazzovalentini.it* 🎫 *€11.50 including booking fee.*

Monumento a Vittorio Emanuele II, or Altare della Patria (*Victor Emmanuel Monument, or Altar of the Nation*). The huge white mass of the "Vittoriano" is an inescapable landmark—Romans say you can avoid its image only if you're actually standing on it. Some have likened it to a huge wedding cake; others, to an immense typewriter. Though not held in the highest esteem by present-day citizens, it was the source of great civic pride at the time of its construction, at the turn of the 20th century. To create this elaborate marble monster and the vast piazza on which it stands, architects blithely destroyed many ancient and medieval buildings and altered the slope of the Capitoline Hill, which abuts it. Built to honor the unification of Italy and the nation's first king, Victor Emmanuel II, it also shelters the eternal flame at the tomb of Italy's Unknown Soldier killed during World War I. The flame is guarded day and night by sentinels, while inside the building there is the (rather dry) Institute of the History of the Risorgimento. You can't avoid the Monumento, so enjoy neo-imperial grandiosity at its most bombastic.

The views from the top are some of Rome's most panoramic. The only way up is by elevator (located to the right as you face the monument); stop at the museum entrances (to the left and right of the structure) to get a pamphlet identifying the sculpture groups on the monument itself and the landmarks you will be able to see once at the top. Opposite the monument, note the enclosed olive-green wooden veranda fronting the palace on the corner of Via del Plebiscito and Via Corso. For the many years that she lived in Rome, Napoléon's mother had a fine view from this spot of the local goings-on. ✉ *Entrance at Piazza Ara Coeli, next to Piazza Venezia, Monti* ☎ *06/0608* 🌐 *www.060608.it* 🎫 *Free, elevator €7* ⏲ *Elevator Mon.–Thurs. 9:30–5:45; Fri. and weekends 9:30–6:45; stairs open winter 9:30–4:30, summer 9:30–5:30.*

Museo-Atelier Canova Tadolini. A gorgeous remnant of Rome's 19th-century artistic milieu, this is the former atelier of Antonio Canova, Europe's greatest Neoclassic sculptor. Fabled for his frostily perfect statues of antique goddesses and fashionable princesses (sometimes in the same work, as in the Galleria Borghese's nearly naked *Principessa Pauline Borghese* posing as a "Victorious Venus"), he was given commissions by the poshest people. Today, his studio—atmospherically crammed to the gills with models, study sketches, and tools of the trade—has become a café and restaurant, so you can ogle Canova's domain for the price of a very expensive meal (or a cheaper coffee at the bar). ✉ *Via del Babuino 150 A/B, Piazza di Spagna* ☎ *06/32110702* 🌐 *www.canovatadolini.com* ⏲ *Café daily 8–midnight, restaurant daily noon–11* Ⓜ *Spagna.*

Fodor's Choice ★ **Palazzo Colonna.** Rome's grandest family built itself Rome's grandest palazzo in the 18th century—it's so immense, it faces Piazza Santi Apostoli on one side and the Quirinal Hill on the other (a little bridge over Via della Pilotta links the palace with the gardens on the hill). While still home to some Colonna patricians, the palace also holds the family picture gallery, open to the public one day a week. The galleria is itself a setting of aristocratic grandeur; you might recognize the **Sala Grande** as the site where Audrey Hepburn meets the press in *Roman Holiday.* At one end looms the ancient red marble column (*colonna* in Italian), which is the family's emblem; above the vast room is the spectacular ceiling fresco of the Battle of Lepanto painted by Giovanni Coli and Filippo Gherardi in 1675—the center scene almost puts the computer-generated special effects of Hollywood to shame. Adding redundant luster to the opulently stuccoed and frescoed salons are works by Poussin, Tintoretto, and Veronese, and a number of portraits of illustrious members of the family such as Vittoria Colonna—Michelangelo's muse and longtime friend—and Marcantonio Colonna, who led the papal forces in the great naval victory at Lepanto in 1577. Lost in the array of madonnas, saints, goddesses, popes, and cardinals is, spoon at the ready, with mouth missing some front teeth, Annibale Carracci's lonely *Bean-eater*. As W.H. Auden put it, "Grub first, art later." At 11:45, there's a guided tour in English, included in your entrance fee. In 2013 the gallery opened a new wing, including its tapestry room, to the public. ✉ *Via della Pilotta 17, Piazza di Spagna* ☎ *06/6784350* 🌐 *www.galleriacolonna.it* 🎫 *€12* ⏲ *Sat. 9–1:15 (tour in English 11:45); private tours available daily on request.*

Fodor's Choice ★ **Palazzo Doria Pamphilj.** Along with the Palazzo Colonna and the Galleria Borghese, this spectacular family palace provides the best glimpse of aristocratic Rome. Here, the main attractions are the legendary Old Master paintings, including treasures by Velázquez and Caravaggio; the splendor of the main galleries; and a unique suite of private family apartments. The beauty of the graceful 18th-century facade of this patrician palace may escape you unless you take time to step to the

DID YOU KNOW?

One of Rome's most popular *passeggiate*, the Via Condotti—seen here from the Spanish Steps—gets its name from conduits that carried water to the Baths of Agrippa.

opposite side of the street for a good view; it was designed by Gabriele Valvassori in 1730. The foundations of the immense complex of buildings probably date from classical times. The current building dates from the 15th century, with the exception of the facade. It passed through several hands before it became the property of the famous seafaring Doria family of Genoa, who had married into the Roman Pamphilj (also spelled Pamphili) clan. As in most of Rome's older patrician residences, the family still lives in part of the palace.

Housed in four wings that line the palace's courtyard, the picture gallery contains 550 paintings, including three by Caravaggio—a young *St. John the Baptist, Mary Magdalene*, and the breathtaking *Rest on the Flight to Egypt*. Off the eyepopping **Galleria degli Specchi** (Gallery of Mirrors)—a smaller version of the one at Versailles—are the famous Velázquez *Pope Innocent X,* considered by some historians to be the greatest portrait ever painted, and the Bernini bust of the same Pamphilj pope. Elsewhere you'll find a Titian, a double portrait by Raphael, and some noted 17th-century landscapes by Claude Lorrain and Gaspar Dughet. The audio guide by Prince Jonathan Doria Pamphilj, the current heir (born in England, he was adopted by the late Principessa Orietta), provides an intimate family history well worth listening to. ✉ *Via del Corso 305, Around Piazza Navona* ☎ *06/6797323* 🌐 *www.doriapamphilj.it* 🎫 *€11* ⏲ *Daily 9–7.*

Palazzetto Zuccaro. The most amusing house in all of Italy, this folly was designed in 1591 by noted painter Federico Zuccaro to form a monster's face. Typical of the outré Mannerist style of the period, the eyes are the house's windows; the entrance portal is through the monster's mouth. Zuccaro (1540–1609)—whose frescoes adorn many Roman churches, including Trinità del Monti just up the block—sank all of his money into his new home, dying in debt before his curious memorial, as it turned out to be, was completed. Today, it is the property of the Biblioteca Hertziana, Rome's prestigious fine-arts library; at press time, it has been sheathed for a long-term renovation project. Leading up to the quaint Piazza Trinità del Monti, Via Gregoriana is a real charmer and has long been one of Rome's most elegant addresses, home to such residents as French 19th-century painter Ingres and famed couturier Valentino's first couture salon. ✉ *Via Gregoriana 30, Piazza di Spagna* ☎ *06/69993242 Biblioteca Hertziana* Ⓜ *Spagna.*

Sant'Andrea delle Fratte. Copies have replaced Bernini's original angels on the Ponte Sant'Angelo, but two of the originals are here, on either side of the choir. The door in the right aisle leads into one of Rome's hidden gardens, where orange trees bloom in the cloister. Borromini's fantastic contributions—the dome and a curious bell tower with its droop-winged angels looking out over the city—are best seen from Via Capo le Case, across Via Due Macelli. ✉ *Via Sant'Andrea delle Fratte 1(Via della Mercede), Piazza di Spagna* ☎ *06/6793191* 🌐 *www.santandreadellefratte.it* ⏲ *Weekdays 6:30–noon and 4–7, weekends 6:30–12:30 and 4–8* Ⓜ *Spagna.*

Fodor's Choice ★ **Sant'Ignazio.** Rome's largest Jesuit church, this 17th-century landmark harbors some of the city's most magnificent trompe-l'oeil. To get the full effect of the marvelous illusionistic ceiling by priest-artist Andrea Pozzo, stand on the small disk set into the floor of the nave. The heavenly vision above you, seemingly extending upward almost indefinitely, represents the *Allegory of the Missionary Work of the Jesuits* and is part of Pozzo's cycle of works in this church exalting the early history of the Jesuit Order, whose founder was the reformer Ignatius of Loyola. The saint soars heavenward, supported by a cast of thousands; not far behind is Saint Francis Xavier, apostle of the Indies, leading a crowd of Eastern converts; a bare-breasted, spear-wielding America in American Indian headdress rides a jaguar; Europe with crown and scepter sits serene on a heftily rumped horse; while a splendid Africa with gold tiara perches on a lucky crocodile. The artist repeated this illusionist technique, so popular in the late 17th century, in the false dome, which is actually a flat canvas—a trompe l'oeil trick used when the budget drained dry. The overall effect of the frescoes is dazzling (be sure to have coins handy for the machine that switches on the lights) and was fully intended to rival that produced by Baciccia in the nearby mother church of Il Gesù. Scattered around the nave are several awe-inspiring altars; their soaring columns, gold-on-gold decoration, and gilded statues make these the last word in splendor. The church is often host to concerts of sacred music performed by choirs from all over the world. Look for posters at the church doors for more information. ✉ *Piazza Sant'Ignazio, Around Piazza Navona* ☎ *06/6794406* 🌐 *www.chiesasantignazio.it* ⏲ *Daily 7:30–12:20 and 3–7:20.*

6

FAMILY **The Spanish Steps.** That icon of postcard Rome, the Spanish Steps (often called simply *la scalinata*—"the staircase"—by Italians) and the Piazza di Spagna from which they ascend both get their names from the Spanish Embassy to the Vatican on the piazza—even though the staircase was built with French funds in 1723. In honor of a diplomatic visit by the king of Spain, the hillside was transformed by architect Francesco de Sanctis to link the church of Trinità dei Monti at the top with the Via dei Condotti below. In an allusion to the church, the staircase is divided by three landings (beautifully banked with azaleas from mid-April to mid-May). For centuries, the scalinata and its neighborhood have welcomed tourists, dukes, and writers in search of inspiration—among them Stendhal, Honoré de Balzac, William Makepeace Thackeray, and Byron, along with today's enthusiastic hordes. Bookending the bottom of the steps are two monuments to the 18th-century days when the English colonized the area: to the right, the Keats-Shelley House, to the left, Babington's Tea Rooms, both beautifully redolent of the Grand Tour era. For weary sightseers, there is an elevator at Vicolo del Bottino 8 (next to the adjacent Metro entrance), but those with mobility problems should be aware that there is still a small flight of stairs after. **■ TIP→ In recent years, a low-grade but annoying scam has proliferated in the piazza. This is the "rose scam," where a man comes up to a female tourist with a rose and insists he's giving it to her for free. When she takes it, he waits a couple of beats and then goes to a gentleman in her party, asking for just a few euros for the flower. Often, everyone concerned is too embarrassed not to pay. If this happens to you, simply firmly refuse the rose from the beginning, or hand it back when you're** asked for money. Unless you want it, of course! ✉ *Intersection of vias Condotti, del Babuino, and Due Macelli, Piazza di Spagna* Ⓜ *Spagna.*

NEED A BREAK?

Antico Caffè Greco. You may prefer to limit your shopping on Via Condotti to the window variety, but there's one thing here that everybody can afford—a stand-up coffee at the bar at the Antico Caffè Greco, set just off the Piazza di Spagna and the Fontana della Barcaccia. With its tiny marble-top tables and velour settees, this 200-year-old institution has long been the haunt of artists and literati; it's closed Sunday. Johann Wolfgang von Goethe, Byron, and Franz Liszt were habitués. Buffalo Bill stopped in when his road show hit Rome. The caffè is still a haven for writers and artists, along with plenty of Gucci-clad ladies. The tab picks up considerably if you decide to sit down to enjoy table service. ✉ *Via Condotti 86, Piazza di Spagna* ☎ *06/6791700* 🌐 *www.anticocaffegreco.eu.*

Il Palazzetto. For the ultimate view from atop the Spanish Steps, you can climb up, take the elevator from inside the Spagna metro . . . or pay for the privilege at the wine bar Il Palazzetto, where an interior elevator takes you to the top terrace. ✉ *Vicolo del Bottino 8, Piazza di Spagna* ☎ *06/699341000* 🌐 *www.ilpalazzettoroma.com.*

WORTH NOTING

Colonna di Marco Aurelio. Inspired by Trajan's Column, this 2nd-century AD column is composed of 27 blocks of marble covered in reliefs recording Marcus Aurelius's victory over the Germans. A bronze statue of St. Paul, which replaced the effigy of Marcus Aurelius in the 16th century, stands at the top. The column is the centerpiece of Piazza Colonna. ✉ *Piazza Colonna, Monti.*

Fontana della Barcaccia (*Leaky Boat Fountain*). At the center of Piazza di Spagna and at the bottom of the Spanish Steps, this curious, half-sunken boat gently spills out water rather than cascading it dramatically; it may have been designed that way to make the most of the area's low water pressure. It was thanks to the Barberini pope Urban VIII, who commissioned the fountain, that there was any water at all in this area, which was becoming increasingly built up during the 17th century. He restored one of the ancient Roman aqueducts that once channeled water here. The bees and suns on the boat constitute the Barberini motif. Some insist that the Berninis (Pietro and his more famous son Gian Lorenzo) intended the fountain to be a reminder that this part of town was often flooded by the Tiber; others claim that it represents the Ship of the Church; and still others think that it marks the presumed site of the emperor Domitian's water stadium in which sea battles were reenacted in the glory days of the Roman Empire. ■ **TIP→ Restoration of the fountain, begun in October 2013, is expected to finish by summer 2014; until then, the fountain is covered in scaffolding.** ✉ *Piazza di Spagna, Piazza di Spagna* Ⓜ *Spagna.*

Gagosian Gallery. One of the most prestigious modern art galleries opened this Rome branch in 2007. In a former bank, temporary

TREVI FOUNTAIN

✉ *Piazza di Trevi, Piazza di Spagna* Ⓜ *Barberini–Fontana di Trevi.*

Alive with rushing waters commanded by an imperious Oceanus, the Fontana di Trevi (Trevi Fountain) earned full-fledged iconic status in 1954 when it starred in 20th-Century Fox's *Three Coins in the Fountain.* As the first color film in Cinemascope to be produced on location, it caused practically half of America to pack their bags for the Eternal City.

From the very start, however, the Trevi has been all about theatrical effects. An aquatic marvel in a city filled with them, the fountain's unique drama is largely due to the site: its vast basin is squeezed into the tight meeting of three little streets (the "tre vie," which may give the fountain its name) with cascades emerging as if from the wall of Palazzo Poli.

The conceit of a fountain emerging full-force from a palace was first envisioned by Bernini and Pietro da Cortona for Pope Urban VIII's plan to rebuild the fountain (which marked the end-point of the ancient Acqua Vergine aqueduct, created in 18 BC by Agrippa).

Only three popes later, under Pope Clement XIII, did Nicolo Salvi finally break ground with his winning design.

Salvi had his cake and ate it, too, for while he dazzles the eye with Baroque pyrotechnics—the sculpted seashells, the roaring seabeasts, the divalike mermaids—he has slyly incorporated them in a stately triumphal arch (in fact, Clement was then restoring Rome's Arch of Constantine).

Salvi, unfortunately, did not live to see his masterpiece completed in 1762: working in the culverts of the aqueduct 11 years earlier, he caught his death of cold and died.

TIPS

- Everyone knows the famous legend that if you throw a coin into the Trevi Fountain you will ensure a return trip to the Eternal City. But not everyone knows how to do it the right way: You must toss a coin with your right hand over your left shoulder, with your back to the fountain. One coin means you'll return to Rome; two, you'll return and fall in love; three, you'll return, find love, and marry. The fountain grosses some €600,000 a year, and aside from incidences of opportunists fishing coins from the water, all of the money goes to charity.
- Even though you might like to reenact Anita Ekberg and Marcello Mastroianni's famous Trevi dip inLa Dolce Vita,be forewarned that police guard the fountain 24 hours a day to keep out movie buffs and lovebirds alike. Transgressors risk a fine of up to €500.
- Around the corner, the Gelateria San Crispino (EVia della Panetteria 42P06/6793924) is for discerning palates, with unusual taste combinations and natural ingredients.

exhibitions include many mega-stars, including Cy Twombly, Damien Hirst, and Jeff Koons. ✉ *Via Francesco Crispi 16, Piazza di Spagna* ☎ *06/42086498* 🌐 *www.gagosian.com* ⏲ *Tues.–Sat. 10:30–7 and by appointment* Ⓜ *Spagna.*

Galleria d'Arte Moderna. After an eight-year renovation, Rome's modern art gallery reopened in 2011. The completely overhauled space—which happens to be the lovely, 18th-century convent of the Discalced Carmelites—perfectly shows off the gem of a collection, which focuses on Roman 19th- and 20th-century paintings, drawings, prints, and sculptures. With more than 3,000 pieces by artists like Giorgio de Chirico, Gino Severini, Scipione, Antonio Donghi, and Giacomo Manzù, the permanent collection is too large all to be on display at once, so exhibits rotate. Regardless of what the particular exhibit is, stop by to soak in another side of the city: one where, in the near-empty halls, tranquillity and contemplation reign. ✉ *Via Francesco Crispi 24, Piazza di Spagna* ☎ *06/0608* 🌐 *www.galleriaartemodernaroma.it* 🎟 *€6.50* ⏲ *Tues.–Sun. 10–6* Ⓜ *Spagna.*

Palazzo Venezia. Centerpiece of the eponymous piazza, this palace was originally built for Venetian cardinal Pietro Barbo, who became Pope Paul II. It was also the backdrop used by Mussolini to harangue crowds with dreams of empire from the balcony over the main portal. Lights were left on through the night during his reign to suggest that the Fascist leader worked without pause. The palace shows a mixture of Renaissance grace and heavy medieval lines; salons include frescoes by Giorgio Vasari and a Bernini sculpture of Pope Clement X. The caffè on the loggia has a pleasant view over the garden courtyard. ✉ *Via del Plebiscito 118, Monti* ☎ *06/69994388* 🌐 *museopalazzovenezia.beniculturali.it* 🎟 *€5* ⏲ *Tues.–Sun. 8:30–7:30.*

Piazza Venezia. The geographic heart of Rome, this is the spot from which all distances from Rome are calculated and the principal crossroads of city traffic. Piazza Venezia stands at what was the beginning of Via Flaminia, the ancient Roman road leading east across Italy to Fano on the Adriatic Sea. The Via Flaminia was, and remains, a vital artery. Its initial tract, from Piazza Venezia to Piazza del Popolo, is now known as Via del Corso, after the horse races (*corse*) that were run here during the wild Roman carnival celebrations of the 17th and 18th centuries. It also happens to be one of Rome's busiest shopping streets. The massive female bust near the church of San Marco in the corner of the piazza, a fragment of the statue of Isis, is known to the Romans as Madama Lucrezia. This was one of the "talking statues" on which anonymous poets hung verses pungent with political satire, a practice that has not entirely disappeared. ✉ *Junction of Via del Corso, Via Plebiscito, and Via Cesare Battisti, Monti.*

Trinità dei Monti. Standing high above the Spanish Steps, this 16th-century church has a rare double-tower facade, suggestive of late-Gothic French style—in fact, the French crown paid for the church's construction. Today, it is beautiful primarily for its dramatic location and magnificent views. ✉ *Piazza Trinità dei Monti, Piazza di Spagna* ☎ *06/6794179* ⏲ *Tues.–Sun. 8–1 and 3–8* Ⓜ *Spagna.*

7

REPUBBLICA AND QUIRINALE

GETTING ORIENTED

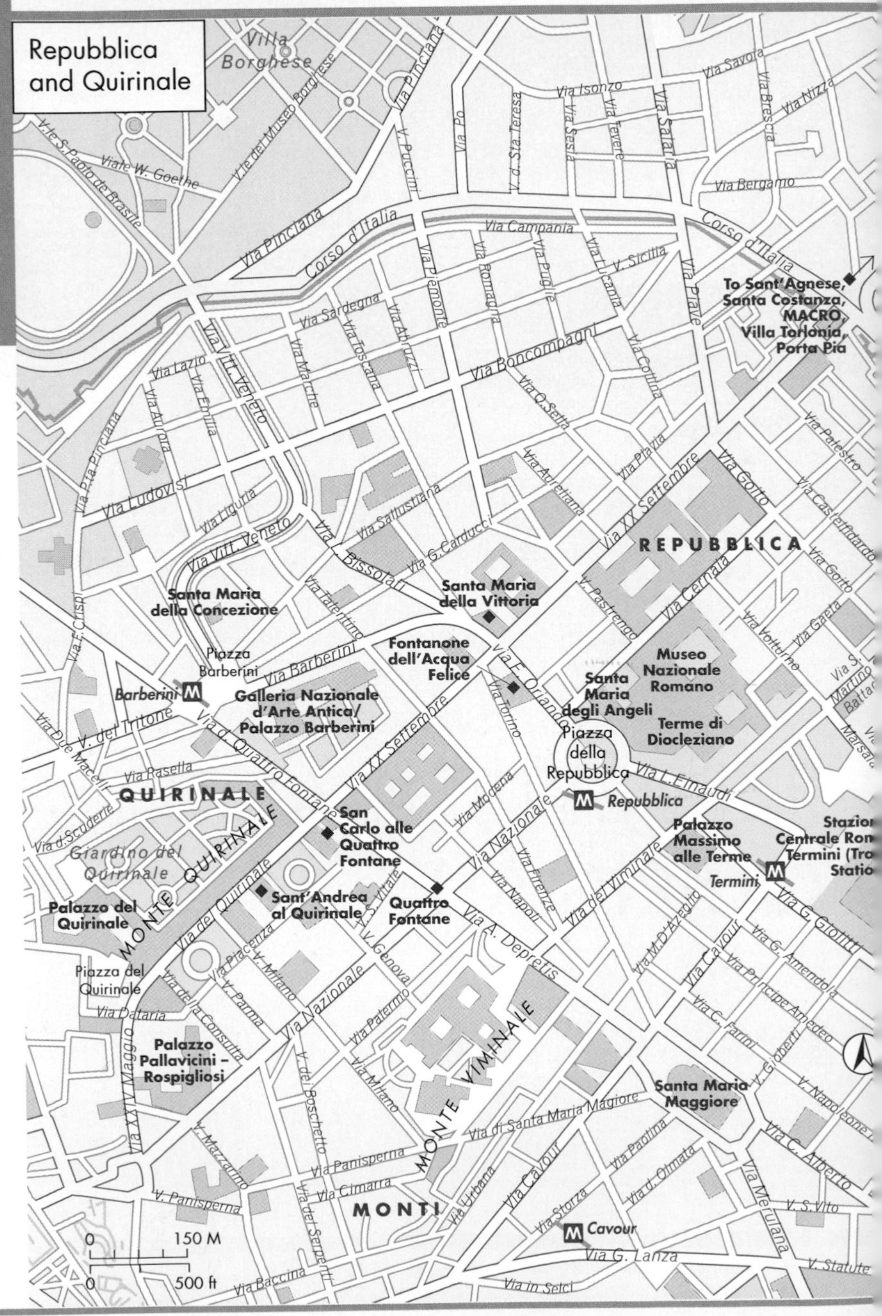

GETTING HERE

Between Termini station and the Spanish Steps, this area is about a 15-minute walk from either. Bus No. 40 will get you from Termini to the Quirinale in two stops; from the Vatican take Bus No. 64. The very busy and convenient Repubblica Metro stop is on the piazza of the same name.

MAKING THE MOST OF YOUR TIME

While slightly off Rome's bustling tourist path, this central (and well-connected) area has a number of intriguing sights, from the stunning sweep of Piazza della Repubblica and the excellent ancient-art collection of the Palazzo Massimo to the bones of the Capuchin Crypt and Bernini's breathtaking sculpture, the *Ecstasy of St. Theresa. It's possible to walk the whole area, but schlepping from one attraction to the other can be a bit of a slog; this part of town is so well-connected by bus and metro that it's sometimes easier to take public transport instead.* When choosing a time of day to visit, remember that many of the churches (like Santa Maria della Vittoria, home of the Bernini sculpture) close in the afternoons, reopening around 4 or 5.

QUICK BITES

Come il Latte. Located just a five-minute walk from Piazza della Repubblica, the two-year-old Come il Latte already has a serious following for its super-creamy, all-natural gelato. The pistachio may be the best in town, although you can't go wrong with any of the flavors, some particularly creative (like rice and cinnamon). Top off your scoop with homemade *panna* (whipped cream) in a variety of flavors and either dark or white chocolate from the shop's chocolate fountain. ✉ *Via Silvio Spaventa 24/26, Repubblica* ☎ *06/42903882* 🌐 *www.comeillatte.it.*

TOP REASONS TO GO

Bernini's Ecstasy of St. Theresa: Admire, or just blush at, the worldly realism of Theresa's allegedly spiritual rapture. Star of the Cappella Cornaro, the sculpture is Bernini's audacious fusion of architecture, painting, and sculpture.

Palazzo Barberini: Take in five centuries of art at one of Rome's greatest family palaces, where you can gape at Rome's biggest 18th-century ballroom and Raphael's *La Fornarina.*

Changing of the Guard: Snap photos of stony-faced guards as they march in formation at the Quirinale presidential palace, which perches atop the highest of ancient Rome's seven hills.

Capuchin Crypt: Contemplate eternity in the creepy-yet-creative crypt under **Santa Maria della Concezione,** "decorated" with the skeletons of 4,000 monks, replete with fluted arches made of collarbones and arabesques of shoulder blades.

On a Clear Day You Can See Forever: Crowning the Quirinale Hill—the loftiest of Rome's seven hills—is the Piazza del Quirinale, with spectacular views over the city, with the horizon marked by "Il Cupolino," the dome of St. Peter's. Framing the vista are the enormous ancient statues of Castor and Pollux, the *Discouri* (Horse-Tamers), which still give the Quirinale its nickname Monte Cavallo ("Horse Hill").

Sightseeing ★★★★
Nightlife ★★
Dining ★★★★
Lodging ★★★★★
Shopping ★★★

Just west of Rome's modern Termini train station, this area offers an extraordinary Roman blend of old and new. Think of this area as the place where work gets done today: the district from Piazza Repubblica to Piazza Barberini swarms with professionals going in and out of office buildings, while much of Rome's political work happens at the Quirinale, home to the president of Italy. Far from just a workaday area, though, this is also one with lots of attractions for travelers, from the bizarre Capuchin Crypt to ancient artworks and great Bernini sculptures.

REPUBBLICA

Updated by Amanda Ruggeri

Climbing the stairs out of the Metro at Piazza della Repubblica feels like stepping into a tornado. The clanging of sirens and car horns, the squeal of brakes, and the roar of mopeds, not to mention the smell of the fast-food joints, may make you want to duck back down underground and get out at another stop. But to do so would be to miss out on a district featuring an array of fascinating attractions, like the one right before you: the piazza's main landmark, the vast ruins of the Baths of Diocletian (Terme di Diocleziano). They were subsequently transformed into a Renaissance monastery and, by Michelangelo's own design, to the church of Santa Maria degli Angeli. The streets here may not be conducive to wandering but the ancient treasures at Palazzo Massimo, Bernini's spectacular Cornaro Chapel, and, farther afield, the modern MACRO museum will always be vying for your attention.

As a gateway, Piazza della Repubblica was laid out to serve as a monumental foyer between the Termini rail station and the rest of the city.

TOP ATTRACTIONS

Museo delle Terme di Diocleziano (*Baths of Diocletian*). Though part of the ancient structure is now the church of Santa Maria degli Angeli, and other parts were transformed into a Carthusian monastery or razed to make room for later urban development, a visit gives you an idea of the scale and grandeur of this ancient bathing establishment. Upon entering the church you see the major structures of the baths, partly covered by 16th- and 17th-century overlay, some of which is by Michelangelo. The monastery cloister is filled with the lapidary collection of the Museo Nazionale Romano while other rooms have archaeological works, along with a virtual representation of Livia's villa, which you can tour with the help of a joystick. ✉ *Viale E. De Nicola 79, Repubblica* ☎ *06/39967700* 🎫 *€7, includes three other Museo Nazional Romano sites (Crypta Balbi, Palazzo Massimo, Palazzo Altemps)* ⏲ *Tues.–Sun. 9–7:45 (ticket office closes at 6:45)* Ⓜ *Repubblica.*

FULL FRONTAL FASHION

Outside the gates of the Palazzo del Quirinale, you can see the changing of the military guard at 4 pm daily, and occasionally you can glimpse the *corazzieri* (presidential guard). All extra-tall, they are a stirring sight in their magnificent crimson-and-blue uniforms, gleaming knee-high boots, and embossed steel helmets adorned with flowing manes.

Fodor's Choice ★ **Palazzo Massimo alle Terme.** Come here to get a real feel for ancient Roman art—the collection rivals even the Vatican's. The Roman National Museum, with a collection ranging from striking classical Roman paintings to marble bric-a-brac, has been organized in four locations: here, Palazzo Altemps, Crypta Balbi, and the Museo delle Terme di Diocleziano. The vast structure of the Palazzo Massimo holds the great ancient treasures of the archaeological collection and also the coin collection. Highlights include the *Niobid*, the famous bronze *Boxer*, and the *Discobolus Lancelloti*. Pride of place goes, however, to the great ancient frescoes on view, stunningly set up to "re-create" the look of the homes they once decorated. These include stuccos and wall paintings found in the area of the Villa della Farnesina (in Trastevere) and the legendary frescoes from Empress Livia's villa at Prima Porta, delightful depictions of a garden in bloom and an orchard alive with birds. Their colors are remarkably well preserved. These delicate decorations covered the walls of cool, sunken rooms in Livia's summer house outside the city. **TIP→ Admission includes entrance to all four national museums, good for three days.** ✉ *Largo Villa Peretti 1, Repubblica* ☎ *06/39967700* 🌐 *www.coopculture.it* 🎫 *€7* ⏲ *Tues.–Sun. 9–7:45* Ⓜ *Repubblica.*

Piazza della Repubblica. Often the first view that spells "Rome" to weary travelers walking from the Stazione Termini, this broad square was laid out in the late 1800s and includes the exuberant **Fontana delle Naiadi** (Fountain of the Naiads). This pièce de résistance is draped with voluptuous bronze ladies wrestling happily with marine monsters. The nudes weren't there when the pope unveiled the fountain in 1870, sparing him any embarrassment. But when the figures were added in 1901, they caused a scandal: It's said that the sculptor, Rutelli, modeled them on the ample figures of two musical comedy stars of the day. The piazza owes its curved lines to the structures of the Terme di Diocleziano; the curving, colonnaded Neoclassical buildings on the southwest side trace the underlying form of the ancient baths. Today, one of them is occupied by the superdeluxe Hotel Exedra—which shows you how much the fortunes of the formerly tatterdemalion part of the city have changed. ✉ *Repubblica* Ⓜ *Repubblica.*

Fodor's Choice ★ **Santa Maria della Vittoria.** Like the church of Santa Susanna across Piazza San Bernardo, this church was designed by Carlo Maderno, but this one is best known for Bernini's sumptuous Baroque decoration of the **Cappella Cornaro** (Cornaro Chapel), on the left as you face the altar, where you'll find his interpretation of heavenly ecstasy in his statue of the *Ecstasy of St. Theresa* (⇨ *For more on Bernini, see our special photo feature, "Baroque and Desperate: The Tragic Rivalry of Bernini and Borromini" in this chapter*). Your eye is drawn effortlessly from the frescoes on the ceiling down to the marble figures of the angel and the swooning saint, to the earthly figures of the Cornaro family (who commissioned the chapel), to the two inlays of marble skeletons in the pavement, representing the hope and despair of souls in purgatory.

As evidenced in other works of the period, the theatricality of the chapel is the result of Bernini's masterly fusion of elements. This is one of the key examples of the mature Roman high Baroque. Bernini's audacious conceit was to model the chapel as a theater: Members of the Cornaro family—sculpted in colored marbles—watch from theater boxes as, center stage, the great moment of divine love is played out before them. The swooning saint's robes appear to be on fire, quivering with life, and the white marble group seems suspended in the heavens as golden rays illuminate the scene. An angel assists at the mystical moment of Theresa's vision as the saint abandons herself to the joys of heavenly love. Bernini represented this mystical experience in what, to modern eyes, may seem very earthly terms. Or, as the visiting dignitary President de Brosses put it in the 19th century, "If this is divine love, I know what it is." No matter what your reaction, you'll have to admit it's great theater. ✉ *Via XX Settembre 17, Largo Santa Susanna, Repubblica* ☎ *06/42740571* 🌐 *www.chiesasmariavittoria.191.it* ⏲ *Daily 7–noon and 3:30–7* Ⓜ *Repubblica.*

FAMILY **Villa Torlonia.** Built for aristocrats-come-lately, the Torlonia family—the Italian Rockefellers of the 19th century—this villa became Mussolini's residence as prime minister under Italy's king and is now a public park. Long neglected, the park's vegetation and buildings are gradually being refurbished. Newly restored is the **Casina Nobile,** the main palace designed by the great architect Giuseppe Valadier. A grand, Neoclassical edifice, it comes replete with a gigantic ballroom, frescoed salons, and soaring templelike facade. While denuded of nearly all their furnishings and art treasures, some salons have important remnants of decor, including the reliefs once fashioned by the father of Italian Neoclassical sculpture, Antonio Canova. In the park, a complete contrast is offered by the **Casina delle Civette** (Little House of Owls), a hypercharming example of the Liberty (Art Nouveau) style of the early 1900s:

DID YOU KNOW?

To increase the hallucinatory impact of the *Ecstasy of St. Theresa*, Bernini hid a window of yellow glass above the pediment to add iridescence to the gilded rays of "divine light."

the gabled, fairy-tale-like cottage-palace now displays majolica and stained-glass decorations, including windows with owl motifs, and is a stunning, overlooked find for lovers of 19th-century decorative arts. Temporary exhibits are held in the small and elegant **Il Casino dei Principi** (The House of Princes), designed in part by Valadier. ✉ *Villa Torlonia, Via Nomentana 70, Repubblica* ☎ *06/0608* 🌐 *www.museivillatorlonia.it* 🎫 *Entrance to Casina delle Civette, Casino Nobile, and Casino dei Principi with temporary exhibit, €10; only Casino Nobile and Casino dei Principi with exhibit, €8.50* ⏲ *Tues.–Sun. 9–7* Ⓜ *Repubblica. Bus 36, 84.*

AURORA'S HOUSE

Palazzo Pallavinici-Rospigliosi. Set just off the Piazza del Quirinale is the Palazzo Pallavinici-Rospigliosi. Originally built for Cardinal Scipione Borghese, it is, unfortunately, closed to the public. However, on the first day of every month except January, 10–noon and 3–5, you are allowed in to see the palace's summer pavilion, which is graced with a legendary ceiling fresco of Aurora painted by Baroque artist Guido Reni—a painting once thought to be the last word in 17th-century style. ✉ *Via XXIV Maggio 43, Quirinale* ☎ *06/83467000* 🌐 *www.casinoaurorapallavicini.it* 🎫 *Free.*

WORTH NOTING

Fontanone dell'Acqua Felice (*Fountain of Happy Water*). When Pope Sixtus V completed the restoration of the Acqua Felice aqueduct toward the end of the 16th century, Domenico Fontana was commissioned to design this commemorative fountain. As the story goes, a sculptor named Prospero da Brescia had the unhappy task of executing the central figure, which was to represent Moses (Sixtus liked to think of himself as, like Moses, having provided water for his thirsting population). The comparison with Michelangelo's magnificent *Moses* in the church of San Pietro in Vincoli was inevitable, and the largely disparaging criticism of Prospero's work is said to have driven him to his grave. A full cleaning, however, has left the fountain, whose Moses in recent years had looked as if he were dipped in soot, sparkling white—and uncovered a great deal of its charm. ✉ *Piazza San Bernardo, Repubblica* Ⓜ *Repubblica.*

MACRO. Formerly known as Rome's Modern and Contemporary Art Gallery, and before that formerly known as the Peroni beer factory, this redesigned industrial space has brought new life to the gallery and museum scene of a city formerly known for its then, not its now. The collection here covers Italian contemporary artists from the 1960s through today. Its sister museum, MACRO Testaccio (*Piazza O. Giustiniani*) is housed in a renovated slaughterhouse in Testaccio district, Rome's "Left Bank," and features temporary exhibits and installations by current artists. The goal of both spaces is to bring current art to the public in innovative spaces, and, not incidentally, to give support and recognition to Rome's contemporary art scene, which labors in the shadow of the city's artistic heritage. After a few days—or millennia—of dusty marble, it's a breath of fresh air. ✉ *Via Nizza 138, intersection with Via Cagliari, Repubblica* ☎ *06/671070400* 🌐 *www.macro.roma.museum* 🎫 *€12.50 combined entrance to MACRO and MACRO*

Testaccio (good for 7 days) ⏲ Tues.–Sun. 11–7, Sun. 11–10. MACRO Testaccio Tues.–Sun. 4–10 Ⓜ Repubblica. Bus 719, 38.

Santa Maria degli Angeli e dei Martiri. The curving brick facade on the northeast side of Piazza della Repubblica is one small remaining part of the colossal Terme di Diocleziano, the largest and most impressive of the baths of ancient Rome. A gift to the city from Emperor Diocletian, it was erected about AD 300 with the forced labor of 40,000 Christians. In 1561 Michelangelo was commissioned to convert the vast *tepidarium,* the central hall of the baths, into a church. His work was altered by Vanvitelli in the 18th century, but the huge transept, which formed the nave in Michelangelo's plan, has remained as he adapted it. The eight enormous monolithic columns of red granite that support the great beams are the original columns of the tepidarium, 45 feet high and more than 5 feet in diameter. The great hall is 92 feet high. ✉ *Via Cernaia 9, Repubblica* ☎ *06/4880812* 🌐 *www.santamariadegliangeliroma.it* ⏲ *Mon.–Sat. 7:30–6:30, Sun. 7:30–8* Ⓜ *Repubblica.*

QUIRINALE

Rome's highest hill, the Quirinale, has hosted ancient Roman senators, Renaissance popes (it was breezier here than at the Vatican), and, with the end of papal rule, Italy's kings.

West from Via Nazionale, the hill is set with various jewels of the Baroque era, including masterpieces by Bernini and Borromini. Nearby stands Palazzo Barberini, a grand and gorgeous 16th-century palace holding five centuries of masterworks.

Crowning the Piazza del Quirinale is the enormous Palazzo del Quirinale, built in the 16th century as a summer residence for the popes. It became the presidential palace in 1946; today you can tour its reception rooms, which are as splendid as you might imagine. The changing of the guard (daily at 4), outside on the piazza with its oversize stairway, is an old-fashioned exercise in pomp and circumstance.

While Bernini's work feels omnipresent in much of the city center, the Renaissance-man range of his work is particularly notable here. The artist as architect considered the church of Sant'Andrea al Quirinale one of his best; Bernini the urban designer and waterworker wrought the muscle-bound sea gods who wrestle in the fountain at the center of Piazza Barberini. And Bernini the master gives religious passion corporeal treatment in what is perhaps his greatest work, the *Ecstasy of St. Theresa,* in the church of Santa Maria della Vittoria.

In this district, the triumvirate of Rome's Baroque—Bernini, Borromini, and Pietro di Cortona—vie, even after four centuries, to amaze the visitor.

TOP ATTRACTIONS

Fodor's Choice ★ **Capuchin Crypt.** Not for the easily spooked, the crypt under the Church of Santa Maria della Concezione holds the bones of some 4,000 dead Capuchin monks. Arranged in odd decorative designs around the shriveled and decayed skeletons of their kinsmen, a macabre reminder of the impermanence of earthly life, the crypt is strangely touching and beautiful. As one sign proclaims: "What you are, we once were. What we are, you someday will be." After a recent renovation, the crypt was reopened to the public with a new museum devoted to teaching visitors about the Capuchin order; the crypt is now located at the end of the museum circuit. Upstairs in the church, the first chapel on the right contains Guido Reni's mid-17th-century *St. Michael Trampling the Devil.* The painting caused great scandal after an astute contemporary observer remarked that the face of the devil bore a surprising resemblance to the Pamphili Pope Innocent X, archenemy of Reni's Barberini patrons. Compare the devil with the bust of the pope that you saw in the Palazzo Doria Pamphilj and judge for yourself. ✉ *Via Veneto 27, Quirinale* ☎ *06/88803695* 🌐 *www.cappucciniviaveneto.it* 🎫 *€6 includes museum and crypt* ⏲ *Fri.–Wed. 9–7* Ⓜ *Barberini.*

Palazzo del Quirinale. Pope Gregory XIII started building this spectacular palace, now the official residence of Italy's president, in 1574. He planned to use it as a summer home. But less than 20 years later, Pope Clement VIII decided to make the palace—safely elevated above the malarial miasmas shrouding the low-lying location of the Vatican—the permanent residence of the papacy. It remained the official papal residence until 1870, in the process undergoing a series of enlargements and alterations. When Italian troops under Garibaldi stormed Rome in 1870, making it the capital of the newly united Italy, the popes moved back to the Vatican; the Quirinale became the official residence of the kings of Italy. After the Italian people voted out the monarchy in 1946, the Quirinal Palace passed to the presidency of the Italian Republic. ■ **TIP→ Visitable only on Sundays, with sometimes a noon concert in the chapel included, the state reception rooms are some of Italy's most majestic.** You already get a fair idea of the palace's splendor from the size of the building, especially the interminable flank of the palace on Via del Quirinale. Behind this wall are the palace gardens, which, like the gardens of Villa d'Este in Tivoli, were laid out by Cardinal Ippolito d'Este when he summered here. Unfortunately, they are open to the public only once a year on Republic Day (June 2). ✉ *Piazza del Quirinale, Quirinale* ☎ *06/46991* 🌐 *www.quirinale.it* 🎫 *€5* ⏲ *Sept.–June, Sun. 8:30–noon* Ⓜ *Barberini.*

Piazza del Quirinale. This strategic location atop the Quirinal Hill has long been of great importance. It served as home of the Sabines in the 7th century BC, then deadly enemies of the Romans, who lived on the Capitoline and Palatine Hills (all of 1 km [½ mile] away). Today it's the foreground for the presidential residence, Palazzo del Quirinale, and home to the **Palazzo della Consulta,** where Italy's Constitutional Court sits. The open side of the piazza has an impressive vista of the rooftops and domes of central Rome and St. Peter's. The **Fontana di Montecavallo,** or Fontana dei Dioscuri, is composed of a huge Roman statuary group and an obelisk from the tomb of the emperor Augustus. The group of the Dioscuri trying to tame two massive marble steeds was found in the Baths of Constantine, which occupied part of the summit of the Quirinal Hill. Unlike just about every other ancient statue in Rome, this group survived the Dark Ages intact and accordingly became one

Continued on page 176

BERNINI & BORROMINI

By Martin Wilmot Bennett

ANGELS & DEMONS

Designed by Bernini, the ten angels of the Ponte Sant'Angelo bridge star along with other Berninis in Dan Brown's *Angels & Demons*, the Rome-based prequel to *The Da Vinci Code*. See Chapter 1 ("What's New") for details.

THE TRAGIC RIVALRY OF BERNINI AND BORROMINI

Consider the famous feuding duos of Lennon vs. McCartney, Mozart vs. Salieri, Michelangelo vs. Raphael. None of them match the rivalry of Gian Lorenzo Bernini vs. Francesco Borromini. In a pitched battle of anything-you-can-do-I-can-do-better, these two great geniuses of the Baroque style transformed 17th-century Rome into a city of spectacle, the "theater of the entire world." While it was Bernini who triumphed and Borromini who wound up taking his own life, the real winner was Rome itself—a banquet for the eyes cooked up by these two Baroque masters.

Borromini's dome in San Carlo alle Quattro Fontane

United in genius, the two could not have been more different in fortune and character. Born within a year of each other at the turn of the 1600s, they spent decades laying out majestic squares, building precedent-shattering churches, all the while outdoing each other in Baroque bravado.

AN ARTISTIC THROWDOWN

Compared and contrasted, the pair form the ultimate odd couple: Bernini, perhaps the greatest master showman of all time, exulted in Technicolor-hued theatricality; Borromini, the purist and reclusive genius, pursued the pure light of geometry, although with an artisan's hankering after detail. Bernini grew into the famed lover and solid family man; Borromini seems not to have had any love life at all. Bernini became a smooth mingler with society's great and worthy ranks; Borromini remained the quirky outsider. Bernini triumphed as the all-rounder, he of the so-called *"bel composto,"* as in the Cornaro Chapel where his talents as sculptor/architect/dramatist come stunningly together. Borromini was an architect, pure and simple. Throughout their lives, they had tried to turn the tables—psychologically as well as architecturally—on each other, a struggle that ended with Borromini's tragic suicide.

OPERATION AMAZEMENT

Both, however, fervently believed in the Baroque style and its mission to amaze, as well as edify. Thanks to the Counter-Reformation, the Catholic church discovered, and exploited, the effects on its congregants of such overtly Baroque tricks-of-the-trade as *chiaroscuro* (light-and-dark) and *trompe l'oeil* (fool-the-eye) techniques. Using emotion and motion, Bernini and Borromini learned how to give stone wing. In Bernini's famed *Pluto and Persephone,* the solid stone seems transmuted into living flesh—sculpted effects previously thought possible only in paint. Together transforming the city into a "giant theater," the rivals thus became the principal dramaturges and stage managers of Baroque Rome.

(preceding page) Bernini's *Pluto and Persephone,* (left) Bernini's *Angel* on the Ponte St. Angelo

BERNINI (1598–1680): THE POPE'S FAVORITE

Born: December 7, 1598, in Naples, southern Italy.

Greatest Works: St. Peter's Square, *Ecstasy of St. Theresa*, Piazza Navona's *Fountain of Four Rivers*, *Apollo and Daphne*, Sant'Andrea al Quirinale.

Personality Profile: Extrovert and fully aware of his genius or, to quote his own mother, "He acts as if he were master of the world."

Scandal: Just imagine the headlines: "Brother Attacked with Crowbar/Costanza Slashed with Razor by Jealous Genius." Bernini went ballistic on learning his wife, Costanza Nonarelli, was having an affair with his brother Luigi. Protected by Pope Urban VIII, Bernini was let off with a fine of 3,000 scudi.

Career Low: Largely on Borromini's expert insistence, the two crack-ridden bell-towers Bernini designed for St. Peter's were subsequently pulled down.

"La Bella Morte": Death in Bernini becomes star performer. His tomb for Urban VIII has a skeleton writing the pope's name in a marble registry of death, while his tomb for Alexander VII has a golden skeleton riffling marble drapery (this pope kept a Bernini-designed coffin in his bedroom).

"An ignorant Goth who has corrupted architecture. . . ."

Bernini on Borromini

Considered the "father of the Baroque," Bernini enjoyed almost too many career highs to count, starting from a drawing done as a youth, for which Pope Paul V awarded him a handful of gold ducats, to his being dubbed with the honorarium of "cavaliere" at age 23 (Borromini only received the same honor when he was past fifty). Born "under a happy star," as he himself put it, Bernini had patrons lining up, starting with church potentate and eventual pope, Maffeo Barberini, and Pope Paul's nephew, cardinal and art-dealer, Scipio Borghese, who claimed a bevy of Bernini's sculptures for his new Roman palace.

Bernini was a genius of self-promotion.

Bernini's *David*

Cupola, Sant'Andrea al Quirinale

Trick No. 1: In an early bust of Cardinal Borghese, there was an unsightly crack across the forehead; as cardinal turns away in disappointment, Bernini whips out a perfect copy, no more crack. Trick No. 2: On inaugurating Piazza Navona's River Fountain, Innocent X is distressed upon realizing that the water isn't running; Bernini explains technical hitch; pope steps away; abracadabra, Bernini switches water on. Bravo, Bernini!?

BORROMINI (1599–1667): THE ICONOCLAST

Born: September 27, 1599 in Bissone near Lake Lugano in Italy's far north, but with the name Castelli, the name-change coming later, partly to honor San Carlo Borromeo, whose San Carlo church will be Borromini's first major commission.

Greatest Works: San Carlo alle Quattro Fontane, Sant' Ivo della Sapienza, Sant'Agnese in Piazza Navona, Palazzo Falconieri.

Personality Profile: If Bernini is the "instant hit," Borromini is the "struggling genius," the introspective loner, and the complex, often misunderstood perfectionist.

Scandal: A young man, caught filching marble, was beaten and left for dead in San Giovanni in Lanterno, evidently on Borromini's orders. He avoids murder charges thanks to Pope Innocent's intervention.

Scale: Arguably his greatest work, San Carlo could be fitted into one of the four giant crossing-piers of the dome in St Peter's (in one of which towers Bernini's statue of St. Longinus).

"La Brutta Morte": His messy suicide was anything but "bella," as his brave note written in the hours it took him to expire after he fell on his sword attests.

"What I mind is not that the money goes to Bernini but that he should enjoy the honor of my labors."

Borromini on Bernini

Usually dressed in Spanish black, Borromini evidently had few attachments beyond his art. He not only had great artistic vision but an astounding command of geometry, an impeccable hankering after detail, and an artisan's willingness to get his hands dirty. The main influences on him range from Hiram, the builder of Solomon's temple in Jerusalem (who also died by falling on his sword) to Milan's Gothic cathedral, whose influence has been traced to S. Ivo's spiraled dome. On Urban VIII's death, Borromini's star began to ascend. The new pope, Innocent X, makes him papal architect, responsible for restructuring the S. Giovanni basilica and turning the S. Agnese church into a papal chapel. Bernini, however, is again waiting in the wings, readying himself for a startling come back.

While he had a long run of patrons, Borromini was often overshadowed by Bernini's showmanship. He is done out of designing the *Four Rivers* fountain after Bernini submits a silver model of his own design to the new pope. After Innocent's death, commissions become scarce and depression followed. His suicide note is famously calm: "I've been wounded like this since half past eight this morning and I will tell you how it happened...." Once forgotten and derided, Francesco Borromini is now considered "the architect's architect."

Church of Sant' Agnese

BERNINI & BORROMINI TOP 20 MASTERPIECES

2

Bernini

1. Apollo and Daphne, Galleria Borghese

2. The Baldacchino, Basilica di San Pietro

3. Ecstasy of Saint Theresa, Santa Maria della Vittoria

4. David, Galleria Borghese

5. Pluto and Persephone, Galleria Borghese

6. Tomb of Pope Urban VIII, Basilica di San Pietro

7. Fountain of the Four Rivers, Piazza Navona

8. Two Angels, Ponte Sant'Angelo

9. Elephant and Obelisk, Piazza Sta Maria sopra Minerva

10. Ludovica Albertoni, San Francesco a Ripa

11. Fontana della Barcaccia, Piazza di Spagna

12. Fontana del Tritone, Piazza Barberini

Borromini

13. San Carlo alla Quattro Fontane, Quirinale

14. Sant' Agnese, Piazza Navona

15. Sant' Ivo alla Sapienza, Piazza Navona

16. Oratory of Saint Phillip Neri, Piazza Chiesa Nuova

17. Palazzo Spada, Piazza Capo di Ferro

18. Palazzo Barberini, Via Barberini

19. Sant'Andrea delle Fratte, Via dell Mercede

20. Palazzo Falconieri, Via Giulia

BERNINI VS. BORROMINI: A MINI-WALK

In Rome, you may become lost looking for the work of one rival, then suddenly find yourself gazing at the work of the other. As though an eerily twinned path was destined for the two giants, several of their greatest works are just a few blocks from each other.

A short street away (Via Orlando) from mammoth Piazza Repubblica stands **Santa Maria della Vittoria,** famed for Bernini's **Cornaro Chapel.** Out of favor with new anti-Barberini Pope Innocent X, Bernini was rescued by a commission from Cardinal Cornaro to build a chapel for his family. Here, as if in a "theater," sculpted figures of family members look down from two marble balconies on the so-called "transverberation" of Carmelite Saint Theresa of Avila being pierced by the arrow of the Angel of Divine Love, eyes shut in agony, mouth open in rapture. Spiritual ecstasy has become shockingly real—to quote the famed comment by President de Brosses, "If this is divine love, I know what it is."

Leave the church and head down Via Barberini to Piazza Barberini where perch three of the largest bees you'll ever see. The **Fountain of the Bees** is Bernini's tribute to his arch-patron from the Barberini family, Pope Urban VIII. The bees were family emblems. Another Bernini masterstroke is the **Triton Fountain** in the center of Piazza Barberini. Turn left up Via delle Quattro Fontane. On your left is spectacular **Palazzo Barberini,** where Bernini and Borromini worked together in an

uneasy partnership. The wonderful winding staircase off to the right is the work of Borromini, while the other more conventionally angled staircase on the left is by Bernini, who also has a self-portrait hanging in the art gallery upstairs.

Borromini's prospects soon took a turn for the better thanks to the Barefoot Spanish Trinitarians, who commissioned him to design **San Carlo alla Quatto Fontane,** set at the crossroads up the road. One of the marvels of architecture, its dome—not much bigger than a down-turned bathtub—is packed immaculately throughout with hexagons, octagons, and crosses. Like jigsaw pieces they diminish upwards until the tiny roof seems anything but: to a space that in another architect might turned out claustrophobic Borromini is able to bring a touch of infinity. In the adjoining cloister, revel in Borromini's rearrangement of columns, which transform what would be a conventional rectangle into an energetic octagon. Don't forget to stop and admire the church's *movementé* facade.

S.M. della Vittoria
Fountain of the Bees
Tritone
Palazzo Barberini
San Carlo
Sant 'Andrea
Via di San Nicola da Tolentino
Via Barberini
Via del Tritone
Via delle 4 Fontane
Via Rasella
Via dei Giardini
Via del Quirinale
Via 20 Settembre
Via Torino

On the same Via del Quirinale stands a famous Bernini landmark, the Jesuits' **Sant' Andrea al Quirinale.** With steps flowing out into the street, it could be viewed as Bernini's response to his rival's nearby masterpiece.

Ironically, the commission for the Jesuit church was originally earmarked for Borromini (but transferred when Pope Alexander VII took over). Note how the hexagons in Bernini's dome diminish upwards to create an illusion of space—in Borrominiesque fashion.

PALAZZO BARBERINI

✉ Via Barberini 18, Quirinale ☎ 06/32810 🌐 www.galleriaborghese.it 🎫 €7 ⏲ Tues.–Sun. 8:30–7 (ticket office closes at 6) Ⓜ Barberini. Bus 52, 56, 60, 95, 116, 175, 492.

TIPS

■ Part of the family of museums that includes the Galleria Borghese, Palazzo Spada, Palazzo Venezia, and Palazzo Corsini, the Palazzo Barberini has gone into marketing in a big way—visit the shop here for some distinctive gifts for Aunt Ethel back home, including tote bags bearing the beloved visage of Raphael's La Fornarina, bookmarks with Caravaggio's Judith slicing off Holofernes's head, and coffee mugs bearing the famous Barberini heraldic bees.

One of Rome's most splendid 17th-century palaces, the recently renovated Palazzo Barberini is a landmark of the Roman Baroque style. Pope Urban VIII had acquired the property and given it to a nephew, who was determined to build an edifice worthy of his generous uncle and the ever-more-powerful Barberini clan. The result was, architecturally, a precedent-shattering affair: a "villa suburbana" set right in the heart of the urban city and designed to be strikingly open to the outdoors. Note how Carlo Maderno's grand facade seems almost entirely composed of window tiers rising up in proto-20th-century fashion.

Ascend Bernini's staircase to the Galleria Nazionale d'Arte Antica, hung with famed paintings including Raphael's *La Fornarina,* a luminous portrait of the artist's lover (a resident of Trastevere, she was reputedly a baker's daughter)—study the bracelet on her upper arm bearing Raphael's name. Also noteworthy are Guido Reni's portrait of the doomed *Beatrice Cenci* (beheaded in Rome for patricide in 1599)—Hawthorne called it "the saddest picture ever painted" in his Rome-based novel, *The Marble Faun*—and Caravaggio's *Judith and Holofernes.*

But the showstopper here is the palace's Gran Salone, a vast ballroom with a ceiling painted in 1630 by the third (and too-often neglected) master of the Roman Baroque, Pietro da Cortona. It depicts the *Glorification of Urban VIII's Reign* and has the spectacular conceit of glorifying Urban VIII as the agent of Divine Providence and escorted by a "bomber squadron" (to quote art historian Sir Michael Levey) of some huge, mutantlike Barberini bees, the heraldic symbol of the family.

of the city's great sights, especially during the Middle Ages. Next to the figures, the ancient obelisk from the Mausoleo di Augusto (Tomb of Augustus) was put here by Pope Pius VI at the end of the 18th century. ✉ *Quirinale* Ⓜ *Barberini.*

Quattro Fontane (*Four Fountains*). The intersection takes its name from its four Baroque fountains, representing the Tiber (on the San Carlo corner), the Arno, Juno, and Diana. Despite the traffic, it's worthwhile taking in the views from this point in all four directions: to the southwest as far as the obelisk in Piazza del Quirinale; to the northeast along Via XX Settembre to the Porta Pia; to the northwest across Piazza Barberini to the obelisk of Trinità dei Monti; and to the southeast as far as the obelisk and apse of Santa Maria Maggiore. The prospect is a highlight of Pope Sixtus V's campaign of urban beautification and an example of the Baroque influence on city planning. ✉ *At intersection of Via Quattro Fontane, Via XX Settembre, and Via del Quirinale, Quirinale* Ⓜ *Barberini.*

Fodor'sChoice ★ **San Carlo alle Quattro Fontane.** Sometimes identified by the diminutive San Carlino because of its tiny size, this is one of Borromini's masterpieces. In a space no larger than the base of one of the piers of St. Peter's Basilica, he created a church that is an intricate exercise in geometric perfection, with a coffered dome that seems to float above the curves of the walls. Borromini's work is often bizarre, definitely intellectual, and intensely concerned with pure form. In San Carlo, he invented an original treatment of space that creates an effect of rippling movement, especially evident in the double-S curves of the facade. Characteristically, the interior decoration is subdued, in white stucco with no more than a few touches of gilding, so as not to distract from the form. Don't miss the **cloister,** a tiny, understated Baroque jewel, with a graceful portico and loggia above, echoing the lines of the church. ⇨ *For more on Borromini and this church, see our special photo feature, "Baroque and Desperate: The Tragic Rivalry of Bernini and Borromini" in this chapter.* ✉ *Via del Quirinale 23, Quirinale* ☎ *06/4883109* 🌐 *www.sancarlino-borromini.it* ⏲ *Weekdays 10–1 and 3–6; Sat. 10–1; Sun. noon–1* Ⓜ *Barberini.*

Sant'Andrea al Quirinale. Designed by Bernini, this is an architectural gem of the Baroque. His son wrote that Bernini considered it one of his best works and that he used to come here occasionally just to sit and enjoy it. Bernini's simple oval plan, a classic of Baroque architecture, is given drama and movement by the church's decoration, which carries the story of St. Andrew's martyrdom and ascension into heaven, starting with the painting over the high altar, up past the figure of the saint over the chancel door, to the angels at the base of the lantern and the dove of the Holy Spirit that awaits on high. ✉ *Via del Quirinale 29, Quirinale* ☎ *06/4740807* 🌐 *www.gesuitialquirinale.it* ⏲ *Mon.–Sat. 8:30–noon and 3:30–7; Sun. 9–noon and 4–7* Ⓜ *Barberini.*

WORTH NOTING

Fontana delle Api (*Fountain of the Bees*). Decorated with the famous heraldic bees of the Barberini family, the upper shell and the inscription are from a fountain that Bernini designed for Pope Urban VIII; the rest was lost when the fountain had to be moved to make way for a new street. The inscription was the cause of a considerable scandal when the fountain was first put up in 1644. It said that the fountain had been erected in the 22nd year of the pontiff's reign, although in fact the 21st anniversary of Urban's election to the papacy was still some weeks away. The last numeral was hurriedly erased, but to no avail—Urban died eight days before the beginning of his 22nd year as pope. The superstitious Romans, who had immediately recognized the inscription as a foolhardy tempting of fate, were vindicated. Thanks to a recent restoration and cleaning, the once-dirty fountain has been returned to its former glory. ✉ *Via Veneto at Piazza Barberini, Quirinale* Ⓜ *Barberini.*

Scuderie del Quirinale. Directly opposite the main entrance of the Palazzo del Quirinale sits the Scuderie Papale, a grand 18th-century stable strikingly remodeled in the late 1990s by architect Gae Aulenti and now host to big temporary art shows. ✉ *Via XXIV Maggio 16, Quirinale* ☎ *06/39967500* 🌐 *www.scuderiequirinale.it* 🎫 *€12* ⏲ *Sun.–Thurs. 10–8, Fri. and Sat. 10 am–10:30 pm* Ⓜ *Barberini. Bus 16, 36, 60, 62, 136, 175.*

Colline Emiliane. Around the corner from Piazza Barberini, this tiny, family-run trattoria serves up something different: excellent dishes from Emilia-Romagna, which some say is the best food region in Italy. It's popular with tourists and locals, so make a reservation for dinner. ✉ *Via degli Avignonesi 22, Piazza di Spagna* ☎ *06/4817538* Ⓜ *Barberini.*

8

VILLA BORGHESE, PIAZZA DEL POPOLO, AND FLAMINIO

GETTING ORIENTED

Villa Borghese, Piazza del Popolo, and Flaminio

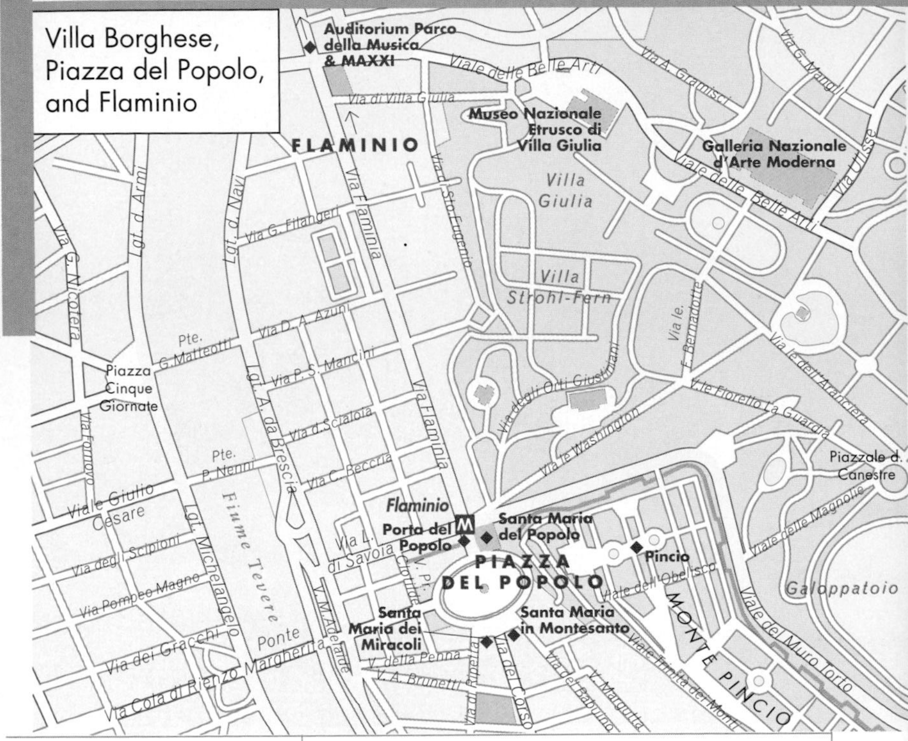

GETTING HERE	TOP REASONS TO GO
The Metro stop for Piazza del Popolo is Line A's Flaminio. The Villa Giulia, the Galleria Nazionale d'Arte Moderna, and Villa Borghese's Biopark are accessible from Via Flaminia, 1 km (½ mile) from Piazza del Popolo. Tram 19 and Bus No. 3 stop at each. Bus No. 119 connects Piazza del Popolo to Piazza Venezia. From the Colosseum or San Giovanni, take No. 117 to Piazza del Popolo. No. 116, starting near the Museo Borghese, is the only bus that goes through the park; it also stops throughout the historic center.	**Piazza del Popolo:** At the end of three of the centro storico's most important streets—Via del Babuino, Via del Corso, and Via di Ripetta—the People's Square, as the name translates, offers a ringside seat for some of Rome's best people-watching. **Villa Borghese:** Drink in the oxygen in central Rome's largest park—stretches of green and plenty of leafy pathways encourage wandering, biking, or just chilling out. **The Pincio:** Stroll through formal gardens in the footsteps of 19th-century fashion plates, aristocrats, and even popes. **Santa Maria del Popolo:** Marvel at the incredible realism of Caravaggio's gritty paintings in the Cerasi Chapel, then savor Raphael's Chigi Chapel. **Galleria Borghese:** Wink at Canova's sexy statue of Pauline Borghese in one of Rome's most spectacularly opulent—and pleasant—museums.

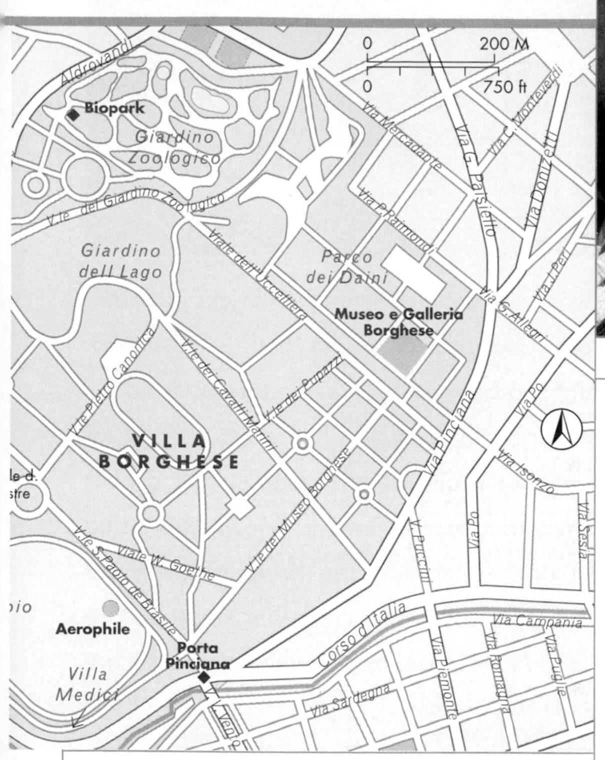

MAKING THE MOST OF YOUR TIME

Explore this area on a clear day: the Villa Borghese park is at its best (and most bustling with strolling Italian families) on beautiful days, while the view from the top of the Pincio hill provides a stunning panorama over Rome's pastel rooftops. The Galleria Borghese, one of several museums within the Villa Borghese, is a Roman gem and a must-see for art lovers; just remember to book your tickets in advance (you can do so online), as walk-ins are rarely accommodated. After your "walk in the park," head down to Piazza del Popolo, one of Rome's loveliest piazzas, and duck into Santa Maria del Popolo for its gorgeous paintings by Baroque master Caravaggio—keeping in mind that, like many of Rome's churches, it's closed in the afternoons.

QUICK BITES

Caffè delle Arti. Attached to the Galleria d'Arte Moderna, this café with a pretty terrace is a favorite all-day rendezvous for Romans and visitors to Villa Borghese park and its museums. This is the place to break up your walk with a gelato or lunch. ✉ *Via Gramsci 73, Villa Borghese* ☎ *06/32651236* 🌐 *www.caffedelleartiroma.it.*

Il Margutta. For a light meal head to one of Rome's few vegetarian restaurants. A chic, elegant spot—the restaurant is also an art gallery—the food is top-quality and mostly organic. ✉ *Via Margutta 118, Piazza del Popolo* ☎ *06/32650577* 🌐 *www.ilmarguttavegetariano.it* Ⓜ *Flaminio.*

Stravinskij Bar. The Hotel de Russie's luxurious Stravinskij Bar isn't cheap, but it offers a leafy courtyard refuge from Rome's cacophony. Visiting Hollywood stars sip martinis and international political movers and shakers clinch deals. ✉ *Hotel de la Russie, Via del Babuino 9, Piazza di Spagna* ☎ *06/32888874* 🌐 *www.hotelderussie.it.*

Sightseeing ★★★★
Nightlife ★
Dining ★★
Lodging ★★
Shopping ★

If beautiful masterpieces are as common as bricks in Rome, parks are far rarer. Happily, although you'll find few ilex and poplars dotting piazzas and streets, a verdant hoard can be found to the north of central Rome's cobblestoned chaos. Here breathes the city's giant green lung: the Villa Borghese park, where residents love to escape for some serious R&R. But don't think you can completely prevent gallery gout: three of Rome's most important museums are inside the park, and Piazza del Popolo (which has some art-crammed churches) is close by.

VILLA BORGHESE

Updated by Amanda Ruggeri

Central Rome's largest open space is filled with playful fountains, sculptured gardens, and picturesque forests of shady pine trees. But that's not the park's only purpose, for on the perimeter lie three of Rome's most important museums: the Galleria Borghese, for the very best of ancient, Renaissance, and Baroque art; the Villa Giulia, for the world's ultimate collection of Etruscan remains; and the Galleria Nazionale d'Arte Moderna, a reminder that the Italians had their Impressionists, too. For theatergoers, there are summer performances of Shakespeare in a replica of London's Globe. All in all, there's enough here to satisfy the most avid culture vulture. For real vultures, and an excellent day out with the children, head for the new Biopark, Rome's zoo.

TOP ATTRACTIONS

Fodor's Choice ★ **Galleria Borghese.** It's a real toss-up as to which is more magnificent: the villa built for Cardinal Scipione Borghese in 1612, or the art that lies within. Despite its beauty, the villa never was used as a residence. Instead, the luxury-loving cardinal built it as a showcase for his fabulous collection of both antiquities and more "modern" works, including those he commissioned from the masters Caravaggio and Bernini. Today, it's a monument to Roman interior decoration at its most extravagant. With the passage of time, however, the building has become less celebrated than the collections housed within, including one of the finest collections of Baroque sculpture anywhere in the world.

WORD OF MOUTH

"The Museo Borghese is the perfect museum, because so few people are allowed in at a time. It is truly an intimate experience. You can move at your own pace, and you won't feel you're on a 'step this way' forced march." —slgass

Like the gardens, the casino and its collections have undergone many changes since the 17th century. Much of the building was redecorated in the late 18th century, when the villa received many of its eye-popping ceiling frescoes (although some original decorations also survive). The biggest change to the collection, however, came thanks to Camillo Borghese. After marrying Napoléon's sister Pauline, he sold 154 statues, 170 bas-reliefs, 160 busts, 30 columns, and a number of vases, all ancient pieces, to his new brother-in-law. Today, those sculptures, including the so-called "Borghese Gladiator" and "Borghese Hermaphrodite," are in the Louvre in Paris. At the end of the 19th century, a later member of the family, Francesco Borghese, attempted damage control with his fellow Romans (outraged that many of their art treasures had been shipped off to Paris) with some new acquisitions; he also transferred to the casino the remaining works of art then housed in Palazzo Borghese. In 1902 the casino, its contents, and the estate were sold to the Italian government.

One of the most famous works in the collection is Canova's Neoclassical sculpture of Pauline Borghese as Venus Victrix. Scandalously, Pauline reclines on a Roman sofa, bare-bosomed, her hips swathed in classical drapery, the very model of haughty detachment and sly come-hither. You can imagine what the 19th-century gossips were saying!

The next three rooms hold three key early Baroque sculptures: Bernini's *David, Apollo and Daphne*, and *Rape of Proserpina.* All were done when the artist was in his 20s, and all illustrate Bernini's extraordinary skill. They also demonstrate the Baroque desire to invest sculpture with a living quality, to imbue inert marble with a sense of real flesh. Whereas Renaissance sculptors wanted to capture the idealized beauty of the human form that they had admired in ancient Greek and Roman sculptures, later sculptors like Bernini wanted movement and drama as well, capturing not an essence but an instant, infused with theatricality and emotion. The *Apollo and Daphne* shows the moment when, to escape the pursuing Apollo, Daphne is turned into a laurel tree. Leaves and twigs sprout from her fingertips as she stretches agonizingly away from Apollo. In the *Rape of Proserpina,* Pluto has just plucked Persephone (or Proserpina) from her flower-picking—or perhaps he's returning to Hades with his prize. (Don't miss the realistic way his grip causes dimples in Proserpina's flesh.) This is the stuff that makes the Baroque exciting—and moving. Other Berninis on view in the collection include a large, unfinished figure called

Verità, or Truth. Bernini began work on this brooding figure after the death of his principal patron, Pope Urban VIII. It was meant to form part of a work titled *Truth Revealed by Time*. The next pope, Innocent X, had little love for the ebullient Urban, and, as was the way in Rome, this meant that Bernini would be excluded from the new pope's favors. However, Bernini's towering genius was such that the new pope came around with his patronage with almost indecent haste.

RISQUÉ BUSINESS

Camillo Borghese seems to have been unconcerned that his princess had posed for Canova's erotic masterpiece, ostensibly a sculpted homage to *Venus Victrix*. Principessa Pauline, on the other hand, was supposedly shocked that her husband took pleasure in showing the work to guests. This coyness seems all the more curious given the reply Pauline is supposed to have made to a lady who asked her how she could have posed for the sculpture: "Oh, but the studio was heated." After the couple's divorce, the statue was locked away but Camillo occasionally showed it at night—by the light of a single candle.

The Caravaggio Room holds works by this hotheaded genius, who died of malaria at age 37. All of his paintings, even the charming *Boy with a Basket of Fruit,* seethe with an undercurrent of darkness. The disquieting *Sick Bacchus* is a self-portrait of the artist who, like the god, had a penchant for wine. *David and Goliath,* painted in the last year of Caravaggio's life—while he was on the lam for murder—includes his self-portrait . . . in the head of Goliath. Upstairs, the Pinacoteca (Picture Gallery) boasts paintings by Raphael (including his moving *Deposition*), Pinturicchio, Perugino, Bellini, and Rubens. Probably the gallery's most famous painting is Titian's allegorical *Sacred and Profane Love,* a mysterious and yet-unsolved image with two female figures, one nude, one clothed.

■ **TIP→ Admission to the Museo is by reservation only.** Visitors are admitted in two-hour shifts 9 am to 5 pm. Prime-time slots can sell out days in advance, so in high season reserve by phone or directly through the Borghese's website. You need to collect your reserved ticket at the museum ticket office a half hour before your entrance. However, when it's not busy you can purchase your ticket at the museum for the next entrance appointment. ✉ *Piazza Scipione Borghese 5, off Via Pinciana, Villa Borghese* ☎ *06/32810 Reservations, 06/8413979 Information* 🌐 *www.galleriaborghese.it* 🎫 *€11, plus a €2 reservation fee; audio guide €5, English tour €6* ⏲ *Tues.–Sun. 8:30–7:30, with sessions at 9, 11, 1, 3, and 5* Ⓜ *Bus 910 from Piazza della Repubblica, or Tram 19 or Bus 3 from Policlinico.*

FAMILY **Pincio.** Redolent of the yesteryears of Henry James and Edith Wharton, the Pincian gardens always have been a favorite spot for strolling. Grand Tourists, and even a pope or two, would head here to see and be seen among the beau monde of Rome. Today, the Pincian terrace remains a favorite spot to cool off overheated locals. The rather formal, early-19th-century style contrasts with the far more elaborate terraced gardens of Lucullus, the Roman gourmand who held legendary banquets here. Today, off-white marble busts of Italian heroes and artists line the pathways. Along with similar busts on the Gianicolo (Janiculum Hill), their noses have been victims of vandalism, perhaps as an attempt to fight ghosts: A belief going back to ancient times held that the nose was the source of breath and therefore of life itself, even after death. By depriving a bust of the same organ, its accompanying spirit would be deprived of oxygen, which evidently spirits need to walk the night.

A stretch of ancient walls separates the Pincio from the southwest corner of Villa Borghese. From the balustraded terrace, you can look down at Piazza del Popolo and beyond, surveying much of Rome. Southeast of the Pincian terrace is the **Casina Valadier,** a magnificently decorated Neoclassical building that was reopened to the public in 2007 after a decade-long renovation. It remains one of Rome's most historic restaurants (*06/69922090* 🌐 *casinavaladier.it*). ✉ *Piazzale Napoleone I and Viale dell'Obelisco, Villa Borghese* Ⓜ *Flaminio (Piazza del Popolo).*

FAMILY **Villa Borghese.** Rome's "Central Park," the Villa Borghese was originally laid out as a pleasure garden in the early 17th century by Cardinal Scipione Borghese, a worldly and cultivated cleric and nephew of Pope Paul V. The word "villa" was used to mean suburban estate, of the type developed by the ancient Romans and adopted by Renaissance nobles. Today's gardens bear little resemblance to the originals. Not only do they cover a much smaller area—by 1630, the perimeter wall was almost 5 km (3 miles) long—but they also have been almost entirely remodeled. This occurred at the end of the 18th century, when a Scottish painter, Jacob More, was employed to transform them into the style of the "cunningly natural" park so popular in 18th-century England. Until then, the park was probably the finest example of an Italian-style garden in the entire country.

8

In addition to the gloriously restored Galleria Borghese, the highlights of the park are Piazza di Siena, a graceful amphitheater, and the botanical garden on Via Canonica, where there is a pretty little lake, a Neoclassical faux-Temple of Aesculapius (a favorite photo-op), the newly designed Biopark zoo, Rome's own replica of London's Globe Theatre, and the Villa Giulia museum.

The recently opened Carlo Bilotti Museum is particularly visitable for De Chirico fans, although there is more modern art in the nearby Galleria Nazionale d'Arte Moderna. The park is dotted with bike, in-line skating, and electric scooter rental concessions and has a children's movie theater (showing films for adults in the evening), as well as a cinema center, Casa del Cinema, where film buffs can screen films or sit at the slick, cherry red, indoor-outdoor caffè (you can find a schedule of events at 🌐 *www.casadelcinema.it*). ✉ *Main entrances at Porta Pinciana, the Pincio, Piazzale Flaminio (Piazza del Popolo), Viale delle Belle Arti, and Via Mercadante, Villa Borghese* Ⓜ *Flaminio (Piazza del Popolo).*

Villa Medici. Purchased by Napoléon to create an academy where artists could hone their knowledge of Italian art and so put it to the (French) national good, the villa originally belonged to Cardinal Ferdinando

Sister of Napoléon, Principessa Pauline Borghese scandalized all Europe by posing as a half-naked Venus for Canova; the statue is on view at the Galleria Borghese.

Medici, who also laid out the immaculate Renaissance garden to set off his sculpture collection. Garden tours in English are offered, allowing you to walk in the footsteps of Velázquez, Fragonard, and Ingres, who all worked here (at what is now officially called the French Academy in Rome). The €9 guided tour is also the only way you can see not only the gardens, but the incredibly picturesque garden facade, which is studded with Mannerist and Rococo sculpted reliefs and overlooks a loggia with a beautiful fountain devoted to Mercury. ✉ *Viale Trinità dei Monti 1, Villa Borghese* ☎ *06/67611* 🌐 *www.villamedici.it* 🎫 *Entrance including garden tour and exhibit, €12* ⏲ *Tues.–Sun. 10:30–12:30 and 2–5:30 (6:30 if there is an exhibition). Tours of the gardens in English at noon* Ⓜ *Spagna.*

WORTH NOTING

Biopark. Especially good for a day out with the children, this zoo has been remodeled along eco-friendly lines—more space for the animals, most brought from other zoos or born from animals already in captivity rather than snatched from the wild. There aren't any rhinos, koalas, pandas, or polar bears, but there are local brown bears from Abruzzo and a Reptilarium. Other features are the Biopark train (€1), a picnic area next to the flamingos, and a farm. ✉ *Piazzale del Giardino Zoologico 1, Villa Borghese* ☎ *06/3608211* 🌐 *www.bioparco.it* 🎫 *€15 adults (€12 children)* ⏲ *Jan.–Mar., daily 9:30–5; Apr.–Sept., weekdays 9:30–6, weekends 9:30–7; Oct., daily 9:30–6; Nov.–Dec., daily 9:30–5* Ⓜ *Tram 19; Bus 3, 88, 95, 490, 495.*

Galleria Nazionale d'Arte Moderna (*National Gallery of Modern Art*). This massive white Beaux Arts building, built for the 1911 World Exposition in Rome, contains one of Italy's leading collections of 19th- and 20th-century works. It's primarily dedicated to the history of Italian modernism, examining the movement's development over the last two centuries, but crowd-pleasers Degas, Monet, Courbet, Van Gogh, and Cézanne put in appearances along with an outstanding Dadaist collection. You can mix coffee and culture at the art nouveau Caffè delle Arti in the columned alcove of the museum. ✉ *Via delle Belle Arti 131, Villa Borghese* ☎ *06/32298221* 🌐 *www.gnam.beniculturali.it* 🎫 *Museum only, €8; exhibition only, €10; museum and exhibition, €12* ⏲ *Tues.–Sun. 8:30–7:30 (last entrance 45 mins before closing)* Ⓜ *Tram 19, 3; Bus 88, 95, 490, 495.*

Globe Theater. Directed by prolific Roman actor Gigi Proietti, this theater replicates the London original inaugurated in 1576. Rome's homage to Shakespeare is built entirely of wood and seats 1,250 with standing room for 420 groundlings (following Elizabethan custom). Performances are from July to September, generally in Italian. Set in the Villa Borghese park, it is roughly between the Biopark and the Carlo Bilotti Museum. ✉ *Silvani Toti Globe Theater, Largo Aqua Felix on the Viale Pietro Canonica, Villa Borghese* ☎ *06/0608* 🌐 *www.globetheatreroma.com.*

Museo Nazionale Etrusco di Villa Giulia. The world's most outstanding collection of Etruscan art and artifacts is housed in Villa Giulia, built around 1551 for Pope Julius III (hence its name). Among the team called in to plan and construct the villa were Michelangelo and his fellow Florentine Vasari. Most of the actual work, however, was done by Vignola and Ammannati. The villa's *nymphaeum*—or sunken sculpture garden—is a superb example of a refined late-Renaissance setting for princely pleasures. No one knows precisely where the Etruscans originated. Many scholars maintain they came from Asia Minor, appearing in Italy about 2000 BC, and creating a civilization that was a dazzling prelude to the ancient Romans. Unfortunately, the exhibitions here are as dry as their subject matter—hundreds of glass vitrines stuffed with objects. Even so, you'll find great artistic treasures. Among the most striking pieces are the terra-cotta statues, such as the *Apollo of Veio* and the serenely beautiful *Sarcophagus of the Wedded Couple.* Dating 530–500 BC, this couple, or Sposi, look at the viewer with almond eyes and archaic smiles, suggesting an openness and joie de vivre rare in Roman art. Also look for the cinematic frieze from a later temple (480 BC) from Pyrgi, looking like a sort of Etruscan Elgin marbles in terra-cotta. Note the fabulous Etruscan jewelry, which makes Bulgari look like your village blacksmith. ✉ *Piazzale Villa Giulia 9, Villa Borghese* ☎ *06/3226571* 🌐 *villagiulia.beniculturali.it* 🎫 *€8* ⏲ *Tues.–Sun. 8:30–7:30 (ticket office closes 1 hr earlier)* Ⓜ *Tram 19, Bus 3.*

8

PIAZZA DEL POPOLO

The formal garden terraces of the Pincio, on the southwestern side of Villa Borghese, give way to a stone staircase down to Piazza del Popolo, a mercifully traffic-free piazza that is one of Rome's best people-watching spots. Very round, very explicitly defined, and very photogenic, the Piazza del Popolo—the People's Square—is one of Rome's biggest. Papal architect Giuseppe Valadier (1762–1839) laid out this square with twin churches (and two adjacent ritzy cafés) at one end and the Porta del Popolo—Rome's northern city gate—at the other. Part of an earlier urban plan, the three streets to the south radiate straight as spokes to other parts of the city, forming the famed "tridente" that nicknames this neighborhood. The center is marked with an obelisk taken from Egypt, one so old it makes the Pantheon look like the Sears Tower: it was carved for Ramses II in the 13th century BC. Today, it is guarded by four water-gushing lions and steps that mark the end of many a sunset *passeggiata* (stroll). The most fascinating pieces of art, however, hide within the northeast corner's often-overlooked church of Santa Maria del Popolo, snuggled against the 400-year-old Porta del Popolo. Here you'll find masterpieces by Raphael and Caravaggio.

If you're looking to rest your feet, there are cafés and restaurant tables aplenty.

TOP ATTRACTIONS

NEED A BREAK?

Buccone. This wine shop serves light snacks at lunchtime and wine by the glass all day long. ✉ ***Via di Ripetta 19, Piazza del Popolo*** ☎ ***06/3612154*** 🌐 ***www.enotecabuccone.com.***

Fodor's Choice ★

Santa Maria del Popolo. Standing inconspicuously in a corner of the vast Piazza del Popolo, this church often goes unnoticed, but the treasures inside make it a must for art lovers, as they include an entire chapel designed by Raphael and one adorned with striking Caravaggio masterpieces. Bramante enlarged the apse of the church, which had been rebuilt in the 15th century on the site of a much older place of worship. Inside, in the first chapel on the right, you'll see some frescoes by Pinturicchio from the mid-15th century; the adjacent **Cybo Chapel** is a 17th-century exercise in marble decoration. Raphael's famous **Chigi Chapel**, the second on the left, was built around 1513 and commissioned by the banker Agostino Chigi (who also had the artist decorate his home across the Tiber, the Villa Farnesina). Raphael provided the cartoons for the vault mosaic—showing God the Father in benediction—and the designs for the statues of Jonah and Elijah. More than a century later, Bernini added the oval medallions on the tombs and the statues of Daniel and Habakkuk, when, in the mid-17th century another Chigi, Pope Alexander VII, commissioned him to restore and decorate the building.

The organ case of Bernini in the right transept bears the Della Rovere family oak tree, part of the Chigi family's coat of arms. The **choir,** with vault frescoes by Pinturicchio, contains the handsome tombs of Ascanio Sforza and Girolamo delle Rovere, both designed by Andrea Sansovino. The best is for last: The **Cerasi Chapel,** to the left of the high altar, holds two Caravaggios, the *Crucifixion of St. Peter* and *Conversion of St. Paul*. Exuding drama and realism, both are key early Baroque works that show how "modern" 17th-century art can appear. Compare their style with the much more restrained and classically "pure" *Assumption of the Virgin* by Caravaggio's contemporary and rival, Annibale Carracci; it hangs over the altar of the chapel. ✉ *Piazza del Popolo 12, near Porta Pinciana, Piazza del Popolo* ☎ *06/3610836* 🌐 *www.santamariadelpopolo.it* ⏲ *Mon.–Sat. 7–noon and 4–7, Sun. 7:30–1:30 and 4:30–7:30* Ⓜ *Flaminio*.

WORTH NOTING

Porta del Popolo (*City Gate*). The medieval gate in the Aurelian walls was replaced in 1561 by the current one. Bernini further embellished it in 1655 for the much-heralded arrival of Queen Christina of Sweden, who had abdicated her throne to become a Roman Catholic. ✉ *Piazza del Popolo and Piazzale Flaminio, Piazza del Popolo* Ⓜ *Flaminio*.

Santa Maria dei Miracoli. A twin to Santa Maria in Montesanto, this church was built in the 1670s by Carlo Fontana as an elegant frame for the entrance to Via del Corso from Piazza del Popolo. ✉ *Via del Corso 528, Piazza del Popolo* ☎ *06/3610250* ⏲ *Weekdays 5–8, Sun. 10:30–1:30* Ⓜ *Flaminio*.

Santa Maria in Montesanto. One of the two bookend churches on the eastern side of Piazza del Popolo, this edifice was built by Carlo Fontana and supervised by his brilliant teacher, Bernini (whose other pupils are responsible for the saints topping the facade). ✉ *Via del Babuino 197, Piazza del Popolo* ☎ *06/3610594* 🌐 *www.chiesadegliartisti.it* ⏲ *Weekdays 5–8, Sun. 10:30–1:30* Ⓜ *Flaminio*.

FLAMINIO

The Flaminio neighborhood, in northern Rome near the Tiber, was the focus of urban renewal plans for many years. Renzo Piano's Auditorium della Musica *(see Nightlife and Performing Arts)* put the area on the map in 2002 and the MAXXI museum, several years later, solidified the area as a destination.

Fodor's Choice ★ **MAXXI—Museo Nazionale delle Arti del XXI Secolo** (*National Museum of 21st-Century Arts*). It took 10 years and cost some €150 million, but for art lovers, Italy's first national museum devoted to contemporary art and architecture was worth it. The building alone impresses, as it should: the design, by Anglo-Iraqi starchitect Zaha Hadid, triumphed over 272 other contest entries. The building plays with lots of natural light, curving and angular lines, and big open spaces, all meant to question the division between "within" and "without" (think glass ceilings and steel staircases that twist through the air). While not every critic adored it at its 2010 unveiling, it's hard not to feel delighted by the surprisingly playful space.

The MAXXI hosts temporary exhibits on art, architecture, film, and more. Past shows have included a retrospective on top Arte Povera artist Michelangelo Pistoletto and an exhibit of works by architect and engineer Pietro Nervi. From the permanent collection, rotated through the museum, more than 350 works represent artists including Andy Warhol, Francesco Clemente, and Gerhard Richter. ✉ *Via Guido Reni 4, Flaminio* ☎ *06/32810* 🌐 *www.fondazionemaxxi.it* 🎫 *€11* ⏲ *Tues.–Fri. and Sun. 11–7, Sat. 11–10 (ticket office closes 1 hr earlier)* Ⓜ *Flaminio, then Tram 2 to Apollodoro; Bus 53, 217, 280, 910.*

MONTE MARIO

In the northwest part of Rome, perched on the city's highest hill, the neighborhood of Monte Mario has fabulous views. Although not the easiest to get to by public transportation there are a few noteworthy hotels and restaurants here.

PARIOLI

The elegant residential neighborhood of Parioli, north of the Villa Borghese, is home to some of the city's poshest hotels and restaurants. It's not especially convenient if you're planning to do sightseeing, though.

TRASTEVERE

GETTING ORIENTED

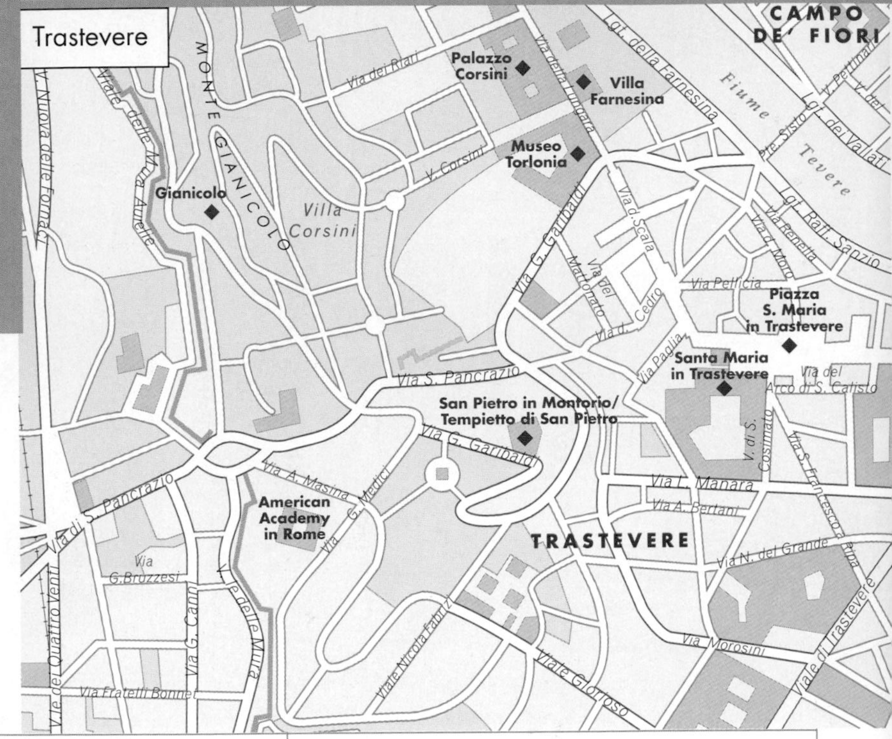

GETTING HERE

From the Vatican or Spanish Steps, expect a 20- to 30-minute walk to reach Trastevere.

From Termini, take the No. 40 Express or the No. 64 bus to Largo Torre Argentina, where you can switch to Tram 8 to get to Trastevere.

As for ascending the very steep Janiculum Hill, take the No. 41 bus from Ponte Sant'Angelo, then enjoy the stately walk down to the northern reaches of Trastevere.

TOP REASONS TO GO

Santa Maria in Trastevere: Tear yourself away from the piazza scene outside to take in the gilded glory of one of the city's oldest and most beautiful churches, fabled for its medieval mosaics.

"Tiber, Father Tiber": Cross over the river on the Ponte Fabricio—the city's oldest bridge—for a stroll on the paved shores of the adorable Isola Tiberina (and don't forget to detour for the lemon ices at La Gratachecca).

I Love the Nightlife: Trastevere has become one of Rome's hottest nighttime scene-arenas, with hipsterious clubs at nearly every turn.

Get a Feel for the Middle Ages: With cobblestone alleyways and medieval houses, the area around Trastevere's Piazza di Piscinula offers a magical dip into Rome's Middle Ages.

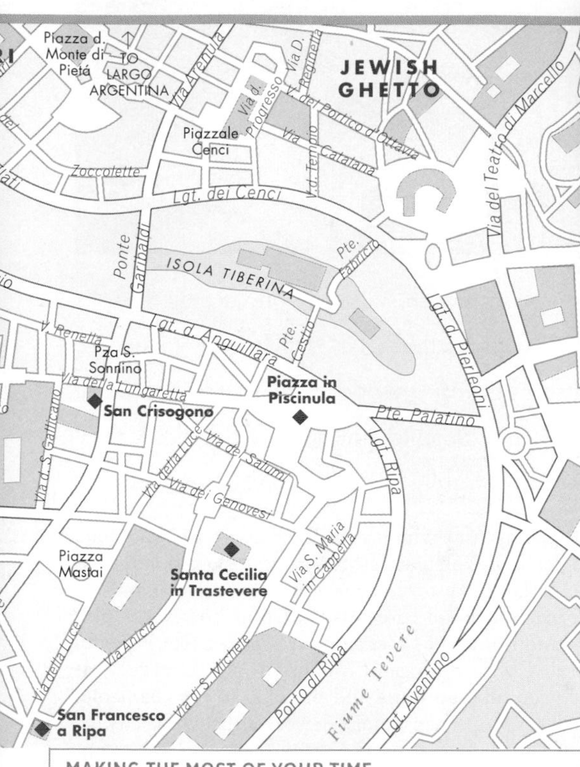

MAKING THE MOST OF YOUR TIME

It's easy to get to Trastevere from Piazza Venezia: take Tram No. 8 to the first stop on the other side of the river. You'll probably want to head right to the Piazza of Santa Maria in Trastevere, the heart of this lively area. Heading to the opposite side of Viale di Trastevere, though, is a treat many tourists miss. The cobblestone streets around Piazza in Piscinula and Via della Luce, with locals peering down from balconies and the smell of fresh-baked bread floating from bakeries, are much more reminiscent of how Trastevere used to be than the touristic area north. Either way, remember that many of Trastevere's lovely small churches close, like others in Rome, for the afternoons. In the evenings, the neighborhood heats up with locals and visitors alike, drinking, eating, and going for passeggiate (strolls)—a not-to-be-missed atmosphere, especially for those with energy to burn.

QUICK BITES

Caffè di Marzio. Over a coffee or a cocktail, sit and gaze upon Santa Maria in Trastevere's glistening golden facade at Caffè di Marzio. Although the outdoor seating is lovely, the interior is warm and welcoming, too. ✉ *Piazza Santa Maria in Trastevere 15, Trastevere* ☎ *06/5816095* 🌐 *www.caffedimarzio.it.*

La Renella (*Forno La Renella*). Snack among locals at La Renella, a no-frills pizzeria and bakery hidden just off Piazza Trilussa. The goods come fresh from the wood-fired oven. As in many traditional bakeries, pizzas and cookies are sold by the kilogram, so get your pizza sliced to the size you want. ✉ *Via del Moro 15, Trastevere* ☎ *06/5817265.*

Rivendita. The full name is Rivendita: Libri Cioccolata e Vino, and that's exactly what you'll find in this charming, trendy Trastevere hole-in-the-wall: books, chocolate, and wine. If you have a sweet tooth, you won't want to miss this. ✉ *Vicolo del Cinque 11/a, Trastevere* ☎ *06/58301868.*

Sightseeing ★★★★★
Nightlife ★★★★
Dining ★★★★
Lodging ★★★
Shopping ★★★

Updated by Amanda Ruggeri

New York has its Greenwich Village, and Rome has its Trastevere (literally, "across the Tiber"). In Trastevere's case, however, the sense of being a world apart goes back more than two millennia and despite galloping gentrification, it remains about the most tightly knit community in Rome.

Perfectly picturesque piazzas, tiny winding medieval alleyways, and time-burnished Romanesque houses all cast a frozen-in-time spell, while grand art awaits at Santa Maria in Trastevere, San Francesco a Ripa, and the Villa Farnesina. The neighborhood's greatest attraction, however, is simply its atmosphere—traditional shops set along crooked streets, peaceful during the day and alive with throngs of restaurant- and partygoers at night. From here, a steep hike up stairs and the road to the Gianicolo, Rome's highest hill, earns you a panoramic view over the whole city.

The inhabitants of Trastevere don't even call themselves Romans but Trasteverini, going on to claim that they, not the citizens north of the river, are the true remaining Romans. No matter: a trip to Trastevere still feels a bit like entering a different time and place. Some call it the world's second-smallest nation (after the Vatican, which is number 1). A living chronology, the district remains an enchanting confusion of past and present.

TOP ATTRACTIONS

FAMILY **Gianicolo** (*Janiculum Hill*). The Gianicolo is famous for offering panoramic views of the city, a noontime cannon, and statues of Giuseppe and Anita Garibaldi (Garibaldi was the guiding spirit behind the unification of Italy in the 19th century; Anita was his long-suffering wife). The view, backdropped by the first slopes of the Appenine Mountains, is especially breathtaking at dusk, when Roman lovers, camera-happy tourists, and tchotchke-selling vendors gather. Small crowd aside, it's fun to pick out Rome's finest buildings, from the Pantheon to St. Peter's, and you'll be surprised at how peaceful and pastel it all looks from up here. At the plaza here there's a free puppet show in Italian on weekends 10:30–noon and 5–7. ✉ *Via Garibaldi and Passeggiata del Gianicolo, Trastevere.*

FAMILY **Piazza Santa Maria in Trastevere.** At the very heart of the Trastevere *rione* (district) lies this beautiful piazza, with its elegant raised fountain and sidewalk café. The showpiece is the 12th-century church of Santa Maria in Trastevere. The striking mosaics on the church's facade—which add light and color to the piazza, particularly when they're spotlighted at night—are believed to represent the Wise and Foolish Virgins. Through innumerable generations, this piazza has seen the comings and goings of tourists and travelers, intellectuals and artists, who lounge on the steps of the fountain or eat lunch at an outdoor table at Sabatini's. At night, it's the center of Trastevere's action, with street festivals, musicians, and gamboling dogs vying for attention from the throngs of people taking the evening air. ✉ *Via della Lungaretta, Via della Paglia, and Via San Cosimato, Trastevere.*

San Pietro in Montorio. Built partly on command of Ferdinand and Isabella of Spain in 1481 near the spot where, tradition says (evidently mistakenly), St. Peter was crucified, this church is a handsome and dignified edifice. It contains a number of well-known works, including, in the first chapel on the right, the *Flagellation* painted by the Venetian Sebastiano del Piombo from a design by Michelangelo, and *St. Francis in Ecstasy,* in the next-to-last chapel on the left, in which Bernini made one of his earliest experiments with concealed lighting effects.

However, the most famous work here is the circular **Tempietto** (Little Temple) in the monastery cloister next door. This sober little building—though tiny, holding only 10 people, it's actually a church in its own right—marks the spot where, legend has it, St. Peter's cross once stood. It remains one of the key Renaissance buildings in Rome. Designed by Bramante (the original architect of the new St. Peter's Basilica) in 1502, it represents one of the earliest and most successful attempts to reproduce an entirely classical building. The basic design came from a circular temple on the grounds of the emperor Hadrian's great villa at Tivoli, outside Rome. ✉ *Piazza San Pietro in Montorio 2 (Via Garibaldi), entrance to cloister and Tempietto at portal next to church, Trastevere* ☎ *06/5813940 San Pietro in Montorio, 06/5812806 Tempietto (Accademia di Spagna)* 🌐 *www.sanpietroinmontorio.it* ⏲ *Church weekdays 8:30–noon and 3–4, weekends 8:30–noon.*

9

Fodor's Choice ★ **Santa Cecilia in Trastevere.** The basilica commemorates the aristocratic St. Cecilia, patron saint of music. One of ancient Rome's most celebrated Early Christian martyrs, she was put to a supernaturally long death by the emperor Diocletian around the year AD 300. After an abortive attempt to suffocate her in the baths of her own house (a favorite means of quietly disposing of aristocrats in Roman days), she was brought before the executioner. But not even three blows of the executioner's sword could dispatch the young girl. She lingered for several days, converting others to the Christian cause, before finally dying. In 1595, her body was exhumed. It was said to look as fresh as if she still breathed—and the heart-wrenching sculpture by eyewitness Stefano Maderno that lies below the main altar was, the sculptor insisted, exactly how she looked. Time your visit to enter the cloistered convent to see what remains of Pietro Cavallini's *Last Judgment,* dating from 1293. It's the only major fresco in existence known to have been painted by Cavallini, a forerunner of

ISOLA TIBERINA

Isola Tiberina can be accessed by the Ponte Fabricio and the Ponte Cestio ✉ Trastevere.

TIPS

■ Sometimes called the world's most beautiful movie theater, the open-air Cinema d'Isola di Tiberina operates from mid-June to early September as part of Rome's big summer festival, Estate Romana (wwww.estateromana.comune.roma.it). The 450-seat Arena unfolds its silver screen against the backdrop of the ancient Ponte Fabricio, while the 50-seat CineLab is set against Ponte Garibaldi facing Trastevere. Screenings usually start at 9:30 pm; admission is €6 for the Arena, €3 CineLab. Call 06/58333113 or go towisoladelcinema.comfor more information.

■ Line up at the kiosk of "La Gratachecca del 1915" (near the Ponte Cestio) for the most yumptious frozen ices in Rome.

It's easy to overlook this tiny island in the Tiber. Don't. In terms of history and sheer loveliness, the charming Isola Tiberina—shaped like a boat about to set sail—gets high marks.

Cross onto the island via Ponte Fabricio, constructed in 62 BC, Rome's oldest remaining bridge; on the north side of the island crumbles the romantic ruin of the Ponte Rotto (Broken Bridge), which dates back to 179 BC. Descend the steps to the lovely river embankment to see the island's claim to fame: a Roman relief of the intertwined-snakes symbol of Aesculapius, the great god of healing. In 291 BC, a temple to Aesculapius was erected on the island. A ship had been sent to Epidaurus in Greece, heart of the cult of Aesculapius, to obtain a statue of the god.

As the ship sailed back up the Tiber, a great serpent was seen escaping from it and swimming to the island—a sign that a temple to Aesculapius should be built here.

In imperial times, Romans sheathed the entire island with marble to make it look like Aesculapius's ship, replete with a towering obelisk as a mast. Amazingly, the ancient sculpted ship's prow still exists. You can marvel at it on the downstream end of the embankment.

Today, medicine still reigns here. The island is home to the hospital of Fatebenefratelli (literally, "Do good, brothers"). Nearby is San Bartolomeo, built at the end of the 10th century by the Holy Roman Emperor Otto III and restored in the 18th century.

Giotto. ✉ *Piazza Santa Cecilia in Trastevere 22, Trastevere* ☎ *06/5899289* 🎫 *Church free; frescoes €2.50; underground €2.50* ⏲ *Basilica and underground, 9:15–12:45 and 4–6; frescoes, 10–12:30.*

Fodor's Choice ★ **Santa Maria in Trastevere.** Originally built sometime before the 4th century, this is certainly one of Rome's oldest, and grandest, churches. With a nave framed by a processional of two rows of gigantic columns (22 in total) taken from ancient Roman temples and an altar studded with gilded mosaics, the interior conjures up the splendor of ancient Rome better than any other in the city. Larger Roman naves exist, but none seem as majestic as this one, bathed in a sublime glow from the 12th- and 13th-century mosaics and Domenichino's gilded ceiling (1617). Supposedly Rome's first church dedicated to the Virgin Mary, it was rebuilt in the 12th century by Pope Innocent II (who hailed from Trastevere). The 19th-century portico draws attention to the facade's 800-year-old mosaics, which represent the parable of the Wise and Foolish Virgins. They enhance the whole piazza, especially at night, when the church front and bell tower are illuminated. Back inside, the church's most important mosaics, Pietro Cavallini's six panels of the *Life of the Virgin,* cover the semicircular apse. Their new sense of realism is said to have inspired the great Giotto. Note the little building labeled "Taberna Meritoria" just under the figure of the Virgin in the Nativity scene, with a stream of oil flowing from it. It recalls the legend that on the day Christ was born, a stream of pure oil flowed from the earth on the site of the piazza, signifying the coming of the grace of God. Off the piazza's northern side lies a little street called Via delle Fonte dell'Olio in honor of this miracle. ✉ *Piazza Santa Maria in Trastevere, Trastevere* ☎ *06/5814802* ⏲ *Daily 7:30 am–9 pm.*

NEED A BREAK?

Trattoria Da Augusto. You can find any kind of eatery in Trastevere, from pubs to pizzerias. But for good, honest *cucina romana* at good, honest prices you can't do better than Trattoria Da Augusto, off to the right before you reach Santa Maria in Trastevere. ✉ *Piazza de Renzi 15, Trastevere* ☎ *06/5803798.*

9

Fodor's Choice ★ **Villa Farnesina.** Money was no object to the extravagant Agostino Chigi, a banker from Siena who financed many a papal project. His munificence is evident in this elegant villa, built for him about 1511. He was especially proud of the delicate fresco decorations in the airy loggias, now glassed in to protect their artistic treasures. When Raphael could steal a little time from his work on the Vatican Stanze, he came over to execute some of the frescoes himself, notably a luminous *Galatea.* In his villa, Agostino entertained the popes and princes of 16th-century Rome. He delighted in impressing his guests at alfresco suppers held in riverside pavilions by having his servants clear the table by casting the precious silver and gold dinnerware into the Tiber. His extravagance was not quite so boundless as he wished to make it appear, however: He had nets unfurled a foot or two under the water's surface to catch the valuable ware.

In the magnificent **Loggia of Psyche** on the ground floor, Giulio Romano and others worked from Raphael's designs. Raphael's lovely *Galatea* is in the adjacent room. On the floor above you can see the trompe l'oeil effects in the aptly named **Hall of Perspectives** by Peruzzi. Agostino Chigi's bedroom, next door, was frescoed by Sodoma with scenes from the life of Alexander the Great, notably the *Wedding of Alexander and Roxanne,* which is considered to be the artist's best work. The palace also houses the **Gabinetto Nazionale delle Stampe,** a treasure-house of old prints and drawings. When the Tiber embankments were built in 1879, the remains of a classical villa were discovered under the Farnesina gardens, and their decorations are now in the Museo Nazionale Romano's collections in Palazzo Massimo alle Terme. ✉ *Via della Lungara 230, Trastevere* ☎ *06/68027268 Information, 06/68027397 Guided tour reservations* 🌐 *www.villafarnesina.it* 🎫 *€6* 🕐 *Mon.–Sat. 9–2.*

WORTH NOTING

Palazzo Corsini. A brooding example of Baroque style, the palace houses part of the 16th- and 17th-century sections of the collection of the Galleria Nazionale d'Arte Antica and is across the road from the Villa Farnesina. Among the most famous paintings in this large, dark collection are Guido Reni's *Beatrice Cenci* and Caravaggio's *St. John the Baptist.* Stop in, if only to climb the 17th-century stone staircase, itself a drama of architectural shadows and sculptural voids. Behind, but separate from, the palazzo is the **Orto Botanico** *(Mon.–Sat. 9:30–6:30 in summer, 4:30 in winter; €8),* Rome's only botanical park, containing 3,500 species of plants. There are various greenhouses around a recently restored stairway/fountain with 11 jets. Or, if you prefer, it's just a peaceful park where kids can run and play. ✉ *Via della Lungara 10, Trastevere* ☎ *06/68802323 Galleria Corsini, 06/32810 Galleria Corsini tickets, 06/49912436 Orto Botanico* 🌐 *www.galleriaborghese.it* 🎫 *€5* 🕐 *Tues.–Sun. 8:30–7:30.*

Piazza in Piscinula. One of Trastevere's most historic and time-burnished squares, this piazza takes its name from some ancient Roman baths on the site (*piscina* means "pool"). The tiny church of **San Benedetto** on the piazza is the smallest church in the city and, despite its 18th-century facade, dates back to the 4th century AD. Opposite is the medieval **Casa dei Mattei** (Mattei House). The rich and powerful Mattei family lived here until the 16th century, when, after a series of murders on the premises, they decided to move out of the district entirely, crossing the river to build their magnificent palace in the Jewish Ghetto. ✉ *Via della Lungaretta, Piazza della Gensola, Via in Piscinula, and Via Lungarina, Trastevere.*

San Francesco a Ripa. Near Trastevere's southern end, this Baroque church attached to a 13th-century Franciscan monastery holds one of Bernini's last works, a statue of the Blessed Ludovica Albertoni. This is perhaps Bernini's most hallucinatory sculpture, a dramatically lighted figure ecstatic at the prospect of entering heaven as she expires on her deathbed. She clutches her breast as a symbol, art historians say, of the "milk of human kindness" and Christian *caritas* (charity). Gracing the altar is Baciccia's *Madonna and St. Anne.* St. Francis is supposed to have stayed at this monastery when visiting the city; to see his cell, ask the Sacristan. The side chapels of the church, including Bernini's, have been restored and are open to the public. ✉ *Piazza San Francesco d'Assisi 88, Trastevere* ☎ *06/5819020* 🌐 *www.sanfrancescoaripa.com* 🕐 *Daily 8–1 and 2–7:30.*

AVENTINO AND TESTACCIO

10

GETTING ORIENTED

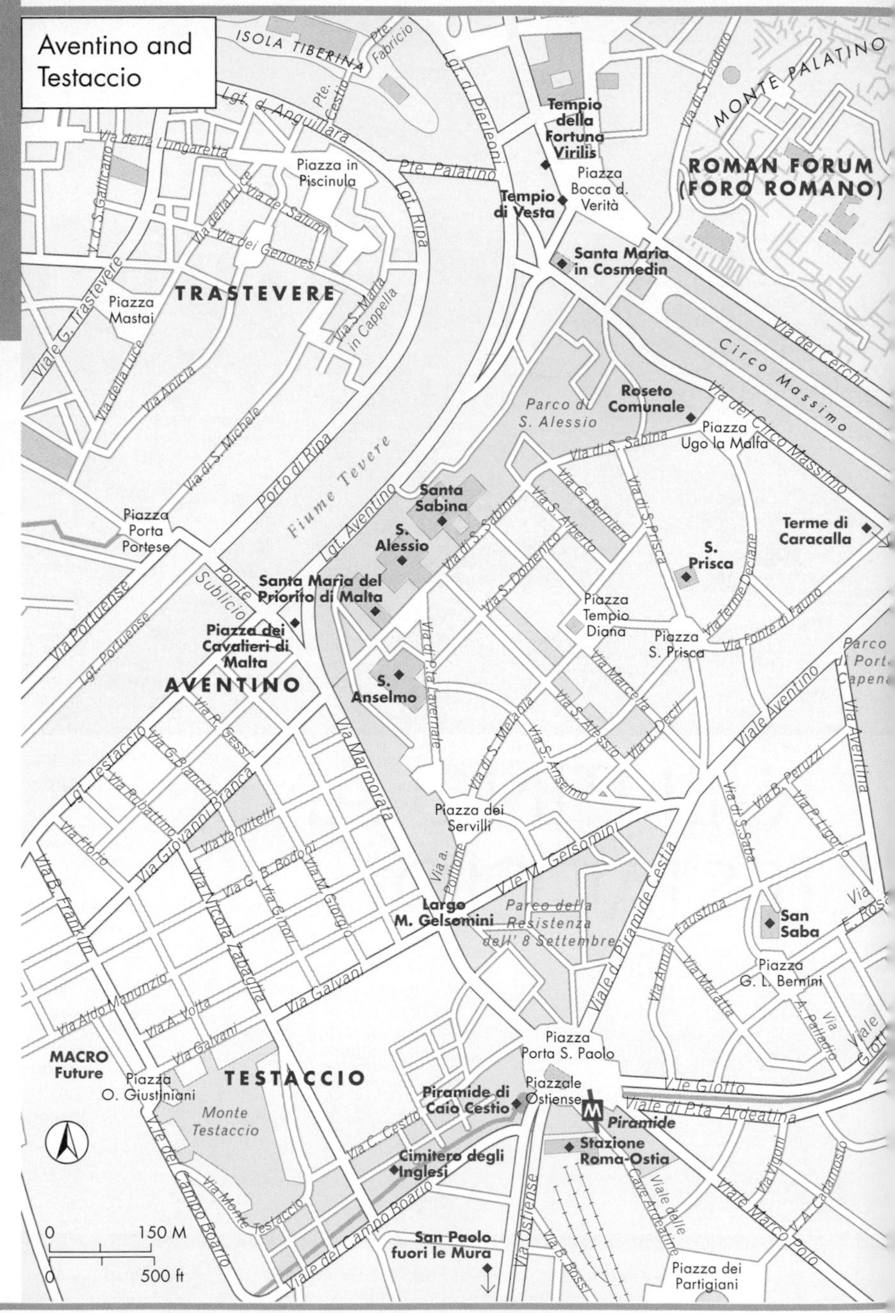

TOP REASONS TO GO

Santa Maria in Cosmedin: Test your truthfulness (or someone else's) at the mouth of the Bocca della Verità.

Cimitero degli Inglesi: Swoon over Keats's body and Shelley's heart in this romantic graveyard.

Piazza Cavalieri di Malta: Peek through the keyhole of the Priorato di Malta for a privileged view—one of Rome's most surprising delights.

Tempting Testaccio: Like New York City's Meatpacking District, this neighborhood is a combination of factories and nightclubs.

Roseto Comunale: Overlooking the Circo Massimo, this rose garden offers a fitting and fragrant vestibule to Rome's most poetic hill.

Baths of Caracalla: South of the lovely Villa Celimontana parks tower the Terme di Caracalla, ruins of one of the most spectacular bathing complexes in ancient Rome.

QUICK BITES

Cristalli di Zucchero. This chic, Parisian-influenced bakery offers delicious macarons, pastries, and cakes (miniatures, too) so pretty, you'll feel bad digging in. Almost. ✉ *Via di San Teodoro 88, Aventino* ☎ *06/69920945* 🌐 *www.cristallidizucchero.it.*

Sicilia e Duci. In the heart of Testaccio, this Sicilian bakery boasts mouthwatering—and gorgeous—pastries, cakes, and cannoli. ✉ *Via Marmorata 87/89, Testaccio* ☎ *06/5743766.*

MAKING THE MOST OF YOUR TIME

Travelers with limited time often see just one sight here: the Bocca della Verità, or "Mouth of Truth." It's a shame, though, as there are some other real gems, especially on a nice day. On the Aventine hill, duck into the Cimitero degli Inglesi, one of the most atmospheric cemeteries in Rome, and don't miss the Giardino degli Aranci (Garden of the Oranges) for its view over the Tiber and Rome. Next to the Giardino is Santa Sabina, one of Rome's finest ancient churches, and the Piazza Cavalieri di Malta, whose keyhole has a special surprise. Visit the Aventine's neighboring quarter, Testaccio, in the evening, when locals take their passeggiata (stroll), and the restaurants and pizzerias heat up with diners. You can stay out until the wee hours here, as this area is one of the most popular for dance clubs and music.

GETTING HERE

It's a a spectacular 20-minute walk through ancient ruins like the Circo Massimo to reach the Aventine hill on foot from either the Roman Forum or the Campidoglio. There's also a metro stop of the same name at the foot of Aventino. Coming from the Colosseum or Trastevere, hop on Bus No. 3. From the Spanish Steps, take Bus No. 160; from Termini, Bus No. 175. For the Testaccio section, use the Piramide (Ostiense) Metro stop.

Sightseeing
★★
Nightlife
★★★
Dining
★★
Lodging
★★★
Shopping
★

While Romans consider these neighborhoods central, they are off the beaten path just enough to be little-known to tourists—and to have retained their unique characters, from the well-heeled, flower-draped residential quarter of the Aventine to the traditional-yet-trendy riverside neighborhood of Testaccio. For travelers with a little extra time (or who simply want to see a Rome beyond the Trevi Fountain and Spanish Steps), making a visit to these areas allows a glimpse into what the Eternal City really means for its residents.

AVENTINO

Updated by Amanda Ruggeri

One of the seven hills on which the city was founded, the Aventine hill enjoys a serenity hard to find elsewhere in Rome. Trills of birdsong win out over the din of traffic. This is highly appropriate, as the hill's name derives from the Latin *avis* ("bird"), the swallows here having once featured in the bird-watching contest whereby Romulus and Remus decided the best site on which to build their city.

This is a rarefied district, where some houses still have their own bell towers and private gardens are called "parks," without exaggeration. Like the emperors of old on the Palatine, the fortunate residents here look out over the Circus Maximus and the river, winding its way far below. And today's travelers still enjoy the great views, including the famous one spotted through the peculiar keyhole at the gates to the headquarters of the Knights of Malta, which may be the most peered-through in the world—take a look and see why.

TOP ATTRACTIONS

Fodor's Choice ★ **Piazza dei Cavalieri di Malta.** Peek through the keyhole of the **Priorato di Malta,** the walled compound of the Knights of Malta, and you'll get a surprising eyeful: a picture-perfect view of the dome of St. Peter's Basilica, far across the city. This priory landmarks the Piazza dei Cavalieri di Malta. Piranesi—18th-century Rome's foremost engraver—is more famous for drawing architecture than creating it, yet the square is his work along with the priory (1765) within. Stone insignia of the Knights notwithstanding, the square's most famed feature is that initially nondescript keyhole in the dark green door of Number 3. Bend slightly and surprise your eyes with a view that is worth walking miles for. As for the Order of the Knights of Malta, it is the world's oldest and most exclusive order of chivalry, founded in the Holy Land during the Crusades. Though nominally ministering to the sick in those early days, a role that has since become the order's raison d'être, the knights amassed huge tracts of land in the Middle East. From 1530 they were based on the Mediterranean island of Malta but in 1798 Napoléon expelled them and, in 1834, they established themselves in Rome. If you want to go inside, you can book a 1.5-hour tour of the headquarters (€15). ✉ *Via Santa Sabina and Via Porta Lavernale, Aventino* ☎ *06/61661527 to book tours* Ⓜ *Circo Massimo. Tram 3; Bus 60, 81, 118, 175, 271, 715.*

Roseto Comunale. As signified by the paths shaped like a menorah, this was once a Jewish cemetery (a tombstone is still visible on the side of the garden across from Valle Murcia, the name for the swamp that once separated this area from the Palatine). The garden is laid out to reflect the history of roses from antiquity to the present day. ✉ *Viale di Valle Murcia, Aventino* ☎ *06/5746810* ⏲ *May–June, daily 8–7:30* Ⓜ *Circo Massimo. Tram 3; Bus 60, 81, 118, 160, 271, 628, 715.*

FAMILY
Fodor's Choice ★

Santa Maria in Cosmedin. Though this is one of Rome's oldest churches, with a haunting, almost exotic interior, it plays second fiddle to the renowned artifact installed in the church portico. The **Bocca della Verità** (Mouth of Truth) is in reality nothing more than an ancient drain cover, unearthed during the Middle Ages. Legend has it, however, that the teeth will clamp down on a liar's hand . . . and to tell a lie with your hand in the fearsome mouth is to risk losing it. Hordes of tourists line up to take the test every day, with kids especially getting a kick out of it. Few churches, inside or out, are as picturesque as this one. The church was built in the 6th century for the city's burgeoning Greek population. Heavily restored at the end of the 19th century, it has the typical basilica form, and stands across from the **Piazza della Bocca della Verità,** originally the location of the Forum Boarium, ancient Rome's cattle market, and later the site of public executions. ✉ *Piazza Santa Maria in Cosmedin, Aventino* ☎ *06/6787759* ⏲ *May–Sept., daily 9:30–5:50; Oct.–Apr., daily 9:30–4:50* Ⓜ *Circo Massimo. Bus 3, 60, 75, 81, 118, 160, 175, 271, 628.*

Santa Sabina. This Early Christian basilica demonstrates the severe—but lovely—simplicity common to churches of its era. Although some of the side chapels were added in the 16th and 17th centuries, the essential form is as Rome's Christians knew it in the 5th century. Once bright with mosaics, today the church only has one: that above the entrance door (its gold letters announce how the church was founded by Peter of Illyria, "rich for the poor," under Pope Celestine I). Meanwhile, the mosaics in the apse have been at least partially reproduced in Taddeo Zuccari's Renaissance fresco of Christ and his apostles. The beautifully carved, 5th-century cedar doors to the left of the outside entrance are the oldest of their kind in existence. ✉ *Piazza Pietro d'Illiria 1, Via di Santa Sabina, Aventino* ☎ *06/579401* ⏲ *Daily 6:30–12:45 and 3:30–6* Ⓜ *Circo Massimo. Tram 3; Bus 60, 75, 81, 118, 160, 175, 715.*

Tempio della Fortuna Virilis. A picture-perfect, if dollhouse-size, Roman temple, this rectangular edifice from the 2nd century BC is built in the Greek style, as was the norm in Rome's early years. It owes its fine state of preservation to the fact that it was consecrated and used as a Christian church. ✉ *Piazza Bocca della Verit, Aventino* Ⓜ *Circo Massimo. Tram 3; Bus 60, 75, 81, 118, 160, 175, 271.*

Tempio di Vesta. Long called the Temple of Vesta because of its similarity in shape to the building of that name in the Roman Forum, it's now recognized as a temple to Hercules Victor. All but one of the 20 Corinthian columns of this evocative ruin remain intact. Like its next-door neighbor, the Tempio della Fortuna Virilis, it was built in the 2nd century BC. Recent city works have given the little park around the temple a new look, with lovely landscaped green space and benches for relaxing. ✉ *Piazza Bocca della Verità, Aventino* Ⓜ *Circo Massimo. Tram 3; Bus 60, 75, 81, 118, 160, 175, 271.*

FAMILY **Terme di Caracalla** (*Baths of Caracalla*). The Terme di Caracalla are some of Rome's most massive—yet least-visited—ruins. They're also a peek into how Romans turned "bathing" into one of the most lavish leisure activities imaginable.

Begun in AD 206 by the emperor Septimius Severus and completed by his son, Caracalla, the 28-acre complex could accommodate 1,600 bathers at a time. Along with an Olympic-size swimming pool and baths, the complex also boasted two different gymnasiums for weight-lifting, boxing, and wrestling, a library with both Latin and Greek texts, and shops, restaurants, and gardens. All of the services depended on slaves, who checked clients' robes, rubbed them down, and saw to all of their needs. Under the magnificent marble pavement of the stately halls, other slaves toiled in a warren of tiny rooms and passages, stoking the fires that heated the water.

Taking a bath was a long and complex process—something that makes more sense if you see it, first and foremost, as a social activity. You began in the *sudatoria,* a series of small rooms resembling saunas. Here you sat and sweated. From these you moved to the *caldarium,* a large, circular room that was humid rather than simply hot. This was where the actual business of washing went on. You used a *strigil,* or scraper, to get the dirt off; if you were rich, your slave did this for you. Next stop: the warm(-ish) *tepidarium,* which helped you start cooling down. Finally, you splashed around in the *frigidarium,* a swimming pool filled with cold water.

Today, the complex is a shell of its former self. While some black-and-white mosaic fragments remain, you have to use your imagination to see the interior as it would have been, filled with opulent mosaics, frescoes, and sculptures, including the famous Farnese Bull. But for getting a sense of the sheer size of ancient Rome's ambitions, few places are better. The walls still tower, the spaces still dwarf, and—if you try—you almost can hear the laughs of long-gone bathers, splashing in the pools. ■ **TIP→ If**

you're here in the summer, don't miss the chance to catch an open-air opera or ballet in the baths, put on by the Teatro dell'Opera di Roma (*€25–€110; 06/48078400*). ✉ *Via delle Terme di Caracalla 52, Aventino* ☎ *06/39967700* 🌐 *www.coopculture.it* 🎫 *€6 (includes Villa dei Quintili and Mausoleo di Cecilia Metella)* 🕒 *Mon. 9–1, Tues.–Sun. 9–4:30* Ⓜ *Circo Massimo.*

WORD OF MOUTH

"In the once-proletariat Testaccio neighborhood, we first visited Volpetti (Via Marmorata 47), perhaps Rome's best food store, famed for its hard-to-find, Slow Food–resurrected Roman foodstuffs." —wrldpeas

WORTH NOTING

Centrale Montemartini. After visiting Rome's many old, art-cluttered palaces, the Centrale Montemartini feels like a breath of fresh air. Rome's first electricity plant, reopened as a permanent museum in 2005, houses the overflow of ancient art from the Capitoline Museum's collection. With Roman sculptures and mosaics set against industrial machinery and pipes, nowhere else in Rome is the contrast between ancient and modern more stark—or enjoyable. A pleasure, too, is the sheer space of the building; even better than the soaring ceilings and high walls is the fact that you're likely to be one of the few visitors here, making it the perfect stop for those feeling claustrophobic from Rome's crowds. Unusually, the collection is organized by the area where the ancient pieces were found. Standout pieces include the 4th-century AD mosaic of a hunting scene, complete with horseman driving his sword into a boar, and the two portrait-heads so well preserved that they still, unusually, retain flakes of the gold that once gilded them. ✉ *Via Ostiense 106, Aventino* ☎ *06/0608* 🌐 *centralemontemartini.org* 🎫 *€6.50* 🕒 *Tues.–Sun. 9–7* Ⓜ *Garbatella. Bus 23, 271, 769, 770.*

San Saba. Formerly a monastery founded by monks of the order of San Saba after they had fled from Jerusalem following the Arab invasion, this is a major monument of Romanesque Rome. Inside, an almost rustic interior harbors a famed Cosmatesque mosaic pavement and a hodgepodge of ancient marble pieces. ✉ *Piazza Gianlorenzo Bernini 20, Via San Saba, Aventino* ☎ *06/64580140* 🌐 *www.sansaba.it* 🕒 *Weekdays and Sat. 8–noon and 4–7:10, Sun. 9:30–1 and 4–7:30* Ⓜ *Circo Massimo.*

TESTACCIO

Testaccio is perhaps the world's only district built on broken pots: the hill of the same name was born from discarded pottery used to store oil, wine, and other goods loaded from the nearby Ripa, when Rome had a port and the Tiber was once a mighty river to an empire. Quiet during the day, but on Saturday buzzing with the very loud music from rows of discos and clubs (this is sometimes hailed as Rome's new "Left Bank" neighborhood), the area is also a must for those seeking authentic and comparatively cheap Roman cuisine.

TOP ATTRACTIONS

Cimitero degli Inglesi (*Non-Catholic or English Cemetery*). Reminiscent of a country churchyard, this famed cemetery was intended for the interment of non-Catholics. This is where you'll find the tomb of John Keats, who tragically died in Rome after succumbing to consumption at age 25 in 1821. The stone is famously inscribed with "Here lies one whose name was writ in water" (the poet said no dates or name should appear). Nearby is the place where Shelley's heart was buried, as well as the tombs of Goethe's son, Italian anarchist Antonio Gramsci, and America's famed beat poet Gregory Corso. It is about a 20-minute walk south from the Arch of Constantine along Via San Gregorio and Viale Aventino, but the easiest way to get here is to catch the Metro B line from Termini, which deposits you almost directly outside the cemetery. ✉ *Via Caio Cestio 6, Testaccio* ☎ *06/5741900* 🌐 *www.cemeteryrome.it* 🎫 *Suggested donation €3* ⏲ *Mon.–Sat. 9–5, Sun. 9–1; if door is closed, ring bell for cemetery custodian* Ⓜ *Piramide. Tram 3; Bus 23, 30, 60, 75, 95, 118, 715.*

FAMILY **Piramide di Caio Cestio.** This monumental tomb was designed in 12 BC for the immensely wealthy praetor Gaius Cestius in the form of a 120-foot-tall pyramid. Though little else is known about him, he clearly had a taste for grandeur—and the then-trendy Egyptian style. The structure was completed in a little less than a year. The pyramid currently is undergoing a much-needed restoration (paid for with a €1 million donation by Japanese fashion tycoon Yazu Yagi) and is covered in scaffolding; the project is expected to finish by the end of 2014. ✉ *Piazzale Ostiense, Testaccio* 🌐 *www.pierreci.it* Ⓜ *Piramide. Bus 3, 30, 60, 75, 95, 118, 130, 175, 719.*

San Paolo fuori le Mura (*St. Paul's Outside the Walls*). For all its dreary location and dull exterior (19th-century British writer Augustus Hare said the church resembled "a very ugly railway station"), St. Paul's is one of Rome's most historic and important churches. Its size, second only to St. Peter's Basilica, allows ample space for the 272 roundels depicting every pope from St. Peter to current Pope Francis (found below the ceiling, with spaces left blank for pontiffs to come). Built in the 4th century AD by Constantine over the site where St. Paul had been buried, St. Paul's was then rebuilt and enlarged. But in July 1823, a fire burned the church to the ground. Although the rebuilt St. Paul's has a sort of monumental grandeur, it's only in the cloisters that you get a real sense of what must have been the magnificence of the original building (for guided tours for a fee of €4, call *06/69880800*). In the middle of the nave is the famous baldachino created by sculptor Arnolfo di Cambio. ✉ *Piazzale San Paolo, Via Ostiense 190, Testaccio* ☎ *06/69880800* 🌐 *www.basilicasanpaolo.org* 🎫 *Church free; cloister €4* ⏲ *Daily 7–6:30; cloister daily 8–6:15* Ⓜ *Piramide.*

MONTI, ESQUILINO, CELIO, AND THE VIA APPIA ANTICA

with Pigneto, San Giovanni, and San Lorenzo

GETTING ORIENTED

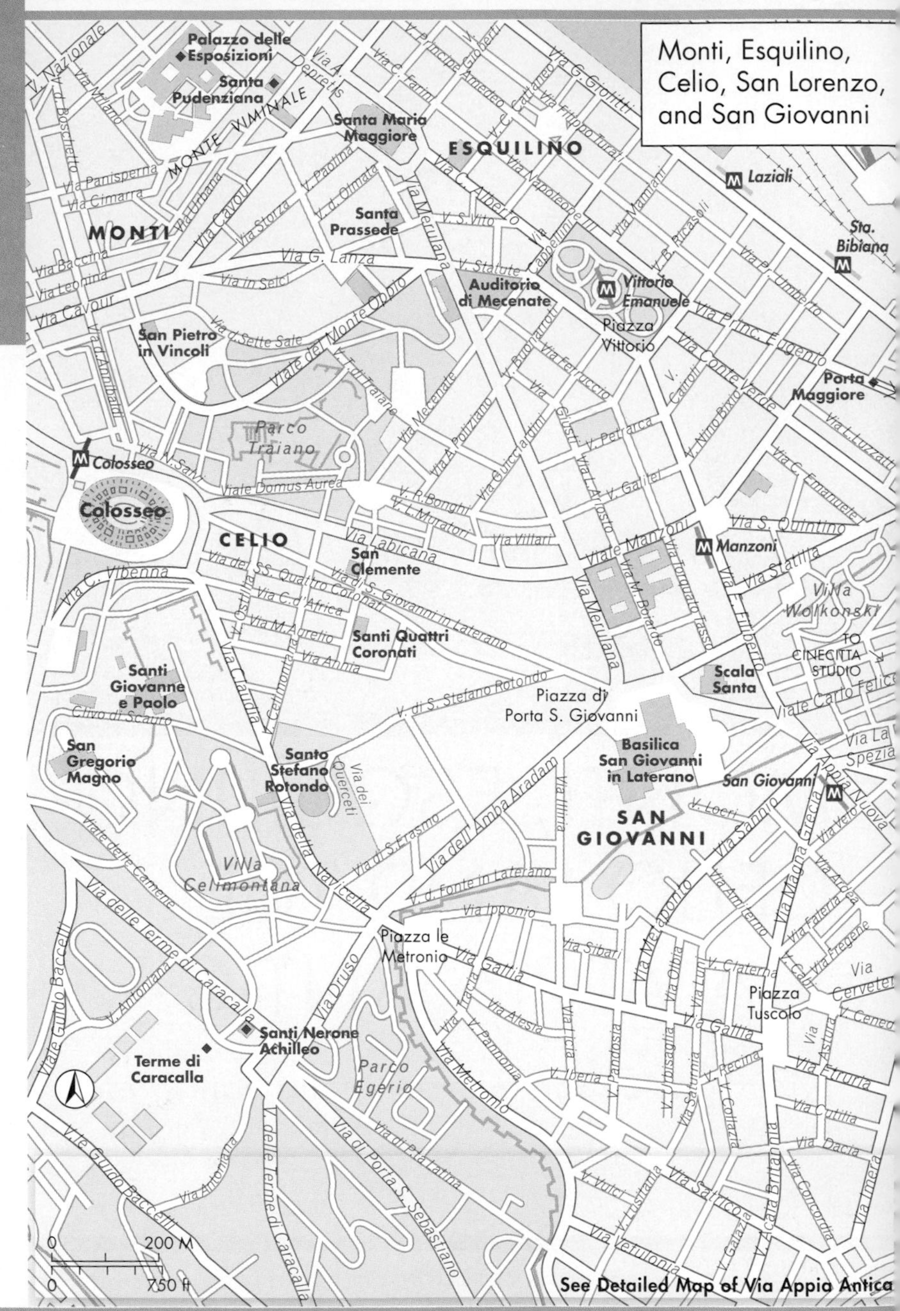

TOP REASONS TO GO

San Pietro in Vincoli: Hike uphill past Lucrezia Borgia's palace to visit Michelangelo's magisterial *Moses.*

San Clemente: Hurtle back through three eras—ancient Roman, Early Christian, and medieval—by descending through four excavated levels of this venerated church.

Magnificent Mosaics: In a neighborhood once home to the first Christians, Santa Pudenziana gleams with a stunning 4th-century mosaic of Christ while Santa Prassede shimmers with Byzantine beauty nearby.

Catacomb Country: Be careful exploring the underground graves of the earliest Christians—one wrong turn and you may only surface days later.

QUICK BITE

Enoteca Il Pentagrappolo. With its exposed-brick arches and soft lighting, Il Pentagrappolo offers an ample spread of cheeses and salamis as well as more than 250 wines. On Thursday, Friday, and Saturday nights, there's live jazz, blues, and bossa nova. ✉ *Via Celimontana 21/B, Celio* ☎ *06/7096301* 🌐 *www.ilpentagrappolo.com.*

GETTING HERE

The Esquilino hill can be reached via the Piazza Vittorio Emanuele subway stop, which is one stop from Termini station. The Monti area (running down one side of the Esquilino to the Roman Forum) can be reached by the Cavour Metro stop on Line B. Bus No. 117 runs from Piazza del Popolo and the Corso to both Celio and Monti districts on the Esquilino. Bus No. 3 from Trastevere and Bus No. 75 from Termini reach Celio, about a 5-minute walk from the Colosseo stop.

MAKING THE MOST OF YOUR TIME

Some of Rome's least touristy and best-loved neighborhoods, these areas also have a great deal to explore—especially in the way of ancient sights. If you have limited time, combine your exploration here with your discovery of the ancient Forum and Colosseum, which are nearby. From those sights, it's a short walk up the hill to see the multilayered Basilica of San Clemente and the gem of a medieval church Santi Quattro Coronati. Head back to the Colosseum area and then toward the Esquiline hill by using the Colosseo Metro steps to reach the grandly scenic Largo Agnesi overlook. On the north side of the Colosseum, in the quarter known as Monti, you'll find San Pietro in Vincoli, home to Michelangelo's *Moses.* As you head farther northeast, don't miss gigantic Santa Maria Maggiore; nearby are wonderful mosaics in San Prassede and Santa Pudenziana. But make sure to give yourself at least a couple of hours to explore the neighborhood of Monti itself, with its artisanal shops, fine trattorias, and high-end boutiques—the best of old and new Rome, all in one tiny, proud *rione* (district).

Sightseeing ★★★★
Nightlife ★★
Dining ★★★
Lodging ★★★★
Shopping ★★

Several neighborhoods come together here, just north of the Roman forum and Colosseum. They range from the bustling, multicultural Esquilino neighborhood to the super-trendy, yet still traditional, ancient rione of Monti. Most travelers will find themselves passing through at least part of the area, either when they come into the Termini train station or pay a visit to Michelangelo's Moses at the Church of San Pietro in Vincoli. Head farther south for the evocative Via Appia Antica, dotted with ruins and ancient catacombs.

MONTI

Updated by Amanda Ruggeri

As the hill starts to slope downward from Termini station, right around Santa Maria Maggiore, the streets become cobblestoned, the palazzos prettier, and the boutiques higher-end. This is the area known as Monti, the oldest rione in Rome. Gladiators, prostitutes, and even Caesar made their homes in this area that stretches from Santa Maria Maggiore down to the Forum. Today, Monti is one of the best-loved neighborhoods in Rome, known for its appealing mix of medieval streets, old-school trattorias, and hip boutiques.

TOP ATTRACTIONS

Palazzo delle Esposizioni. Since its 2007 reopening, the Palazzo delle Esposizioni has been bombarding Rome with singularly amazing exhibitions such as New York State of Mind, Rothko, Calder, Darwin, and even Bulgari jewelry. The complex also has an expansive coffee bar and a restaurant with a late-evening bar. ✉ *Via Nazionale 194, Monti* ☎ *06/39967500* 🌐 *www.palazzoesposizioni.it.*

San Pietro in Vincoli. Michelangelo's *Moses*, carved in the early 16th century for the never-completed tomb of Pope Julius II, has put this church on the map. The tomb was to include dozens of statues and stand nearly 40 feet tall when installed in St. Peter's Basilica. But only three statues—*Moses* and the two that flank it here, *Leah* and *Rachel*—had been completed when Julius died. Julius's successor as pope, from a rival family, had other plans for Michelangelo, and the tomb was abandoned unfinished. The fierce power of this remarkable sculpture dominates its setting. People say that you can see the sculptor's profile in the lock of Moses's beard right under his lip, and that the pope's profile is also there somewhere. As for the rest of the church, St. Peter takes second billing to Moses. The reputed chains (*vincoli*) that bound St. Peter during his imprisonment by the Romans in Jerusalem are in a bronze and crystal urn under the main altar. Other treasures in the church include a 7th-century mosaic of St. Sebastian, in front of the second altar to the left of the main altar, and, by the door, the tomb of the Pollaiuolo brothers, two lesser 15th-century Florentine artists. ✉ *Piazza San Pietro in Vincoli, Monti* ☎ *06/97844952* ⏲ *Apr.–Sept., daily 8–12:30 and 3–7; Oct.–Mar., daily 8–12:30 and 3–6* Ⓜ *Cavour.*

A CALENDAR MIX-UP

Every August 5, a special mass in Santa Maria Maggiore's Cappella Sistina commemorates the miracle that led to the founding of the basilica: the Virgin Mary appeared in a dream to Pope Liberio and ordered him to build a church in her honor on the spot where snow would fall on the night of August 5 (an event about as likely in a Roman August as snow in the Sahara). The Madonna of the Snows is celebrated with a shower of white rose petals from the ceiling.

Santa Maria Maggiore. The exterior of the church, from the broad sweep of steps on Via Cavour to the more elaborate facade on Piazza Santa Maria Maggiore, is that of a gracefully curving 18th-century building, a fine example of the Baroque architecture of the period. But Santa Maria Maggiore is one of the oldest churches in Rome, built around 440 by Pope Sixtus III. One of the four great pilgrimage churches of Rome, it's also the city center's best example of an Early Christian basilica—one of the immense, hall-like structures derived from ancient Roman civic buildings and divided into thirds by two great rows of columns marching up the nave. The other six major basilicas in Rome (San Giovanni in Laterano and St. Peter's Basilica are the most famous) have been entirely transformed, or even rebuilt. Paradoxically, the major reason why this church is such a striking example of Early Christian design is that the same man who built the incongruous exteriors about 1740, Ferdinando Fuga, also conscientiously restored the interior, throwing out later additions and, crucially, replacing a number of the great columns.

Precious 5th-century mosaics high on the nave walls and on the triumphal arch in front of the main altar are splendid testimony to the basilica's venerable age. Those along the nave show 36 scenes from the Old Testament (unfortunately, tough to see clearly without binoculars), and those on the arch illustrate the Annunciation and the Youth of Christ. The resplendent carved wood ceiling dates from the early 16th century; it's supposed to have been gilded with the first gold brought from the New World. The inlaid marble pavement (called Cosmatesque after the family of master artisans who developed the technique) in the central nave is even older, dating from the 12th century.

TO MARKET, TO MARKET

For a piece of the new buzzing Esquiline Hill action, try one of Rome's most distinctive luncheon options: the Piazza Vittorio Emanuele, a historic Roman square and its famed food market nearby on Via Principe Amadeo. The surrounding streets are chockablock with international food stores and offer a glimpse at the emerging immigrant scene in the city.

The **Cappella Sistina** (Sistine Chapel), which opens onto the right-hand nave, was created by architect Domenico Fontana for Pope Sixtus V in 1585. Elaborately decorated with precious marbles "liberated" from the monuments of ancient Rome, the chapel includes a lower-level museum in which some 13th-century sculptures by Arnolfo da Cambio are all that's left of what was the once richly endowed chapel of the *presepio* (Christmas crèche), looted during the Sack of Rome in 1527.

Directly opposite, on the church's other side, stands the **Cappella Paolina** (Pauline Chapel), a rich Baroque setting for the tombs of the Borghese popes Paul V—who commissioned the chapel in 1611 with the declared intention of outdoing Sixtus's chapel across the nave—and Clement VIII. The **Cappella Sforza** (Sforza Chapel) next door was designed by Michelangelo and completed by della Porta. Just right of the altar, next to his father, lies Gian Lorenzo Bernini; his monument is an engraved slab, as humble as the tombs of his patrons are grand. ■ **TIP→ Above the loggia, the outside mosaic of Christ raising his hand in blessing is one of Rome's most beautiful sights, especially when lit up at night.** ✉ *Piazza Santa Maria Maggiore, Monti* ☎ *06/69886802* 💳 *Free; museum €4* ⏲ *Daily 7–6:45; museum daily 9:30–6:30* Ⓜ *Termini.*

Santa Prassede. This small, inconspicuous 9th-century church is known above all for the exquisite **Cappella di San Zenone,** just to the left of the entrance. It gleams with vivid mosaics that reflect their Byzantine inspiration. Though much less classical and naturalistic than the earlier mosaics of Santa Pudenziana, they are no less splendid, and the composition of four angels hovering on the sky-blue vault is one of the masterstrokes of Byzantine art. Note the square halo over the head of Theodora, mother of St. Pasquale I, the pope who built this church. It indicates that she was still alive when she was depicted by the artist. The chapel also contains one curious relic: a miniature pillar, supposedly part of the column at which Christ was flogged during the Passion. It was brought to Rome in the 13th century. Over the main altar, the magnificent mosaics on the arch and apse are also in rigid Byzantine style. In them, Pope Pasquale I wears the square halo of the living and holds a model of his church. ✉ *Via di Santa Prassede 9/a, Monti* ☎ *06/4882456* ⏲ *Daily 7–noon and 4–6:30* Ⓜ *Cavour.*

Fodor's Choice ★ **Santa Pudenziana.** Outside of Ravenna, Rome has some of the most opulent mosaics in Italy and this church has one of the most striking examples. Commissioned during the papacy of Innocent I, its late 4th-century apse mosaic represents "Christ Teaching the Apostles" and sits high on the wall perched above a Baroque altarpiece surrounded by a bevy of florid 18th-century paintings. Not only is it the largest Early Christian apse mosaic extant, it is remarkable for its iconography. At the center sits Christ Enthroned, looking a bit like a Roman emperor, presiding over his apostles. Each apostle faces the spectator, literally rubs shoulders with his companion (unlike earlier hieratic styles where each figure is isolated), and bears an individualized expression. Above the figures and a landscape that symbolizes the Heavenly Jerusalem float the signs of the four evangelists in a blue sky flecked with an orange sunset, all done in thousands of tesserae. This extraordinary composition seems a sort of paleo-Christian forerunner of Raphael's *School of Athens* in the Vatican.

To either side of Christ, Sts. Praxedes and Pudenziana hold wreaths over the heads of Sts. Peter and Paul. These two women were actually daughters of the Roman senator Pudens (probably the one mentioned in 2 Timothy 4:21), whose family befriended both apostles. During the persecutions of Nero, both sisters collected the blood of many martyrs and then suffered the same fate. Pudenziana transformed her house into a church, but this namesake church was constructed over a 2nd-century bathhouse. Beyond the sheer beauty of the mosaic work, the size, rich detail, and number of figures make this both the last gasp of ancient Roman art and one of the first monuments of early Christianity. ✉ *Via Urbana 160, Monti* ☎ *06/4814622* ⏲ *Daily 8:30–noon and 3–6* Ⓜ *Termini.*

ESQUILINO

Rome's most sprawling hill—the Esquiline—lies at the edge of the tourist maps. Even Imperial Rome could not have matched this minicosmopolis for sheer internationalism. Right around Termini, sons of the soil, the so-called "romani romani," mingle with Chinese, Sri Lankans, Sikhs, and a hundred nationalities in between. A highlight is the Nuovo Mercato Esquilino, a covered market hall where goods from the four corners of the earth are sold in a multitude of languages. This is also where you can find some of the city's best ethnic restaurants and cheapest B&Bs—but not the cobblestone-street atmosphere that most think of when they think of Rome.

EXPLORING

Porta Maggiore (*Main Gate*). The massive 1st-century AD monument is not only a *porta* (city gate), but part of the Acqua Claudia aqueduct. It gives you an idea of the grand scale of ancient Roman public works. On the Piazzale Labicano side of the portal, to the east, is the curious **Baker's Tomb,** erected in the 1st century BC by a prosperous baker, shaped like an oven to signal the deceased's trade. The site is especially accessible given that Rome's first tram depot (going back to 1889) is just nearby. ✉ *Junction of Via Eleniana, Via di Porta Maggiore, and Via Casilina, Esquilino* Ⓜ *Tram 3, 5, 14, 19.*

PIGNETO

This is the latest up-and-coming hip neighborhood in Rome, with lots of young people and gritty but cool restaurants and cafés. It a bus ride from the Termini stations.

CELIO

On the border of Monti, from the Colosseum west toward Piazza San Giovanni, the neighborhood of Celio is a tranquil, lovely residential area replete with medieval churches and ruins. Sights not to miss here include the Basilica of San Clemente, the church of Santi Quattro Coronati, and the church of Santo Stefano Rotondo.

TOP ATTRACTIONS

Case Romane del Celio. Formerly accessible only through the church of San Giovanni e Paolo, this important ancient Roman excavation was opened in 2002 as a full-fledged museum. An underground honeycomb of rooms, this comprises the lower levels of a so-called "insula," or apartment tower, the heights of which were a wonder to ancient Roman contemporaries. Through the door on the left of the Clivo di Scauro lane a portico leads to the Room of the Genie, where painted figures grace the walls as if untouched by two millennia. Farther on is the Confessio altar of Sts. John and Paul, officials at Constantine's court who were executed under Julian the Apostate. Still lower is the Antiquarium, where state-of-the-art lighting showcases amphorae, pots, and stamped ancient Roman bricks, the stamps so fresh they might've been imprinted yesterday. ✉ *Clivus Scauri, Celio* ☎ *06/70454544* 🌐 *www.caseromane.it* 🎟 *€6* 🕒 *Thurs.–Mon. 10–1 and 3–6* Ⓜ *Colosseo. Bus 60, 75, 81, 117, 118, 175; Tram 3.*

Fodor's Choice ★ **San Clemente.** One of the most impressive archaeological sites in Rome, San Clemente is a historical triple-decker. A 12th-century church was built on top of a 4th-century church, which in turn was built over a 2nd-century pagan temple to the god Mithras and 1st-century Roman apartments. The layers were rediscovered in 1857, when a curious prior, Friar Joseph Mullooly, started excavations beneath the present basilica. Today, you can descend to explore all three.

The upper church (at street level) is a gem even on its own. In the apse, a glittering 12th-century mosaic shows Jesus on a cross that turns into a living tree. Green acanthus leaves swirl and teem with small scenes of everyday life. Early Christian symbols, including doves, vines, and fish, decorate the 4th-century marble choir screens. In the left nave, the Castiglioni chapel holds frescoes painted around 1400 by the Florentine artist Masolino da Panicale (1383–1440), a key figure in the introduction of realism and one-point perspective into Renaissance painting. Note the large Crucifixion and scenes from the lives of Sts. Catherine, Ambrose, and Christopher, plus an Annunciation (over the entrance).

To the right of the sacristy (and bookshop), descend the stairs to the 4th-century church, used until 1084, when it was damaged beyond repair during a siege of the area by the Norman prince Robert Guiscard. Still intact are some vibrant 11th-century frescoes depicting stories from the life of St. Clement. Don't miss the last fresco on the left, in what used to be the central nave. It includes a particularly colorful quote—including "Go on, you sons of harlots, pull!"—that's not only unusual for a religious painting, but one of the earliest examples of written vernacular Italian.

Descend an additional set of stairs to the mithraeum, a shrine dedicated to the god Mithras. His cult spread from Persia and gained a hold in Rome during the 2nd and 3rd centuries AD. Mithras was believed to have been born in a cave and was thus worshipped in underground, cavernous chambers, where initiates into the all-male cult would share a meal while reclining on stone couches, some visible here along with the altar block. Most such pagan shrines in Rome were destroyed by Christians, who often built churches over their remains, as happened here. ✉ *Via San Giovanni in Laterano 108, Celio* ☎ *06/7740021* 🌐 *www.basilicasanclemente.com* 🎫 *Archaeological area €5* ⏲ *Mon.–Sat. 9–12:30 and 3–6; Sun. noon–6* Ⓜ *Colosseo.*

Fodor's Choice ★ **Santi Giovanni e Paolo.** Perched up the incline of the Clivus di Scauro—a magical time-machine of a street where the dial seems to be stuck somewhere in the 13th century—Santi Giovanni e Paolo is an image that would tempt most landscape painters. Landmarked by one of Rome's finest Romanesque bell towers, it looms over a poetic piazza. Underneath, however, are other treasures, whose excavations can be seen in the new Case Romane del Celio museum (see above). A basilica erected on the spot was, like San Clemente, destroyed in 1084 by attacking Normans. Its half-buried columns, near the current church entrance, are visible through misty glass. The current church has its origins at the start of the 12th century, but the interior dates mostly from the 17th century and later. The lovely, incongruous chandeliers are a hand-me-down from New York's Waldorf-Astoria hotel, a gift arranged by the late Cardinal Francis Spellman of New York, whose titular church this was. Spellman also initiated the excavations here in 1949. ✉ *Piazza Santi Giovanni e Paolo 13, Celio* ☎ *06/772711* ⏲ *Oct.–Apr., 8:30–noon and 3:30–6; May–Sept., 8:30–12:30 and 3:30–6:30* Ⓜ *Colosseo.*

Fodor's Choice ★ **Santi Quattro Coronati.** One of those evocative cul-de-sacs in Rome where history seems to be holding its breath, this church is strongly imbued with the sanctity of the Romanesque era. Marvelously redolent of the Middle Ages, this is one of the most unusual and unexpected corners of Rome, a quiet citadel that has resisted the tides of time and traffic. The church, which dates back to the 4th century, honors the Four Crowned Saints—the four brothers Severus, Severianus, Carpophorus, and Victorinus, all Roman officials who were whipped to death for their faith by Emperor Diocletian (284–305). After its 9th-century reconstruction, the church was twice as large as it is now. The abbey was partially destroyed during the Normans' sack of Rome in 1084, but reconstructed about 30 years later. This explains the inordinate size of the apse in relation to the small nave. Don't miss the **cloister,** with its well-tended gardens and 12th-century fountain. The entrance is the door in the left nave; ring the bell if it's not open.

There's another medieval gem hidden away off the courtyard at the church entrance: the **Chapel of San Silvestro.** (Enter the door marked "Monache Agostiniane" and ring the bell at the left for the nun; give her the appropriate donation through a grate, and she will press a button to open the chapel door automatically.) The chapel has remained, for the most part, as it was when consecrated in 1246. Some of the best-preserved medieval frescoes in Rome decorate the walls, telling the story of the Christian emperor Constantine's recovery from leprosy thanks to Pope Sylvester I. Note, too, the delightful *Last Judgment* fresco above the door, in which the angel on the left neatly rolls up sky and stars like a backdrop, signaling the end of the world. ✉ *Via Santi Quattro Coronati 20, Celio* ☎ *06/70475427* *Church and cloister free; Chapel of St. Sylvester €1 donation* ⌚ *Basilica, daily 6:30–12:45 and 3–6:45; San Silvestro Chapel, daily 8:30–1:45 and 4–5:45; cloister, daily 10–11:45 and 4–5:45* Ⓜ *Colosseo.*

Santo Stefano Rotondo. This 5th-century church likely was inspired by the design of the church of the Holy Sepulchre in Jerusalem. Its unusual round plan and timbered ceiling set it apart from most other Roman churches. So do the frescoes, which lovingly depict the goriest martyrdoms of 34 different Catholic saints. You've been warned: these are not for the fainthearted, cataloging, above the names of different emperors, every type of violent death conceivable. ✉ *Via Santo Stefano Rotondo 7, Celio* ☎ *06/421199* ⌚ *End of Oct.–Mar., Tues.–Sat. 9:30–12:30 and 3–6, Sun. 9:30–12:30; Apr.–Oct., Tues.–Sat. 9:30–12:30 and 2–5, Sun. 9:30–12:30* Ⓜ *Colosseo.*

WORTH NOTING

San Gregorio Magno. Set amid the greenery of the Celian Hill, this church wears its Baroque facade proudly. Dedicated to St. Gregory the Great (who served as pope 590–604), it was built about 750 by Pope Gregory II to commemorate his predecessor and namesake. The church of San Gregorio itself has the appearance of a typical Baroque structure, the result of remodeling in the 17th and 18th centuries. But you can still see what's said to be the stone slab on which the pious Gregory the Great slept; it's in the far right-hand chapel. Outside are three chapels. The right chapel is dedicated to Gregory's mother, St. Sylvia, and contains a Guido Reni fresco of the *Concert of Angels*. The chapel in the center, dedicated to St. Andrew, contains two monumental frescoes showing scenes from the saint's life. They were painted at the beginning of the 17th century by Domenichino (*The Flagellation of St. Andrew*) and Guido Reni (*The Execution of St. Andrew*). It's a striking juxtaposition of the sturdy, if sometimes stiff, classicism of Domenichino with the more flamboyant and heroic Baroque manner of Guido Reni. ✉ *Piazza San Gregorio, Celio* ☎ *06/7008227* 🌐 *www.camaldolesiromani.it* ⌚ *Daily 9–1 and 3:30–7* Ⓜ *Colosseo.*

SAN GIOVANNI

The crown jewel of Giovanni, just west of Celio, is the Basilica of San Giovanni, Rome's main cathedral. Today, it is largely a residential neighborhood with 19th- and 20th-century apartment buildings and modern shops. Reach San Giovanni by walking south down Via Merulana from the Colosseum.

TOP ATTRACTIONS

San Giovanni in Laterano. The official cathedral of Rome, it's actually San Giovanni in Laterano, not St. Peter's, that serves as the ecclesiastical seat of the bishop of Rome—also known as the pope. San Giovanni dates back to the 4th century, when Emperor Constantine obtained the land from the wealthy Laterani family and donated it to the Church. But thanks to vandals, earthquakes, and fires, today's building owes most of its form to 16th- and 17th-century restorations, including an interior designed by Baroque genius Borromini. Before you go inside, look up: At the top of the towering facade, done for Pope Clement X in 1736, 15 colossal statues (the 12 apostles plus Christ, John the Baptist, and John the Evangelist) stand watch over the suburbs spreading from Porta San Giovanni.

Despite the church's Baroque design, some earlier fragments do remain. Under the portico on the left stands an ancient statue of Constantine, while the central portal's ancient bronze doors were brought here from the Forum's Curia. Inside, the fragment of a fresco on the first pillar is attributed to the 14th-century Florentine painter Giotto; it depicts Pope Boniface VIII proclaiming the first Holy Year in 1300. The altar's rich Gothic tabernacle—holding what the faithful believe are the heads of Sts. Peter and Paul—dates from 1367. Head to the last chapel at the end of the left aisle to check out the **cloister.** Encrusted with 12th-century Cosmatesque mosaics by father-and-son team the Vassallettos, it's a break from Baroque . . . and from the big tour groups that tend to fill the church's interior. Around the corner, meanwhile, stands one of the oldest Christian structures in Rome. Emperor Constantine built the **Baptistery** in AD 315. While it's certainly changed over time, thanks to several restorations, a 17th-century interior redecoration, and even a Mafia-related car bombing in 1993, the Baptistery remains much like it would have been in ancient times. ✉ *Piazza di Porta San Giovanni, San Giovanni* ☎ *06/69886433* 🎫 *Church free, cloister €3, museum €4* ⏲ *Church daily 7–6:30. Vassalletto Cloister daily 9–6. Museum daily 9–1. Baptistery daily 7:30–12:30 and 4–6:30* Ⓜ *San Giovanni.*

WORTH NOTING

Scala Santa. According to tradition, the Scala Santa was the staircase from Pilate's palace in Jerusalem—and, therefore, one trodden by Christ himself. St. Helena, Emperor Constantine's mother, brought the 28 marble steps to Rome in 326. As they have for centuries, pilgrims still come to climb the steps on their knees. At the top, they can get a glimpse of the **Sancta Sanctorum** (Holy of Holies), the richly decorated private chapel of the popes containing an image of Christ "not made by human hands." You can sneak a peek, too, by taking one of the (non-sanctified) staircases on either side. ✉ *Piazza San Giovanni in Laterano, San Giovanni* ☎ *06/69886433* ⏲ *Oct.–Mar., weekdays and Sat. 6–noon and 3–6:15, Sun. 7–12:30 and 3–6:30; Apr.–Sept., weekdays and Sat. 6–noon and 3:30–6:45, Sun. 7–12:30 and 3:30–7* Ⓜ *San Giovanni.*

SAN LORENZO

This traditionally working-class neighborhood north of the Termini station has become inundated with students. The area is lively in the evenings.

VIA APPIA ANTICA

Far south of the Celio lies catacomb country—the haunts of the fabled underground graves of Rome's earliest Christians, arrayed to either side of the Queen of Roads, the Via Appia Antica (Appian Way). Strewn with classical ruins and dotted with grazing sheep, the road stirs images of chariots and legionnaires returning from imperial conquests. It was completed in 312 BC by Appius Claudius, who laid it out to connect Rome with settlements in the south, in the direction of Naples. Here Christ allegedly stopped Peter, as commemorated by the Domine Quo Vadis church. Though time and vandals have taken their toll on the ancient relics along the road, the catacombs remain to cast their spirit-warm spell. Although both Jews and pagans used the catacombs, the Christians expanded the idea of underground burials to a massive scale. Persecution of Christians under pagan emperors made martyrs of many, whose bones, once interred underground, became objects of veneration. Today, the dark, gloomy catacombs contrast strongly with the Appia Antica's fresh air, verdant meadows, and evocative classical ruins.

The initial stretch of the Via Appia Antica is not pedestrian-friendly—there is fast, heavy traffic and no sidewalk all the way from Porta San Sebastiano to the Catacombe di San Callisto. To reach the catacombs, one route is Bus No. 218 from San Giovanni in Laterano. Alternatively, take Metro line A to Colli Albani and Bus No. 660 to the Tomb of Cecilia Metella. A more expensive option is No. 110 Archeobus from Piazza Venezia; with an open-top deck the big green buses allow you to hop on and off as you please at a price of €12 for two days. An attractive alternative is to hire a bike.

TOP ATTRACTIONS

Catacombe di San Callisto (*Catacombs of St. Calixtus*). Burial place of many popes of the 3rd century, this is the oldest and best-preserved underground cemetery. One of the (English-speaking) friars who act as custodians of the catacomb will guide you through its crypts and galleries, some adorned with Early Christian frescoes. Watch out for wrong turns: this is a five-story-high catacomb! ✉ *Via Appia Antica 110/126, Via Appia Antica* ☎ *06/5310151* 🌐 *www.catacombe.roma.it* 🎫 *€8* ⏲ *Mar.–mid-Jan., Thurs.–Tues. 9–noon and 2–5* Ⓜ *Bus 118, 218.*

Walk in the footsteps of St. Peter along the Via Appia Antica, stretches of which seem barely altered from the days of the Caesars.

Catacombe di San Sebastiano (*Catacombs of St. Sebastian*). The 4th-century church was named after the saint who was buried in the catacomb, which burrows underground on four different levels. This was the only Early Christian cemetery to remain accessible during the Middle Ages, and it was from here that the term "catacomb" is derived—it's in a spot where the road dips into a hollow, known to the Romans as *catacumbas* (Greek for "near the hollow"). The Romans used the name to refer to the cemetery that had existed here since the 2nd century BC, and it came to be applied to all the underground cemeteries discovered in Rome in later centuries. ✉ *Via Appia Antica 136, Via Appia Antica* ☎ *06/7850350* 🌐 *www.catacombe.org* 🎫 *€8* ⏲ *Mid-Dec.–mid-Nov., Mon.–Sat. 10–4:30* Ⓜ *Bus 118, 218, 660.*

Domine Quo Vadis? (*Church of Lord, Where Goest Thou?*). This church was built on the spot where tradition says Christ appeared to St. Peter as the apostle was fleeing Rome and persuaded him to return and face martyrdom. A paving stone in the church bears an imprint said to have been made by the feet of Christ. ✉ *Via Appia Antica at Via Ardeatina, Via Appia Antica* ☎ *06/5120441* ⏲ *Daily 8–6 (summer until 7).*

Fodor's Choice ★ **Tomba di Cecilia Metella.** For centuries, sightseers have flocked to this famous landmark, one of the most complete surviving tombs of ancient Rome. One of the many round mausoleums that once lined the Appian Way, this tomb is a smaller version of the Mausoleum of Augustus, but impressive nonetheless. It was the burial place of a Roman noblewoman, wife of the son of Crassus, one of Julius Caesar's rivals and known as the richest man in the Roman Empire (infamously entering the English language as "crass"). The original decoration

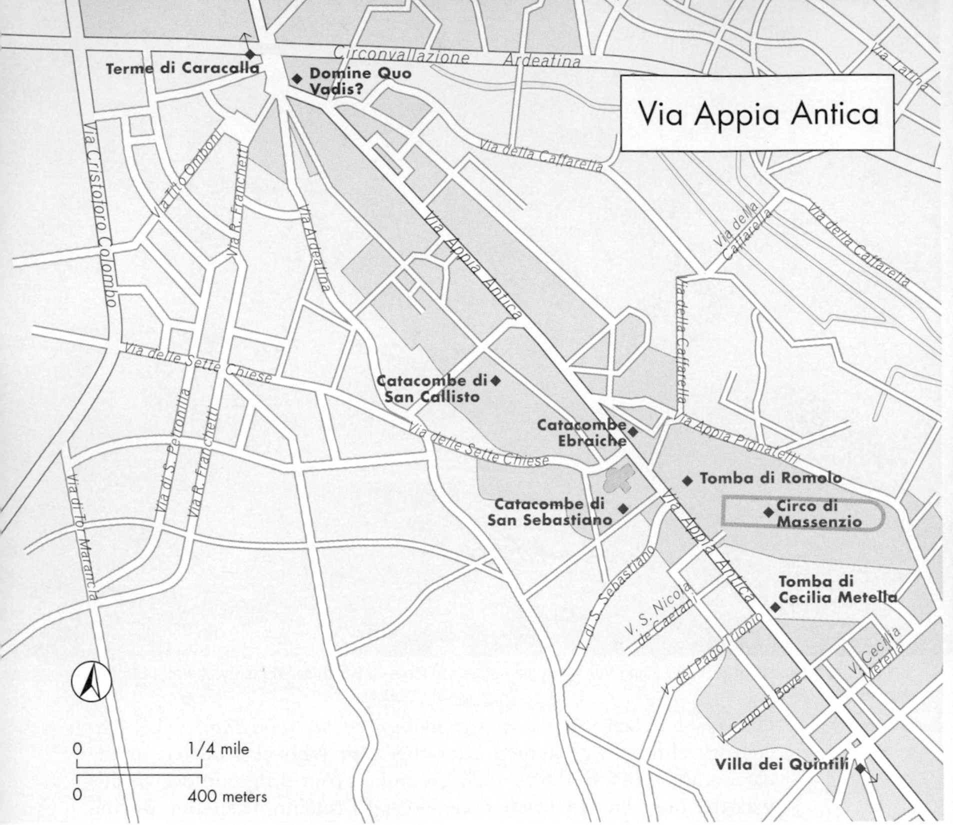

includes a frieze of bulls' skulls near the top. The travertine stone walls were made higher and the medieval-style crenellations added when the tomb was transformed into a fortress by the Caetani family in the 14th century. An adjacent chamber houses a small museum of the area's geological phases. ✉ *Via Appia Antica 162, Via Appia Antica* ☎ *06/39967700* 🌐 *archeoroma.beniculturali.it* 🎟 *€7, includes Terme di Caracalla and Villa dei Quintili* 🕙 *Tues.–Sun. 9–4:30; ticket office closes 1 hr earlier.*

NEED A BREAK?

Appia Antica Caffè. Placed strategically at the bus stop, the Appia Antica Caffè is a bar rare for its sound of birdsong. It also offers lunch and hires out bikes, which is an economical way of exploring the catacombs and other monuments to the right, spread as they are over several miles (if you're heading leftward, opt for the bus as those bike routes can be blocked off). ✉ ***Via Appia Antica 175, Via Appia Antica*** ☎ ***06/89879575*** 🌐 ***www.appiaanticacaffe.it.***

WORTH NOTING

OFF THE BEATEN PATH

Cinecittà Studios. Film lovers will want to make the trip out to Cinecittà Studios, stomping ground of Fellini, Audrey Hepburn, and Elizabeth Taylor and home to such classics as *Roman Holiday*, *Cleopatra*, and

La Dolce Vita. Another draw is the set built for the recent BBC/HBO series *Rome*, which includes movie versions of ancient homes, temples, and streets. You can take a guided tour of the sets and see the exhibition *Cinecittà Shows Off, w*ith its displays of memorabilia like Elizabeth Taylor's *Cleopatra* gown and the dolphin-shaped statue that marked the chariot laps in *Ben-Hur*. Cinecittà is located about 20 minutes southeast on Line B from the Colosseo stop. ✉ *Via Tuscolana 1055, Cinecittà* ☎ *06/722931* 🌐 *www.cinecittastudios.it* 🎟 *€10 exhibition, €20 exhibition and tour* ⏲ *Daily 9:30–5:30; guided tours in English daily at 11:30 and 3:15* Ⓜ *Cinecittà.*

Circo di Massenzio. Of the Circus of Maxentius, built in AD 309, remain the towers at the entrance; the *spina,* the wall that divided it down the center; and the vaults that supported the tiers of seating for the spectators. The obelisk now in Piazza Navona was found here. The adjacent **Mausoleo di Romolo** is a huge tomb built by the emperor for his son Romulus, who died young. The tomb and circus were on the grounds of the emperor's villa. ✉ *Via Appia Antica 153, Via Appia Antica* ☎ *06/0608* 🌐 *www.villadimassenzio.it* 🎟 *€5* ⏲ *Tues.–Sun. 10–4* Ⓜ *Bus 118.*

Villa dei Quintili. Even in ruins, this splendid, 52-room villa gives a real sense of ancient Rome's opulence. Even today, two millennia later, it remains clear why Emperor Commodus—the villain in *Gladiator*—coveted the sumptuous property. To get the villa from its owners, the Quintili, he accused the family of plotting against him, and had them executed before moving in himself. He may have used the exedra for training for his fights with ostriches back in the Colosseum. **■ TIP→ Note that the villa is best included in a separate itinerary from the catacombs, being 5 km (3 miles) away and accessible by a different route.** ✉ *Via Appia Nuova 1092, Via Appia Antica* ☎ *06/39967700* 🎟 *€7 (includes entrance to Terme di Caracalla and Mausoleo di Cecilia Metella)* ⏲ *Tues.–Sun. 9–1 hr before sunset (last entrance 1 hr before closing time)* Ⓜ *Bus 664 from Colli Albani Metro A.*

WHERE TO EAT

EAT LIKE A LOCAL

In Rome tradition is dominant feature of the cuisine, with the focus on freshness and simplicity, so when Romans continue ordering the standbys, it's easy to understand why. That noted, Rome *is* the capital city, and the influx of residents from other regions of the country allows for many variations on the Italian theme.

Artichokes

If there's one vegetable Rome is known for, it's the artichoke, or *carciofo*. In Rome, there are two well-known preparations. One, the classic *carciofo alla Romana,* is stuffed with wild mint, garlic, and pecorino and then braised in olive oil, white wine, and water. The other is *carciofo alla Giudia*, in which the artichoke is deep-fried twice, so that it opens like a flower, the outer leaves crisp and golden brown in color, while the thistle's heart remains tender. Either option is wonderful. When artichokes are in season—late winter through the spring—they're served everywhere.

Bucatini all'amatriciana

It might appear to the naked eye as spaghetti with red sauce but *bucatini all'amatriciana* has much more to it. It's a spicy, rich, and complex dish that owes its flavor to an important ingredient: *guanciale,* or cured pork jowl. Once you taste a meaty, guanciale-flavor dish, you'll understand why Romans swear by it. In *amatriciana,* along with guanciale, the simple sauce features crushed tomatoes and red pepper flakes. It's served over *bucatini,* a hollow, spaghetti-like pasta, and topped with grated pecorino Romano cheese.

Coda alla vaccinara

Rome's largest slaughterhouse in the 1800s was housed in the Testaccio neighborhood. That's where you'll find dishes like *coda alla vaccinara,* or "oxtail in the style of the cattle butcher." This dish is made from ox or veal tails stewed with tomatoes, carrots, celery, and wine, and seasoned with cinnamon, pancetta, and myriad other flavorings. The stew cooks for hours then is finished with a sweet-and-sour element—often raisins and pine nuts or bittersweet chocolate.

Gelato

For many travelers, the first taste of gelato is one of the most memorable moments of their Italian trip. With a consistency that's a cross between regular American ice cream and soft-serve, gelato's texture is dense but softer than hard ice cream because it's kept at a higher temperature. The best gelato is extremely flavorful, and made daily. In Rome a few common flavors are *caffè* (espresso), *pistacchio* (pistachio), *nocciola* (hazelnut), *fragola* (strawberry), and *cioccolato fondant* (dark chocolate).

Pizza

Roman pizza comes in two types: *pizza al taglio* (by the slice) and *pizza tonda* (round pizza). The former has a thicker focaccia-like crust and is cut into squares. These slices are sold by weight and available all day. In Rome, the typical pizza tonda has a very thin crust.

It's cooked in wood-burning ovens that reach extremely high temperatures. Since they're so hot, the ovens are usually fired up in the evening, which is why Roman pizzerias are only open for dinner.

Peppery Pasta

Cacio e pepe is a simple pasta dish from the *cucina povera,* or rustic cooking, tradition. It's also a favorite Roman primo, usually made with tagliatelle (a long, flat noodle), *tonnarelli* (a narrower squarish noodle), or spaghetti, which is then coated with pecorino cheese and a generous amount of freshly ground black pepper. Some restaurants serve the dish in an edible bowl of paper-thin, baked cheese, for added delicious effect.

Updated by Dana Klitzberg

In Rome, the Eternal(ly culinarily conservative) City, simple yet traditional cuisine reigns supreme. Most chefs prefer to follow the mantra of freshness over fuss, and simplicity of flavor and preparation over complex cooking methods.

Rome has been known since ancient times for its grand feasts and banquets, and though the days of Saturnalia feasts are long past, dining out is still a favorite Roman pastime. But even the city's buongustaii (gourmands) will be the first to tell you Rome is distinguished more by its good attitude toward eating out than by a multitude of world-class restaurants. Romans like Roman food, and that's what you'll find in the majority of the city's trattorias and *osterie* (wine bars). For the most part, today's chefs cling to the traditional and excel at what has taken hundreds, sometimes thousands, of years to perfect. This is why the basic trattoria menu is more or less the same wherever you go. And it's why even the top Roman chefs feature their versions of simple trattoria classics like pasta all'amatriciana with a tomato, Roman bacon, chili pepper, and pecorino cheese sauce—sometimes with onion, although for some that's an issue of debate. To a great extent, Rome is still a town where the Italian equivalent of "what are you in the mood to eat?" translates to "pizza or pasta?"

Nevertheless, Rome is the capital of Italy, and because people move here from every corner of the Italian peninsula, there are more variations on the Italian theme in Rome than you'd find elsewhere in Italy: Sicilian, Tuscan, Pugliese, Bolognese, Marchegiano, Sardinian, and northern Italian regional cuisines are all represented. And reflecting the increasingly cosmopolitan nature of the city, you'll find a growing number of good-quality international food here as well—particularly Japanese, Indian, and Ethiopian.

Oddly enough, though, for a nation that prides itself on la bella figura ("looking good"), most Romans don't care about background music, other people's personal space, the lighting, or the fanfare of decor. But who needs interior design when so much of Roman life takes place outdoors, and dining alfresco in Rome can take place in the middle of a glorious ancient site or centuries-old palazzo?

PLANNING

RESTAURANT TYPES

Until relatively recently, there was a distinct hierarchy delineated by the names of Rome's eating places. A **ristorante** was typically elegant and expensive; a **trattoria** served more traditional, home-style fare in a relaxed atmosphere. An **osteria** was even more casual, essentially a wine bar and gathering spot that also served food, although the latest species of wine bars generally goes under the moniker of **enoteca.** All these terms still exist but the distinction has blurred considerably. Now, an osteria in the center of town may be pricier than a ristorante across the street.

For many travelers, stopping in a **gelaterie** for a taste of *gelato*—Italian ice cream—is one of the most memorable moments of their Italian trip. Along with the listings here, you can find a number of gelaterias in Via di Tor Millina, a street off the west side of Piazza Navona, where there are also a couple of good places for frozen yogurt and delicious *frullati*—shakes made with milk, crushed ice, and fruit of your choosing.

Although Rome may not boast the grand **cafés** of Paris or Vienna, it does have hundreds of small places on pleasant side streets and piazzas. The coffee is routinely of high quality. Locals usually stop in for a quickie at the bar, where prices are much lower than for the same drink taken at the table.

HOW TO ORDER: FROM PRIMO TO DOLCE

In a Roman sit-down restaurant, whether a ristorante, trattoria, or osteria, you're expected to order at least a two-course meal. It could be a *primo* (first course, usually pasta or an appetizer) with a *secondo* (second course, which is really a "main course" in English parlance, usually meat or fish); an *antipasto* (starter) followed by a primo or secondo; or a secondo and a *dolce* (dessert). Many people consider a full meal to consist of a primo, a secondo, and a dolce. If you're in a rush, however, many people only order two of these three courses.

In a pizzeria, it's common to order just one dish. The handiest places for a snack between sights are bars, cafés, and *pizza al taglio* (by the slice) shops. Bars are places for a quick coffee and a sandwich, rather than drinking establishments. A café is a bar but usually with more seating. If you place your order at the counter, ask if you can sit down: some places charge more for table service. Often you'll pay a cashier first, then give your *scontrino* (receipt) to the person at the counter who fills your order.

MEAL TIMES AND CLOSURES

Breakfast (*la colazione*) is usually served from 7 am to 10:30 am, lunch (*il pranzo*) from 12:30 pm to 2:30 pm, dinner (*la cena*) from 7:30 pm to 11 pm. Peak times are around 1:30 pm for lunch and 9 pm for dinner.

Enotecas are sometimes open in the morning and late afternoon for snacks.

Most pizzerias open at 8 pm and close around midnight or 1 am. Most bars and cafés are open from 7 am to 8 or 9 pm.

Almost all restaurants close one day a week (in most cases Sunday or Monday) and for at least two weeks in August. The city is zoned, however, so that there are always some restaurants in each zone that remain open, to avoid tourists (and residents) getting stuck without any options.

Keep in mind that the laws are in the process of changing in Rome, giving proprietors more leeway in their opening and closing hours. The law is meant to enable places to stay open later, to make more money in a down economy, and to offer patrons longer hours and more time to eat, drink, and be merry. It has yet to be seen whether or not Italians will find the law "flexible" and use it as an excuse to also close early when they feel like it. *E' tutto possible*: anything's possible in Rome.

PRICES, TIPPING, AND TAXES

Prices in the dining reviews are the average cost of a main course at dinner, or, if dinner is not served, at lunch.

All prices include tax and service *(servizio),* unless indicated otherwise on the menu. It's customary to leave a small tip in cash (from a euro to 10% of the bill) in appreciation of good service. Most restaurants have a "cover" charge, usually listed on the menu as *pane e coperto*. It should be modest (€1–€2.50 per person) except at the most expensive restaurants. Some instead charge for bread, which should be brought to you (and paid for) only if you order it. When in doubt, ask before ordering.

Note that the price of fish dishes is often given by weight (before cooking); the price on the menu will be for 100 grams (*l'etto*), not for the whole fish. An average fish portion is about 300 grams.

WITH KIDS

In restaurants and trattorias you may find a high chair or a cushion for the child to sit on, but there's rarely a children's menu. Order a *mezza porzione* (half portion) of any dish, or ask the waiter for a *porzione da bambino* (child's portion).

WHAT TO WEAR

We mention dress only when men are required to wear a jacket or a jacket and tie. Keep in mind that Italian men rarely wear shorts in a restaurant or enoteca and infrequently wear sneakers or running shoes or baseball caps, no matter how humble the establishment. The same "rules" apply to ladies' casual shorts, running shoes, and flip-flops. Shorts are acceptable in pizzerias and cafés.

RESTAURANT REVIEWS

Listed alphabetically within neighborhoods. Use the coordinate (⊕ 1:B2) at the end of each listing to locate a property on the Where to Eat and Stay in Rome atlas at the end of this chapter.

VILLA BORGHESE, PIAZZA DEL POPOLO & FLAMINIO
upscale dining & tourist traps
AROUND THE VATICAN: BORGO & PRATI
residential, refined neighborhood favorites
PIAZZA DI SPAGNA & QUIRINALE
celebrity hot spots & shopping-spree respites
REPUBBLICA & SAN LORENZO
student haunts & innovative regional cuisine
NAVONA
hot young chefs' outposts; traditional pizza joints
CAMPO DE' FIORI
trattorias featuring market-fresh ingredients
MONTI & ESQUILINO
ethnic spots & hip up-and-comers
JEWISH GHETTO
traditional Roman & Jewish Roman fare among the ruins
TRASTEVERE
cheap joints, local favorites
AVENTINO & TESTACCIO
old-school Roman eateries meet club/ lounge scene
Villa Giulia
Villa Strohl Fern
Parco D.Daini
Giardino D.Lago
Villa Borghese
Villa Medici
Via Salaria
Corso d'Italia
Via Flaminia
Lgt. d. Armi
Lgt. A. da Brescia
Fiume Tevere
Lgt. Michelangelo
Viale del Muro Torto
Lgt. Prati
Lgt. Marzio
Lgt. Castello
Lgt. Tor di Nona
C. so Vittorio Emanuele II
Lgt. Gianicolense
Lgt. Sangallo
Lgt dei Tebaldi
Lgt. della Farnesina
Lgt. dei Vallati
Lgt. dei Cenci
Lgt. Raff Sanzio
Lgt. d. Anguillara
Lgt. di Pierleoni
Via Nazionale
Via A. Depretis
Via dei Fori
Parco Traiano
Via Labicana
Villa Corsini
Villa Sciarra
Viale G. Trastevere
Porto di Risa
Via Marmorata
Fiume Tevere
Parco Della Resistenza Dell'8 Sett.
Viale d. Pir. Cestia
Viale di Trastevere
Viale Aventino
Via delle Terme di Caracalla
Parco Di Porta Capena
Villa Celimontana
Via Druso

BEST BETS FOR ROME DINING

With thousands of restaurants to choose from, how will you decide where to eat? Fodor's writers and editors have selected their favorite restaurants here, by price, cuisine, and experience. Or find details in the full reviews.

Fodor's Choice ★

Angelina, $$, p. 257
Agata e Romeo, $$$$, p. 260
Alle Fratte di Trastevere, $$, p. 253
Antico Arco, $$$, p. 254
Ba' Ghetto, $$, p. 245
Cul de Sac, $, p. 236
Del Frate, $$, p. 233
Etablì, $$, p. 237
Filetti di Baccalà, $, p. 242
Flavio al Velavevodetto, $$, p. 258
Grano, $$, p. 237
Il Convivio, $$$$, p. 238
Il Leoncino, $, p. 248
Il Pagliaccio, $$$$, p. 239
Il Sanlorenzo, $$$$, p. 242
La Ciambella, $$, p. 239
La Gensola, $$$, p. 255
La Pergola, $$$$, p. 253
La Veranda dell'Hotel Columbus, $$$, p. 232
Nino, $$$, p. 249
Osteria dell'Ingegno, $$, p. 240
Pierluigi, $$$, p. 243
Porto Fluviale, $, p. 258
Roscioli, $$$, p. 244
San Teodoro, $$$, p. 246
Settembrini, $$, p. 233
Trattoria Monti, $$, p. 259
Uno e Bino, $$$, p. 262

Best by Price

$

Cul de Sac, p. 236
Da Baffetto, p. 241
Dar Poeta, p. 254
Filetti di Baccalà, p. 242
Panattoni, p. 256
Remo, p. 258

$$

Acchiappafantasmi, p. 241
Alle Fratte di Trastevere, p. 253
Etablì, p. 237
Obikà, p. 240
Osteria dell'Ingegno, p. 240
Taverna Angelica, p. 232
Tram Tram, p. 261
Trattoria Moderna, p. 244
Trattoria Monti, p. 259
Urbana 47, p. 260

$$$

Antico Arco, p. 254
La Gensola, p. 255
La Veranda dell'Hotel Columbus, p. 232
San Teodoro, p. 246
Uno e Bino, p. 262

$$$$

Agata e Romeo, p. 260
Il Convivio, p. 238
Il Sanlorenzo, p. 242
La Pergola, p. 253
La Rosetta, p. 239

Best by Cuisine

CAFÉ

GiNa, $, p. 247
Sant'Eustachio, $, p. 236
Tazza d'Oro, $, p. 240

CENTRAL ITALIAN

Dal Bolognese, $$$$, p. 252
Trattoria Monti, $$, p. 259

MODERN ITALIAN

Agata e Romeo, $$$$, p. 260
Il Bacaro, $$$, p. 238
Il Convivio, $$$$, p. 238
Il Pagliaccio, $$$$, p. 239
La Pergola, $$$$, p. 253
Osteria dell'Ingegno, $$, p. 240
Settembrini, $$, p. 233
Taverna Angelica, $$, p. 232
Uno e Bino, $$$, p. 262

OSTERIA/TRATTORIA

Alle Fratte di Trastevere, $$, p. 253
Armando al Pantheon, $, p. 234
Flavio al Velavevodetto, $$, p. 258
Nino, $$$, p. 249

RISTORANTE

Il Convivio, $$$$, p. 238
Il Pagliaccio, $$$$, p. 239
La Pergola, $$$$, p. 253

MEAT

Angelina, $$, p. 257
Bellacarne, $$, p. 245
Dal Toscano, $$, p. 233
Il Ciak, $$, p. 255
Il Simposio di Costantini, $$$, p. 233
Tullio, $$$, p. 250

Best by Experience

AROUND THE VATICAN: BORGO AND PRATI

BORGO

Many tourists think the area around the Vatican is rip-off central when it comes to drinking and dining. Although there are an overwhelming number of tourist trap-torias, the Borgo area, just outside the Vatican walls, is home to some genuinely good restaurants off the usual tourist radar.

$ ITALIAN **Cremeria Ottaviani.** This old-fashioned gelateria is noted for its excellent *granita di caffè.* *Average main: €3 Via Leone IV 83/85, Vatican 06/37514774 Closed Wed. 1:C2.*

$$$ ROMAN Fodor's Choice ★ **La Veranda dell'Hotel Columbus.** Deciding where to sit at La Veranda isn't easy, since both the shady courtyard, torch-lit at night, and the frescoed dining room are among Rome's most spectacular settings. While La Veranda is known for classic Roman cuisine, some dishes are served with refreshing twists on the familiar. The seasonal menu may include an eggplant *caponata* with *burrata* (fresh cheese made from mozzarella and cream) and *bottarga* (salted fish roe) from Sardinia; Piedmontese oxtail soup; or a risotto with Barolo wine, blue cheese, and quail carpaccio with mustard seeds. Call ahead, especially on Saturday, because the hotel often hosts weddings, which close the restaurant. *Average main: €25 Hotel Columbus, Borgo Santo Spirito 73, Borgo 06/6872973 www.laveranda.net Reservations essential Closed Mon. 1:D3.*

$$ MODERN ITALIAN **Taverna Angelica.** The Borgo area near St. Peter's Basilica hasn't been known for culinary excellence, but this is starting to change, and Taverna Angelica was one of the first of a handful of more refined dining outposts in this part of town. The dining room is small, which allows the chef to create a menu that's inventive without being pretentious. Dishes such as warm scampi with artichokes and tomatoes are more about taste than presentation. Spaghetti with crunchy pancetta and leeks is practically addictive, as is the warm seafood soup. Fresh sliced tuna in a pistachio crust with orange sauce is light and delicious. And desserts here go beyond the same-old tiramisu and panna cotta. *Average main: €22 Piazza A. Capponi 6, Borgo 06/6874514 www.tavernaangelica.it Reservations essential No lunch Mon.–Sat. M Ottaviano 1:D2.*

PRATI

Also near the Vatican, Prati is slightly farther up the river than Borgo and has become a bit of a hotbed for interesting niche foodie spots.

$ CAFÉ **Al Settimo Gelo.** Located in Prati, this spot has been getting rave reviews for both classic flavors and newfangled inventions such as cardamom, chestnut, and ginger. *Average main: €5 Via Vodice 21/a, Prati 06/3725567 www.alsettimogelo.it 1:A1.*

$$ TUSCAN **Cesare.** An old standby in Prati, Cesare is a willing slave to tradition. Classic fish dishes like fresh marinated anchovies and sardines, and mixed seafood salad, quell seafood cravings. Homemade pasta with meat sauce is the primo to order, and *saltimbocca* (thinly sliced veal with prosciutto and sage) or the thick Florentine steaks are the ultimate meat-lover's dishes. Also try the €40 "menu toscano"—a great, multicourse value. The general menu's tendency toward stick-to-the-ribs

comfort food makes it a great place to go in the autumn and winter, when the cooler weather ushers in heartier dishes featuring truffles and game. *Average main: €20 Via Crescenzio 13, Prati 06/6861227 www.ristorantecesare.com Closed 3 weeks in Aug., Easter wk, Christmas day 1:E2.*

$$ TUSCAN
Dal Toscano. An open wood-fired grill and classic dishes such as *ribollita* (a thick bread and vegetable soup) and *pici* (fresh, thick pasta) with wild hare sauce are the draw at this great family-run Tuscan trattoria near the Vatican. The cuts of beef visible at the entrance tell you right away that the house special is the prized *bistecca alla fiorentina*—a thick grilled steak seared on the outside and rare in the middle, with its rub of gutsy Tuscan olive oil and sea salt forming a delicious crust to keep in the natural juices. Seating outside on the sidewalk in warm weather is a nice touch. *Average main: €22 Via Germanico 58/60, Prati 06/39725717 www.ristorantedaltoscano.it Closed Mon. and 3 wks in Aug. M Ottaviano–San Pietro–Musei Vaticani 1:C2.*

$$ Fodor's Choice ★
Del Frate. This impressive wine bar, adjacent to one of Rome's noted wineshops, matches sleek and modern decor with creative cuisine and three dozen wines available by the glass. The house specialty is marinated meat and fish, and you can also get cheeses, smoked meats, and composed salads. Try a risotto or braised oxtail–stuffed tortelli in a celery sauce for primi, and a monkfish alla cacciatore with bitter Roman *puntarelle* (a type of chicory) as a main. For dessert, try the molten chocolate cake with banana cream. *Average main: €19 Via degli Scipioni 118, Prati 06/3211612 Closed 3 wks in Aug., Sun. No lunch Mon. M Ottaviano 1:C1.*

$$$ MODERN ITALIAN
Il Simposio di Costantini. At the most upscale wine bar in town you come for the wine, but return for the food. Everything here is appropriately *raffinato* (refined): marinated and smoked fish, composed salads, and top-quality salumi and other cured meats and pâtés. There are plenty of dishes with classic Roman leanings, including artichokes prepared three ways. Main courses favor meat, as in roast lamb, a fillet with foie gras, or game (like pigeon, in season), and complement the vast offering of top-notch red wines. The restaurant boasts 80 assorted cheeses to savor with your dessert wine. *Average main: €30 Piazza Cavour 16, Prati 06/32111131 www.pierocostantini.it Reservations essential Closed Sun. and last 2 wks of Aug. No lunch Sat. 1:E2.*

$ PIZZA
L'Isola della Pizza. Right near the Vatican metro stop, the "Island of Pizza" is also known for its copious antipasti. Simply ask for the house appetizers, and a waiter will swoop down with numerous plates of salad, seafood, bruschetta, prosciutto, and crispy pizza bianca. Though it's easy to fill up on these starters—you can order just one, or selection for a fixed price—the pizza is dependably good, and meat-lovers can get a decent steak. *Average main: €14 Via degli Scipioni 45, Prati 06/39733483 www.isoladellapizza.com Closed Wed., Aug., and Christmas wk 1:C2.*

$$ MODERN ITALIAN Fodor's Choice ★
Settembrini. The modern, intimate dining room hints at what's to come from the kitchen and the staff: elegant and restrained cooking, friendly yet unobtrusive service, and an interesting and well-curated wine list. Whipped salt cod on citrus polenta is a light and airy affair,

and *moscardini* (baby Mediterranean octopus) in a wine-and-tomato broth on crostini is also a great starter. Pastas, including thin tagliolini with crab, zucchini, and mandarin orange or fettucine with a lamb and porcini ragu, are creative. Main dishes range from land (Kobe-style beef with mushrooms and radicchio) to sea (cod with cabbage and spicy *'nduja* sausage). This is a gem in a quiet neighborhood. *Average main: €21 Via Luigi Settembrini 27, Prati, Roma 06/3232617 www.viasettembrini.it/index.php Reservations essential Closed Sun. No lunch Sat. Lepanto 1:C1.*

PIAZZA NAVONA, CAMPO DE' FIORI, AND THE JEWISH GHETTO

PIAZZA NAVONA

The narrow, cobblestone *vicoli* (alleys) around Piazza Navona house a vast range of dining options. You'll find everything from casual pizzerias, where hurried waiters scribble your bill on a paper tablecloth, to several of the city's most revered gourmet temples, featuring star chefs and inventive cuisine with decidedly higher bills placed on the finest high-thread-count damask tablecloths. The area around the Pantheon is rife with classic, old-school trattorias and mid-range to upscale restaurants, including many in gorgeous piazzas that could double as opera sets. You'll feel the grandeur of Rome here, sometimes with prices to match.

$ ROMAN **Armando al Pantheon.** In the shadow of the Pantheon, this trattoria, open since 1961, delights the tourists who tend to come for lunch. There's an air of authenticity, witnessed by Roman antiques shop owners who've been regulars here for a generation—to wit, well-dressed older gentlemen who come here to enjoy a leisurely meal . . . and scold the waitress, by name, when she brings coffee before the profiteroles. This is the place to try Roman artichokes or *vignarola* (a fava bean, asparagus, pea, and guanciale stew) in the spring, or the wild boar bruschetta in winter. Pastas are filling and great, and secondi deliver all the Roman staples: oxtail, baby lamb chops, tripe, meatballs, and other hearty fare. *Average main: €15 Salita dei Crescenzi 31, Piazza Navona 06/68803034 www.armandoalpantheon.it Closed Sun. No dinner Sat. Closed Dec.–Jan. 6 4:E3.*

$ NORTHERN ITALIAN **Birreria Peroni.** With its long wooden tables, hard-back booths, and free-flowing beer, this casual restaurant in a 16th-century palazzo might seem more like a Munich beer hall than a popular Roman hangout that's been around since 1906. But remember that in the far northern reaches of Italy, locals speak as much German as they do Italian, and that's where Birreria Peroni draws its inspiration. The goulash and the many sausage specialties certainly provide a respite from pasta and tomato sauce. The bonus is that this is one of the few places in the historic center of Rome where you can fill up on protein for very few euros. *Average main: €10 Via di San Marcello 19, Piazza Navona 06/6795310 www.anticabirreriaperoni.it Reservations not accepted Closed Sun. and Aug. No lunch Sat. 4:G3.*

$ CAFÉ **Caffè della Pace.** With its sidewalk tables taking in Santa Maria della Pace's beautiful jewel of a piazza, Caffè della Pace has long been the

CLOSE UP

La Cucina Romana

Hearty, unflinching, and proud, *la cucina romana* originates from all of the various geographic and cultural influences on the city over the course of more than 2,000 years. Since Rome's Testaccio area was once a central zone for the butcher trade in this part of the country, the city's cuisine relies heavily on meat dishes and meat products—as reflected in the ubiquity of guanciale (cured pork jowl) in Roman pastas, as well as meat dishes like abacchio (baby lamb) and porchetta (roast pork).

CLASSIC DISHES

From this butchering tradition grew the famed (or notorious) old-school Roman dishes of the quinto quarto, or "fifth quarter": offal and throw-away parts that were left after the butchers had sold the best cuts to paying customers. This gave birth to *coda* alla vaccinara (oxtail stewed with celery and tomatoes), pasta with pajata (baby lamb or calf intestines with the mother's milk still inside), coratella (a mix of lamb innards including heart), and trippa alla romana (tripe boiled in a savory tomato sauce).

But Roman cuisine takes as much from the sea as it does from land, as the Mediterranean—Ostia and Fiumicino are the closest beach towns—is only 25 km (15 miles) from the city center. A variety of fish, including seabass, turbot, and gilthead bream, is served in local restaurants, cooked simply (and often whole) in the oven, on the grill, or baked in a salt crust. And crustaceans, from gamberetti (baby shrimp) to scampi (langoustines) to spiny lobster are served alongside a family of calamari, cuttlefish, octopus, and small and large versions of everything in between.

LOCAL PRODUCE

Ah, Roman farmers' markets! Heading to an outdoor market anywhere in the city will educate you on exactly what is in season at the moment, and what the bounties of Italy, and particularly the Lazio region (where Rome is located), have to offer. Rome has always loved its greens, whether it's chicory or spinach, arugula or dandelion, beet or broccoli greens. Not to mention beans (string, fava, and broad, to name a few), as well as squash, zucchini, pumpkins, broccoli, and agretti, a staunchly Roman green that resembles sturdy chives and tastes more like spinach. If you ask for agretti outside of Rome, vendors will most likely look at you as if you come from another planet. But perhaps the most famous Roman vegetable is the globe artichoke, or carciofo romano, in season late winter through the spring

Speaking of outside of Rome, the most delicious strawberries (and teeny, fragrant wild strawberries) of the region come from Nemi, a hill town in the Castelli Romani outside of the city. Rome in the summer has an abundance of stone fruits and seasonal treats (fresh plums, apricots, and figs are nothing like their dried counterparts, and should be tasted to be believed), and great citrus in cooler months, like the sweet-tasting, beautiful blood oranges arriving daily from Sicily, which are often fresh-squeezed and served in tall glasses at Roman cafés.

haunt of Rome's *beau monde*. Set on a quiet street near Piazza Navona, it also has two rooms filled with old-world personality and paparazzi-worthy patrons. The neighborhood is currently hipper than ever, creating clogged *vicoli*, so a table here is now an especially prized commodity. Dinner is more of a light meal than a dining "experience," but it's worth coming for the vibe—particularly for postprandial sips. *Average main: €12 ✉ Via della Pace 3, Piazza Navona ☎ 06/6861216 🌐 www.caffedellapace.it ✣ 4:C2.*

$ CAFÉ **✕ Caffè Sant'Eustachio.** Traditionally frequented by Rome's literati, this has what is generally considered Rome's best cup of coffee. Servers are hidden behind a huge espresso machine, vigorously mixing the sugar and coffee to protect their "secret method" for the perfectly prepared cup. (If you want your *caffè* without sugar here, ask for it *amaro*). *Average main: €2 ✉ Piazza Sant'Eustachio 82, Piazza Navona ☎ 06/68802048 🌐 www.santeustachioilcaffe.it ✣ 4:E3.*

$ ITALIAN **✕ Cremeria Monteforte.** Immediately beside the Pantheon is Cremeria Monteforte, which has won several awards for its flavors. Also worth trying is its chocolate sorbetto—it's an icier version of the gelato without the dairy (except, of course, for the whipped cream you'll want them to plop on top)! *Average main: €3 ✉ Via della Rotonda 22, Piazza Navona ☎ 06/6867720 ⊗ Closed Mon. Closed mid-Dec.–mid-Jan. ✣ 4:E2.*

$ WINE BAR Fodor's Choice ★ **✕ Cul de Sac.** This popular wine bar near Piazza Navona is among the city's oldest and offers a book-length selection of wines from Italy, France, the Americas, and elsewhere. The food is eclectic, ranging from a huge assortment of Italian meats and cheeses (try the delicious *lonza*, cured pork loin, or *speck*, a northern Italian smoked prosciutto), and various Mediterranean dishes, including delicious baba ghanoush, a tasty Greek salad, and a spectacular wild boar pâté. Outside tables get crowded fast, so arrive early, or come late—they serve until about 12:30 am, though they're closed from about 4 pm to 5:30 pm. *Average main: €14 ✉ Piazza Pasquino 73, Piazza Navona ☎ 06/68801094 🌐 web.tiscali.it/culdesac ⇨ Reservations not accepted ✣ 4:D3.*

$ ITALIAN **✕ Della Palma.** Close to the Pantheon on a street just north of the Piazza della Rotonda, Della Palma serves 100 flavors of gelato, and for sheer gaudy display and range of choice it's a must. It also offers a colorful selection of bulk candy, as well as several flavors of *granita* (ice slush) on rotation. *Average main: €3 ✉ Via della Maddalena 20/23, Piazza Navona ☎ 06/68806752 🌐 www.dellapalma.it ✣ 4:E2.*

$ ITALIAN **✕ Enoteca Corsi.** Very convenient to the historic center for lunch or an afternoon break, this little hole-in-the-wall looks like it missed the revolution; renovations were done a few years back but it's hard to imagine unless you knew the place *before*. Prices and decor are *come una volta* (like once upon a time) when the shop sold—as the sign says—wine and oil. You can still get wine here by the liter, or choose from a good variety of fairly priced bottles. The place is packed at lunch, when a few specials—classic pastas and some second dishes like veal roast with peas—are offered. *Average main: €12 ✉ Via del Gesù 88, Piazza Navona ☎ 06/6790821 🌐 www.enotecacorsi.com ⊗ Closed Sun. No dinner Sat.–Wed. ✣ 4:F4.*

An *alimentari* is a specialty food shop. Visit one to stock up on lunch or picnic fixings; some will give you samples to taste.

$$ MEDITERRANEAN Fodor's Choice ★

Etablì. On a narrow *vicolo* (alley) off beloved Piazza del Fico, this multifunctional space has a beautifully finished lounge-bar done in modern Italian farmhouse chic, with vaulted wood beam ceilings, wrought-iron touches, plush leather sofas, and chandeliers. In the restaurant section, it's minimalist Provençal hip (*etabli* is French for the regionally typical tables within). The food is clean and Mediterranean, with touches of Asia in the raw fish appetizers. Pastas are more traditional Italian, and the secondi run the gamut from land to sea. The place fills up by *dopo cena* ("after dinner") when it becomes a popular spot for sipping and posing, usually overlooking the tiny cobblestone street out front. *Average main: €22* *Vicolo delle Vacche 9/a, Piazza Navona* *06/97616694* *www.etabli.it* *No lunch* *4:C2.*

$ CAFÉ

Fiocco di Neve. Don't miss the fabulous *granita di caffè* (coffee ice slush) here as well as a big scoop of gelato—the chocolate chip and After Eight (mint chocolate chip) flavors are delicious. Seasonal flavors like pear-cinnamon are worth experiencing. *Average main: €3* *Via del Pantheon 51, Piazza Navona* *06/6786025* *4:F2.*

$ CAFÉ

Giolitti. For years Giolitti was considered the best gelateria in Rome, and it's still worth a stop if you're near the Pantheon. It's best known for its variety of fresh seasonal fruit flavors, which taste like the essence of the fruits themselves. *Average main: €3* *Via degli Uffici del Vicario 40, Piazza Navona* *06/6991243* *www.giolitti.it* *4:F2.*

$$ MODERN ITALIAN Fodor's Choice ★

Grano. Light, bright, and happy: that's the setting for this restaurant in a pretty piazza down the street from the Pantheon. Start with a nice wine from the well-stocked cellar and you're off, with inventive starters like the *polpetti di brasato* (slow-cooked braised beef made into breaded meatballs topped with a zingy green sauce). The first courses really shine, mingling meat, seafood, and vegetables with aplomb (the gnocchi with clams and sea beans is fresh and delicious). Second courses are simpler, including tuna steak with caponata and roast chicken. Desserts are tasty and the setting calls for dessert wines and post-prandial *digestivi.* *Average main: €17 Piazza Rondanini 53, Piazza Navona 06/68192096 www.ristorantegrano.it 4:G3.*

$$$$ MODERN ITALIAN **Hostaria dell'Orso.** Back in the Hollywood-on-the-Tiber 1950s, this was *the* place to be. Everyone from Sophia Loren to Aristotle Onassis reveled in the historic 15th-century palazzo. After several fallow decades, the restaurant reopened a decade ago and deals in top-quality ingredients like baby pig and black cod, and the chefs tease out maximum flavors using classic techniques and some esoteric ingredients. Highlights include a *cacio e pepe* ("cheese and pepper") ravioli primo with potato cream and crispy bacon, or an artfully presented secondo of pigeon cooked in myrtle leaves with lemon sauce and crispy chestnut-herb bread. Desserts are delightful: perhaps crème brûlée with coffee parfait, chocolate ice-cream, or cotton candy? Elegant dress is recommended. *Average main: €40 Via dei Soldati 25c, Piazza Navona 06/68301192 www.hdo.it Reservations essential Closed Sun. No lunch Mon. 4:D1.*

$$$ MODERN ITALIAN **Il Bacaro.** With a handful of choice tables set outside against an ivy-draped wall, this tiny candlelit spot not far from the Pantheon makes for an ideal evening, equally suited for a romantic twosome or close friends and convivial conversation. Pastas—like *orecchiette* (little ear-shaped pasta) with prosciutto *crudo* and radicchio, a dish that lip-smacks of Puglia—are star players. As a bonus, the kitchen keeps its clients from picking at each other's plates by offering side dishes of all the pastas ordered among those at the table. The choice main courses are mostly meat—the Argentine beef with balsamic vinegar or London broil–style marinated in olive oil and rosemary are winners. *Average main: €25 Via degli Spagnoli 27, Piazza Navona 06/6872554 www.ilbacaro.com Reservations essential No lunch weekdays. Closed 3 wks at Christmas/New Year's 4:E2.*

$$$$ MODERN ITALIAN Fodor's Choice ★ **Il Convivio.** In a tiny, nondescript alley north of Piazza Navona, the three Troiani brothers—Angelo in the kitchen, and brothers Giuseppe and Massimo presiding over the dining room and wine cellar—have quietly been redefining the experience of Italian eclectic *alta cucina* (haute cuisine) for many years. Antipasti include a selection of ultra-fresh raw seafood preparations in the mixed *crudi*, while a "carbomare" pasta is a riff on tradition, substituting pancetta with fresh fish roe and house-cured *bottarga* (salted fish roe). Or opt for one of the famed signature dishes, including a fabulous version of a cold-weather pigeon main course. Service is attentive without being overbearing, and the wine list is exceptional. *Average main: €41 Vicolo dei Soldati 31, Piazza Navona 06/6869432 www.ilconviviotroiani.it Reservations essential Closed Sun. and 2 wks in Aug. No lunch 4:D1.*

$$$$ MODERN ITALIAN Fodor's Choice ★ ✕ **Il Pagliaccio.** To find some of the latest spins on Roman *alta cucina* (haute cuisine), you should head to this hidden back street nestled between upscale Via Giulia and popular Campo de' Fiori. This is where widely-traveled chef Anthony Genovese came to roost a few years ago. Born in France to Calabrese parents, and having worked in Japan and Thailand, it's no surprise that Genovese has a love of unusual spices and "foreign" ingredients and preparations. These have gained him a loyal following *and* prized Michelin stars. As a result, prices here are exorbitant, but dishes are worth it, like pasta bundles filled with onion, tapioca, and red currants in a saffron broth or duck with black salsify, caramelized pear, and chocolate sauce. Desserts by Alsatian Marion Lichtle are also expertly executed. *Average main: €48 ✉ 129 Via dei Banchi Vecchi, Piazza Navona ☎ 06/68809595 ⊕ www.ristoranteilpagliaccio.com Reservations essential ⊗ Closed Sun., Mon., 3 wks in Aug., and 10 days in Feb. No lunch Tues. ⊕ 4:B3*

$$ ITALIAN Fodor's Choice ★ ✕ **La Ciambella.** The sprawling space evokes a U.S. restaurant, with a bar up front and a bartender mixing specialty cocktails, but the structure itself is all Roman, with brick archways, high ceilings, and a skylight in one of the dining rooms that allows guests to gaze at the fantastic Roman sky. The emphasis here is on high-quality primary ingredients and Italian culinary traditions, evident in the incomparable Pugliese burrata cheese, thin-crust pizzas, flavorful pastas (both classic and seasonal specialties), and grilled meats on offer. Thursdays offer an added benefit at aperitivo hour: live jazz music. *Average main: €17 ✉ Via dell'Arco della Ciambella 20, Piazza Navona, Roma ☎ 06/6832930 ⊕ www.laciambellaroma.com ⊕ 4:E4.*

$ PIZZA FAMILY ✕ **La Montecarlo.** Run by the niece of the owner of the pizzeria Da Baffetto, La Montecarlo has a similar menu and is almost as popular as its relative around the corner. Pizzas are super-thin and a little burned around the edges—the sign of a good wood-burning oven. This is one of few pizzerias open for both lunch and dinner. *Average main: €12 ✉ Vicolo Savelli 13, Piazza Navona ☎ 06/6861877 No credit cards ⊗ Closed 2 wks in mid-Aug. and Mon. Nov.–Apr. ⊕ 4:C3.*

$$$$ SEAFOOD ✕ **La Rosetta.** Chef-owner Massimo Riccioli took the nets and fishing gear off the walls of his parents' trattoria to create what is widely known as *the* place to go in Rome for first-rate seafood. But beware: the staff may be friendly and the fish may be of high quality, but the preparations are generally very simple, and the prices can be startlingly high. If you come though, start with the justifiably well-known selection of marinated seafood appetizers, like carpaccios of fresh, translucent fish drizzled with olive oil and perhaps a fresh herb. Pastas tend to mix varieties of shellfish, usually with a touch of oil, white wine, and lemon. Simple dishes such as the classic *zuppa di pesce* (fish soup) deserve star billing under the title of *secondi*—and command star prices. *Average main: €50 ✉ Via della Rosetta 9, Piazza Navona ☎ 06/6861002 ⊕ www.larosetta.com Reservations essential Jacket required ⊗ Closed Sun. and 3 wks in Aug. ⊕ 4:E2*

$$ ROMAN ✕ **Maccheroni.** This boisterous, convivial trattoria north of the Pantheon makes for a fun evening out. The decor is basic: white walls with wooden shelves lined with wine bottles, blocky wooden tables covered in white

butcher paper—but there's an "open" kitchen (with even the dishwashers in plain view of the diners) and an airy feel that attracts a young clientele. The menu sticks to Roman basics such as simple pasta with fresh tomatoes and basil, or rigatoni *alla gricia* (with bacon, sheep's-milk cheese, and black pepper). Probably the best choice on the menu is the *tagliata con rughetta*, a juicy, two-inch-thick steak sliced thinly and served over arugula. *Average main: €22 ✉ Piazza delle Coppelle 44, Piazza Navona ☎ 06/68307895 🌐 www.ristorantemaccheroni.com Reservations essential ✣ 4:E2.*

$$ ITALIAN

Obikà. There's no sushi here but this "mozzarella bar" is based on the idea of a sushi bar, with chefs working behind a "mozzarella counter" and the mozzarella platters presented like sushi. Even the decor is modern Japanese minimalism–meets–ancient Roman grandeur. But here the cheese, in all its varieties, is the focus of the dishes: the familiar cow's milk, the delectable water buffalo milk varieties, and the sinfully rich *burrata* from Puglia (fresh cow's milk mozzarella encasing a creamy center of unspun curds and fresh cream). They're all served with various accompanying cured meats, vegetables, sauces, and breads. An outdoor deck is a great spot for dining alfresco. Also visit other locations in Campo de' Fiori (corner of Via dei Baullari, 06/68802366) and in Parioli (Via Guido d'Arezzo 49, 06/685344184). *Average main: €15 ✉ Piazza di Firenze 26, Piazza Navona ☎ 06/6832630 🌐 www.obika.it ✣ 4:E1.*

$$ MODERN ITALIAN Fodor's Choice ★

Osteria dell'Ingegno. This casual, trendy place is a great spot to enjoy a glass of wine or a gourmet meal in an ancient piazza in the city center, but the modern interior decor—vibrant with colorful paintings by local artists—brings you back to the present day. The simple but innovative menu includes dishes like *panzanella* (Tuscan bread salad), beef tagliata with red wine reduction, and a perfectly cooked duck breast with seasonal fruit sauce. Outdoor tables from April to October make you feel as if you're on an opera stage set, since your perch looks out over the Tempio d'Adriano (AD 145). If ever there was a place to linger outdoors over limoncello, this is it. *Average main: €19 ✉ Piazza di Pietra 45, Piazza Navona ☎ 06/6780662 ⏲ Closed Sun. and 2 wks in Aug. ✣ 4:F2.*

$ CAFÉ

Tazza d'Oro. Many admirers contend this is the city's best cup of coffee. The hot chocolate in winter, all thick and gooey goodness, is a treat. And in warm weather, the coffee granita is the perfect cooling alternative to a regular espresso. *Average main: €4 ✉ Via degli Orfani 84, Piazza Navona ☎ 06/6789792 🌐 www.tazzadorocoffeeshop.com ✣ 4:F2.*

CAMPO DE' FIORI

Campo de' Fiori has one of Rome's biggest open-air produce markets, and is historically the secular crossroads of the city: even in ancient Rome, pilgrims gathered here to eat, drink, and be merry. Today's shoppers at the market include local chefs who head here to concoct menus based on what looks good.

$$ SOUTHERN ITALIAN FAMILY
Acchiappafantasmi. This popular pizzeria near Campo de' Fiori offers pizza and much more. In addition to the traditional margherita you'll find their prizewinning version with buffalo mozzarella and cherry tomatoes, shaped like a ghost (a theme throughout, hence the name, which means "Ghostbusters"). Appetizers feature traditional fried items and Calabrese specialties, and secondi include a variety of items not standard to pizzerias, such as a version of eggplant Parmesan with prosciutto and egg. True to the owners' Calabrian roots, they offer spicy homemade *'nduja,* a spreadable sausage condiment comprised of pork and chili pepper at a ratio of 50:50—not for the weak of constitution! *Average main: €15 Via dei Cappellari 66, Campo de' Fiori 06/6873462 www.acchiappafantasmi.it Closed Mon. and 2 wks in Aug. 4:C3.*

$ CAFÉ
Alberto Pica. This artisan is renowned for his gelato production and the selection of seasonal *sorbetti* and *cremolate* (like sorbetto but made with the fruit pulp, not the juice). An interesting gelato flavor to try here is the *riso a cannella,* like a cinnamon rice pudding. These are possibly the grumpiest bar owners in Rome, so remember: in, out, and nobody gets hurt. *Average main: €4 Via della Seggiola 12, Campo de' Fiori 06/6868405 Closed Sun. and 2 wks in Aug. 4:D5.*

$$$ MODERN ITALIAN
Boccondivino. The structure is built around ancient Roman pillars but when you walk through the 16th-century door, it's clear that Boccondivino ("divine mouthful") is of the moment, with animal-print chairs and a glass-fronted dining room. The outdoor seating in the intimate piazzetta out front is a great summer spot. Start, perhaps, with a smoked swordfish served with peppery Roman arugula, candied citrus, and parmigiano cheese, then move on to a delicious pasta with pesto, shrimp, and cherry tomatoes. For a secondo, try the southern Italian *pezzogna* (like a plump snapper fish) in *acqua pazza*—a fish broth seasoned with tomato and a pinch of chili pepper. *Average main: €25 Piazza Campo Marzio 6, Campo de' Fiori 06/68308626 www.boccondivino.it Closed Sun. and 3 wks in Aug. 4:E2.*

$ PIZZA
Da Baffetto. On a cobblestone street not far from Piazza Navona, this is one of Rome's most popular pizzerias and a summer favorite for street-side dining. There is constand debate over whether this spot is overrated, but as with all the "great" pizzerias in Rome, it's hard to argue with the line that forms outside the door on weekends (the wait can be up to an hour). Happily, outdoor tables—enclosed and heated in winter—provide much-needed additional seating and turnover is fast; lingering is not encouraged. (Note: Baffetto 2, at Piazza del Teatro di Pompeo 18, also offers pasta and *secondi,* and doesn't suffer from the same overcrowding, plus you can reserve a table). *Average main: €12 Via del Governo Vecchio 114, Campo de' Fiori 06/6861617 www.pizzeriabaffetto.it No credit cards Closed Tues. and Aug. No lunch Mon.–Fri. 4:C3.*

$$ ITALIAN
Ditirambo. Don't let the country-kitchen ambience fool you. At this little spot off Campo de' Fiori, the constantly changing selection of offbeat takes on Italian classics is a step beyond ordinary Roman fare. Antipasti can be delicious and unexpected, like Gorgonzola-pear soufflé drizzled with aged balsamic vinegar, or a mille-feuille of mozzarella,

sundried tomatoes, and fresh mint. But people really love this place for rustic dishes like roast lamb, suckling pig, and hearty pasta with guinea fowl and porcini mushrooms. Vegetarians will adore the cheesy potato gratin with truffle shavings. Desserts can be skipped in favor of a *digestivo*. $ *Average main: €16* ✉ *Piazza della Cancelleria 74, Campo de' Fiori* ☎ *06/6871626* 🌐 *www.ristoranteditirambo.it* ⏲ *Closed 2 wks in Aug. No lunch Mon.* ✥ *4:D4.*

$ ITALIAN Fodor's Choice ★ **Filetti di Baccalà.** For years, Dar Filettaro a Santa Barbara (to use its official name) has been serving just that—battered, deep-fried fillets of salt cod—and not much else. You'll find no-frills starters such as *bruschette al pomodoro* (garlic-rubbed toast topped with fresh tomatoes and olive oil), and sautéed zucchini. In winter months, the cod is served alongside *puntarelle,* chicory stems tossed with a delicious anchovy-garlic-lemon vinaigrette. The location, down the street from Campo de' Fiori in a little piazza in front of the beautiful Santa Barbara church, begs you to eat at one of the outdoor tables, weather permitting. $ *Average main: €12* ✉ *Largo dei Librari 88, Campo de' Fiori* ☎ *06/6864018* ▬ *No credit cards* ⏲ *Closed Sun. and Aug. No lunch* ✥ *4:D4.*

$$$$ SEAFOOD Fodor's Choice ★ **Il Sanlorenzo.** This gorgeous space—think chandeliers and soaring original brickwork ceilings—houses one of the better seafood spots in the Eternal City. Tempting tasting menus are available, as well as à la carte items like a wonderful series of small plates including the *crudo* (raw fish) appetizer, which can include a perfectly seasoned fish tartare trio, sweet *scampi* (local langoustines), and a wispy-thin carpaccio of red shrimp. The restaurant's version of spaghetti with sea urchin is exquisite and delicate; follow up with a main course of freshly caught seasonal fish prepared to order. $ *Average main: €36* ✉ *Via dei Chiavari 4/5, Campo de' Fiori* ☎ *06/6865097* 🌐 *www.ilsanlorenzo.it* ✍ *Reservations essential* ⏲ *No lunch Sat.–Mon.* ✥ *4:D4.*

$$ WINE BAR **L'Angolo Divino.** There's something about this cozy wine bar that feels as if it's in a small university town instead of a bustling metropolis. Serene blue-green walls lined with wood shelves of wines from around the Italian peninsula add to the warm atmosphere. Along with several hot plates including fresh pasta, you can order smoked fish, cured meats, cheeses, and salads to make a nice lunch or light dinner. The kitchen stays open until the wee hours on weekends. $ *Average main: €15* ✉ *Via dei Balestrari 12, Campo de' Fiori* ☎ *06/6864413* 🌐 *www.angolodivino.it* ⏲ *Closed 1 wk in Aug.* ✥ *4:D5.*

$$ SEAFOOD **Monserrato.** In a high-rent area dense with design stores and antiques shops, this simple spot is just a few steps from elegant Piazza Farnese and yet happily devoid of throngs of tourists. Monserrato's signature dishes feature seafood: *carpaccio di pesce* (fresh fish carpaccio with lemon and arugula), *insalatina di seppie* (cuttlefish salad), *bigoli con gamberi e asparagi* (homemade pasta with shrimp and asparagus), and simple-but-satisfying grilled fish. There's also a nice antipasto assortment so you can eat your share of veggies. Select a nice white from the Italo-centric wine list and when the weather heats up, you can enjoy it all alfresco at umbrella-covered tables on the adjacent piazza. $ *Average*

main: €22 ✉ Via di Monserrato 96, Campo de' Fiori ☎ 06/6873386 ⏲ Closed Mon. and 1 wk at Christmas ✥ 4:C4.

$ ITALIAN ✕ **Open Baladin.** The craft beer movement has really taken hold in Italy of late. The Baladin label owns this casual beer-and-burger joint in a gorgeous, sprawling space down the road from Campo de' Fiori. Staff members take their jobs—and brews—seriously, and they're helpful with recommendations from the more than 40 interesting options on tap, from Baladin's own domestic beers to imports from Belgium, Germany, and beyond. There are also over 100 bottled beers on offer. The kitchen has yet to conquer the beauty of a simple burger done well and the classic accompaniment of french fries are sorely missed, but Italian options like antipasti, salads, and fresh mozzarella are good choices. [$] *Average main: €14 ✉ Via Degli Specchi 5-6, Campo de' Fiori, Roma ☎ 06/6838989 🌐 www.baladin.it ✥ 4:E5.*

$$ ROMAN ✕ **Osteria La Quercia.** Diners can sit under a gorgeous looming oak tree at this casual trattoria. The menu is simple—the usual suspects include fried starters like stuffed zucchini flowers, as well as Roman pasta dishes like spaghetti carbonara. Main dishes include *saltimbocca alla romana* (veal with prosciutto and sage) and meatballs in tomato sauce. The ubiquitous Roman sautéed *cicoria* (chicory) with olive oil and chili pepper is a good choice for a green side. Service is friendly and allows for lingering on balmy Roman afternoons and evenings—so close, and yet so seemingly far from the chaos of nearby Campo de' Fiori. [$] *Average main: €15 ✉ Piazza della Quercia 23, Campo de' Fiori ☎ 06/68300932 ✥ 4:C4.*

$$ SOUTHERN ITALIAN ✕ **Pesci Fritti.** This cute jewel box of a restaurant on the amphitheater-shaped street behind Campo de' Fiori serves the namesake fried fish, and much more. It feels like an escape to Capri, Amalfi, or one of the Pontine Islands off the Rome/Naples coast, all whitewashed with touches of pale sea blue. Much of the cuisine echoes this, with fish served *all'amalfitana*, (Amalfi style, with fresh lemon and white wine) or *in guazetto* (usually some variation on seafood broth with fresh tomato and wine). Also delicious are the baby octopus on toast, pasta with clams, and fish prepared many different ways. The few missteps happen when the cooks try to get too creative, so stick to the southern classics and enjoy this virtual seaside escape. [$] *Average main: €19 ✉ Via della Grottapinta 8, Campo de' Fiori, Roma ☎ 06/68806170 ⏲ Closed Sun. and Mon. ✥ 4:D4*

$$$ ITALIAN Fodor's Choice ★ ✕ **Pierluigi.** This perennial seafood favorite is quite the scene on balmy summer evenings, and interior renovations have made Pierluigi a year-round dining destination. As at many Italian fish *ristoranti*, antipasti featuring *crudi* (raw fish selections) are smart choices here: delicious tartare, carpaccio, shrimp, clams, and oysters are all in abundance. So are pastas and risotto with seafood, and mains like roasted turbot with potatoes, cherry tomatoes, and black olives are delicious. Traditional Roman meat dishes are also on offer for the landlubbers among the group. No matter your preference, ask for a nice *sgroppino* (lemon sorbet, vodka, and prosecco) to end the meal. [$] *Average main: €28 ✉ Piazza de Ricci 144, Campo de' Fiori, Roma ☎ 06/6861302 🌐 www.pierluigi.it/e_index.asp ✍ Reservations essential ⏲ Closed Mon. ✥ 4:B4*

$$$ ITALIAN Fodor's Choice ★ **Roscioli.** More like a Caravaggio painting than a place of business, this food shop and wine bar is dark and decadent. The store in front beckons with top-quality comestibles: wild Alaskan smoked salmon, hand-sliced prosciutto from Italy and Spain, more than 300 cheeses, and a dizzying array of wines. Venture farther inside to a cavelike room where you can sit and order artisanal cheeses and smoked meats, as well as an extensive selection of unusual dishes and interesting takes on classics. Try the burrata cheese with Norwegian herring caviar, pasta with sardines, or Sicilian linguini with red prawns and cumin. The menu features meats, seafood (including a nice selection of raw fish preparations), and vegetarian-friendly items. ■ **TIP→ Reserve a table in the cozy wine cellar beneath the dining room. After your meal, head around the corner to their bakery for rightfully famous breads and sweets.** *Average main: €30 Via dei Giubbonari 21/22, Campo de' Fiori 06/6875287 www.anticofornoroscioli.com Reservations essential Closed Sun. 4:D4.*

INSTEAD OF PORK . . .

Variations on cured pork, such as *guanciale* (cured pork jowl), *prosciutto* (smoked ham), and *pancetta* (bacon), are signature flavorings for Roman dishes. When Jewish culinary culture started intermingling with Roman, it was discovered that Jewish cooks used *alici* (anchovies) to flavor dishes the way Romans used cured pork. For excellent-quality anchovies, check out the Jewish *alimentari* (food shops) in the Ghetto.

$$ ITALIAN **Trattoria Moderna.** The space is as the name implies—modern, with high ceilings, done in neutral shades—with an oversize chalkboard displaying daily specials, such as a delicious chickpea and *baccalà* (salt cod) soup. The food runs toward the traditional but with a twist, like a pasta *all'amatriciana* with kosher beef instead of the requisite pork *guanciale* (cured pork jowl). Main courses are more creative but can be hit or miss. The friendly serving staff and reasonable prices are pluses, as is the outdoor seating—a few tables surrounded by greenery, off a lovely cobblestone street. *Average main: €16 Vicolo dei Chiodaroli 16, Campo de' Fiori 06/68803423 Closed Mon. 4:E4.*

JEWISH GHETTO

Across Via Arenula from the Campo de' Fiori, the Ghetto is home to Europe's oldest Jewish population, living in Rome uninterrupted for more than 2,000 years. There are excellent restaurants not just along its main drag, Via del Portico d'Ottavia, but also hidden in the narrow backstreets that wind between the river, Via Arenula, and Piazza Venezia.

$$$ ROMAN **Al Pompiere.** The entrance on a narrow side street leads upstairs to the main dining room of this neighborhood favorite where those in the know can enjoy dining on classic Roman fare under arched ceilings. Fried zucchini flowers, battered salt cod, and gnocchi are all consistently good, as are some nice, historic touches, like a beef-and-citron stew from an ancient Roman recipe of Apicius. If the *porchetta* (roasted suckling pig) is on the menu, order it immediately. Back in 2004, there was a terrible fire in a shop below the restaurant, but the kitchen was soon

back in business, though the irony here is as thick as the chef's tomato sauce: *Al Pompiere* means "the fireman." *Average main: €25 ✉ Via Santa Maria dei Calderari 38, Jewish Ghetto ☎ 06/6868377 www.alpompiereroma.com Closed Sun. and Aug. ↔ 4:E5.*

$$ ISRAELI Fodor's Choice ★ **Ba' Ghetto.** This hot spot on the main promenade in the Jewish Ghetto has been going strong for years. The smart black-and-white with turquoise decor makes the inside as pleasant as the outdoor seating in warmer months. The kitchen is kosher (many places featuring Roman Jewish fare are not), serving meat dishes, and features an assortment of Roman Jewish delights as well as Mediterranean–Middle Eastern Jewish fare. Enjoy starters like phyllo "cigars" stuffed with ground meat and spices, or the mixed dip platter with hummus. Forego pasta for a couscous (the spicy fish is delicious), or *baccalà* (dried salted cod) with raisins and pinenuts. Down the street is **Ba'Ghetto Milky** (Via del Portico d'Ottavia 2/a), the kosher dairy version of the original. *Average main: €22 ✉ Via del Portico d'Ottavia 57, Jewish Ghetto ☎ 06/68892868 www.kosherinrome.com No dinner Fri. No lunch Sat. ↔ 4:F5.*

$$ ROMAN **Bellacarne.** *Bellacarne* means "beautiful meat," and that's the focus of this Jewish Ghetto newcomer, though the double entendre is that it's also what a Jewish Italian grandmother might say while pinching her grandchild's cheek. The kosher kitchen makes its own pastrami—a decent version of what one might find in Jewish delis in NYC. The difference is that the meat is served on its own, thinly sliced, at room temperature, and on a platter with mustard—much like cured meats are served in Italy. It's culturally on point, though it might leave you longing for two slices of rye bread to make a sandwich. Try the fried artichokes, the shawarma with hummus, and chopped Israeli salad. The dining room is tranquil and lovely, but the kitchen is still working out a few kinks. *Average main: €22 ✉ Via Portico d'Ottavia 51, Jewish Ghetto, Roma ☎ 06/6833104 bellacarne.it No dinner Fri., no lunch Sat. Closed Jewish holidays ↔ 4:F5.*

$ CAFÉ **Pasticceria Boccioni.** *Forno* means "oven" in Italian, but it's also the word for a bakery that specializes in bread and simple baked goods, like biscotti and pine nut tarts. A pasticceria, on the other hand, specializes in more complicated Italian sweets, like fruit tarts, *montebianco* (a chestnut-cream creation resembling an alpine mountain), and *millefoglie* (puff pastry layered with pastry cream). Straddling the line between a forno and a pasticceria, on the "main drag" of the Ghetto, Pasticceria Boccioni—commonly known as Forno del Ghetto (aka "The Burnt Bakery," for the dark brown crust most everything here seems to have)—is famed for being the only establishment that makes Roman Jewish specialties. Try the delicious ricotta cheesecake, filled with cherries or chocolate, baked in an almondy crust. Get here early on Friday as they sell out before closing for the Sabbath. *Average main: €4 ✉ Via del Portico d'Ottavia 1, Jewish Ghetto ☎ 06/6878637 ↔ 4:F5.*

$$$ ROMAN **Piperno.** *The* place to go for Rome's extraordinary *carciofi alla giudia* (fried whole artichokes), Piperno has been in business since 1860. The location, up a tiny hill in a piazza tucked away behind the palazzi of the Jewish Ghetto, lends the restaurant a rarefied air. Try the exquisite

prosciutto and buffalo mozzarella plate, the *fiori di zucca ripieni e fritti* (fried stuffed zucchini flowers), and *filetti di baccalà* (fillet of cod) to start. The display of fresh local fish is enticing enough to lure diners to try offerings from sea instead of land. Service is in the old school style of dignified formality. This is a very popular destination for Sunday lunch. *Average main: €25 ✉ Monte dei Cenci 9, Jewish Ghetto ☎ 06/68806629 www.ristorantepiperno.it Reservations essential Closed Mon. and Aug. No dinner Sun. ✣ 4:E5.*

$$$ SEAFOOD Fodor's Choice ★ ✕ **San Teodoro.** The setting: a pair of enclosed piazzas, ivy-covered walls, nestled by the Roman Forum and Campidoglio. The specialty: refined Roman cuisine, including Roman Jewish fare and specializing in seafood. In spring and summer there's a lovely outdoor dining deck, and in cooler months, the bright rooms decorated with contemporary art offer pleasant surroundings. The menu includes classic fried artichokes (among the city's best), ravioli *con cipolla di Tropea* (filled with red onion and tossed in balsamic vinegar), and favorite local fish turbot, adorned with perfectly roasted potatoes. Everything down to the last bite (make your dessert choice the chocolate medley) is a pleasure, even if it doesn't come cheaply. An adjacent café is open at breakfast and lunch. *Average main: €33 ✉ Via dei Fienili 50–51, Jewish Ghetto ☎ 06/6780933 www.st-teodoro.it Reservations essential Closed Sun. ✣ 4:H6.*

$$$ ROMAN ✕ **Sora Lella.** It may not be the most original spot in town, but Sora Lella can boast that it's the only restaurant on Isola Tiberina, the wonderously picturesque island set in the middle of the Tiber river between the Jewish Ghetto and Trastevere, that's open year-round. The dining rooms on two floors are elegant, and service is discreet. As for the food, try the delicious prosciutto and mozzarella to start, and move on to classics like pasta *all'amatriciana,* meatballs in tomato sauce, or Roman baby lamb chops. The stuffed calamari in white wine sauce is worthy of *facendo una scarpetta*—taking a piece of bread to sop up the savory sauce. *Average main: €26 ✉ Via di Ponte Quattro Capi 16, Jewish Ghetto ☎ 06/6861601 www.soralella.com Reservations essential Closed 3 wks in Aug. ✣ 3:D1.*

$$$ SEAFOOD ✕ **Vecchia Roma.** Though the frescoed dining rooms are lovely, the choice place to dine is outside on the piazza, under the big white umbrellas, in the shadow of Santa Maria in Campitelli. For appetizers, the seafood selection may include an assortment of fresh anchovies in vinegary goodness, seafood salad, or baby shrimp. Chef Raffaella generally doles out large portions, so select one of her wonderful pasta dishes or skip straight to the secondi. Seafood is the specialty, and simple southern Italian preparations, such as fresh white flaky fish in a potato crust with cherry tomatoes, are excellent no-fail choices. House-made fruit desserts provide a light(ish) finish to the meal. *Average main: €28 ✉ Piazza Campitelli 18, Jewish Ghetto ☎ 06/6864604 www.ristorantevecchiaroma.com Reservations essential No lunch. Closed Wed. ✣ 4:F5.*

PIAZZA DI SPAGNA

The area around the Spanish Steps is a hotbed for tourists, serious shoppers, and work-week office dwellers during the day. It gets significantly quieter at night and, as a result, it's easy to fall into tourist traps and overpriced hotel dining. Stick to recommended restaurants.

$ CAFÉ **Antico Caffè Greco.** Pricey Antico Caffè Greco is a national landmark; its red-velvet chairs, marble tables, and neoclassical sculpted busts have hosted the likes of Byron, Shelley, Keats, Goethe, and Casanova, the antique artwork lining the walls lending it the air of a gorgeously romantic, bygone era. Located in the middle of the shopping madness on the upscale Via Condotti, this place is indeed filled with tourists, but there are some locals who love to breathe the air of history—more than 250 years of it—within these dark-wood walls. Coming at off-hours is your best bet to glimpse authenticity. *Average main: €12* *Via dei Condotti 86, Piazza di Spagna* *06/6791700* *www.anticocaffegreco.eu* *1:H2.*

$$$ NORTHERN ITALIAN **Caffè 'Gusto and Rotisserie 'Gusto.** This offshoot of the 'Gusto Empire focuses specifically on what can be dubbed Italian brasserie fare: basics, including pizza, with an emphasis on casual café eats. Look for pizza and sandwiches during the day and typical Roman dinner fare at night, including rich pasta with black truffle and rotisserie-cooked meats from central-north Italian traditions. The space is a soaring modern spot, like the rest of the 'Gusto siblings, with a vibe of urban smart. Service can be a bit slow, but hey, the waiters are serious about their *bella figura,* meaning they look good, so you might not notice. *Average main: €25* *Piazza Augusto Imperatore 28, Piazza di Spagna* *06/68134221* *www.gusto.it* *1:G2.*

$$$ ECLECTIC **Caffè Romano dell'Hotel d'Inghilterra.** One of Rome's most soigné hotels, the d'Inghliterra houses this symphony in beige marbles and classic columns. This spot is geared towards jet-setters and hotel guests—it's got *orario continuato,* or nonstop operating hours, from 10 am, so snacking or having a late lunch is a possibility here. Though its menu is "global," some of the dishes are simply international misfires, so it's best to select from among the authentic northern Italian meat and southern Italian seafood dishes. Safe bets include glazed boar with polenta, seafood soup, or a classic pasta dish. Tables are close together, but perhaps you won't mind eavesdropping on your supermodel neighbor. *Average main: €28* *Via Borgongna 4M, Piazza di Spagna* *06/69981500* *www.royaldemeure.com* M *Spagna* *1:H2.*

$ CAFÉ **GiNa.** "Homey minimalism" isn't a contradiction at this whitewashed café with a modern edge. The block seats and sleek booths, white chandeliers, and multiplicity of mirrors make this small but multilevel space a tiny gem. The menu offers various bruschette, mixed salads, and sandwiches, making this a great spot for a light lunch or aperitivo at a reasonable price (considering the high-end neighborhood). And the sweets are top-notch: gelato, pastries, fruit with yogurt, and even some American pies and cheesecake, along with the best hot chocolate in Rome during the winter. In warmer months, fully stocked gourmet picnic baskets are ready for pick up on your way to Villa Borghese park.

$ *Average main: €10* ✉ *Via San Sebastianello 7A, Piazza di Spagna* ☎ *06/6780251* 🌐 *www.ginaroma.com* Ⓜ *Spagna* ✣ *1:H2.*

$$ WINE BAR ✕ **'Gusto.** There's an urban-loft feel to this trendy two-story space, a bit like a Pottery Barn exploded in Piazza Augusto Imperatore. The ground floor trattoria has a busy, buzzing atmosphere and serves typically Roman and Italian staples, done well. The ground-floor wine bar in the back has a casual-but-hopping vibe, where a rotating selection of wines by the glass and bottle are served alongside a vast array of cheeses, salumi, and breads. Lunchtime features a great-value salad bar. And for the kitchen enthusiast, the 'Gusto "complex" includes a store, selling everything from cookware to cookwear. Upstairs is a more upscale restaurant, where some dishes work, some don't. $ *Average main: €22* ✉ *Piazza Augusto Imperatore 9, Piazza di Spagna* ☎ *06/3226273* 🌐 *www.gusto.it* ✣ *1:G2.*

$$$ ITALIAN ✕ **'Gusto – Osteria.** The second sibling in the 'Gusto empire focuses on hearty traditional Roman fare. And why not? Romans are traditionalists and regionalists, so, when in Rome.... You may want to begin by choosing from the vast selection of 400 cheeses kept in the basement cellar, then from the various *fritti* (fried items), and moving on to pastas such as sheep's milk cheese and pepper spaghetti. Secondi are meats or grilled seafood items, highlighting the simplicity of the *cucina romana*. The atmosphere is predictably buzzy, and the loft-like airy space is a refreshing change from the often dour standard found elsewhere. $ *Average main: €26* ✉ *Via della Frezza 16, Piazza di Spagna* ☎ *06/32111482* 🌐 *www.gusto.it* ✍ *Reservations essential* ✣ *1:G2.*

$ CAFÉ ✕ **Il Gelato di San Crispino.** Perhaps the most celebrated gelato in all of Italy is created here at San Crispino. Without artificial colors or flavors, these scoops are worth crossing town for. Flavors like chocolate rum, armagnac, and ginger-cinnamon keep taste buds tap-dancing. And to preserve the "integrity" of the flavor, the ice cream is only served in paper cups. Some naysayers claim it's overrated. But either way, additional locations behind the Pantheon (Piazza della Maddalena 3) and San Giovanni (Via Acaia 56) are proof that the word is getting out and the empire is growing. $ *Average main: €4* ✉ *Via della Panetteria 42, Piazza di Spagna* ☎ *06/6793924* 🌐 *www.ilgelatodisancrispino.it* ⏲ *Closed Tues.* ✣ *4:H2.*

$ PIZZA Fodor's Choice ★ ✕ **Il Leoncino.** Lines out the door on weekends attest to the popularity of this fluorescent-lighted pizzeria in the otherwise big-ticket neighborhood around Piazza di Spagna. This is one of the few pizzerias open for lunch as well as dinner. $ *Average main: €12* ✉ *Via del Leoncino 28, Piazza di Spagna* ☎ *06/6867757* ⏲ *Closed Wed. and Aug. No lunch weekends* ✣ *1:G3.*

$$ WINE BAR ✕ **L'Enoteca Antica di Via della Croce.** This wine bar is always crowded, and for good reason. It's long on personality: colorful ceramic-tile tables are filled with locals and foreigners, as is the half moon–shaped bar where you can order from the large selection of salumi and cheeses on offer. Peruse the chalkboard highlighting the special wines by-the-glass for that day to accompany your nibbles. There's waiter service at the tables in back and out front on the bustling Via della Croce, where people-watching is in high gear. $ *Average main: €20* ✉ *Via della Croce 76/b,*

Piazza di Spagna ☎ *06/6790896* 🌐 *www.anticaenoteca.com* ⏲ *Closed 2 wks in Aug.* Ⓜ *Spagna* ✥ *1:G2.*

$$$ MODERN ITALIAN ✕ **Moma.** Almost a sister in spirit to the Hotel Aleph, a favorite of the design *trendoisie* across the street, Moma is modern, moody, and very "concept." The menu has hits and misses, and attempts to raise the nouvelle bar in Rome—foie gras *millefoglie* with apple slices and cider vinegar gelée, anyone? Seared scallops, plump and sweet, are a find, and the rigatoni all'amatriciana is tasty. Mains like lamb with spices and yogurt and a Jerusalem artichoke salad are flavorful twists on classics. There are several basic desserts, of which the molten chocolate cake is probably the best, served with pear sorbetto and chocolate sauce. $ *Average main: €25* ✉ *Via San Basilio 42/43, Piazza di Spagna* ☎ *06/42011798* 🌐 *www.ristorantemoma.it* ✍ *Reservations essential* ⏲ *Closed Sun. and 2 wks in Aug.* Ⓜ *Barberini–Fontana di Trevi* ✥ *2:C2.*

$$$ ITALIAN Fodor's Choice ★ ✕ **Nino.** A favorite among international journalists and the rich and famous for decades (Tom Cruise and Katie Holmes had their celeb-studded rehearsal dinner here), Nino is Rome's best loved dressed-up trattoria. The interior is country rustic *alla Tuscana,* and, along with its look (and waiters!), Nino sticks to the classics when it comes to its food—basically Roman and Tuscan staples. Start with a selection from the fine antipasto spread, or go for the cured meats or warm *crostini* (toasts) spread with liver pâté. Move on to pappardelle *al lepre* (a rich hare sauce) or hearty Tuscan ribollita soup, and go for the gold with a piece of juicy grilled beef. ⚠ **If you're not Italian, or a regular, or a celebrity, the chance of brusque service multiplies—insist on good service and you'll win the waiters' respect.** $ *Average main: €28* ✉ *Via Borgognona 11, Piazza di Spagna* ☎ *06/6786752, 06/6795676* 🌐 *www.ristorantenino.it* ⏲ *Closed Sun. and Aug.* Ⓜ *Spagna* ✥ *1:H2.*

$$$ TUSCAN ✕ **Papá Baccus.** Italo Cipriani takes his meat as seriously as any Tuscan, using real Chianina beef for the house specialty, the *bistecca alla fiorentina,* a thick grilled steak served on the bone and rare in the center. Cipriani brings many ingredients from his hometown on the border of Emilia-Romagna and Tuscany. Try the sweet and delicate prosciutto from Pratomagno or the *ribollita,* a traditional bread-based minestrone soup. Anything that says "cinta senese" refers to a special breed of pig—and is worth eating. The welcome is warm, the service excellent, and the glass of prosecco (gratis) starts the meal on the right foot. $ *Average main: €28* ✉ *Via Toscana 36, Piazza di Spagna* ☎ *06/42742808* 🌐 *www.papabaccus.com* ✍ *Reservations essential* ⏲ *Closed Sun. and 2 wks in Aug. No lunch Sat.* ✥ *2:C1.*

REPUBBLICA AND QUIRINALE

REPUBBLICA

The areas around Piazza Repubblica and Termini station aren't known as gastronomic hot spots, but there are some classic Roman wine bars.

$$ WINE BAR ✕ **Trimani Il Winebar.** Operating nonstop from 11 am to midnight, this wine bar serves hot food at lunch and dinner. The interior is in minimalist style, and the second floor provides a subdued, candlelit space to sip wine. There's always a choice of soup and pasta plates, as well

CLOSE UP

Refueling the Roman Way

Staggering under the weight of a succession of three-course meals, you may ask yourself, how do the Romans eat so much, twice a day, every day? The answer is, they don't.

If you want to do as the Romans do, try lunch at a *tavola calda* (literally, hot table), a cross between a café and a cafeteria where you'll find fresh food in manageable portions.

There's usually a selection of freshly prepared pastas, cooked vegetables such as *bietola all'agro* (cooked beet greens with lemon), roasted potatoes, and grilled or roasted meat or fish.

Go to the counter to order an assortment and quantity that suits your appetite, and pay by the plate, usually about €5 plus drinks. Tavole calde aren't hard to find, particularly in the city center, as they're often marked with "tavola calda" or "self-service" signs.

The other ubiquitous options for a light lunch or between-meal snack are pizza *al taglio* (by the slice) shops, bars, and enoteche (wine bars). At bars throughout Italy, coffee is the primary beverage served (drinking establishments are commonly known as pubs or American bars); at them you can curb your appetite with a panino (a simple sandwich) or tramezzino (triangular sandwich on crustless, untoasted white bread, usually heavy on the mayonnaise).

Wine bars vary widely in the sophistication and variety of food available, but you can count on cheese and cured meats, at the very least.

as second courses and *torte salate* (savory tarts). Around the corner is a wineshop, one of the oldest in Rome, of the same name. Call about wine tastings and classes (in Italian). $ *Average main: €15* ✉ *Via Cernaia 37/b, Repubblica* ☎ *06/4469630* 🌐 *www.trimani.com* ⏲ *Closed Sun. and 2 wks in Aug.* M *Castro Pretorio* ✣ *2:E2.*

QUIRINALE

This area has lots of government offices, hotels, and museums, and the tourist traps and expense account stalwarts that go with them. There are some reasonable standouts though.

$$$ TUSCAN ✕ **Tullio.** Just off Piazza Barberini sits this Tuscan-accented upscale trattoria. The decor is basic wood paneling and white linens, with the requisite older—and often grumpy—waiters. The menu is heavy on Tuscan classics such as white beans and the famed *bistecca alla fiorentina,* a carnivore's dream. Meat dishes other than beef, such as lamb and veal, are also dependably good. The homemade pappardelle *al cinghiale* (wide, flat noodles in a wild boar sauce) are delectable. A few key Roman dishes and greens are offered, like *brocoletti,* sauteéd to perfection with garlic and olive oil. The wine list favors robust Tuscan reds and thick wallets. $ *Average main: €32* ✉ *Via San Nicola da Tolentino 26, Quirinale* ☎ *06/4745560* 🌐 *www.tullioristorante.it* ✍ *Reservations essential* ⏲ *Closed Sun. and Aug.* M *Barberini–Fontana di Trevi* ✣ *2:C3.*

VILLA BORGHESE, PIAZZA DEL POPOLO, FLAMINIO, AND MONTE MARIO

VILLA BORGHESE

One of Rome's two large parks borders the famed-but-faded Via Veneto, the former haunt of the Hollywood-on-the-Tiber scene. The upscale neighborhood is home to historic dining destinations as well as the café culture that formed the main scene for those living La Dolce Vita.

$$$ ITALIAN **Al Ceppo.** The well-heeled, the business-minded, and those of more refined palate frequent this outpost of tranquility. Its owners hail from Le Marche, the region northeast of Rome that encompasses inland mountains and the Adriatic coastline. These ladies dote on their customers as you'd wish a sophisticated Italian *mamma* would. There's always a selection of dishes from their native region, such as *olive ascolane* (green olives stuffed with ground meat, breaded, and fried), fresh pasta dishes, succulent roast lamb, and a delicious *marchigiano*-style rabbit. Other temptations include a beautiful display of seafood and a wide selection of meats ready to be grilled in the fireplace in the front room. *Average main: €32 Via Panama 2, Villa Borghese 06/8419696 www.ristorantealceppo.it Reservations essential Closed Mon. and 2 wks in Aug. 2:C1.*

$$$$ ITALIAN **Casina Valadier.** Every Hollywood movie filmed in Rome had a scene set here: a splendid pavilion in the Villa Borghese park, designed by the great neoclassical architect Giuseppe Valadier. "The most beautiful restaurant in Rome" finally underwent a major renovation in 2007, but with mixed results. The bar area and terrace are still delightful, but the setting (gorgeous, but even the refurbished interiors could use some upkeep) and magnificent view are not matched by what the kitchen puts out, as quality is inconsistent. Fresh tagliatelle with capon, sweetbreads, and black truffle are truly delicious, but a seafood *fregola* (Sardinian couscous) is fishy. The wine list is surprisingly moderate on cost and offers nice variety. *Average main: €36 Piazza Bucarest, Villa Borghese 06/69922090 www.casinavaladier.it Reservations essential Closed Mon. and 2 wks in Aug. 1:H1.*

$$$ AMERICAN **Duke's.** It dubs itself a California-style restaurant and bar, although the California rolls contain tuna and carrot and they've added mint leaves to the Caesar salad. Truth be told, after a stretch of Italian-only bingeing, you may actually want *the entire menu*. Perhaps a nice, juicy beef fillet, and the finishing touch of a warm apple pie served with gelato. The decor is Malibu beach house, with a patio out back: consummately SoCal chic. Up front, opening out onto the street, the beautiful people from the neighborhood (read: plenty of unnatural blondes) gather at the bar, sipping frozen cocktails, the whir of blenders and music blaring in the background. *Average main: €26 Viale Parioli 200, Villa Borghese 06/80662455 www.dukes.it Reservations essential June–Sept. closed weekends; Sept.–May closed Sun. and Mon. Closed 2 wks in Aug. No lunch 2:C1.*

PIAZZA DEL POPOLO

This high-traffic shopping and tourist zone has both casual *pizzerie* and upscale eateries, as well as classic cafés where one can have a restorative espresso and light bite.

$$$$ EMILIAN **Dal Bolognese.** The darling of the media, film, and fashion communities, this classic restaurant off Piazza del Popolo is not only a perennial hot spot, but a convenient lunch break mid-shopping spree. The offerings adhere to the hearty tradition of Bologna, so start with a plate of sweet prosciutto di Parma, then move on to the traditional egg pastas of Emilia-Romagna. Secondi include the famous *bollito misto,* a steaming tray of an assortment of boiled meats (some recognizable, some indecipherable) served with its classic accompaniment, a tangy, herby *salsa verde* (green sauce). Linger for dessert and take in the passing parade of destination diners as they air kiss their way around the room. *Average main: €35 Piazza del Popolo 1, Piazza del Popolo 06/3611426 dalbolognese.it Reservations essential Closed Mon. and 3 wks in Aug. Flaminio 1:G1.*

$$ WINE BAR **Il Brillo Parlante.** Il Brillo Parlante's location near Piazza del Popolo makes it convenient for lunch or dinner after a bit of shopping in the Via del Corso area. Choose from 20 wines by the glass at the bar or eat downstairs in one of several wood-panel rooms. The menu is extensive for a wine bar; choose from cured meats, *crostini* (toasted bread with various toppings such as pâté or prosciutto), pastas, grilled meats, and even pizzas. *Average main: €16 Via della Fontanella 15, Piazza del Popolo 06/3243334 www.ilbrilloparlante.com Closed Mon. and 1 wk in mid-Aug. No lunch 1:G1.*

$ VEGETARIAN **Il Margutta.** Parallel to posh Via del Babuino, Via Margutta has long been known as the street where artists have their studios in Rome. How fitting, then, that the rare Italian vegetarian restaurant, with changing displays of modern art, sits on the far end of this gallery-lined street. Here it takes on a chic and cosmopolitan air, where you'll find meat-free versions of classic Mediterranean dishes as well as more daring tofu concoctions. Lunch is essentially a pasta/salad bar to which you help yourself, while dinner offers à la carte and prix-fixe options. *Average main: €14 Via Margutta 118, Piazza del Popolo 06/32650577 www.ilmarguttavegetariano.it 1:G1.*

$ CAFÉ **Rosati.** You can sit yourself down and watch the world go by at Rosati, where tourists and locals have met for decades to sip and be seen. This is a stalwart of Roman café culture, open since 1922. *Average main: €12 Piazza del Popolo 5, Piazza del Popolo 06/3225859 www.barrosati.com Flaminio 1:G1.*

FLAMINIO

This area is largely residential, with a few destination dining spots.

$$$ SEAFOOD **Acquolina.** Chef-proprietor of Il Convivio Angelo Troiani has branched out, heading out of the city center to the Flaminio area, and specializing here in high-quality seafood. He tapped chef Giulio Terrinoni to head the kitchen, and the results are delicious and understated, with some dishes reflecting the time-honored Italian tradition of letting great seafood speak for itself. The crudo is ultra-fresh, and pastas like

the seafood carbonara and the *cacio e pepe* (cheese and pepper) with skate and zucchini flowers are upscale aquatic riffs on Roman classics. Main dishes range from fish stew to *gran fritto misto* (deep-fried seafood platter). Desserts are surprisingly sophisticated. Service is helpful and thorough, but beware of the sometimes slow kitchen. *$ Average main: €28 ✉ Via Antonio Serra 60, Flaminio ☎ 06/3337192 ⊕ www.acquolinahostaria.it ⊙ Closed Sun. No lunch ✣ 1:F1.*

MONTE MARIO

This hilltop neighborhood has Rome's fanciest restaurants.

$$$$ MODERN ITALIAN Fodor's Choice ★

✕ **La Pergola.** La Pergola's rooftop location offers a commanding view of the city and a three-Michelin-star experience. The difficulty comes in choosing from among Chef Heinz Beck's *alta cucina* (haute cuisine) specialties, though most everything will prove to be incredibly special. Lobster is perfectly poached, and fish is cooked properly—including a delicious black cod with a curried crust and celery sauce. The dessert course is extravagant, including tiny petits fours, and the wine list is as thrilling as one might expect from such a high-class establishment. *$ Average main: €50 ✉ Rome Cavalieri hotel, Via Cadlolo 101, Monte Mario ☎ 06/35092152 ⊕ www.romecavalieri.com/lapergola.php ✍ Reservations essential 👔 Jacket and tie ⊙ Closed Sun., Mon., 2 wks in Aug., and most of Jan. No lunch ✣ 1:A1.*

TRASTEVERE

Trastevere has always been known for its Left Bank bohemian appeal. A hip expat enclave with working-class Roman roots, the neighborhood is now lined with so many trattorias and wine bars that it's starting to feel like a Roman gastro-theme park. The Gianicolo is more subdued, with a few restaurants at the top worth the hike up the hill (not to mention the breathtaking view).

$$ ROMAN FAMILY Fodor's Choice ★

✕ **Alle Fratte di Trastevere.** Here you find staple Roman trattoria fare as well as dishes with a southern slant. This means *spaghetti alla carbonara* (with pancetta, eggs, and cheese) shares the menu with penne *alla Sorrentina* (with tomato, basil, and fresh mozzarella). For starters, the bruschette here are exemplary, as is the pressed octopus carpaccio on a bed of arugula. As for *secondi,* you can again look to the sea for a grilled sea bass with oven-roasted potatoes, or go for the meat with a fillet *al pepe verde* (green peppercorns in a brandy cream sauce). Service is always with a smile, as owner Francesco and his trusted staff make you feel at home. *$ Average main: €15 ✉ Via delle Fratte di Trastevere 49/50, Trastevere ☎ 06/5835775 ⊕ www.allefratteditrastevere.com ⊙ Closed Wed. and 2 wks in Aug. ✣ 3:B2.*

$ SICILIAN

✕ **Antica Focacceria San Francesco.** The people behind this Sicilian restaurant, which has roots that go back as far as 1834 in Palermo, have teamed with the Feltrinelli Group (essentially the Italian Barnes & Noble) to open locations of this fun, modern-rustic restaurant in Rome and Milan in the past few years. There are Sicilian classics on the menu, but the thing to focus on here is the street food called *schiticchi.* These savory bites include chickpea pancakes, fried dough, fried risotto balls, eggplant caponata, and breaded stuffed sardines. Otherwise, the focaccia is well made, the pastas are decent, and the seafood secondi passable. Sicilian sweets are always a highlight, and here the young crowd comes to devour the delicious cannoli and pistachio mousse. *Average main: €14 Piazza San Giovanni della Malva 14, Trastevere, Roma 06/5819503 www.afsf.it 3:B1.*

$$$ MODERN ITALIAN Fodor's Choice ★ **Antico Arco.** Founded by three friends with a passion for wine and fine food (the team leader is Patrizia Mattei), Antico Arco attracts foodies from Rome and beyond with its refined culinary inventiveness. The location on top of the Janiculum hill provides a charming setting, and recent renovations updated the dining rooms into plush, modern spaces: whitewashed brick walls, dark floors, and black velvet chairs. The seasonal menu offers delights such as amberjack tartare with lime, ginger, and a salad of chicory stems; classic pasta alla carbonara enriched with black truffle; and a duck with artichokes and foie gras. The molten chocolate cake is justly famous among chocoholics the city over. *Average main: €28 Piazzale Aurelio 7, Trastevere 06/5815274 www.anticoarco.it Reservations essential Closed Sun. and 2 wks in Aug. 3:A1.*

$ CAFÉ **Bar San Calisto.** Walk toward Viale di Trastevere and discover the small and wonderfully down-at-the-heels Bar San Calisto, immensely popular with the old local community and expat crowd. The drinks are as inexpensive as the neighborhood gets and the same could be said about the institutional lighting; the crowd wavers between bohemian and just plain unshowered and drunk. Don't miss the super hot chocolate in winter and the chocolate gelato in summer, both of which are as rich as the beer is cheap. *Average main: €4 Piazza San Calisto 4, Trastevere 06/5895678 Reservations not accepted 3:B1.*

$ ROMAN **Da Lucia.** There's no shortage of old-school trattorias in Trastevere, but Da Lucia seems to have a strong following among them. Both locals and expats enjoy the brusque "authentic" service and hearty Roman fare, like classic *bombolotti* (short, fat tubed pasta) all'amatriciana and spaghetti *cacio e pepe* (cheese and pepper), and meat dishes like beef *involtini* with peas and Roman-style tripe. Snag a table outside in warm weather for the true Roman experience of dining on the cobblestones. *Average main: €14 Vicolo del Mattonato 2b, Trastevere, Roma 06/5803601 www.trattoriadalucia.com Closed Mon. 3:A1*

$ PIZZA **Dar Poeta.** Romans drive across town for great pizza from this neighborhood institution on a small street in Trastevere. Maybe it's the dough—it's made from a secret blend of flours that's reputed to be easier to digest than the competition. They offer both thin-crust pizza and a thick-crust (*alta*) Neapolitan-style pizza with any of the given toppings. For dessert, there's a ridiculously good calzone with Nutella chocolate-hazelnut spread and ricotta cheese, so save some room. Service from the owners and friendly waitstaff is smile-inducing. *Average main: €12 Vicolo del Bologna 45, Trastevere 06/5880516 www.darpoeta.com No lunch 4:B6.*

$$$ ITALIAN **Ferrara.** This key corner of Trastevere real estate has become "the Ferrara block": what was once an enoteca has expanded into a restaurant, wine bar, and gastronomic boutique. The renovations have resulted in an airy, modernist destination, with the original space as it was, all

wooden chairs and ceramic-tiled tables. Service can be iffy to slow, and, in the end, the results coming out of the kitchen are inconsistent. A fine starter is ricotta-and-herb-stuffed zucchini flowers with crispy pancetta. Secondi include pigeon-quail *alla diavola* (spicy) with onions glazed in raspberry vinegar. But true to its enoteca roots, it's the award-winning wine selection that impresses here. *Average main: €25 Piazza Trilussa 41, Trastevere 06/58333920 www.enotecaferrara.it Reservations essential No lunch 4:C6.*

$ CAFÉ **Gelateria alla Scala.** This may be a tiny place but don't let the size fool you. It does a good business offering artisanal gelato prepared in small batches, so when one flavor runs out on any given day, it's finished. *Average main: €3 Via della Scala 51, Trastevere 06/5813174 Closed Dec. and Jan. 4:B6.*

$$$$ MODERN ITALIAN **Glass Hostaria.** After 14 years in Austin, Texas, Glass chef Cristina Bowerman returned to Rome to reconnect with her Italian roots. Her cooking is as innovative as the building she works in, which has received numerous recognitions for its design since opening in 2004. Bowerman still abides by some cardinal Italian kitchen rules, such as the use of fresh, local, seasonal ingredients. The menu changes frequently, featuring dishes like tagliatelle pasta with eggplant, prunes, and ricotta *affumicata* (smoked); scallops with brussels sprouts, lentils, and radishes in dashi broth; and for dessert, a passion fruit frozen custard with lychees, cornbread, and popcorn granita. Need help pairing wine? Glass offers more than 600 labels for interested oenophiles. *Average main: €35 Vicolo del Cinque 58, Trastevere 06/58335903 www.glass-restaurant.it Reservations essential Closed Mon. No lunch 4:C6.*

$$ TUSCAN **Il Ciak.** This Tuscan staple in Trastevere is a carnivore's delight. Specializing in the Tuscan *chianina* beef as well as the many game and pork dishes of the region, Il Ciak prepares reliably tasty fare. It's probably best appreciated during the autumn and winter months, when hunter's dishes—such as wild boar sausage or the pasta with wild hare sauce—get accompaniments like porcini mushrooms and truffles with polenta. Be prepared to share the pleasure of your oversize fiorentina steak—prepared *al sangue* (rare), of course. *Average main: €22 Vicolo del Cinque 21, Trastevere 06/5894774 ristoranteilciak.com Reservations essential No lunch Mon.–Sat. 4:C6.*

$$ INDIAN **Jaipur.** Named after the pink city in India, this restaurant meets the standards of the most discerning Londoners, who know a thing or two about their curries. Here, in this large space just off the main Viale di Trastevere, you'll find a vast, high-ceilinged dining room decked in retina-burning yellow with festive Indian decorations on the huge walls (there's also dining outside when the weather calls for it). Portions are small but made for sharing, so go ahead and get a variety of dishes to "divide and conquer." *Average main: €16 Via di San Francesco a Ripa 56, Trastevere 06/5803992 www.ristorantejaipur.it No lunch Mon. 3:C2.*

$$$ SICILIAN Fodor's Choice ★ **La Gensola.** For Italian "mainlanders," going out for Sicilian fare is a culinary adventure involving out-of-the-ordinary tastes and flavor combinations, many thanks to the island's interesting mix of Arab, African, and Mediterranean influences. Antipasti include fresh tuna "meatballs"

or gratineéd scallops with squid ink. Pastas, like a homemade tagliatelle with sun-dried tomatoes, baby calamari, and spicy peperoncino, are zippy on the palate. Sicily is Italy's largest island, so it's no surprise that its cuisine leans heavily on the bounty of the sea; a fresh fish like turbot with tomatoes, red onion, and capers is a wonderful choice. And for dessert, don't pass up an opportunity to try a cannolo or a piece of cassata cake. *Mmm, buono!* *Average main: €26* *Piazza della Gensola 15, Trastevere* *06/5816312* *www.osterialagensola.it* *Reservations essential* *3:C1.*

$ WINE BAR **Ombre Rosse.** Set on lovely Piazza Sant'Egidio in the heart of Trastevere, this open-day-and-night spot is a great place to pass the time. You can have a morning cappuccino and read one of their international newspapers; have a light lunch (soups and salads are fresh and delicious) while taking in some sun or working on your laptop (free Wi-Fi); enjoy an aperitivo and nibbles at an outdoor table; or finish off an evening with friends at the bar. Ombre Rosse bustles with regulars and expats who know the value of a well-made cocktail and an ever-lively atmosphere. *Average main: €12* *Piazza Sant'Egidio 12, Trastevere* *06/5884155* *www.ombrerossecaffe.it* *Reservations not accepted* *No lunch Sun.* *3:B1.*

$ PIZZA FAMILY **Panattoni.** Nicknamed "L'Obitorio" (the morgue) for its marble-slab tables, Panattoni is actually about as lively as you can get. Packed every night, it serves crisp pizzas that come out of the wood-burning ovens at top speed. The fried starters here, like a nice *baccalà* (cod), are light and tasty. Panattoni stays open well past midnight, convenient for a late meal after the theater or a movie nearby. *Average main: €12* *Viale Trastevere 53–57, Trastevere* *06/5800919* *Reservations not accepted* *No credit cards* *Closed Wed. and 3 wks in mid-Aug. No lunch* *3:C2.*

$$$ ITALIAN **Ripa 12.** This classic Roman seafood spot is an old standard in the neighborhood, and renovations a few years ago spiffed it up and made the environs as elegant as the food. Fresh ingredients and simple preparations make this a great place for going for broke with a mixed antipasto of crudi, including delicious tartares, carpaccios, and the like. Or, pick fresh shellfish and mollusks to slurp down with some spumante, always the perfect accompaniment to light, bright seafood. Pastas like a classic spaghetti *con le vongole* (white clam sauce) are expertly prepared, and main courses are inventive, like black cod cooked on a rock with pistachios and pink salt. *Average main: €28* *Via San Francesco a Ripa 12, Trastevere, Roma* *06/5809098* *www.ripa12.com* *Reservations essential* *Closed Sun.* *3:B2*

$$ ITALIAN **Spirito di Vino.** At this restaurant on the less-traveled side of Viale Trastevere, diners can enjoy an evening of historical and culinary interest. The restaurant was rebuilt on the site of a 12th-century Jewish synagogue, so the spot is rich with history—several ancient sculptures, now in the Vatican and Capitoline museums, were unearthed in the basement. The food ranges from inventive (marinated duck salad with grapes, walnuts, and pomegranate seeds) to traditional (spaghetti with pecorino and pepper), to historical (braised pork shoulder with apples and leeks, an ancient Roman recipe). The proud owner is happy to

explain every dish on the menu, and offers a postdinner tour of the wine cellar—and that basement. $ *Average main: €18* ✉ *Via dei Genovesi 31, Trastevere* ☎ *06/5896689* 🌐 *www.spiritodivino.com* ⏲ *Closed Sun. and 2 wks in Aug.* ✥ *3:C2.*

TESTACCIO

Testaccio is a true Roman working-class neighborhood, where the old slaughterhouses once stood and butchers invented the (in)famous meat and *quinto quarto* (offal) dishes you can still find in authentic Roman spots.

$$ ITALIAN Fodor's Choice ★

✕ **Angelina.** Via Galvani is prime real estate in the hip nabe of Testaccio, and at Angelina, you're one or two stories above all the riff-raff, eating grilled pizzas and steaks, or sipping drinks among the treetops that line the street. Or you're inside, in one of Angelina's whitewashed dining rooms pungently perfumed with the smell of the grill. Starters range from salumi to fried veggies, and first courses are hearty Roman staples like rigatoni all'amatriciana. But the focus here is on meat *alla brace*—everything grilled, from sausages to steaks to lamb. It's a scene here, from aperitivo through *dopocena* (postdinner), so get ready to enjoy the party. Another location that's more of a casual bar-café, called Angelina Trevi, is near the Trevi Fountain at Via Poli 27. $ *Average main: €18* ✉ *Via Galvani 24a, Testaccio* ☎ *06/57283840* 🌐 *www.ristoranteangelina.com* ✥ *3:C4.*

$$$ ROMAN

✕ **Checchino dal 1887.** Literally carved out of a hill of ancient shards of amphorae, Checchino remains an example of a classic, upscale family-run Roman restaurant, with one of the best wine cellars in the region. Though the slaughterhouses of Testaccio are long gone, an echo of their existence lives on in the restaurant's soul food—mostly offal and sundry cuts like *trippa* (tripe), *pajata* (intestine with the mother's milk still inside), and *coratella* (sweetbreads and beef heart) are all still on the menu for Roman purists. For the less adventuresome, house specialties include braised milk-fed lamb with seasonal vegetables. It's always a classic, but note that Checchino is really beginning to show its age. $ *Average main: €30* ✉ *Via di Monte Testaccio 30, Testaccio* ☎ *06/5746318* 🌐 *www.checchino-dal-1887.com* ✍ *Reservations essential* ⏲ *Closed Sun., Mon., Aug., and 1 wk at Christmas* ✥ *3:C5.*

$ ROMAN

✕ **Da Oio a Casa Mia.** Some turn their noses up at this classic Roman trattoria, but it has all the usual suspects, including locals straight out of central casting and gruff but good-natured service. The classic local pastas here are good bets, with delicious versions of carbonara, amatriciana, and rigatoni with a *coda alla vaccinara* (stewed oxtail) tomato sauce. Secondi like meatballs, chicken hunter's style, and stewed tripe are all excellent options. The grilled eggplant preserved in olive oil and vinegar, with a nice kick of peperoncino, is a killer side dish not to be overlooked. Outdoor seating in warm months is the way to go. $ *Average main: €14* ✉ *Via Galvani 43–45, Testaccio* ☎ *06/5782680* ⏲ *Closed Sun.* M *Piramide* ✥ *3:C4.*

$$ ROMAN Fodor's Choice ★ ✕ **Flavio al Velavevodetto.** It's all the things you want a real Roman eating experience to be: authentic, in a historic setting, filled with Italians eating good food at good prices. In this very "romani di Roma" working-class neighborhood, and surrounded by discos and bars sharing Monte Testaccio, you can enjoy a meal of classic Roman pasta dishes (carbonara, amatriciana, etc.) or a delicious fettucine with baby calamari and cherry tomatoes, along with some very good antipasti (try the mixed vegetable plate), and great meat mains like meatballs and beef stew. It's simple, seasonal, and served with a smile, either in the cozy cavelike indoor dining rooms or outside under the umbrellas. *Average main: €16 Via di Monte Testaccio 97, Testaccio, Roma 06/5744194 www.flavioalvelavevodetto.it Reservations essential No lunch weekends. No dinner Sun. Piramide 3:C5.*

$$ ROMAN ✕ **Perilli.** In this restaurant dating from 1911, the old Testaccio remains, as proven by the interior style. A seasonal antipasto table starts things off, offering specialties like stewed Roman artichokes and *puntarelle* (curled chicory stems in a garlicky vinaigrette with lemon and anchovy). The waiters wear crooked bow ties and are just a little bit too hurried—until, that is, you order classics like pasta *all'amatriciana* and carbonara, which they relish tossing in a big bowl, tableside. *Secondi* are for meat-eaters only, and the house wine is a golden enamel-remover from the Castelli Romani. *Average main: €18 Via Marmorata 39, Testaccio 06/5742415 Closed Wed. Piramide 3:D4.*

$ ITALIAN Fodor's Choice ★ ✕ **Porto Fluviale.** This massive structure is on a stretch of street that's gone from gritty clubland to popular night spot, thanks largely to Porto Fluviale's arrival here. It means all things to all people: bar-café, pizzeria and lunch buffet, lively evening restaurant, and private dining spot. And, in true Italian fashion, it features cuisine from up and down the peninsula, with service as organized as one might expect in a cavernous space in Rome (which is to say, not very). Still, it's quite a convivial spot, and the food is tasty, from pizza made in wood-burning ovens to pasta and grilled meats and interesting salads. Cocktails at the bar, if you can swing a spot, are a fun option. *Average main: €14 Via del Porto Fluviale 22, Testaccio, Roma 06/5743199 www.portofluviale.com 3:D6.*

$ PIZZA ✕ **Remo.** Expect a wait at this perennial favorite in Testaccio frequented by students and locals. You won't find tablecloths or other nonessentials, just classic Roman pizza—going simple with a *margherita* is best—and boisterous conversation. *Average main: €10 Piazza Santa Maria Liberatrice 44, Testaccio 06/5746270 No credit cards Closed Sun., Aug., and Christmas wk. No lunch 3:C4.*

MONTI, ESQUILINO, AND SAN LORENZO

MONTI

Monti is a chic, slightly bohemian neighborhood with a great variety of ethnic offerings and an ever-diversifying food scene.

$$ ROMAN ✕ **Ai Tre Scalini.** A traditional restaurant by the Colosseum, Ai Tre Scalini is old-school Roman with touches of the Sicilian. The seating outside in warm weather is pleasant, and some dishes highlight the chef's

Naples may lay claim to the invention of pizza, but to many pizza purists Rome perfected it. Roman pizza has a thin crust, with just the right ratio of crisp-to-chewy.

playfulness, like the unusual radicchio and cheese-stuffed *zagnolotti* (small ravioli) in a lobster sauce. A wide variety of second courses, from gilthead bream topped with paper-thin potato rounds, to simple beef with rosemary, are indeed what they seem, served by waiters who have clearly been around for quite some time. $ *Average main: €20* ✉ *Via SS. Quattro 30, Monti* ☎ *06/7096309* ✉ *infoai3scalini.com* 🌐 *www.ai3scalini.com* ⏲ *Closed Mon. and 10 days in Sept.* ✥ *3:G1.*

$ WINE BAR ✕ **Cavour 313.** Wine bars are popping up all over the city, but Cavour 313 has been around much longer than most. With a tight seating area in the front, your best bet is to head to the large space in the rear, which is divided into sections with booths that give this bar a rustic feel, halfway to a beer hall. Open for lunch and dinner, it serves an excellent variety of cured meats, cheeses, and salads, with a focus on DOP, organic, and artisanal products. Choose from about 25 wines by the glass or uncork a bottle (there are more than 1,200) and stay a while. $ *Average main: €14* ✉ *Via Cavour 313, Monti* ☎ *06/6785496* 🌐 *www.cavour313.it* ⏲ *Closed Aug. No lunch weekends. Closed Sun. and June 15–Sept.* ✥ *2:B5.*

$$ ITALIAN Fodor's Choice ★ ✕ **Trattoria Monti.** Not far from Santa Maria Maggiore, Trattoria Monti is one of the most dependable, moderately priced trattorias in the city, featuring the cuisine of Le Marche, an area to the northeast of Rome. There are surprisingly few places specializing in this humble fare, but served up by the Camerucci family, it's hearty and simple. Staples include various roasted meats and game and a selection of generally vegetarian timbales and soufflés that change seasonally. The region's rabbit dishes are much loved, and here the *timballo di coniglio con patate* (rabbit casserole with potatoes) is no exception. $ *Average main:*

€17 ✉ *Via di San Vito 13a, Monti* ☎ *06/4466573* *Reservations essential* ⊙ *Closed Aug., 1 wk at Easter, and 10 days at Christmas* Ⓜ *Vittorio Emanuele* ✥ *2:E5.*

$$
MODERN ITALIAN

✕ **Urbana 47.** Urbana 47 is open from breakfast through dinner and represents a relatively new concept for Rome's culinary landscape: a restaurant highlighting local ingredients from the surrounding Lazio region, called *kilometro zero*, referring to the lack of distance food items travel to get to the kitchen and onto your plate. This appeals to local hipsters and the boho Monti crowd. In the morning there is a Continental or "American" breakfast with free Wi-Fi; lunch means tasty "fast slow food" options like grain salads and healthy panini. From 6 pm onward there are tapas and drinks, plus leisurely dinners like homemade pasta with broccoli, anchovies, and orange zest, or a local free-range chicken stuffed with potatoes and chicory. $ *Average main: €17* ✉ *Via Urbana 47, Monti* ☎ *06/47884006* 🌐 *www.urbana47.it* Ⓜ *Cavour* ✥ *2:C5.*

ESQUILINO

Esquilino is Rome's main multicultural artery, containing Mercato Esquilino, a great covered market for Italian, Asian, and African specialties. Tourist traps abound, but you can find some authentic Roman food.

$$$$
MODERN ITALIAN
Fodor's Choice ★

✕ **Agata e Romeo.** For the perfect marriage of fine dining, creative cuisine, and rustic Roman tradition, the husband-and-wife team of Agata Parisella and Romeo Caraccio is the top. Chef Agata was perhaps the first in the capital to put a gourmet spin on Roman ingredients and preparations, elevating dishes like *cacio e pepe* (cheese and pepper) with the addition of an even richer Sicilian aged cheese and saffron to the pecorino; "*baccalà* 5 ways" showcases salt cod of the highest quality; and many dishes are the best versions of classics you can get. Prices are steep, but for those who appreciate extremely high-quality ingredients, an incredible wine cellar, and warm service, dining here is a real treat. $ *Average main: €42* ✉ *Via Carlo Alberto 45, Esquilino* ☎ *06/4466115* 🌐 *www.agataeromeo.it* *Reservations essential* ⊙ *Closed Sun. and 2 wks in Aug. No lunch Sat. and Mon.* Ⓜ *Vittorio Emanuele* ✥ *2:E5.*

$$
PIZZA

✕ **La Gallina Bianca.** This pizzeria's location right down the road from Termini station makes it a perfect place for a welcome-to-Rome meal. A bright, country-cute, noisy locale, La Gallina Bianca attracts a young crowd and serves classic thin-crust pizzas. Try the "full-moon" specialty, perfect for cheese lovers, with ricotta, Parmesan, mozzarella, ham, and tomato. There are other menu items available from the trattoria menu for those who may be trying to stick to proteins. $ *Average main: €16* ✉ *Via A. Rosmini 5, Esquilino* ☎ *06/4743777* 🌐 *www.lagallinabiancaroma.com* ⊙ *Closed Aug.* Ⓜ *Termini* ✥ *2:D4.*

$$
SOUTHERN ITALIAN

✕ **Monte Caruso.** The regional delicacies of certain areas of Italy are grossly underrepresented in Rome. Monte Caruso is truly a standout, as its menu focuses on food from Lucania, an area of Italy divided between the southern regions of Basilicata and Calabria. Homemade pastas have strange-sounding names, such as *cautarogni* (large cavatelli with Sicilian broccoli) and *cauzuni* (enormous ricotta-stuffed ravioli), but the dishes are generally simple and hearty. $ *Average main: €18* ✉ *Via Farini*

12, Esquilino ☎ *06/483549* 🌐 *www.montecaruso.com* ✍ *Reservations essential* ⏱ *Closed Sun. and Aug. No lunch Mon.* Ⓜ *Termini* ✥ *2:D4.*

PIGNETO

Pigneto is Rome's rough-around-the-edges, up-and-coming *zona*—gritty cafés, artsy bars, and youth-driven, modern Italian restaurants is what you'll find.

$$ ITALIAN ✕ **Primo.** In Pigneto, an up-and-coming hipster neighborhood compared to Brooklyn's Bushwick, Primo is a trendsetting modern Italian restaurant highlighting local ingredients. But while the name *Primo* may reference the primary ingredients that are the focus of the menu, it could just as easily refer to the *prime* people-watching. The young patrons sip from a selection of 250 wines and nibble hand-sliced prosciutto, anchovy-and-broccoli gratin, and salads with goat cheese and radicchio. Pastas include artichoke tortelli with marjoram and pecorino, and seafood mains like grilled swordfish with a pistachio sauce. Those with more carnivorous desires can sink their teeth into dishes like the provolone-and-herb-stuffed veal. The neighborhood is a 10-minute bus ride from Termini station. [$] *Average main: €18* ✉ *Via del Pigneto 46, Pigneto* ☎ *06/7013827* 🌐 *www.primoalpigneto.it* ✍ *Reservations essential* ⏱ *Closed Mon. No lunch Tues.–Sat.* ✥ *2:H6.*

SAN LORENZO

San Lorenzo is a gritty-but-fun university quarter, where student budgets dictate low prices and good value. There are also a few hidden gourmet gems here.

$$ ETHIOPIAN ✕ **Africa.** Ethiopia was the closest thing Italy ever had to a "colony" at one point. As a result, what Indian food is to London, Ethiopian/Eritrean food is to Rome. Interesting offerings include braised meat main courses, yogurt-based breakfasts, and vegetarian-friendly stews—all under the category of utensil-free dining. [$] *Average main: €20* ✉ *Via Gaeta 26/28, San Lorenzo* ☎ *06/4941077* ▭ *No credit cards* ⏱ *Closed Mon.* Ⓜ *Castro Pretorio* ✥ *2:E2.*

$ PIZZA ✕ **Formula 1.** Its location in the trendy San Lorenzo neighborhood makes this a particularly convenient stop for dinner before checking out some of the area's funky, gritty bars. The atmosphere here is casual and friendly—posters of Formula 1 cars and drivers past and present attest to the owner's love for auto racing—and draws students from the nearby university as well as pizza lovers from all over the city. [$] *Average main: €12* ✉ *Via degli Equi 13, San Lorenzo* ☎ *06/4453866* ▭ *No credit cards* ⏱ *Closed Sun. and Aug. No lunch* ✥ *2:G5.*

$$ SOUTHERN ITALIAN ✕ **Tram Tram.** The name refers to its proximity to the tram tracks, but could also describe its size, as it's narrow-narrow and often stuffed to the rafters-rafters (in warmer weather, happily, there's a "side car" of tables enclosed along the sidewalk). The cuisine is mostly rooted in Puglia, with an emphasis on seafood and vegetables—maybe prawns with saffron-kissed sautéed vegetables—as well as pastas of very particular shapes. Try the homemade *orecchiette*, ear-shaped pasta, made here with clams and broccoli. Meats tend toward traditional Roman offerings. [$] *Average main: €20* ✉ *Via dei Reti 44/46, San Lorenzo*

☎ 06/490416 ⊕ *www.tramtram.it* ✍ *Reservations essential* ⊗ *Closed Mon. and 1 wk in mid-Aug.* ✚ *2:H4.*

$$$ MODERN ITALIAN Fodor's Choice ★ ✕ **Uno e Bino.** The setting is simple: wooden tables and chairs on a stone floor with little more than a few shelves of wine bottles lining the walls for decor. Giampaolo Gravina's restaurant in this artsy corner of the San Lorenzo neighborhood is popular with foodies and locals alike, as the kitchen turns out inventive cuisine inspired by the family's Umbrian and Sicilian roots. Dishes like octopus salad with asparagus and carrots, and spaghetti with swordfish, tomatoes, and capers are specialties. The Parmesan soufflé is a study in lightness, all silky, salty perfection. Delicious and simple, yet upscale, this small establishment offers one of the top dining deals—and pleasurable meals—in Rome. [$] *Average main: €26* ✉ *Via degli Equi 58, San Lorenzo* ☎ *06/4460702* ✍ *Reservations essential* ⊗ *Closed Mon. and Aug. No lunch* ✚ *2:G5.*

VIA APPIA ANTICA

$$$ ITALIAN ✕ **L'Archeologia.** In this farmhouse just beyond the catacombs, you dine indoors beside the fireplace in cool weather or in the garden under age-old vines in summer. The atmosphere is friendly and intimate. Specialties include fettuccine al finocchio salvatico (with wild fennel), abbacchio alla scottadito, and fresh seafood. But remember that the food here is secondary: you're paying for the view and the setting more than any culinary adventure or excellence with the classics. [$] *Average main: €26* ✉ *Via Appia Antica 139, Via Appia Antica* ☎ *06/7880494* ⊕ *www.larcheologia.it* ⊗ *Closed Tues.* ✚ *2:E6.*

ROME DINING AND LODGING ATLAS

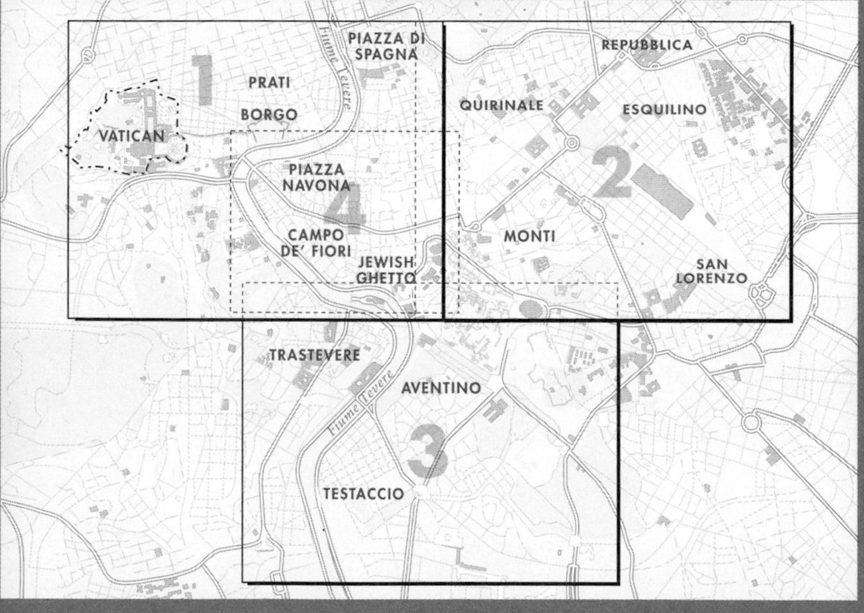

KEY

- Hotels
- Restaurants
- Restaurant in Hotel

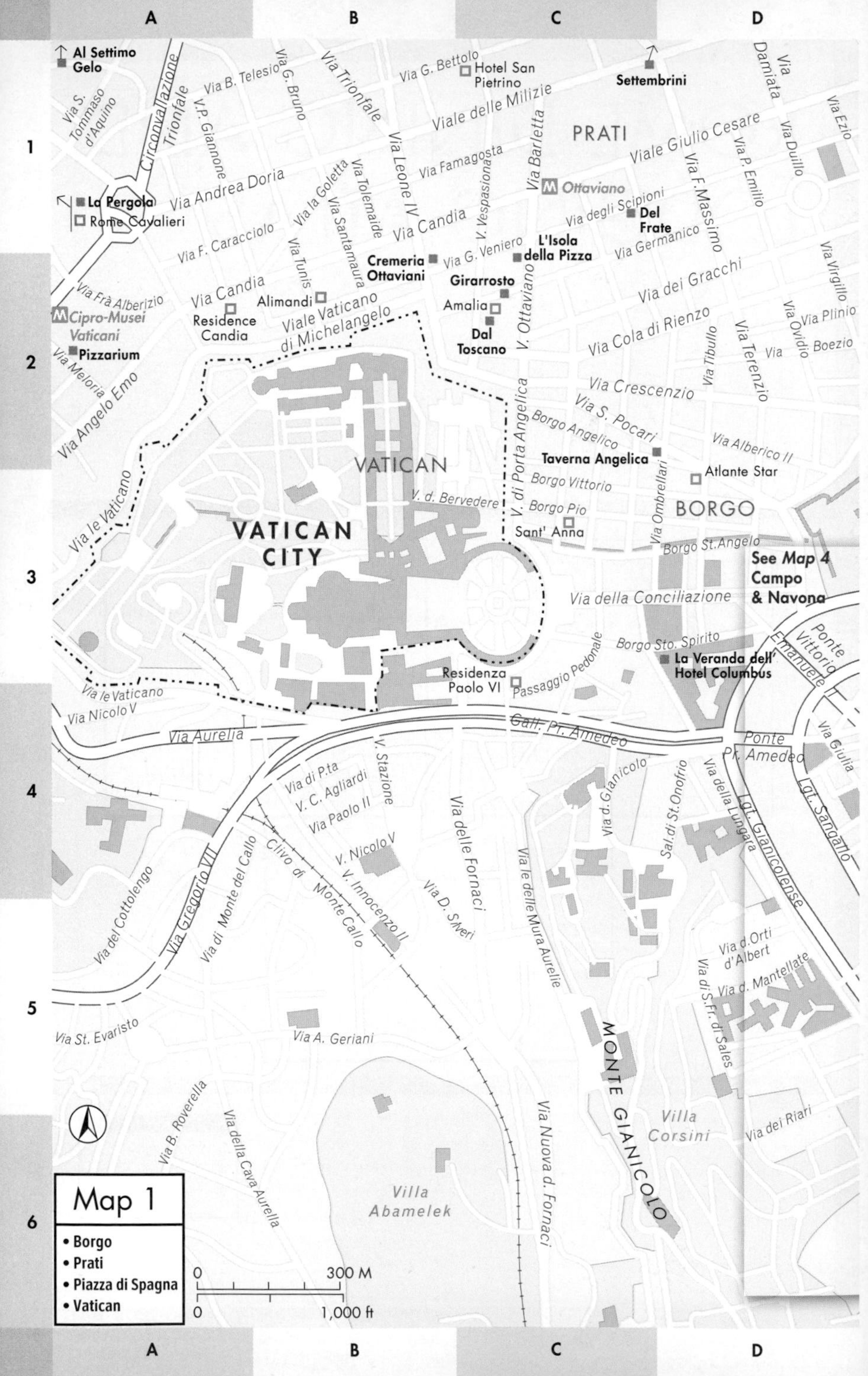

Map 1
• Borgo
• Prati
• Piazza di Spagna
• Vatican
VATICAN CITY
VATICAN
PRATI
BORGO
MONTE GIANICOLO
Villa Abamelek
Villa Corsini
Al Settimo Gelo
Hotel San Pietrino
Settembrini
La Pergola
Rome Cavalieri
Ottaviano
Del Frate
L'Isola della Pizza
Cremeria Ottaviani
Girarrosto
Amalia
Dal Toscano
Alimandi
Residence Candia
Cipro-Musei Vaticani
Pizzarium
Taverna Angelica
Atlante Star
Sant' Anna
Residenza Paolo VI
La Veranda dell' Hotel Columbus
See Map 4 Campo & Navona
Viale Giulio Cesare
Viale delle Milizie
Via Andrea Doria
Via Candia
Via dei Gracchi
Via Cola di Rienzo
Via Crescenzio
Via della Conciliazione
Borgo St.Angelo
Borgo Sto. Spirito
Via Aurelia
Gall. Pr. Amedeo
Ponte Pr. Amedeo
Ponte Vittorio Emanuele
Via Gregorio VII
Via delle Fornaci
Via Nuova d. Fornaci
Via le delle Mura Aurelie
Lgt. Gianicolense
Lgt. Sangallo
Via della Lungara
Via dei Riari
Viale Vaticano di Michelangelo
Via Trionfale
Via Leone IV
Via le Vaticano
Via Angelo Emo
Circonvallazione Trionfale
0 300 M
0 1,000 ft

A B C D
1 2 3 4 5 6

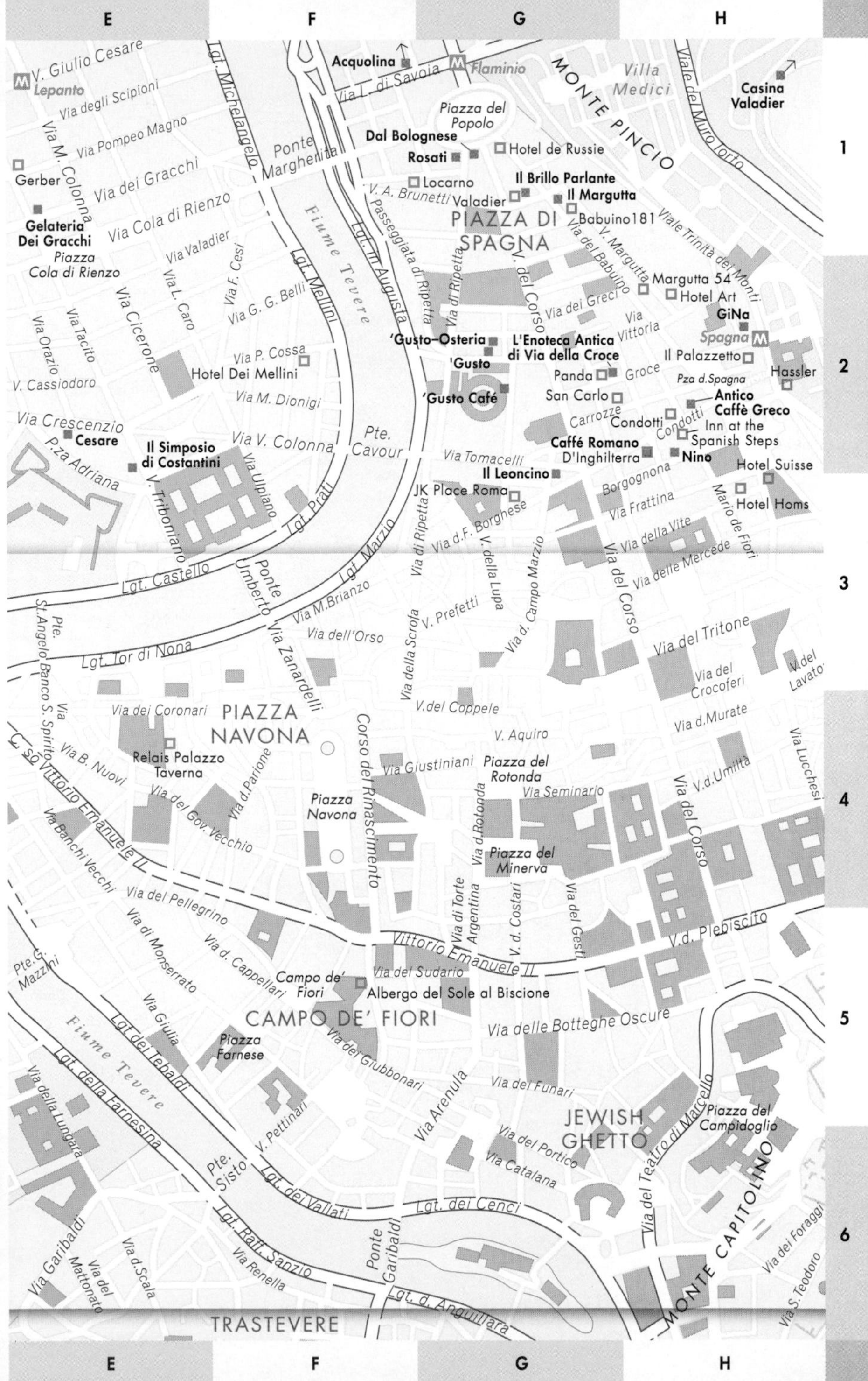
E
F
G
H
1
2
3
4
5
6
Acquolina
Flaminio
MONTE PINCIO
Villa Medici
Casina Valadier
Lepanto
Piazza del Popolo
Dal Bolognese
Rosati
Hotel de Russie
Gerber
Locarno
Il Brillo Parlante
Valadier
Il Margutta
Babuino181
Gelateria Dei Gracchi
PIAZZA DI SPAGNA
Margutta 54
Hotel Art
GiNa
Spagna
'Gusto-Osteria
L'Enoteca Antica di Via della Croce
'Gusto
Il Palazzetto
Hotel Dei Mellini
Panda
Hassler
'Gusto Café
San Carlo
Antico Caffè Greco
Condotti
Inn at the Spanish Steps
Cesare
Caffé Romano
D'Inghilterra
Nino
Il Simposio di Costantini
Il Leoncino
Hotel Suisse
JK Place Roma
Hotel Homs
PIAZZA NAVONA
Relais Palazzo Taverna
Piazza Navona
Piazza del Rotonda
Piazza del Minerva
Campo de' Fiori
Albergo del Sole al Biscione
CAMPO DE' FIORI
Piazza Farnese
JEWISH GHETTO
Piazza del Campidoglio
MONTE CAPITOLINO
TRASTEVERE
Fiume Tevere
Via Cola di Rienzo
Via del Corso
Via del Tritone
Corso del Rinascimento
Vittorio Emanuele II
Via delle Botteghe Oscure
Via Arenula
Ponte Garibaldi
Pte. Sisto
Ponte Umberto
Pte. Cavour
Ponte Margherita
E
F
G
H

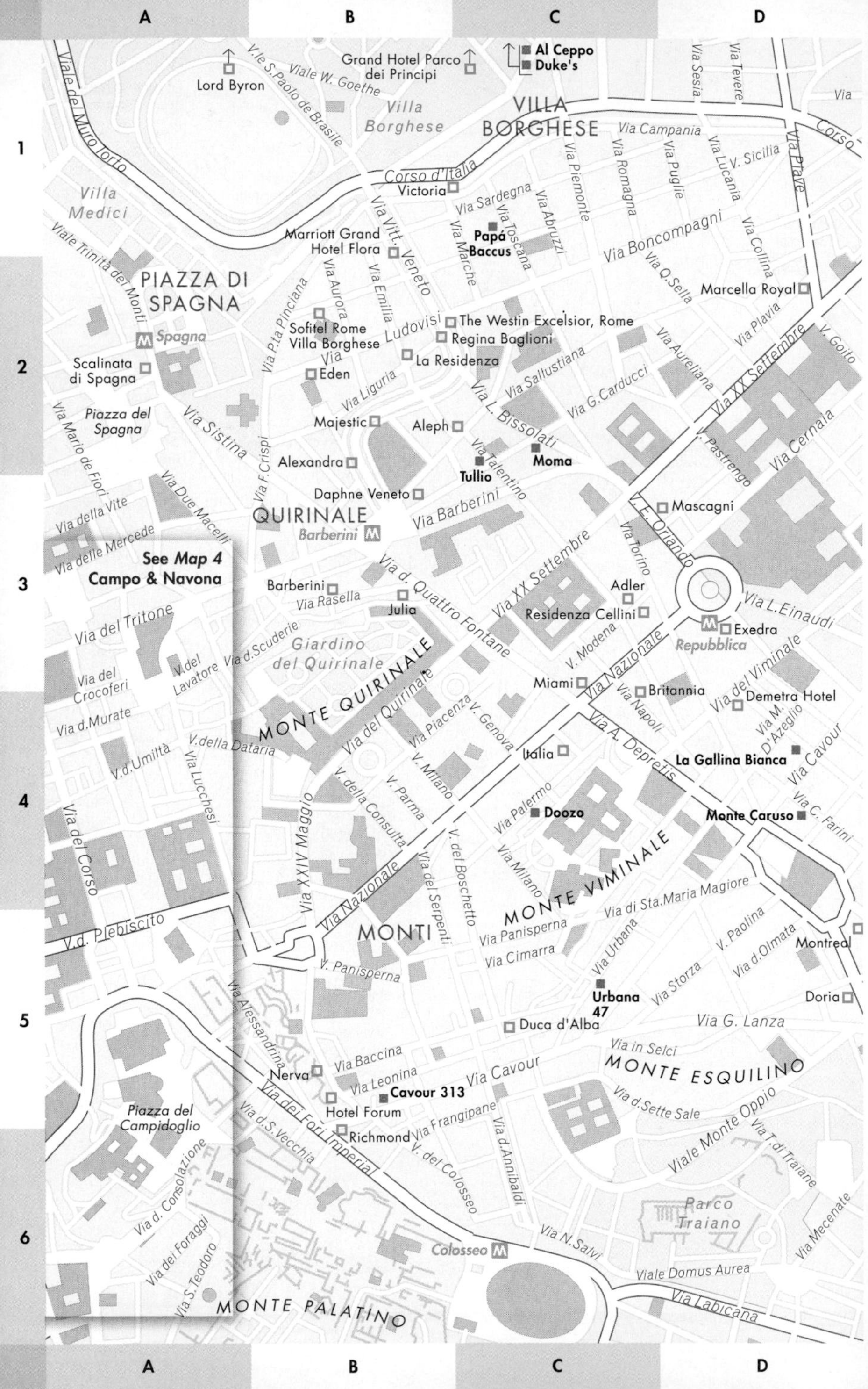

A
B
C
D
1
2
3
4
5
6
Lord Byron
Grand Hotel Parco dei Principi
Al Ceppo
Duke's
VILLA BORGHESE
Villa Borghese
Villa Medici
PIAZZA DI SPAGNA
Spagna
Scalinata di Spagna
Piazza del Spagna
Victoria
Marriott Grand Hotel Flora
Papá Baccus
Marcella Royal
Sofitel Rome Villa Borghese
The Westin Excelsior, Rome
Regina Baglioni
La Residenza
Eden
Majestic
Aleph
Alexandra
Tullio
Moma
Daphne Veneto
QUIRINALE
Barberini
Mascagni
See Map 4
Campo & Navona
Barberini
Julia
Adler
Residenza Cellini
Exedra
Repubblica
Giardino del Quirinale
MONTE QUIRINALE
Miami
Britannia
Demetra Hotel
Italia
La Gallina Bianca
Doozo
Monte Caruso
MONTE VIMINALE
MONTI
Montreal
Urbana 47
Doria
Duca d'Alba
Nerva
Cavour 313
Hotel Forum
Richmond
MONTE ESQUILINO
Piazza del Campidoglio
Parco Traiano
Colosseo
MONTE PALATINO
Viale del Muro Torto
V.le S.Paolo de Brasile
Viale W. Goethe
Corso d'Italia
Via Campania
Via Sesia
Via Tevere
Via Piave
Corso
V. Sicilia
Via Piemonte
Via Romagna
Via Puglie
Via Lucania
Via Sardegna
Via Toscana
Via Abruzzi
Via Vitt. Veneto
Via Marche
Via Boncompagni
Via Q.Sella
Via Collina
Viale Trinità dei Monti
Via Aurora
Via Emilia
Via P.ta Pinciana
Via Ludovisi
Via Plavia
V. Goito
Via Aureliana
Via XX Settembre
Via Sallustiana
Via G.Carducci
Via Liguria
Via L. Bissolati
V. Pastrengo
Via Cernaia
Via Mario de Fiori
Via Sistina
Via F.Crispi
Via Talentino
Via Due Macelli
Via della Vite
Via delle Mercede
Via Barberini
V.E. Orlando
Via Torino
Via d. Quattro Fontane
Via Rasella
Via L.Einaudi
Via del Tritone
Via d.Scuderie
V.del Lavatore
Via del Crocoferi
V. Modena
Via Nazionale
Via del Viminale
Via Napoli
Via M. D'Azeglio
Via d.Murate
Via del Quirinale
Via Piacenza
V. Genova
Via A. Depretis
Via Cavour
V.della Dataria
V.d.Umiltà
Via Lucchesi
V. della Consulta
V. Parma
V. Milano
Via Palermo
Via C. Farini
Via del Corso
Via XXIV Maggio
Via del Serpenti
V. del Boschetto
Via Milano
Via di Sta.Maria Magiore
V.d. Plebiscito
Via Panisperna
Via Cimarra
Via Urbana
V. Paolina
Via d.Olmata
V. Panisperna
Via Alessandrina
Via Storza
Via G. Lanza
Via in Selci
Via Baccina
Via Leonina
Via dei Fori Imperial
Via d.S.Vecchia
Via Frangipane
Via d.Annibaldi
Via d.Sette Sale
Viale Monte Oppio
Via T.di Traiane
Via d. Consolazione
V. del Colosseo
Via Mecenate
Via dei Foraggi
Via N.Salvi
Via S.Teodoro
Viale Domus Aurea
Via Labicana

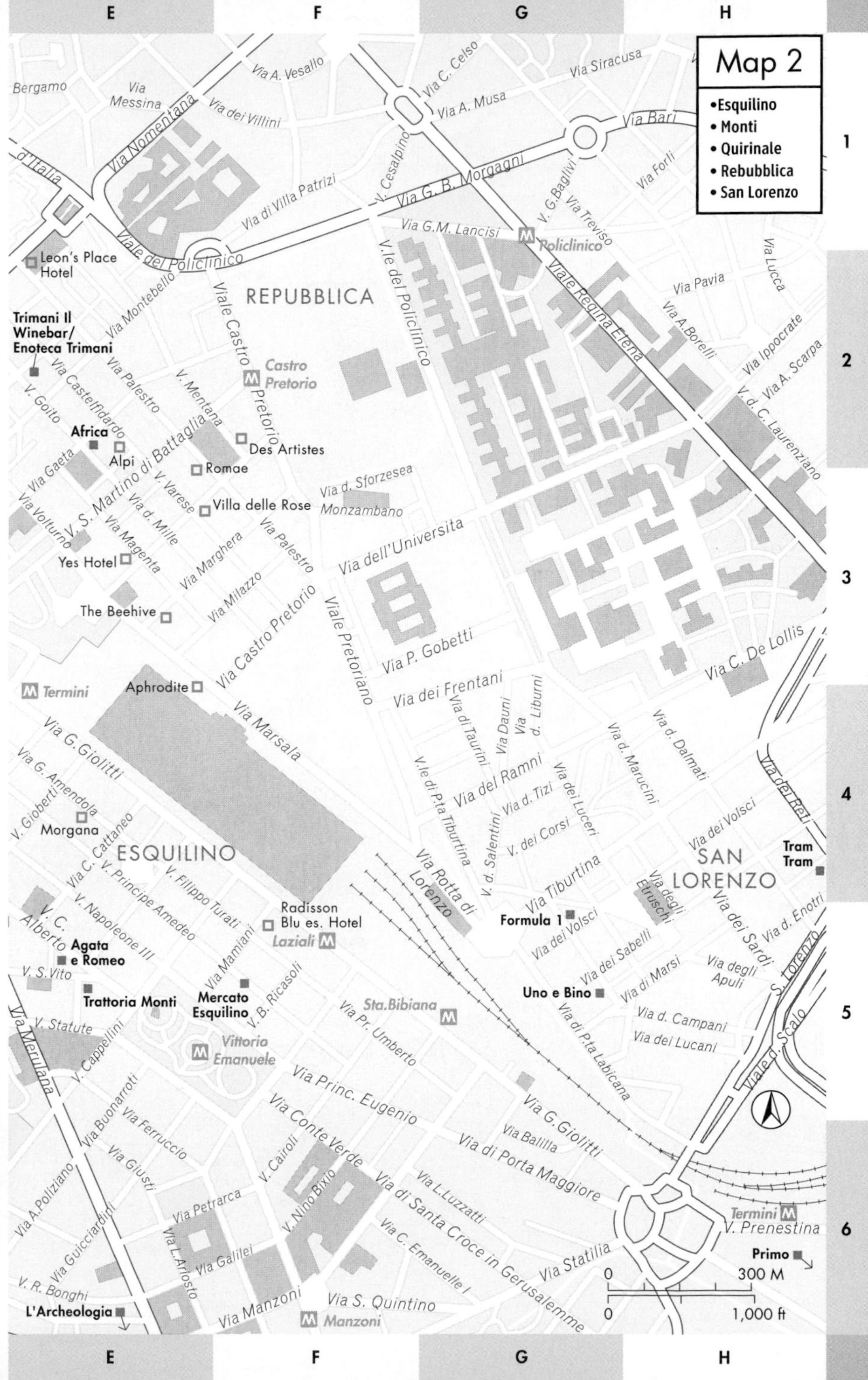
E
F
G
H
Map 2
•Esquilino
• Monti
• Quirinale
• Rebubblica
• San Lorenzo
1
2
3
4
5
6
Bergamo
Via Messina
Via Nomentana
Via A. Vesallo
Via dei Villini
Via C. Celso
Via A. Musa
Via Siracusa
Via Bari
d'Italia
V. Cesalpino
Via G. B. Morgagni
Via di Villa Patrizi
V. G.Baglivi
Via Forlì
Via Treviso
Via G.M. Lancisi
Policlinico
Leon's Place Hotel
Viale del Policlinico
Via Montebello
Viale Castro Pretorio
REPUBBLICA
V.le del Policlinico
Viale Regina Elena
Via Pavia
Via Lucca
Trimani Il Winebar/ Enoteca Trimani
Via Castelfidardo
Via Palestro
V. Mentana
Castro Pretorio
Via A.Borelli
Via Ippocrate
Via A. Scarpa
V. d. C. Laurenziano
V. Goito
Africa
Alpi
V. S. Martino di Battaglia
Des Artistes
Romae
Via Gaeta
V. Varese
Via d. Sforzesea
Monzambano
Via Volturno
Via d. Mille
Villa delle Rose
Via Magenta
Via Palestro
Via Marghera
Via dell'Universita
Yes Hotel
Via Milazzo
Via Castro Pretorio
Viale Pretoriano
The Beehive
Via P. Gobetti
Via C. De Lollis
Termini
Aphrodite
Via dei Frentani
Via Marsala
Via di Taurini
Via Dauni
Via d. Liburni
Via G.Giolitti
Via d. Marucini
Via d. Dalmati
Via dei Reti
Via G. Amendola
V.le di P.ta Tiburtina
Via del Ramni
Via dei Luceri
V. Gioberti
Morgana
Via d. Tizi
V. d. Salentini
V. dei Corsi
Via dei Volsci
ESQUILINO
Via C. Cattaneo
V. Principe Amedeo
V. Filippo Turati
Via Rotta di Lorenzo
SAN LORENZO
Tram Tram
Via Tiburtina
Via degli Etruschi
V. Napoleone III
Radisson Blu es. Hotel
Laziali
Formula 1
Via dei Volsci
Via dei Sardi
Via d. Enotri
V. C. Alberto
Agata e Romeo
Via Mamiani
V. S.Vito
Via dei Sabelli
Via degli Apuli
Trattoria Monti
Mercato Esquilino
V. B. Ricasoli
Uno e Bino
Via di Marsi
S. Lorenzo
Sta.Bibiana
Via Pr. Umberto
Via di P.ta Labicana
Via d. Campani
Via Merulana
V. Statute
V. Cappellini
Vittorio Emanuele
Via dei Lucani
Viale d. Scalo
Via Princ. Eugenio
Via G. Giolitti
Via Buonarroti
Via Ferruccio
Via Conte Verde
Via Balilla
Via di Porta Maggiore
Via Giusti
V. Cairoli
Via A.Poliziano
Via L.Luzzatti
V. Nino Bixio
Via di Santa Croce in Gerusalemme
Via Petrarca
Termini
V. Prenestina
Via Guicciardini
Via L.Ariosto
Via C. Emanuelle I
Via Statilia
Primo
Via Galilei
0
300 M
V. R. Bonghi
0
1,000 ft
L'Archeologia
Via Manzoni
Via S. Quintino
Manzoni

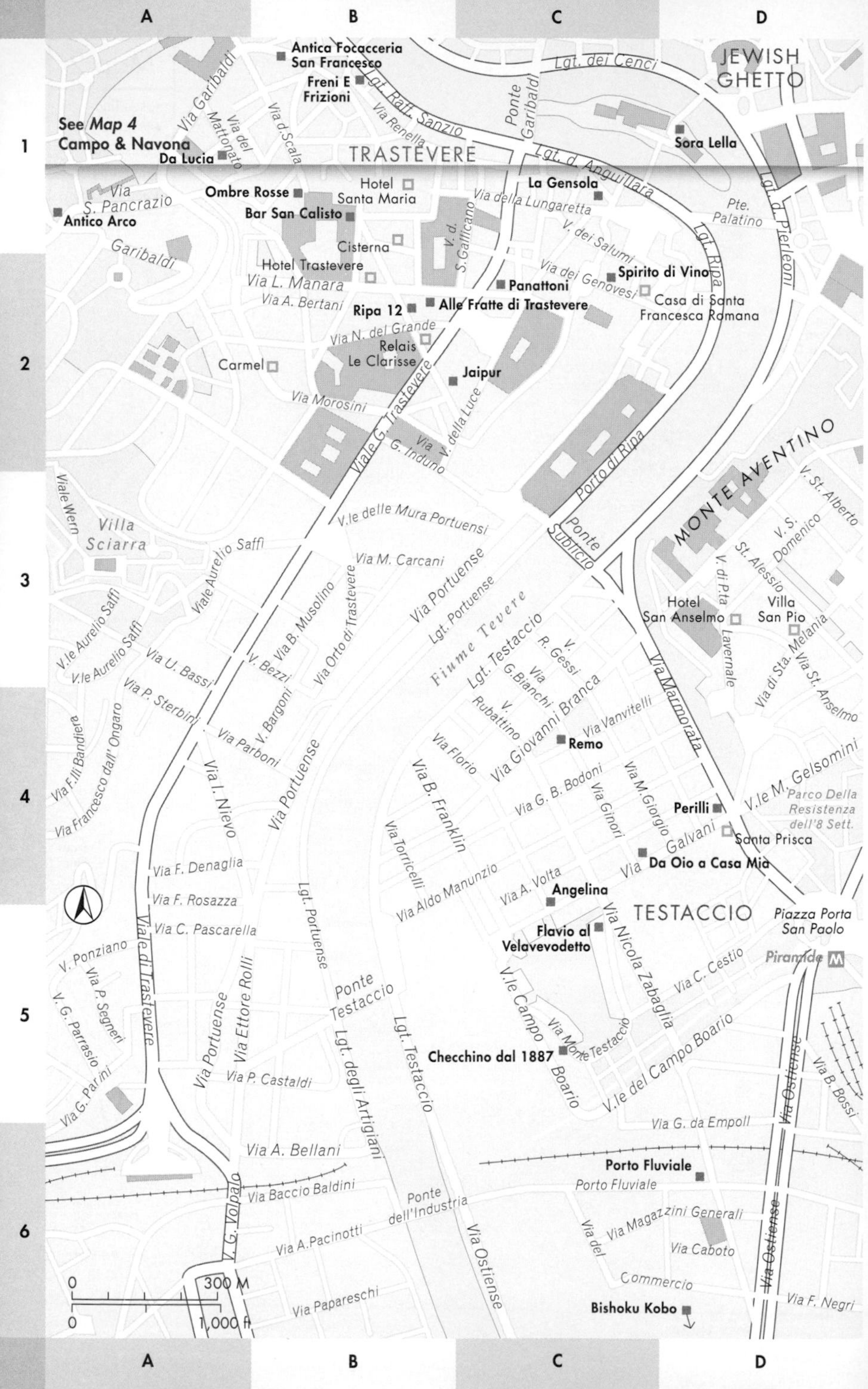
A
B
C
D
1
2
3
4
5
6
See Map 4
Campo & Navona
JEWISH GHETTO
TRASTEVERE
MONTE AVENTINO
TESTACCIO
Antica Focacceria San Francesco
Freni E Frizioni
Da Lucia
Sora Lella
Ombre Rosse
Hotel Santa Maria
La Gensola
Antico Arco
Bar San Calisto
Cisterna
Hotel Trastevere
Spirito di Vino
Panattoni
Casa di Santa Francesca Romana
Ripa 12
Alle Fratte di Trastevere
Relais Le Clarisse
Carmel
Jaipur
Hotel San Anselmo
Villa San Pio
Remo
Perilli
Santa Prisca
Da Oio a Casa Mia
Angelina
Flavio al Velavevodetto
Piazza Porta San Paolo
Piramide
Checchino dal 1887
Porto Fluviale
Bishoku Kobo
Parco Della Resistenza dell'8 Sett.
Villa Sciarra
Fiume Tevere
Lgt. dei Cenci
Lgt. Raff. Sanzio
Ponte Garibaldi
Lgt. d. Anguillara
Via Garibaldi
Via del Mattonato
Via d.Scala
Via Renella
Via S. Pancrazio
Garibaldi
Via della Lungaretta
V. d. S.Gallicano
V. dei Salumi
Via dei Genovesi
Lgt. Ripa
Lgt. d. Pierleoni
Pte. Palatino
Via L. Manara
Via A. Bertani
Via N. del Grande
Via Morosini
Viale G. Trastevere
Via V. della Luce
Via G. Induno
Porto di Ripa
Ponte Sublicio
Viale Werri
V.le delle Mura Portuensi
Via M. Carcani
Via Portuense
Lgt. Portuense
Viale Aurelio Saffi
V.le Aurelio Saffi
Via U. Bassi
Via P. Sterbini
V. Bezzi
Via B. Musolino
Via Orto di Trastevere
V. Bargoni
Via Parboni
Lgt. Testaccio
V. R. Gessi
Via G.Bianchi
V. Rubattino
Via Giovanni Branca
Via Vanvitelli
Via Marmorata
V. St. Alberto
V. S. Domenico
St. Alessio
V. di P.ta Lavernale
Via di Sta. Melania
Via St. Anselmo
V.le M. Gelsomini
Via F.lli Bandiera
Via Francesco dall' Ongaro
Via I. Nievo
Via Florio
Via B. Franklin
Via G. B. Bodoni
Via Ginori
Via M.Giorgio
Via Galvani
Via Torricelli
Via Aldo Manunzio
Via A. Volta
Via F. Denaglia
Via F. Rosazza
Via C. Pascarella
Viale di Trastevere
V. Ponziano
Via P. Segneri
V. G. Parrasio
Via G. Parini
Via Portuense
Via Ettore Rolli
Lgt. Portuense
Ponte Testaccio
Via P. Castaldi
Lgt. degli Artigiani
Lgt. Testaccio
V.le Campo Boario
Via Nicola Zabaglia
Via Monte Testaccio
Via C. Cestio
V.le del Campo Boario
Via Ostiense
Via B. Bossi
Via G. da Empoli
Via A. Bellani
Via Baccio Baldini
V. G. Volpato
Ponte dell'Industria
Via A.Pacinotti
Via Ostiense
Porto Fluviale
Via del Commercio
Via Magazzini Generali
Via Caboto
Via Papareschi
Via F. Negri
0
300 M
0
1,000 ft
A
B
C
D

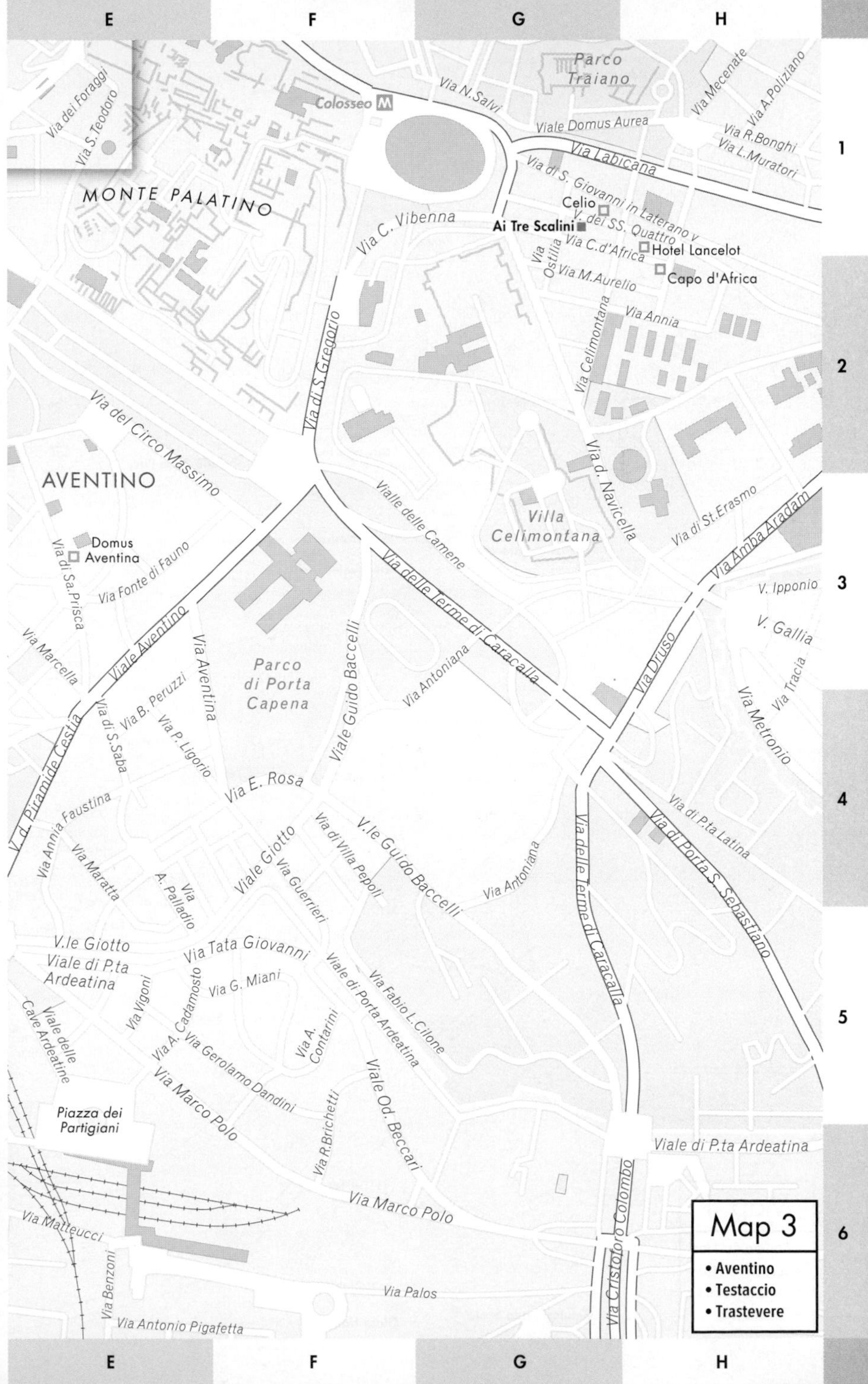
E
F
G
H
1
2
3
4
5
6
Map 3
• Aventino
• Testaccio
• Trastevere
MONTE PALATINO
AVENTINO
Parco Traiano
Colosseo
Via dei Foraggi
Via S.Teodoro
Via N.Salvi
Viale Domus Aurea
Via Labicana
Via Mecenate
Via A.Poliziano
Via R.Bonghi
Via L.Muratori
Via di S. Giovanni in Laterano
Celio
V. dei SS. Quattro
Ai Tre Scalini
Via C.d'Africa
Hotel Lancelot
Via Ostilia
Via M.Aurelio
Capo d'Africa
Via C. Vibenna
Via di S.Gregorio
Via Celimontana
Via Annia
Via del Circo Massimo
Via d. Navicella
Villa Celimontana
Vialle delle Camene
Via di St.Erasmo
Via Amba Aradam
Domus Aventina
Via di Sa.Prisca
Via Fonte di Fauno
Via delle Terme di Caracalla
V. Ipponio
V. Gallia
Via Tracia
Via Marcella
Viale Aventino
Via Aventina
Parco di Porta Capena
Viale Guido Baccelli
Via Antoniana
Via Druso
Via Metronio
Via B. Peruzzi
Via di S.Saba
Via P. Ligorio
V.d. Piramide Cestia
Via E. Rosa
Via Annia Faustina
Via Maratta
Via A. Palladio
Viale Giotto
Via Guerrieri
Via di Villa Pepoli
V.le Guido Baccelli
Via Antoniana
Via delle Terme di Caracalla
Via di P.ta Latina
Via di Porta S. Sebastiano
V.le Giotto
Viale di P.ta Ardeatina
Via Tata Giovanni
Via G. Miani
Via Vigoni
Via A. Cadamosto
Viale di Porta Ardeatina
Via Fabio L.Cilone
Via A. Contarini
Viale delle Cave Ardeatine
Via Gerolamo Dandini
Via Marco Polo
Viale Od. Beccari
Piazza dei Partigiani
Via R.Brichetti
Viale di P.ta Ardeatina
Via Marco Polo
Via Cristoforo Colombo
Via Matteucci
Via Benzoni
Via Palos
Via Antonio Pigafetta
E
F
G
H

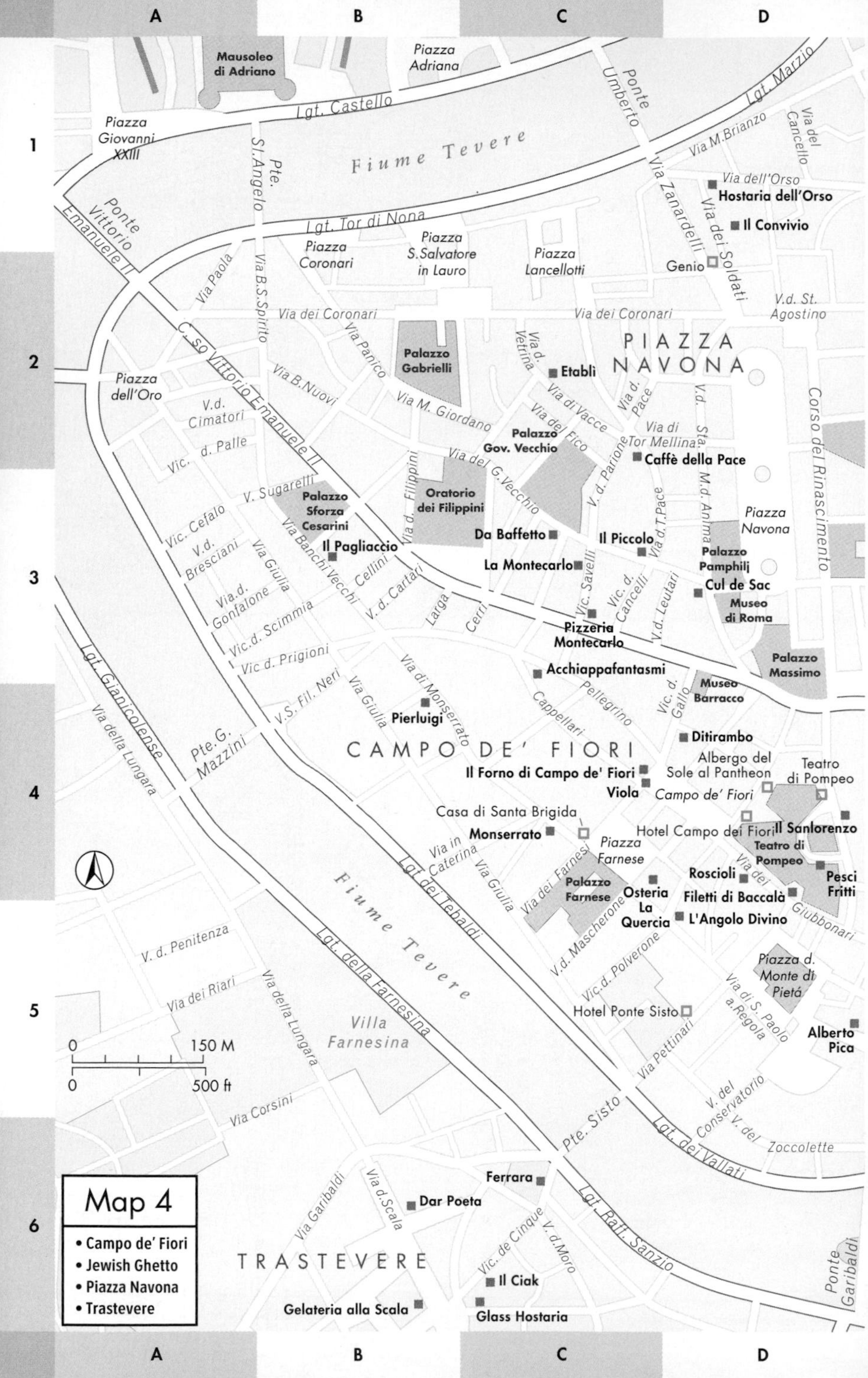

A
B
C
D
1
2
3
4
5
6
Mausoleo di Adriano
Piazza Adriana
Lgt. Castello
Ponte Umberto
Lgt. Marzio
Piazza Giovanni XXIII
Pte. S.Angelo
Fiume Tevere
Via M.Brianzo
Via del Cancello
Via dell'Orso
Hostaria dell'Orso
Il Convivio
Ponte Vittorio Emanuele II
Lgt. Tor di Nona
Via Zanardelli
Via dei Soldati
Piazza Coronari
Piazza S.Salvatore in Lauro
Piazza Lancellotti
Genio
Via Paola
Via B.S.Spirito
V.d. St. Agostino
Via dei Coronari
Via dei Coronari
C.so Vittorio Emanuele II
Via Panico
Palazzo Gabrielli
Via d. Vetrina
PIAZZA NAVONA
Etablì
Piazza dell'Oro
Via B.Nuovi
Via M. Giordano
Via di Vacce
Via d. Pace
V.d. Cimatori
Via del Fico
Palazzo Gov. Vecchio
Via di Tor Mellina
Corso del Rinascimento
Vic. d. Palle
Via d. Filippini
Via del G.Vecchio
V. d. Parione
Caffè della Pace
V.d. Sta. M.d. Anima
V. Sugarelli
Palazzo Sforza Cesarini
Oratorio dei Filippini
Vic. Cefalo
V.d. Bresciani
Via Giulia
Via Banchi Vecchi
Il Pagliaccio
Da Baffetto
Il Piccolo
Via d.T.Pace
Piazza Navona
Palazzo Pamphilj
La Montecarlo
Cellini
V. d. Cartari
Vic. Savelli
Vic. d. Cancelli
Via d.Gonfalone
Vic.d. Scimmia
Larga
Cerri
V.d. Leutari
Cul de Sac
Museo di Roma
Pizzeria Montecarlo
Vic d. Prigioni
Palazzo Massimo
Acchiappafantasmi
Lgt. Gianicolense
Via di Monserrato
Via Giulia
V.S. Fil. Neri
Cappellari
Pellegrino
Vic. d. Gallo
Museo Barracco
Pierluigi
Via della Lungara
Pte. G. Mazzini
Ditirambo
CAMPO DE' FIORI
Albergo del Sole al Pantheon
Teatro di Pompeo
Il Forno di Campo de' Fiori
Viola
Campo de' Fiori
Casa di Santa Brigida
Monserrato
Hotel Campo dei Fiori
Il Sanlorenzo
Via in Caterina
Piazza Farnese
Teatro di Pompeo
Via dei Farnesi
Roscioli
Via dei Giubbonari
Pesci Fritti
Palazzo Farnese
Osteria La Quercia
Filetti di Baccalà
Via Giulia
Lgt. dei Tebaldi
V.d. Mascherone
L'Angolo Divino
V. d. Penitenza
Lgt. della Farnesina
Vic.d. Polverone
Piazza d. Monte di Pietá
Via di S. Paolo a.Regola
Via dei Riari
Via della Lungara
Hotel Ponte Sisto
Villa Farnesina
Alberto Pica
0
150 M
0
500 ft
Via Pettinari
V. del Conservatorio
Via Corsini
Pte. Sisto
Lgt. dei Vallati
V. del Zoccolette
Ferrara
Via Garibaldi
Via d.Scala
Dar Poeta
Lgt. Raff. Sanzio
Vic. de Cinque
V. d.Moro
TRASTEVERE
Il Ciak
Ponte Garibaldi
Gelateria alla Scala
Glass Hostaria
Map 4
• Campo de' Fiori
• Jewish Ghetto
• Piazza Navona
• Trastevere

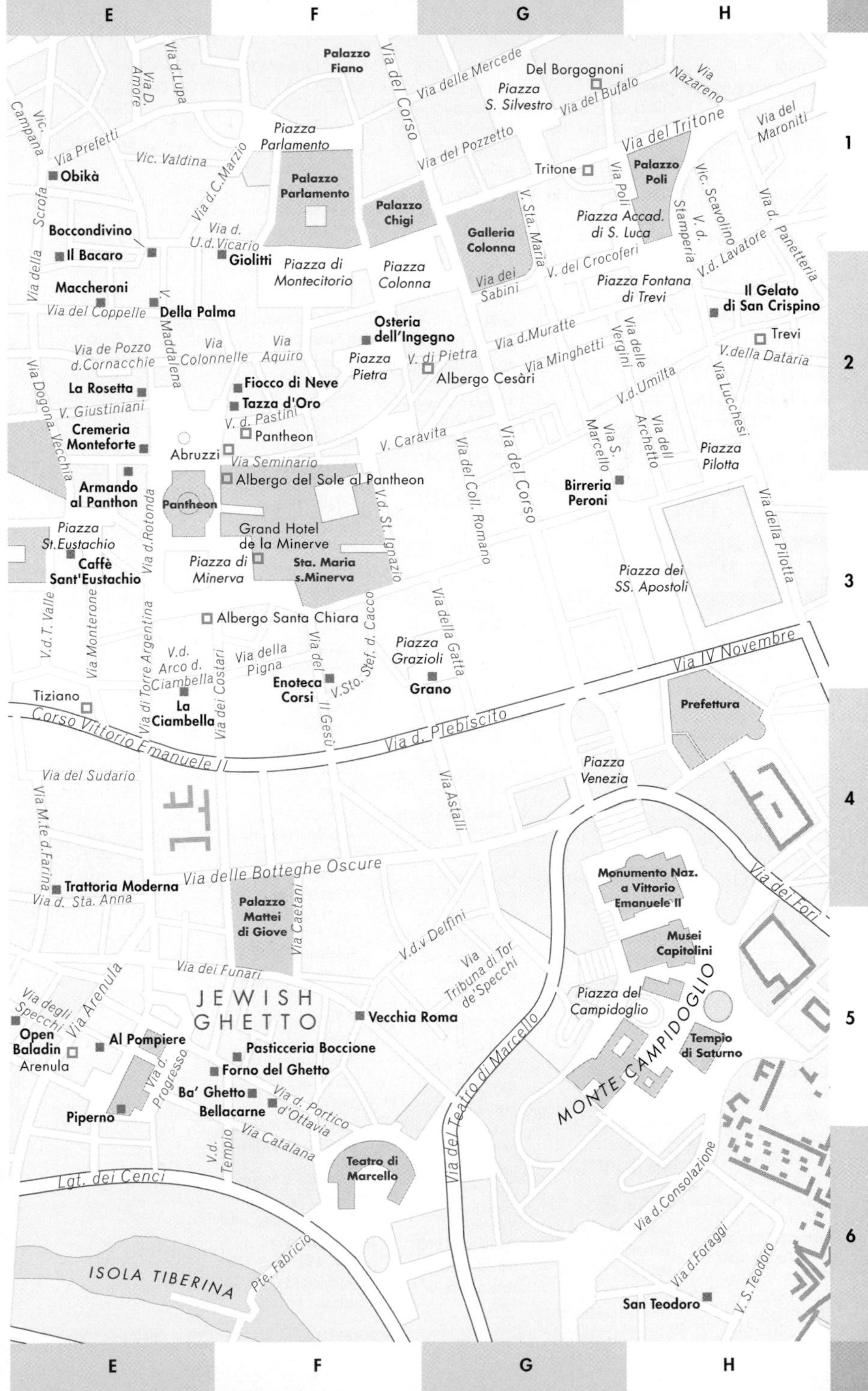

E
F
G
H
1
2
3
4
5
6
Palazzo Fiano
Via del Corso
Via delle Mercede
Del Borgognoni
Piazza S. Silvestro
Via del Bufalo
Via Nazareno
Via D. Amore
Via d.Lupa
Vic. Campana
Via Prefetti
Piazza Parlamento
Via del Pozzetto
Via del Tritone
Via del Maroniti
Vic. Valdina
Via d.C.Marzio
Palazzo Parlamento
Palazzo Chigi
Tritone
Via Poli
Palazzo Poli
Obikà
Via della Scrofa
Via d. U.d.Vicario
Galleria Colonna
V. Sta. Maria
Piazza Accad. di S. Luca
Vic. Scavolino
V. d. Stamperia
Via d. Panetteria
Boccondivino
Il Bacaro
Giolitti
Piazza di Montecitorio
Piazza Colonna
Via dei Sabini
V. del Crocoferi
V.d. Lavatore
Maccheroni
Via del Coppelle
V. Maddalena
Della Palma
Piazza Fontana di Trevi
Il Gelato di San Crispino
Osteria dell'Ingegno
Trevi
Via de Pozzo d.Cornacchie
Via Colonnelle
Via Aquiro
Piazza Pietra
V. di Pietra
Via d.Muratte
Via Minghetti
Via delle Vergini
V.della Dataria
Albergo Cesàri
Via Dogona Vecchia
La Rosetta
Fiocco di Neve
Tazza d'Oro
V.d.Umilta
V. Giustiniani
V. d. Pastini
Via Lucchesi
Cremeria Monteforte
Pantheon
V. Caravita
Via S. Marcello
Via dell Archetto
Abruzzi
Via Seminario
Piazza Pilotta
Albergo del Sole al Pantheon
Via del Coll. Romano
Via del Corso
Birreria Peroni
Armando al Panthon
Pantheon
V.d. St. Ignazio
Via d.Rotonda
Via della Pilotta
Piazza St.Eustachio
Grand Hotel de la Minerve
Caffè Sant'Eustachio
Piazza di Minerva
Sta. Maria s.Minerva
Piazza dei SS. Apostoli
V.d.T. Valle
Via Monterone
Via di Torre Argentina
Albergo Santa Chiara
V.Sto. Stef. d. Cacco
Via della Gatta
V.d. Arco d. Ciambella
Via della Pigna
Via dei Costari
Via del Il Gesù
Piazza Grazioli
Via IV Novembre
Enoteca Corsi
Grano
Tiziano
La Ciambella
Prefettura
Corso Vittorio Emanuele II
Via d. Plebiscito
Via del Sudario
Piazza Venezia
Via Astalli
Via M.te d.Farina
Via delle Botteghe Oscure
Monumento Naz. a Vittorio Emanuele II
Trattoria Moderna
Via d. Sta. Anna
Palazzo Mattei di Giove
Via Caetani
Via dei Fori
V.d.v Delfini
Musei Capitolini
Via Tribuna di Tor de'Specchi
Via dei Funari
Via Arenula
Via degli Specchi
JEWISH GHETTO
Piazza del Campidoglio
Vecchia Roma
Open Baladin
Al Pompiere
Arenula
Pasticceria Boccione
Tempio di Saturno
Via d. Progresso
Forno del Ghetto
MONTE CAMPIDOGLIO
Via del Teatro di Marcello
Ba' Ghetto
Bellacarne
Via d. Portico d'Ottavia
Piperno
Via Catalana
V.d. Tempio
Teatro di Marcello
Lgt. dei Cenci
Via d.Consolazione
ISOLA TIBERINA
Pte. Fabricio
Via d.Foraggi
V. S.Teodoro
San Teodoro
E
F
G
H

Dining

Lodging

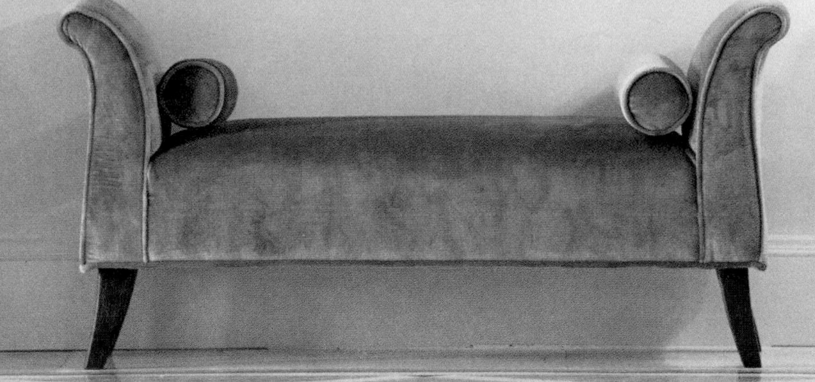

WHERE TO STAY

Updated by Nicole Arriaga

It's the click of your heels on inlaid marble, the whisper of 600-thread count Frette sheets, the murmured *buongiorno* of a coat-tailed porter bowing low as you pass. It's a rustic attic room with wood-beamed ceilings, a white umbrella on a roof terrace, a 400-year-old palazzo. Maybe it's the bird-song warbling into your room as you swing open French windows to a sun-kissed view of the Colosseum, a timeworn piazza, a flower-filled marketplace.

When it comes to accommodations, Rome offers a wide selection of high-end hotels, bed-and-breakfasts, designer boutique hotels, and quiet options that run the gamut from whimsical to luxurious. Whether you want a simple place to rest your head or a complete cache of exclusive amenities, you have plenty to choose from.

Luxury hotels like the Eden, the Hassler, and the Hotel de Russie are justly renowned for sybaritic comfort: postcard views over Roman rooftops, white linen and silver at a groaning-table breakfast buffet, and the fluffiest towels. But in other categories, especially moderate and inexpensive, standards vary considerably. That's a nice way of saying that very often, Rome's budget hotels are not up to the standards of space, comfort, quiet, and service that are taken for granted in the United States: you'll still find places with tiny rooms, lumpy beds, and anemic air-conditioning. Happily, the good news is that if you're flexible there are happy mediums aplenty.

One thing to figure out before you arrive is which neighborhood you want to stay in. There are obvious advantages to staying in a hotel within easy walking distance of the main sights. If a picturesque location is your main concern, stay in one of the small hotels around Piazza Navona or Campo de' Fiori. If luxury is a high priority, head for Piazza di Spagna or beyond the city center, where price-to-quality ratios are higher and some hotels have swimming pools. Most of Rome's good budget hotels are concentrated around Termini station, but here accommodations can vary widely, from fine to seedy, and you'll have to use public transportation to get to the historic part of town.

PLANNING

RESERVATIONS

Unless you don't mind flying by the seat of your pants, it's best to book ahead. This is especially true for May and June, when the Eternal City is virtually bursting at the seams; the same goes for major Catholic holidays such as Easter and Christmas. The city is never empty, but July and August and January and February are slower months. These are the best times to find rock-bottom rates as well.

Be as specific as possible about the accommodations you desire. Request the room size (single, double, or triple), type (standard, deluxe, or suite), and whether you want air-conditioning, a no-smoking room, a private bathroom with a shower or tub (or both), a terrace or balcony, or a view of the city (and ask whether there are extra costs associated with any of these). You may be required to leave a deposit; get a statement from the hotel about its refund policy before releasing your credit card number or mailing a money order. Insist on a written confirmation from the hotel stating the duration of your stay, room rate, any extras, location, room size, and type.

CHECKING IN

As soon as you get to Rome, you'll notice the leisurely pace of life here, which extends to hotel check-in times. If you arrive early in the morning (as is often the case with North American flights), you may find that your room is not ready yet (after 2 pm is pretty standard for most hotels, big and small). In this case, most hotels will store your luggage and encourage you to go out sightseeing. If you think you'll arrive later in the day, mention this before booking to make sure someone will be on hand to check you in. Some smaller hotels don't have a round-the-clock staff, and it's best to avoid unpleasant surprises. Check-out times are a little stricter, between 10 am and noon. If you need more time than that, the hotel may try to charge you for an extra night. However, if you just want to store your luggage for a few hours on your last day, most hotels will accommodate this request.

FACILITIES

The most expensive hotels have all the amenities you would expect at top levels and rates, with full services, spacious lounges, bars, restaurants, and some fitness facilities. Midrange hotels may have refrigerators, in-room safes, and double-glazed windows to keep out street noise. Budget hotels will have in-room direct-dial telephone and TV, and most will have air-conditioning. In less expensive places, you may have to pay extra for air-conditioning, and the shower may be the drain-in-the-floor type that hovers over the toilet and drenches the whole bathroom.

Unless stated in the review, hotels are equipped with elevators, and all guest rooms have air-conditioning, TV, and telephones.

WHERE SHOULD I STAY?

	Neighborhood Vibe	Pros	Cons
Around the Vatican: Borgo and Prati	Touristy near the Vatican but also with some upmarket restaurants and cafés. Not especially atmospheric.	Close to the Vatican, pretty quiet at night.	Pretty far from the other tourist attractions and nightlife.
Piazza Navona, Campo de' Fiori, and Jewish Ghetto	The areas around the Piazza Navona and Campo de' Fiorio are filled with good restaurants and most of Rome's major attractions. The Ghetto is quieter.	Everything you need is within walking distance: good eats, shopping, and many of Rome's museums and monuments.	This is the height of hustle and bustle in Rome, convenient, but often pricey. Street noise may be an issue.
Piazza di Spagna	Home to Rome's crème de la crème of hotels and shopping.	Where all the high rollers and A-listers like to reside.	Everything is expensive. Not very close to central hot spots.
Repubblica and Quirinale	Repubblica, with its beautiful piazza, is near Termini station without feeling grungy.	Hotels are much cheaper than elsewhere in Rome. Close to Termini train station. Great restaurants and hip bars.	Cheap, basic accommodations. The area surrounding Termini station can be iffy.
Villa Borghese and Piazza del Popolo	Somewhat removed from the hubbub, the area is a bit more refined, with fancy boutiques and hotels.	Close to the Piazza di Spagna and shopping. Lots of dining options not far away.	Pricey and a bit remote from Piazza Navona and Campo de' Fiori.
Trastevere	Village-like Trastevere has winding cobbled alleys, beautiful churches, and authentic mom-and-pop trattorias.	Fun area with great restaurants and cafés.	General area gets busy at night, can be rowdy and rambunctious on the weekends. Full of students.
Aventino and Testaccio	Aventino is a relaxing hilltop retreat. Working-class Testaccio is the heart of Rome's nightlife.	Tranquility, amazing views, and spacious rooms in Aventino. Party like a rock star in Rome's famous nightlife district, Testaccio.	Transportation difficult on the Aventine Hill. Testaccio is crowded on weekends.
Monti, Esquilino, and San Lorenzo	These are some of the more chic and funky neighborhoods in Rome. San Lorenzo is the university district.	Hotels are cheaper here than elsewhere in Rome. It's also close to Termini train station.	Areas are more local, but far from main tourist attractions. San Lorenzo not easily accessed by public transport.

WITH KIDS

Italians love kids, and many hotels go out of their way to accommodate families, with programming, special games, and other perks. Although hotels often allow children to stay in their parents' room for free, keep in mind that hotel rooms in Italy tend to be very small by American standards. It's a good idea to inquire about triples, connecting rooms, or suites, or consider taking a short-term apartment rental or residence hotel for the duration of your stay.

PRICES

In 2011, the city of Rome implemented a new tax for all overnight stays. Guests in bed-and-breakfasts, vacation apartment rentals, and 1-, 2-, and 3-star hotels will incur an additional €2 surcharge per person per night for a maximum of 10 nights. In 4- and 5-star hotels, the surcharge is €3 per person per night for a maximum of 10 nights. In the off-season months of late January, February, July, and August, prices can be considerably discounted (sometimes up to half off the regular rate). Inquire about specials and weekend deals, and you may be able to get a better rate per night if you are staying a week or longer. Rates are inclusive of service, but it's customary to tip porters, waiters, maids, and concierges. *Prices in the reviews are the lowest cost of a standard double room in high season.*

HOTEL REVIEWS

The following reviews are listed alphabetically within neighborhoods.

For expanded hotel reviews, visit Fodors.com.

Use the coordinate (⊕ 1:B2) at the end of each listing to locate a property on the Where to Eat and Stay in Rome atlas in the previous chapter.

AROUND THE VATICAN: BORGO AND PRATI

BORGO

Just east of the Vatican, the Borgo area has medieval charm but can be overrun by tourists (and tourist traps). However, there are a few appealing and atmospheric hotels here, and you can't beat the location for soaking up the Vatican sights.

$$$ HOTEL **Atlante Star.** The lush rooftop-garden terrace with a center-stage view of St. Peter's Basilica is one reason to stay here; you'll also enjoy the proximity to the Vatican and superb shopping and dining. **Pros:** close to St. Peter's; impressive view from the restaurant and some of the rooms. **Cons:** some rooms are nicer than others; the area can feel a bit residential; service is iffy. *Rooms from: €280 ✉ Via Vitelleschi 34, Borgo ☎ 06/6873233 ⊕ www.atlantestarhotel.com ⇨ 65 rooms, 10 suites 🍴 Breakfast Ⓜ Ottaviano ⊕ 1:D3.*

$$$$ HOTEL Fodor's Choice ★ **Residenza Paolo VI.** Set in a former monastery that is still an extraterritorial part of the Vatican and magnificently abutting Bernini's colonnade of St. Peter's Square, the Paolo VI (pronounced Paolo Sesto, Italian for Pope Paul VI) is unbeatably close to St. Peter's. **Pros:** unparalleled views of St. Peter's from the roof terrace; quiet rooms; huge breakfast spread. **Cons:** the small rooms are really small; bathrooms are small; the atmosphere at night is a little too quiet. *Rooms from: €320 ✉ Via Paolo VI 29, Borgo ☎ 06/684870 ⊕ www.residenzapaolovi.com ⇨ 35 rooms 🍴 Breakfast Ⓜ Ottaviano ⊕ 1:C4.*

$$ HOTEL **Sant'Anna.** In the picturesque, medieval Borgo neighborhood in the shadow of St. Peter's, this fashionable small hotel is good value.

BEST BETS FOR ROME LODGING

Fodor's offers a selective listing of quality lodging experiences at every price range, from the city's best budget motel to its most sophisticated luxury hotel. Here, we've compiled our top recommendations by price and experience.

Fodor's Choice ★

Albergo Santa Chiara, $$$, p. 280
Aleph, $$$, p. 283
The Beehive, $, p. 289
Britannia, $$$, p. 297
Casa di Santa Brigida, $$, p. 282
Casa di Santa Francesca Romana, $$, p. 293
Daphne Veneto, $$$, p. 285
D'Inghilterra, $$$$, p. 285
Eden, $$$$, p. 285
Exedra, $$$$, p. 290
The Hassler, $$$$, p. 285
Hotel de Russie, $$$$, p. 292
Hotel Ponte Sisto, $$$, p. 282
Hotel San Pietrino, $, p. 278
Hotel Santa Maria, $$$, p. 294
Il Palazzetto, $$$$, p. 286
Margutta 54, $$$$, p. 287
Relais Le Clarisse, $$$, p. 294
Residenza Paolo VI, $$$$, p. 277
Scalinata di Spagna, $$$, p. 288
Yes Hotel, $$, p. 291

By Price

$

The Beehive, p. 289
Hotel San Pietrino, p. 279
Hotel Trastevere, p. 294
Santa Prisca, p. 295

$$

Alimandi, p. 279
Casa di Santa Brigida, p. 282
Casa di Santa Francesca Romana, p. 293
Hotel Lancelot, p. 296
Italia, p. 296
Yes Hotel, p. 291

$$$

Albergo Santa Chiara, p. 280
Aleph, p. 283
Britannia, p. 297
Capo d'Africa, p. 295
Condotti, p. 285
Daphne Veneto, p. 285
Hotel Santa Maria, p. 294
Relais Le Clarisse, p. 294
Scalinata di Spagna, p. 288

$$$$

Dei Borgognoni, p. 285
Eden, p. 285
Exedra, p. 290
The Hassler, p. 285
Hotel Campo de' Fiori, p. 282
Hotel de Russie, p. 292
JK Place Roma, p. 287
Pantheon, p. 281

Best by Experience

BEST DESIGN

Aleph, $$$, p. 283
Capo d'Africa, $$$, p. 295
Hotel Art, $$$$, p. 286
Radisson Blu es. Hotel, $$$, p. 298

BEST CONCIERGE

The Beehive, $, p. 289
Daphne Veneto, $$$, p. 285
Demetra Hotel, $$$, p. 290
Hotel Lancelot, $$, p. 296
Majestic, $$$$, p. 287
Mascagni, $$$$, p. 290

BEST POOL

Exedra, $$$$, p. 290
Hotel de Russie, $$$$, p. 292
Grand Hotel Parco dei Principi, $$$, p. 292
Radisson Blu es. Hotel, $$$, p. 298
Rome Cavalieri, $$$$, p. 293

BEST SPA

Aleph, $$$, p. 283
Exedra, $$$$, p. 290
Hotel de Russie, $$$$, p. 292
Radisson Blu es. Hotel, $$$, p. 298
The Westin Excelsior, Rome, $$$$, p. 289

MOST KID-FRIENDLY

Hotel de Russie, $$$$, p. 292
Hotel Lancelot, $$, p. 296
Mascagni, $$$$, p. 290
The Westin Excelsior, Rome, $$$$, p. 289

MOST ROMANTIC

Daphne Veneto, $$$, p. 285
Hotel San Anselmo, $$$, p. 295
Inn at the Spanish Steps, $$$$, p. 286

Pros: Borgo Pio is a pedestrian-only zone during the day; beds are comfy; staff is friendly. **Cons:** no in-hotel bar or restaurant, and many nearby restaurants are tourist traps; the neighborhood is dead at night. *Rooms from: €160 Borgo Pio 134, Borgo 06/68801602 www.santannahotel.net 20 rooms Breakfast Ottaviano 1:C3.*

PRATI

This calm residential neighborhood north of the Vatican is convenient to sightseeing and shopping but removed from the chaotic centro storico. Here you'll find small, friendly hotels that don't break the bank.

$$ HOTEL **Alimandi.** A stone's throw away from the Vatican Museums, this family-run hotel offers good service and prices, with all sorts of perks. **Pros:** friendly staff; roof-top terrace; near reasonably priced restaurants and shops. **Cons:** breakfast is a good spread but it goes quickly; rooms are small; not much of interest besides the Vatican. *Rooms from: €160 Via Tunisi 8, Prati 06/39723948 www.alimandi.it 35 rooms Breakfast Ottaviano, Cipro 1:B2.*

$$ HOTEL **Amalia.** Convenient to St. Peter's, the Vatican, and Prati's Cola di Rienzo shopping district (and just a block from the Ottaviano stop of Metro line A), this small, family-run hotel is crisp and smart. **Pros:** good location for visiting the Vatican and shopping; 24-hour turnaround on laundry services; large beds; air-conditioning. **Cons:** sometimes hot water in bathrooms runs out quickly; Wi-Fi is only free when you book rooms directly through their website. *Rooms from: €150 Via Germanico 66, Prati 06/39723356 www.hotelamalia.com 33 rooms, 26 with bath, 1 suite Breakfast Cipro, Lipanto 1:C2.*

$$ HOTEL **Gerber.** Across the river from Piazza del Popolo on a quiet side street in the Prati neighborhood, this intimate, unpretentious hotel offers friendly service and simple, pleasant rooms. **Pros:** good value for your money; great service; comfortable beds and big bathrooms. **Cons:** elevator is tiny; you'll probably need to take a taxi or public transport for some of the sightseeing. *Rooms from: €170 Via degli Scipioni 241, Prati 06/3216485 www.hotelgerber.it 27 rooms Breakfast Lepanto 1:E1.*

$$$ HOTEL **Hotel Dei Mellini.** On the west bank of the Tiber between the Spanish Steps and St. Peter's Basilica (a five-minute stroll from Piazza del Popolo), this modern luxury hotel is tucked away from the chaos of the centro but still close enough for convenient sightseeing. **Pros:** spacious and spotless rooms; turndown service; the quiet neighborhood means a good night's rest. **Cons:** not for those who want to be in the center of the action; few dining options right nearby. *Rooms from: €280 Via Muzio Clementi 81, Prati 06/324771 www.hotelmellini.com 80 rooms Breakfast 1:F2.*

$ HOTEL Fodor's Choice ★ **Hotel San Pietrino.** This cute, simple hotel on the third floor of a 19th-century palazzo offers rock-bottom prices a five-minute walk from the Vatican. **Pros:** heavenly prices near the Vatican; high-speed Internet; close to Rome's famous farmers' market, Mercato Trionfale. **Cons:** a couple of Metro stops away from the center of Rome; no breakfast; no bar. *Rooms from: €100 Via Giovanni Bettolo 43, Prati 06/3700132 www.sanpietrino.it 12 rooms No meals Ottaviano 1:C1.*

$ RESORT **Residence Candia.** Located in the Prati area just behind the Vatican Museums, this place, which offers both hotel-style rooms and apartments with kitchenettes, is the perfect solution for those looking to be just outside the chaotic centro district but close enough to all the major sights. **Pros:** Wi-Fi in all rooms; owner sometimes hosts free dinners for his guests and provides free papal mass tickets. **Cons:** the residence tends to be noisy when student groups are staying there. *Rooms from: €120 ✉ Via Candia 135/B, Prati ☎ 06/39721046 www.residencecandia.it 55 rooms No meals Ⓜ Cipro ✣ 1:A2.*

PIAZZA NAVONA, CAMPO DE' FIORI, AND THE JEWISH GHETTO

PIAZZA NAVONA

Thanks to its Baroque palazzi, Bernini fountains, and outdoor cafés, Piazza Navona is one of Rome's most popular squares. The nearby Pantheon area, equally as beautiful but not as lively, offers great restaurants and shops. Hotels in this area offer postcard views of Rome and personalized service.

$$$ HOTEL **Abruzzi.** This friendly, comfortable family-run hotel has magnificent views of the Pantheon at a relatively gentle price. **Pros:** views of the Pantheon; sizeable bathrooms; the piazza is a hot spot. **Cons:** the area can be somewhat noisy; rooms are on the small side; it's about a 15-minute walk from the Barberini metro stop. *Rooms from: €260 ✉ Piazza della Rotonda 69, Piazza Navona ☎ 06/97841351 www.hotelabruzzi.it 29 rooms Breakfast Ⓜ Barberini ✣ 4:F2.*

$$$ HOTEL **Albergo Cesàri.** On a pedestrian-only street near the Pantheon, this lovely little hotel has an air of warmth and serenity, and a rooftop bar with great views. **Pros:** prime location and soundproofed from the street noise; free Wi-Fi; friendly staff. **Cons:** some of the bathrooms could use renovating; air-conditioning is not especially strong. *Rooms from: €260 ✉ Via di Pietra 89/a, Piazza Navona ☎ 06/6749701 albergocesari.it 48 rooms Breakfast Ⓜ Barberini ✣ 4:F2.*

$$$ HOTEL **Albergo del Sole al Pantheon.** The granddaddy of Roman hotels and one of the oldest in the world—the doors first opened in 1467—this charming hotel is adjacent to the Pantheon and right in the middle of the lovely Piazza della Rotonda. **Pros:** complimentary newspaper delivered to your room daily; rich breakfast buffet. **Cons:** rooms are a bit small; despite the double-glazed windows, street noise can be an issue. *Rooms from: €270 ✉ Piazza della Rotonda 63, Piazza Navona ☎ 06/6780441 www.hotelsolealpantheon.com 33 rooms Breakfast Ⓜ Barberini ✣ 4:D4.*

$$$ HOTEL Fodor's Choice ★ **Albergo Santa Chiara.** If you're looking for a good location (right behind the Pantheon) and top-notch service at great prices—not to mention comfortable beds and a quiet stay—look no further than this historic hotel, run by the same family for some 200 years. **Pros:** great location; free Wi-Fi; lovely terrace/sitting area in front, overlooking the piazza. **Cons:** some rooms in need of updating; service is iffy; some rooms can be noisy. *Rooms from: €240 ✉ Via Santa Chiara 21,*

Piazza Navona ☎ *06/6872979* 🌐 *www.albergosantachiara.com* *96 rooms, 3 suites, 3 apartments* 🍴 *Breakfast* Ⓜ *Barberini* ✥ *4:E3.*

$$ HOTEL **Genio.** Just outside one of Rome's most beautiful piazzas—Piazza Navona—this pleasant hotel has a lovely rooftop terrace perfect for enjoying a cappuccino or glass of wine and taking in the view. **Pros:** staff is very friendly; breakfast buffet is abundant; elegant bathrooms. **Cons:** rooms facing the street can be noisy; hot water unreliable at times. *Rooms from: €160* ✉ *Via Giuseppe Zanardelli 28, Piazza Navona* ☎ *06/6832191* 🌐 *www.hotelgenioroma.it* *60 rooms* 🍴 *Breakfast* ✥ *4:D2.*

$$$$ HOTEL **Grand Hotel de la Minerve.** Once one of Rome's landmark fixtures, this 17th-century palazzo used to be a favorite address for everyone from Stendhal to Sartre along with a bevy of crowned (and uncrowned—Carlotta, the deposed empress of Mexico resided here for a while) heads. **Pros:** right by the Pantheon yet set on quiet Piazza della Minerva; staff is friendly and accommodating; some rooms have terraces. **Cons:** some rooms need updating and lack common five-star-hotel amenities; Internet can be spotty. *Rooms from: €400* ✉ *Piazza della Minerva 69, Piazza Navona* ☎ *06/695201* 🌐 *www.grandhoteldelaminerve.com* *119 rooms, 17 suites* 🍴 *No meals* ✥ *4:F3.*

$$$$ HOTEL **Pantheon.** On a quiet street around the corner from the Pantheon, this little hotel is warm and inviting. **Pros:** proximity to the Pantheon; big, clean bathrooms; friendly staff. **Cons:** some rooms are on the small side and need restyling; rooms can feel a bit stuffy. *Rooms from: €320* ✉ *Via dei Pastini 131, Piazza Navona* ☎ *06/6787746* 🌐 *www.hotelpantheon.com* *12 rooms, 1 suite* 🍴 *Breakfast* ✥ *4:F2.*

$$ HOTEL **Relais Palazzo Taverna.** This little hidden gem on a side street behind the lovely Via dei Coronari is a good compromise for those looking for boutique-style accommodations on a budget. **Pros:** centrally located; boutique-style at moderate prices. **Cons:** staff is on duty only until 11 pm (they can be contacted after hours in an emergency). *Rooms from: €180* ✉ *Via dei Gabrielli 92, Piazza Navona* ☎ *06/20398064* 🌐 *www.relaispalazzotaverna.com* *6 rooms* 🍴 *Breakfast* ✥ *1:E4.*

CAMPO DE' FIORI

If you're looking to be in the cuore of Vecchia Roma (heart of Old Rome), there's no better place than Campo de' Fiori, a gorgeous piazza that's lively with merchants, outdoor cafés, and bars. The hotels here are not generally as lovely as their surroundings, however—many are cramped and could use updating.

$$ HOTEL **Albergo del Sole al Biscione.** This affordable and comfortable hotel, centrally located in the heart of Campo de' Fiori and built atop the ruins of the ancient Theater of Pompey, has warm, cozy decor and a rooftop terrace with a stunning view of Sant'Andrea delle Valle. **Pros:** parking garage in the hotel; reasonable rates for the location; nice rooftop terrace. **Cons:** some rooms are small and without a/c; no elevator at the entrance of hotel; the area can be a bit noisy. *Rooms from: €130* ✉ *Via del Biscione 76, Campo de' Fiori* ☎ *06/68806873* 🌐 *www.solealbiscione.it* *59 rooms* *No credit cards* 🍴 *No meals* Ⓜ *Barberini* ✥ *4:D4.*

13

$$ B&B/INN Fodor's Choice ★ **Casa di Santa Brigida.** The friendly sisters of Santa Brigida oversee simple, straightforward, and centrally located accommodations in one of Rome's loveliest convents, with a rooftop terrace overlooking Palazzo Farnese. **Pros:** no curfew in this historic convent; insider papal tickets; location in the Piazza Farnese. **Cons:** weak a/c; no TVs in the rooms (though there is a common TV room); breakfast is unexciting. *Rooms from: €180 ✉ Piazza Farnese 96, entrance around the corner at Via Monserrato 54, Campo de' Fiori ☎ 06/68892596 ⊕ www.brigidine.org 20 rooms Multiple meal plans ✣ 4:C4.*

$$$$ HOTEL **Hotel Campo de' Fiori.** This handsome, ivy-draped hotel is a romantic refuge located right in the heart of Campo de' Fiori. **Pros:** free Wi-Fi; rooftop terrace; a 5% discount if you pay in cash. **Cons:** rooms are on the small side; some apartments are too close to the area's noisy bar scene. *Rooms from: €350 ✉ Via del Biscione 6, Campo de' Fiori ☎ 06/68806865 ⊕ www.hotelcampodefiori.it 23 rooms, 12 apartments Breakfast ✣ 4:D4.*

$$$ HOTEL Fodor's Choice ★ **Hotel Ponte Sisto.** Situated in a restored Renaissance palazzo with one of the prettiest patio-courtyards in Rome, this hotel is a relaxing retreat inches from Trastevere and Campo de' Fiori. **Pros:** staff is friendly; rooms with views (and some with balconies and terraces); luxury bathrooms; beautiful courtyard garden. **Cons:** street-side rooms can be a bit noisy; some rooms are on the small side; aside from breakfast, restaurant only caters to groups and must be booked in advance. *Rooms from: €250 ✉ Via dei Pettinari 64, Campo de' Fiori ☎ 06/6863100 ⊕ www.hotelpontesisto.it 103 rooms, 4 suites Breakfast ✣ 4:D5.*

$$$ HOTEL **Teatro di Pompeo.** Have breakfast under the ancient stone vaults of Pompey's Theater, the site of Julius Caesar's assassination, and sleep under restored beamed ceilings that date from the days of Michelangelo at this hotel with simple (and perhaps a bit dated) rooms and wonderful, genuinely helpful staff. **Pros:** great location near Campo de' Fiori; helpful staff; an old-school Roman feel. **Cons:** rooms can be a bit noisy; rooms are small and some are a bit musty; Wi-Fi is very spotty. *Rooms from: €220 ✉ Largo del Pallaro 8, Campo de' Fiori ☎ 06/68300170 ⊕ www.hotelteatrodipompeo.it 12 rooms Breakfast ✣ 4:D4.*

$$$ HOTEL **Tiziano.** With Campo de' Fiori, Piazza Navona, and the Pantheon all at your doorstep, this 18th-century hotel in a former palace—the once grand Palazzo Pacelli—makes an ideal base from which to explore, though the decor could use an update. **Pros:** a very "European" feel; excellent value and location; computer terminal with Internet access at the reception for guests to use. **Cons:** some rooms are noisy; especially when hosting student university groups; breakfast offerings are modest; not exactly 4-star quality. *Rooms from: €230 ✉ Campo Vittorio Emanuele II 110, Campo de' Fiori ☎ 06/6865019 ⊕ www.tizianohotel.it 51 rooms Breakfast ✣ 4:E4.*

JEWISH GHETTO

Next to Campo de' Fiori and across the river from Trastevere, the Jewish Ghetto is filled with kosher restaurants and bakeries, shops, and the city's biggest synagogue.

$$ HOTEL **Arenula.** A hefty bargain by Rome standards, Hotel Arenula has an almost unbeatable location, an imposingly elegant stone exterior, and simple but comfortable rooms with pale-wood furnishings and double-glazed windows, but alas, no elevator. **Pros:** a real bargain; conveniently located, close to Campo de' Fiori and Trastevere; spotless. **Cons:** totally no-frills accommodations; no elevator; can still be a bit noisy despite the double-glazed windows. *Rooms from: €140 Via Santa Maria dei Calderari 47, off Via Arenula, Jewish Ghetto 06/6879454 www.hotelarenula.com 50 rooms Breakfast 4:E5.*

PIAZZA DI SPAGNA

If being right in the heart of Rome's shopping district and within walking distance of the major sights is a priority, this is the place to stay. You'll find a range of accommodations here—exclusive boutique hotels with over-the-top amenities but also moderately priced urban B&Bs and pensioni with clean, comfortable rooms.

$$$ HOTEL Fodor's Choice ★ **Aleph.** If you're wondering where the beautiful people are, look no further than the Aleph, the most unfalteringly fashionable of Rome's design hotels. **Pros:** free access to the spa for hotel guests; award-winning design; free Wi-Fi. **Cons:** rooms are too petite for the price; cocktails are expensive. *Rooms from: €300 Via San Basilio 15, Piazza di Spagna 06/422901 aleph-roma.boscolohotels.com 90 rooms, 6 suites No meals Barberini–Fontana di Trevi 2:C2.*

$$ HOTEL **Alexandra.** For nearly a century, Hotel Alexandra has been a family affair, and distinguished style and moderate prices allow it to hold its own against its flashier big brothers and sisters on the Via Veneto. **Pros:** great location near Piazza Barberini for sightseeing, restaurants, and transportation; decorated with authentic antiques; free Wi-Fi. **Cons:** mostly tiny rooms and tinier bathrooms; breakfast is just the standard fare. *Rooms from: €175 Via Veneto 18, Piazza di Spagna 06/4881943 www.hotelalexandraroma.com 60 rooms Breakfast Barberini–Fontana di Trevi 2:B2.*

$$$ HOTEL **Barberini.** This elegant 4-star hotel, housed in a 19th-century palazzo near Palazzo Barberini, has old-world luxury and charm an easy distance from the Metro, the Trevi Fountain, and plenty of good restaurants. **Pros:** beautiful view from the roof terrace; located on a quiet side street close to several important attractions; attentive staff with deals for theater tickets and other events; spa facilities. **Cons:** some rooms are on the small side; not all rooms have bathtubs. *Rooms from: €285 Via Rasella 3, Piazza di Spagna 06/4814993 www.hotelbarberini.com 35 rooms, 4 suites Breakfast Barberini–Fontana di Trevi 2:B3.*

$$$$ HOTEL **Babuino 181.** Named for its street known for high-end boutiques and antiques shops, this stylish hotel with spacious, loftlike suites offers top-notch amenities, ultimate privacy, and personalized service. **Pros:** iPod/iPhone docks and other handy in-room amenities; Nespresso coffee machines; spacious suites. **Cons:** the rooms can be a bit noisy; breakfast is nothing special. *Rooms from: €430 Via Babuino 181, Piazza di*

CLOSE UP

Renting an Apartment in Rome

The saying "Two's company and three's a crowd" definitely holds true in Roman hotel rooms. If you're traveling with a larger group, consider renting a short-term apartment. Apartments are generally rented out the old-fashioned way by their owners, though in some cases a realtor or management company is involved. A three-night minimum is the norm. Prices will vary, but expect them to be higher in the historic city center, the Vaticano/Borgo, the Campo de' Fiori, and Trastevere areas. ■ **TIP→ Keep in mind that there's sometimes an extra charge involved for final cleaning, utilities, and Internet access when renting an apartment.** When seeking a holiday home in Rome, start your research online. Rome's official tourism website (🌐 *www.turismoroma.it*) offers a search function for a number of different housing options.

Wanted in Rome (🌐 *www.wantedinrome.com*) is a popular English language expat magazine that features an extensive classifieds section on their website. The Bed & Breakfast Association of Rome (🌐 *www.b-b.rm.it*) offers an online apartment rental search in addition to their B&B search. They personally inspect all properties on their site. Cross-Pollinate (🌐 *www.cross-pollinate.com*), an accommodation service owned by the people who run the Beehive Hotel, gives visitors the information to seek out their own accommodations. They personally screen all properties. San Francisco–based Craigslist hosts classifieds for 450 cities worldwide, including Rome. Craigslist Rome lists postings for apartments, houses, swaps, sublets, and other vacation rentals at 🌐 *rome.en.craigslist.it*.

HOTELS WITH APARTMENTS

More and more hotels in Rome now offer their prospective guests a selection of apartments (either located on the grounds or just nearby), in addition to rooms and suites.

Albergo Santa Chiara Apartments. 3 apartments. ✉ *Via Santa Chiara 21, Piazza Navona* ☎ *06/6872979* 🌐 *www.albergosantachiara.com* ✣ *4:E3.*

Hotel Campo de' Fiori Apartments. 12 apartments. [$] *Rooms from: €380* ✉ *Via del Biscione 6, Campo de' Fiori* ☎ *06/68806865* 🌐 *www.hotelcampodefiori.it* ✣ *4:D4.*

Italia Apartments. 1 apartment. ✉ *Via Venezia 18, Monti* ☎ *06/4828355* 🌐 *www.hotelitaliaroma.it* ✣ *2:C4.*

Julia Apartments. 2 apartments. ✉ *Via Rasella 29, Piazza di Spagna* ☎ *06/4881637* 🌐 *www.hoteljulia.it* ✣ *2:B3.*

Mecenate Palace Hotel Apartments. 2 apartments. [$] *Rooms from: €430* ✉ *Via Carlo Alberto 3, Esquilino* ☎ *06/44702024* 🌐 *www.mecenatepalace.com* ✣ *2:D5.*

Trastevere Apartments. 3 apartments. ✉ *Via Luciano Manara 24a–25, Trastevere* ☎ *06/5814713* 🌐 *www.hoteltrastevere.net* ✣ *3:B2.*

Spagna ☎ *06/32295295* 🌐 *www.romeluxurysuites.com/babuino* 🛏 *14 rooms* 🍴 *No meals* Ⓜ *Flaminio, Spagna* ✥ *1:G1.*

$$$ B&B/INN **Condotti.** Near the most expensive shopping street in Rome, Via dei Condotti, and one block from the Spanish Steps, this delightful little hotel is all about peace, comfort, and location. **Pros:** soundproof rooms with terraces; individual climate control. **Cons:** small rooms; tiny elevator. 💲 *Rooms from: €230* ✉ *Via Mario de' Fiori 37, Piazza di Spagna* ☎ *06/6794661* 🌐 *www.hotelcondotti.com* 🛏 *16 rooms, 2 suites* 🍴 *Breakfast* Ⓜ *Spagna* ✥ *1:H2.*

13

$$$ B&B/INN Fodor's Choice ★ **Daphne Veneto.** This "urban B&B" is run by people who love Rome and want to make sure you do, too—the staff will happily act as your personal travel planner, helping you map out your destinations, plan day trips, choose restaurants, and organize transportation. **Pros:** the opportunity to see Rome "like an insider"; beds have Simmons mattresses and fluffy comforters; free Wi-Fi. **Cons:** no TVs; some bathrooms are shared; Visa or MasterCard required to hold bookings (though you can actually pay with an AmEx). 💲 *Rooms from: €230* ✉ *Via di San Basilio 55, Piazza di Spagna* ☎ *06/87450087* 🌐 *www.daphne-rome.com* 🛏 *7 rooms, 2 suites* 🍴 *Breakfast* Ⓜ *Barberini–Fontana di Trevi* ✥ *2:B3.*

$$$$ HOTEL **Dei Borgognoni.** Travelers with shopping on their minds will appreciate the position of this quietly chic hotel set in a centuries-old palazzo near Piazza San Silvestro, a short walk from the Spanish Steps. **Pros:** reasonably priced but still very central; some rooms have private balconies or terraces. **Cons:** some rooms are small for the price; breakfast lacks variety; Wi-Fi in the rooms isn't free. 💲 *Rooms from: €320* ✉ *Via del Bufalo 126, Piazza di Spagna* ☎ *06/69941505* 🌐 *www.hotelborgognoni.it* 🛏 *51 rooms* 🍴 *Breakfast* Ⓜ *Barberini* ✥ *4:G1.*

$$$$ HOTEL Fodor's Choice ★ **D'Inghilterra.** Situated in a 17th-century guesthouse, Hotel D'Inghilterra has been one of Rome's most fashionable hotels since it opened in 1845. **Pros:** distinct character and opulence; turndown service (with chocolates!); genuinely friendly and attentive staff. **Cons:** elevator is small and slow; bathrooms are surprisingly petite; the location, despite soundproofing, is still noisy. 💲 *Rooms from: €550* ✉ *Via Bocca di Leone 14, Piazza di Spagna* ☎ *06/699811* 🌐 *www.hoteldinghilterraroma.it* 🛏 *81 rooms, 7 suites* 🍴 *No meals* Ⓜ *Spagna* ✥ *1:H2.*

$$$$ HOTEL Fodor's Choice ★ **Eden.** A recent refurbishment of the Hotel Eden has put it back in the running for one of Rome's top luxury lodgings: once a favorite haunt of Hemingway, Ingrid Bergman, and Fellini, this superlative hotel combines dashing elegance, exquisitely lush decor, and stunning vistas of Rome with true Italian hospitality. **Pros:** gorgeous mirrored roof terrace restaurant; you could be rubbing elbows with the stars; 24-hour room service. **Cons:** breakfast not included in the price (and quite expensive); Wi-Fi is expensive; some say the staff can be hit-or-miss. 💲 *Rooms from: €440* ✉ *Via Ludovisi 49, Piazza di Spagna* ☎ *06/478121* 🌐 *www.lhw.com/Eden* 🛏 *121 rooms, 13 suites* 🍴 *No meals* Ⓜ *Spagna* ✥ *2:B2.*

$$$$ HOTEL Fodor's Choice ★ **The Hassler.** When it comes to million-dollar views, this exclusive hotel atop the Spanish steps has the best seats in the house, so it's no surprise that generations of fans, many rich and famous (Tom Cruise, Jennifer Lopez, Gwenyth Paltrow, and the Beckhams included), are

willing to pay top dollar to stay here. **Pros:** charming Old World feel; prime location and panoramic views; near some of the best shopping in the world. **Cons:** VIP prices; many think the staff is too standoffish; spa facilities are far from 5-star material. *Rooms from: €780 Piazza Trinità dei Monti 6, Piazza di Spagna 06/69934755, 800/223–6800 Toll-free from the U.S. www.hotelhasslerroma.com 82 rooms, 14 suites No meals Spagna 1:H2.*

$$$$ HOTEL **Hotel Art.** High Fashion Rome meets Chic Contemporary Gallery at this hotel that sits on Via Margutta, "the street of painters." **Pros:** hotel has an ultra-hip art gallery feel; close to the metro; comfortable beds. **Cons:** the glass floors are noisy at night; the courtyard bar crowd may keep you awake; the staff can be iffy. *Rooms from: €320 Via Margutta 56, Piazza di Spagna 06/328711 www.hotelart.it 44 rooms, 2 suites Breakfast Spagna 1:H2.*

$$ HOTEL **Hotel Homs.** Tucked away on a quiet street steps from the Spanish Steps, this midsize hotel is convenient to great cafés, serious shopping, and all the sights. **Pros:** walking distance to Piazza di Spagna; steps away from a big bus hub and close to the metro; helpful staff. **Cons:** breakfast not included; small rooms and bathrooms. *Rooms from: €200 Via della Vite 71–72, Piazza di Spagna 06/6792976 www.hotelhoms.it 53 rooms, 5 suites, 1 apartment No meals Barberini–Fontana di Trevi, Spagna 1:H3.*

$$ HOTEL **Hotel Suisse.** Located on a picturesque street around the corner from the Spanish Steps is a warm and inviting hotel that's been run by the same family for three generations. **Pros:** good value for reasonable price; the rooms are obviously cared for; great location. **Cons:** breakfast selection isn't that ample and is served in your room; bathrooms are on the small side. *Rooms from: €185 Via Gregoriana 54, Piazza di Spagna 06/6783649 www.hotelsuisserome.com 12 rooms Breakfast Barberini–Fontana di Trevi, Spagna 1:H3.*

$$$$ B&B/INN Fodor's Choice ★ **Il Palazzetto.** This 15th-century house, once a retreat for one of Rome's richest noble families, is one of the most intimate and luxurious hotels in Rome, with gorgeous terraces where you can watch the never-ending theater of the Scalinatella. **Pros:** location and view; free Wi-Fi; guests have full access of The Hassler's services. **Cons:** restaurant is often rented out for crowded special events; bedrooms do not access the communal terraces. *Rooms from: €350 Vicolo del Bottino 8, Piazza di Spagna 06/699341000 www.ilpalazzettoroma.com 4 rooms No meals Spagna 1:H2.*

$$$$ B&B/INN **Inn at the Spanish Steps.** This quaint yet cushy hotel, which occupies the upper floors of a centuries-old town house it shares with Casanova's old haunt, Antico Caffè Greco, wins a gold star for its sharp design and smart decor. **Pros:** the best of high-end and boutique shopping at your fingertips; rooms with superb views of the Spanish Steps; afternoon snacks and outstanding breakfast buffet. **Cons:** interior rooms are claustrophobic; the area can be noisy due to crowds at the Spanish Steps; rooms located in the annex don't always receive the same attention as those located directly in the hotel. *Rooms from: €355 Via Condotti 85, Piazza di Spagna 06/69925657 www.atspanishsteps.com 22 suites Breakfast Spagna 1:H2.*

$$$$ HOTEL **JK Place Roma.** This beautiful, intimate boutique hotel in the heart of the *centro* is dripping with luxury and has breathtaking views from the rooftop bar and lounge. **Pros:** staff is eager to please; excellent meals at rooftop lounge; complimentary mini-bar. **Cons:** no fitness center; not all rooms have a balcony; some rooms are on the small side. *Rooms from: €700 Via Monte d'Oro, 30, Piazza di Spagna 06/982634 www.jkroma.com 30 Spagna 1:G3.*

$$ HOTEL **Julia.** This small three-star hotel, situated on a small cobblestone street just behind Piazza Berberini and a short walk to the Trevi Fountain, offers clean, comfortable rooms in the center of Rome that won't break the bank. **Pros:** safe neighborhood; convenient to sights and transportation; quiet location. **Cons:** no frills; very basic accommodations; some of the rooms are dark. *Rooms from: €190 Via Rasella 29, Piazza di Spagna 06/4881637 www.hoteljulia.it 33 rooms, 30 with bath, 2 suites, 3 apartments Breakfast Barberini–Fontana di Trevi 2:B3.*

13

$$$ HOTEL **La Residenza.** This cozy hotel in a converted town house near Via Veneto is widely popular with American travelers thanks to its American-style breakfast and helpful staff. **Pros:** big American breakfast with eggs, pancakes, and sausage; spacious rooms with balconies; friendly staff. **Cons:** the building's exterior doesn't compare to its interior; located on a street with some "gentleman's" clubs; rooms are in need of restyling. *Rooms from: €210 Via Emilia 22, Piazza di Spagna 06/4880789 www.hotel-la-residenza.com 29 rooms Breakfast Spagna 2:B2.*

$$$$ HOTEL **Majestic.** The first luxury hotel built on the Via Veneto, in 1889, the luxurious Majestic was a favorite among Rome's royalty and social climbers (it was a backdrop in Fellini's film *La Dolce Vita*) and is still a grand old-world hotel. **Pros:** silky linens on big, plush beds; some rooms have private balconies overlooking Via Veneto; 24-hour fitness center. **Cons:** breakfast is especially expensive; not all rooms are spacious. *Rooms from: €495 Via Vittorio Veneto 50, Veneto, Piazza di Spagna 06/421441 www.hotelmajestic.com 98 rooms, 13 suites No meals Spagna 2:B2.*

$$$$ B&B/INN Fodor's Choice ★ **Margutta 54.** Tucked away on a quiet, leafy street known for its art galleries, this four-suite property is like your very own hip, New York style loft in the center of old-world Rome, with top-drawer amenities, contemporary design, and an ivy-draped courtyard. **Pros:** studio loft feel in center of town; notable former occupants (like Picasso); complete privacy; deluxe furnishings. **Cons:** breakfast is an additional €20 per person and is served at sister hotel Babuino 181; no staff available on-site after 8 pm. *Rooms from: €390 Via Margutta 54, Piazza di Spagna 06/69921907 www.romeluxurysuites.com/margutta 4 suites No meals Spagna 1:H2.*

$$$$ HOTEL **Marriott Grand Hotel Flora.** This handsome hotel at the top of Via Veneto next to the Villa Borghese park is something of a beacon on the Rome landscape, and no expense has been spared in decorating the rooms and suites, among the largest in the Eternal City. **Pros:** convenient location and pleasant staff; spectacular view from the terrace; free Internet. **Cons:** breakfast finishes fast; sometimes the noise from Via Veneto

drifts in; crowded with businessmen and big tour groups. *Rooms from: €400 Via Veneto 191, Veneto, Piazza di Spagna 06/489929 www.hotelfloraroma.com 155 rooms, 21 suites Breakfast Barberini–Fontana di Trevi, Spagna 2:B1.*

$ HOTEL **Panda.** You couldn't possibly find a better deal in Rome than here at the Panda, especially given its key location just behind the Spanish Steps. **Pros:** discount if you pay cash; free Wi-Fi; on a quiet street, but still close to the Spanish Steps. **Cons:** not all rooms have private bathrooms; no elevator directly to floor; breakfast is not included in the price. *Rooms from: €110 Via della Croce 35, Piazza di Spagna 06/6780179 www.hotelpanda.it 28 rooms, 20 with bath No meals Spagna 1:G2.*

$$$$ HOTEL **Regina Baglioni.** A former playground of kings and poets, the Regina Baglioni, which enjoys a prime spot on the Via Veneto, is a favorite among today's international jetsetters. **Pros:** nice decor; refurbished rooms; Brunello Lounge and Restaurant. **Cons:** some rooms need restyling; staff is hit-or-miss; Internet is spotty; some rooms are noisy. *Rooms from: €430 Via Veneto 72, Piazza di Spagna 06/421111 www.reginabaglioni.com 136 rooms, 7 suites No meals Barberini–Fontana di Trevi 2:B2.*

$$$ HOTEL **San Carlo.** This renovated 17th-century mansion–turned–hotel offers modern comforts at reasonable prices, right around the corner from the Spanish Steps and the best shopping in Rome. **Pros:** some rooms have terraces and views of historic Rome; rooftop garden; attentive staff. **Cons:** some rooms are on the small side; rooms can be noisy. *Rooms from: €225 Via delle Carrozze 92–93, Piazza di Spagna 06/6784548 www.hotelsancarloroma.com 50 rooms, 2 suites Breakfast Spagna 1:G2.*

$$$ B&B/INN Fodor's Choice ★ **Scalinata di Spagna.** Perched atop the Spanish Steps, this charming boutique hotel makes guests fall in love over and over again—in fact, it's often booked far in advance. **Pros:** friendly and helpful concierge; fresh fruit in the rooms; free Wi-Fi throughout. **Cons:** it's a hike up the hill to the hotel; no porter and no elevator. *Rooms from: €250 Piazza Trinità dei Monti 17, Piazza di Spagna 06/45686150 www.hotelscalinata.com 16 rooms Breakfast Spagna 2:A2.*

$$$ HOTEL **Sofitel Rome Villa Borghese.** Set in a refurbished 1902 Victorian palace, the Hotel Sofitel—which has a long-standing reputation with business travelers—exudes old-world elegance, albeit with a modern design sensibility. **Pros:** luxury lodging off the main drag (but not far from it); first-rate concierge and porter. **Cons:** luxury chain with business clientele could feel a little stuffy; some say the air-conditioning could be stronger; the showers are a bit leaky. *Rooms from: €280 Via Lombardia 47, Piazza di Spagna 06/478021 www.sofitel.com 113 rooms, 4 suites Breakfast Spagna 2:B2.*

$$$ HOTEL **Trevi.** Location, location, location: at this delightful place tucked away down one of Old Rome's quaintest alleys near the Trevi Fountain, the smallish rooms are bright and clean, and you can eat marvelous pasta at the arborlike roof-garden restaurant as you peer at the city below. **Pros:** pass the Trevi Fountain each day as you come and go; comfortable rooms. **Cons:** area can be very noisy due to foot

traffic around the Trevi Fountain; some rooms are in need of restyling. *Rooms from: €250* *Vicolo del Babbuccio 20/21, Piazza di Spagna* *06/6789563* *www.hoteltrevirome.com* *29 rooms* *Breakfast* *Barberini–Fontana di Trevi* *4:H2.*

$$$ HOTEL **Tritone.** This trusty hotel offers modern rooms in a great location steps from Rome's majestic Trevi Fountain. **Pros:** walking distance to major attractions; modern decor; friendly staff. **Cons:** rooms can be noisy despite soundproofing, breakfast is standard fare; Wi-Fi isn't free. *Rooms from: €220* *Via del Tritone 210, Piazza di Spagna* *06/69922575* *www.tritonehotel.com* *43 rooms* *Breakfast* *Barberini–Fontana di Trevi* *4:G1.*

13

$$$ HOTEL **Victoria.** Just across the street from Villa Borghese is this four-star boutique hotel that's popular with American travelers on business in Rome. **Pros:** view of the gardens; quiet and comfortable; rooftop bar and restaurant; great personalized service. **Cons:** it's a schlep to most sights; rooms are small. *Rooms from: €230* *Via Campania 41, Piazza di Spagna* *06/423701* *www.hotelvictoriaroma.com* *110 rooms* *No meals* *2:C1.*

$$$$ HOTEL FAMILY **The Westin Excelsior, Rome.** Ablaze with lights at night, this seven-layer-cake hotel—topped off by its famous cupola, a landmark nearly as famous as the American Embassy palazzo across the street—is popular with visiting diplomats, celebrities, and American business conference groups. **Pros:** elegant period furnishings and decor; celeb-sightings; health club and indoor pool. **Cons:** some rooms are in need of updating; Wi-Fi is expensive; reception staff can be a little off-putting. *Rooms from: €420* *Via Veneto 125, Piazza di Spagna* *06/47081* *www.westinrome.com* *319 rooms, 32 suites* *No meals* *Barberini–Fontana di Trevi, Spagna* *2:C2.*

REPUBBLICA

With its beautiful piazza and fountain, Repubblica is the place to stay if you want to be near, but not *too* near, Termini station, Rome's central train hub. You'll find lodging here in all price ranges, along with cafés and shops. Rooms tend to be better value in this part of town.

$$$ HOTEL **Alpi.** You'll feel right at home from the moment you waltz into Hotel Alpi, where high ceilings with elegant chandeliers, white walls, and marble floors lend both elegance and warmth—right around the corner from Termini station. **Pros:** clean and comfortable; lovely terraces and restaurant for dining and relaxing. **Cons:** not all rooms are created equal; slow elevator; you'll need to take transportation to most sights. *Rooms from: €240* *Via Castelfidardo 84, Repubblica* *06/4441235* *www.hotelalpi.com* *48 rooms* *Breakfast* *Castro Pretorio, Termini* *2:E2.*

$ B&B/INN Fodor's Choice ★ **The Beehive.** Living the American dream *dolce vita* style is exactly what one Los Angeles couple started to do in 1999, when they opened the Beehive, a hip, alternative budget hotel near Termini station. **Pros:** massage and other therapies offered on-site; organic brunches and dinners on weekends; convenient to Termini station. **Cons:** some rooms do not have private baths; standard rooms lack TV and air-conditioning;

breakfast is not included in the room rate. *Rooms from: €100* ✉ *Via Marghera 8, San Lorenzo* ☎ *06/44704553* 🌐 *www.the-beehive.com* *8 rooms, 1 dormitory, 3 apartments* *No meals* Ⓜ *Termini* ✣ *2:E3.*

$$$ HOTEL **Demetra Hotel.** This hotel, which opened in 2012 between the Termini station and Piazza Repubblica, has modern comforts and a great concierge, all at moderate prices. **Pros:** free Wi-Fi if you book directly through hotel's website; convenient to Termini station; soundproof rooms. **Cons:** basic breakfast buffet; some rooms are on the small side; no in-hotel bars or restaurants. *Rooms from: €220* ✉ *Via del Viminale, 8, Repubblica* ☎ *06/45494943* 🌐 *www.demetrahotelrome.com* *27 rooms; 1 suite* Ⓜ *Repubblica* ✣ *2:D4.*

$$ HOTEL **Des Artistes.** This lovely hotel near Termini (really in Castro Pretorio rather than Repubblica) is a perfect example of a family establishment: the three Riccioni brothers put their hearts and souls into running the place, while their parents oversee housekeeping and maintenance. **Pros:** good value; decent-size rooms; relaxing roof garden. **Cons:** breakfast room is small; Wi-Fi is free in common areas but not in rooms. *Rooms from: €145* ✉ *Via Villafranca 20, Repubblica* ☎ *06/4454365* 🌐 *www.hoteldesartistes.com* *48 rooms* *Breakfast* Ⓜ *Castro Pretorio* ✣ *2:F2.*

$$$$ HOTEL Fodor's Choice ★ **Exedra.** Located in one of the most spectacular piazzas in the city, this is the It-Girl of Rome's hotel scene, where highrollers come to party by the rooftop pool and pamper themselves in the spa. **Pros:** spacious and attractive rooms; great spa and pool; terrace with cocktail service; close to Termini station. **Cons:** food and beverages are expensive; beyond the immediate vicinity of many sights. *Rooms from: €385* ✉ *Piazza della Repubblica 47, Repubblica* ☎ *06/489381* 🌐 *www.exedra-roma.boscolohotels.com* *220 rooms, 18 suites* *Breakfast* Ⓜ *Repubblica, Termini* ✣ *2:D3.*

$$$ HOTEL **Leon's Place Hotel.** If you like a lot of bling for your buck, this stylish design hotel that looks like it belongs on the pages of Italian *Vogue* magazine is the place for you. **Pros:** several rooms have balconies with panoramic views of the city; free Wi-Fi; top-quality toiletries; affordable prices. **Cons:** not very central; some rooms face the courtyard; Wi-Fi spotty in the rooms. *Rooms from: €225* ✉ *Via XX Settembre 90/94, Repubblica* ☎ *06/890871* 🌐 *www.leonsplacehotel.it* *50 rooms, 4 suites* *Breakfast* Ⓜ *Barberini, Repubblica* ✣ *2:E2.*

$$ HOTEL **Marcella Royal.** You can do your sightseeing from the rooftop terrace of the Marcella, a midsize hotel with the feel of a smaller, more intimate establishment, where all the guest rooms are furnished with flair. **Pros:** breakfast in the roof garden; aperitivo at the piano bar; staff goes the extra kilometer to help guests. **Cons:** small rooms; Internet is spotty; not very close to major attractions. *Rooms from: €200* ✉ *Via Flavia 106, Repubblica* ☎ *06/42014591* 🌐 *www.marcellaroyalhotel.com* *85 rooms, 2 suites* *Repubblica* *Breakfast* ✣ *2:D2.*

$$$$ HOTEL FAMILY **Mascagni.** Situated on a side street around the corner from one of Rome's most impressive piazzas (Piazza della Repubblica), this friendly hotel has staff that go out of their way to make you feel at home, public spaces cleverly styled with contemporary art pieces, and wood fixtures and furnishings accentuated by warm colors in the guest rooms. **Pros:**

staff is friendly and attentive; evening lounge serves light fare; great for families with kids. **Cons:** elevator is too small and takes a while; weak a/c; some bathrooms are smallish. *Rooms from: €315 Via Vittorio Emanuele Orlando 90, Repubblica 06/48904040 www.mascagnihotelrome.it 40 rooms Breakfast Repubblica 2:C3.*

$$ HOTEL **Miami.** Rooms at this low-key hotel, in a dignified 19th-century building on Rome's busy Via Nazionale, are soundproof and tastefully styled, but the main draw is the hotel's location on main bus lines and near Termini station and the Metro. **Pros:** pleasant staff; soundproof windows; strong a/c; Wi-Fi. **Cons:** bathrooms are on the small side; small breakfast room. *Rooms from: €170 Via Nazionale 230, Repubblica 06/4817180 www.hotelmiami.com 42 rooms, 4 suites, 1 apartment Breakfast Barberini–Fontana di Trevi, Termini, Repubblica 2:C3.*

13

$$ B&B/INN **Residenza Cellini.** Fresh flowers in the foyer and personal attention from the staff help make this small, family-run residence close to Termini station feel like a gracious home. **Pros:** close to Termini station; Jacuzzi bathtubs and Hydrojet showers; personalized care from the staff. **Cons:** not close to the main attractions; the orthopedic mattresses may be too firm for some; breakfast is the standard Continental fare. *Rooms from: €200 Via Modena 5, Repubblica 06/47825204 www.residenzacellini.it 6 rooms Breakfast Repubblica, Termini 2:C3.*

$$ HOTEL **Romae.** Clean, comfortable rooms with perks like a free mini-bar and fresh fruit attract guests to this hotel, as does its location—between the better side of Termini station and the Nomentana district. **Pros:** spacious rooms; free mini-bar if you book directly from their site; international newspapers available; free Internet access. **Cons:** breakfast is served at the bar across the street; not much nightlife nearby; smallish. *Rooms from: €140 Via Palestro 49, Repubblica 06/4463554 www.hotelromae.com 40 rooms Breakfast Castro Pretorio, Termini 2:E3.*

$$ HOTEL **Villa delle Rose.** When the Eternal City becomes too chaotic for you, head to this relaxing retreat in a charming 19th-century palazzo minutes away from Termini station. **Pros:** delightful garden with blooming roses and jasmine; free parking; free Wi-Fi. **Cons:** some of the rooms are small (ask for a larger one); the elevator is small; breakfast pickings are modest. *Rooms from: €130 Via Vicenza 5, Repubblica 06/4451788 www.villadellerose.it 37 rooms No meals Termini 2:E3.*

$$ HOTEL Fodor's Choice ★ **Yes Hotel.** This chic hotel may fool you into thinking these digs are expensive, but the contemporary coolness of Yes Hotel, located around the corner from Termini station, comes at a bargain rate. **Pros:** close to the Termini station; discount if you pay cash; great value and doesn't feel budget. **Cons:** rooms are small; extra fee for Wi-Fi in rooms. *Rooms from: €170 Via Magenta 15, San Lorenzo 06/44363836 www.yeshotelrome.com 38 rooms, 2 suites Breakfast Termini, Castro Pretorio 2:E3.*

VILLA BORGHESE, PIAZZA DEL POPOLO, MONTE MARIO, AND PARIOLI

VILLA BORGHESE

The area around the Villa Borghese gardens is a relaxing retreat from the hustle of the Eternal City. You won't get tired of waking up to views of the park.

$$$ HOTEL **Grand Hotel Parco dei Principi.** The 1960s-era facade of this large, seven-story hotel contrasts with the turn-of-the-20th-century Italian court decor and the extensive botanical garden outside, resulting in a combination of traditional elegance and contemporary pleasure. **Pros:** quiet location on Villa Borghese; nice pool. **Cons:** beyond the city center; private events held at hotel some weekends can be noisy; a bit of a hike to cafés and restaurants. *Rooms from: €300 Via G. Frescobaldi 5, Villa Borghese 06/854421 www.parcodeiprincipi.com 179 rooms, 24 suites, 1 apartment Breakfast 2:C1.*

PIAZZA DEL POPOLO

While Piazza del Popolo is still quite close to the centro action, it's just removed enough to feel relaxing after a day of sightseeing. Here, amidst high-end boutiques and galleries, you'll find several smart, stylish hotels.

$$$$ HOTEL FAMILY Fodor's Choice ★ **Hotel de Russie.** A ritzy retreat for government bigwigs and Hollywood high rollers, the de Russie is just steps away from the famed Piazza del Popolo and occupies a 19th-century hotel that once hosted royalty, Picasso, and Cocteau. **Pros:** big potential for celebrity sightings; activities for children; extensive gardens (including a butterfly reserve); first-rate luxury spa. **Cons:** some rooms need updating; breakfast is not included; avoid street-side rooms. *Rooms from: €800 Via del Babuino 9, Piazza del Popolo 06/328881 www.hotelderussie.it 89 rooms, 33 suites No meals M Flaminio 1:G1.*

$$$ HOTEL **Locarno.** This hotel has been a longtime choice for art and cinema aficionados (it even inspired Bernard Weber's 1978 film *Hotel Locarno*), but everyone can appreciate its charm, intimate feel, and central location off Piazza del Popolo. **Pros:** luxurious (you might feel like you're in a movie); spacious rooms; free bicycles. **Cons:** some rooms are dark; the annex doesn't compare to the main hotel; staff may not go out of their way to help you. *Rooms from: €275 Via della Penna 22, Piazza del Popolo 06/3610841 www.hotellocarno.com 64 rooms, 2 suites Breakfast M Flaminio 1:G1.*

$$$$ HOTEL **Valadier.** In the heart of the *centro*, just steps away from the prominent Piazza del Popolo and a few minutes' walk from the Spanish Steps, is this luxury hotel—known for comfortable rooms with marble and travertine bathrooms and a superb location—that has captured the hearts of elite travelers over the years. **Pros:** excellent American-style breakfast buffet; piano bar; flat-screen TVs; good a/c. **Cons:** cocktails don't come cheap; rooms are smaller than you'd expect for a luxury hotel; the lighting in rooms is very dim. *Rooms from: €330 Via della Fontanella 15, Piazza del Popolo 06/3611998 www.hotelvaladier.com 60 rooms Breakfast M Flaminio 1:G1.*

MONTE MARIO

Travelers looking for a relaxing getaway well away from the city center will appreciate staying in Monte Mario, but beware, public transportation is sparse in this area. Some hotels offer shuttles (it's a 20- to 30-minute drive to the centro, and as much as an hour on public transport). If you don't want to rely on shuttles and/or taxis, consider renting a car.

$$$$ RESORT **Rome Cavalieri.** One of Rome's ritziest resorts, the Rome Cavalieri is a hilltop oasis far from the hustle and bustle of the centro, with magnificent views, lush gardens, an Olympic-size pool, and a palatial spa. **Pros:** beautiful bird's-eye view of Rome; complimentary shuttle to the city center; three-Michelin-star dining. **Cons:** you definitely pay for the luxury of staying here—everything is expensive; outside the city center; not all rooms have the view. *Rooms from: €450 ✉ Via Cadlolo 101, Monte Mario ☎ 06/35091 www.romecavalieri.com 345 rooms, 25 suites Breakfast ✣ 1:A1.*

PARIOLI

Rome's poshest residential neighborhood attracts a well-heeled international crowd who are happy to be away from the centro hubub. Luxurious lodgings and a great night's sleep might make you feel like you're in an elegant country home. Public transportation is limited in this area, but some hotels offer shuttles to major attractions.

$$$ HOTEL **Lord Byron.** Rome's first boutique hotel, this Art Deco retreat has a jewel-like charm inside and feels like a small country manor where you are the lord. **Pros:** luxury bathrobes and slippers; friendly and helpful staff; free shuttle to some of the major tourist attractions. **Cons:** too far to walk to sights; not many cafés and shops in the area; cabs to the centro are expensive. *Rooms from: €300 ✉ Via Giuseppe de Notaris 5, Parioli ☎ 06/3220404 www.lordbyronhotel.com 23 rooms, 9 suites Breakfast ✣ 2:A1.*

TRASTEVERE

This former working-class neighborhood, once the stomping ground of artists and artisans, is now home to many of Rome's expats and exchange students. Its village-like charm makes it an appealing place to stay, and you'll find plenty of moderately priced accommodations here, including converted convents and small family-run hotels.

$ HOTEL **Carmel.** In the heart of Trastevere and across the Tiber from the main synagogue is Rome's only kosher hotel, a friendly and budget-friendly place to stay. **Pros:** good budget choice; kosher-friendly; short walk to Jewish Ghetto; free Wi-Fi. **Cons:** no frills; a/c is noisy; breakfast is not exciting; reception closes after 8 pm. *Rooms from: €115 ✉ Via Goffredo Mameli 11, Trastevere ☎ 06/5809921 www.hotelcarmel.it 10 rooms, 8 with bath, 1 suite No credit cards Breakfast ✣ 3:B2.*

$$ HOTEL Fodor's Choice ★ **Casa di Santa Francesca Romana.** In the heart of Trastevere but tucked away from the hustle and bustle of the medieval quarter, this cheap, clean, comfortable hotel in a former monastery is centered on a lovely green courtyard. **Pros:** the price can't be beat; excellent restaurants

nearby; away from rowdy side of Trastevere. **Cons:** thin walls; interior is a bit bland; Wi-Fi is spotty. *Rooms from: €130 Via dei Vasceillari 61, Trastevere 06/5812125 www.sfromana.it 37 rooms Breakfast Piramide, Circo Massimo 3:C2.*

$ HOTEL **Cisterna.** On a quiet street in the very heart of medieval Trastevere, this basic but comfortable hotel is ideally located for getting to know Rome's most authentic neighborhood, a favorite of artists and bohemians for decades. **Pros:** simple accommodations for budget travelers; good location in trendy Trastevere. **Cons:** staff is very iffy; street-side rooms are noisy; some bathrooms need updating. *Rooms from: €120 Via della Cisterna 7–8–9, Trastevere 06/5817212 www.cisternahotelrome.com 20 rooms Breakfast 2:B1.*

$$$ HOTEL Fodor's Choice ★ **Hotel Santa Maria.** A Trastevere treasure with a pedigree going back four centuries, this ivy-covered, mansard-roofed, rosy-brick-red, erstwhile Renaissance-era convent—just steps away from the glorious Santa Maria in Trastevere church and a few blocks from the Tiber—has sweet and simple guest rooms: a mix of brick walls, "cotto" tile floors, modern oak furniture, and matching bedspreads and curtains. **Pros:** a quaint and pretty oasis in a central location; relaxing courtyard; stocked wine bar; free bicycles to use during your stay. **Cons:** hotel is tricky to find; some of the showers drain slowly; finding a cab is not always easy in Trastevere. *Rooms from: €230 Vicolo del Piede 2, Trastevere 06/5894626 www.hotelsantamariatrastevere.it 20 rooms Breakfast 3:B1.*

$ HOTEL **Hotel Trastevere.** This tiny hotel captures the villagelike charm of the Trastevere district and offers basic, clean, comfortable rooms in a great location. **Pros:** cheap with a good location; convenient to transportation; free Wi-Fi; friendly staff. **Cons:** no frills; rooms are a little worn on the edges; few amenities. *Rooms from: €105 Via Luciano Manara 24/a–25, Trastevere 06/5814713 www.hoteltrastevere.net 18 rooms Breakfast 3:B2.*

$$$ B&B/INN Fodor's Choice ★ **Relais Le Clarisse.** Set within the former cloister grounds of the Santa Chiara order, with beautiful gardens, Le Clarisse makes you feel like a personal guest at a friend's villa, thanks to the comfortable size of the accommodations and personalized service. **Pros:** spacious rooms with comfy beds; high-tech showers/tubs with good water pressure; complimentary Wi-Fi. **Cons:** this part of Trastevere can be noisy at night; rooms fill up quickly; reception unavailable after 11 pm. *Rooms from: €220 Via Cardinale Merry del Val 20, Trastevere 06/58334437 www.leclarisse.com 13 rooms, 3 suites Breakfast 3:B2.*

AVENTINO AND TESTACCIO

AVENTINO

This affluent neighborhood, set on Aventine Hill, attracts travelers looking for a green oasis removed from the centro. Hotels take advantage of the extra space, with gardens and courtyards where you can enjoy alfresco R&R, and the only noise you'll hear in the morning is birdsong.

$$$ HOTEL **Domus Aventina.** The best part of this quaint, friendly hotel is that it's situated between two of Rome's loveliest gardens—a municipal rose

garden and Rome's famous Orange Garden—in the heart of the historic Aventine district not far from the Temple to Mithras and the House of Aquila and Priscilla (where St. Peter touched down). **Pros:** quiet location; walking distance to tourist attractions; complimentary Wi-Fi throughout. **Cons:** no elevator; small showers; some rooms are very dark; Wi-Fi can be spotty. *Rooms from: €220 Via di Santa Prisca 11/b, Aventino 06/5746135 www.hoteldomusaventina.com 26 rooms Breakfast Circo Massimo 3:E3.*

13

$$$ HOTEL **Hotel San Anselmo.** This refurbished 19th-century villa is a romantic retreat from the city, set in a molto charming garden atop the Aventine Hill. **Pros:** free Wi-Fi; historic building with artful interior; great showers with jets; a garden where you can enjoy breakfast. **Cons:** a bit of a hike to sights; limited public transportation. *Rooms from: €280 Piazza San Anselmo 2, Aventino 06/570057 www.aventinohotels.com 38 rooms Breakfast Circo Massimo 3:D3.*

TESTACCIO

Next to Aventino is this lively working-class neighborhood, filled with great Roman trattorias, *mercati all'aperto* (open-air markets), and gourmet food shops. The buzzing nightlife makes it attractive to budget-conscious travelers looking for a bit more action after dinner.

$ HOTEL **Santa Prisca.** Off the beaten path, this clean and comfortable hotel has been welcoming guests for more than 50 years. **Pros:** near public transportation (trams and metro); complimentary Wi-Fi; outside terrace with chairs and tables for relaxing; Internet point available for guests without computers. **Cons:** some say the breakfast is mediocre; the school next door can be a little noisy on weekdays; a bit of a trek from the main sights. *Rooms from: €110 Largo M. Gelsomini 25, Testaccio 06/5741917 www.hotelsantaprisca.it 49 rooms, 2 suites Breakfast Piramide 3:D4.*

MONTI, ESQUILINO, AND SAN LORENZO

MONTI

A charming neighborhood with winding cobblestone streets, Monti attracts an artsy, boho-chic crowd thanks to its abundance of funky bars, good Roman and ethnic eateries, and cool vintage shops and boutiques. The area around the Colosseum makes a fine base for exploring the sights of the ancient city, but many of the restaurants here are tourist traps. Hotels in both areas tend to be better value than in swankier parts of town, whether budget or luxury.

$$$ HOTEL **Capo d'Africa.** Many find the modern look and feel of Capo d'Africa—not to mention its plush beds and deep bathtubs—refreshing after a long day's journey through ancient Rome: each room is decorated in warm, muted tones with sleek furniture, stylish accents, and contemporary art. **Pros:** quiet, comfortable rooms; fitness center; great food served at the hotel. **Cons:** hotel lacks a great view of Colosseum despite proximity; not a lot of restaurants in the immediate neighborhood. *Rooms from: €300 Via Capo d'Africa 54, Monti 06/772801 www.hotelcapodafrica.com 64 rooms, 1 suite Breakfast Colosseo 3:H2.*

$$$ HOTEL **Celio.** There's much more to brag about than proximity to the Colosseum at this chic boutique hotel. **Pros:** rooftop garden; nice decor; comfortable beds; gym. **Cons:** very small bathrooms; service can be iffy. *Rooms from: €230 Via dei Santissimi Quattro 35/c, Monti 06/70495333 www.hotelcelio.com 20 rooms, 2 suites Breakfast Colosseo 3:G1.*

$$$ HOTEL **Duca d'Alba.** In Italy, it's all about the *bella figura* (making a good impression), so when you step into this lovely little boutique hotel near the Colosseum, you'll know you've hit the jackpot: between the marble decor and reproductions of antiquated paintings, the Duca d'Alba tells the traveler that their stay will be a clean and comfortable one, and the hotel's attentive staff and reasonable rates make it a good value to boot. **Pros:** great breakfast selection; fitness center; deep discounts if you book directly on their site. **Cons:** some rooms are cramped and worn around the edges; late-night revelers from the Irish pub across the way. *Rooms from: €240 Via Leonina 14, Monti 06/484471 www.hotelducadalba.com 27 rooms, 1 suite Breakfast Cavour 2:C5.*

$$$$ HOTEL **Hotel Forum.** A longtime favorite, this converted 18th-century convent has a truly unique setting on one side of the Fori Imperiali with a cinematic view of ancient Rome across the avenue. **Pros:** bird's-eye view of ancient Rome; "American" bar on the rooftop terrace. **Cons:** small rooms; noisy pub-crawlers congregate in the street below; food and drinks are expensive; Wi-Fi isn't free. *Rooms from: €310 Via Tor de' Conti 25–30, Monti 06/6792446 www.hotelforum.com 80 rooms Breakfast Cavour, Colosseo 2:B5.*

$$ HOTEL FAMILY **Hotel Lancelot.** This home away from home in a quiet residential area close to the Colosseum has been run by the same family since 1970 and is quite popular: its carefully and courteously attentive staff go the extra mile for their guests, and the clean and comfortable rooms are bright and airy, with big windows. **Pros:** hospitable staff; secluded and quiet; very family-friendly. **Cons:** some bathrooms are on the small side; no refrigerators in the rooms; thin walls mean you can sometimes hear your neighbors. *Rooms from: €196 Via Capo d'Africa 47, Monti 06/70450615 www.lancelothotel.com 60 rooms Breakfast Colosseo 3:H1.*

$$ HOTEL **Italia.** Just a block from bustling Via Nazionale, this hotel feels like a classic pensione: low budget with a lot of heart. **Pros:** free Wi-Fi and Internet point for guests without a laptop; great price; individual attention and personal care. **Cons:** can be a bit noisy; Wi-Fi can be hit or miss. *Rooms from: €140 Via Venezia 18, Monti 06/4828355 www.hotelitaliaroma.com 35 rooms, 1 apartment Breakfast Repubblica 2:C4.*

$$$ HOTEL **Nerva.** Step out of this charming, clean, and well-run hotel and you'll feel like you're literally in the middle of an ancient imperial stomping ground. **Pros:** a stone's throw from the Forum and the lovely Monti neighborhood; friendly staff; free Wi-Fi. **Cons:** some showers are tiny; view of the Forum is obstructed by a wall. *Rooms from: €220 Via Tor de' Conti 3/4, Monti 06/6781835 www.hotelnerva.com 19 rooms Breakfast Cavour, Colosseo 2:B5.*

$$ HOTEL **Richmond.** Right at the beginning of Via Cavour, this charming little hotel—ideally situated for visits to the Forum, the Colosseum, and all the major sites of Ancient Rome—has an attractive rooftop terrace with panoramic views. **Pros:** impressive views of the Forum; friendly and courteous staff; modern bathrooms. **Cons:** rooms are small and some need restyling; climate control in the rooms is difficult to operate; rooms that face the street are noisy. *Rooms from: €180 Largo Corrado Ricci 36, Monti 06/69941256 www.hotelrichmondrome.com 23 rooms Breakfast Colosseo 2:B6.*

ESQUILINO

Budget-conscious travelers who want to be near Rome's major transport hub, Termini station, often stay here. There are a number of cheap, clean, no-frills hotels and pensions, as well as a few more stylish options.

$ B&B/INN **Adler.** This tiny *pensione*, run by the same family for more than three decades, provides a comfortable stay—rooms are basic, but impeccably clean—on a quiet street near the main station for reasonable prices. **Pros:** breakfast on the terrace; free Internet point in the lobby; strong a/c. **Cons:** some rooms are dark; showers are tiny; no safes in the rooms. *Rooms from: €125 Via Modena 5, Esquilino 06/484466 www.hoteladler-roma.com 8 rooms Breakfast Repubblica 2:C3.*

$$ HOTEL **Aphrodite.** This hotel, which recently had a design makeover, is one of the nicest options right near Termini. **Pros:** panache for a low price; big bathrooms with mosaic tiles; rooftop terrace. **Cons:** not near historic center; small rooms. *Rooms from: €150 Via Marsala 90, San Lorenzo 06/491096 www.hotelaphrodite.com 50 rooms Breakfast Termini 2:E3.*

$$$ HOTEL Fodor's Choice ★ **Britannia.** Situated in an elegant Art Nouveau *palazzo* dating back to 1876, this charming hotel feels like a luxurious private home, with all the modern amenities. **Pros:** spacious; comfortable rooms with free Wi-Fi; some pets are allowed; good service. **Cons:** rooms can be noisy for light sleepers; not very close to the city's main attractions. *Rooms from: €205 Via Napoli 64, Esquilino 06/4883153 www.hotelbritannia.it 33 rooms, 1 suite Breakfast Repubblica 2:C4.*

$$ HOTEL **Doria.** A convenient location close to the grand Basilica di Santa Maria Maggiore and Termini station, and reasonable rates, are the advantages of this diminutive hotel. **Pros:** smart use of space; breakfast on the rooftop terrace. **Cons:** minuscule elevator; small reception area; tiny bathrooms. *Rooms from: €130 Via Merulana 4, Esquilino 06/4465888 www.doriahotel.it 20 rooms Breakfast Cavour, Termini, Vittorio Emanuele 2:D5.*

$$ B&B/INN **Montreal.** A good choice for budget travelers, this modest hotel on a central avenue across the square from Santa Maria Maggiore, three blocks from Stazione Termini, occupies a totally renovated older building and offers bright, fresh-looking (though small) rooms. **Pros:** helpful staff provides maps and good recommendations; bathrooms are spacious; great garden area for relaxing; private garage with limited parking space for guests. **Cons:** can be noisy at night; need to take a bus or a metro to get to most of the sights. *Rooms from: €130 Via Carlo*

Alberto 4, Esquilino ☎ 06/4457797 🌐 www.hotelmontrealrome.com 🛏 27 rooms 🍽 Breakfast Ⓜ Vittorio Emanuele ✣ 2:D5.

$$ HOTEL **Morgana.** A stylish hotel just a stone's throw from Termini sounds like some sort of a miracle, but, complete with unbeatable prices, the Morgan welcomes guests with chic rooms and top amenities. **Pros:** special deals if you book directly; pet-friendly; breakfast is abundant. **Cons:** neighborhood is run-down; removed from most sightseeing; some bathrooms are on the small side. *$ Rooms from: €170 ✉ Via Filippo Turati 33/37, Esquilino ☎ 06/4467230 🌐 www.hotelmorgana.com 🛏 121 rooms, 2 suites 🍽 Breakfast Ⓜ Termini ✣ 2:E4.*

$$$ HOTEL **Radisson Blu es. Hotel.** Design aficionados will enjoy this hotel, which has the feeling of a chic big-city modern art museum, complete with large windows that light up at night. **Pros:** distinctive design; convenient to Termini station; friendly and helpful staff. **Cons:** Termini area can be a little sketchy at night; see-through bathrooms don't allow for much privacy. *$ Rooms from: €250 ✉ Via Filippo Turati 171, Esquilino ☎ 06/444841 🌐 www.radissonblu.com/eshotel-rome 🛏 232 rooms, 27 suites 🍽 Breakfast Ⓜ Vittorio Emanuele ✣ 2:F5.*

14

NIGHTLIFE AND THE ARTS

Update by
Erica Firpo

Rome has always been Italy's go-to city for epic evening adventures. Whether it's a romantic rooftop drink, dinner in a boisterous restaurant, or dancing into the wee hours, Roman nightlife has always been a scene set for a movie.

Director Federico Fellini immortalized nocturnal Rome in his many films about life in the Eternal City. *Satyricon* showcased Lucullan all-night banquets (and some more naughty entertainments) of the days of the emperors, while *La Dolce Vita* flaunted nightclubs and *paparazzi* of the city's Hollywood-on-the-Tiber era. And as the director lovingly showed in *Fellini's Roma*, the city's streets and piazzas offered the best place for parties and alfresco dinners. Many visitors would agree with Fellini: Rome, the city, is entertainment enough. The city's piazzas, fountains, and delicately colored palazzos make impressive backdrops for Rome's living theater. And Rome is a flirt, taking advantage of its spectacular cityscape, transforming ancient, Renaissance, and contemporary monuments into settings for the performing arts, whether outdoors in summer or in splendid palaces and churches in winter. Held at locations such as Villa Celimontana, Teatro dell'Opera, the Baths of Caracalla, or the church of Sant'Ignazio, the venue often steals the show.

Of all the performing arts, music is what Rome does best to entertain people, whether it's opera, jazz, or disco. The cinema is also a big draw, particularly for Italian-language speakers, and there's a fantastic array of other options. Toast the sunset with prosecco while overlooking a 1st-century temple. Enjoy an evening reading in the Roman Forum or a live performance of Shakespeare in the Globe theater in Villa Borghese park. Top off the night in your choice of Rome's many bars and dance clubs. When all else fails, there's always late-night café-sitting, watching the colorful crowds parade by on a gorgeous piazza—it's great fun, even if you don't speak the language. Little wonder Rome inspired Fellini to make people-watching into an art form in his famous films.

PLANNING

HOW DO I FIND OUT WHAT'S GOING ON THIS WEEK?

With its foot firmly in the 21st century, Rome has a pantheon of publications heralding its cultural events. For city-sponsored events, Rome's official website 🌐 *www.comune.roma.it* tries to remain as au courant as any governmental entity can. A broader range of event listings can be found in the *Cronaca* and *Cultura* section of Italian newspapers, as well as in *Metro*, the free newspaper found at Metro stops and on trams.

On the Internet, check out 🌐 *www.inromenow.com*, an events site written exclusively for the English-speaking community, along with expat favorite *The American* (🌐 *www.theamericanmag.com*). Their Italian-language counterpart Roma 2night (🌐 *2night.it*) has an even more robust selection of nightlife, along with food spots. Rome's top cultural, news, and events websites, *06blog* (🌐 *www.06blog.it*) and *RomaToday* (🌐 *www.romatoday.it*), add postings practically hourly. The monthly English-language periodical (with accompanying website) *Wanted in Rome* (🌐 *www.wantedinrome.com*) is available at many newsstands and has good coverage of arts events. For simple factual information, such as addresses, *060608* (🌐 *www.060608.it*) has listings of every cultural site (monument, church, museum, art space) in the city.

14

WHAT TIME DO PEOPLE GO OUT?

Discoteche open after 10 pm, but punctuality isn't important. The scene doesn't heat up until later in the evening so never arrive before midnight.

For early evening outings, *enoteche* aperitivi hour, from 6:30 to 9 pm, is the quintessential scene of Roman life where Italians and non-Italians mix together for wine tasting and cocktails.

FEES AND TICKETS

Most clubs charge a cover charge, between €10 and €20, which often includes the first drink.

Depending on the venue, concert tickets can cost between €7 and €50, and as much as several hundred euros for an exclusive, sold-out event.

Often, you can find seating that is unreserved (identified in Italian as *posti non numerati*), or even last-minute tickets. Inquire about this option when ticket shopping; you may have to arrive early to get a good seat.

Purchase opera and concert tickets in advance at the box office, or just before the performance.

Orbis. An in-person, cash-only ticket vendor, Orbis stocks a wide array of tickets for music, cultural, and performance events. ✉ *Piazza dell'Esquilino 37, Repubblica* ☎ *06/4827403*.

Ticketone. Ticketone is the the go-to spot for all cultural event listings—whether tickets to archaeological sites and museums or tickets to stand-alone events—in Rome. Online reservations require tenacity. 🌐 *www.ticketone.it*.

VivaTicket. One of Italy's largest ticket vendors (both online and at ticket offices), VivaTicket covers major musical performances and cultural events in Rome and throughout Italy. 🌐 *www.vivaticket.it*.

NIGHTLIFE

Toast the sunset with prosecco while overlooking a 1st-century temple. Enjoy an evening reading in the Roman Forum or a live performance of Shakespeare in the Globe theater in Villa Borghese park. Top off the night in your choice of Rome's many bars and discoteches. When all else fails, find a café (and your inner Fellini) and watch the colorful crowds parade by in a gorgeous piazza.

E mo' che fammo? ("And now what do we do?")... For a great night out in Rome, all you need to do is to wander, because easy entertainment will find you on every corner. It's important to follow Rome's rule of thumb: if you see an enoteca—those quaint wine bars—stop in. Though most enoteche are tiny and offer a limited antipasto menu, they cover more ground in their wine lists and often have a charming gang of regulars. For the linguistically timid, there are also several stereotypical English and Irish pubs peppered around the city, complete with a steady stream of Guinness, darts, and rugby on their satellite televisions. The oversize flat screens also show American football, baseball, and basketball—ideal for those who don't want to miss a playoff game.

Although Rome offers a cornucopia of evening bacchanalia, from ultra-chic to super cheap, all that glitters is not gold. Insiders and visitors alike understand that finding "the scene" in Rome is the proverbial needle in the haystack: it requires patience and pursuit. Your best asset will be your ability to talk, since word-of-mouth is the most accurate source. Entertainment guides like Roma 2night provide great logistical information including up-to-date listings of bars and clubs. Most visitors head out to the centro storico to find some fun. Piazza Navona, Pantheon, Campo de' Fiori, and even Trastevere may be filled with tourists, but more recently, several niche and boutique bars have opened. (The Spanish Steps neighborhood is a ghost town by 9 pm.) If you want to get out of the comfort zone, head to the Testaccio, San Lorenzo, and Pigneto areas. Remember, Romans love an after-party—after dinner, of course—so plenty of nightlife doesn't start until midnight.

When it comes to clubs, discos, and DJs in Rome, you have two choices: Testaccio—considered a mecca for clubs, discotheques, and bars, and perhaps your best choice for disco roulette—and everywhere else, since discoteche can be found in any Rome neighborhood. Testaccio's Via Galvani is Rome's Sunset Strip, where hybrid restaurant-clubs largely identical in music and crowd jockey for top ranking. On average, drinks range between €10 and €15, and one is often included with the entrance (€10–€20). In summer, many clubs relocate to the beach or the Tiber, so call ahead to confirm location and hours.

LISTINGS BY NEIGHBORHOOD

PRATI

The Prati area, right outside the Vatican, is best known for its high saturation of clergy and families, so expect the evening scene to be tamer than other neighborhoods.

LIVE MUSIC

Alexanderplatz. The black-and-white checkered floors of Alexanderplatz, Rome's most important live jazz and blues club, are reminiscent of Harlem's 1930s jazz halls, and Alexanderplatz loves to promote this image with excellent jazz programming of Italian and international performers. The bar and restaurant are always busy, so reservations are suggested. ✉ *Via Ostia 9, Prati* ☎ *06/39742171* 🌐 *www.alexanderplatz.it.*

14

Fonclea. In a cellar fit to hide a cardinal, and conveniently just around the corner from Castel Sant'Angelo, Fonclea jams with live music venue every night of the week—from jazz to Latin American to rhythm and blues. ✉ *Via Crescenzio 82/a, Prati* ☎ *06/6896302* 🌐 *www.fonclea.it.*

PIAZZA NAVONA AND CAMPO DE' FIORI

PIAZZA NAVONA

Piazza Navona is where you can find just about anything, from sophisticated café life and flirty cocktail bars to dance clubs and chess games. Expect to be easily understood, as there is a high concentration of tourist traffic.

BARS

Fodor's Choice ★ **Antico Caffè della Pace.** It doesn't get any more Rome than this: a cappuccino or cocktail al fresco at a turn-of-the-20th-century-style café nestled in the picturesque side streets behind Piazza Navona. Celebrities and literati hang out at the coveted outdoor tables of Antico Caffè della Pace, also known as Bar della Pace, where the atmosphere ranges from peaceful to percolating. Its location is equally enchanting, in the *piazzatina* (tiny piazza) of Santa Maria della Pace, by Baroque architect Pietro da Cortona. ✉ *Via della Pace 3/7, Piazza Navona* ☎ *06/6861216* 🌐 *www.caffedellapace.it.*

Bar del Fico. Bar del Fico looks a lot different from the days of yore when raucous chess outdoor matches accompanied cocktails at the once barebones local hangout. Though the chess tables are still sitting in the shade of the historic fig tree, Bar del Fico is now a charming bar, restaurant, evening cocktail spot, and late-night hangout. ✉ *Piazza del Fico 26, Piazza Navona* ☎ *06/68808413* 🌐 *www.bardelfico.com.*

Fluid. Fluid's looking-glass front window lures in the crowds for creative aperitivi and great music. Standing room only. ✉ *Via del Governo Vecchio 46/47, Piazza Navona* ☎ *06/6832361* 🌐 *www.fluideventi.com.*

Fodor's Choice ★ **Les Affiches.** Not just for the itinerant francophile, Les Affiches has French country-chic decor that makes it a charming spot for brunch, and a very busy cocktail crowd from early evening through late night. ✉ *Via dell'Anima 52, Piazza Navona* ☎ *06/64760715.*

CLOSE UP

The City of Eternal Festivals

The City of Eternal Festivals, Rome has gone from "provincial" to "provocative" thanks in large part to its bevy of internationally recognized festivals. In the fall and spring especially, you'll see the best of local and international talent in some of the most beautiful venues in the city.

ART AND DESIGN

RomaContemporary. An annual contemporary art fair where Italy-based gallerists and their international colleagues showcase artists and artwork at the MACRO Testaccio exhibition space, RomaContemporary is a three-day event that is announced several months in advance, so be sure to check the website for updates. ✉ *Piazza Orazio Giustiniani 4* 🌐 *www.romacontemporary.it.*

RomaEuropa. For six weeks in early fall, the RomaEuropa festival ignites stages and theaters as a collective, multivenue avant-garde performing and visual arts program showcasing international artists, installations, film, and performance. ✉ *Via dei magazzini generali 20A* ☎ *06 45553050* 🌐 *www.romaeuropa.net.*

FILM

Da Venezia a Roma Festival. Immediately following the finale of the Venice Film Festival in September, Rome's cinemas host Da Venezia a Roma, a two-week screening of Venice's award-nominated films. Widely distributed films and art house specials make fleeting screen appearances months before their international release. Films are shown in their original languages with Italian subtitles when necessary. 🌐 *www.agisanec.lazio.it/festival.html.*

Festival Internazionale del Film di Roma. In the fall, cinephiles head to Rome for the International Festival of Film, a packed two weeks of cinema and celebrity spotting. The festival showcases homegrown Italian indie and experimental films, art house films and shorts, as well as technical lectures. Each genre has an awards ceremony for best films and silver-screen icons both past and present. ✉ *Viale Pietro De Coubertin 10, Flaminio* 🌐 *www.romacinemafest.it*

Notti di Cinema. This is a summer-long outdoor film festival between mid-July and September 1st. Piazza Vittorio becomes an open-air cinema, screening Italian and international films. ✉ *Piazza Vittorio, Monti, Roma* 🌐 *www.agisanec.lazio.it/notti_cinema.html.*

MUSIC

From mid-spring through summer, Rome becomes an alfresco theater, with stages hosting internationally recognized musicians of all genres.

Estate Romana. Estate Romana is a summer-long city-sponsored cultural event series. Many events are free and take place outdoors along the Tiber River and in piazzas in and around the city. Events include cinema, art programs, theater, book fairs, and guided tours of some of Rome's monuments by night. ⊕ *www.estateromana.comune.roma.it.*

Fiesta!. Fiesta! is Rome's mega summer-long music party with more than 4,000 hours of Latin and Caribbean music, jazz, and blues. Fiesta! hosts international stars, exhibits related to Latin American culture, and gastro-events with delectables from all over the world. ✉ *Ippodromo delle Capannelle, Via Appia Nuova 1245, Appia* ☎ *06/66183792* ⊕ *www.fiesta.it.*

I Concerti nel Parco. *I Concerti nel Parco* is a beautiful evening-concert series held under the stars in Rome's largest park, Villa Doria Pamphilj. From June through August, the concerts are held at sunset and last late into the evening, showcasing a variety of musical genres from classical to contemporary. *I Concerti nel Parco* has also added winter events, including Christmas concerts, to its programming. ✉ *Piazza Porta di San Pancrazio, Monteverde* ⊕ *www.iconcertinelparco.it.*

Il Tempietto. Unforgettable concerts series are organized throughout the year in otherwise inaccessible sites, such as the 1st-century Teatro di Marcello. Music covers the entire scope from classical to contemporary. ✉ *Teatro di Marcello, Via Teatro di Marcello, Jewish Ghetto* ☎ *06/45615180* ⊕ *www.tempietto.it.*

Rock in Roma. June through August, the Ippodromo, Stadio Olimpico, and other stages become the heart of rock and roll with summer concert series Rock in Roma. Headliners have included David Guetta, Kings of the Stone Age, The Lumineers, Metallica, Radiohead, Subsonica, the Cure, and the Killers. ✉ *Ippodromo delle Capannelle, Via Appia Nuova 1245, Appia* ☎ *06/45496350* ⊕ *www.rockinroma.com.*

Roma Incontra il Mondo. Roma Incontra il Mondo is one of Europe's most impressive world-music festivals for its consistently world-class headliners and its beautiful location in Villa Ada, a former monarch's residence. The summer concert series is held in the middle of the park and begins at 10 pm, followed by dancing until 2 am. More recently, a pop-up village sells handmade goods and food from around the world. ✉ *Laghetto di Villa Ada, Parioli* ⊕ *www.villaada.org.*

Villa Celimontana Jazz Festival. Villa Celimontana can boast the longest-running jazz festival in Europe. The summer-long jazz series showcases the broad scope of jazz from contemporary electronic and acid to more classic styles. Held at the bucolic Villa Celimantona, a Baroque-era villa and park near the Colosseum, the setting is decidedly romantic, a perfect backdrop for listening to music or enjoying a little Roman cuisine at its bar/restaurant. ✉ *Piazza della Navicella, San Giovanni* ☎ *06/39721867* ⊕ *www.villacelimontanajazzfestival.com.*

Fodor's Choice ★ **Roof Garden Bar at Grand Hotel della Minerve.** During the warm months, this lofty perch offers up perhaps the most inspiring view in Rome—directly to the Pantheon's dome. The Roof Garden has an equally impressive cocktail menu. Take advantage of summer sunsets and park yourself in a front-row seat as the dome glows. ✉ *Grand Hotel della Minerve, Piazza della Minerve 69, Piazza Navona* ☎ *06/695201* 🌐 *www.grandhoteldelaminerve.com.*

Shari Vari. Shari Vari has reinvented itself into a sumptuous supper club, lounge, and disco. Its bistro and champagnerie are stocked with delicious delicacies and sought-after vintages. Its night club covers every genre of music from electronic, underground, and vinyl to hip-hop, lounge, and international. ✉ *Via dei Nari 14, Piazza Navona* ☎ *06/68806936* 🌐 *www.sharivari.it.*

Terrace Bar of the Hotel Raphael. Want to sneak a peak at Rome's rooftops? Head to the Terrace Bar at the Hotel Raphael, noted for its bird's-eye view of the campaniles and palazzos of Piazza Navona. This is one of Rome's most romantic spots for a proposal. ✉ *Largo Febo 2, Piazza Navona* ☎ *06/682831* 🌐 *www.raphaelhotel.com* ⏲ *Summer only.*

Fodor's Choice ★ **Vinoteca Novecento.** A fantastic and tiny enoteca with a very old-fashioned vibe, Vinoteca Novecento has a seemingly unlimited selection of wines, proseccos, vin santos, and grappas along with salami-and-cheese tasting menus. Inside is standing-room only; in good weather, sit outside on one of the oak barriques. ✉ *Piazza Delle Coppelle 47, Piazza Navona* ☎ *06/6833078.*

DANCE CLUBS

Fodor's Choice ★ **La Cabala.** Atop the medieval Hostaria dell'Orso, La Cabala is an after-dinner club and late-night dance party whose VIP room hosts wanna-be models. Depending on the evening, vibe can be chic, hipster, or clubby. Rome's version of a supper club, La Cabala is part of the Hostaria dell'Orso trio of restaurant, disco, and piano bar. Dress code is stylish. ✉ *Hostaria dell'Orso, Via dei Soldati 23, Piazza Navona* ☎ *06/68301192* 🌐 *www.hdo.it.*

JAZZ CLUB

Charity Café. An intimate jazz club with live music performances nightly, Charity hosts local and international jazz musicians in a relaxed atmosphere. ✉ *Via Panisperna 68, Monti* ☎ *06/47825881* 🌐 *www.charitycafe.it.*

CAMPO DE' FIORI

With college bars and brawls, Campo de' Fiori is Rome's magnet for the study-abroad scene.

BARS

Il Goccetto. A rustic wine bar with a copious amount of elusive vintages, Il Goccetto specializes in wines from smaller vineyards from Sicily to Venice. Stay for a snack—its carefully curated menu of Italian delicacies (meats and cheeses) represents the entire Italian peninsula. Il Goccetto is always busy and never accepts reservations. ✉ *Via dei Banchi Vecchi 14, Campo de' Fiori* ☎ *06/6864268* 🌐 *ilgoccetto.com.*

DID YOU KNOW

The Parco della Musica's "Cavea" holds events year-round. Spring to fall, the Greco-Roman–style amphitheater hosts concerts, fashion shows, festivals, and public talks; in winter, ice skating takes over.

L'Angolo Divino. Nestled on a quiet sidestreet around the corner from the ever vivacious Campo de' Fiori, this wood-paneled enoteca is a hidden treasure of wines. Its extensive selection lists over 1,000 labels to go along quite nicely with its quaint menu of delicious homemade pastas and local antipasti. ✉ *Via dei Balestrari 12, Campo de' Fiori* ☎ *06/6864413* 🌐 *www.angolodivino.it.*

Rooftop Lounge Bar at the St. George Hotel. St. George's rooftop terrace has a 360-degree view of the Eternal City, so it's not surprise that this is one of Rome's favorite spots for a late-afternoon cocktail. Head downstairs to St. George's Wine Bar and Cigar Room in the cooler months when the rooftop is closed. ✉ *Via Giulia 62, Campo de' Fiori* ☎ *06/686611* 🌐 *www.stgeorgehotel.it.*

GAY VILLAGE

From the end of May through mid-September, Gay Village (🌐 *www.gayvillage.it*) hosts an outdoor mega-party held in a different central location each year. Every time more amazing than the last, Gay Village is larger than life with great bars, clubs, pop-up shops, and an international line-up of DJs and performance artists.

PIAZZA DI SPAGNA

After 9 pm, Piazza di Spagna holds the title for being the quietest area in the historical center. Don't expect a party here, but do come to seek out some lovely enotecas.

BARS

Antica Birreria Peroni. For beer lovers, the art nouveau–style halls of Antica Birreria Peroni will enchant you with their turn-of-the-century atmosphere, not to mention the always-flowing taps. Expect filling canteen-style meals and big steins, with several taps featuring Peroni favorites. Best place for hot dogs in Rome, though presentation may be a bit tasteless. ✉ *Via di San Marcello 19, Corso* ☎ *06/6795310* 🌐 *www.anticabirreriaperoni.net.*

Antica Enoteca. Piazza di Spagna's staple wine bar literally corners the market on prime people-watching. In addition to a vast selection of wine, Antica Enoteca has delectable antipasti, perfect for a snack or a light lunch. ✉ *Via della Croce 76/b, Piazza di Spagna* ☎ *06/6790896* 🌐 *www.anticaenoteca.com.*

Fodor's Choice ★ **Enoteca Palatium.** Just down the street from the Piazza di Spagna hub is this quiet gem run by Lazio's Regional Food Authority as a chic showcase for the best of Lazio's pantry and wine cellar. You can sample fine vintages, olive oils, cheeses, and meats, and also a full seasonal menu of Lazio cuisine. Located where famed aesthete and poet Gabriele d'Annunzio once lived, this is not your garden-variety corner wine bar. ■ **TIP→ Stop by during aperitivo hour, from 6:30 pm onward (reservations recommended) to enjoy this burst of local flavor.** ✉ *Via Frattina 94, Piazza di Spagna.*

h club> doney at the Westin Excelsior. Nattily dressed businesspeople and harried tourists enjoy fresh-fruit aperitifs at the street-side h club>

doney, Via Veneto's grand dame, in front of the Westin Excelsior. The indoor Orvm bar is a return to the Jazz Age and Roaring Twenties in decor, with excellent cocktails served all day. ✉ *Westin Excelsior, Via Vittorio Veneto 145, Piazza di Spagna* ☎ *06/0647082805* 🌐 *www.restaurantdoney.com.*

Wine Bar at the Palazzetto. The prize for perfect aperitivo spot goes to the Palazzetto, with excellent drinks and appetizers and a breathtaking view of Rome's domes and rooftops, all from its 5th-floor rooftop overlooking Piazza di Spagna. Keep an eye on the sky, as any chance for a rainy day will close the terrace. ✉ *Palazzetto, Piazza Trinità di Monti, Piazza di Spagna* ☎ *06/69934711* 🌐 *www.ilpalazzettoroma.com* Ⓜ *Spagna.*

SUMMER LOVIN'

From June through August, many of Rome's bars and clubs shut down and the owners get out of town to avoid the summer heat. Other hangouts open temporary clubs on the beaches of Ostia and Fregene, about 20 minutes outside the city. Even more conveniently, *Estate Romana* (Roman Summer) 🌐 *www.estateromana.comune.roma.it* brings beach nightlife to the banks of the Tiber River, with miniversions of some familiar bars, restaurants, and clubs along the Tiber banks.

DANCE CLUBS

Gilda. Every year, historic disco Gilda reinvents herself to continue the never-ending party near the Spanish Steps. Recent incarnations have added a piano bar and restaurant just off the dance floors. Expect a younger crowd. ✉ *Via Mario de' Fiori 97, Piazza di Spagna* ☎ *06/6784838* 🌐 *www.gildabar.it* Ⓜ *Spagna.*

Jackie O'. A dip into Rome's dolce vita is not complete without a visit to the historic Jackie O', a retro-hip disco and restaurant off Via Veneto. The small lounge area is where you want to be, and don't arrive before 11 pm. ✉ *Via Boncompagni 11, Piazza di Spagna* ☎ *06/42885457* 🌐 *www.jackieoroma.com.*

Piazza della Repubblica is by far one of Rome's prettiest and largest piazzas, but its proximity to the central station means the nightlife scene can be a bit scruffy. There are few spots worth visiting, though.

BARS

Fodor's Choice ★ **Champagnerie Tazio.** A chic champagne bar named after the original Italian *paparazzo* Tazio Secchiaroli, this spot brings a very *dolce vita* vibe with its red, black, and white lacquered interior with crystal chandeliers. The favorite pastime at Tazio is sipping champagne while watching the people parade through the colonnade of the lobby. In summer, the hotel's rooftop Posh bar is the place to be, with its infinity pool and terrace view overlooking downtown. ✉ *Hotel Exedra, Piazza della Repubblica 47* ☎ *06/48938061* 🌐 *exedra-roma.boscolohotels.com* Ⓜ *Repubblica–Teatro dell'Opera.*

Trimani Il Winebar. Perhaps Rome's best-stocked enoteca/wine shop, this never-ending cantina proudly boasts over 4,000 labels. The bi-level Trimani Il Winebar is a favorite for wine tasting. Sommeliers frequent

Trimani daily to stock up their restaurants. ✉ *Via Cernaia 37/b, Repubblica* ☎ *06/4469661* 🌐 *www.trimani.com.*

PIAZZA DEL POPOLO

Like nearby Piazza di Spagna, Piazza del Popolo takes a turn for quiet once the sun sets.

BARS

Stravinskij Bar at the Hotel de Russie. The Stravinskij Bar, in the Hotel de Russie's garden, is the best place to catch a glimpse of la dolce vita. Celebrities, blue bloods, and VIPs hang out in the private courtyard garden where mixed drinks and cocktails are well above par, as are the prices. ✉ *Hotel de Russie, Via del Babuino 9, Popolo* ☎ *06/328881* 🌐 *www.hotelderussie.it* Ⓜ *Flaminio.*

TRASTEVERE

Trastevere is no longer the rough-around-the-edges neighborhood where visitors used to come to get a glimpse of "real" Rome. Years of gentrification have made this medieval "country within a town" a mecca for tourists and students. Its nightlife is a fun mix of overflowing piazzas filled with creative buskers, busy pubs, and great hole-in-the-wall restaurants.

BARS

Fodor's Choice ★ **Freni e Frizioni.** This hipster hangout has a cute artist vibe, great for an afternoon coffee, tea or aperitifs, or late-night socializing. In warmer weather, the crowd overflows the large terrazzo overlooking the Tiber and the side streets of Trastevere. ✉ *Via del Politeama 4, Trastevere* ☎ *06/45497499* 🌐 *www.freniefrizioni.com.*

Grazia e Graziella. A charming wine bar and restaurant, "G e G" has an atmosphere reminiscent of the 1960s, from the dolce vita decor to the relaxed vibe. ✉ *Largo F. Biondi 5, Trastevere* ☎ *06/5880398* 🌐 *www.graziaegraziella.it.*

LIVE MUSIC

Art Cafe. At Rome's most fashionable (and flashy) nightclub, the lust for luxe is complemented by great DJs and even better cocktails. Don't arrive before midnight, and dress to impress. ✉ *Viale del Galoppatoio, 33, Villa Borghese* ☎ *06/3220994* 🌐 *www.art-cafe.it.*

Big Mama. The recently renovated Big Mama is Trastevere's homegrown institution for live music including jazz, blues, rhythm and blues, international, and rock. ✉ *Vicolo San Francesco a Ripa 18, Trastevere* ☎ *06/5812551* 🌐 *www.bigmama.it.*

AVENTINO AND TESTACCIO

AVENTINO

Aventino is a niche residential neighborhood with no nightlife activity in its central area. However, the peripheral streets, especially Viale Aventino, have recently been blossoming with new restaurants and bars.

TESTACCIO

Testaccio is the usual go-to neighborhood for nightlife, in particular discos and clubs. The via Galvani is choc-a-bloc with clubs featuring every genre of music, which means weekends are congested with party-goers. More recently, the neighborhood has evolved as a hot bed for the restaurant and bar scene with some of Rome's newest hangouts opening up here.

DANCE CLUBS

l'Alibi. One of Testaccio's longest-running clubs, l'Alibi hosts parties daily including its much-anticipated Thursday Gloss Party. The crowd crosses all boundaries and the music knows no limits at what is often considered Rome's most famous gay disco. In summer, the open terrace is a large dance space. ✉ *Via di Monte Testaccio 40* ☎ *06/5743448* 🌐 *www.lalibi.it.*

The Manhattan. A new entry to Testaccio's club line up on Via Galvani, The Manhattan combines lounge style with disco vibes. Great for late-night dancing. ✉ *Via Galvani 20* ☎ *39/3931818498* 🌐 *www.themanhattan.it.*

MONTI, ESQUILINO, AND SAN LORENZO

MONTI

Lately, Monti has been wearing the crown as the "it" neighborhood, reigning supreme as an all-ages hipster hang out with trendy bars, restaurants, shops, and hangouts, as well as picturesque piazzas.

BARS

Ai Tre Scalini. A rustic wine bar in the center of Monti, Rome's boho 'hood, Ai Tre Scalini has a warm and cozy menu of delicious antipasti and light entrées to go along with its enticing wine list. ✉ *Via Panisperna 251* ☎ *06/48907495* 🌐 *www.aitrescalini.org* Ⓜ *Cavour.*

Caffè Propaganda. Propaganda is reminiscent of Parisian brasseries of the 1930s, with its charming bar design, clever cocktail menu and creative Italian/French cuisine—not to mention its delicious desserts. For a glimpse of Rome's super-stylish, park yourself at Propaganda's bar for a few hours. ✉ *Via Claudia 15/19* ☎ *06/94534255* 🌐 *www.caffepropaganda.it.*

DANCE CLUBS

Casa Clementina. A homey lounge with DJs, aperitivi, and cocktails, Casa Clementina creates an ersatz home with kitchen, living room, dining room, and bedroom for your disposal. ✉ *Via Clementina 9* ☎ *06/48913254.*

ESQUILINO

Monti's neighbor Esquilino is lined up and ready for the next urban renaissance. The area has been enjoying the Monti hipster spillover, opening more and more bars and restaurants. If there was one phrase to describe Esquilino, it would be "coming soon."

BARS

Fiddler's Elbow. The oldest Irish pub in Rome, proud Fiddler's Elbow is a rustic, traditional pub that probably hasn't changed since it first installed its wood panels in 1976. Expect raucous nights of beer and singing. ✉ *Via dell'Olmata 43, Esquilino* ☎ *06/4872110* 🌐 *www.thefiddlerselbow.com.*

SAN LORENZO

Literally the other side of the tracks, just beyond Termini train station, San Lorenzo is a traditional university area with lots of inexpensive bars and restaurants, as well as art spaces. Evenings are always brimming with people and activity

DANCE CLUBS

Micca Club. In a cave-like former warehouse, Micca Club has one of Rome's best bartenders to go alongside its multi-genre programming from DJs and burlesque to live music, hip-hop, and lounge. ✉ *Via Pietro Micca 7a, Esquilino* ☎ *39/33236244* 🌐 *www.miccaclub.com.*

THE PERFORMING ARTS

One of the pleasures of Rome is seeing a performance in one of the city's stunning venues, ancient or modern. This is the city where you might experience classical music in a centuries-old structure or see a contemporary performance at the Renzo Piano–designed Auditorium Parco della Musica. There is plenty to take your breath away.

DANCE

Rome's classical and modern dance scene may play understudy to Milan and Bologna, but dance is flourishing in the Eternal City. Teatro dell'Opera and the Auditorium Parco della Musica, as well as other theaters, have enriched their programming to include more performances, feature international performers, and showcase contemporary along with classical dance. Each year, the city hosts the six-week-long RomaEuropa Festival, which includes various performance artists. RomaEuropa also continues with select programming throughout the year.

Corps de Ballet, Teatro dell'Opera. Rome's Corps de Ballet performs throughout the year at the lovely Belle Epoque opera house, with leading international guest stars. During the summer season, ballet performances are held under the stars at the Baths of Caracalla, mixing contemporary set design with the classic structure. ✉ *Teatro dell'Opera, Piazza Beniamino Gigli 7, Esquilino* ☎ *06/48160255* 🌐 *www.operaroma.it*

Museo Nazionale degli Strumenti Musicali. On the grounds of Museo Nazionale degli Strumenti Musicali (National Museum of Musical Instruments), classical and contemporary dance festivals take place from June through August. ✉ *Piazza di Santa Croce in Gerusalemme 9/a, San Giovanni* ☎ *06/7014796* 🌐 *www.museostrumentimusicali.it.*

Teatro Greco. As part of Rome's rich and intense performance circuit, the Teatro Greco features international contemporary dance performances and, on occasion, hosts the Festa della Danza in the fall. ✉ *Via Ruggero Leoncavallo 10, Roma Nord* ☎ *06/8607513* 🌐 *www.teatrogreco.it.*

Teatro Olimpico. Part of Rome's theater circuit, the 1930s-era Teatro Olimpico is one of the main venues for contemporary dance companies, visiting international ballet companies, touring Broadway shows, and TedX Roma. ✉ *Piazza Gentile da Fabriano 17, Flaminio* ☎ *06/3265991* 🌐 *teatroolimpico.it.*

FILM

Andiamo al cinema! Rome has dozens of movie houses, where you'll find both blockbuster and art house films. All films, unless noted "V.O." in the listing, which means *versione originale* (original version or original language), are shown in Italian.

Most international films are dubbed in Italian, *grazie a Mussolini,* who insisted on this approach in order to instill pride in the native language. Dubbing has since become an art form—voice-over actors receive recognition and awards, and consistently dub their silver screen counterparts. Unless stated otherwise, non-Italian films are not viewed in the original language.

For show times, see the entertainment pages of daily newspapers, *roma c'è,* or Rome's English-language publications. Check out 🌐 *www.inromenow.com* for the most up-to-date reviews of all English-language films or visit 🌐 *www.mymovies.it* or 🌐 *www.cinemadelsilenzio.it* for a list of current features and theaters. Tickets range in price from €4.50 for matinees and some weekdays, up to €10 for weekend evenings.

Alcazar. The small Cinema Alcazar in Trastevere is known for its more international, art house films. English-speaking guests flock here for its original language programming. It's best to contact the Alcazar in advance for confirmation on film showings. ✉ *Via Merry del Val 14, Trastevere* ☎ *06/5880099* 🌐 *www.cinemaz.com/film-e-orari/orari-e-programmazione/cinema/roma/alcazar.html.*

Casa del Cinema. Casa del Cinema is Rome's hub for all things film, with multiple screening rooms, a resource center with DVD library, laptops for private viewings, plus a café and restaurant. Yearly programming includes new and retro films from its vast archives; original language films are often showcased from several festivals, including Venice Film Festival and Roma Cinema Fest (🌐 *www.romacinemafest.it*). In summer, the cinema heads outdoors to show a wide array of movies, sometimes in original language. ✉ *Largo Marcello Mastroianni 1, Villa Borghese* ☎ *06/423601* 🌐 *www.casadelcinema.it.*

Nuovo Olimpia. Just off Rome's Via del Corso in the center of the city, Nuovo Olimpia shows classic and current films in original language and subtitled in Italian. Wednesday night tickets are half-price. ✉ *Via in Lucina 16/b, Piazza Navona* ☎ *06/6861068* 🌐 *circuitocinema.it/nuovo_olimpia/.*

MUSIC

CLASSICAL

Since 2002 Rome has had its very own state-of-the-art auditorium a 10-minute tram ride north of Piazza del Popolo—the Parco della Musica (or Music Park), splashed over the pages of glossy magazines everywhere. However, if you prefer smaller or quirkier venues, Rome does not disappoint. Classical music concerts take place at numerous places throughout the city, and you're likely to see memorable performances in smaller halls and churches, often for free. This is true particularly at Christmas and Easter, especially busy concert seasons in Rome. Some churches that frequently host afternoon and evening concerts are Sant'Ivo alla Sapienza, San Francesco a Ripa, and San Paolo entro le Mura. Look for posters outside churches announcing free performances, particularly at Sant'Ignazio (✉ Piazza Sant'Ignazio, Pantheon ☎ 06/6794560 🌐 *www.amicimusicasacra.com*), which hosts concerts in a spectacular setting. Or try the summertime concerts at the ancient Theatre of Marcello (✉ *Via del Teatro Marcello, Ghetto* ☎ *06/488991*).

One of the charming things about Rome is that, with all the little side streets tucked behind quiet piazzas, not to mention the nearly 1,000 churches throughout the Eternal City, it's quite easy to stumble upon a choir rehearsing, or a chorus performing for just a few churchgoers. Sometimes all it takes is some wandering around, and serendipitous luck, to trip over a memorable concert experience.

Accademia Filarmonica Romana. Nearly two centuries old, this is one of Rome's historic concert venues featuring classical music. The garden hosts occasional outdoor performances. ✉ *Via Flaminia 118, Flaminio* ☎ *06/3201752* 🌐 *www.filarmonicaromana.org*.

Accademia di Santa Cecilia. Part of Rome's amazing and well-versed musical circuit, this venue has a program of performances ranging from classical to contemporary and a lineup of world-renowned artists. The futurist Auditorium Parco della Musica hosts Santa Cecilia's concerts. ⇨ *Auditorium Parco della Musica.* ✉ *Via Pietro de Coubertin 34, Flaminio* ☎ *06/8082058* 🌐 *www.santacecilia.it*

Teatro Eliseo. Hosting musical performances and the work of historical and contemporary playwrights throughout the year, Teatro Eliseo also offers innovative programming for children, including English-language programs. ✉ *Via Nazionale 183, Repubblica* ☎ *06/488721, 06/48872222* 🌐 *www.teatroeliseo.it*.

Il Tempietto. Music festivals and concerts are organized throughout the year in otherwise inaccessible sites, such as the Teatro di Marcello, Church of San Nicola in Carcere and Villa Torlonia. Music covers the entire scope from classical to contemporary. ✉ *Piazza Campitelli 9, Jewish Ghetto* ☎ *06/45615180* 🌐 *www.tempietto.it*.

Fodor's Choice ★ **Oratorio del Gonfalone.** A small concert hall with an internationally recognized music series of Baroque classics, the Oratorio del Gonfalone's mid-16th-century frescoed walls are painted in high Mannerist style—a beautiful accompaniment to the music. ✉ *Via del Gonfalone 32/a, Campo de' Fiori* ☎ *06/6875952* 🌐 *www.oratoriogonfalone.com*.

Orto Botanico. Rome's historic botanical garden spans 30 acres in Trastevere, at the base of the Janiculum hill. In the spring and summer, this bucolic settings becomes a stage for a series of art and concert programming. ✉ *Largo Cristina di Svezia 23/a, Trastevere* ☎ *06/49917108* 🌐 *sweb01.dbv.uniroma1.it.*

ROCK, POP, AND JAZZ

Local and smaller-act rock, pop, and jazz concerts are frequent in Rome, with big-name acts coming through less frequently—almost exclusively during warmer weather, although even these performances may not be well advertised. Some locales are outside the city center, and sometimes as far as Tivoli, so it's worth asking about transportation before you buy your tickets. The Estate Romana (Roman Summer) program, organized by the local and regional governments, has been growing every year. The program now includes a diverse offering of well-publicized and well-organized cultural events, most set outdoors and all free or reasonably priced. In addition to Estate Romana, both Rock in Roma and Fiesta are cultural series with a heavy focus on music in places such as the Stadio Olimpico, Hippodrome, and even on the Tiber banks.

Events spread from the center of town to the periphery and usually run from early June to early September. They include music of every sort, as well as outdoor cinema, theater, and other events, such as book fairs and guided tours of some of Rome's monuments by night. The city administration has really made the push for important music acts to give free concerts, and the crowds at these gigs prove that music is, in fact, an international language. James Taylor gave a heartfelt free performance in lovely Piazza del Popolo. Record crowds once filled the Via dei Fori Imperiali, from Piazza Venezia down to the stage in front of a brightly lighted Colosseum, for free concerts by no less than Paul McCartney and Simon & Garfunkel, respectively.

PalaLottomatica. Built for the 1960 Rome Olympics for basketball and boxing events, the PalaLottamatica is now a concert venue for big names like Italian favorites Zucchero and Renato Zero, as well international superstars like Bruce Springsteen and Elton John. It's in the EUR neighborhood (about 15 minutes out of the city center), which means bring extra cab fare. ✉ *Palazzetto dello Sport, Piazzale dello Sport, Flaminio* ☎ *06/540901* 🌐 *www.palalottomatica.it.*

OPERA

Rome may be a tiny star in Italy's opera constellation, but with an increasing emphasis on quality productions, along with its never-ending supply of performances, this little star is twinkling. The historic Teatro dell'Opera, Rome's center for lyrical performances, has upped its brilliance by adding famed maestro Riccardo Muti as Music Director for select productions. Its season runs from late fall through spring, and showcases summertime alfresco performances at the Baths of Caracalla. There are also several churches and smaller venues that host operas, often for free.

Fodor's Choice ★ **Teatro dell'Opera.** Rome has recently stepped into the spotlight for opera aficionados thanks to Maestro Riccardo Muti's ongoing support of

AUDITORIUM PARCO DELLA MUSICA

✉ *Viale Pietro de Coubertin 30, Flaminio* ☎ *06/80241281 information, 06/60060900 information and tickets* 🌐 *www.auditorium.com.*

TIPS

■ To get to the Auditorium from Rome's Termini train station, take Bus M or No. 910, which stops directly in front of the complex at Viale Pietro de Coubertin. If you're coming from the city center, walk to Piazzale Flaminio (the other side of Piazza del Popolo) and hop on Tram #2 for six stops. Using the Metro, take Line A to Flaminio, and aboveground to Tram #2, again six stops. Access the Auditorium's underground parking using Viale Maresciallo Pilsudski and Via Giulio Gaudini.

■ To book guided tours, email: visiteguidate@musicaperroma.it. Keep in mind that a summertime visit means outdoor concerts and festivals.

Rome became an arts contender when world-renowned architect Renzo Piano conceived and constructed the Parco della Musica, fondly known as the Auditorium. The futuristic music complex is made up of three enormous pod-shaped concert halls, which have heard the live melodies of Luciano Pavarotti, Philip Glass, Tracy Chapman, Peter Gabriel, Burt Bacharach, Woody Allen, and many more.

Likened to anything from beetles to computer "mice," the musical pods are consistently jammed with people: the Sala Santa Cecilia is a massive hall for grand orchestra and choral concerts; the Sala Sinopoli is more intimately scaled for smaller troupes; and the Sala Petrassi was designed for alternative events. All three are arrayed around the "Cavea," a vast Greco-Roman–style theater.

The auditorium is more than just music. The music park also includes seasonal festivals (including the International Film Festival of Rome, a Christmas Village, and a springtime science, math, and philosphy festival). The grounds have a charming café, restaurants, a bookstore, outdoor amphitheater, archaeological site, and an outstanding children's playground. Located in the Flaminio/Villaggio Olimpico neighborhood, the Auditorium is just 10 minutes from the city center, reachable by local tram transport.

CLOSE UP

Opera Alfresco

Opera buffs know that the best performances and most exquisite surroundings for opera are to be found at Milan's La Scala, Venice's newly reconstructed La Fenice, and at Verona's Arena (outdoor amphitheater). But Rome is Italy's capital, and so although its opera company does not have the renown of the aforementioned landmarks, it has a healthy following. Rome's spring opera season runs from November or December to May. During the summertime exodus of many of the city's pubs, restaurants, and discos to outdoor venues, opera heads outside for its summer season. Rome's many opera companies commandeer church courtyards, ancient villas, and soccer *campi* (fields) with performances that range from mom-and-poperas to full-scale, large-budget extravaganzas. Quality is generally quite high, even for smaller, low-budget productions. Tickets cost €15 to €40. To find these productions, listen closely or look for the old-fashioned posters advertising classic operas like *Tosca* and *La Traviata.* The weekly *roma c'è,* the monthly *Wanted in Rome,* and the website 🌐 *www.inromenow.com* also have complete lists of performances.

14

Rome's Teatro dell'Opera. Though considered a far younger sibling of Milan's La Scala and Venice's La Fenice, the company commands an audience during its mid-November to May season. In the hot summer months, the company moves to the Baths of Caracalla for its outdoor opera series. As can be expected, the oft-preferred performance is *Aïda* for its spectacle, which has been known to include real elephants. The company has taken a new direction, using projections atop the ancient ruins to create cutting-edge sets. ✉ *Piazza Beniamino Gigli 8, Repubblica* ☎ *06/481601, 06/48160255 tickets* 🌐 *www.operaroma.it* Ⓜ *Repubblica–Teatro dell'Opera.*

Terme di Caracalla ballet and opera. The 3rd-century AD bath complex Terme di Caracalla is the spectacular backdrop for summer performances of the Teatro dell'Opera's ballet and opera series. *Aïda* is the most sought-after performance, for its melodramatic flair and amazing props, including live elephants. Along with traditional pieces, many of the performances have contemporary elements such as the stage design, which uses projections atop the ancient ruins to create cutting-edge sets. ✉ *Via Antoniniana 14, Aventino* ☎ *06/481601* 🌐 *www.operaroma.it.*

THEATER

Italian film director Federico Fellini's *La Dolce Vita* immortalized Rome's vivacious nightclubs and pernicious paparazzi to introduce Rome as Hollywood-on-the-Tiber. Though the Eternal City's cinematic dominance has waxed and waned, Cinecittà—one of the world's largest film studios (*see Exploring*)—and Rome itself are positioned as choice locations for international film productions, such as Woody Allen's *To Rome with Love,* Wes Anderson's *Life Aquatic,* Martin Scorsese's *Gangs of New York,* HBO/BBC Production's series *Rome,* as well as

Paolo Sorrentino's *The Great Beauty.* With the presence of so many actors, the city has also reinvigorated its theater productions.

English Theatre of Rome. The oldest English-language theater group in town, English Theatre of Rome has a repertoire of original and celebrated plays. Performances are held at John Cabot University and Teatro Arciliuto. ✉ *Piazza Montevecchio, 5, Piazza Navona* ☎ *06/4441375* 🌐 *www.rometheatre.com.*

Miracle Players. Looking for a bit of English humor? With an obvious penchant for Monty Python, the Miracle Players are Rome's most vocal English-language comedy troupe performing original plays. Head to the Roman Forum on Friday afternoons in summer for their free, live performances. ✉ *Largo Romolo e Remo, Monti* 🌐 *www.miracleplayers.org.*

Fodor's Choice ★ **Teatro Argentina.** A gorgeous, turn-of-the-last-century theatre, Teatro Argentina evokes glamour and sophistication with its velvet upholstery, large crystal chandeliers, and beautifully dressed theatre-goers who come to see international productions of stage and dance performances. ✉ *Largo di Torre Argentina 52, Campo de' Fiori* ☎ *06/684000311* 🌐 *www.teatrodiroma.net.*

Rock in Roma. From June through August, the Ippodromo, Stadio Olimpico, and other stages become the heart of rock and roll with summer concert series Rock in Roma. Headliners have included David Guetta, Kings of the Stone Age, The Lumineers, Metallica, Radiohead, Subsonica, the Cure, and the Killers. 🌐 *www.rockinroma.com.*

15

SHOPPING

WHAT TO SHOP FOR IN ROME

Handmade leather goods are among the best things to splurge on in Rome—excellent workmanship and attention to detail are the norm, and you'll find beautifully constructed jackets, shoes, gloves, handbags, and more. You can even have items made to order at artisan workshops.

Antiques and Prints

Rome is one of Italy's happiest hunting grounds for antiques and bric-a-brac. You'll find streets lined with shops groaning with gilded Rococo tables, charming Grand Tour memorabilia, fetching 17th-century *veduti* (view) engravings, and curios—perhaps even Lord Byron's snuff spoon.

CERAMICS AND DECORATIVE ARTS

Italy has always been beloved for its wonderful craftsmanship and decorative arts. In Rome, sometimes the best treasures are found not in its galleries but in artisan shops tucked away in the city's numerous winding alleyways. Whether you fancy a typical Roman mask or a bust or even a copy of the popular Roman relic La Bocca della Verità, you're bound to find something worth shipping home.

FLEA MARKET FINDS

Treasure-seekers and bargain-hunters alike will appreciate Rome's *mercati all'aperto* (open air markets). Flea markets are great spots to gain insight into the thrift-shopping spirit of the capital. Every Sunday it seems that all of Trastevere comes out for the bustling Porta Portese flea market, where tents overflow with cheap luggage, new and used clothes, vintage World War II memorabilia, and everything else imaginable. Make sure to watch your valuables, as pickpockets abound.

GLOVES

You just wouldn't be an Italian signora without a pair of fashionable handmade gloves, and you'll find plenty to choose from in Rome. Whether you're looking for cashmere, silk, lambskin, or other types of leather, there is a sea of colors to chose from. Gloves make wonderful presents, too.

HANDBAGS, LUGGAGE, AND LEATHER GOODS

Really good bags—the classic kind that you can carry for years—don't come cheap. Whether you're in the market for something high fashion that the Hollywood A-listers are wearing or a one-of-a-kind travel bag, you'll find plenty of splurge-inducing shops. You'll find other types of well-made leather goods in Rome, too, like wallets, belts, and jackets.

SHOES

When it comes to stylish slingbacks, strappy sandals, and cult-status heels, Rome has a *scarpa* (shoe) to fit every Cinderella. Whet your appetite in the swanky Spagna area, but you may not want to buy the first pair you fall in love with. If you have a dream shoe in mind, consider ordering something bespoke. *Scarpe Diem!*

CLOTHING

Italians know fashion; it's indisputable. There are plenty of up-market flagships in Rome if you have the means for Prada, Biagiotti, or Valentino spend, but make sure to browse the smaller boutiques. You're sure to find a piece of two to liven up your wardrobe.

VINTAGE CLOTHING

Looking good needn't mean looking like everyone else. Rome has a wide range of vintage shops where you can find some great couture from the Dolce Vita days and other classic time periods. Spend some time going through the racks, you never know what treasures you might find.

Updated by Nicole Arriaga

In Rome shopping is an art form. Perhaps it's the fashionably bespeckled Italian wearing Giorgio Armani as he deftly zips through traffic on his Vespa or all those Anita Ekberg, Audrey Hepburn, and Julia Roberts films that make us want to be Roman for a day. But with limited time and no Hollywood studio backing you, the trick is to find what you're looking for and still not miss out on the city's museums and monuments—and have enough euros left to enjoy the rest of your trip.

These days, many shop-'til-you-droppers heading over to the Trevi Fountain may be forgiven for humming that immortal song, "Three Coins in a Cash Register." Yes, the Eternal City is awash in fountains and iconographic Roman rituals: gazing at Saint Peter's Basilica through a secret keyhole on the Aventine; putting your hand inside the Bocca della Verità, the city's ancient lie detector; and tossing that fateful coin over your shoulder into the Fontana di Trevi. All are customs that will buy you a classic photo opportunity, but none will bring you as much pleasure or stay with you longer than the purchases you make in Rome's appealing and overflowing emporia.

There may be no city that takes shopping quite as seriously as Rome, and no district more worthy of your time than Piazza di Spagna, with its abundance of shops and designer powerhouses like Fendi and Armani. The best of them are clumped tightly together along the city's three primary fashion arteries: Via dei Condotti, Via Borgognona, and Via Frattina. From Piazza di Spagna to Piazza Navona and on to Campo de' Fiori, shoppers will find an explosive array of shops within walking distance of one another. A shop for fine handmade Amalfi paper looks out upon the Pantheon, while slick boutiques anchor the corners of 18th-century Piazza di Spagna. Across town in the colorful hive that is Monti, a second-generation mosaic-maker creates Italian masterpieces on a street named for a pope who died before America was even discovered. Even in Trastevere, one can find one of Rome's rising shoe designers creating next-century *nuovo chic* shoes nestled on a side street beside one of the city's oldest churches.

This chapter will help shopaholics choose the perfect souvenir for someone back home, find a vintage poster, choose a boutique for those *molto* chic Versace sandals, or rustle up truffles. When you're done filling your bags with memories of Mamma Roma, you can be sure of two things: that you'll be nostalgic for Caput Mundi long after you arrive back home, and that you've saved a few coins—to throw into that fabulous famous fountain.

PLANNING

OPENING HOURS

When planning your shopping adventure, it's important to be flexible. Small, family-run businesses may close a few hours for lunch (approximately 1 or 1:30 to 4 or 4:30) and one day a week. Major retailers and chains open between 9 and 10 am and stay open until 7:30 or 8 pm; these larger shops tend to stay open all day. Most clothing stores adhere to the general operating hours listed above but close Sunday and Monday mornings. Banks are generally open weekdays from 8:30 to 1:30 and from 2:30 to 3:30 pm. Summer travelers should be aware that most small shops close for two to three weeks just before or after August's Ferragosto holiday.

COUNTERFEITS

Piracy, in any form, is now considered a serious offense in Italy. This not only applies to citizens, but also to tourists visiting the country. According to Italian law, anyone caught buying counterfeit goods—DVDs, CDs, sunglasses, or those impossibly discounted "Fendi" and "Gucci" bags—sold by illegal sidewalk vendors is subject to a fine of no less than €1,000. While the police in Rome enforce this law to varying degrees, travelers are advised to purchase products only from stores and licensed retailers that give out a receipt, to avoid unknowingly buying counterfeit goods or committing tax evasion.

DUTY-FREE SHOPPING

Value-added tax (IVA) is 23% on clothing and luxury goods, but is already included in the amount on the price tag for consumer goods. All non–EU citizens visiting Italy are entitled to a reimbursement of this tax when purchasing nonperishable goods that total more than €180 in a single transaction. If you buy goods in a store that does not participate in the "Tax-Free Italy" program, ask the cashier to issue you a special invoice known as a *fattura,* which must be made out to you and includes the phrase *Esente IVA ai sensi della legge 38 quater.* The bill should indicate the amount of IVA included in the purchase price. Present this invoice and the goods purchased to the Customs Office on your departure from Italy to obtain your tax reimbursement.

ITALIAN SIZES

Italian sizes are not uniform, so always try on or measure items. If you wear a size small, you may be surprised to learn that the shirt you like needs to be a medium. Children's sizes are all over the place and though they usually go by age, sizes are calibrated to Italian children. (Average size-per-age standards vary from country to country.) Check washing instruction labels on all garments as many are dry-clean-only or not meant for the dryer. When in doubt about the proper size, ask the shop attendant; most will have an international size chart handy. At open-air markets, where there often isn't any place to try on garments, you'll have to take your best guess; if you're wrong, you may or may not be able to find the vendor the next day to exchange.

SALES

Saldi (end-of-season sales) mean big bargains in clothing and accessories and they occur twice a year in Italy. Rome's main sale periods run January 7 through February and late July to mid-September. Unlike in many other countries, most stores adopt a no-exchange, all-sales-final policy on sale goods. Others might even go as far as not allowing you to try on items on the "sales" rack. At other times of year, a *liquidazione* sign indicates a close-out sale, but take a hard look at the goods; they may be bottom-of-the-barrel or may carry stipulations that preclude the shopper from trying them on first.

If your trip is truly a shopping holiday or time is of the essence, consider scheduling your own personal shopping assistant through Context Rome (☎ *06/96727371* 🌐 *www.contexttravel.com*).

LISTINGS BY NEIGHBORHOOD

AROUND THE VATICAN: BORGO AND PRATI

BORGO

Slightly upriver from Prati, just outside the Vatican, Borgo also has plenty of shops selling religious relics.

Savelli Arte e Tradizione. For a selection of holier than thou gifts and sacred trinkets Savelli Arte e Tradizione is the place to go in Rome. The religious relics store has been a Roman landmark since 1878. The Savelli name belongs to an old Roman family with four popes among its ancestors: Benedict II, Gregory II, Honorius III, and Honorius IV. The shop specializes in everything from rosaries and crosses to religious artwork, statues and other souvenirs. ✉ *Via Paolo VI, 27, Borgo* ☎ *06/68307017* 🌐 *www.savellireligious.com.*

PRATI

Just a hop, skip, and jump from the Vatican, you'll find an array of religious relic shops plus department stores and specialty food and wine shops.

DEPARTMENT STORES

Coin. A perfect place for upscale merchandise in a proper department store atmosphere, Coin has convenient locations in the center of Rome. Customers can select from trendy merchandise, including clothing separates, lingerie, and sportswear for men, women, and children. Searching for a pressure-driven espresso machine, a simpler stove-top Bialetti model, or a mezzaluna? You can find these and other high-quality, stylish cookware items that are difficult to find back home. If you are hopping a train from Termini station be sure to check out the smaller version of this store, which has a fabulous emphasis on hip fashions. ✉ *Via Cola di Rienzo 173, Prati* ☏ *06/36004298* 🌐 *www.coin.it* Ⓜ *Lepanto, Ottaviano–San Pietro–Musei Vaticani*

FOOD AND WINE

Fodor's Choice ★ **Castroni.** The legend over the door reads Castroni Droghe Coloniali, but for years this international food emporium has been known by the single moniker Castroni. Opening its flagship shop near the Vatican in 1932, this gastronomic paradise has long been Rome's port of call for decadent delicacies from around the globe; there are now other locations throughout the city. Jonesing expatriates and study-abroad students pop in for their Fauchon products from Paris, their Twinings teas, or tins of their special smoked Spanish paprika. Travelers will want to stock up on exquisite Italian goodies like Sardinian Bottarga, aromatic Alba white truffles, or their in-house roasted espresso (some of the best coffee in Rome is also served at the bar here). Just be sure to bring an extra suitcase: you will want to buy everything. ✉ *Via Cola di Rienzo 196, Prati* ☏ *06/6874383* 🌐 *www.castroni.it* Ⓜ *Lepanto, Ottaviano–San Pietro–Musei Vaticani*

MUSIC STORES

Remix. An underground favorite for famous producers and distributors of legendary Roman vinyl labels like Sounds Never Seen, ACV, and many others, Remix specializes in techno. The shop also has a great back catalogue—all at prices that will make new collectors smile. The store also houses a production studio. ✉ *Via Luigi Rizzo 110, Prati* ☏ *06/3216514* 🌐 *www.re-mix.it* Ⓜ *Cipro.*

SHOES AND ACCESSORIES

Serafini Ferruccio Pelletteria. For more than 70 years, artisan Ferruccio Serafini has been churning out handmade leather bags, shoes, and belts in Rome. Only a handful of these true saddler artisans still exist today. Marlon Brando, Liz Taylor, and the Kennedy brothers were all faithful followers of Serafini's design and work in the 1960s. Today, the Serafini brand is managed by Francesca, Ferruccio Serafini's youngest daughter, and the laboratory continues to work the leather just as Ferruccio did since beginning his career in the 1940s. Choose from their premade stock or select your own style and accompanying leathers. ✉ *Via Caio Mario 14, Prati* ☏ *06/3211719* 🌐 *www.serafinipelletteria.it* Ⓜ *Ottaviano.*

PIAZZA NAVONA AND CAMPO DE' FIORI

PIAZZA NAVONA

The area around Piazza Navona is filled with vintage boutiques and tiny artisan shops. This is a great place to look for unique gifts, like delicate Florentine stationery or hand-blown Murano glass. Near the Pantheon, you'll also find old-fashioned Italian toys like wooden Pinocchios and cuckoo clocks.

ANTIQUES

Galleria Biagiarelli. In a superb setting in the former chapel of the Pre-Renaissance Palazzo Capranica, where the windows still have the cardinal's coat of arms, Rome's leading antiques dealer of 18th- and 19th-century Russian icons and English watercolors has also amassed a collection of Eastern European antique china figurines as well as Soviet-era artwork. ✉ *Piazza Capranica 97, Piazza Navona* ☎ *06/6784987* 🌐 *biagiarelli.it.*

Nardecchia. In the heart of Piazza Navona, in front of Bernini's Fountain of the Four Rivers, Nardecchia knows there are three major considerations when it comes to antique prints and etchings: value, aesthetics, and rarity. The shop showcases some of its beautiful 19th-century prints, old photographs, and watercolors, giving browsers a hint at what Rome looked like in centuries past. Can't afford an 18th-century etching? They have refined postcards, too. ✉ *Piazza Navona 25, Piazza Navona* ☎ *06/6869318.*

BEAUTY PRODUCTS AND PERFUME

Fodor's Choice ★ **Ai Monasteri.** Among dark-wood paneling, choirlike alcoves, and painted angels, at Ai Monasteri you'll find traditional products made by Italy's diligent friars and monks. Following century-old recipes, the herbal decoctions, liqueurs, beauty aids, and toiletries offer a look into the time-honored tradition of monastic trade. The Elixir dell'Amore (love potion) is perfect for any well-deserving valentine, or, if it isn't true love, you can opt for a bottle of the popular Elixir of Happiness. There are myriad products, ranging from colognes for children to quince-apple and Cistercian jams, made exclusively with organic produce and Royal Jelly honey. ✉ *Corso del Rinascimento 72, Piazza Navona* ☎ *06/68802783* 🌐 *www.emonasteri.it.*

Antica Erboristeria Romana. Complete with hand-labeled wooden drawers holding its more than 200 varieties of herbs, flowers, and tinctures including aper, licorice, and hellbane, Antica Erboristeria Romana has maintained its old-world apothecary feel (it's the oldest shop of its kind in Rome, dating back to 1752). The shop stocks an impressive array of herbal teas and infusions, more than 700 essential oils, bud derivatives, and powdered extracts. ✉ *Via Torre Argentina 15, Piazza Navona* ☎ *06/6879493* 🌐 *www.anticaerboristeriaromana.it.*

CERAMICS AND DECORATIVE ARTS

Arte del Vetro Natolli Murano. Specializing in handblown Venetian art glass pieces, including Murano glass jewelry (necklaces and pendants), tableware, glass vases, and extravagant chandeliers, at Arte del Vetro Natolli Murano every individual piece is handcrafted from the furnaces of master glassmakers using ancient techniques kept alive by the island's artisans since 1291. Some limited-edition designs show not only the craftsman's mastery of the art form but the artisan's love for the vibrant aesthetic of the glassmaking tradition. ✉ *Corso Rinascimento 37/45, Piazza Navona* ☎ *06/68301170* 🌐 *www.natollimurano.com.*

Fodor's Choice ★ **IN.OR. dal 1952.** For more than 50 years, Romans have registered their bridal china and gifts under the frescoed ceilings of IN.OR. dal 1952, a grand silver and china store occupying the piano nobile of an 18th-century palazzo in the characteristic Campo Marzo area, in hopes of receiving something elegant. With seven rooms for browsing, the shop specializes in work handcrafted by the silversmiths of Pampaloni in Florence and Bellotto of Padua. ✉ *Via della Stelletta 23, Piazza Navona* ☎ *06/6878579* 🌐 *www.inor.it.*

CLOTHING

Arsenale. Arsenale has a sleek layout and a low-key elegance that stands out, even in Rome. Rest your feet awhile in an overstuffed chair before sifting through the racks. Whether you are looking for a wedding dress or a seductive bustier, you are bound to find something unconventional here. Designer and owner Patriza Pieroni creates many of the pieces on display, all cleverly cut and decidedly captivating. ✉ *Via del Pellegrino 172, Piazza Navona* ☎ *06/68802424* 🌐 *www.patriziapieroni.it.*

15

Le Tartarughe. Designer Susanna Liso, a Rome native, adds suggestive elements of playful experimentation to her haute couture and ready-to-wear lines, which are much loved by Rome's aristocracy and intelligentsia. With intense and enveloping designs, she mixes raw silks or cashmere and fine merino wool together to form captivating garments that are a mix of seduction and linear form. ✉ *Via Piè di Marmo 17, Piazza Navona* ☎ *06/6792240* 🌐 *www.letartarughe.eu.*

Mado. Still a leader in nostalgia styling, Mado has been vintage cool in Rome since 1969. The shop is funky, glamorous, and often over-the-top wacky. Whether you are looking for a robin's-egg-blue empire-waist dress or a '50s gown evocative of a Lindy Hop, Mado understands the challenges of incorporating vintage pieces into a modern wardrobe. ✉ *Via del Governo Vecchio 89/a, Piazza Navona* ☎ *06/6798660.*

Maga Morgana. Maga Morgana is a family-run business where everyone's nimble fingers contribute to producing the highly original clothes and accessories. From hippie-chick to bridal-chic, designer Luciana Iannace creates lavishly ornate clothes that are as inventive as they are distinguished. In addition to her own designs, she also sources inventive items from Paris and Florence. ✉ *Via del Governo Vecchio 27, Piazza Navona* ☎ *06/6879995.*

Replay. A typical example of young Italians' passion for American trends, Replay has jeans and T-shirts with American sports teams emblazoned on them that have that little extra kiss of Italian styling that transforms sloppy hip into fashionable casual chic. Styles range from punk to hip-hop. Strictly for those under 30, with cash to spare. ✉ *Via della Rotonda 24, Piazza Navona* ☎ *06/68301212* 🌐 *www.replay.it.*

Taro. Designed by owners Marisa Pignataro and Enrico Natoli, Taro's chic handmade knitwear in unusual yarns and striking colors is handmade in Rome. Selections from their casual, easy-to-wear line include luxuriously textured tunics, loose sleeveless jackets, and shawls and pants. ✉ *Via della Scrofa 50, Piazza Navona* ☎ *06/6896476.*

Vestiti Usati Cinzia. There's a fun, unique, and diverse inventory of 1960s- and '70s-style apparel and googly sunglasses at Vestiti Usati Cinzia, beloved by private clients, costume designers, and fashion designers and stylists alike. You'll find lots of flower power, embroidered tops, and psychedelic clothing here, along with trippy boots and dishy bubblegum pink shoes that Twiggy would have loved. ✉ *Via del Governo Vecchio 45, Piazza Navona* ☎ *06/6832945.*

CLOTHING: MEN'S

Davide Cenci. For the discerning shopper, Davide Cenci is a Roman classic for high-quality clothing and accessories for every occasion. For most visitors on a short holiday, purchasing custom-designed clothing is not an option. Cenci's clothiers will adjust and tailor most anything to fit your body like a glove and have it delivered to your hotel within three days. The label is famous for its sinful cashmere, sailing sportswear, and trench coats, and you will appreciate their customer service and attention to detail. ✉ *Via Campo Marzio 1-7, Piazza Navona* ☎ *06/6990681* 🌐 *www.davidecenci.com.*

SBU. In a city famous for classically sharp suits, it can be a challenge to find hip menswear in Rome, but SBU (Strategic Business Unit) suavely fills the void. In a 19th-century former draper's workshop, it's the place where Rome's VIPS buy their soft and supple vintage low-cut Japanese denims. Behind the old wooden counters, stacked drawer chests, and iron columns, SBU offers a sophisticated range of casual clothing, sportswear, shoes, and upscale accessories. The small hidden garden around back offers a relaxing moment between shopping sprees. ✉ *Via di San Pantaleo 68–69, Piazza Navona* ☎ *06/68802547* 🌐 *www.sbu.it.*

FOOD AND WINE

Enoteca al Parlamento Achilli. The tantalizing smell of truffles from the snack counter, where a sommelier waits to organize your wine-tasting session, is enough alone to lure you into Enoteca al Parlamento Achilli, filled with gastronomic treasures. The proximity of this traditional enoteca to Montecitorio, the Italian Parliament building, makes it a favorite with journalists and politicos, who often stop in for a glass of wine after work, making its prices not for the faint of heart. Ask to take a look at the wine shop's most prized possessions: bottles of the Brunello di Montalcino vintages 1891 and 1925, strictly not for sale. ✉ *Via dei Prefetti 15, Piazza Navona* ☎ *06/6873446* 🌐 *www.enotecaalparlamento.it.*

Moriondo e Gariglio. The Willy Wonka of Roman chocolate factories opened its doors in 1850. The shop uses the finest cocoa beans and adheres strictly to family recipes passed down from generation to generation. Known for rich, gourmet chocolates, they soon were the favored chocolatier to the House of Savoy. In 2009, the shop partnered with Bulgari and placed 300 pieces of jewelry in their Easter eggs to benefit cancer research. While you may not find diamonds in your bonbons, marrons glacés, or dark-chocolate truffles, you'll still delight in choosing from more than 80 delicacies. ✉ *Via Piè di Marmo 21, Piazza Navona* ☎ *06/6990856.*

HOME DECOR

Society. Have decorator envy? Everything you need for do-it-yourself Italian home couture can be found at Society, the flagship store for Limonta, one of the most prestigious and historic textile brands made in Italy. With a carefully edited collection of inspiring designs, the store sports a free-spirited, lived-in bohemian interior with a multitude of innovations to dress up any area of your home. Centering on the rarest and most sought-after fabrics, their designs give the appearance they come from a different era (the 18th, 19th, and 20th centuries). ✉ *Piazza di Pasquino 4, Piazza Navona* ☎ *06/6832480* 🌐 *www.societylimonta.com.*

Tebro. First opened in 1867 and listed with the Associazione Negozi Storici di Roma (Association of Historic Shops of Rome), Tebro is a classic Roman department store that epitomizes quality. It specializes in household linens and sleepwear, and you can even find those 100-percent cotton, Italian waffle-weave bath sheets that are synonymous with Italian hotels. ✉ *Via dei Prefetti 46, Piazza Navona* ☎ *06/6864851* 🌐 *www.tebro.it.*

JEWELRY

Delfina Delettrez. When your great grandmother is Adele Fendi, it's not surprising that creativity runs in your genes. In her early 20s, Delfina Delettrez creates edgy, conceptual collections. Using human body–inspired pieces blending skulls, wild animals, and botanical elements, she daringly merges gold, silver, bone and glass, crystals and diamonds to create gothic, edgy styles worthy of Fritz Lang's *Metropolis* or *Blade Runner.* Don't be put off by her signature goth-glam designs in the window: this dazzling emporium, with its innumerable drawers filled with baubles, has something saucy and refined for everyone's sensibilities. ✉ *Via Governo Vecchio 67, Piazza Navona* ☎ *06/68136362* 🌐 *www.delfinadelettrez.com.*

MMM—Massimo Maria Melis. Drawing heavily on ancient Greek, Roman, and Etruscan designs, Massimo Maria Melis jewelry will carry you back in time. Working with 21-carat gold, he often incorporates antique coins acquired by numismatists or pieces of ancient bronze and polychromatic glass. Some of his pieces are done with an ancient technique much loved by the Etruscans in which tiny gold droplets are soldered together to create intricately patterned designs. ✉ *Via dell'Orso 57, Piazza Navona* ☎ *06/6869188* 🌐 *www.massimomariamelis.com.*

Quattrocolo. This historic shop dating to 1938 showcases exquisite antique micro-mosaic jewelry painstakingly crafted in the style perfected by the masters at the Vatican mosaic studio. You'll also find 18th- and 19th-century cameos and beautiful engraved stones. Their small works were beloved by cosmopolitan clientele of the Grand Tour age and offer modern-day shoppers a taste of yesteryear's grandeur. ✉ *Via della Scrofa 48, Piazza Navona* ☎ *06/68801367* 🌐 *www.quattrocolo.com.*

SHOES AND ACCESSORIES

Spazio IF. In a tiny piazza alongside Rome's historic Via dei Coronari, designers Irene and Carla Ferrara have created a tantalizing hybrid between fashion paradise and art gallery. Working with unconventional designers and artists who emphasize Sicilian design, the shop has more to say about the style of Sicily and the creativity of the island's inhabitants than flat caps, puppets, and rich pastries. Perennial favorites include handbags cut by hand in a *putia* (shop) in Palermo, swimsuits, designer textiles, jewelry, and sportswear. ✉ *Via dei Coronari 44a, Piazza Navona* ☎ *06/64760639* 🌐 *www.spazioif.it.*

Superga. Superga, which celebrated its 100th anniversary in 2011, sells those timeless sneakers that every Italian wears at some point, in classic white or—yum—a rainbow of colors. Their 2750 model has been worn by everyone from Kelly Brook to Katie Holmes. If you are a sneakerhead who has been stuck on Converse, give these Italian brethren a look. Just remember not to wear socks with them. ✉ *Via dei Coronari 17, Piazza Navona* ☎ *06/68300481* 🌐 *www.superga.com* Ⓜ *Spagna.*

STATIONERY

Fodor's Choice ★ **Cartoleria Pantheon dal 1910.** An absolute Aladdin's cave for scribblers and those inspired by the blank page, the simply sumptuous Cartoleria Pantheon dal 1910 has unique leather journals and fine handmade paper to write a special letter. Writers and artists can choose from simple, stock paper to artisanal sheets of handcrafted Amalfi paper and from among hand-bound leather journals in an extraordinary array of colors and sizes. The store has two other locations in the neighborhood. ✉ *Via della Rotonda 15, Piazza Navona* ☎ *06/6875313* 🌐 *www.pantheon-roma.it* Ⓜ *Barberini–Fontana di Trevi.*

Il Papiro. One of Rome's preferred shops for those who appreciate exquisite writing materials and papermaking techniques that are almost extinct, Il Papiro sells hand-decorated marbleized papers made using the 17th-century technique called *a la cuve.* Their stationery and card stock are printed with great care using exacting standards. Whether you are searching for unique lithography, engraving, or delicate watermarked paper, you'll find some indulgence here. They also carry a fine selection of wax seals, presses for paper embossing, Venetian glass pens, and ink stamps. ✉ *Via del Pantheon 50, Piazza Navona* ☎ *06/6795597* 🌐 *www.ilpapirofirenze.it.*

TOYS

Al Sogno. If you're looking for quality toys that encourage imaginative play and learning, look no farther than Al Sogno. With an emphasis on the artistic as well as the multisensory, the shop has a selection of toys that are both discerning and individual, making them perfect for children of all ages. Carrying an exquisite collection of fanciful puppets, collectible dolls, masks, stuffed animals, and illustrated books, this Navona jewel is crammed top to bottom with beautiful and well-crafted playthings. If you believe that children's toys don't have to be high-tech, you will adore reliving some of your best childhood memories here. ✉ *Piazza Navona 53, corner of Via Agonale, Piazza Navona* ☎ *06/6864198* 🌐 *www.alsogno.net.*

Fodor's Choice ★ **Bartolucci.** Bartolucci attracts shoppers with a life-size Pinocchio pedaling furiously on a wooden bike. Inside is a shop that would have warmed Gepetto's heart. For more than 60 years and three generations, this family has been making whimsical, handmade curiosities out of pine, including clocks, bookends, bedside lamps, and wall hangings. You can even buy a child-size vintage car entirely made of wood, including the wheels. ✉ *Via dei Pastini 98, Piazza Navona* ☎ *06/69190894* 🌐 *www.bartolucci.com.*

Bertè. One of the oldest toy shops in Rome, Bertè carries a large selection of stuffed animals, dolls, Legos, and other collectibles. It specializes in dolls, both the crying, eating, and talking types, as well as the ribbon-bedecked old-fashioned beauties. ✉ *Piazza Navona 108, Piazza Navona* ☎ *06/6875011.*

La Città del Sole. La Città del Sole is the progressive parent's ideal store, chock-full of fair-trade and eco-friendly toys that share shelf space with retro and vintage favorites. With educational toys arranged by age, the store is a child-friendly browser's delight crammed with puzzles, gadgets, books, and toys in safe plastics and sustainable wood. The knowledgeable sales staff can help you choose. ✉ *Via della Scrofa 65, Piazza Navona* ☎ *06/68803805* 🌐 *www.cittadelsole.it.*

15

CAMPO DE' FIORI

Campo de' Fiori, one of Rome's most captivating piazzas, comes to life early in the morning, when merchants theatrically sell their best tomatoes, salami, artichokes, blood oranges, herbs, and spices. Around the piazza, labyrinthine streets are crowded with small shops to suit any budget.

BOOKS AND STATIONERY

Libreria del Viaggiatore. *Viaggiatore* means traveler, and this lovely little bookstore located on a quaint side street off Campo de' Fiori welcomes wandering, curious travelers. The shop stocks guidebooks, maps, travel journals, and poetry from all over the world, in English as well as French and Italian. ✉ *Via del Pellegrino 78, Campo de' Fiori* ☎ *06/68801048* 🌐 *www.libreriadelviaggiatore.com.*

CHILDREN'S CLOTHING

Rachele. Rachele is a small, charming shop tucked down a small alley not far from the Campo de' Fiori piazza. Most of the items of clothing are handmade by Rachele herself, and she only makes two of each piece, so you're getting something truly original. Choose from whimsical crocheted hats and a cute selection of pants, skirts, and rainbow-colored tops for tykes up to age 12. ✉ *Vicolo del Bollo 6–7, Campo de' Fiori* ☎ *06/6864975* 🌐 *www.racheleartchildrenswear.it.*

CLOTHING

Angelo di Nepi. This Roman designer makes women's pantsuits, dresses, and blouses in rich fabrics, bright colors, and bold patterns. There are two other shops in town, on Via Cola Di Rienzo and Via Frattina. ✉ *Via dei Giubbonari 28, Campo de' Fiori* ☎ *06/68133441* 🌐 *www.angelodinepi.it.*

SHOES, HANDBAGS, AND LEATHER GOODS

Ibiz–Artigianato in Cuoio. In business since 1970, this father-and-daughter team creates colorful, stylish leather handbags, purses, belts, and sandals. Choose from the premade collection or order something made to measure; the family workshop is right next door to the boutique. ✉ *Via dei Chiavari 39, Campo de' Fiori* ☎ *06/68307297.*

PIAZZA DI SPAGNA

The Piazza di Spagna area is considered to be the heart and soul of shopping in Rome, with all the international chains as well as independent shops. If your budget isn't big enough to binge at the high-end fashion houses along Via dei Condotti, try the more moderate shops down Via del Corso, where young Romans come to shop for jeans and inexpensive, trendy clothes. As you move towards Piazza del Popolo, at one end of Via del Corso, you'll find more antiques shops and galleries.

ANTIQUES

Antica Farmacia Pesci dal 1552. Likely Rome's oldest pharmacy, the Antica Farmacia is run by a family of pharmacists. The shop's 18th-century furnishings, herbs, and vases evoke Harry Potter's Diagon Ally; and while they don't carry Polyjuice Potion, the pharmacists can whip up a just-for-you batch of composite powders, syrups, capsules, gels, and creams to soothe what ails you. ✉ *Piazza Trevi 89* ☎ *06/6792210* Ⓜ *Barberini–Fontana di Trevi.*

Fratelli Alinari. The gallery store of the world's oldest photography firm, Fratelli Alinari was founded by brothers Leopoldo, Giuseppe, and Romualdo Alinari in 1852. Patrons can browse through a vast archive of prints, books, rare collotypes, and finely detailed reproductions of historical images, drawings, and paintings. ✉ *Via Alibert 16/a* ☎ *06/6792923* 🌐 *www.alinari.it* Ⓜ *Spagna.*

Galleria Benucci. With carved and gilded late Baroque and Empire period furniture and paintings culled from the noble houses of Italy's past, Galleria Benucci is a treasure trove. An establishment favored by professionals from Europe and abroad, this elegant gallery has a astonishing selection of objects in a hushed atmosphere where connoisseurs will find the proprietors only too happy to discuss their latest finds. ✉ *Via del Babuino 150/C* ☎ *06/36002190* 🌐 *www.galleriabenucci.it* Ⓜ *Spagna.*

BEAUTY AND PERFUME

Castelli Profumerie. Castelli Profumerie is a straightforward Italian perfume shop with one distinct advantage. Besides being a perfumed paradise offering an array of perfumes like Acqua di Parma, Bois 1920, Bond No. 9, and Comme de Garçons, their precise and courteous staff speak multiple languages and know their merchandise, making the experience a lot more pleasant than a dash through duty-free. There are several other locations around the city. ✉ *Via Frattina 18 & 54* ☎ *06/6790339* 🌐 *www.profumeriecastelli.com* Ⓜ *Spagna.*

Pro Fvmvm. The Durante family lives by the motto that a scent can be more memorable than a photograph. Started in 1996 by the grandchildren of Celestino Durante, Pro Fvmvm is fast on its way to becoming a new cult classic in Italian fragrance design. Each of the 20 scents is designed to be unisex and comes complete with a poem that describes the intention of the artisans. Pricey but worth it, some of their top-selling perfumes are Acqva e Zvcchero, Fiore d'Ambra, Thvndra, Volo Az 686 (named after a direct flight from Rome to the Caribbean), and Ichnvsa. There are four locations around the city. ✉ *Via Ripetta 10* ☎ *06/3200306* 🌐 *www.profumum.com.*

BOOKS AND STATIONERY

Anglo-American Book Co. A large and friendly English-language bookstore with more than 45,000 books, Anglo-American Book Co. has been a mecca for English-language reading material in Rome for more than 25 years. Whether you are a study-abroad student in need of an art history or archaeology textbook, or a visitor searching for a light read for the train, there is something for everyone here. Among shelves stuffed from floor to ceiling and sometimes several rows deep, book lovers can find British and American editions and easily spend hours just looking. The bilingual staff pamper browsers and do not rush or hover. ✉ *Via della Vite 102* ☎ *06/6795222* 🌐 *www.aab.it* Ⓜ *Spagna.*

Ex Libris. Founded in 1931 and one of the oldest antiquarian bookshops in Rome, Ex Libris has a distinctive selection of scholarly and collectible books from the 16th to 21st centuries that will make bookworms drool. The selection includes rare editions on art and architecture, music and theater, and literature and humanities, as well as maps and prints. ✉ *Via dell' Umiltà 77/a* ☎ *06/6791540* 🌐 *www.exlibrisroma.it* Ⓜ *Barberini–Fontana di Trevi.*

La Feltrinelli. As Rome's biggest bookseller, La Feltrinelli's main attraction is the Piazza Colonna flagship store. Ensconced in the elegant 19th-century Galleria Alberto Sordi, this mega-bookstore fills three floors with books, music, postcards, holiday items, and small gifts. A great place to explore Italian-style book shopping, there are 12 branches peppered throughout the city. The Torre Argentina shop also has a ticketing office for music and cultural events and a café tucked upstairs with refreshing snacks and good coffee. The Repubblica branch carries a large section of titles in many languages as well as a well-stocked foreign film selection. ✉ *Piazza Colonna 31/35* ☎ *06/69755001* 🌐 *www.lafeltrinelli.it* Ⓜ *Barberini–Fontana di Trevi.*

CERAMICS AND DECORATIVE ARTS

Le IV Stagioni. Le IV Stagioni stocks a colorful selection of traditional Italian pottery from well-known manufacturers like Capodimonte, Vietri, Deruta, Caltagirone, and Faenza. If you're looking for something alla Romana, opt for the brown glazed pots with a lacy white border and charming flower basket wall ornaments, made in the Rome area. ✉ *Via dell' Umiltà 30/b* ☎ *06/69941029* Ⓜ *Barberini–Fontana di Trevi.*

Marmi Line Gifts. For a wide variety of marble and alabaster objets d'art, Marmi Line offers three locations in central Rome. Beautifully worked into familiar shapes, their mesmerizing pieces of fruit make centerpieces that would make Caravaggio proud. If you want something distinctly Roman, choose a practical or whimsical item made from travertine, the stone used to build the Colosseum and Bernini's St. Peter's Colonnade. ✉ *Via dei Pastini 113* ☎ *06/69200711* Ⓜ *Barberini–Fontana di Trevi.*

Musa. Musa is the place to shop if you're looking for decorative ceramic accents. Be sure to pop up to the second floor, where you can find a fine array of extravagant hand-painted ceramic tiles from Vietri, a region renowned for the quality of its clays and artisanal ceramic tradition. Shipping can be arranged. Whether you're planning to tile an entire bathroom or just pick up a few pieces to use in your kitchen as hot plates, your house will have an Italian villa feel when you are done. ✉ *Via di Campo Marzio 39* ☎ *06/6871202* 🌐 *www.ceramichemusa.it.*

CHILDREN'S CLOTHING

Bonpoint. Bonpoint brings a little of Paris to Rome in fine French children's wear. The crème de la crème when it comes to styling, refinement, and price, Bonpoint's casual and classic children's clothing are both picture-perfect and fashion-forward. Well-heeled mums will appreciate their soft, cuddly onesies, and hand-stitched party dresses. ✉ *Piazza San Lorenzo in Lucina 25* ☎ *06/6871548* 🌐 *www.bonpoint.com.*

La Cicogna. A well-known designer children's clothier found throughout Italy with clothing for little ones from birth to age 14, La Cicogna is one-stop, name-brand shopping for antsy kids and tired parents. The stores carry clothes, shoes, baby carriages, and nursery supplies as well as child-size versions of designer names like Armani, Burberry, Guru, Timberland, Replay, Blumarine, and DKNY. ✉ *Via Frattina 138* ☎ *06/6791912.*

Pinco Pallino. Founded by Imelde Bronzieri and Stefano Cavalleri in 1980, Pinco Pallino has extraordinary clothing for boys and girls, be it a sedate tulle petal jumper or savvy sailor wear. Moms will find their latest lines for babies and tots absolutely delicious. ✉ *Via del Babuino 115* ☎ *06/69190549* 🌐 *www.pincopallino.it* Ⓜ *Spagna.*

Pùre Sermoneta. The mothership for fashionistas in the making, Pùre carries designer brands that include Fendi, Diesel, Dior, Juicy Couture, Nolita, and Miss Blumarine. The store has plush carpet to crawl on and children's clothes for newborns to age 12. ✉ *Via Frattina 111* ☎ *06/6794555* 🌐 *www.puresermoneta.it.*

CLOTHING

Dolce & Gabbana. Dolce and Gabbana met in 1980 when both were assistants at a Milan fashion atelier and opened their first store in 1982. With a modern aesthetic that screams sex appeal, the brand has always thrived on its excesses. The Rome store can be more than a little overwhelming with its glossy glamazons, but at least there is plenty of eye candy, masculine and feminine, with a spring line heavy of stars and sequins as well as enthusiastic fruits, flowers, and veggies. There's a second location on Via Condotti. ✉ *Piazza di Spagna 94–95* ☎ *06/6991592* 🌐 *www.dolcegabbana.it* Ⓜ *Spagna.*

Elena Mirò. Elena Mirò is an absolutely delectable Italian atelier making its mark designing clothes specifically for those who don't have the proportions of a 14-year-old. If your DNA gave you the curves of Mad Men's Joan Holloway, you will love the fact that this designer specializes in beautifully sexy clothes for curvy, European-styled women size 46 (U.S. size 12, UK size 14) and up. There are four locations in Rome. ✉ *Via Frattina 11–12* ☎ *06/6784367* 🌐 *www.elenamiro.it* Ⓜ *Spagna.*

Fodor's Choice ★ **Fendi.** Fendi has been a fixture of the Roman fashion landscape since "Mamma" Fendi first opened shop with her husband in 1925. With an eye for crazy genius, she hired Karl Lagerfeld, who began working with the group at the start of his career. His furs and runway antics have made him one of the world's most influential designers of the 20th century and brought international acclaim to Fendi along the way. Recent Lagerfeld triumphs include new collections marrying innovative textures, fabrics (cashmere, felt, and duchesse satin) with exotic skins like crocodile. Keeping up with technology, they even have an iPad case that will surely win a fashionista's seal of approval. The atelier, now owned by the Louis Vuitton group, continues to symbolize Italian glamour at its finest, though the difference in owners is noticeable. ✉ *Largo Carlo Goldoni 419–421* ☎ *06/3344501* 🌐 *www.fendi.com* Ⓜ *Spagna.*

Galassia. Galassia has ingenious and avant-garde women's styles by an A-list of designers including Gaultier, Westwood, Issey Miyake, and Yamamoto. If you're the type who dares to be different and in need of some closet therapy, you will love the extravagant selection, which gives the store a look that cannot be found elsewhere. ✉ *Via Frattina 20* ☎ *06/6797896* 🌐 *www.galassiaroma.com* Ⓜ *Spagna.*

15

Giorgio Armani. One of the most influential designers of Italian haute couture, Giorgio Armani creates fluid silhouettes and dazzling evening gowns with décolletés so deep they'd make a grown man blush, his signature cuts made with the clever-handedness and flawless technique that you only achieve working with tracing paper and Italy's finest fabrics over the course of a lifetime. His menswear collection uses traditional textiles like wide-ribbed corduroy and stretch jersey in nontraditional ways while staying true to a clean, masculine aesthetic. It's true that exotic runway ideas and glamorous celebrities give Armani saleability, but his staying power is casual Italian elegance with just the right touch of whimsy and sexiness. Want to live la bella vita for longer than your Roman holiday? Armani is also selling luxury apartments in Rome at Cavour 220, complete with his personalized interiors. ✉ *Via Condotti 77* ☎ *06/6991460* 🌐 *www.giorgioarmani.com* Ⓜ *Spagna.*

Fodor's Choice ★ **Gucci.** As the glamorous fashion label turns 90, the success of the double-G trademark brand is unquestionable. Survival in luxury fashion depends on defining market share, and creative director Frida Giannini has proven she knows the soul of the House of Gucci. Tom Ford may have made Gucci the sexiest brand in the world, but it's today's reinterpreted horsebit styles and Jackie Kennedy scarves that keep the design house on top. And while Gucci remains a fashion must for virtually every A-list celebrity, their designs have moved from heart-stopping sexy rock star to something classically subdued and retrospectively feminine. There's another store on Via Borgognona. ✉ *Via Condotti 8* ☎ *06/6790405* 🌐 *www.gucci.com* Ⓜ *Spagna.*

Krizia. Designer Mariuccia Mandelli borrowed the name Krizia from the title of Plato's unfinished dialogue on women's vanity to market her designs by. Born in 1933, she began designing dresses for her dolls at age 8. The designer's collections have gone through many top stylists and have recently returned to their original stylized roots. The current prêt-à-porter line emphasizes the use of black and dove grey, mixed with animal prints; it's dramatic, yet classy: wearing Krizia will get you noticed. ✉ *Piazza di Spagna 87* ☎ *06/6793772* 🌐 *www.krizia.it* Ⓜ *Spagna.*

Fodor's Choice ★ **Laura Biagiotti.** For 40 years Laura Biagiotti has been a worldwide ambassador of Italian fashion. Considered the Queen of Cashmere, her soft-as-velvet pullovers have been worn by Sophia Loren and her snow-white cardigans were said to be a favorite of the late Pope John Paul II. Princess Diana even sported one of Biagiotti's cashmere maternity dresses. Be sure to indulge in her line of his-and-her perfumes. ✉ *Via Mario de' Fiori 26* ☎ *06/6791205* 🌐 *www.laurabiagiotti.it* Ⓜ *Spagna.*

Mariella Burani. Highly wearable and never boring, Mariella Burani has classy yet sensual ready-to-wear that borrows judiciously from several of the company's other principal lines. Recently they have begun adding jewelry and accessories to complete their fashion portfolio. ✉ *Via Borgognona 29* ☎ *06/6790630* 🌐 *www.mariellaburani.com.*

Missoni. Notable for its bohemian knitwear designs with now-legendary patterns of zigzags, waves, and stripes (some of which are influenced by folk art), as well as elegant eveningwear and must-have swimsuits, Missoni is unlike other Italian fashion families: in three generations there have been neither vendettas nor buyouts by huge multinational conglomerates to stain their colorful history. And while their eye-popping designs have polarized critics, they continue to deliver exquisite collections, mesmerizing the buying public. ✉ *Piazza di Spagna 78* ☎ *06/6792555* 🌐 *www.missoni.it* Ⓜ *Spagna.*

Fodor's Choice ★ **Patrizia Pepe.** One of Florence's best-kept secrets for up-and-coming fashions, Patrizia Pepe emerged on the scene in 1993 with designs both minimalist and bold, combining classic styles with low-slung jeans and jackets with oversize lapels that are bound to draw attention. Her line of shoes are hot-hot-hot for those who can walk in stilts. It's still not huge on the fashion scene as a stand-alone brand, but take a look at this shop before the line becomes the next fast-tracked craze. ✉ *Via Frattina 44* ☎ *06/6781851* 🌐 *www.patriziapepe.com.*

Fodor's Choice ★ **Prada.** Not just the devil, but also serious shoppers wear Prada season after season, especially those willing to sell their souls for one of their ubiquitous handbags. If you are looking for that blend of old-world luxury with a touch of fashion-forward finesse, you'll hit pay dirt here. Recent handbag designs have a bit of a 1960s Jackie Kennedy feel, and whether you like them will hinge largely on whether you find Prada's signature retro-modernism enchanting. You'll find the Rome store more service-focused than the New York City branches—a roomy elevator delivers you to a series of thickly carpeted rooms where a flock of discreet assistants will help you pick out dresses, shoes, lingerie, and fashion accessories. The men's store is located at Via Condotti 88/90, and women's is at down the street at 92/95. ✉ *Via Condotti 88/90 & 92/95* ☎ *06/6790897* 🌐 *www.prada.com* Ⓜ *Spagna.*

Renard. A leather boutique that scrupulously selects from superior quality leather hides, Renard carries leathers tanned with natural extracts—not chemicals—a slow and natural process that maintains the hides' original properties. Choose from classic leather blazers, trench coats, and skirts in sporty and sophisticated colors and styles. Be sure to eye their racy motorcycle styles, perfect for windswept and gutsy Ducati rides. ✉ *Via dei Due Macelli 53* ☎ *06/6797004* Ⓜ *Cavour*.

Salvatore Ferragamo. One of the top-10 most-wanted men's footwear brands, Salvatore Ferragamo has been providing Hollywood glitterati and discerning clients with unique handmade designs for years. Ferragamo fans will think they have died and followed the white light when they enter this store. The Florentine design house also specializes in handbags, small leather goods, men's and women's ready-to-wear, and scarves and ties. Men's styles are found at Via Condotti 65, women's at 73/74. Want to sleep in Ferragamo style? Their splendid luxury Portrait Suites Hotel is on the upper floors. ✉ *Via Condotti 65 & 73/74* ☎ *06/6781130* 🌐 *www.ferragamo.com* Ⓜ *Spagna*.

15

Save the Queen!. A hot Florentine design house with exotic and creative pieces for women and girls with artistic and eccentric frills, cut-outs, and textures, Save the Queen! has one of the most beautiful shops in the city, with window displays that are works of art unto themselves. The store is chock-full of Baroque-inspired dresses, shirts, and skirts that are ultrafeminine and not the least bit discreet. Pieces radiate charming excess, presenting a portrait of youthful chic. ✉ *Via del Babuino 49* ☎ *06/36003039* 🌐 *www.savethequeen.com* Ⓜ *Spagna*.

Trussardi. A classic design house moving in a youthful direction, Trussardi has been symbolized by its greyhound logo since 1973. Today, with Gaia Trussardi at the helm and following in her father and brother's footsteps, the line is making use of leather accent pieces like suede tunics and wider belts. Tru Trussardi (in Galleria Alberto Sordi) addresses a modern woman's need for both luxury and comfort in upscale daily wear. ✉ *Via Condotti 49/50* ☎ *06/6780280* 🌐 *www.trussardi.com* Ⓜ *Spagna*.

Fodor's Choice ★

Valentino. Since taking the Valentino reins a few years ago, creative directors Maria Grazia Chiuri and Pier Paolo Piccioli have faced numerous challenges, the most basic being keeping Valentino true to Valentino after the designer's retirement in 2008. Both served as accessories designers under Valentino for more than a decade and understand exactly how to make the next generation of Hollywood stars swoon. Spagna's sprawling boutiques showcase designs with a romantic edginess: think kitten heels and or a show-stopping prêt-à-porter evening gown worthy of the Oscars. ✉ *Via Condotti 15* ☎ *06/6739420* 🌐 *www.valentino.com* Ⓜ *Spagna*.

Versace. Occupying the ground floor of a noble palazzo with wrought-iron gratings on the windows and mosaic pavement, Versace is as imaginative as the store is ostentatious. Here shoppers will find apparel, jewelry, watches, fragrances, cosmetics, and home furnishings. The designs are as flamboyant as Donatella and Allegra (Gianni's niece), drawing heavily on the sexy rocker gothic underground vibe. Be sure to check out the Via Veneto location for prêt-à-porter and jewelry; there's also another boutique in Piazza di Spagna with clothes, shoes, and sexy handbags. ✉ *Via Bocca di Leone 23* ☎ *06/6691773* 🌐 *www.versace.com* Ⓜ *Spagna.*

CLOTHING: MEN'S

Fodor's Choice ★ **Brioni.** Founded in 1945 and hailed for its impeccable craftsmanship and flawless execution, the Brioni label is known for attracting and keeping the best men's tailors in Italy where the exacting standards require that custom-made suits are designed from scratch and measured to the millimeter. For this personalized line, the menswear icon has 5,000 spectacular fabrics to select from. As thoughtful as expensive, one bespoke suit made from wool will take a minimum of 32 hours to create. Their prêt-à-porter line is also praised for peerless cutting and stitching. Past and present clients include Clark Gable, Donald Trump, Barack Obama, and, of course, James Bond. And they say clothing doesn't make the man? There's another location on Via Condotti. ✉ *Via Barberini 79, Piazza di Spagna* ☎ *06/484517* 🌐 *www.brioni.com* Ⓜ *Barberini–Fontana di Trevi.*

Eddy Monetti. Eddy Monetti is a conservative but upscale men's store featuring jackets, sweaters, slacks, and ties made out of wool, cotton, and cashmere. Sophisticated and pricey, the store carries a range of stylish British- and Italian-made pieces. The women's store is at Via Borgognona 35. ✉ *Via Borgognona, 5/B-6/A, Piazza di Spagna* ☎ *06/6783794* 🌐 *www.eddymonetti.com* Ⓜ *Spagna.*

Ermenegildo Zegna. Ermenegildo Zegna, of the unpronounceable name, is a 100-year-old powerhouse of men's clothing. Believing that construction and fabric are the key, Zegna is the master of both. Most of the luxury brand's suits cost in the €1,500–€2,500 range, with the top of the line, known as "Couture," costing considerably more. But don't despair if your pockets aren't that deep: their ready-to-wear dress shirts are suit-defining. ✉ *Via Condotti 58* ☎ *06/69940678* 🌐 *www.zegna.com* Ⓜ *Spagna.*

DEPARTMENT STORES

La Rinascente. Italy's best-known department store, La Rinascente is where Italian fashion mogul Giorgio Armani got his start as a window dresser. Recently relocated inside the Galleria Alberto Sordi, the store has a phalanx of ready-to-wear designer sportswear and blockbuster handbags and accessories. The upscale clothing and accessories are a hit with the young and well dressed, while retail turf is geared toward people on lunch breaks and the ubiquitous tourist. The Piazza Fiume location has more floor space and a wider range of goods, including a housewares department. ✉ *Galleria Alberto Sordi, Piazza Colonna* ☎ *06/6784209* 🌐 *www.rinascente.it* Ⓜ *Spagna.*

FLEA MARKETS

Soffitta Sotto i Portici. Held every first and third Sunday of the month from 9 am until sunset, this colorful vintage has more than 100 stands selling antique jewelry, furniture, artworks, and collector's items. ✉ *Piazza Augusto Imperatore* ☎ *06/36005345* Ⓜ *Spagna.*

FOOD AND WINE

Buccone. A landmark wine shop inside the former coach house of the Marquesse Cavalcabo, Buccone has 10 layers of shelves packed with quality wines and spirits ranging in price from a few euros to several hundred for rare vintages. The old atmosphere has been preserved with the original wood-beamed ceiling and an antique till. You can also buy sweets, biscuits, and packaged candy perfect for inexpensive gifts. Lunch is available daily and dinner is served Friday and Saturday (reservations essential). Book a week in advance, and they can also give you a guided wine tasting, highlighting vintages from many of Italy's important wine-producing regions. ✉ *Via di Ripetta 19/20, Piazza di Spagna* ☎ *06/3612154* 🌐 *www.enotecabuccone.com.*

HOME DECOR

Cesari. Since 1946 Cesari is where Italian brides traditionally buy their trousseaux. Precious velvets, silks, cottons, damasks, and taffeta abound and are shippable internationally. Famous for their personalized line of bedspreads, tablecloths, lingerie, and embroidered linens, they supply high-end hotels as well as old-fashioned girls of all ages. ✉ *Via del Babuino 195* ☎ *06/3613456* 🌐 *www.cesari.com* Ⓜ *Spagna, Flaminio.*

Frette. Classic, luxurious, colorful, timeless, and fun, there is nothing like Frette's bed collections. A leader in luxurious linens and towels for the home and hotel industry since 1860, their sophisticated bed linens in cotton satine, percale, and silk are just what the doctor ordered for a great night's sleep. Be sure to look for their Dreamscapes collection, which introduces a romantic, fantastical theme seen in the surreal landscapes of Fellini films, such as *8 1/2* and *Voice of the Moon*. There are a few locations around the city. ✉ *Piazza di Spagna 11* ☎ *06/6790673* 🌐 *www.frette.com.*

JEWELRY

Borsalino Boutique. Borsalino fedoras and Panama hats have donned the heads of many silver screen icons including Humphrey Bogart and Gary Cooper. They may be expensive, but there is a reason for the exorbitant prices. Considered by many to be the Cadillac of fedoras, the dashing Borsolino has been a staple of the fashionable Italian man since 1857. Today, Borsalino retains its unmistakable class, style, and elegance. Few hats are made with such exacting care and attention, and the company's milliners still use machines that are more than 100 years old. Borsalino also has boutiques near the Pantheon and Piazza di Spagna. ✉ *Piazza del Popolo 20* ☎ *06/32650838* 🌐 *www.borsalino.it* Ⓜ *Flaminio.*

Bulgari. Every capital city has its famous jeweler, and Bulgari is to Rome what Tiffany is to New York and Cartier is to Paris. The jewelry giant has developed a reputation for meticulous craftsmanship melded with noble metals and precious gems. In the middle of the 19th century, the great-grandfather of the current Bulgari brothers began working as a silver jeweler in his native Greece and is said to have moved to Rome with less than 1,000 lire in his pocket. Today the megabrand emphasizes colorful and playful jewelry as the principal cornerstone of its aesthetic. Popular collections include Parentesi, Bulgari-Bulgari and B.zero1. ✉ *Via Condotti 10* ☎ *06/696261* 🌐 *www.bulgari.com* Ⓜ *Spagna.*

LINGERIE

Brighenti. Brighenti looks like what it is—a traditional Roman shop from a gentler era, replete with a marble floor and a huge crystal chandelier suspended overhead. Sensual silk nightgowns and exquisite peignoirs that have a vintage silver screen feel are displayed downstairs. Upstairs are sumptuous vintage-inspired swimsuits that will make you feel like Marlene Dietrich. There's a second location nearby on Via Borgognona. ✉ *Via Frattina 7/8* ☎ *06/6791484* 🌐 *www.brighentiboutique.it* Ⓜ *Barberini–Fontana di Trevi, Spagna.*

Marisa Padovan. The place to go for exclusive, made-to-order lingerie and bathing suits, Marisa Padovan has been sewing for Hollywood starlets like Audrey Hepburn and the well-heeled women of Rome for more than 40 years. Whether you want to purchase a ready-made style trimmed with Swarovski crystals and polished turquoise stones or design your own bespoke bikini or one-piece, their made-to-measure precision will have you looking like Rita Hayworth. ✉ *Via delle Carrozze 81–82* ☎ *06/6793946* 🌐 *www.marisapadovan.it* Ⓜ *Spagna.*

La Perla. La Perla is the go-to for beautifully crafted lingerie and glamorous underwear for that special night, a bridal trousseau, or just to spoil yourself on your Roman holiday. In partnership with Jean Paul Gaultier, the brand has just launched a swimwear line alongside his second lingerie collection. If you like decadent finery that is both stylish and romantic, you will find something here to make you feel like a goddess. There are silk boxers and briefs for gents here, too. ✉ *Via Bocca di Leone 28* ☎ *06/69941934* 🌐 *www.laperla.com* Ⓜ *Spagna.*

Yamamay. Specializing in sophisticated lingerie for the fashion-conscious woman, Yamamay designs are a perfect combination of femininity and sexiness. Branches of the store are located throughout the city. ✉ *Via del Corso 309* ☎ *06/6991196* 🌐 *www.yamamay.com* Ⓜ *Spagna.*

SHOES, HANDBAGS, AND LEATHER GOODS

A. Testoni. Amedeo Testoni was born in 1905 in Bologna, the heart of Italy's shoemaking territory. In 1929 he opened his first shop and began producing shoes as artistic as the Cubist and Art Deco artwork of the period. His shoes have adorned the art-in-motion feet of Fred Astaire and proved that lightweight shoes could be comfortable and luxurious and still make heads turn. Today the Testoni brand includes an extraordinary women's collection and a sports line that is relaxed without losing its artistic heritage. The soft, calfskin sneakers are a dream, as are the matching messenger bags. ✉ *Via Condotti 80* ☎ *06/6788944* 🌐 *www.testoni.com* Ⓜ *Spagna.*

Fodor's Choice ★

Braccialini. Founded in 1954 by Florentine stylist Carla Braccialini and her husband, Braccialini—currently managed by their sons—makes bags that are authentic works of art in delightful shapes, such as little gold taxis or Santa Fe stagecoaches. The delightfully quirky beach bags have picture postcard scenes of Italian resorts made of brightly colored appliquéd leather: Be sure to check out their eccentric Temi (Theme) creature bags; the opossum-shaped handbag made out of crocodile skin makes a richly whimsical fashion statement. There's a second location at the Galleria Alberto Sordi. ✉ *Via Mario De' Fiori 73* ☎ *06/6785750* 🌐 *braccialini.it* Ⓜ *Spagna.*

Bruno Magli. Bruno Magli has high-end, well-crafted, classically styled shoes for both men and women. Magli and his siblings Marino and Maria learned the art of shoemaking from their father and grandfather. From its humble family origins to the corporate design powerhouse it has become today, Bruno Magli footwear always has kept the focus on craftsmanship: it's not uncommon for 30 people to touch each shoe during the course of its manufacture. ✉ *Via Condotti 6* ☎ *06/69292121* 🌐 *www.brunomagli.it* Ⓜ *Spagna.*

Di Cori. Di Cori packs a lot of gloves into a tiny space, offering a rainbow of color choices. Made of the softest lambskin, and lined with silk, cashmere, rabbit fur, or wool, a pair of these gloves will ensure warm and fashionable hands. They also carry a smaller selection of unlined, washable versions. ✉ *Piazza di Spagna 53* ☎ *06/6784439* 🌐 *www.dicorigloves.it* Ⓜ *Spagna.*

15

Fausto Santini. Fausto Santini gives a hint of extravagance in minimally decorated shoes that fashion mavens love. For almost 20 years, Santini has successfully attracted an avant-garde clientele of both men and women who flock to his preppy-hipster/nerdy-chic shoes, which are bright and colorful and sport deconstructed forms in plush, supple leathers that scream to be tried on. ■ **TIP→ A second shop at Via Cavour 106 sells last season's shoes at a deep discount.** ✉ *Via Frattina 120* ☎ *06/6784114* 🌐 *www.faustosantini.it* Ⓜ *Spagna.*

Fratelli Rossetti. An old-world company with modern aspirations, Fratelli Rossetti is well known to shoe hounds for their captivatingly comfortable Jasper loafers and discreet women's pumps. Their motto has long been sophisticated yet discreet, but while continuing to offer classic power elegance with an emphasis on quality, luxury, and craftsmanship, their new line is a bit more playful. Be sure to check out their new blue suede shoes designed by a Southern California designer. ✉ *Via Borgognona 5/a* ☎ *06/6782676* 🌐 *www.rossetti.it* Ⓜ *Spagna.*

Furla. Furla has 15 franchises in Rome alone. Its flagship store, to the left of the Spanish Steps, sells bags like hot cakes. Be prepared to fight your way through crowds of passionate handbag lovers, all anxious to possess one of the delectable bags, wallets, or watch straps in ice-cream colors. ✉ *Piazza di Spagna 22* ☎ *06/69200363* 🌐 *www.furla.com* Ⓜ *Spagna.*

Gherardini. In business since 1885, Gherardini has taken over a deconsecrated church and slickly transformed it into a showplace for their label, which is known for its retro handbags and logo-stamped synthetic materials. Gherardini's leather totes, sling bags, and soft luggage have become classics and are worth the investment. Be sure to take a look at their limited edition Japanese flag bag "Gherardini for Japan"; proceeds will go to the Japanese Red Cross supporting those affected by the 2011 Tōhoku earthquake. ✉ *Via Belsiana 48* ☎ *06/6795501* 🌐 *www.gherardini.it.*

La Coppola Storta. La Coppola Storta describes a type of Sicilian beret and the jaunty way it was worn by Mafiosi. They say the more the hat was twisted to the side, the more connected the wearer was to organized crime. In defiance of Mafia influence across Sicily, activist Guido Agnello helped to open a factory in San Giuseppe specializing in the manufacture of these colorful caps, giving jobs to local sewers, many of whom were previously unemployed or connected to the black market. With the help of some of Italy's best designers, they have created a line of dapper Coppola for adults, children, and even puppies, which have become a sought-after fashion accessory and an unexpected ambassador for the anti-mafia struggle all over the world. With every color and fabric imaginable, hat prices start at €55. ✉ *Via Frattina 52, Piazza di Spagna* ☎ *06/69191079* 🌐 *www.lacoppolastorta.it* Ⓜ *Spagna.*

Fodor's Choice ★ **Saddlers Union.** Reborn on the mythical artisan's street, Via Margutta, across the street from Federico Fellini's old house, Saddlers Union first launched in 1957 and quickly gained a cult following among those who valued Italian artistry and the traditional aesthetic. Jacqueline Kennedy set the trend of classical elegance by sporting Saddlers Union's rich saddle-leather bucket bag. Closed in 2004, one of Italy's finest labels is back, representing everything for which Rome leatherwork has become famous. If you're searching for a sinfully fabulous handbag in a graceful, classic shape or that "I have arrived" attorney's briefcase, you will find something guaranteed to inspire envy. Items are made on-site with true artistry and under the watchful eye of Angelo Zaza, one of Saddlers Union's original master artisans. The prices are high, but so is the quality. ✉ *Via Margutta 11, Piazza di Spagna* ☎ *06/32120237* 🌐 *www.saddlersunion.com* Ⓜ *Flaminio, Spagna.*

Schostal. At the end of the 19th century when ladies needed petticoats, corsets, bonnets, or white or colored stockings made of cotton thread, wool, or silk, it was inevitable for them to stop at Schostal. A Piazza di Spagna fixture since 1870, the shop still preserves that genteel ambience. Fine-quality shirts come with spare collars and cuffs. Ultraclassic underwear, handkerchiefs, and pure wool and cashmere are available at affordable prices. There's a second location at Piazza Euclide. ✉ *Via Fontanella Borghese 29* ☎ *06/6791240* 🌐 *www.schostalroma.com* Ⓜ *Spagna.*

Sermoneta. Sermoneta allures with its stacks of nappa leather, deerskin, and pigskin gloves in all colors. To produce one pair of gloves requires the skill and precision of at least 10 artisans. To satisfy demand, they carry a diverse selection of hand-stitched gloves (lined or unlined) for men and women. You can even find opera-length gloves for those special evenings or you can have your purchases personalized with initials, logos, and other designs. ✉ *Piazza di Spagna 61* ☎ *06/6791960* 🌐 *www.sermonetagloves.com.*

Fodor's Choice ★ **Tod's.** With just 30 years under its belt, Tod's has grown from a small family brand into a global powerhouse so wealthy that it has donated €20 million to renovate the Colosseum. Tod's has gathered a cult following among style mavens worldwide, due in large part to owner Diego Della Valle's equally famous other possession: Florence's soccer team. The shoe baron's trademark is his simple, understated designs. Sure to please are his light and flexible slip-on Gommini driving shoes with rubber-bottomed soles for extra driving-pedal grip. Now you just need a Ferrari. There are also locations on Via Condotti and Via Borgogona. ✉ *Via Fontanella di Borghese 56a–57* ☎ *06/68210066* 🌐 *www.tods.com* Ⓜ *Spagna.*

STATIONERY

Fodor's Choice ★ **Pineider.** Pineider has been making exclusive stationery in Italy since 1774; this is where Rome's aristocratic families have their wedding invitations engraved and their stationery personalized. For stationery and desk accessories, hand-tooled in the best Florentine leather, it has no equal. There's a second location on Via dei Due Macelli. ✉ *Via di Fontanella Borghese 22, Piazza di Spagna* ☎ *06/6878369* 🌐 *www.pineider.com* Ⓜ *Spagna.*

REPUBBLICA

In this neighborhood you'll find bookstores, souvenir shops, and places to shop for decorative pieces like Roman masks or busts.

BOOKS AND STATIONERY

Libreria IBS. If you like discounts on remainder stock and secondhand books, come to Libreria IBS (formerly Mel Bookstore). Browse through the large basement and find a treasure trove of marked-down merchandise as well as a modest selection of English-language paperbacks. Upstairs, shop for books in Italian on a variety of subjects or pick up a DVD of Roman Holiday. Afterward, relax with your purchases while you treat yourself to a coffee and dessert in the spacious art deco–style café. ✉ *Via Nazionale 254–255, Repubblica* ☎ *06/4885405* 🌐 *www.ibs.it* Ⓜ *Repubblica.*

CERAMICS AND DECORATIVE ARTS

Il Giardino di Domenico Persiani. Nestled in a cool courtyard garden under the shade of an expansive oak tree is refreshing open-air terra-cotta shop Il Giardino di Domenico Persiani. Whether you're looking for a chubby cherub, a replica of Bacchus, or your very own Bocca della Verità, this is your chance to bring a little piece of Rome home to your garden. With a large selection of handmade Roman masks, busts, flower pots, and vases, there is something here for anyone with a green thumb. ✉ *Via Torino 92, Repubblica* ☎ *06/4883886* Ⓜ *Repubblica–Teatro dell'Opera.*

FOOD AND WINE

Trimani Vinai a Roma dal 1821. For more than 180 years Trimani Vinai a Roma dal 1821, occupying an entire block near the Termini train station, has had the city's largest selection of wines, champagne, spumante, grappa, and other liqueurs. With more than 1,000 bottles to choose from and knowledgeable wine stewards, Trimani will give you the opportunity to explore Europe's diverse wine regions without leaving the city. ✉ *Via Goito 20, Repubblica* ☎ *06/4469661* 🌐 *www.trimani.com* Ⓜ *Castro Pretorio.*

SHOPPING MALLS

Il Forum Termini. Rome's handiest central shopping mall is Il Forum Termini, a cluster of shops that stay open until 10 pm (even on Sunday), conveniently located directly inside Rome's biggest train station, Stazione Termini. In a city not known for its convenient shopping hours, this "shop before you hop/buy before you fly" hub is a good spot for last-minute goodies or a book for your train or airplane ride. There are more than 50 shops, including the ever-popular United Colors of Benetton, L'Occitane, Sephora, and Optimissimo, which has more than 3,000 super-stylish glasses and sunglasses by top Italian designers. There is even a supermarket for your picnic lunch on the train. ✉ *Stazione Temini, Repubblica* 🌐 *www.romatermini.com* Ⓜ *Termini.*

TRASTEVERE

Across the Tiber from the city center, Trastevere, one of Rome's most charming neighborhoods, is filled with authentic trattorias, ivy-draped buildings, funky boutiques, lively wine bars and pubs, and the biggest open-air flea market in Rome. The neighborhood attracts a lot of tourist traffic and an American college student crowd thanks to the bustling nightlife, but it's also a local favorite.

BOOKSTORES

Almost Corner Bookshop. This Trastevere bookstore is a well-loved meeting point for English-speaking residents and visitors to this lively neighborhood. Owner Dermot O'Connell, from Kilkenny, Ireland, stocks an inviting selection ranging from translated Italian classics to today's latest bestsellers. With a reputation for being able to find anything a customer requests, the small shop is a good place to special order books, and it has a wonderful selection of obscura if you've got the time to poke around. There's now a second shop near Campo dei Fiori. ✉ *Via del Moro 45, Trastevere* ☎ *06/5836942.*

CERAMICS AND DECORATIVE ARTS

Polveri del Tempo. This is the place to go if you are looking for decorative timepieces. At Polveri del Tempo you will find sundials and handcrafted hourglasses—including a giant 18-hour model that is quite memorable. The owner, architect and craftsman Adrian Rodriguez, will tell you how monks once used marked candles, like those on sale here, to note the passage of time. ✉ *Via del Moro 59, Trastevere* ☎ *06/05880704* 🌐 *www.polvereditempo.com.*

FLEA MARKETS

Fodor's Choice ★ **Porta Portese.** Rome's biggest flea market is at Porta Portese, which welcomes 100,000 visitors every Sunday from 7 am until 2 pm. Larger than the St-Ouen in Paris, this mecca of flea markets is easily accessible with Tram 8. Like one vast yard sale, the market disgorges mountains of new and secondhand clothing, furniture, pictures, old records, used books, vintage clothing, and antiques—all at rock-bottom prices (especially if you're adept at haggling). There is a jovial atmosphere, with an aroma of foods wafting in the air and people crowding around the stalls, hoping to pick up a 1960s Beatles album or a rare Art Deco figurine. Bring your haggling skills, and cash—stallholders don't accept credit cards and the nearest ATM is a hike. ■ **TIP→ Keep your valuables close; pickpockets lurk around here.** ✉ *Via Portuense and adjacent streets between Porta Portese and Via Ettore Rolli, Trastevere.*

FOOD AND WINE

Antica Caciara Trasteverina. The fresh ricotta cheese in the windows of this old-world Trastevere deli catches your eye, enticing you to come inside. Behind the counter you will find heaping helpings of ham, salami, Sicilian anchovies, and burrata cheese from Puglia, as well as Parmigiano-Reggiano and local wines. ✉ *Via San Francesco a Ripa 140a/b, Trastevere* ☎ *06/5812815* 🌐 *www.anticacaciara.it.*

SHOES AND ACCESSORIES

Fodor's Choice ★ **Joseph DeBach.** The best-kept shoe secret in Rome and open only in the evenings, when Trastevere diners begin to strut their stuff, Joseph DeBach has weird and wonderful creations that are more art than footwear. Entirely handmade from wood, metal, and leather in his small and chaotic studio, his abacus wedge is worthy of a museum. Styles are outrageous "wow" and sometimes finished with hand-painted strings, odd bits of comic books, newspapers, or other unexpected baubles. Individually signed and dated, his shoes are distributed, in very small numbers, in London, Paris, Tokyo, and New York. ✉ *Vicolo del Cinque 19, Trastevere* ☎ *06/5562756.*

15

TESTACCIO

Testaccio is foodie-land, with specialty food and wine shops, as well as an abundance of great Roman eateries.

FOOD AND WINE

Fodor's Choice ★ **Volpetti.** A Roman institution, Volpetti sells excellent, if pricey, cured meats and salami. Its rich aromas and flavors are captivating from the moment you enter the store. Food selection includes genuine buffalo-milk mozzarella, Roman pecorino, salami, sauces, spreads, oils, balsamic vinegars, desserts, gift baskets, and much more. ✉ *Via Marmorata 47* ☎ *06/5742352* 🌐 *www.volpetti.com* Ⓜ *Piramide.*

MONTI, SAN LORENZO, AND SAN GIOVANNI

MONTI

Today, Rome's oldest quarter is a lively neighborhood for the boho-chic thirtysomethings of Rome. You'll find fun, eclectic shops here selling homemade chocolate, tea, and other gourmet goodies, clothing, antique watches, and more.

CLOTHING

Anteprima. Anteprima is filled with revolutionary ready-to-wear separates that make a bold statement. Carrying a large selection of day and evening wear constructed with lustrous fabrics, the style here is offbeat. A deliberate contradiction of colors make the clothing dazzlingly original. Friendly and helpful staff have a unique eye for putting together accessories and shoes from their ever-changing collection. ✉ *Via delle Quattro Fontane 38–40* ☎ *06/4828445* 🌐 *www.anteprimadimoda.com* Ⓜ *Repubblica.*

Hydra. An avant-garde clothing shop for older teens and twentysomethings who believe clothing should make a statement, Hydra has styles that range from voluptuous Betty Boop retro dresses to indie underground to in-your-face T-shirts that would make your grandmother blush. ✉ *Via Urbana 139* ☏ *06/48907773* 🌐 *www.hydra2.it* Ⓜ *Cavour.*

Fodor's Choice ★ **Le Gallinelle.** This tiny boutique lives in a former butcher's shop—hence the large metal hooks. Owner Wilma Silvestri transforms vintage, ethnic, and contemporary fabrics into retro-inspired clothing with a modern edge without smelling like mothballs from your great aunt Suzie's closet. ✉ *Via Panisperna 61* ☏ *06/4881017* 🌐 *www.legallinelle.it* Ⓜ *Cavour.*

CLOTHING: MEN'S

Mimmo Siviglia. Eighty-year-old Mimmo Siviglia is shirtmaking at its apex. The epitome of an old-world master tailor, he has been one of Rome's best-kept secrets for more than 50 years. To achieve a perfectly smooth look, Siviglia knows he has to cut the pattern just right, accounting for the person's shoulder to ensure there are no wrinkles around the collarbone. If you know your fine cloth, you'll enjoy discussing the merits of high-end fabrics such as Alumo, Albini, or Riva. Dress-shirt aficionados will be impressed by his attention to each customer and precise dedication to each order. Once his daughter has your size in the computer, future orders can be shipped anywhere in the world. ✉ *Via Urbana 14a* ☏ *06/48903310, 34/88710079 (English speaking)* 🌐 *www.mimmosiviglia.com* Ⓜ *Cavour.*

FOOD AND WINE

La Bottega del Cioccolata. At the first shop you'll smell when walking down this picturesque street, master chocolate maker Maurizio Proietti and his father before him have been making chocolates as mouth-watering and beautiful as those seen in the famous film *Chocolat*. There's a second location near Piazza del Popolo. ✉ *Via Leonina 82* ☏ *06/4821473* 🌐 *www.labottegadelcioccolato.it* Ⓜ *Cavour.*

JEWELRY

Art Privé. Just off Monti's principal square is the small jewelry shop where Tiziana Salzano makes multistrand torsade necklaces using the finest silverworks and a combination of boldly hued raw rubies and other semiprecious gemstones. Each piece is unique and cannot be exactly duplicated, so if you see a piece that steals your heart be sure to grab it. ✉ *Via Leonina 8* ☏ *06/47826347* Ⓜ *Cavour.*

Orologi e Design. Orologi e Design specializes in nostalgic mechanical watches and chronographs from the 1900s through the 1970s. Whether you are looking for a solid gold dress watch or a vintage World War II military pilot's chronograph, chances are you'll find the piece you are looking for here. Have an heirloom piece that has stopped working or that needs a little tuning? Two expert watchmakers have the parts and skilled precision to clean, regulate, and repair your grandfather's vintage timepiece and get it tick-tocking again in no time. ✉ *Via Urbana 123, Monti* ☏ *06/4742284* Ⓜ *Cavour.*

SAN LORENZO

This university district is a good place to hunt for unique boho-chic clothing and Roman pottery.

CERAMICS AND DECORATIVE ARTS

Le Terre di AT. Le Terre di AT is a modern potters' workshop nestled in the belly of San Lorenzo, Rome's burgeoning university district. Working on the premises, artist Angela Torcivia creates vases, cups, ceramic jewelry, and necklaces. Her pieces have an otherworldly style, combining ancient shapes with fiery contrasting colors, and are modern while still paying homage to the rich history of Roman clay pottery. **■ TIP→ You must call to make an appointment before visiting the shop.** ✉ *Via degli Ausoni 13* ☎ *3406916969* 🌐 *www.leterrediat.it.*

CLOTHING

Fodor's Choice ★ **L'Anatra all'Arancia.** Repetto ballerinas, roomy handbags, and funky dresses make L'Anatra all'Arancia one of the best local secrets of boho San Lorenzo. Its window display showcases innovative designer clothes from Marina Spadafora, Antik Batik, See by Chloé, and Donatella Baroni (the store's owner and buyer). Leaning towards the alternative with an eclectic selection of handpicked Italian and French labels, Donatella carries sinful perfumes from L'Artisan Parfumeur and beautiful jewelry from the line of Serge Thoraval. ✉ *Via Tiburtina 105* ☎ *06/4456293* Ⓜ *Termini, Castro Pretorio.*

Pifebo. A sensational vintage-clothing emporium packed with thousands of items, fire-engine red Pifebo has a loyal following of university students, offbeat musicians, and even the occasional costume designer. Specializing in '70s, '80s and '90s clothes and shoes, the prices are great, the feel is welcoming, and the merchandise turns over quickly. The shop has two other locations—one in Monti and in San Giovanni. ✉ *Via dei Volsci 101* ☎ *06/64870813* 🌐 *www.pifebo.com.*

Red Frame Shop. A small and somewhat hard-to-find boutique that is identified only by its red-brick framed door, Red Frame Shop is open odd hours, so don't be afraid to knock if the door is locked. The shop is filled with wool and cotton sweaters and skirts, each handmade with attention to detail. If you don't find your size or color, let the owner know and they can make it for you. ✉ *Via degli Equi 70.*

SAN GIOVANNI

San Giovanni has a wide selection of department stores and chains, as well as a great market.

FLEA MARKET

Via Sannio. Though not strictly a flea market, the *mercato* Via Sannio is entirely without pretension. Here you can find military surplus, leather jackets, cosmetics, and many other bargains. Also expect great deals on shoes—you can buy good-quality name-brand shoes that have served their time only as shop-window displays. Open Monday through Saturday 8 am–2 pm. ✉ *Near La Basilica di San Giovanni in Laterano* Ⓜ *Como San Giovanni.*

16

SIDE TRIPS FROM ROME

WELCOME TO SIDE TRIPS FROM ROME

TOP REASONS TO GO

★ **Ostia Antica:** Perhaps even more than Pompeii, the excavated port city of ancient Rome conveys a picture of everyday life in the days of the empire.

★ **Tivoli's Villa d'Este:** Hundreds of fountains cascading and shooting skyward (one even plays music on organ pipes) will delight you at this spectacular garden.

★ **Castelli Romani:** Be a Roman for a day and enjoy an escape to the ancient hilltop wine towns on the city's doorstep.

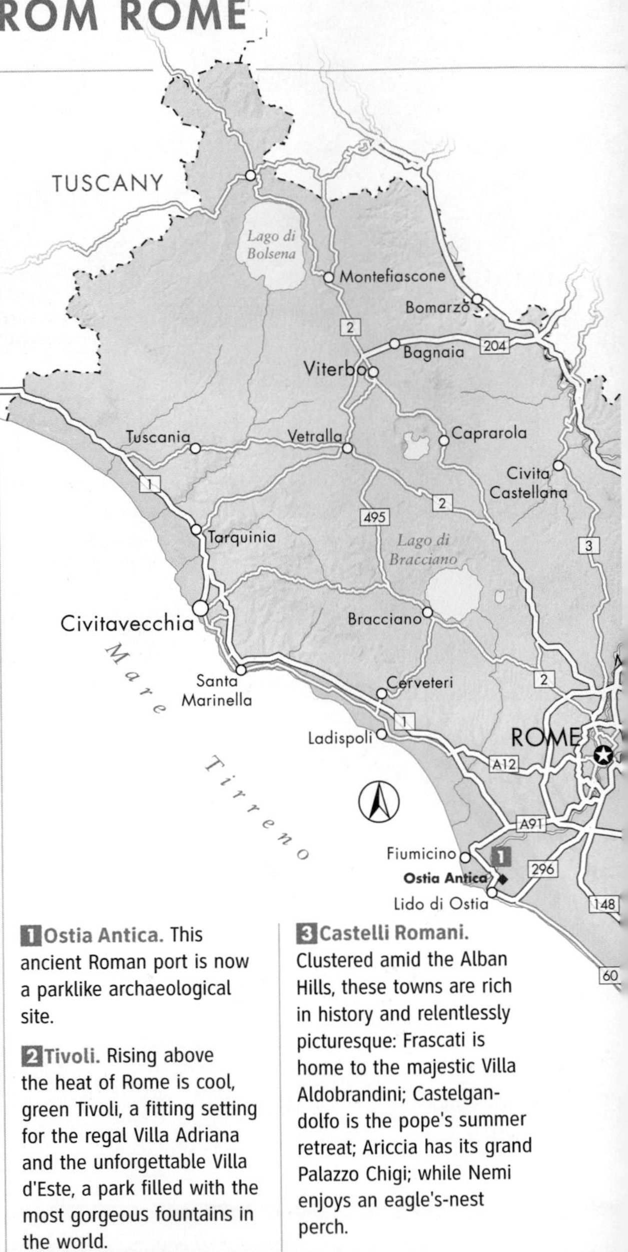

1 Ostia Antica. This ancient Roman port is now a parklike archaeological site.

2 Tivoli. Rising above the heat of Rome is cool, green Tivoli, a fitting setting for the regal Villa Adriana and the unforgettable Villa d'Este, a park filled with the most gorgeous fountains in the world.

3 Castelli Romani. Clustered amid the Alban Hills, these towns are rich in history and relentlessly picturesque: Frascati is home to the majestic Villa Aldobrandini; Castelgandolfo is the pope's summer retreat; Ariccia has its grand Palazzo Chigi; while Nemi enjoys an eagle's-nest perch.

GETTING ORIENTED

All roads may indeed lead to Rome, but for thousands of years emperors, popes, and princes have been heading *fuori porta* (beyond the gates) for a change of pace from city life. To the west lies ancient Ostia Antica. East of Rome is Tivoli, famed for retreats ranging from the noble—the Villa d'Este—to the imperial—Villa Adriana (Hadrian's Villa). South lie the enchanting towns of the Castelli Romani.

Updated by Margaret Stenhouse

Lazio, the region that encompasses Rome, the capital, is often bypassed by foreign visitors. This is a pity, as the area, which stretches from the Apennine mountain range to the Mediterranean coast, holds dozens of fascinating towns and villages, as well as scenic lakes, national parks, and forests. A trip outside of Rome introduces you to a more intimate aspect of Italy, where local customs and feast days are still enthusiastically observed, and local gastronomic specialties take pride of place on restaurant menus. Despite these small towns' proximity to the capital and the increased commuter traffic congestion of today, they still each manage to preserve their individual character.

Ostia Antica, ancient Rome's seaport, is one of the region's top attractions—it rivals Pompeii in the quality of its preservation, and for evocativeness and natural beauty, it easily outshines the Roman Forum. Emperors, cardinals, and popes have long escaped to green and verdant retreats in nearby Tivoli and the Alban Hills, and their amazing villas, palaces, and gardens add to nature's allure. So if the screeching traffic and long lines at the Colosseum start to wear on you, do as the Romans do—get out of town. There's plenty to see and do.

PLANNING

MAKING THE MOST OF YOUR TIME

Ostia Antica is in many ways an ideal day trip from Rome: it's fascinating, it's not far from the city, it's reachable by public transit, and it takes about half a day to do. Villa d'Este and Villa Adriana in Tivoli also make for a manageable, though fuller, day trip. There's so much to see at these two sights alone, but be sure to also visit Tivoli's picturesque

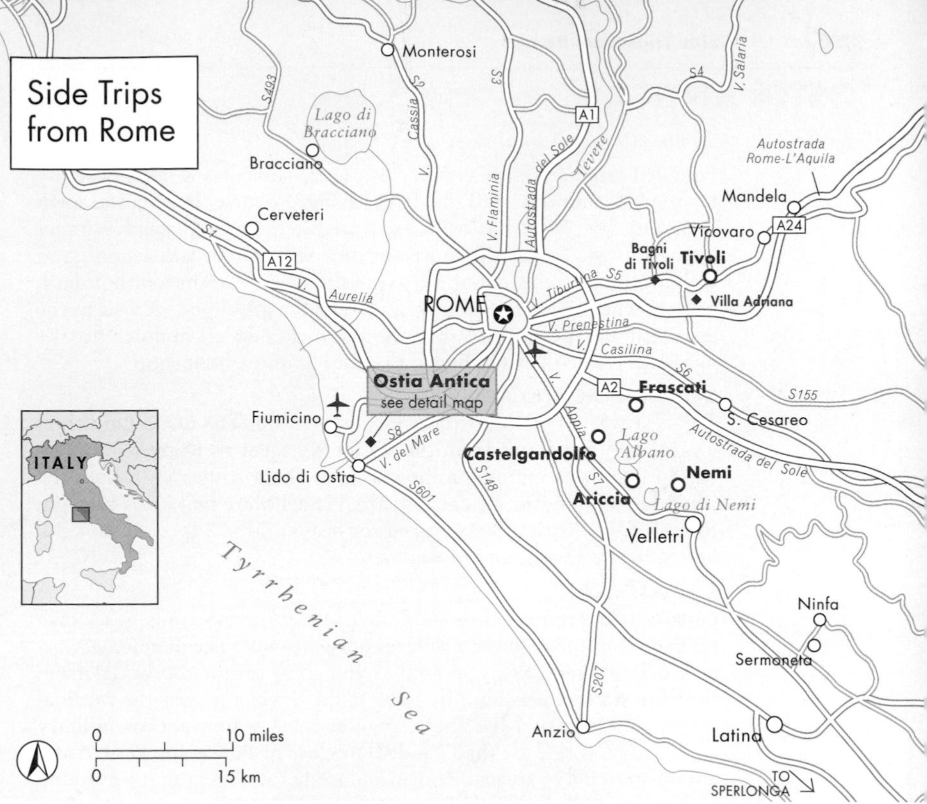

gorge, which is strikingly crowned by an ancient Roman temple to Vesta (now it's part of the famed Sibilla restaurant).

GETTING HERE AND AROUND

There's reliable public transit from Rome to Ostia Antica or Tivoli. For other destinations in the region, a car is a big advantage—going by train or bus can add hours to your trip, and the routes and schedules are often puzzling.

COTRAL. This is the regional bus company. ☎ *800/174471* 🌐 *www.cotralspa.it.*

Trenitalia. Also known as Ferrovie dello Stato. National and regional rail service. ☎ *892021* 🌐 *www.trenitalia.com.*

RESTAURANTS

Prices in the dining reviews are the average cost of a main course at dinner, or, if dinner is not served, at lunch.

HOTELS

Former aristocratic houses with frescoed ceilings, agriturismi farmhouses, luxury spas, and cozy bed-and-breakfasts are just a few of the lodging options here. You won't find much in the way of big chain hotels, though.

Prices in the reviews are the lowest cost of a standard double room in high season.

OSTIA ANTICA

30 km (19 miles) southwest of Rome.

Founded around the 4th century BC, Ostia served as Rome's port city for several centuries until the Tiber changed course, leaving the town high and dry. What has been excavated here is a remarkably intact Roman town. To get the most out of a visit, fair weather and good walking shoes are essential. To avoid the worst extremes of hot days, be here when the gates open or go late in the afternoon. A visit to the excavations takes two to three hours, including 20 minutes for the museum. Inside the site, there's a snack bar and a bookshop.

GETTING HERE AND AROUND

The best way to get to Ostia Antica is by train. The Ostia Lido train leaves every half hour from the station adjacent to Rome's Piramide Metro B subway station, stopping off at Ostia Antica en route. The trip takes 35 minutes. By car, take the Via del Mare that leads off from Rome's EUR district. Be prepared for heavy traffic, especially at peak hours, on weekends, and in summer.

EXPLORING

Castello della Rovere. Before exploring Ostia Antica's ruins, it's worth taking a tour through the medieval *borgo* (town). The distinctive Castello della Rovere, easily spotted as you come off the footbridge from the train station, was built by Pope Julius II when he was the cardinal bishop of Ostia in 1483. Its triangular form is unusual for military architecture. Inside are (badly faded) frescoes by Baldassare Peruzzi and a small museum of ancient Roman and medieval pottery that was found on the site. ✉ *Piazza della Rocca* ☎ *06/56358013* 🌐 *www.ostiaantica.net* 🎫 *Free* 🕓 *Tours Thurs.–Sat. 11, Sun. 11 and noon.*

Fodor's Choice ★ **Scavi di Ostia Antica** (*Ostia Antica excavations*). Tidal mud and wind-blown sand covered the ancient port town, which lay buried until the beginning of the 20th century, when it was extensively excavated. A cosmopolitan population of rich businessmen, wily merchants, sailors, slaves, and their respective families once populated the city. The great warehouses were built in the 2nd century AD to handle huge shipments of grain from Africa; the *insulae* (forerunners of the modern apartment building) provided housing for the city's growing population. Due to the combined assaults of the barbarians and the malaria-carrying mosquito, as well as the Tiber changing course, the port was eventually abandoned. The Ostiense Museum inside the ruined city displays sculptures, mosaics, and objects of daily use found on the site. A cafeteria is at the entrance. ✉ *Viale dei Romagnoli 717* ☎ *06/56350215* 🌐 *www.ostiaantica.beniculturali.it* 🎫 *€8, includes Museo Ostiense* 🕓 *Tues.–Sun. 8:30–1 hr before sunset.*

WHERE TO EAT

$ ITALIAN ✕ **Cipriani.** Under the shadow of the castle in the medieval town, this welcoming trattoria is decorated with reproductions of fresco fragments from a Roman palace. The prix-fixe menu, which has a choice of three first courses, three second courses, fruit, and coffee, is a good value. The owner, Fabrizio Ciprian, speaks English and will be happy

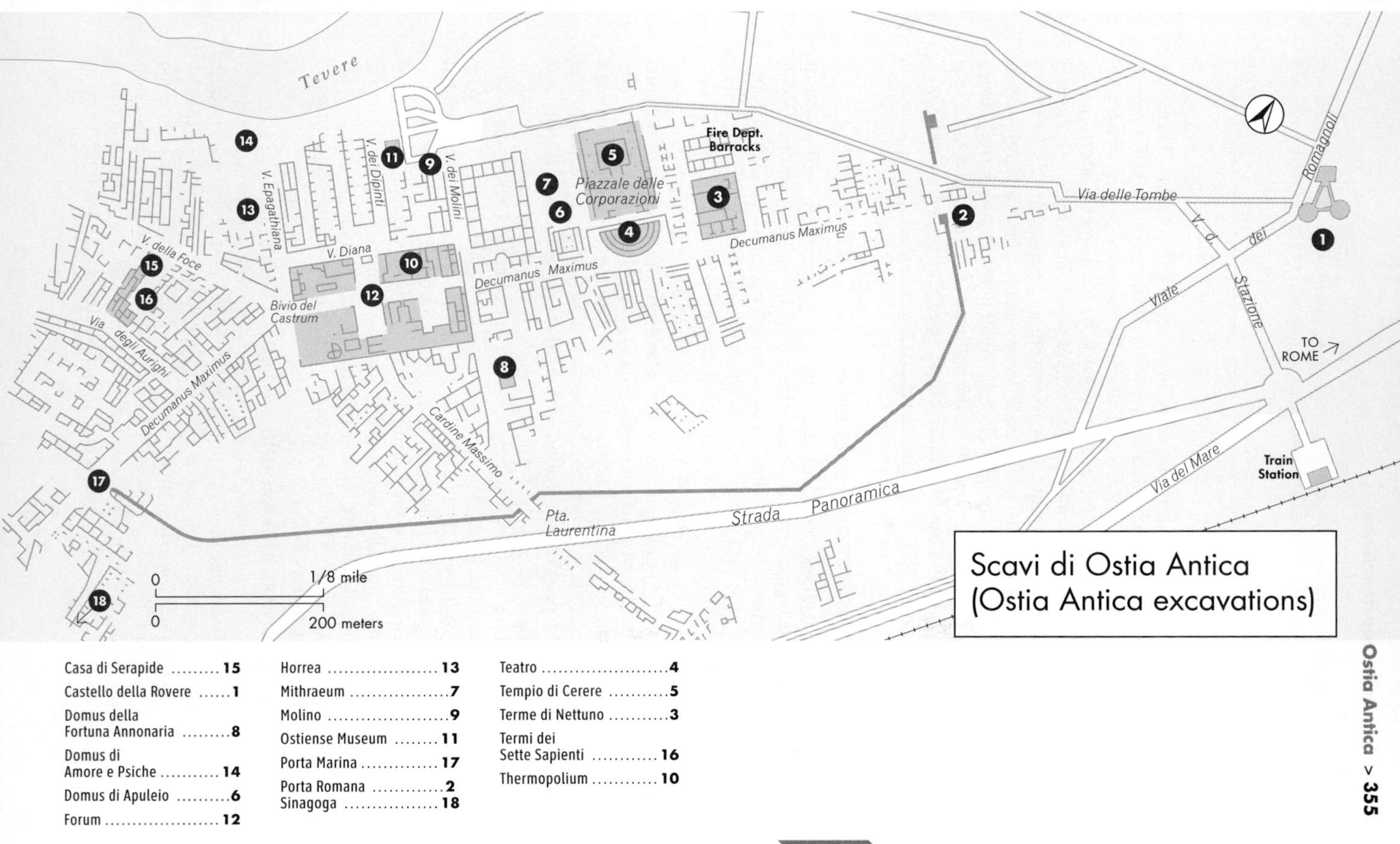
Scavi di Ostia Antica
(Ostia Antica excavations)
Tevere
Fire Dept. Barracks
Piazzale delle Corporazioni
Romagnoli
Via delle Tombe
V. d.
dei
Viale
Stazione
TO ROME
Train Station
Via del Mare
Strada Panoramica
Pta. Laurentina
Cardine Massimo
Decumanus Maximus
Decumanus Maximus
V. Diana
V. dei Dipinti
V. dei Molini
V. Epagathiana
V. della Foce
Via degli Aurighi
Decumanus Maximus
Bivio del Castrum
0
1/8 mile
0
200 meters
Casa di Serapide 15
Castello della Rovere 1
Domus della Fortuna Annonaria 8
Domus di Amore e Psiche 14
Domus di Apuleio 6
Forum 12
Horrea 13
Mithraeum 7
Molino 9
Ostiense Museum 11
Porta Marina 17
Porta Romana 2
Sinagoga 18
Teatro 4
Tempio di Cerere 5
Terme di Nettuno 3
Termi dei Sette Sapienti 16
Thermopolium 10

to guide you in your choice. *Average main: €10* *Via del Forno 11* *06/56352956* *www.ristoranteciprian i.com* *Closed Wed. No lunch Sun.*

TIVOLI

Tivoli is a five-star draw, its attractions being its two villas. There's an ancient one in which Hadrian reproduced the most beautiful monuments in the then-known world, and a Renaissance one, in which Cardinal Ippolito d'Este put a river to work for his delight. Unfortunately, the Via Tiburtina from Rome to Tivoli passes through miles of industrial areas with chaotic traffic. Grit your teeth and persevere. It'll be worth it. In the heart of this gritty shell lie two pearls that are rightly world famous. You'll know you're close to Tivoli when you see vast quarries of travertine marble and smell the sulfurous vapors of the little spa, Bagni di Tivoli. Both sites in Tivoli are outdoors and entail walking.

TIVOLI

36 km (22 miles) northeast of Rome.

In ancient times just about anybody who was anybody had a villa in Tivoli, including Crassus, Trajan, Hadrian, Horace, and Catullus. Tivoli fell into obscurity in the medieval era until the Renaissance, when popes and cardinals came back to the town and built villas showy enough to rival those of their extravagant predecessors.

Nowadays Tivoli is small but vibrant, with winding streets and views over the surrounding countryside. The deep Aniene River gorge runs right through the center of town, and comes replete with a romantically sited bridge, cascading waterfalls, and two jewels of ancient Roman architecture that crown its cliffs—the round Temple of Vesta (or the Sybil, the prophetess credited with predicting the birth of Christ) and the ruins of the rectangular Temple of the hero-god Tibur, the mythical founder of the city. These can be picturesquely viewed across the gorge from the Villa Gregoriana park, named for Pope Gregory XVI, who saved Tivoli from chronic river damage by diverting the river through a tunnel, weakening its flow. An unexpected side effect was the creation of the Grande Cascata (Grand Cascade), which shoots a huge jet of water into the valley below. You may also want to set your sights on the Antico Ristorante Sibilla, set right by the Temple of Vesta. From its dining terrace you can take in one of the most memorably romantic landscape views in Italy.

GETTING HERE AND AROUND

Unless you have nerves of steel, it's best not to drive to Tivoli. Hundreds of businesses line the Via Tiburtina from Rome and bottleneck traffic is nearly constant. You can avoid some, but not all, of the congestion by taking the Roma–L'Aquila toll road. Luckily, there's abundant public transport. Buses leave every 15 minutes from the Ponte Mammolo stop on the Metro A line. The ride takes an hour. Regional Trenitalia trains connect from both Termini and Tiburtina stations and will have you in

Tivoli in under an hour. Villa d'Este is in the town center, and there is a bus service from Tivoli's main square to Hadrian's Villa.

VISITOR INFORMATION

PIT (Punto Informativo Turistico) (*Tivoli tourist office*). ✉ *Piazzale Nazioni Unite* ☎ *0774/313536* 🌐 *www.comune.tivoli.rm.it/pit* ⏲ *Tues.–Sun. 10–1 and 4–6.*

EXPLORING

Villa Adriana (*Hadrian's Villa*). This astonishingly grand 2nd-century villa was an emperor's theme park: an exclusive retreat below the ancient settlement of Tibur where the marvels of the classical world were reproduced for a ruler's pleasure. Hadrian, who succeeded Trajan as emperor in AD 117, was a man of genius and intellectual curiosity, fascinated by the accomplishments of the Hellenistic world. From AD 125 to 134, architects, laborers, and artists worked on the villa, periodically spurred on by the emperor himself when he returned from another voyage full of ideas for even more daring constructions (he also gets credit for Rome's Pantheon). After his death in AD 138 the fortunes of his villa declined as it was sacked by barbarians and Romans alike. Many of his statues and decorations ended up in the Vatican Museums, but the expansive ruins are nonetheless compelling. It's not the single elements but the delightful effect of the whole that makes Hadrian's Villa so great. Oleanders, pines, and cypresses growing among the ruins heighten the visual impact. To help you get your bearings, get a map, which is issued free with the audio guides (€5). A visit here takes at least two hours. In summer visit early to take advantage of cool mornings. ✉ *Bivio di Villa Adriana off Via Tiburtina, 6 km (4 miles) southwest of Tivoli* ☎ *0774/382733 reservations* 🎫 *€8* ⏲ *Daily 9–1 hr before sunset.*

16

Fodor's Choice ★ **Villa d'Este.** Created by Cardinal Ippolito d'Este in the 16th century, this villa in the center of Tivoli was the most amazing pleasure garden of its day: it still stuns visitors with its beauty. Este (1509–72), a devotee of the Renaissance celebration of human ingenuity over nature, was inspired by the excavation of Villa Adriana. He paid architect Pirro Ligorrio an astronomical sum to create a mythical garden with water as its artistic centerpiece. To console himself for his seesawing fortunes in the political intrigues of his time (he happened to be cousin to Pope Alexander VI), he had his builders tear down part of a Franciscan monastery to clear the site, then divert the Aniene River to water the garden and feed the fountains—and what fountains: big, small, noisy, quiet, rushing, running, and combining to create a late-Renaissance masterpiece in which sunlight, shade, water, gardens, and carved stone create an unforgettable experience. To this day, several hundred fountains cascade, shoot skyward, imitate birdsong, and simulate rain. The musical **Fontana dell'Organo** has been restored to working order: the organ plays a watery tune every two hours from 10:30 to 6:30 (until 2:30 in winter). Romantics will love the night tour of the gardens and floodlit fountains, available on Friday and Saturday from July until September. Allow at least an hour for the visit, and bear in mind that there are a lot of stairs to climb. ✉ *Piazza Trento 1* ☎ *0774/312070* 🌐 *www.villadestetivoli.info* 🎫 *€8* ⏲ *Tues.–Sun. 8:30–1 hr before sunset.*

WHERE TO EAT

$$$ ITALIAN Fodor's Choice ★ **Antico Ristorante Sibilla.** This famed restaurant should be included among the most beautiful sights of Tivoli. Built in 1730 beside the circular Roman Temple of Vesta and the Sanctuary of the Sybil, the terrace garden has a spectacular view over the deep gorge of the Aniene River, with the thundering waters of the waterfall in the background. The food, wine, and service standards are all high, and seasonal produce and local dishes are a major part of the menu. Be sure to sample the house specialty—a lavish choice of antipasti served on individual triple-tiered trays that resemble old-fashioned cake stands. Dishes for the first course may include pappardelle made with spelt and dressed with garlic, olive oil, and tiny "datterini" tomatoes. For the second course, local lamb; sucking pig; and a salad with ricotta, herbs, honey, and prunes may all make an appearance. The desserts are equally strong contenders for your attention. *Average main: €25 ✉ Via della Sibilla 50 ☎ 0774/335281 ⊕ www.ristorantesibilla.com ⊗ Closed Mon.*

WHERE TO STAY

$ B&B/INN **Adriano.** The guest rooms in this converted 19th-century mansion tend to be small, with an overabundance of chintz drapes, but the position right next to the ruins of the Emperor Hadrian's palatial residence is ample compensation. **Pros:** wonderful location; peaceful garden; attentive service. **Cons:** busloads of tourists disembark under the windows; restaurant can be crowded. *Rooms from: €80 ✉ Largo Yourcenar 2, Via di Villa Adriana 194 ☎ 0774/382235 ⊕ www.hoteladriano.it 10 rooms ⊗ Closed in Jan. Breakfast.*

$ HOTEL **Hotel Torre Sant'Angelo.** A former monastery and residence of the Massimo princes now offers comfortable guest rooms well equipped with modern amenities; best of all, it overlooks the old town, the Aniene Falls, and the Temple of the Sybil. **Pros:** 21st-century comfort in a historic mansion house; pool; competitive rates. **Cons:** isolated location a mile out of town. *Rooms from: €100 ✉ Via Quintilio Varo ☎ 0774/332533 ⊕ www.hoteltorresangelo.it 25 rooms, 10 suites Breakfast.*

THE CASTELLI ROMANI

The "castelli" aren't really castles, as their name would seem to imply. They're little towns that are scattered on the slopes of the Alban Hills near Rome. And the Alban Hills aren't really hills, but extinct volcanoes. There were castles here in the Middle Ages, however, when each of these towns, fiefs of rival Roman lords, had its own fortress to defend it. Some centuries later, the area became given over to villas and retreats, notably the pope's summer residence at Castelgandolfo, and the 17th- and 18th-century villas that transformed Frascati into the Beverly Hills of Rome. Arrayed around the rim of an extinct volcano that encloses two crater lakes, the string of picturesque towns of the Castelli Romani are today surrounded by vineyards, olive groves, and chestnut woods—no wonder overheated Romans have always loved to escape here.

Ever since Roman times the Castelli towns have been renowned for their wine. In the narrow, medieval alleyways of the oldest parts you can still find old-fashioned taverns where the locals sit on wooden benches, quaffing the golden nectar straight from the barrel. Traveling around the countryside, you can also pop into some of the local vineyards, where they will be happy to give you a tasting of their wines. Exclusive local gastronomic specialties include the bread of Genzano, baked in traditional wood-fire ovens, the *porchetta* (roast suckling pig) of Ariccia, and the *pupi* biscuits of Frascati, shaped like women or mermaids with three or more breasts (an allusion to ancient fertility goddesses). Each town has its own feasts and saints' days, celebrated with costumed processions and colorful events. Some are quite spectacular, like Marino's annual Wine Festival in October, where the town's fountains flow with wine; or the Flower Festival of Genzano in June, when an entire street is carpeted with millions of flower petals, arranged in elaborate patterns.

FRASCATI

20 km (12 miles) south of Rome.

It's worth taking a stroll through Frascati's lively old center. Via Battisti, leading from the Belvedere, takes you into Piazza San Pietro with its imposing gray-and-white cathedral. Inside is the cenotaph of Prince Charles Edward, last of the Scottish Stuart dynasty, who tried unsuccessfully to regain the British Crown, and died an exile in Rome in 1788. A little arcade beside the monumental fountain at the back of the piazza leads into Market Square, where the smell of fresh baking will entice you into the Purificato family bakery to see the traditional pupi biscuits, modeled on old pagan fertility symbols.

Take your pick from the cafés and trattorias fronting the central Piazzale Marconi, or do as the locals do—buy fruit from the market gallery at Piazza del Mercato, then get a huge slice of porchetta from one of the stalls, a hunk of *casareccio* bread, and a few *ciambelline frascatane* (ring-shaped cookies made with wine), and take your picnic to any one of the nearby *cantine* (homey wine bars), and settle in for some sips of tasty, inexpensive vino.

GETTING HERE AND AROUND

An hourly train service along a single-track line through vineyards and olive groves takes you to Frascati from Termini station. The trip takes 45 minutes. By car, take the Via Tuscolano, which branches off the Appia Nuova road just after St. John Lateran in Rome, and drive straight up.

VISITOR INFORMATION

Frascati Point (tourism office) ✉ *Piazza G. Marconi 5* ☎ *06/94015378* 🌐 *www.prontocastelli.it/frascati* ⏲ *Weekdays 8–8, weekends 10–8.*

EXPLORING

Abbey of San Nilo. In Grottaferrata, a busy village a couple of miles from Frascati, the main attraction is a walled citadel founded by St. Nilo, who brought his group of Basilian monks here in 1004, when he was 90. The order is unique in that it's Roman Catholic but observes Greek Orthodox rites.

The fortified abbey, considered a masterpiece of martial architecture, was restructured in the 15th century by Antonio da Sangallo for the future Pope Julius II. The abbey church, inside the second courtyard, is a jewel of oriental opulence, with glittering Byzantine mosaics and a revered icon set into a marble tabernacle designed by Bernini. The Farnese chapel, leading from the right nave, contains a series of frescoes by Domenichino.

If you make arrangements in advance you can visit the library, which is one of the oldest in Italy. The abbey also has a famous laboratory for the restoration of antique books and manuscripts, where Leonardo's *Codex Atlanticus* was restored in 1962 and more than a thousand precious volumes were saved after the disastrous Florence flood in 1966. ✉ *Corso del Popolo 128, Grottaferrata* ☎ *06/9459309* 🌐 *www.abbaziagreca.it* 🎫 *Free* 🕒 *Daily 6:30–12:30 and 3:30–6:30.*

Villa Aldobrandini. Frascati was a retreat of prelates and princes, who built magnificent villas on the sun-drenched slopes overlooking the Roman plain. The most spectacular of these is the 16th-century Villa Aldobrandini, which dominates Frascati's main square from the top of its steeply sloped park.

The villa itself is not open to the public, but the garden is now a public park, and you can walk in to admire the sweeping pathways lined with stone balustrades, box hedges, and the spectacular Baroque Teatro d'Acqua, the sort of showy sculpture group with water features that was a must-have garden adornment for every 16th-century millionaire, in this case Cardinal Pietro Aldobrandini, Pope Clement VIII's favorite nephew. The half circle of sculptures of mythical figures that adorn the "theater" reflect the grandeur and wealth of a prince of the church who thought nothing of diverting the entire water supply of the surrounding area to make his fountains perform. These days, the fountains only play on special occasions. To get into the gardens, you have to use a side entrance, which is on the road going up the left side of the villa. You can also see another former water theater on the grounds of nearby Villa Torlonia, which is also a public park. ✉ *Via Cardinale Massaia* ☎ *06/9421434* 🎫 *Free* 🕒 *Garden: Mon.–Fri. 9–5, 9–6 in summer.*

WHERE TO EAT

$$$ ROMAN ✕ **Antica Fontana Grottaferrata.** Across the road from the Abbey of San Nilo lies one of Grottaferrata's most esteemed restaurants, run by the Consoli family since 1989. The decor is rustic but elegant, with plants hanging from the ceiling and rows of polished antique copper pans and molds decorating the walls. Tables are well spaced, and the soft lighting helps make meals here relaxing and congenial. In summer, you can eat outside. Try the specialty antipasti, the fettuccine with porcini, or the gnocchi with radicchio. 💲 *Average main: €25* ✉ *Via Domenichino 24–26, Grottaferrata* ☎ *06/9413687* ✍ *Reservations essential* 🕒 *Closed Mon.*

$ ROMAN ✕ **Il Grottino Frascati.** This former wine cellar just beyond Frascati's market square is now an old-fashioned and cheerful trattoria serving traditional Roman dishes. The pasta and gnocchi are all homemade, and you'll also find old favorites on the menu like pasta carbonara, fettuccine with porcini, and saltimbocca, all lovingly supervised by the owner, Alfredo. In summer you can sit under an awning outside, where you can enjoy the sweeping view over the plain and hills of the Roman countryside. 💲 *Average main: €10* ✉ *Viale Regina Margherita 41–43* ☎ *06/94289772* 🌐 *www.trattoriailgrottino.it* 💳 *No credit cards* 🕒 *Closed Thurs.*

$$$ ITALIAN **Osteria Del Fico Vecchio.** This coaching inn, dating to the 16th century, is on an old Roman road a couple of miles outside Frascati. It has a charming garden shaded by the old fig tree that gave the place its name. The dining room has been tastefully renovated, preserving many of old-fashioned features. The menu offers a wide choice of typical Roman dishes, such as spaghetti *cacio e pepe* (spaghetti with sheep's cheese and pepper) and *abbacchio allo scottadito* (literally "burn your fingers grilled lamb"). Do not confuse this with the more modern Ristorante Al Fico across the road. *Average main: €25* *Via Anagnini 257* *06/9459261* *www.alfico.it.*

$$ HOTEL Fodor's Choice ★ **Park Hotel Villa Grazioli.** One of the region's most famous residences, this elegant patrician villa halfway between Frascati and Grottaferrata is now a first-class hotel, though the standard-issue guest rooms are a bit of a letdown amid the frescoed salons. **Pros:** wonderful views of the countryside; elegant atmosphere; professional staff. **Cons:** difficult to find; some rooms could do with some renovation. *Rooms from: €160* *Via Umberto Pavoni 19, Grottaferrata* *06/9454001* *www.villagrazioli.com* *60 rooms, 2 suites* *Breakfast.*

16

CASTELGANDOLFO

8 km (5 miles) southwest of Frascati, 25 km (15 miles) south of Rome.

This little town is the pope's summer retreat. It was the Barberini Pope Urban VIII who first headed here, eager to escape the malarial miasmas that afflicted summertime Rome; before long, the city's princely families also set up country estates around here.

The 17th-century **Villa Pontificia** has a superb position overlooking Lake Albano and is set in one of the most gorgeous gardens in Italy; unfortunately, neither the house nor the park is open to the public (although crowds are admitted into the inner courtyard for papal audiences). On the little square in front of the palace there's a fountain by Bernini, who also designed the nearby Church of San Tommaso da Villanova, which has works by Pietro da Cortona.

The village has a number of interesting craft workshops and food purveyors, in addition to the souvenir shops on the square. On the horizon, the silver astronomical dome belonging to the Specola Vaticana observatory—one of the first in Europe—where the scientific Pope Gregory XIII indulged his interest in stargazing, is visible for miles around.

GETTING HERE AND AROUND

There's an hourly train service for Castelgandolfo from Termini station (Rome–Albano line). Otherwise, buses leave frequently from the Anagnina terminal of the Metro A subway. The trip takes about 30 minutes. By car, take the Appian Way from San Giovanni in Rome and follow it straight to Albano, where you branch off for Castelgandolfo (about an hour, depending on traffic).

EXPLORING

FAMILY **Lakeside Lido.** Lined with restaurants, ice-cream parlors, and cafés, this is favorite spot for Roman families to relax. No motorized craft are allowed on the lake, but you can rent paddleboats and kayaks. In summer, you can also take a short guided boat trip to learn about the geology and history of the lake, which lies at the bottom of an extinct volcanic crater. The waters are full of swans, herons, and other birds, and there is a nature trail along the wooded end of the shore for those who want to get away from the throng. Deck chairs are available for rent; you might also want to stop for a plate of freshly prepared pasta or a gigantic Roman sandwich at one of the little snack bars under the oak and alder trees. There's also a small, permanent fairground for children. ✉ *Lake Albano.*

WHERE TO EAT

$$$ ITALIAN **✕ Antico Ristorante Pagnanelli.** One of most refined restaurants in the Castelli Romani has been in the same family since 1882. The present generation—Aurelio Mariani, his Australian wife, Jane, and their four sons—has lovingly restored this old railway inn perched high above Lake Albano. The dining-room windows open onto a breathtaking view across the lake to the conical peak of Monte Cavo. In winter a log fire blazes in a corner; in summer you can dine on the flower-filled terrace. Many of the dishes are prepared with produce from the family's own farm. The wine cellar, carved out of the local tufa rock, boasts more than 3,000 labels. [$] *Average main: €25* ✉ *Via Gramsci 4* ☎ *06/9361740* 🌐 *www.pagnanelli.it.*

ARICCIA

8 km (5 miles) southwest of Castelgandolfo, 26 km (17 miles) south of Rome.

Ariccia is a gem of Baroque town planning. When millionaire banker Agostino Chigi became Pope Alexander VII, he commissioned Gian Lorenzo Bernini to redesign his country estate to make it worthy of his new station. Bernini consequently restructured not only the existing 16th-century palace, but also the town gates, the main square, with its loggias and graceful twin fountains, and the round church of Santa Maria dell'Assunzione (the dome is said to be modeled on the Pantheon). The rest of the village was coiled around the apse of the church down into the valley below.

Ariccia's splendid heritage was largely forgotten in the 20th century, and yet it was once one of the highlights of every artist's and writer's Grand Tour. Corot, Ibsen, Turner, Longfellow, and Hans Christian Andersen all came to stay here.

GETTING HERE AND AROUND

For Ariccia, take the COTRAL bus from the Anagnina terminal of the Metro A underground line. Buses on the Albano–Genzano–Velletri line stop under the monumental bridge that spans the Ariccia Valley, where an elevator whisks you up to the main town square. If you take a train to Albano, you can proceed by bus to Ariccia or go on foot (it's just under 3 km [2 miles]). If you're driving, follow the Appian road to Albano and carry on to Ariccia.

EXPLORING

Palazzo Chigi. This is a true rarity—a Baroque residence whose original furniture, paintings, drapes, and decorations are still mostly intact. Italian film director Luchino Visconti used the villa for most of the interior scenes in his 1963 film *The Leopard*. The rooms contain intricately carved pieces of 17th-century furniture, as well as textiles and costumes from the 16th to the 20th centuries. The Room of Beauties is lined with paintings of the loveliest ladies of the day, and the Nuns' Room with portraits of 10 Chigi sisters, all of whom took the veil. On weekends you can also visit the suites of rooms that belonged to the pleasure-loving Cardinal Flavio Chigi. The upper floors contain the Museo del Barocco, with an important collection of 17th-century paintings. The park stretching behind the palace is the last remnant of the ancient Latium forest, where herds of deer still graze under the trees. Book ahead for tours in English. ✉ *Piazza di Corte 14* ☎ *06/9330053* 🌐 *www.palazzochigiariccia.it* *€7 (piano nobile), €11 piano nobile + Cardinal's Rooms + Museo del Barocco* ⏲ *Tours: Apr.–Sept., Tues.–Fri. at 11, 4, and 5:30; weekends at 10:30, 11:30, 12:30, 3, 4, 5, 6, 7 on the hour; Oct.–Mar., Tues.–Fri. at 11, 4, and 5:30; weekends at 10.30, 11:30, 12:30, 3, 4, 5, 6.*

WHERE TO EAT

A visit to Ariccia isn't complete without tasting the local gastronomic specialty: porchetta, a delicious roast whole pig stuffed with herbs. The shops on the Piazza di Corte will make up a sandwich for you, or you can do what the Romans do: head for one of the *fraschette* wine cellars, which also serve cheese, cold cuts, pickles, olives, and sometimes a plate of pasta. You sit on a wooden bench at a trestle table covered with simple white paper, but there's no better place to make friends and maybe join in a sing-along.

16

$ ROMAN **Da Ciccio.** Tucked away in a corner of Ariccia's centro storico stands this friendly little trattoria, which is run with loving care and attention to quality. The ingredients include certified specialty products such as pasta di Gragnano, mozzarella *di bufala*, and Parma ham. The mixed antipasti are not to be missed. Main dishes center on traditional Roman cuisine, like rigatoni *alla matriciana, pinze* (a type of pizza), and *coda alla vaccinara* (stewed oxtail). And the desserts are all homemade. *Average main: €10* ✉ *Piazza Domenico Sabatini 18* ☎ *06/93393160* *No credit cards* ⏲ *Closed Tues.*

$ ITALIAN **L'Ariccarola.** This is a great place for people-watching, which you can do while enjoying a platter of cold cuts and mixed cheeses, washed down with a carafe of local Castelli wine. It's in a corner under the Galloro bridge at the side of Palazzo Chigi. Informality is the keynote. You'll be sitting on wooden benches with a paper tablecloth, surrounded by Roman families who come specially to Ariccia for its famous porchetta. Be sure to try it! *Average main: €8* ✉ *Via Borgo S. Rocco 9* ☎ *06/9334103* ⏲ *Closed Mon.*

NEMI

8 km (5 miles) west of Ariccia, 34 km (21 miles) south of Rome.

A bronze statue to Diana the Huntress greets you at the entrance to Nemi, the smallest and prettiest village of the Castelli Romani. It's perched on a spur of rock 600 feet above the little oval-shaped lake of the same name, which is formed from a volcanic crater. Nemi has an eagle's-nest view over the rolling Roman countryside as far as the coast, some 18 km (11 miles) away. The one main street, Corso Vittorio Emanuele, takes you to the baronial Castello Ruspoli (not open to the public), where there's an 11th-century watchtower, and the quaint Piazza Umberto 1, lined with outdoor cafés serving the tiny wood strawberries harvested from the crater bowl.

If you continue on through the arch that joins the castle to the former stables, you come to the entrance of the dramatically landscaped public gardens, which curve steeply down to the panoramic **Belvedere terrace,** with a café that's open in summer. A pedestrian-only road runs down the crater side to the Roman Ships Museum. Otherwise, car access is from the town of Genzano on the opposite side of the lake.

GETTING HERE AND AROUND

Nemi is difficult to get to unless you come by car. Buses from the Anagnina Metro A station go to the town of Genzano, where a local bus travels to Nemi every two hours. If the times aren't convenient, you can take a taxi or walk the 5 km (3 miles) around Lake Nemi. By car, take the panoramic route known as the Via dei Laghi (Road of the Lakes). Follow the Appia Nuova from St. John Lateran and branch off on the well-signposted route after Ciampino airport. Follow the Via dei Laghi toward Velletri until you see signs for Nemi.

EXPLORING

Museo delle Navi Romani (*Roman Ship Museum*). Nemi may be small, but it has a long and fascinating history. In Roman times it was an important sanctuary dedicated to the goddess Diana: it drew thousands of pilgrims from all over the Roman Empire. In the 1930s the Italian government drained the lake in order to recover two magnificent ceremonial ships, loaded with sculptures, bronzes, and art treasures, that were submerged for 2,000 years.

The Museo delle Navi Romani, on the lakeshore, was built to house the ships, but they were burned during World War II. Inside are scale models and a collection of finds from the sanctuary and the area nearby. There's also a colossal statue of the infamous Roman Emperor Caligula, who had the ships built. Italian police snatched it just in time from tomb robbers as they were about to smuggle it out of the country. ✉ *Via del Tempio di Diana 9* ☎ *06/9398040* 🎫 *€3* 🕑 *Mon.–Sat. 9–6:30, Sun. 9–1.30.*

WHERE TO EAT

$ ITALIAN ✕ **Specchio di Diana.** Halfway down the main street is the town's most historic inn—Byron may have stayed here when visiting the area. A wine bar and café are on street level, while the restaurant proper on the second floor offers marvelous views, especially at sunset. Mega-pizzas (they stretch over two plates) are a specialty of the house, but don't neglect Nemi's regional specialties: *fettucine al sugo di lepre* (fettucine with hare sauce), roasted porcini mushrooms, and the little wood-strawberries with whipped cream. [$] *Average main: €14* ✉ *Corso Vittorio Emanuele 13* ☎ *06/9368805* 🌐 *www.specchiodidiana.it.*

TRAVEL SMART ROME

GETTING HERE AND AROUND

Almost all the main attractions in the *centro storico* (historic center) can be covered on foot, or by bus or Metro (subway).

The first thing you should know, especially when moving around the historic city center, is that most street names are posted on ceramiclike plaques on the side of buildings, which can be hard to see. Addresses are fairly straightforward: the street is followed by the street number. It's worth noting that the streets of Rome, even in the newer outskirts, are numbered erratically. Numbers are usually even on one side of the street and odd on the other, but sometimes numbers are in ascending consecutive order on one side of the street and descending order on the other side.

AIR TRAVEL

Flying time to Rome is 7½–8½ hours from New York, 10–11 hours from Chicago, 12–13 hours from Los Angeles, and 2½ hours from London.

Although the trend with international flights is to drop reconfirmation requirements, many airlines still ask you to reconfirm each leg of your international itinerary. Failure to do so may result in your reservations being canceled. When flying out of Italian airports, always check with the airport or tourist agency about upcoming transport strikes (sciopero), which are frequent in Italy and can affect air travel.

Airlines and Airports Airline and Airport Links.com. Airline and Airport Links.com has links to many of the world's airlines and airports. 🌐 *www.airlineandairportlinks.com.*

Airline Security Issues Transportation Security Administration. Transportation Security Administration has answers for almost every question that might come up. ☎ *866/289–9673* ✉ *TSA-ContactCenter@dhs.gov* 🌐 *www.tsa.gov.*

Transportation Security Administration (*TSA*). 🌐 *www.tsa.gov.*

AIRPORTS

The principal airport for flights to Rome is Leonardo da Vinci Airport, more commonly known as Fiumicino (FCO). It's 30 km (19 miles) southwest of the city, on the coast. There is a direct train link with Rome's Termini station on the Leonardo Express train, and a local train to Trastevere and Ostiense stations. Rome's other airport is Ciampino (CIA), on Via Appia Nuova, 15 km (9 miles) south of downtown. Ciampino is hub to most low-cost airlines that fly both nationally and internationally. There are no trains linking the Ciampino airport to downtown Rome but there are a number of shuttle buses running daily.

Airport Information Ciampino ☎ *06/65951* 🌐 *www.adr.it.* **Leonardo da Vinci Airport/ Fiumicino** ☎ *06/65951* 🌐 *www.adr.it.*

TRANSFERS BETWEEN FIUMICINO AND DOWNTOWN

When approaching by car, follow the signs for Rome and the GRA (the ring road that circles Rome). The direction you take on the GRA depends on where your lodging is located. If you're staying in the historic center areas, follow indications for Roma Centro. Get a map and directions from the car-rental service, and if you aren't using one on your phone, considering renting a GPS as well.

A new law implemented by the Comune di Roma requires all Rome taxi drivers to charge a fixed fare of €48, including luggage handling, if your destination is within the Aurelian walls (this covers the centro storico, most of Trastevere, most of the Vatican area, and parts of San Giovanni). To make sure your hotel falls within the Aurelian walls, ask when you book your room. If your hotel is outside of the walls, the cab ride will run you about €60 plus *supplementi* (extra charges) for luggage. (Of course, this also depends on traffic.) The ride from the airport to the city center takes about 30–45 minutes. Private limousines can be booked at booths in the Arrivals hall; they charge more than taxis but can carry more passengers. The Comune di Roma now has a representative in place outside the International Arrivals hall (Terminal 2), where the taxi stand is located, to help assist tourists get into a taxi cab safely (hopefully without getting ripped off). Use only licensed white or older yellow taxis. When in doubt, always ask for a receipt and write the cab company and taxi's license number down (it's written on a metal plate on the inside of the passenger door). Avoid drivers who may approach you in the Arrivals hall; they charge exorbitant, unmetered rates and are most often unauthorized taxi drivers.

Airport Shuttle has shuttles that cost €25 (for one person) and €6 for each additional passenger. The fee includes two bags per person. Airport Connection Services charges €39 for two people and luggage.

Two trains link downtown Rome with Fiumicino—a non-stop express and a local. Inquire at the APT tourist information counter in the International Arrivals hall (Terminal 2) or train information counter near the tracks to determine which takes you closest to your destination in Rome. The 30-minute nonstop Airport–Termini express (called the Leonardo Express) goes directly to Track 25 at Termini station, Rome's main train station, which is well served by taxis and is a hub of Metro and bus lines. The ride to Termini takes about 30 minutes; departures are every half hour beginning at 6:38 am from the airport, with a final departure at 11:38 pm. Trains depart Termini from Tracks 23 and 24 to the airport starting at 5:50 am and the last train leaves at 10:50 pm. Tickets cost €14.

FM1, the local train, leaves from the same tracks and runs to Rome and beyond, serving commuters as well as air travelers.

NAVIGATING ROME

Remember, Rome wasn't built in a day and no one expects you to see it one either. At the center of a huge city, the historic districts of Rome are quite large. Streets can be quaint and adorable but there are zillions of them, so pace yourself accordingly; as much as visitors feel they can proudly stride across the city in one glorious day, this would leave them in bad need of a week's rest. Happily, if all roads no longer lead to Rome, many streets in the city lead to Termini station, or Stazione Centrale, Rome's main train station and the city's main transportation hub.

Make sure the bus you're waiting for actually runs during that part of the day or on that particular day of the week. For example, notturno buses (late-night buses), which can be distinguished by the "N" sign just above the bus number, don't run until after midnight and only a few times per hour. Tourists often get confused while waiting at the bus stop, since the notturno bus schedules are listed side by side with the regular day bus schedules.

Also, be aware that *deviata* buses run on bus lines that have been rerouted due to road construction or public demonstrations. And *festivi* buses are ones that only run on Sunday and holidays. Both notturno buses and festivi buses don't run as often as other buses do on weekdays and Saturdays.

Regular buses will either say *feriali*, which means "daily," or won't have any special distinction.

The Metro A (red) line will take you to a chunk of the main attractions in Rome: Piazza di Spagna, Piazza del Popolo, St. Peter's Square, and the Vatican Museums. The B (blue) line will take you to the Colosseum, Circus Maximus, and also lead you to the heart of Testaccio, Rome's nightlife district.

The main stops in Rome are at Trastevere (27 minutes), Ostiense (30 minutes), and Tiburtina (45 minutes); at each you can find taxis and public transport connections to other areas of Rome. FM1 trains run from Fiumicino between 5:57 am and 11:27 pm, with departures every 30 minutes; the schedule is similar going to the airport. Tickets cost €8. For either train, buy your ticket at a vending machine or at ticket counters at the airport and at some stations (Termini, Trastevere, Tiburtina). At the airport, stamp the ticket at the gate. Remember when using the train at other stations to stamp the ticket in the little yellow or red machine near the track before you board. If you fail to stamp your ticket before you board, you could receive a hefty fine, as much as €100.

At night, take COTRAL buses from the airport to Tiburtina station in Rome (45 minutes); they depart from in front of the International Arrivals hall at 1:15, 2:15, 3:30, 5, 10:55 am, noon, and 3:30 pm. Buses leave Tiburtina station for the airport at 12:30, 1:15, 2:30, 3:45, 9:30, 10:30 am, 12:35 pm, and 5:30 pm. Tickets either way cost €5 (a few euros more if purchased onboard).

TRANSFERS BETWEEN CIAMPINO AND DOWNTOWN

By car, go north on the Via Appia Nuova into downtown Rome.

The new taxi fare law implemented by the Comune di Roma that affects Fiumicino applies to this airport, too. All taxi drivers are supposed to charge a fixed fare of €30, including luggage handling, if your destination is within the Aurelian walls (this covers the centro storico, Trastevere, the Vatican area, and parts of San Giovanni). If your hotel is outside the walls, the cab ride will run you about €60, plus *supplementi* (extra charges) for luggage. The ride takes about 25 minutes. Take only official cabs with the "taxi" sign on top; unofficial cabs often overcharge disoriented travelers.

Airport Connection Services has shuttles that cost €39 for the first two passengers. Airport Shuttle charges €25 for the first person, and €5 for each additional passenger.

A COTRAL bus connects Ciampino airport with Termini station. Buses depart from in front of the airport terminal around 25 times a day between 6 am and 11:40 pm. The fare is €3.90 and tickets can be bought on the bus. Travel time is approximately 40 minutes.

TRANSFERS BETWEEN AIRPORTS

It's not easy to move from one airport to another in Rome—the airports aren't connected by a railway system or by the Metro. The only way to make the transfer is by car, taxi, or a combination of bus, Metro, and train. The latter option is not advisable because it would take you at least two to three hours to get from one airport to the other.

A taxi ride from Fiumicino Leonardo Da Vinci Airport to Ciampino Airport will take approximately 45 minutes and could cost roughly €60–€70, plus *supplementi* (extra charges) for luggage.

Contacts Airport Connection Services ☎ *06/3383221, 3921540713 emergency phone in case you cannot find the driver, 213/985–3045 from the U.S., 44/2071933062 from the U.K.* 🌐 *www.airportconnection.it.* **Airport Shuttle** ☎ *06/42013469, 06/4740451* ✉ *airportshuttle@airportshuttle.it* 🌐 *www.airportshuttle.it.*

GETTING FROM THE AIRPORT TO CENTRO HISTORICO		
Mode of Transport	Duration	Price
Taxi	20 minutes from Ciampino, 30–40 minutes from Fiumicino	€30 from Ciampino, €48 from Fiumicino
Leonardo Express Train	30 minutes	€14
Car	20 minutes from Ciampino, 30–40 minutes from Fiumicino	N/A

BUS TRAVEL

An extensive network of bus lines that covers all of Lazio (the surrounding geographical region in which Rome is the capital) is operated by COTRAL (Consorzio Trasporti Lazio). There are several main bus stations. Long-distance and suburban COTRAL bus routes terminate either near Tiburtina station or at outlying Metro stops, such as Rebibbia and Ponte Mammolo (Line B) and Anagnina (Line A).

ATAC, Rome's city transport service, offers reasonable fares for travel in and around Rome, especially with the BIRG (Bigiletto Integrale Regionale Giornali), which allows you to travel on all the lines (and some railroad lines) up to midnight on the day of the ticket's first validation. The cost of a BIRG depends upon the distance to your destination and how many "zones" you travel through. Because of the extent and complexity of the system, it's a good idea to consult with your hotel concierge, review ATAC's website (*www.aci.it*), or to telephone COTRAL's central office when planning a trip. COTRAL buses and other similar bus companies such as SENA are good options for taking short day trips from Rome. There are several buses that leave daily from Rome's Ponte Mammolo (Line B) Metro station for the town of Tivoli, where Hadrian's Villa and Villa D'Este are located. SENA buses leave from Rome's Tiburtina Metro and train station (Line B) and will take you to Siena and other towns in Tuscany.

While the bus may be an affordable way of moving around, keep in mind that buses can be crowded due to commuter traffic. Just because you've managed to purchase a ticket doesn't mean you're guaranteed a seat. Make sure to arrive early and stand your ground in line. If you are not able to procure a seat, you may be standing for the entire ride.

Bus Information COTRAL *800/174471* *www.cotralspa.it.* **SENA** *0577/208282* *www.sena.it.*

CAR TRAVEL

The main access routes from the north are A1 (Autostrada del Sole) from Milan and Florence and the A12–E80 highway from Genoa. The principal route to or from points south, including Naples, is the A2. All highways connect with the Grande Raccordo Anulare Ring Road (GRA), which channels traffic into the city center. Markings on the GRA are confusing: take time to study the route you need. Be extremely careful of pedestrians and scooters when driving: Romans are casual jaywalkers and pop out frequently from between parked cars. People on scooters tend to be the worst and most careless drivers, as they tend to weave in and out of traffic.

For driving directions, check out *www.tuttocitta.it*.

GASOLINE

Only a few gas stations are open on Sunday, and most close for a couple of hours at lunchtime and at 7 pm for the night. Many, however, have self-service pumps that accept both currency and credit cards and are operational 24 hours a day. Most service stations have attendants that pump the gas for you, though self-service pumps are also available. After-hours at self-service stations, it is not uncommon to find someone who will pump your gas for you. While they're not official employees of the gas station, a small tip is usually expected (about €0.50 is acceptable). Gas stations on autostrade are open 24 hours. Gas costs about €1.8 per liter. Diesel costs about €1.70 per liter.

PARKING

Be warned: parking in Rome can be a nightmare. The situation is greatly compounded by the fact that private cars without permits are not allowed access to the entire historic center during weekdays (6:30 am to 6 pm), Saturdays (2 pm to 6 pm), and the centro storico area, Trastevere, Monti, and Testaccio on Friday and Saturday evenings (11 pm to 3 am). These areas, known as Zona Traffico Limitato (ZTL), are marked by electric signs and bordering streets have video cameras for photographing license plates. Fines are sent directly to car rental companies and added to your bill. There is limited free parking in Rome; most parking is metered, on a pay-by-the-hour basis. Spaces with white lines are free parking, while spaces with yellow lines are for the handicapped only. Spaces with blue lines are paid parking. All other color-coded spaces are usually reserved for residents, disabled drivers, or carpooling and require special permits. If you park in one of these spaces without a permit, your car could be ticketed or towed. Make sure to check with your hotel regarding appropriate places to park nearby. Meter parking costs €1–€1.20 per hour (depending on what area you're in) with limited stopping time allowed in many areas; however, if you pay for four consecutive hours, you will get eight hours of meter time for just €4. Parking facilities near the historic sights exist at the Villa Borghese underground car park (entrance at Viale del Muro Torto) and the Vatican (entrance from Piazza della Rovere).

ROAD CONDITIONS

Italians drive fast and are impatient with those who don't, a tendency that can make driving on the congested streets of Rome a hair-raising experience. Traffic is heaviest during morning and late-afternoon commuter hours, and on weekends. Watch out for mopeds.

ROADSIDE EMERGENCIES

There are phone boxes on highways to report breakdowns. Major rental agencies often provide roadside assistance, so check your rental agreement if a problem arises. Also, ACI (Auto Club of Italy) Service offers 24-hour road service. Dial ☎ *803–116* from any phone, 24 hours a day, to reach the nearest ACI service station. When speaking to ACI, ask and you will be transferred to an English-speaking operator. Be prepared to tell the operator which road you're on, the direction you're going, for example, "*verso* (in the direction of) Pizzo," and the *targa* (license plate number) of your car.

Auto Club of Italy (*ACI*). ☎ *803–116, 39/06491115 from abroad* ✉ *infoturismo@aci.it* 🌐 *www.aci.it*.

RULES OF THE ROAD

Driving is on the right. Regulations are largely similar to those in Britain and the United States, except that the police have the power to levy on-the-spot fines. Although honking abounds, the use of horns is forbidden in many areas; a large sign, "zona di silenzio," indicates where. Speed limits are 50 kph (31 mph) in Rome, 130 kph (80 mph) on autostrade, and 110 kph (70 mph) on state and provincial roads, unless otherwise marked. Talking on a cell phone while driving is strictly prohibited, and if caught, the driver will be issued a fine. Not wearing a seat belt is also against the law. The blood-alcohol content limit for driving is 0.5 gr/l with fines up to €5,000 and the possibility of six months' imprisonment for surpassing the limit. Fines for speeding are uniformly stiff: 10 kph (6 mph) over the speed limit can warrant a fine of up to €500; over 10 kph, and your license could be taken away from you.

Whenever the city decides to implement an "Ecological Day" in order to reduce smog levels, commuters are prohibited from driving their cars during certain hours of the day and in certain areas of the city. These are usually organized and announced ahead of time; however, if you're planning to rent a car during your trip, make sure to ask the rental company and your hotel if there are any planned, because the traffic police won't cut you any breaks, even if you say you're a tourist.

CAR RENTAL

When you reserve a car, ask about cancellation penalties, taxes, drop-off charges (if you're planning to pick up the car in one city and leave it in another), and surcharges (for being under or over a certain age, for additional drivers, or for driving across regional or country borders or beyond a specific distance from your point of rental). All these things can add substantially to your costs. Request car seats and extras such as GPS when you book. Make sure to ask the rental car company if they require you to obtain an International Driver's Permit beforehand (most do). These can generally be obtained for a fee through AAA in the United States. Rates are sometimes—but not always—better if you book in advance or reserve through a rental agency's website. There are other reasons to book ahead, though: for popular destinations, during busy times of the year, or to ensure that you get certain types of cars (vans, SUVs, exotic sports cars).

■TIP→ Make sure that a confirmed reservation guarantees you a car. Agencies sometimes overbook, particularly for busy weekends and holiday periods.

Rates in Rome begin at around $75 a day for an economy car with air-conditioning, a manual transmission, and unlimited mileage. This includes the 20% tax on car rentals. Note that Italian legislation now permits certain rental wholesalers, such as Auto Europe, to drop the value-added tax (V.A.T.). All international car-rental agencies in Rome have a number of locations.

It's usually cheaper to rent a car in advance through your local agency than to rent on location in Italy. Or book ahead online—you can save as much as $10 per day on your car rental. Within Italy, local rental agencies and international ones offer similar rates. Whether you're going with a local or international agency, note that most cars are manual; automatics are hard to find, so inquire about those well in advance.

In Italy your own driver's license is acceptable. An International Driver's Permit is a good idea; it's available from the American or Canadian Automobile Association and, in the United Kingdom, from the Automobile Association or Royal Automobile Club. These international permits are universally recognized, and having one in your wallet may save you a problem with the local authorities.

In Italy you must be 21 years of age to rent an economy or subcompact car, and most companies require customers under the age of 23 to pay by credit card. Upon rental, all companies require credit cards as a warranty; to rent bigger cars (2,000 cc or more), you must often show two credit cards. Debit or check cards are not accepted. Call local agents for details. There are no special restrictions on senior-citizen drivers.

Car seats are required for children under three and must be booked in advance. The rental cost is €5 upward, depending on the type of car.

The cost for an additional driver is about €5–€7 per day.

CAR INSURANCE

Everyone who rents a car wonders whether the insurance that the rental companies offer is worth the expense. No one—including us—has a simple answer. It all depends on how much regular insurance you have, how comfortable you are with risk, and whether or not money is an issue.

If you own a car, your personal auto insurance may cover a rental to some degree, though not all policies protect you abroad; always read your policy's fine print. If you don't have auto insurance, then seriously consider buying the collision- or loss-damage waiver (CDW or LDW) from the car-rental company, which eliminates your liability for damage to the car. If you choose not to purchase the CDW coverage, you could be liable for the first €500 worth of damage. Some credit cards offer CDW coverage, but it's usually supplemental to your own insurance and rarely covers SUVs, minivans, luxury models, and the like. If your coverage is secondary, you may still be liable for loss-of-use costs from the car-rental company. But no credit-card insurance is valid unless you use that card for *all* transactions, from reserving to paying the final bill. All companies exclude car rental in some countries, so be sure to find out about the destination to which you are traveling.

Some rental agencies require you to purchase CDW coverage; many will even include it in quoted rates. All will strongly encourage you to buy CDW—possibly implying that it's required—so be sure to ask about such things before renting. In most cases it's cheaper to add a supplemental CDW plan to your comprehensive travel-insurance policy than to purchase it from a rental company. That said, you don't want to pay for a supplement if you're required to buy insurance from the rental company.

MOPED TRAVEL

As bikes are to Beijing, so mopeds are to Rome; that means they are everywhere. Riders are required to wear helmets, and traffic police are tough in enforcing this law. Producing your country's driver's license should be enough to convince most rental firms that they're not dealing with a complete beginner; but if you're unsure of exactly how to ride a moped, think twice, as driving a scooter in Rome is not like you see it in the movies. It can be very dangerous, and Roman drivers tend to be ruthless; at least ask the assistant for a detailed demonstration. If you don't feel up to braving the Roman traffic on a moped, you can hire an electric car to scoot around the city. The MELEX is a four-seater, golf-cart-style car, with battery power lasting up to eight hours. To rent a MELEX, you need a valid driver's license. The cost is €18 per hour.

Rental Agencies Free Rome (MELEX cars) ✉ *Via Ludovisi 60, Via Veneto* ☎ *335/8357590* ✎ *info@freerome.it* 🌐 *www.freerome.it.* **Scoot-a-Long** ✉ *Via Cavour 302, Colosseo* ☎ *06/6780206.* **Treno e Scooter** ✉ *Piazza dei Cinquecento, in the parking lot in front of the train station, Termini* ☎ *06/48905823* 🌐 *www.trenoescooter.com.*

PUBLIC TRANSPORTATION: BUS, TRAM, AND METROPOLITANA

Although most of Rome's sights are in a relatively circumscribed area, the city is too large to be seen solely on foot. Try to avoid rush hours when taking the Metro (subway) or a bus, as public transport can be extremely crowded. Midmorning or the middle of the day up until early afternoon tends to be less busy. Otherwise, it's best to take a taxi to the area you plan to visit if it is across town. You should always expect to do a lot of walking in Rome (especially considering how little ground the subway actually covers) and so plan on wearing a pair of comfortable, sturdy shoes to cushion the impact of the *sampietrini* (cobblestones). Get away from the noise and polluted air of heavily trafficked streets by taking parallel streets whenever possible. You can get free city and transportation-route maps at municipal information booths.

Rome's integrated transportation system includes buses and trams (ATAC), Metropolitana (subway, often nicknamed the Metro), suburban trains and buses (COTRAL), and some other suburban trains (Trenitalia) run by the state railways. A ticket (BIT) valid for 100 minutes on any combination of buses and trams and one entrance to the Metro costs €1.50.

Tickets are sold at tobacco shops, newsstands, some coffee bars, automatic ticket machines in Metro stations, some bus stops, in machines on some buses, and at ATAC ticket booths. You can purchase individual tickets or buy in quantity. It's always a good idea to have a few tickets handy so you don't have to hunt for a vendor when you need one. All tickets must be validated by time-stamping in the yellow meter boxes aboard buses and in underground stations, and immediately prior to boarding. Failure to validate your ticket will result in an on-the-spot fine of €50. Pay the ticket controllers on the spot; otherwise, it'll cost you €100 or more to pay it later.

A BIG ticket—or *Biglietto integrato giornaliero* (integrated daily ticket)—is valid for one day (the date it is stamped, not 24 hours) on all public transport and costs €6. A three-day pass (BTI)—or *Biglietto turistico integrato*—costs €16.50. A weekly ticket (*settimanale,* also known as CIS) costs €24 and gives unlimited travel on ATAC buses, COTRAL urban bus services, trains for the Lido and Viterbo, and subway (Metro). There's an ATAC kiosk at the bus terminal in front of Termini station.

If you're going farther afield, or planning to spend more than a week in Rome, think about getting a BIRG regional ticket or a CIRS (regional weekly ticket) from the railway station. These give you unlimited travel on all state transport throughout the region of Lazio. This can take you as far as the Etruscan city of Tarquinia or medieval Viterbo.

The Metropolitana (or Metro) is the easiest and fastest way to get around Rome (⇨ *see our Metro map*). There are stops near most of the main tourist attractions (street entrances are marked with red "M" signs). The Metro has two lines—A and B—which intersect at Termini station. Line A runs from the eastern part of the city, with stops, among others, at San Giovanni in Laterano, Piazza Barberini, Piazza di Spagna, Piazzale Flaminio (Piazza del Popolo), and Ottaviano/San Pietro, near the Basilica di San Pietro and the Musei Vaticani. Line B has stops near the Colosseum, the Circus Maximus, the Pyramid (Ostiense station and trains for Ostia Antica), and the Basilica di San Paolo Fuori le Mura. The Metro opens at 5:30 am, and the last trains leave the last station at either end at 11:30 pm (on Friday and Saturday nights the last train leaves at 1:30 am).

Although not as fast as the Metropolitana, bus travel is more scenic. With reserved bus lanes and numerous tramlines, surface transportation is surprisingly efficient, given the volume of Roman traffic. At peak times, however, buses can be very crowded. If the distance you have to travel is not too great, walking can be a more comfortable alternative. ATAC city buses are orange, gray-and-red, or blue-and-orange; trams are orange or green. Remember to board at the rear and to exit at the middle: some bus drivers may refuse to let you out the front door, leaving you to scramble through the crowd to exit the middle or rear doors. Don't forget you must buy your ticket before boarding, and stamp it in a machine as soon as you enter. If you find the bus too crowded to get to the ticket machine, write the date and time you boarded on the ticket where you would normally validate it. The ticket is good for a transfer and one Metro trip within the next 75 minutes. Buses and trams run from 5:30 am to midnight, plus there's an extensive network of night buses throughout the city.

The bus system is a bit complicated to navigate due to the number of lines, but ATAC has a website (🌐 *www.atac.roma.it*) that will help you calculate the number of stops and bus route needed, and even give you a map directing you to the appropriate stops. To navigate the site, look for the British flag in the upper right-hand corner to change the website into English.

TICKET/PASS	PRICE
Single Fare	€1.50
Weekly Pass	€24
Monthly Unlimited Pass	€35

Information ATAC urban buses ☎ *06/57003* 🌐 *www.atac.roma.it.* **COTRAL** ☎ *800/174471, 06/72057205* 🌐 *www.cotralspa.it.* **Trenitalia suburban trains** ☎ *892021, 06/68475475 from abroad* 🌐 *www.trenitalia.it.*

TAXI TRAVEL

The etiquette in Rome is generally to hire a taxi at a taxi stand. Taxis do not cruise, but if free they may stop if you flag them down. They wait at stands but can also be called by phone, in which case you're charged a supplement (the meter will already been running when you're picked up). The various taxi services are considered interchangeable and are referred to by their phone numbers rather than names. Taxicabs can be reserved the night before only if you're traveling to and from the airport or the train station. Only some taxis are equipped to take credit cards. Inquire when you phone to make the booking.

The meter starts at €3 during the day, €6.50 after 10 pm, and €4.50 on Sunday and holidays.

Supplemental charges, such as for luggage or even for pick up at Termini station, are added to the meter fare. When in doubt, always ask for a receipt (*ricevuta*). This will encourage the taxicab driver to be honest and charge you the correct amount. Between 10 pm and 6 am, women traveling alone via taxi are entitled to a 10% discount. Make sure to ask for it. Use only licensed, metered white or yellow cabs, identified by a numbered shield on the side, an illuminated taxi sign on the roof, and a plaque next to the license plate reading "servizio pubblico." Avoid unmarked, unauthorized, unmetered gypsy cabs (numerous at Rome airports and train stations), whose drivers actively solicit your trade and may demand astronomical fares.

Taxi Companies Cab ☎ *06/6645, 06/3570, 06/8822, 06/5551, 06/4157* 🌐 *www.3570.it.*

TRAIN TRAVEL

State-owned Trenitalia trains are part of the Metrebus system and also serve some destinations on side trips outside Rome. The main Trenitalia stations in Rome are Termini, Tiburtina, Ostiense, and Trastevere. Suburban trains use all of these stations. The Ferrovie COTRAL line departs from a terminal in Piazzale Flaminio, connecting Rome with Viterbo.

Only Trenitalia trains such as Frecciarossa, Frecciargento, Eurostar, and Intercity Plus have first- and second-class compartments. Local trains can be crowded early morning and evening as many people commute to and from the city, so try to avoid these times. Be ready to stand if you plan to take one of these trains and don't arrive early enough to secure a seat. On long-distance routes (to Florence and Venice, for instance), you can either travel by the cheap (but slow) *regionale* trains, or the fast, but more expensive *Intercity, Eurostar,* Frecciarossa, or Frecciargento, which require seat reservations, available at the station when you buy your ticket, online, or through a travel agent.

For destinations within 200 km (124 miles) of Rome, you can buy a *kilometrico* ticket. Like bus tickets, they can be purchased at some newsstands and in ticketing machines, as well as at Trenitalia ticket windows. Buy them in advance so you won't waste time in line at station ticket booths. Like all train tickets, they must be date-stamped in the little yellow or red machines near the track before you board. Within a range of 200 km (124 miles) they're valid for six hours from the time they're stamped, and you can get on and off at will at stops in between for the duration of the ticket's validity.

The state railways' excellent and user-friendly site at 🌐 *www.trenitalia.it* will help you plan any rail trips in the country.

Since 2012, Italy's rails have had a private competitor, Italo, whose gorgeous and very fast trains travel between large cities including Naples, Rome, Florence, Bologna, Milan, Venice, and Torino. In Rome, Italo trains stop at Tiburtina and Ostiense stations—not Termini.

Information Italo Treno–Nuovo Trasporto Viaggiatori ☎ *06/0708* 🌐 *www.italotreno.it.* **Trenitalia** ☎ *892/2021 within Italy, 199/892021 within Italy, 06/68475475 from abroad* 🌐 *www.trenitalia.it.*

ESSENTIALS

COMMUNICATIONS

INTERNET

Getting online in Rome isn't difficult: public Internet stations and Internet cafés are common. Prices differ from place to place, so spend some time to find the best deal. This isn't always readily apparent: a place might have higher rates, but because it belongs to a chain you won't be charged an initial flat fee again when you go to a different location of the same chain.

If you have a phone with an Italian SIM card, you can access various free Wi-Fi hotspots around the city through DigitRoma (*www.digitroma.it*), Romawireless (*www.romawireless.com*), and Provincia Wifi (*www.mappawifi.provincia.roma.it*), which also accepts a credit card for identity verification if you don't have an Italian phone number. After you register with one of these providers, your phone should recognize the company's free Wi-Fi hotspots, but you will be required to enter login and password.

Many hotels have free Wi-Fi or in-room modem lines, but, as with phones, using the hotel's line is relatively expensive. Always check modem rates before plugging in. You may need an adapter for your computer for the European-style plugs. As always, if you're traveling with a laptop, carry an adapter. Never plug your computer into any socket before asking about surge protection. IBM sells a pea-size modem tester that plugs into a telephone jack to check whether the line is safe to use.

Internet Cafés Cybercafes. Cybercafes lists more than 4,000 Internet cafés worldwide. *www.cybercafes.com.* **Mail Office** *Corso Vittorio Emanuele II 274/a, Piazza Navona* *06/68192051.* **Pantheon Internet Point** *Via di Santa Caterina da Siena 40, Piazza Navona* *06/69200501.*

Cafés with Wi-Fi Friends Café *Piazza Trilussa 34, Trastevere* *06/5816111* *www.cafefriends.it.* **The Library** *Vicolo della Cancelleria 7, Piazza Navona* *333/3517581, 06/97275442* *www.thelibrary.it.*

PHONES

The good news is that you can now make a direct-dial telephone call from virtually any point on earth. The bad news? You can't always do so cheaply. Calling from a hotel is almost always the most expensive option; hotels usually add huge surcharges to all calls, particularly international ones. Calling cards usually keep costs to a minimum, but only if you purchase them locally. In Italy, you can also place international calls from call centers. And then there are mobile phones (*⇨ Mobile Phones*)—as expensive as mobile phone calls can be, they are still usually a much cheaper option than calling from your hotel.

The country code for Italy is 39. The area code for Rome is 06. When dialing an Italian number from abroad, do not drop the initial 0 from the local area code.

The country code is 1 for the United States and Canada, 61 for Australia, 64 for New Zealand, and 44 for the United Kingdom.

CALLING WITHIN ITALY

When calling within Italy to an Italian number, always include city dialing code such as 06 for Rome, 02 for Milan, and 055 for Florence. If you need help, dial *176* for general information in English. To place international telephone calls via operator-assisted service (or for information), dial *170*.

You will notice that only cell phones have a set number of digits, whereas landlines can range from 6 to 10. Calls within Rome are preceded by the city code 06, with the exception of three-digit numbers (113 is for general emergencies) and cell phone numbers. Emergency numbers can be called for free from pay phones.

LOCAL DO'S AND TABOOS

GREETINGS

Italians greet friends with a kiss, usually first on the right cheek, and then on the left. When you meet a new person, shake hands and say *piacere* (*pee*-ah-*cher*-ay).

SIGHTSEEING

Italy is teeming with churches, many with significant works of art in them. Because they are places of worship, care should be taken with appropriate dress. Shorts, cropped tops, miniskirts, and bare midriffs are taboo at St. Peter's in Rome, and in many other churches throughout Italy. When touring churches—especially in summer when it's hot and no sleeves are desirable—it's wise to carry a sweater, or scarf, to wrap around your shoulders before entering the church. Do not enter a church while eating or drinking—keep all food items in a bag. Avoid entering when a service is being held. All cell phones must be on silent. If there are signs saying *no photography* or *no flash photography,* abide by these rules.

OUT ON THE TOWN

In Italy, almost nothing starts on time except for (sometimes) a theater, opera, or movie showing. Italians even joke about a "15-minute window" before actually being late somewhere.

LANGUAGE

You can always find someone who speaks at least a little English in Rome, albeit with a heavy accent. When you do encounter someone who speaks English, it's polite to speak slowly and phonetically so the person can understand you better. Remember that the Italian language is pronounced exactly as it's written—many Italians try to speak English as it's written, with bewildering results.

You may run into a language barrier in the countryside, but a phrase book and close attention to the Italians' astonishing use of pantomime and expressive gestures will go a long way.

Try to master a few phrases for daily use, and familiarize yourself with the terms you'll need to decipher signs and museum labels. Some museums have exhibits labeled in both English and Italian, but this is the exception rather than the rule.

Most exhibitions have multi-language headphones you can rent, and English-language guidebooks are generally available at museum shops.

Many newsstands and bookstores stock a useful guide called *Rome, Past & Present.* It has photos of the most famous ancient monuments, together with drawings of what they originally looked like, and is particularly useful to get children interested in what seems (to them) just heaps of old stones.

A phrase book and language-CD set can help get you started. Fodor's *Italian for Travelers* (available at bookstores everywhere) is excellent.

Private language schools and U.S.- and U.K.-affiliated educational institutions offer a host of Italian language study programs in Rome.

Language Schools American University of Rome ✉ *Via Pietro Rosselli 4, Monteverde* ☎ *06/58330919* 🌐 *www.aur.edu.* **Berlitz** ✉ *Via Fabio Massimo 95, Prati* ☎ *06/6872561* 🌐 *www.berlitz.it.* **Centro Linguistico Italiano Dante Alighieri** ✉ *Piazza Bologna 1* ☎ *06/44231490* 🌐 *www.clidante.it.* **Ciao Italia** ✉ *Via delle Frasche 5, Repubblica* ☎ *06/4814084* 🌐 *www.ciao-italia.it.* **Dilit International House** ✉ *Via Marghera 22, Termini* ☎ *06/4462593* 🌐 *www.dilit.it.* **Fodor's Choice★ Scuola Leonardo da Vinci** ✉ *Piazza dell'Orologio 7, Piazza Navona* ☎ *06/68892513* 🌐 *www.scuolaleonardo.com.*

Calling to cities outside of Rome follows the same procedure: city dialing code plus number.

CALLING OUTSIDE ITALY

Avoid making international and long-distance calls from hotels as they tend to overcharge. If you do not have a cellphone with international cell plan, purchase an international phone card, which supplies a local number to call and offers a low rate. You can make collect calls from any phone by dialing ☎ *800/172444*, which will get you an English-speaking AT&T operator. To make an international call, you must dial 00 and then the country code.

Access Codes AT&T Direct ☎ *800/172444.* **MCI WorldPhone** ☎ *800/905825.* **Sprint International Access.** From cell phones call 892–176. ☎ *800/172–405.*

CALLING CARDS

Most payphones now only accept *schede telefoniche* (phone cards), not coins. You can buy cards of varying values (€5, €10, and so forth) at post offices, newsstands (called *edicole*), and tobacconists. Tear off the corner of the card and insert it in the slot. When you dial, its value appears in the window. After you hang up, the card is returned so you can use it until its value runs out.

MOBILE PHONES

If you have a multiband phone (some countries use different frequencies from those used in the United States) and your service provider uses the world-standard GSM network (as do T-Mobile, AT&T, and Verizon), you can probably use your phone abroad. Depending on how much you want to use your phone, it may be best to add an international package with some combination of calls, texts, and data—consult your service provider before your trip. Otherwise, roaming fees can be steep. For those with unlocked phones, consider buying an Italian SIM card and prepaid service plan. Or else rent an Italian phone (via a domestic provider) with an unlimited plan. Look into rentals carefully though—there are often hidden fees, and if you're not planning to make a lot of calls, it may be cheaper and simpler to stick with your own cell phone.

Contacts Cellular Abroad. Cellular Abroad rents and sells GMS phones and sells SIM cards that work in many countries. ☎ *800/287–5072, 310/862–7100, 800/36233333 toll-free within Italy* 🌐 *www.cellularabroad.com.* **Mobal.** Mobal rents mobiles and sells GSM phones (starting at $29) that will operate in 140 countries. Per-call rates vary throughout the world. ☎ *888/888–9162* 🌐 *www.mobalrental.com.* **Planet Fone.** Planet Fone rents cell phones, but the per-minute rates are expensive. ☎ *888/988–4777* 🌐 *www.planetfone.com.*

CUSTOMS AND DUTIES

You're always allowed to bring goods of a certain value back home without having to pay any duty or import tax. But there's a limit on the amount of tobacco and liquor you can bring back duty-free, and some countries have separate limits for perfumes; for exact figures, check with your customs department. The values of so-called "duty-free" goods are included in these amounts. When you shop abroad, save all your receipts, as customs inspectors may ask to see them as well as the items you purchased. If the total value of your goods is more than the duty-free limit, you'll have to pay a tax (most often a flat percentage) on the value of everything beyond that limit.

Of goods obtained anywhere outside the European Union or goods purchased in a duty-free shop within an EU country, the allowances are as follows: (1) 200 cigarettes or 100 cigarillos or 50 cigars or 250 grams of tobacco; (2) 2 liters of still table wine or 1 liter of spirits over 22% volume or 2 liters of spirits under 22% volume or 2 liters of fortified and sparkling wines; and (3) 50 ml of perfume and 250 ml of toilet water.

Of goods obtained (duty and tax paid) within another EU country, the allowances are (1) 800 cigarettes or 400 cigarillos (under 3 grams) or 200 cigars or 1 kilogram of tobacco; (2) 90 liters of still table wine or 10 liters of spirits over 22% volume or 20 liters of spirits under 22% volume or 110 liters of beer.

Information in Rome Italian Customs, Fiumicino Airport ✉ *Via Bragadin, Fiumicino* ☎ *06/65956366, 06/65956949.*

U.S. Information U.S. Customs and Border Protection ☎ *877/227–5511 from the U.S., 703/526–4200 from abroad* 🌐 *www.cbp.gov.*

ELECTRICITY

The electrical current in Italy is 220 volts, 50 cycles alternating current (AC); wall outlets take Continental-type plugs, with two or three round prongs.

Consider making a small investment in a universal adapter, which has several types of plugs in one lightweight, compact unit. Most laptops and mobile phone chargers are dual voltage (i.e., they operate equally well on 110 and 220 volts), so require only an adapter. These days the same is true of small appliances such as hair dryers. Always check labels and manufacturer instructions to be sure. Don't use 110-volt outlets marked "for shavers only" for high-wattage appliances such as hair dryers.

Note that straightening irons from the United States don't heat up very well and tend to blow a fuse even with correct adapters—as do American hair dryers.

Contacts Walkabout Travel Gear. Walkabout Travel Gear has good coverage of electricity under "adapters." ☎ *800/852–7085 U.S. toll-free number* 🌐 *www.walkabouttravelgear.com.*

EMERGENCIES

No matter where you are in Italy, dial ☎ *113* for all emergencies, or ask somebody (your concierge, a passerby) to call for you, as not all 113 operators speak English. Key words to remember for emergency situations are *Aiuto!* (Help!, pronounced ah-*you*-toh) and *Pronto soccorso*, which means "first aid." When confronted with a health emergency, head straight for the Pronto Soccorso department of the nearest hospital or dial ☎ *118*. To call a Red Cross ambulance (*ambulanza*), dial ☎ *06/5510.* If you just need a doctor, ask for *un medico*; most hotels will be able to refer you to a local doctor (*medico*). Ask the physician for *una fattura* (an invoice) to present to your insurance company for reimbursement. Alternatively, the city of Rome has a medical clinic dedicated to sick tourists (flu, fever, minor aches and pains, etc.). The Nuovo Regina Margherita Hospital offers a 24-hour tourist medical service and is staffed by one medical doctor and two nurses. The tourist medical service is free of charge every weeknight from 8 pm to 8 am, and on weekends. On weekdays (8 am to 8 pm), there is a charge of €20.66. Patients under six years old or over 65 are always treated for free. The tourist service is located at the Nuovo Regina Margherita Hospital on Via Morosini 30 (Trastevere); the phone number is ☎ *06/58441*.

Other useful Italian words to use are *Fuoco!* (Fire!, pronounced *fwoe*-co) and *Ladro!* (Thief!, pronounced *lah*-droh).

Italy has a national military police force (*carabinieri*) as well as local police (*polizia*). Both are armed and have the power to arrest and investigate crimes. Always report any theft or the loss of your passport to either the carabinieri or the police, as well as to your embassy. Local traffic officers are known as *vigili* (though their official name is *polizia municipale*)—they are responsible for, among other things, giving out parking tickets and clamping cars. Should you find yourself involved in a minor car accident, you should contact the vigili. Call the countrywide toll-free number 113 if you need the police.

Most pharmacies are open Monday–Saturday 8:30 am–1 pm and 4 pm–8 pm; though some are open later or even 24 hours. A schedule posted outside each pharmacy indicates the nearest pharmacy open during off-hours (afternoons, through the night, and Sunday). Farmacia Internazionale Capranica, Farmacia Internazionale Barberini (open 24 hours), and Farmacia Cola di Rienzo are pharmacies that have some English-speaking staff. The hospitals listed here have English-speaking doctors. Rome American Hospital is about 30 minutes by cab from the center of town.

For a full listing of doctors and dentists in Rome who speak English, consult the English Yellow Pages at 🌐 *www.englishyellowpages.it* or visit your Embassy's webpage.

Doctors and Dentists **Aventino Medical Group** ✉ *Via Sant'Alberto Magno 5, Aventino* ☎ *06/57288349, 06/57288329* 🌐 *www.aventinomedicalgroup.com.* **Roma Medica (weekends, house calls)** ☎ *338/6224832 24-hour service* 🌐 *www.romamedica.com.*

General Emergency Contacts **Emergencies** ☎ *113.* **Polizia (Police)** ☎ *113.* **Ambulance** ☎ *118.*

Hospitals and Clinics **Rome American Hospital** ✉ *Via Emilio Longoni 69, Tor Sapienza* ☎ *06/22551* 🌐 *www.rah.it.* **Salvator Mundi International Hospital** ✉ *Viale delle Mura Gianicolensi 67, Monteverde* ☎ *06/588961, 800/402323 toll-free within Italy* 🌐 *www.salvatormundi.it.*

Hotlines **Highway Police** ☎ *06/22101.* **Roadside Assistance** ☎ *116.* **Women's Rights and Abuse Prevention** ☎ *06/4882832, 800/001122* 🌐 *www.azzurrorosa.it.*

Pharmacies **Farmacia Cola di Rienzo** ✉ *Via Cola di Rienzo 213/215, San Pietro* ☎ *06/3243130, 06/3244476* 🌐 *www.farmaciacoladirienzo.com.* **Farmacia Internazionale Barberini** ✉ *Piazza Barberini 49, Barberini* ☎ *06/4825456, 06/4871195* 🌐 *www.farmint.it.* **Farmacia Internazionale Capranica** ✉ *Piazza Capranica 96, Piazza Navona* ☎ *06/6794680.*

HEALTH

Smoking is banned in Italy in all public places. This includes trains, buses, offices, hospitals, and waiting rooms, as well as restaurants, pubs, and discotheques (unless the latter have separate smoking rooms). If you want to smoke inside a restaurant, ask before booking; very few have smoking sections. Fines for breaking the law are exorbitant. Sit inside if the smoke in outdoor seating areas bothers you. Many restaurants are now equipped with air-conditioning.

It's always best to travel with your own trusted medications. Should you need medication while in Italy, you should speak with a physician to make sure it is the proper medicine and in case a prescription is necessary. Aspirin (*l'aspirina*) can be purchased at any pharmacy, as can over-the-counter medicines such as ibuprofen and Aleve. Other over-the-counter remedies, including cough syrup, antiseptic creams, and headache pills, are only sold in pharmacies.

HOURS OF OPERATION

Banks are typically open weekdays 8:30–1:30 and 2:45–3:45 or 3–4. Exchange offices are open all day, usually 8:30–8.

Post offices are open Monday–Saturday 8–2; central and main district post offices stay open until 7 or 8 on weekdays for some operations. You can buy stamps (*francobolli*) at tobacconists.

Most gas stations are open from Mondays through Saturdays, with only a few open on Sunday, and most close during weekday lunch hours and at 7 pm for the night. Many, however, have self-service pumps that are operational 24 hours a day, and gas stations on autostrade are open 24 hours.

Museum hours vary and may change with the seasons. Many important national museums are closed one day a week, often on Monday. The Roman Forum, other sites, and some museums may be open until late in the evening during the summer. Always check locally.

Most churches are open from early morning until noon or 12:30, when they close for two hours or more; they open again in the afternoon, generally around 4 pm, closing about 7 pm or later. Major cathedrals and basilicas, such as the Basilica di San Pietro, are open all day. Note that sightseeing in churches during religious rites is usually discouraged. Be sure to have some coins handy for the *luce* (light) machines that illuminate the works of art in the perpetual dusk of ecclesiastical interiors. A pair of binoculars will help you get a good look at painted ceilings and domes. Many churches do not allow you to take pictures inside. When permitted, use of flash is prohibited.

A tip for pilgrims and tourists keen to get a glimpse of the pope: avoid the weekly general audience on Wednesday morning in Piazza di San Pietro, and go to his Sunday angelus instead. This midday prayer service tends to be far less crowded (unless beatifications or canonizations are taking place) and is also mercifully shorter, which makes a difference when you're standing.

Most pharmacies are open Monday–Saturday 8:30–1 and 4–8; some are open all night. A schedule posted outside each pharmacy indicates the nearest pharmacy open during off-hours (afternoons, through the night, and Sunday).

Shop hours vary. Many shops in downtown Rome are open all day during the week and also on Sunday, as are some department stores and supermarkets. Alternating city neighborhoods also have general once-a-month Sunday opening days. Otherwise, most shops throughout the city are closed on Sunday. Shops that take a lengthy lunch break are open 9:30–1 and 3:30 or 4–7:30 or 8. Many shops close for one half day during the week: Monday morning in winter and Saturday afternoon in summer.

Food shops are open 8–2 and 5–7:30, some until 8, and most are closed on Sunday. They also close for one half day during the week, usually Thursday afternoon from September to June and Saturday afternoon in July and August.

Termini station has a large, modern shopping mall with more than a hundred stores, many of which are open late in the evening. Pharmacies, bookstores, and boutiques, as well as cafés, bathrooms, ATMs, and money-exchange services, a first-aid station, and an art gallery and exhibition center can all be found here. The Drug Store here (which oddly doesn't sell medicine) is open every day between 6 am and midnight. It sells sandwiches, fresh fruit, gourmet snacks, toiletries, gifts, and things like cameras, electric razors, and bouquets of fresh flowers (useful if you get an unexpected invitation to someone's home).

HOLIDAYS

If you can avoid it, don't travel at all in Italy in August, when much of the population is on the move, especially around Ferragosto, the August 15 national holiday, when cities such as Rome are deserted and many restaurants and shops are closed.

National holidays are New Year's Day (January 1); Epiphany (January 6); Easter Sunday and Monday; Liberation Day (April 25); Labor Day (May 1); Republic Day (June 2); Ferragosto (August 15); All Saint's Day (November 1); Immaculate Conception (December 8); Christmas Day and the feast of Saint Stephen (December 25 and 26). Rome-specific holidays are Rome's birthday (April 21) and St. Peter and Paul Day (June 29).

MAIL

The Italian mail system has improved tremendously with the introduction of a two-tier postal system. A *posta prioritaria* stamp (first-class stamp) within Italy costs €0.60; to EEC destinations, it costs €0.85 and usually guarantees delivery within three days. Mailing a letter or a postcard from Italy to the United States requires two of these posta prioritaria stamps. When you mail letters, pay attention to the mail slot on the mailbox. The red mailboxes have two slots: the slot on the left is for Rome mail, and the slot on the right is for all other destinations, including abroad. Blue mailboxes are for foreign (*estero*) mail only.

The Vatican postal service has a reputation for efficiency and many foreigners prefer to send their mail from there, with Vatican stamps. You can buy these in the post offices on either side of Piazza di San Pietro, one next to the information office and the other under the colonnade opposite. During peak tourist seasons a Vatican Post Office mobile unit is set up in Piazza di San Pietro. All letters with Vatican stamps can only be mailed from the Vatican Post Office or Vatican mailboxes located near San Pietro.

Letters and postcards to the United States and Canada cost €1.60 for up to 20 grams and automatically go airmail. Letters and postcards to the United Kingdom cost €0.65. You can buy stamps at tobacco shops.

American Express also has a general-delivery service. There's no charge for cardholders, holders of American Express traveler's checks, or anyone who booked a vacation with American Express.

If you can avoid it, try not to have packages sent to you while you're in Rome or in Italy. Packages sent from abroad are notorious for being stopped by the Italian Customs Office or "Ufficio Dogonale." If your package gets stuck in customs, not only will you likely have to pay hefty customs fees but it could also take weeks for you to receive it. Sending medicine and even vitamins through the mail is highly unadvisable, and if discovered your package will definitely be held up in customs for inspection.

Main Branches Poste Italiane (Main Post Office) ✉ *Piazza San Silvestro 19, Piazza di Spagna* ☎ *06/6797398* 🌐 *www.poste.it.*

MONEY

Rome's prices are comparable to those in other major capitals, such as Paris and London. Unless you dine in the swankiest places, you'll still find Rome one of the cheapest European capitals in which to eat. Clothes and leather goods are also generally less expensive than in northern Europe. Public transport is relatively cheap.

A Rome 2-km (1-mile) taxi ride costs €8. An inexpensive hotel room for two, including breakfast, is about €120; an inexpensive dinner for two is €45. A simple pasta item on the menu is about €8 to €12, pizzas from €6 to €9, a ½-liter carafe of house wine is around €5, and a cappuccino can cost €1.20. A movie ticket is approximately €7.50, and the cheapest seat at the opera is €17, while full fare admission to the Musei Vaticani is €15.

Though most places accept credit cards, cash is still preferred. This holds especially true for street markets and small mom-and-pop stores and restaurants.

ITEM	AVERAGE COST
Cup of Coffee	€0.80–€1
Glass of Wine or Beer	€3–€8
Sandwich	€2.50–€5
One-Mile Taxi Ride	€8
Museum Admission	€8–€15

Prices throughout this guide are given for adults. Substantially reduced fees are almost always available for children, students, and senior citizens when it comes to entrances to monuments and museums.

TIP→ Banks never have every foreign currency on hand, and it may take as long as a week to order. If you're planning to exchange funds before leaving home, don't wait until the last minute.

ATMS AND BANKS

Your own bank will probably charge a fee for using ATMs abroad; the foreign bank you use may also charge a fee. Some banks, such as Citibank, which has a branch in Rome (near Via Veneto), don't charge extra fees to customers who use the Citibank ATM. Other banks may have similar agreements with Italian or foreign banks in Rome where customers won't get charged a transaction fee. Check with your bank to see if they have any agreements before your trip. Nevertheless, you'll usually get a better rate of exchange at an ATM than you will at a currency-exchange office or even when changing money in a bank. And extracting funds as you need them is a safer option than carrying around a large amount of cash.

TIP→ PIN numbers with more than four digits are not recognized at ATMs in many countries. If yours has five or more, remember to change it before you leave.

ATMs are common in Rome and are the easiest way to get euros. The word for ATM in Italian is *bancomat,* for PIN, *codice segreto*. Four-digit PINs are the standard, though in some machines longer numbers will work. When using an ATM or *bancomat,* always use extra caution when punching in your PIN and collecting your money.

CREDIT CARDS

Always inform your credit card company and bank that you'll be traveling or spending some time abroad, especially if don't travel internationally very often. Otherwise, the credit-card company or even your bank might put a hold on your card owing to unusual activity—not a good thing halfway through your trip. Record all your credit-card numbers—as well as the phone numbers to call if your cards are lost or stolen—in a safe place, so you're prepared should something go wrong. Both MasterCard and Visa have general numbers you can call (collect if you're abroad) if your card is lost, but you're better off calling the number of your issuing bank, since MasterCard and Visa usually just transfer you to your bank; your bank's number is usually printed on your card.

If you plan to use your credit card for cash advances, you'll need to apply for a PIN at least two weeks before your trip. Although it's usually cheaper (and safer) to use a credit card abroad for large purchases (so you can cancel payments or be reimbursed if there's a problem), note that some credit-card companies *and* the banks that issue them add substantial percentages to all foreign transactions, whether they're in a foreign currency or not. Check on these fees before leaving home, so there won't be any surprises when you get the bill.

Although increasingly common, credit cards aren't accepted at all establishments, and some require a minimum expenditure. If you want to pay with a card in a small hotel, store, or restaurant, it's a good idea to ask before conducting your business. Visa and MasterCard are preferred to American Express, but in tourist areas American Express is usually accepted. Diners Club is rarely accepted.

Some credit card companies require that you obtain a police report if your credit card was lost or stolen. In this case, you should go to the police station at Termini train station or at Rome's central police station on Via San Vitale 15.

Reporting Lost Cards American Express ☎ *800/874333 toll free, 06/72282 within Italy* 🌐 *www.americanexpress.com.* **Diners Club** ☎ *800/393939 toll-free in Italy* 🌐 *www.dinersclub.com.* **MasterCard** ☎ *914/249-2000 collect from abroad, 800/870866 toll-free in Italy* 🌐 *www.mastercard.com.* **Visa** ☎ *800/581-9994 in U.S., 303/967-1096 collect from abroad, 800/877232 toll-free in Italy* 🌐 *www.visaeu.com.*

CURRENCY AND EXCHANGE

The euro is the main unit of currency in Italy, as well as in 12 other European countries. Under the euro system, there are eight coins: 1, 2, 5, 10, 20, and 50 *centesimi* (at 100 centesimi to the euro), and 1 and 2 euros. Note: The 1 and 2 euro coins look very similar. Therefore, pay close attention when using these so that you don't overpay. There are seven notes: 5, 10, 20, 50, 100, 200, and 500 euros.

At this writing, the exchange rate was about €0.72 to the U.S. dollar; €0.66 to the Canadian dollar; €1.21 to the pound sterling; €0.66 to the Australian dollar; and €0.60 to the New Zealand dollar.

TIP→ Even if a currency-exchange booth has a sign promising no commission, rest assured that there's some kind of huge, hidden fee. (Oh, that's right. The sign didn't say no fee.) And as for rates, you're almost always better off getting foreign currency at an ATM or exchanging money at a bank.

Currency Conversion Google. Google does currency conversion. Just type in the amount you want to convert and an explanation of how you want it converted (e.g., "14 euro") and then voila. *www.google.com.* **Oanda.com.** Oanda.com also allows you to print out a handy table with the current day's conversion rates. *www.oanda.com.* **XE.com.** XE.com is a good currency conversion website. *www.xe.com.*

PACKING

Plan your wardrobe in layers, no matter what the season. Rome generally has mild winters and hot, sticky summers. Heavy rain showers are common in spring and late fall, so bring some fashionable rain boots. Take a medium-weight coat for winter; a lightweight all-weather coat for spring and fall; and a lightweight jacket or sweater for summer evenings, which may be cool. Brief summer thunderstorms are common, so take a folding umbrella, and keep in mind that anything more than light cotton clothes is unbearable in the humid heat. Few public buildings in Rome, including museums, restaurants, and shops, are air-conditioned. Interiors can be cold and sometimes damp in the cooler months, so take woolens or flannels.

Dress codes are strict for visits to the Basilica di San Pietro, the Musei Vaticani, and some churches: for both men and women, shorts, scanty tops, bare midriffs, and sometimes even flip-flops are taboo. Shoulders must be covered. Women should carry a scarf or shawl to cover bare arms if the custodians insist. Those who do not comply with the dress code are refused admittance. Although there are no specific dress rules for the huge outdoor papal audiences, you'll be turned away if you're in shorts or a revealing outfit. The Vatican Information Office in Piazza di San Pietro will tell you the dress requirements for smaller audiences.

Most public and private bathrooms are often short on toilet paper. Therefore, it's best to always carry a small packet of tissues with you.

PASSPORTS AND VISAS

All U.S., Canadian, U.K., Australian, and New Zealand citizens, even infants, need a valid passport to enter Italy for stays of up to 90 days. Visas are not required for stays under 90 days.

TIP→ Before your trip, make two copies of your passport's data page (one for someone at home and another for you to carry separately). Or scan the page and email it to someone at home and/or yourself.

U.S. Passport Information U.S. Department of State 877/487–2778 *travel.state.gov/passport.*

U.S. Passport and Visa Expediters A. Briggs Passport & Visa Expeditors *800/806–0581, 202/338–0111* *www.abriggs.com.* **American Passport Express** *800/455–5166, 800/841–6778* *americanpassport.com.* **Passport Express** *800/362–8196* *www.passportexpress.com.* **Travel Document Systems** *800/874–5100, 877/874–5104* *www.traveldocs.com.* **Travel the World Visas** *866/886–8472, 202/223–8822* *www.world-visa.com.*

RESTROOMS

Public restrooms are a rare commodity in Rome, and when found, they are often undesirable. Although there are public toilets in Piazza San Pietro, Piazza di Spagna, on the Palatine Hill, and in a few other strategic locations (often with a token service charge €0.50–€0.70), consider taking well-timed pit stops at a local bar. Most bars will allow you to use the restroom if you ask politely, though it is courteous to buy something such as a bottle of water or espresso—in exchange for access to the facilities. Standards of cleanliness and comfort vary greatly. Restaurants, hotels, department stores like La Rinascente and Coin, and McDonald's restaurants tend to have the cleanest restrooms. Pubs and bars rank among the worst. It's a good idea to carry a packet of tissues with you, as you can't rely on most places having any toilet paper at all. There are bathrooms in all museums, airports, train stations, and in most subway stations. In major train stations you'll also find well-kept pay toilets for €0.70. Carry a selection of coins, as some turnstiles do not give change. There are also facilities at highway rest stops and gas stations: a small tip to the cleaning person is always appreciated. There are no bathrooms in churches nor post offices.

SAFETY

Wear a bag or camera slung across your body bandolier style, and don't rest your bag or camera on a table or underneath your chair at a sidewalk café or restaurant. If you have to bring a purse, make sure to keep it within sight by wearing it toward the front. Women should avoid wearing purses that don't have a zipper or that don't snap shut. Men should always keep their wallet in one of their front pockets with their hand in the same pocket. In Rome, beware of pickpockets on buses, especially Line 64 (Termini–St. Peter's train station); the Line 40 Express, which takes a faster route, and Bus 46 which takes you closer to St. Peter's Basilica; on subways and in subway stations; and on trains, when making your way through the corridors of crowded cars. Pickpockets often work in teams and zero in on tourists who look distracted or are in large groups. Pickpockets may be active wherever tourists gather, including the Roman Forum, the Spanish Steps, Piazza Navona, and Piazza di San Pietro. Purse snatchers work in teams on a single motor scooter or motorcycle: one drives and the other grabs.

Groups of gypsy children and young women (often with babies in arms and a scarf or a shawl wrapped around their shoulders) are present around sights popular with tourists and on buses and are adept pickpockets. One well-tried method is to approach a tourist and proffer a piece of cardboard with writing on it. While the unsuspecting victim attempts to read the message *on* it, the children's hands are busy *under* it, trying to make off with wallets and valuables. If you see such a group, do not even allow them near you—they are quick and know more tricks than you do. The phrases *Vai via!* (Go away!) and *Chiamo la polizia* (I'll call the police) usually keep them at bay. The colorful characters dressed as Roman legionaries, who hover around the Colosseum and other monuments, expect a tip if you photograph them. A €5 tip is quite sufficient.

The difficulties encountered by women traveling alone in Italy are often overstated. Younger women have to put up with much male attention, but it's rarely dangerous or hostile. Ignoring whistling and questions is the best way to get rid of unwanted attention. Women who care to avoid uncomfortable eye contact with strangers tend to wear big sunglasses. Women should also be aware that smiling at others can sometimes be viewed as a sign of flirtation in Italy. Do be careful of gropers on the Metro and on Buses 64 and 46 (Vatican buses) and 218 and 660 (Catacombs). They're known to take advantage of the cramped space. React like the locals: forcefully and loudly. **■ TIP→ Distribute your cash, credit cards, IDs, and other valuables between a deep front pocket, an inside jacket or vest pocket, and a hidden money pouch. Don't reach for the money pouch once you're in public.**

TAXES

The service charge and IVA, or value-added tax (V.A.T.), are included in the rate except in five-star deluxe hotels, where the IVA (15% on luxury hotels) may be a separate item added to the bill at departure.

Many, but not all, Rome restaurants have eliminated extra charges for service and for *pane e coperto* (a cover charge that includes bread, whether you eat it or not). If it is an extra, the service charge may be 12%–15%. Only part, if any, of this amount goes to the waiter, so an additional tip is customary *(⇨ Tipping)*.

Always ask for an itemized bill and a *scontrino,* or receipt. Officially you have to keep this receipt with you for 600 feet from the restaurant, bar, or store and be able to produce it if asked by the tax police. Sound absurd? It's something of a desperate measure for the country with the highest taxes in Europe and the highest levels of tax evasion/avoidance, and there have been cases of unwitting customers falling foul of the law, even though this practice is meant to catch noncompliant restaurants.

Be advised that the vendors selling imitation knock-off purses, sunglasses, and other accessories are unauthorized street vendors. If caught buying from any of these street vendors, you could be served with a hefty fine by Italy's tax police (Guardia di Finanza). Value-added tax (IVA in Italy, V.A.T. to English-speakers) is 23% on luxury goods, clothing, and wine. On most consumer goods, it's already included in the amount shown on the price tag; on services, such as car rentals, it's an extra item. If a store you shop in has a "euro tax free" sign outside and you make a purchase above €155 (before tax), present your passport and request a "Tax Free Shopping Check" when paying, or at least an invoice itemizing the article(s), price(s), and the amount of tax.

To get an IVA refund when you're leaving Italy, take the goods and the invoice to the customs office at the airport or other point of departure and have the invoice stamped. (If you return to the United States or Canada directly from Italy, go through the procedure at Italian customs; if your return is, say, via Britain, take the Italian goods and invoice to British customs.) Once back home—and within 90 days of the date of purchase—mail the stamped invoice to the store, which will forward the IVA rebate to you.

V.A.T. Refunds Global Blue ☎ *800/566-9828, 0331/1778 000 within Italy* 🌐 *www.global-blue.com.*

TIME

Rome is one hour ahead of London, six ahead of New York, seven ahead of Chicago, and nine ahead of Los Angeles. Rome is nine hours behind Sydney and 11 behind Auckland. Like the rest of Europe, Italy uses the 24-hour (or "military") clock, which means that after 12 noon you continue counting forward: 13:00 is 1 pm, 23:30 is 11:30 pm.

Time Zones Timeanddate.com. Timeanddate.com can help you figure out the correct time anywhere. 🌐 *www.timeanddate.com/worldclock.*

TIPPING

Many Rome restaurants have done away with the service charge of about 12%–15% that used to appear as a separate item on your check—now service is almost always included in the menu prices. It's customary to leave an additional 5%–10% tip, or a couple of euros, for the waiter, depending on the quality of service. Tip checkroom attendants €1 per person, restroom attendants €0.50. In both cases tip more in expensive hotels and restaurants. Tip €0.05–€0.10 for whatever you drink standing up at a coffee bar, €0.25 or more for table service in a café. At a hotel bar, tip €1 and up for a round or two of cocktails, more in the grander hotels.

For tipping taxi drivers, it is acceptable if you round up to the nearest euro. Railway and airport porters charge a fixed rate per bag. Tip an additional €0.50, more if the porter is very helpful. Not all theater ushers expect a tip; if they do, tip €0.25 per person, more for very expensive seats. Give a barber €1–€1.50 and a hairdresser's assistant €1.50–€4 for a shampoo or cut, depending on the type of establishment and the final bill; 5%–10% is a fair guideline.

On sightseeing tours, tip guides about €1.50 per person for a half-day group tour, more if they're very good. In museums and other places of interest where admission is free, a contribution is expected; give anything from €0.50 to €1 for one or two people, more if the guardian has been especially helpful. Service station attendants are tipped only for special services.

In hotels, give the *portiere* (concierge) about 15% of his bill for services, or €2.50–€5 if he has been generally helpful. For two people in a double room, leave the chambermaid about €1 per day, or about €4–€6 a week, in a moderately priced hotel; tip a minimum of €1 for valet or room service. Increase these amounts by one half in an expensive hotel, and double them in a very expensive hotel. In very expensive hotels, tip doormen €0.50 for calling a cab and €1 for carrying bags to the check-in desk, bellhops €1.50–€2.50 for carrying your bags to the room, and €2–€2.50 for room service.

TOURS AND GUIDES

ORIENTATION TOURS

Some might consider them campy and kitschy, but guided bus tours can prove a blissfully easy way to enjoy a quick introduction to the city's top sights—if you don't feel like being on your feet all day. Sitting in a bus, with friendly tour guide commentary (and even friendlier fellow sightseers, many of whom will be from every country under the sun), can make for a delightful and fun experience—so give one a whirl *even* if you're an old Rome hand. Of course, you'll want to savor these incredible sights at your own leisure later on.

Appian Line, Carrani, Vastours (in collaboration with American Express), and other operators offer half-day and full-day tours in air-conditioned buses with English-speaking guides. The four main itineraries are: "Ancient Rome," "Classic Rome," "Christian Rome," and "The Vatican Museums and Sistine Chapel." Half-day tours cost around €35 and full-day tours (including lunch and entrance fees) are between €100 and €137. The Musei Vaticani tour costs €60, but offers the advantage of not having to line up (sometimes for an hour or more) at the museum doors, awaiting your turn for admission. All the companies pick you up at centrally located hotels.

All operators can provide a luxury car for up to three people, a limousine for up to seven, or a minibus for up to nine, all with an English-speaking driver, but guide service is extra. Almost all operators offer "Rome by Night" tours, with or without dinner and entertainment. You can book tours through travel agents.

Various sightseeing buses following a continuous circle route through the center of town operate daily. Stop-'n'-Go has eight daily departures and makes 14 scheduled stops at important sites, where you can get on and off at will. Check with the Rome tourist information kiosks or inquire at your hotel for prices and further information.

The least expensive organized sightseeing tour of Rome is that run by ATAC, the municipal bus company. Double-decker Bus 110 leaves from Piazza dei Cinquecento, in front of Termini station, but you can pick it up at any of its 10 stopover points. A day ticket costs about €18 and allows you to stop off and get on as often as you like. The price includes an audio guide system in six languages. The total tour takes about two hours and covers the Colosseum, Piazza Navona, St. Peter's, the Trevi Fountain, and Via Veneto. Tickets can be bought on board. Two-day and three-day tickets are also available. Tours leave from Termini station every 20 minutes between 9 am and 8:30 pm.

The Archeobus, which takes you to the Old Appian Way, the Catacombs, and the new Park of the Aqueducts in the open countryside, also operates with the stop 'n' go formula. Little 15-seater buses leave from Piazza della Cinquecento every hour between 10 am and 4 pm. Tickets cost €12 and are valid all day. A combined 110 and Archeobus ticket costs €25 and is valid for one day.

Of course, you get a real bargain if you do your sightseeing "tours" of Rome by public transport. Many buses and trams pass major sights. With a single €1.50 ticket you can get in 100 minutes of sightseeing (or an entire day, with a €6 *giornaliero* ticket). Time your ride to avoid rush hours. The little electric Bus 116 scoots through the heart of Old Rome, with stops near the Pantheon, the Spanish Steps, and Piazza del Popolo, among others. The route of Bus 117 takes in San Giovanni in Laterano, the Colosseum, and the Spanish Steps.

Since certain parts of the historic center are open to pedestrians only, some walking is involved in most escorted bus tours of the city. Don't forget to dress appropriately for visits to churches (⇨ *Sightseeing*).

Tour operators can also organize minibus tours for small parties.

Bus Line ATAC ☎ *06/57003* 🌐 *www.atac.roma.it.*

Tour Operators American Express ☎ *06/67642250* 🌐 *www.americanexpress.com/italy.* **Appian Line** ☎ *06/48786601* 🌐 *www.appianline.it.* **Carrani** ✉ *Via Vittorio Emanuele Orlando 95, Repubblica* ☎ *06/4742501* 🌐 *www.carrani.com.* **Ciao Roma Trolley Tour** ☎ *06/47824580* 🌐 *ciaoromaopenbus.com.*

Stop-'n'-Go City Tours ☎ *06/48905729.* **Vastours** ☎ *06/4814309* 🌐 *www.vastours.it.*

SPECIAL-INTEREST TOURS

You can make your own arrangements (at no cost) to attend a public papal audience at the Vatican or at the Pope's summer residence at Castel Gandolfo. The easiest way is to request them online through the Santa Susanna Church, the American Catholic Church of Rome (🌐 *www.santasusanna.org*). You can also book through a travel agency for a package that includes coach transportation to the Vatican for the audience and some sightseeing along the way, returning you to your hotel, for about €35. The excursion outside Rome to Castel Gandolfo on summer Sundays for the pope's blessing costs about €45. Agencies that arrange these tours include Appian Line and Carrani.

Tourvisa Italia organizes lunch and dinner boat trips on the Tiber, departing and returning to Ponte Sant'Angelo. Boats leave four times daily for a cruise that covers all of the main historical bridges of Rome and other important sights. Tickets cost approximately €39 for lunch and €58 for dinner. The company also does combined bus and boat tours lasting 2½ hours.

A ride in a horse-drawn carriage is the Rome equivalent of a gondola ride in Venice. Coachmen can be contacted directly at popular sights like St. Peter's Square and the Colosseum. An hour's ride for four passengers to view the fountains of

Rome will cost around €150, depending on your bargaining skills.

Centro Studi Cassia organizes courses in Italian cooking, art, music, and current events in simple Italian. This is an enjoyable way to learn to speak some of the language and, at the same time, find out more about the culture and traditions of the country.

Tour Operators **Appian Line** ☎ *06/487861* 🌐 *www.appianline.it.* **Carrani** ✉ *Via Vittorio Emanuele Orlando 95, Repubblica* ☎ *06/4742501* 🌐 *www.carrani.com.* **Centro Studi Cassia** ☎ *06/33253852* 🌐 *www.centrostudicassia.it.* **Tourvisa Italia** ☎ *06/448741* 🌐 *www.tourvisa.it.*

WALKING TOURS

In Rome, there are tours and there are *tours*. Why pay to be led around by someone who just memorizes some lines and gives you the run-of-the-mill tour, when you can learn firsthand from the experts? Context Rome is an organization formed by a group of architects, archaeologists, art historians, sommeliers, and professors that give specialized walking seminars to small intimate groups (no more than six people) in and around Rome. Every day of the week offers five or six theme walks, which might include Imperial Rome: Architecture and History of the Archaeological Center; Underground Rome: The Hidden City; Baroque Rome: The Age of Bernini; Vatican Collections; and even Rome Shopping. Prices range €55–€75 per person. If you want to graduate "summa cum laude" as a serious Rome tourist and aficionado, the walking tours of Context Rome—with more than 50 academic scholars in its ranks—can't be beat. Similar to Context, Walks of Italy focuses on sustainable travel and also gives specialized tours of Rome in small, intimate groups.

All About Rome, Enjoy Rome, Through Eternity, and Argiletum Tour also offer some fascinating walking tours of the city and its sights. Argiletum and the cultural association Genti e Paesi offer regular walking tours and museum visits in English, including private tours of the Sistine Chapel before all the hordes arrive. Book at least one day in advance. For a popular food tour that's off the beaten path, check out Eating Italy Food Tours, in Testaccio. Owner Kenny Dunn takes you behind the scenes at the Testaccio open-air food market, various mom-and-pop restaurants, and specialty food shops and explains the history of this working-class neighborhood and the slow-food movement in Italy. If you have a reasonable knowledge of Italian, you can take advantage of the free guided visits and walking tours organized by Rome's cultural associations and the city council for museums and monuments. These usually take place on weekends. Programs are announced in the daily papers and in the weekly magazine *roma c'è*.

Those who want to see everything during their trip to Rome without eliminating their daily run or workout might consider hiring a guide from Sight Jogging Tours. The company consists of highly experienced trainers that give tours of Rome based on the level of difficulty chosen by the client. Routes may take in Villa Borghese, Imperial Forum and Colosseum, St. Peter's Basilica, and many other sights. Trainers meet tourists at their hotel and take them back after the run is over. Most tours take 45–60 minutes and cost about €85 per person per hour.

Tour Operators **Argiletum Tour** ✉ *Via Madonna dei Monti 49, Monti* ☎ *06/45438906* 🌐 *www.argiletumtour.com.* **Context Rome** ✉ *Via Santa Maria Maggiore 145, Santa Maria Maggiore* ☎ *06/97625204 within Italy, 800/691–6036 within the U.S.* 🌐 *www.contexttravel.com.* **Eating Italy Food Tours** ☎ *800/838–3006 from the U.S. or Canada, 800/4118881 within Europe* 🌐 *www.eatingitalyfoodtours.com.*

Enjoy Rome ✉ *Via Marghera 8/A, Termini* ☎ *06/4451843* 🌐 *www.enjoyrome.com.* **Genti e Paesi** ✉ *Via Adda 111, Parioli* ☎ *06/85301755* 🌐 *www.gentiepaesi.it.*

Sightjogging ☎ *347/3353185* 🌐 *www.sightjogging.it.* **Through Eternity** ☎ *06/7009336* 🌐 *www.througheternity.com.* **Walks of Italy** ☎ *334/9744274 within Italy, 202/684–6916 within the U.S.* 🌐 *www.walksofitaly.com.*

EXCURSIONS

Most operators offer half-day excursions to Tivoli to see the fountains and gardens of Villa D'Este. Appian Line's afternoon tour to Tivoli includes a visit to Hadrian's Villa, with its impressive ancient ruins, as well as the many-fountained Villa D'Este. Most operators also have full-day excursions to Assisi, to Pompeii and/or Capri, and to Florence.

Tour Operator Appian Line ✉ *Piazza Esquilino 6/7, Esquilino* ☎ *06/48786601* 🌐 *www.appianline.it.*

PERSONAL GUIDES

You can arrange for a personal guide through the main APT (Azienda Per Turismo) Tourist Information Office.

Tour Operator APT ✉ *Via Parigi 11, Repubblica* ☎ *06/51687240.*

VISITOR INFORMATION

Rome has an APT (Azienda Per Turismo) Tourist Information Office in the city center. Green APT information kiosks called Punti Informativi Turistici (P.I.T.), with multilingual personnel, are near the most important sights and squares, as well as at Termini station and Leonardo da Vinci and Ciampino airports. They're open 9–1 and 3–7:30 and provide information about cultural events, museums, opening hours, city transportation, and so on. You can also pick up free tourist maps and brochures.

In Rome 060608 (Tourist Information and Tickets). City-sponsored cultural resources portal ☎ *06/0608* 🌐 *www.060608.it.* **TurismoRoma** ☎ *06/0608* 🌐 *www.turismoroma.it/?lang=en.*

WORD OF MOUTH

After your trip, be sure to rate the places you visited and share your experiences and travel tips with us and other Fodorites in the Forums on 🌐 *www.fodors.com.*

ONLINE RESOURCES

The Turismo Roma website is 🌐 *www.turismoroma.it* and is packed with information about events and places to visit. For more information specifically on Italy, visit 🌐 *www.italiantourism.com*, 🌐 *www.initaly.com*, and 🌐 *www.wel.it*. Another particularly useful site is 🌐 *www.romeguide.it*, which has an English version. Particularly provocative, fascinating, and up-to-date are the monthly Web issues of *The American*, a popular English magazine based in Rome; their website is 🌐 *www.theamericanmag.com*. Magnificent is the only word to describe this passionate writer's ode to the city's treasures of art and architecture, replete with hundreds of photos and little-known facts: 🌐 *www.romeartlover.it*. An official website for many of Rome's most famous sights, and a place to make ticket reservations, is 🌐 *www.060608.it*. If you're particularly curious about the history of food and where to get the best of it in Rome, check out food writer Katie Parla's comprehensive blog, 🌐 *www.parlafood.com*. One example of a top website devoted to one sight in Rome is 🌐 *www.capitolium.org*. Two handy guides to the bus lines threading Rome and its surrounding areas are 🌐 *www.atac.roma.it* and 🌐 *www.cotralspa.it*.

ITALIAN VOCABULARY

	ENGLISH	ITALIAN	PRONUNCIATION
BASICS			
	Yes/no	Sí/No	see/no
	Please	Per favore	pear fa-**vo**-ray
	Yes, please	Sí grazie	see **grah**-tsee-ay
	Thank you	Grazie	**grah**-tsee-ay
	You're welcome	Prego	**pray**-go
	Excuse me, sorry	Scusi	**skoo**-zee
	Sorry!	Mi dispiace!	mee dis-spee-**ah**-chay
	Good morning/ afternoon	Buongiorno	bwohn-**jor**-no
	Good evening	Buona sera	**bwoh**-na **say**-ra
	Good-bye	Arrivederci	a-ree-vah-**dare**-chee
	Mr. (Sir)	Signore	see-**nyo**-ray
	Mrs. (Ma'am)	Signora	see-**nyo**-ra
	Miss	Signorina	see-nyo-**ree**-na
	Pleased to meet you	Piacere	pee-ah-**chair**-ray
	How are you?	Come sta?	**ko**-may **stah**
	Very well, thanks	Bene, grazie	**ben**-ay **grah**-tsee-ay
	Hello (phone)	Pronto?	**proan**-to
NUMBERS			
	one	uno	**oo**-no
	two	due	**doo**-ay
	three	tre	tray
	four	quattro	**kwah**-tro
	five	cinque	**cheen**-kway
	six	sei	say
	seven	sette	**set**-ay
	eight	otto	**oh**-to
	nine	nove	**no**-vay
	ten	dieci	dee-**eh**-chee
	twenty	venti	**vain**-tee

ENGLISH	ITALIAN	PRONUNCIATION
thirty	trenta	**train**-ta
forty	quaranta	kwa-**rahn**-ta
fifty	cinquanta	cheen-**kwahn**-ta
sixty	sessanta	seh-**sahn**-ta
seventy	settanta	seh-**tahn**-ta
eighty	ottanta	o-**tahn**-ta
ninety	novanta	no-**vahn**-ta
one hundred	cento	**chen**-to
one thousand	mille	**mee**-lay
ten thousand	diecimila	dee-eh-chee-**mee**-la

USEFUL PHRASES

Do you speak English?	Parla inglese?	**par**-la een-**glay**-zay
I don't speak Italian.	Non parlo italiano.	non **par**-lo ee-tal-**yah**-no
I don't understand.	Non capisco.	non ka-**peess**-ko
Can you please repeat?	Può ripetere?	pwo ree-**pet**-ay-ray
Slowly!	Lentamente!	**len**-ta-men-tay
I don't know.	Non lo so.	non lo **so**
I'm American.	Sono americano(a).	**so**-no a-may-ree-**kah**-no(a)
I'm British.	Sono inglese.	so-no een-**glay**-zay
What's your name?	Come si chiama?	**ko**-may see kee-**ah**-ma
My name is . . .	Mi chiamo . . .	mee kee-**ah**-mo
What time is it?	Che ore sono?	kay **o**-ray **so**-no
How?	Come?	**ko**-may
When?	Quando?	**kwan**-doe
Yesterday/today/ tomorrow	Ieri/oggi/domani	**yer**-ee/**o**-jee/ do-**mah**-nee
This morning/	Stamattina/Oggi	sta-ma-**tee**-na/**o**-jee
afternoon	pomeriggio	po-mer-**ee**-jo

ENGLISH	ITALIAN	PRONUNCIATION
Tonight	Stasera	sta-**ser**-a
What?	Che cosa?	kay **ko**-za
Why?	Perché?	pear-**kay**
Who?	Chi?	kee
Where is . . .	Dov'è . . .	doe-**veh**
the bus stop?	la fermata dell'autobus?	la fer-**mah**-ta del ow-toe-**booss**
the train station?	la stazione?	la sta-tsee-**oh**-nay
the subway	la metropolitana?	la may-tro-po-lee-**tah**-na
the terminal?	il terminale?	eel ter-mee-**nah**-lay
the post office?	l'ufficio postale?	loo-**fee**-cho po-**stah**-lay
the bank?	la banca?	la **bahn**-ka
the . . . hotel?	l'hotel . . .?	lo-**tel**
the store?	il negozio?	eel nay-**go**-tsee-o
the cashier?	la cassa?	la **kah**-sa
the . . . museum?	il museo . . .?	eel moo-**zay**-o
the hospital?	l'ospedale?	lo-spay-**dah**-lay
the elevator?	l'ascensore?	la-shen-**so**-ray
the restrooms?	Dov'è il bagno?	do-**vay** eel **bahn**-yo
Here/there	Qui/là	kwee/la
Left/right	A sinistra/a destra	a see-**neess**-tra/a **des**-tra
Straight ahead	Avanti dritto	a-**vahn**-tee **dree**-to
Is it near/far?	È vicino/lontano?	ay vee-**chee**-no/ lon-**tah**-no
I'd like . . .	Vorrei . . .	vo-**ray**
a room	una camera	**oo**-na **kah**-may-ra
the key	la chiave	la kee-**ah**-vay
a newspaper	un giornale	oon jor-**nah**-lay
a stamp	un francobollo	oon frahn-ko-**bo**-lo
I'd like to buy . . .	Vorrei comprare . . .	vo-**ray** kom-**prah**-ray

ENGLISH	ITALIAN	PRONUNCIATION
How much is it?	Quanto costa?	**kwahn**-toe **coast**-a
It's expensive/cheap.	È caro/economico.	ay **car**-o/ ay-ko-**no**-mee-ko
A little/a lot	Poco/tanto	**po**-ko/**tahn**-to
More/less	Più/meno	pee-**oo/may**-no
Enough/too (much)	Abbastanza/troppo	a-bas-**tahn**-sa/tro-po
I am sick.	Sto male.	sto **mah**-lay
Call a doctor.	Chiama un dottore.	kee-**ah**-mah oondoe-**toe**-ray
Help!	Aiuto!	a-**yoo**-toe
Stop!	Alt!	ahlt
Fire!	Al fuoco!	ahl **fwo**-ko
Caution/Look out!	Attenzione!	a-ten-**syon**-ay

DINING OUT

A bottle of . . .	Una bottiglia di . . .	**oo**-na bo-**tee**-lee-ah dee
A cup of . . .	Una tazza di . . .	**oo**-na **tah**-tsa dee
A glass of . . .	Un bicchiere di . . .	oon bee-key-**air**-ay dee
Bill/check	Il conto	eel **cone**-toe
Bread	Il pane	eel **pah**-nay
Breakfast	La prima colazione	la **pree**-ma ko-la-**tsee**-oh-nay
Cocktail/aperitif	L'aperitivo	la-pay-ree-**tee**-vo
Dinner	La cena	la **chen**-a
Fixed-price menu	Menù a prezzo fisso	may-**noo** a **pret**-so **fee**-so
Fork	La forchetta	la for-**ket**-a
I am diabetic.	Ho il diabete.	o eel dee-a-**bay**-tay
I am vegetarian.	Sono vegetariano/a.	**so**-no vay-jay-ta-ree-**ah**-no/a
I'd like . . .	Vorrei . . .	vo-**ray**
I'd like to order.	Vorrei ordinare.	vo-**ray** or-dee-**nah**-ray

ENGLISH	ITALIAN	PRONUNCIATION
Is service included?	Il servizio è incluso?	eel ser-**vee**-tzee-o ay een-**kloo**-zo
It's good/bad.	È buono/cattivo.	ay **bwo**-no/ka-**tee**-vo
It's hot/cold.	È caldo/freddo.	ay **kahl**-doe/**fred**-o
Knife	Il coltello	eel kol-**tel**-o
Lunch	Il pranzo	eel **prahnt**-so
Menu	Il menù	eel may-**noo**
Napkin	Il tovagliolo	eel toe-va-lee-**oh**-lo
Please give me . . .	Mi dia . . .	mee **dee**-a
Salt	Il sale	eel **sah**-lay
Spoon	Il cucchiaio	eel koo-kee-**ah**-yo
Sugar	Lo zucchero	lo **tsoo**-ker-o
Waiter/Waitress	Cameriere/cameriera	ka-mare-**yer**-ay/ ka-mare-**yer**-a
Wine list	La lista dei vini	la **lee**-sta **day**-ee **vee**-nee

INDEX

D

E

F

M

N

O

P

PHOTO CREDITS

Front cover: SIME/eStock Photo [Description: Colosseum]. Back cover (from left to right): europhotos/ Shutterstock; Hedda Gjerpen/iStockphoto; Joan Coll/iStockphoto. Spine: cdascher/iStockphoto.

1, Corbis.2–3, Paul D'Innocenzo. 5, Scala/Art Resource. Chapter 1: Experience Rome: 8–9, Luciano Mortula/Shutterstock.com , 10, Angelo Campus. 12, Angelo Campus. 13 (left), Angelo Campus. 13(right), Paul D'Innocenzo. 16 (left), Angelo Campus. 16 (top center), Paul D'Innocenzo. 16 (bottom center). Iakov Kalinin/Shutterstock.com. 16 (top right), Viacheslav Lopatin/Shutterstock. 16 (bottom right), Angelo Campus. 17 (top left), Viacheslav Lopatin/Shutterstock. 17(bottom left), Kostiantyn Ablazov/Shutterstock.com. 17 (bottom center), Brian Kinney/Shutterstock.com, 17 (right), Public Domain. 18, Public Domain, 19. Angelo Campus. 21, Angelo Campus. 23 (left), Paul D'Innocenzo., 23 (right), Angelo Campus. 24, Paul D'Innocenzo. 25, Paul D'Innocenzo. 26, Anton Balazh/Shutterstock. Chapter 2: Rome's Best Walks: 27, Angelo Campus. 28, Paul D'Innocenzo. 32, Angelo Campus. 34, Anthony Majanlahti. 38–39, Angelo Campus. 42, Richard Goerg/iStockphoto. 47, Corbis. Chapter 3: Ancient Rome: 49, Frank/ age fotostock. 51, Paul D'Innocenzo. 52, Paul D'Innocenzo. 54, Paul D'Innocenzo. 65, Paul D'Innocenzo. 66, Amy Nichole Harris/Shutterstock. 67, Javarman/Shutterstock. 68–69, Altair4 Multime– dia Roma, www.altair4. com. 70–71, Angelo Campus. 72 (top), Paul D'Innocenzo. 72 (middle), Amy Nichole Harris/Shutterstock. 72 (bottom right), Paul D'Innocenzo. 72 (bottom left), INTERFOTO Pressebildagentur/ Alamy. 73 (top left), Angelo Campus. 73 (top right), Eugene Mogilnikov/Shutterstock. 73(bottom), PhotoBliss/ Alamy. 74, Angelo Campus. 75 (top left), Marek Slusarczyk/Shutterstock. 75 (top right), Eugene Mogilnikov/ Shutterstock. 75 (middle), Paul D'Innocenzo. 75 (bottom), Wikimedia Commons. 76, Paul D'Innocenzo. 77 (left), Howard Hudson. 77 (right), Alvaro Leiva. 82, Iakov Kalinin/Shutterstock. Chapter 4: The Vatican: 85, Doco Dalfiano. 87, Angelo Campus.88, Stockphoto. 100, Paul D'Innocenzo. 106–107, Paul D'Innocenzo. 109, Paul D'Innocenzo. 110–111, SuperStock. 110 (bottom), public domain. 112, Russell Mountford/ age fotostock. 114–117, Dave Drapak. 118 (top left, top middle, top right, bottom middle, bottom right), Public Domain. 118 (bottom left), Superstock. 119, Gianni Giansanti/Sygmal/Corbis. Chapter 5: Navona and Campo: 121, Nikada/iStockphoto. 123, Angelo Campus. 124, Paul D'Innocenzo. 129, Sorin Colac/ Shutterstock. 134–135 (top), Paul D'Innocenzo. 135 (center), Nataliya Pergudova/shutterstock. 135 (bottom), Paul D'Innocenzo. 136 (top left), Kathy deWitt/Alamy. 136 (top right and center), Paul D'Innocenzo. 136 (bottom), RomanHoliday (7) by Lisa Larsson. http://www.flickr.com/photos/ljcy bergal/641393954/ Attribution–ShareAlike License. 137 (top left), Interfoto Pressebildagentur/¬Alamy. 137 (top right), Paul D'Innocenzo. 137 (bottom left), Russell Mountford/age fotostock. 137 (bottom right), Caro/¬Alamy. 138, Paul D'Innocenzo. Chapter 6: Piazza da Spagna: 145, Alvaro Leiva/ age fotos– tock.147, Angelo Campus. 148, DEA/ M BORCHI/age fotostock. 153, Cosmo Con– dina/ Alamy. 157, Paul D'Innocenzo. Chapter 7: Repubblica and Quirinale: 159, Superstock/age fotostock. 161, Peter beim Graben/ Wikimedia Commons/CC Attribution–Share age footstock. 162, daniele caporale. 165, adam eastland/Alamy. 169, Scala/Art Resource. 170, GUIZIOU Franck/age fotostock. 171, Achim Bednorz/age fotostock. 172 (top), Public Domain. 172 (center), Xavier Florensa/age fotostock. 172 (bottom), Superstock. 173 (top), Public Domain. 173 (bottom), Achim Bednorz/age fotostock. 174, piotrwzk/Shutterstock. 175(top left), Achim Bednorz/age fotostock. 175 (bottom left) Public Domain. 175(top center), Wojtek Buss/age fotostock. 175 (bottom center), Rough Guides/Alamy. 175 (right), Superstock. 176, Public Domain. Chapter 8: Villa Borghese and Piazza del Popolo: 179, Alvaro Leiva/age fotostock. 181, Public Domain. 182, adam eastland/Alamy. 186, Public Domain. Chapter 9: Trastevere and the Ghetto: 191, Robert Harding Picture Library Ltd/Alamy. 193, Angelo Campus. 194, Paul D'Innocenzo. 196, Paul D'Innocenzo. Chapter 10: Aventino: 199, Angelo Campus. 201, Angelo Campus. 202, Paul D'Innocenzo. Chapter 11: Monti, Esquilino and Celio, and the Via Appia Antica: 207, Xavier Florensa/age fotostock. 209, peter mills rymer/iStockphoto. 210, Sylvain Grandadam/age fotostock. 219, Angelo Campus. Chapter 12: Where to Eat: 223, Art Kowalsky/Alamy. 224, John Ferro Sims/Alamy. 225 (bottom left, top right), Angelo Campus. 226, Cagri Özgür/iStockphoto. 237, adam eastland/Alamy. 259, Erica Duecy. Chapter 13: Where to Stay: 273, Alvaro Leiva/age fotostock. 274, Hotel Majestic. Chapter 14: Nightlife and the Arts: 299, Angelo Campus. 300, daniele caporale/age fotostock. 304, Luis Rosario. 307, Agnese Sanviat, Alamy. 316, Luis Rosario. Chapter 15: Shopping: 319, CuboImages srl/ Alamy. 320, Erica Duecy. 321 (top right), Erica Duecy. 321 (bottom left), Delfina Delettrez. 322, Angelo Campus. Chapter 16: Side Trips from Rome: 349, Art Kowalsky/Alamy. 351, Valeria73/Shutterstock352, avatra images/Alamy.

NOTES

museums best @
noon → 2:00

NOTES

NOTES

NOTES

NOTES

NOTES

NOTES

NOTES

NOTES

NOTES

NOTES

ABOUT OUR WRITERS

After her first Italian coffee and her first Italian *bacio* in 1999, **Nicole Arriaga** just knew she'd have to find a way to make it back to Rome and she moved to the Eternal City in 2003 to earn her Master's in political science. Nicole's freelance work has appeared in various travel publications including *Romeing, 10Best,* Eurocheapo, and *The American.* When not writing, Nicole works as a programs coordinator for an American Study Abroad organization based in Rome. For this edition, she updated our our Shopping and Where to Stay chapters.

Erica Firpo likes to cross lines between art and culture, writing about art, lifestyle, fashion, and food for a variety of magazines, books, and online publications. She is a contributing editor to Fathom and is a regular contributor to *Forbes Travel, Huffington Post, Travel + Leisure,* and Cathay Pacific's *Discovery Magazine.* In 2005, she created a series of bilingual restaurant guides *Little Black Book* for Rome and Copenhagen. She is also the author of *Rome Select* (Insight Guides) and boss of (🌐 *www.ericafirpo.com*). She has been contributing to Fodor's since 2005. For this edition, she updated our Nightlife and Performing Arts chapter and the Travel Smart chapter.

Dana Klitzberg is a chef and culinary expert from New York City. Since 1990, her travels frequently took her to Italy, and included a college semester in Florence. Years later, after a career in public relations working with Italian clients in food, wine, and fashion, Ms. Klitzberg switched gears and received her degree from culinary school in New York City, (and earned her cooking chops in top Italian eatery San Domenico NY). In 2000, Ms. Klitzberg moved to Rome. Once top toque in various Roman restaurants, she now works in several culinary areas through her company Blu Aubergine (🌐 *www.bluaubergine.com*), offering catering, private chef services, restaurant consulting, cooking instruction, and culinary tours around The Eternal City. She now splits her time between Manhattan and Rome. Also a food and travel writer, this University of Virginia grad updated the Where to Eat chapter, which she originally penned years back.

Journalist and editor **Amanda Ruggeri** returned to the United States in 2014, after nearly five years living in Rome, where she wrote about travel across Italy and Europe for the *New York Times,* the BBC, the *Globe and Mail, National Geographic Traveler, Travel + Leisure,* and *AFAR*, among other publications. Her popular blog on Rome (🌐 *www.revealedrome.com*) features tips, tricks, and things not to miss in the Eternal City. She also has appeared on the History Channel as a documentary host and provides travel consulting sessions to Italy-bound travelers. She now lives in New York City, where she is the BBC's travel editor at large, works as a freelance journalist, and returns to Italy often. She updated all of the Exploring Neighborhood chapters for this edition, right before she moved to NYC.

An award-winning travel writer, **Margaret Stenhouse** has written for *The Herald* and the *International Herald Tribune's* "Italy Daily" supplement, and updates the website 🌐 *www.italyupdate.it* with cultural, gastronomic, and tourism events. She is also the author of *The Goddess of the Lake: Legends and Mysteries of Nemi.* Margaret updated the Experience Rome and the Side Trips from Rome chapters for this edition.

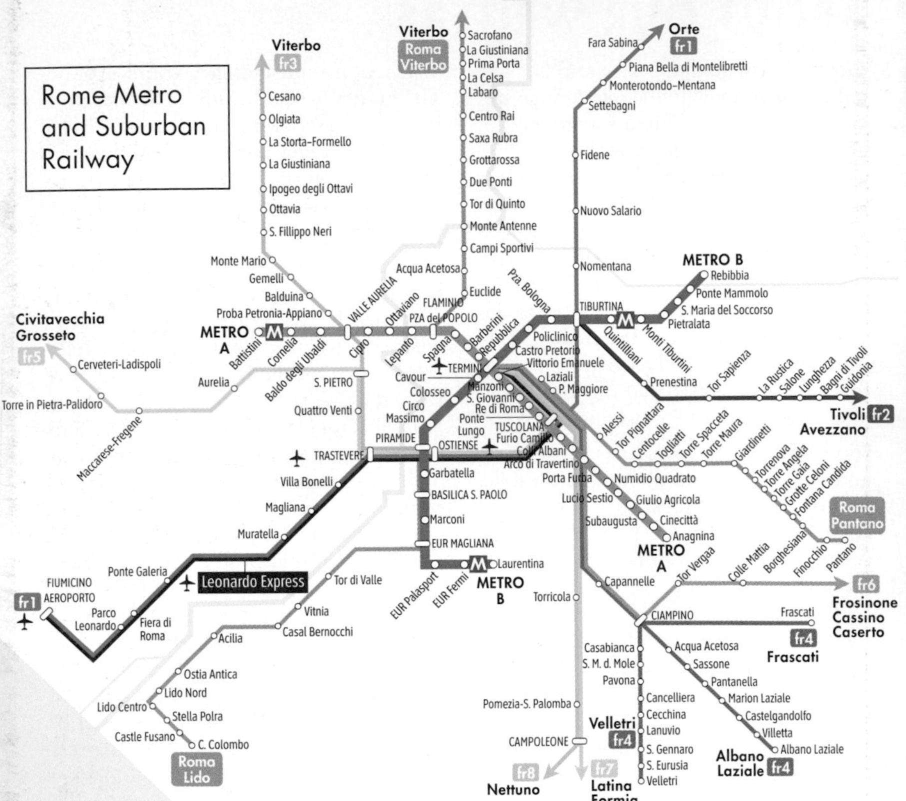

Tickets

A ticket (BIT) valid for 100 minutes on any combination of buses and trams and one entrance to the metro costs €1.50. Tickets are sold at newsstands, some coffee bars, ticket machines in metro stations, and ATAC and COTRAL ticket booths. Time-stamp your ticket when boarding the first vehicle, and stamp it again when boarding for the last time within 75 minutes. You stamp the ticket at Metro sliding electronic doors, and in the little yellow machines on buses and trams.

Fare fees	Price
Single fare	€1.50
Biglietto integrato giornaliero (Integrated Daily Ticket) BIG	€6
Biglietto turistico integrato (Three-Day Pass) BTI	€16.50
Weekly pass	€24
Monthly unlimited pass	€35